D1593303

Architects of Empire

Architects of Empire

The Duke of Wellington and His Brothers

John Severn

University of Oklahoma Press : Norman

Also by John Severn

A Wellesley Affair: Richard Marquess Wellesley and the Conduct of Anglo-Spanish Diplomacy, 1809–1812 (Tallahassee, 1981)

Library of Congress Cataloging-in-Publication Data

Severn, John Kenneth, 1948–
Architects of empire : the Duke of Wellington and his brothers / John Severn.
p. cm.
Includes bibliographical references and index.
ISBN-13: 978-0-8061-3810-7 (alk. paper)
ISBN-10: 0-8061-3810-6 (alk. paper)
1. Wellington, Arthur Wellesley, Duke of, 1769–1852—Family. 2. Wellesley family. 3. Great Britain—History—18th century. 4. Great Britain—History—19th century. 5. Politicians—Great Britain—Biography. 6. Gentry—Ireland—Biography. I. Title. II. Title: Duke of Wellington and his brothers.

DA68.12.W4S48 2007
941.07'0922—dc22

2006028181

Text Design by CF Graphics

The paper in this book meets the guidelines for permanence and durability of the Committee on Production Guidelines for Book Longevity of the Council on Library Resources, Inc. ∞

1 2 3 4 5 6 7 8 9 10

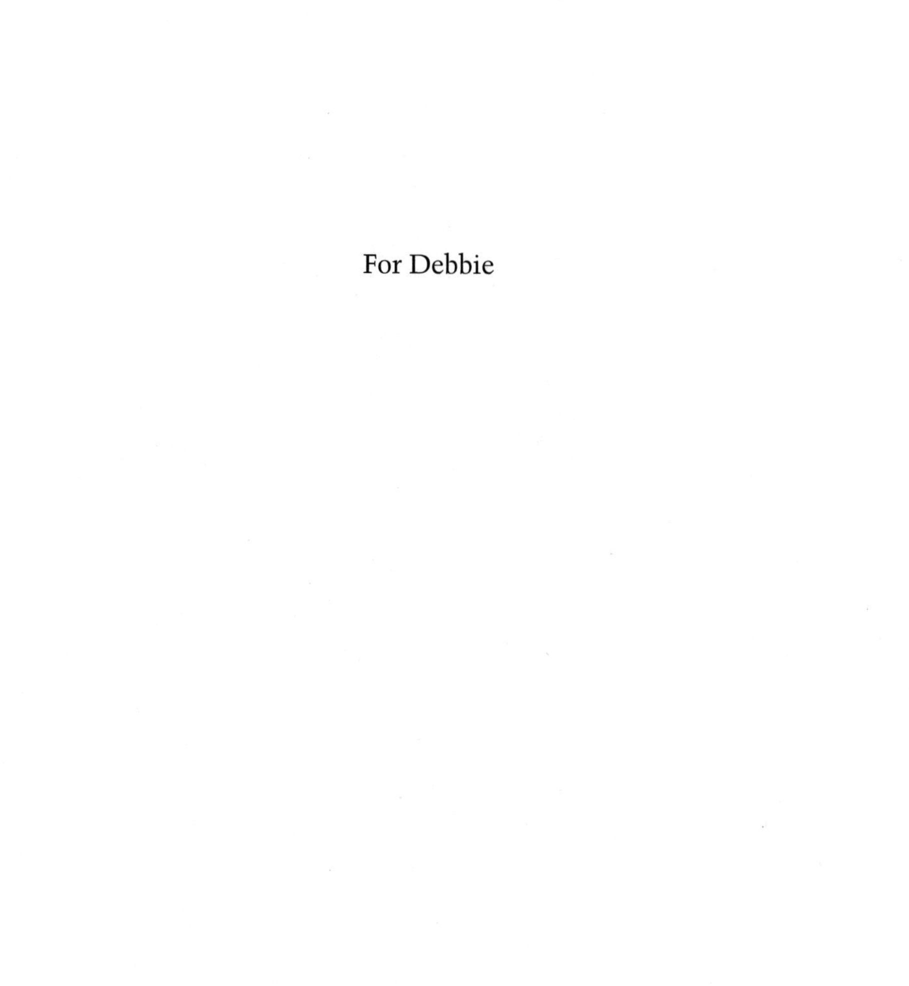

For Debbie

Contents

ILLUSTRATIONS

PLATES

Maps

Preface

This project had its origins in necessity. On completion of my study of the Marquess Wellesley's term as foreign secretary, I cast about for a new avenue of research. At the time, I was a schoolmaster with precious little time and fewer resources; embarking on something entirely new made little sense. Because the Wellesleys continued to interest me, I considered a study of the youngest Wellesley brother, Henry, who became Lord Cowley. It soon became apparent that his career was of insufficient import and interest to justify a comprehensive examination, at least for me at that stage of my career. Instead I began a study of all five Wellesley brothers, with Wellington as the centerpiece, at a time when I became both a preparatory school administrator and an admirer of C. P. Snow. School life required working daily with a variety of personalities, often in resolving conflict, usually at great cost to my emotional well being; Snow, who captured my imagination with his observations of human interaction in confined settings, led me to think more and more how the Wellesleys' personal lives might have affected their careers and vice versa.

The literature on the Duke of Wellington is vast, yet he continues to engage scholarly and popular attention. The Countess of Longford's two-volume biography is still a standard, and Neville Thompson's *Wellington after Waterloo* is excellent. Christopher Hibbert's *Personal History* is engaging and well told, and more focused studies of the duke have made their way into print with regularity. This book considers the career of the duke and his brothers in light of who they were as a family and the significance of a lifetime of interaction. All the brothers had respectable careers. The eldest, Richard, was on the verge of greatness when he wrecked on the shoals of crippling personal shortcomings. It is not my purpose to knock the brothers off their historical perches; rather, they should be considered as human beings who had to deal (or not) with their personal inadequacies. That they could be generous and supportive and then turn around and be insensitive, even cruel, does not diminish them. One cannot understand human behavior without examining the personal dimensions of life, and nothing is as personal as family. Finally, while the Wellesleys are interesting in themselves, their lives provide a unique window on Britain's history between 1750 and 1850. Looking through it, one sees not only a political, diplomatic, and military landscape but also a social, legal, religious, and economic backdrop.

I have benefited more than most from the support of friends and colleagues. I say this because I labored for years in the shadows of academic life. For a high school teacher to engage in the academic world is not easy; one needs help. For me this aid came first from my mentor, Donald Horward, recently retired as director of the Institute on Napoleon and the French Revolution at Florida State University, who is a most determined advocate for his students. A little later, I was fortunate to meet Charles R. Middleton (currently president of Roosevelt University in Chicago), an irrepressible man who took me under his wing and introduced me to many of North America's British historians, put me on conference panels, and urged me on whenever I showed signs of quitting. Very special thanks go to my friends Edward Ingram and Jim J. Sack—both superb scholars who encourage rather than compete—who egged me on, read the manuscript at various stages, and offered timely and helpful critical advice.

In 1991 I left Breck School in Minneapolis to join the History Department at the University of Alabama in Huntsville, thanks to the determined support of the chair, John C. White. My fifteen years in Huntsville have been the happiest and most rewarding of my career because of superb colleagues, fine students, and a supportive dean, Sue Kirkpatrick. My friend and colleague Carolyn White, now retired, not only read the opening chapters but also offered clearheaded advice when I encountered problems.

I thank the University of Alabama in Huntsville for research grants, the university's Humanities Center (under directors Johanna Shields and then Brian Martine), for travel funds when I needed them, and Breck School for supporting my research for eight years simply because it was the right thing to do. I also thank the staff of the British Library, London, particularly the manuscript room; the former India Office Library, All Souls College Library, Oxford; the Archivo Histórico Nacional, Madrid; the Hartley Institute at the University of Southampton and its director, Christopher Woolgar; the Public Record Office of Great Britain; the Staffordshire Record Office for the use of the Hatherton Papers; the Gwent Record Office in Cwmbrân and Lord Raglan for the use of the Raglan Papers; and His Grace the Duke of Wellington, for the use of papers held at Stratfield Saye. Last, I thank Bernard Cornwell for his helpful advice on the labyrinthine world of British publishing.

These expressions of gratitude cannot conclude without a mention of Iris Butler Portal, a friend of thirty years who died in 2002 at the age of ninety-seven. Iris and I became friends by mail shortly after she published a biography of the Marquess Wellesley. Although I visited her as often as possible, our friendship was maintained through the post. I am at a loss as to why she befriended me, but from her I learned history, literature, and politics, and above all, what it means to be a human being. She continues to live in my soul.

And what do I say to my long-suffering wife, Deborah, who has been hearing about Wellesleys for thirty years and anticipating this book for the past fifteen? Thank you, my dear, you are a saint.

Architects of Empire

1

The Wellesleys of County Meath

On 18 November 1852, more than a million people lined London's streets as the funeral cortege of England's greatest soldier-statesman made its way slowly, awkwardly towards St. Paul's Cathedral. Headed for enshrinement next to the other hero of the age, Horatio, Vice-Admiral Viscount Nelson, was the body of the Arthur Wellesley, first Duke of Wellington. Long forgotten were the trials and tribulations of the war with revolutionary France and the troubling uncertainties of the years that followed. A proud legacy of military glory remained, along with the mythology of a defiant Britannia whose resolve and nobility of purpose had led to victory over Napoleon Bonaparte at Waterloo. The Great Duke, to whom the nation bade farewell on that sorrowful day, symbolized both the glory and the myth. Wellington had been strong, bold, honest, enterprising, and predictable. More important, he had never lost a battle. To most Britons, he defined the national character; his funeral was thus both the celebration of a great man's achievements and the nation's affirmation of its own greatness. Nothing could detract from the solemnity. Londoners stood in tribute, numbed by the cold and the realization that an era had come to a close. The other great statesmen of the age—Pitt, Fox, Grenville, Grey, Liverpool, Sidmouth, Castlereagh, and Canning—had all preceded Wellington to the grave, as had three kings. He was the last of his generation.

Lost in the drama of the moment was the fact that Wellington was also the last of a generation of Wellesleys. There had been five Wellesley brothers, the "Gracchi" (a reference to the Gracchus brothers of Rome), as the outspoken Henry, Lord Brougham, called them: Richard, William, Arthur, Gerald, and Henry. Their careers very nearly embodied Great Britain's history in the late eighteenth and early nineteenth centuries. They were politicians, scholars, empire builders, soldiers, diplomats, and clerics. There were no artists or businessmen among them, though Wellington became very rich. Like the Pitts, they were of the meritocracy, for a striking feature of these several careers is that they began in relative obscurity. As Brougham pointed out, four of them sat in the House of Lords, "not by inheritance but by merit raised to that proud eminence."[1] Richard became Baron Wellesley in the English peerage in 1797; Arthur followed in 1809 as Viscount Wellington; William in 1821 as Baron Maryborough; and Henry in 1828 as Baron Cowley. The remaining brother, Gerald, took holy orders and nearly occupied a bishop's seat in the Lords. They were of Anglo-Irish stock, members of the Irish Ascendancy, and though they were born into what appeared to be comfortable circumstances, the family hovered near bankruptcy and possessed neither social nor political influence. They grew up on the fringe of Britain's oligarchy. For the Gracchi, the road to success was neither straight nor smooth, and the fact that they traversed it is a testament to their talent and character.

Britain's history is filled with the names of great families who either saved the country in times of crisis or contributed in an extraordinary fashion to the development of the nation and the enhancement of its security: Churchill, Cecil, and Pitt are but three that come quickly to mind. The Wellesleys fit quite comfortably into that list. They were a remarkable family, and taken as a single generation, the brothers' contributions to British history are unparalleled. Yet other than Wellington, they have largely been forgotten, obscured by his giant shadow and either trivialized or ignored. This observation is not intended to suggest that any of Wellington's four brothers was his equal or that the Great Duke is given more than his due. It is merely a lament that the family's story—which reads like both a saga and a sensational novel—has yet to be told. Glory and grandeur, fortunes won and lost, exultation and despair, honor and scandal: the brothers were an improbable mix of complementary and conflicting talents, personalities, ambitions, and emotions, and while they built their success on mutual loyalty and support, all too often they staggered under the withering blows of jealousy and betrayal. At the end, they stood together, old men basking in one another's glory. It is a remarkable story, one which warrants the telling.

The Wellesleys became a part of England's history in Ireland when one of their number went there as Henry II's standard-bearer. Consequently, they acquired land, but not until the fourteenth century did the family come to live exclusively in Ireland.[2] They were what historians have labelled the "Old English." The English who went to Ireland in the twelfth century were actually Anglo-Normans. They arrived as conquerors and stayed as feudal lords, settling in the eastern part of the island. In the Middle Ages, conquest of this sort was nothing new. England was the product of conquest, and the Old English saw the relationship with the Gaelic Irish as that of lord and vassal, not conqueror and conquered. It was a feudal arrangement typical of the times. During these early years of England's presence in Ireland, the Irish had no sense of nationhood. Culture and politics were local, not national, which in part explains Ireland's vulnerability. Nonetheless, to the Irish, the English were intruders—unwelcome colonizers—and deep-seated antipathies took root.[3]

The fate of the Gaelic people looked much like that of the Saxons: both strained under the Anglo-Norman yoke. Ireland, however, was not England. A rough and wild land where communications were, at best, hazardous, Ireland possessed a culture organized along family lines with clans dominating defined and isolated areas of the country. The Old English found conquest of the whole island impossible, even undesirable, and eventually they settled around Dublin in an area that came to be known as the English Pale. What emerged, literally and figuratively, was a garrison state. Language and cultural differences defined the political arrangement.[4]

As is the case with nearly all colonizers, the Old English believed that they were capable of managing their own affairs without help from London. Ireland had been "conquered" in the name of the king, and the Old English were quick to express devotion and allegiance to him. Beyond that, they declared themselves self-sufficient. The king had his governor in Ireland, the lord lieutenant, but the Anglo-Irish would elect their own parliament. This awkward political condition formed the Anglo-Irish character. The Old English were an exclusive ruling class, a despised minority surrounded by a resentful majority.

They would stick together to preserve themselves and the sociopolitical system that supported them. They considered themselves Irish, much as American colonials considered themselves Americans. But they were Irish of English blood, not Gaelic. This important distinction separated them from both native Irish and the English born.

Such exclusivity had many consequences, including the determination never to compromise their distinctiveness. As a governing class, their behavior towards the native Irish tended to exhibit aggressive arrogance. The Anglo-Irish believed that any sign of weakness could prove fatal. Within the community, society functioned much as in England: it was a layered society, in which families intermarried roughly according to their rank.[5] The community's size bred familiarity, and pride of place led the Anglo-Irish to frown upon new settlers. The English born, viewed with suspicion and thought to be interlopers with an economic or political agenda, were not readily accepted. Within this tight-knit community the Wellesleys took root. They were not among the elite but were respectable and counted among their number a Keeper of the Castles of Kildare and Carbery, Sheriff of Kildare, and Justice Itinerant. In other words, they were modest office holders. They married into families with names such as Plunket, Fitzgerald, Cusack, and Colley, names that regularly appear in Irish (and Wellesley) history. The Colleys, who are central to the story of the Wellesley brothers, probably arrived in Ireland in the fifteenth century, about the time the family established itself in county Meath.[6]

The Reformation profoundly changed Ireland. The Anglo-Irish viewed with interest and concern Henry VIII's quarrel with the pope. It stood to reason that the native Irish would not be interested in the English king's views on the church. They were comfortable with what they had, mostly because it was theirs. As for the Old English, they resented the king's insistence on unequivocal adherence to the religious settlement, but their lack of enthusiasm stemmed from the absence of a substantive quarrel with the church. Consequently, some chose loyalty to both the king and the Roman church. This dualism did not sit well with the Tudors of the sixteenth century, and it combined with the issue of Irish autonomy to make relations tense. Henry VIII considered opposition to the Act of Supremacy from any quarter a challenge to his authority. Nevertheless, he was reluctant to commit precious resources to Ireland at a vulnerable time in England's history. The same could be said for Elizabeth I. Eventually, however, both monarchs employed force in Ireland. For Henry and Elizabeth, recognition of their spiritual and temporal authority seemed natural and just, reflecting the standards of other European monarchs. And for them, the issue was more than that of authority; it was a matter of national security. England's continental adversaries had discovered that Ireland constituted Britain's vulnerable flank. Therefore, in the interest of national security, the crown sought to establish firm control in Ireland. This made certain an increased English military and administrative presence, which in turn compromised Irish autonomy.[7] The crown equated security with loyalty and therefore considered loyalty both a political and a religious matter.

The Old English faced the complex task of defining their role in this new arrangement. Rejection of the Anglican settlement meant political suicide. Nor would the consequences end there. The monarch planned to confiscate the lands of religiously rebellious Gaelic and Old English lords for distribution among Protestants recruited from England. Thus began the plantation system, whereby land and government would fall into the hands of English and, later, Scottish Protestants.[8] The situation taxed the flexibility and ingenuity of the Old English, presenting them with uncomfortable choices. Many chose the moral high ground of defending their faith and lost everything to the "New English"; four centuries of political dominion disappeared in a couple of generations.

The pace of this process accelerated in the seventeenth century with the coming of the Stuarts. Ireland remained calm under James I and Charles I, who, though Protestants, were Scotsmen and therefore less onerous to the Irish. Old English Catholics found that they had an ear in London and began to feel more secure, but relations with the New English remained strained because Protestants were eager to continue the process of dispossessing Catholics of property and influence. In 1641, on the cusp of civil war, Catholic landowners concluded that they could no longer rely on the king for support and that they were at the mercy of Protestants. They rose in violent rebellion. The civil war prevented intervention and intensified the struggle between Catholics and Protestants. Clearly, ethnicity alone no longer constituted the point of dispute in Irish politics; religion and economics became essential ingredients of the proverbial Irish stew.[9]

With the victory of parliamentary forces, Oliver Cromwell went to Ireland to pacify the country and to exact revenge for the rebellion of

1641. In the end, the Catholics were overpowered and their property confiscated. Even some Catholics who could prove noninvolvement in the rebellion were moved to marginal lands west of the Shannon River. Cromwell's activities set off a new wave of immigration to strengthen the Protestant community. The restoration of Charles II in 1660 did not significantly alter the Cromwellian settlement, though some Protestants and Catholics who could prove loyalty to the crown were restored to their original holdings.

But the accession of James II fortified Catholics and gave rise to a growing restiveness and militancy. The Glorious Revolution put an end to that. The Protestant William of Orange took an army to Ireland and snuffed out the Catholic movement one more time in 1690. In the end, Ireland was left in the hands of first-generation, Protestant, English settlers, the descendants of settlers from the reigns of Elizabeth I and James I, and the Scottish landowners in Ulster. Only a few descendants of the Old English, who had adjusted to the changing political and religious conditions, remained as landowners and in positions of influence. The Wellesleys and the Colleys were among this group. How, why, and when they made the switch to Anglicanism is unclear, and whether they were sincere Protestants or mere opportunists can never be determined. But to classify them as opportunists would seem unfair. The decision to abandon a community to which they had belonged since the twelfth century could not have been easy.[10]

What is clear is that the Wellesleys were among the few Old English survivors, which speaks volumes on them. Ireland in the sixteenth and seventeenth centuries was a perilous place. To endure required resourcefulness, courage and quick-wittedness, and a large measure of luck. The Wellesleys must have had all these. They were not prominent people, and perhaps their insignificance served them well. Yet despite their best efforts, even they were not invulnerable to sudden misfortune. During the reign of Charles I, for example, the Wellesley patriarch, Valerian, was one of those who had his estates confiscated. Whether Valerian was a Catholic backslider, politically unreliable, or a victim of circumstance is unclear. In any case, his heir, Garret, successfully petitioned Charles II for the return of the family's property.[11] A sobering experience, it must have impressed upon the Wellesleys the fragility of their situation. As the eighteenth century dawned with the victory of the Williamites, even the Anglo-Irish of recent origin had reason to feel insecure. Having gone to Ireland to claim gifts of land and the right to govern, they were fully aware of Ireland's mercurial nature following the experiences of 1641 and 1690. The Wellesleys, and other Old English families like them, were not a part of this group and therefore had to have been even less certain of their place in the new Ireland. They would become a part of Ascendancy Ireland, but their only true security came from the family. The Wellesley brothers were a product of this experience; as they scrambled up the social and political ladders in the late eighteenth century, they remained remarkably clannish. In the midst of adversity, their first instinct was to band together in support of one another.

The Ireland that emerged from the Glorious Revolution was, from the beginning, schizophrenic. The ruling class, known as the Ascendancy, based their commanding position on the simple facts that they were Protestant and owned most of the land. Thus they were juxtaposed with Catholic Irish and Old English, who were mostly landless and powerless. The fact that the few dominated the many, economically and politically, did not make Ireland an anomaly in eighteenth-century Europe, nor did it represent a dramatic departure from Ireland's recent and distant past. However, that the underclass viewed the ruling class as conquerors, both ethnically and religiously oppressive, made Ireland unique. Although the Ascendancy aped the British ruling class, they could not have felt confident in their supremacy; memories of the events of the seventeenth century were fresh. To protect themselves, they responded legislatively and symbolically, passing laws excluding Catholics from the political life of Ireland and limiting and regulating property ownership and inheritance. Many of these laws—petty and mean and usually not enforced—were there to define place. They did just that. Protestant and Catholic attitudes were fixed in mutual antipathy. Such being the case, the Ascendancy, like the Old English before them, were conservative in their governance of Ireland. For them, change threatened stability.[12]

The desire for stability led the Ascendancy to re-create in Dublin the political life of London. The center of Dublin politics, therefore, became the Irish parliament (though it lacked real legislative power), along with the lord lieutenant. The institutional replication was matched in mortar and stone by the construction of Parliament House at College Green. This extraordinary structure became the symbol of Ascendancy Ireland, and it prompted a general renovation of the city into a modern European capital. Here is where the schizophrenia set in. On the one hand, the Ascendancy was defined by its relationship with Catholic Ireland; on the other, by its relationship with London. The first was simple and clear, the second murky and complicated. It was an old problem. While seeking stability through the trappings of the English, the Anglo-Irish also tried to define a separate identity. They sought legislative independence from England while declaring allegiance to the king. In a sense, they saw themselves as caught between two very different forces: the resentful Catholic Irish and the condescending English. One they sought to repress; the other they regarded as repressive.

So the Wellesleys were products of two different traditions: the Old English and the Ascendancy, both of them alien minorities ruling over an indigenous majority. The former, however, experienced a dramatic loss of both power and place as a consequence of political and religious forces that they neither understood nor controlled. Those who survived by joining the New English were cognizant of a proud past and sensitive to their diminished role. As members of the Ascendancy, they pandered to English styles and mores while chafing at their second-class status. If they bothered to think of it, the Wellesleys of Ascendancy Ireland must have known that in the British world they suffered the liability of being Anglo-Irish, and in Ascendancy Ireland they suffered the liability of being Old English.

The Wellesleys emerge into the clear light of history during the Ascendancy period, and what becomes apparent is that they were a confluence of Wellesley and Colley blood. The families had been tied by marriage for generations, so it is no surprise that the childless Garret Wellesley bequeathed his estates in Meath and his name to his first cousin Richard Colley in 1728.[13] This Richard Colley Wellesley belonged to a large and relatively prosperous family, but had it not been for Garret's generous gift, Richard could not have looked forward to a particularly bright future. Like many of his fellow Irish gentry, Richard had attended Trinity College, Dublin. There is nothing to suggest intellectual prowess, but he acquired refined tastes and exhibited an advanced sociability. He married Elizabeth Sale in 1719 at the age of twenty-nine, and they settled into a modest house just outside Dublin.[14] Nine years later he came into his inheritance. The amiable Richard appreciated his good fortune, rather like the winner of a lottery, and he enthusiastically adopted an expansive generosity. Richard was both gentleman farmer and member of the Irish parliament for the borough of Trim, but these were only sidelines. He spent his time entertaining his friends and enlarging, remodeling, and embellishing Dangan Castle and its extensive grounds.

Wellesley's obsession with socializing and improving his estates reflected the values of Ascendancy Ireland. The rise of elegant Georgian country houses mirrored the rebuilding of Dublin. Historian R. F. Foster writes, "The Ascendancy built in order to convince themselves not only that they had arrived, but that they would remain. Insecurity and the England-complex remained with them to the end."[15] It is safe to say that Richard Wellesley (who appears to have been governed more by emotion and instinct than by reason) never thought much about the reasons for his actions. Thrilled to be a man of means and the owner of a large estate, he also had the good fortune to take charge of his property at the onset of a long-term economic boom. In short, there was plenty of money, and it allowed Wellesley not only to build but also to follow the Ascendancy upper crust to London to partake of the city's social amenities. Wellesley loved people and a good time. The only obstacle to his enthusiasm was Elizabeth, who preferred a quiet life.[16]

Dangan Castle rose out of the rolling, fertile lands of county Meath, twenty miles from Dublin and seven miles from Trim. The region lacked the rugged natural beauty of other Irish counties, and contemporary accounts of it are not flattering. From this nondescript landscape, Richard Wellesley tried to create an earthly paradise. Early on, he began to plant trees; next came the ornamental water. By the time he finished, his park boasted a lake of twenty-six acres, containing islands, waterfowl, and miniature ships and fortifications. Spreading out over six hundred acres, the park, accessed by gravel walks, was laid out in eighteenth-century style. Progressing through it, one encountered statues of Roman gods, temples, and obelisks. It was an extravagant project that occupied Wellesley for a lifetime.[17] Unfortunately, it was not only costly but also wasteful. Six hundred acres devoted to garden and park meant six hundred acres that were not in meaningful production. Even the agriculturalist and author Arthur Young, during his tour of Ireland, commented on it.[18]

As for Dangan Castle, it was more in keeping with Wellesley's status as a country gentleman—not inconsequential but far from grand. Mrs. Delany, a close family friend who visited Dangan on several occasions, described it as "convenient" while lavishing praise on the grounds and the hospitality. Along with the hospitality came music:

an organ and a harpsichord stood prominently in the great hall, and Wellesley at any moment might pick up a violin. The music is significant. It captured the imagination and interest of Wellesley's heir, Garret.

The long-awaited Garret arrived on 19 July 1735, preceded by two doting sisters. All the Wellesleys must have considered Garret something of a miracle, being born sixteen years after Richard and Elizabeth's marriage. Elizabeth enjoyed little time with her son, however, as she died three years later. The family recovered quickly from her death. A shy and awkward sort, she had played little part in her husband's social life. Her daughters, by contrast, resembled their father: happy, eager, sociable, and warmhearted. In short order, they stood in as mother to Garret.[19] From the start, they indulged the boy. But this is understandable in a house without a mother, inhabited by sweet-tempered people who apparently worried about little. Garret began listening to and playing music at a young age, which pleased his father, who made every effort to promote this interest and develop his son's talent. For Garret was a prodigy.

One cannot help but be amazed by the lifestyle of these Wellesleys. In an artificial dreamland created out of the rolling countryside of county Meath, they simply enjoyed life, oblivious to the world around them. Richard sat for Trim in the Irish House of Commons, but there is little to suggest that he took that responsibility seriously. Were he and his family frivolous? Perhaps, but naive might be a better description. Neither malicious nor pretentious, they followed the fun, and if they could not find it, they made it. Of course they were lucky; they could afford to live in idle bliss. Their ignorance of Ireland's stormy history and their disregard for the future are curious. In their style of life, as in other things, perhaps they reflected the times.

Young Garret, meanwhile, grew up nicely. At least he pleased Mrs. Delany: "My godson, Master Wellesley, is a most extraordinary boy; he was thirteen last month, he is a very good scholar, and whatever study he undertakes he masters it most surprisingly. . . . He is a child among children, and as tractable and complying to his sisters, and all that should have any authority over him, as the little children can be to you."[20] He was, in short, not a rebellious child and showed none of the aggressiveness (or ambition) of his forebears or descendants.

On 9 July 1748, after years at the center of Irish social and political life, Richard Wellesley was rewarded with an Irish peerage as Baron Mornington of Meath.[21] He took his seat in the Irish House of Lords at a good time, with his daughters married and Garret about to enter Trinity College. Garret progressed through Trinity smoothly; he completed the B.A. in 1754 and the M.A. in 1757. Trinity was the melting pot of Ascendancy Ireland, and Garret would be associated with it for most of his life. That fact—along with his talent, his pleasing personality, and his father's social and political connections—gave him a place in Dublin society. He had a reputation as an outstanding musician and composer, and his glees and church music proved popular in both England and Ireland.

Lord Mornington died on 31 January 1758, and Garret succeeded to the title and the Dangan estates. He was twenty-three years old. After a period of mourning, the new Lord Mornington might easily be imagined as feeling smug: he possessed ample means, had an attractive estate, and moved easily in Ascendancy society. He was, however, brought up short in his search for a wife. In 1758 he proposed marriage to Lady Louisa Lennox, third daughter of the third Duke of Richmond, the lord lieutenant. The daughter of a duke was above Mornington's touch, even if he, lacking a sense of place, did not realize it. When Lady Louisa received a better offer, he was dismissed with the explanation that she did not love him.[22]

Not given to sulk, Garret wooed the eldest daughter of a Dublin banker, Arthur Hill (later, Lord Dungannon). Not much is known of the genesis of this curious match. From the daughter of the lord lieutenant and a duke to that of a banker with no fortune and little social clout is a gigantic step downward. But Garret (who had few social or practical sensibilities) was unperturbed by the course of events and happy with his selection of the sixteen-year-old Anne.

Anne Hill was a mere girl when she married Garret. Mrs. Delany, although generous in her description of Anne's physique, observed that she was "rather a little clumsy" and was troubled by her spontaneous, even giddy personality:

> I believe Mrs. Hill has been very careful in the common way of the education of her daughters; they are in very good order, and civil. What I think L. M. [Lady Mornington] may be wanting in, is what few people have attained at her age, who have not had some real superiority of understanding and a little experience of the manners of the world; nor *could she learn* from her mother that politeness of behavior and address, which is not

> only *just but right.* She is pretty, excessively good-natured, and happy in her present situation; but I own I think my godson required a wife that knew more the punctilios of *good breeding,* as he is *much wanting* in them *himself,* and those things *should not* be wanting in men of rank and fortune.[23]

This is hardly a ringing endorsement of either husband or wife. Mrs. Delany did not see them as ready for the world, and she despaired for the future because in neither did she find a foundation on which to build. There were no strengths in one to compensate for the deficiencies in the other. Perhaps what she saw was the contrast between the gentrified, rural culture of the Wellesleys and the commercial, urban background of the Hills. One wonders, from Anne's later social aspirations, whether she believed, as did Mrs. Delany, that Garret had married beneath himself.

True to the precedent set by his father, Garret provided generously for his bride. He promised a jointure of £1,400 a year and annual pin money in the amount of £500. Garret (with an income of £8,000 a year from his estate) could well afford the expense initially.[24] The Morningtons married on 6 February 1759 and made Dangan Castle their primary residence. They also had the Dublin house on Grafton Street and the occasional sojourn in London. Life must have seemed bright to Anne, and she should be excused her "giddiness." She was, after all, very young, and to all appearances, she had fallen into the lap of prosperity and security. While she occupied herself bearing and raising children, Garret attended to his music.

Here too the future appeared bright. Mornington enjoyed success in his chosen field. Respected as a musician and composer both in Dublin and in London, his compositions (including "When for the World's Repose My Chloe Sleeps," "Come Fairest Nymph," and "Here in Cool Grot") were well known. To call Lord Mornington a genius would be stretching the point, but he possessed some of the eccentricities of genius. He is said to have been the first nobleman seen on the streets of London carrying a violin. Mornington became doctor and professor of music at Trinity College, Dublin. Successful as he was, his musical pursuits brought little remuneration, but so long as his income was substantial he could not have cared.

Though Mornington was intelligent and talented, he was also focused on his music and seems to have been blithely unaware of everyday practicalities and especially ignorant of the business of estate management. There is something of the absent-minded professor about him. He and his young wife got blissfully on with life and left the management of the estate in the hands of others just when Ireland entered a period of economic decline. In time, that decline diminished the family's income, a fact that Mornington was slow to appreciate. The consequence was increasing debt as the family failed to accommodate to its changing circumstances.

Although other Anglo-Irish families found themselves in similar straits, the Morningtons stood out for their irresponsibility. Their eldest son, Richard, later described them as "frivolous and careless," a judgment that may be close to the truth.

Undeniably true is the fact that two generations of Wellesley good fortune were about to run out, and Lord and Lady Mornington seem to have been aware of it. There is something reminiscent of Louis XV in Garret Wellesley; *"Aprez-moi le deluge"* seems an apt description of his attitude. Perhaps incompetence in matters of business paralyzed him. Whatever the case, not only was the Wellesley fortune spent, but Garret and Anne demonstrated little of the *joie de vivre* that characterized the first Lord Mornington and his family or the resourcefulness and determination of earlier Wellesleys and Colleys. The next generation of Wellesleys were both resourceful and determined.

Lord and Lady Mornington wasted little time attending to the serious business of producing an heir. On 20 June 1760, in the family's Dublin house, Anne gave birth to her first child, and to him went the family name Richard Colley Wellesley. Not long after, Lord Mornington was elevated to an earldom. Anne was a very young woman when she became a parent and entered the adult world, but suggesting that she was not ready for her new station would be presumptuous. Motherhood clearly thrilled her, and Richard (though followed by eight siblings) remained her favorite. Nothing would be spared in the raising of the heir; he would have the best of everything, beginning with his education. At the same time, the responsibilities of parenthood changed Anne.

As parents tend to see in their children the future, and their legacy, Lady Mornington can be excused for seeing her son as extraordinary. In reality, his world did not extend beyond Dangan Castle. Garret was an Irish peer; his world was far from cosmopolitan; and the Wellesleys were not a prominent family. None of this caused his lordship much discomfort. One of his most remarkable traits, which he shared with his father, was his complacency. Happy as he was, not a hint of pretentiousness shadowed his character. Unfortunately, neither did a hint of ambition.

Anne would make up for that. In maturity Lady Mornington was not an endearing character. Because she became cold and demanding, none of her children much loved her—not even Richard, on whom she doted. She nonetheless raised a remarkable brood: the brothers' talent and intellect came from both parents, but their ambition and energy came from Anne. There is, however, a very narrow line between ambition and pretense, and it is impossible to tell on which side of that line Lady Mornington stood. Her aspirations for her children, especially the eldest, increased with age and the number of children she bore. She developed an almost fanatical determination to see them move up in the world. Reconstructing the relationship between Anne and Garret is impossible, but when their children arrived, the personalities of Lord and Lady Mornington went in opposite directions. There is no question that Anne dominated the marriage; what one wonders is whether Garret conceded gracefully or whether his wife's domination became a source of tension between them. Benjamin Disraeli, perpetuating gossip in his *Reminiscences* a generation later, suggests the latter:

> The Duke of Wellington's mother, the old Countess of Mornington, was one of the wickedest women that ever lived, a female tyrant of the Middle Ages, or what we sometimes read of in oriental history—the temper of a daemon heartless & debauched. When Lord Mornington woke in the morning he rang for his valet & used to say "Has your lady rung her bell?" "Yes; my Lord." "How is she?" "Well my Lord I hear she is very crump." "Oh! then you lock my door, & go away with the key in your pocket."[25]

In any case, Anne's life changed dramatically at age seventeen, when she gave birth to Richard; no sooner had she become accustomed to one child than a second, the first Arthur, arrived in January 1762, followed by William in May 1763. The short-lived Francis came in 1765, and Anne in 1768. By that time, Lady Mornington had placed Richard and Arthur in a nearby boarding school in the village of Portarlington.

The school, run by Miss Susanna Towers, was fashionable, attended by other scions of the Irish aristocracy. It taught writing and mathematics, along with spoken French. Little is known of the first Arthur, but Richard, by all accounts, was a delicate, even fragile boy. He kept close to Miss Towers and did not play the more active games. From an early age, he must have possessed charm and a captivating intellect, because Miss Towers and others at the school favored him. The attention he received perhaps increased when Arthur died at the school of smallpox. Certainly the proprietors would have felt an increased obligation to the Morningtons after such a misfortune.[26] In any case, Richard enjoyed his days at Portarlington.

The picture is one of a boy who, by the age of six or seven, was already self-important. He tutored his classmates and regaled them with extemporaneous mimicry of visitors passing through the school. That he maintained some of the friendships that he made at Portarlington into adulthood suggests that he must not have been insufferable, however. By age eleven, it was time to move on; those close to him knew that he possessed brilliance, something that Anne more than likely took for granted. In the meantime, she had given birth to the second Arthur, the future Duke of Wellington, in 1769, followed by Gerald in 1770. At this moment, the course of Wellesley history changed dramatically, when Richard was sent to finish his schooling in England.

No Wellesley before him had done this; an Irish education had sufficed. It hardly seems possible that the break with family tradition came from Garret, but if Anne was the source, what would have been her motives? After thirteen years of marriage to Garret, Anne had become keenly aware of her family's limitations in the world of Irish aristocracy, mostly because of her husband's lack of social ambition. Rightly or wrongly, she believed that the best way to break out of this restricted world was through her children. She would provide them with an English education.

It was a bold and expensive step. Not only would a fashionable English education be costly, but so too would moving the family to London to be closer to Richard and his brothers at school. Regardless, the family moved to London when Richard enrolled at Harrow, where he suffered an inglorious and brief career. His first year coincided with the death of the headmaster, the Reverend Robert Sumner, in 1771. Sumner was replaced by an Eton man, Benjamin Heath, selected over Samuel Parr, a popular assistant master at Harrow. Several students, including young Richard, rose in protest, giving scant thought to the gravity of their actions; the result was expulsion.[27]

There is no record of Richard's or his parents' reaction to this event, but one can imagine their consternation. In the first place, it revealed lack of judgment, if not character, which neither Richard nor his parents would have been willing to concede. More important, it gave rise to the quandary of what to do next. Were other suitable schools, such as Winchester and Eton, likely to accept the young miscreant? Or would the family have to go home to Dangan Castle? The unease in the Wellesley household must have been palpable.

Fortunately, Eton opened its doors to young Richard, who never looked back. He loved Eton; it became the object of wistful reminiscences in the years to come. His remains lie beneath the antechapel, over which, as his biographer Iris Butler points out, Etonians ever since have trod.[28] That Richard should have so loved Eton reveals an interesting side to his character. Preparatory school was a daunting experience intellectually, physically, and emotionally. As Richard in his early years was a delicate soul, he might have buckled under the pressure. Instead he thrived, energized by the environment. No doubt he fully expected to succeed, but there was more to it than this. Richard's keen and active mind, both disciplined and imaginative, responded to the curriculum and the society. He had the best tutors: first Jonathan Davies, who in 1773 became headmaster, and then John Norbury. He boarded with Mrs. Mary Young, who had long been associated with Eton and was considered the best of Eton "dames."[29]

At Eton, Richard enjoyed the best of everything, just as his mother had planned. That the situation worked out this way is remarkable, however, because the Morningtons were not noteworthy people, to say the least, and England's elite constituted Eton's clientele. Richard was probably unaware of his status, as yet. He was, after all, considered a nobleman, and he found out very quickly that he was an intellectual match for anyone. He made fast friendships, the most important of which was with William Grenville, two years his senior. This friendship endured into middle age, when it faded because of political disagreements, Richard's fragile ego, and William's peculiar character. What held them together was enthusiasm for the classics and vivid imaginations. Eton's intellectual leaders were generally destined for great things, and the two engaged in schoolboy speculations on how they would run the world.[30]

But what of the rest of the family? William was just three years behind his redoubtable eldest brother, and he too was destined for

Eton. William was probably first educated at the diocesan school in Trim. As the trusted confidant of his brother Arthur, William later led an active political life, but his early history is obscure, perhaps because he was an undistinguished student.[31] Like his grandfather, he was chosen by a cousin (in this case, William Pole of Ballyfin) as his heir. William, who would be well provided for, was not in need of a thorough education. He entered Eton in 1774, and though his tutor and dame are not noted, one must assume that he followed Richard in the care of Norbury and Young. In 1776, when the Morningtons were beginning to feel the pinch of Ireland's declining economy and their own extravagance, he left Eton and joined the navy to have something to do until he came into his inheritance in 1778. He then added "Pole" to his name.[32]

The Morningtons placed their daughter Anne in the hands of a governess for instruction in etiquette and French. Her letters reveal her as intelligent and proud but resentful of her brothers' successes. She forever asked for money, pointing out that she never had their opportunities. This probably grated on them, but they never rejected her. She was one of them—she was a Wellesley.

The younger boys (Arthur, Gerald, and Henry, who was born in 1773) took their early educations either at Trim or at Brown's School in Chelsea while awaiting their turns at Eton. They are unlikely to have been particularly challenged or made ready for Eton. Wellington biographer Lady Longford believes that Arthur received and achieved very little at Brown's.[33] All the while, they grew up in Richard's shadow, joined by another sister, the Morningtons' last child, Mary.

These years in London must not have been easy. Here was a large, ambitious family transplanted from Ireland. With shrinking revenues from the Irish estates and dramatically increased expenses from choosing to live in London and enrolling the children in the country's most expensive schools, the family lurched towards bankruptcy. Garret was a likable sort, but his unambitious nature did nothing to halt the precipitous decline in the family's fortunes.

Anne Wellesley, wife and mother to this collection of souls, had given birth to nine children (seven of whom survived childhood) in sixteen years. In her one finds the guts of the family. She envisioned her family moving upward and onward. In the absence of documentary evidence, one can only speculate about her thinking based on the decisions she made. She realized that though her husband enjoyed a good reputation in the Anglo-Irish community, real advancement—let alone power and influence—would not be the result of a musical career. Poorly educated but very clever, Anne discovered that few took her husband seriously. Moreover, she came from the bourgeoisie. Her father was a banker, and though he and his family were acquainted with Dublin society, they did not belong to it. While that society would have appeared very attractive to a sixteen-year-old girl who knew nothing about it, upon marriage she discovered just how small and confining it was. At that point, she concluded three things: that she wanted a broader world for her children, that a broader world could only be found in England, and that if the family were to join that broader world, she would have to be the driving force behind it. There were, after all, no incentives for Lord Mornington to go to London. He had been made doctor and professor of music at Trinity, an institution that had been so much a part of his formative years. His father had made Dangan Castle a comfortable place, and he had acquired a new house in Dublin where he and his wife could join society when they felt the need. Why would he want to leave? Why would anyone want more?

Anne wanted more, however, and young Richard offered the opportunity to obtain it. Their diminishing fortune could be restored only by the children. Nevertheless, if she believed that an English education would provide an automatic entrée into English society, she miscalculated. More was needed: talent, wealth, and a patron. Here were her blind spots. She understood English society no better than Irish. The doors to the noble house of the British oligarchy, kept locked, required special keys to open them. Such keys were hard to obtain. Be that as it may, Anne grimly pushed her family onward and upward; in the process she became a hard woman. What she accomplished was very nearly heroic: she bore nine children, supported a husband who needed as much care and direction as the children, and successfully promoted her family despite diminishing means. When the young Wellesleys reached school age, she patched together the family's resources as best she could, and she did so very dispassionately.

The children must have felt this formidable woman's drive. The message she conveyed, spoken or unspoken, was that the future lay in England, in working hard, and in taking advantage of every opportunity. She instilled a sense of family solidarity, convincing her children that only from one another could they derive reliable support. And she stressed that in Richard lay the family's destiny. This was, after all, the eighteenth century. In a family such as the Wellesleys, only the heir had the remotest chance of making a serious mark. The rest could hope only for respectability. And if the eldest did make a name for himself, he might be able to make his siblings' progress easier.

Gerald and Henry were bright, eager boys. Arthur, however, was an enigma. As a youngster, he resembled his father more than his mother. Neither particularly energetic nor ambitious, he took an interest in music, which must have pleased his father. Arthur learned to play the violin, though how well is uncertain. His mother was not pleased. She knew from firsthand experience the unprofitability of a career in music. Unfortunately, to her mind, Arthur apparently exhibited no interests other than music. More to the point, she believed him to be a dull boy. The Wellesleys rarely spoke of their childhoods and how they got on with one another, but judging from their clannishness as adults, relations between them must have been reasonably good. Richard, nine years older than Arthur, played the role of senior sibling well. He visited his brothers at school and gave them little, patronizing gifts. The three youngest brothers looked up to him.

Richard left Eton in 1778 and went up to Christ Church, Oxford, in December. He took with him a legendary reputation as a classical scholar. On one occasion, when George III dropped by the school with the celebrated actor David Garrick to hear speeches from the boys, Richard delivered Buckingham's scaffold speech to great effect. When an enthralled Garrick commented, "You have done more than I could ever do, you have drawn tears from the King," Richard replied matter-of-factly: "You never spoke before his Majesty in the character of a fallen, favorite, arbitrary Minister."[34] It is not surprising, then, that his tutor was the brilliant William Jackson, destined to be Regius Professor of Greek and Bishop of Oxford: superb training for a superb mind. At Oxford, Richard rejoined his friend from Eton, William Grenville, who had matriculated two years earlier and whose scholarly reputation equaled his. They were joined by Henry Bathurst (then Lord Apsley and the future Earl Bathurst) and Henry Addington, the future Viscount Sidmouth. More than Addington and Bathurst, Wellesley and Grenville were scholars. With an eye to the future, Richard worked hard. In July 1780, encouraged by William Jackson, he competed for the University

Prize for Latin Verse, which he won with an elegy on the death of Captain Cook. He and Grenville celebrated together, as William had won the previous year. A formidable duo, they might have been insufferable. Their portraits to this day guard the doors to the hall at Christ Church. There was time for socializing and a normal dose of college mischief making, but that was secondary. Wellesley was a natural student, so much so that an academic life would have suited him well.

The Marchioness Stafford observed in 1787, "I have a notion that at Oxford, if they are good scholars, they contract High Ideas of themselves, which wear off when they come to live with the rest of the world."[35] Unfortunately, Richard's "high ideas" of himself would never wear off. He had, after all, been led to believe that he was destined for greatness. As it happened, he would come to "live with the rest of the world" sooner than he expected. In May 1781, his father died unexpectedly at the young age of forty-five. It would be easy to make the cynical suggestion that Garret Wellesley did not die of stress. From outward appearances, he was a contented man, happily engaged with his music and uninvolved in the trials and tribulations of raising a large family. We do not know much about him as a father, because only Richard, William, and Anne were old enough to appreciate him as such. Garret, however, had had a warm relationship with his father, so why would he not have had the same with his own children? One cannot imagine him as a stern and demanding parent. No one in his own family—his mother, father, siblings—was ever harsh, and besides, that role fell to Anne. One would hope that he loved and was loved by his enormous brood. Was he ignorant of his declining fortunes? This is hardly likely, since he gradually mortgaged the estate in Ireland to keep up with mounting expenses. Garret had to sign off on each transaction and certainly knew that he and Anne had squandered a respectable fortune. Such a realization might cause stress in even the most unflappable of people. Upon reflection, Garret is a tragic figure. He would have preferred Ireland, moving between Dangan Castle, Trinity College, and Dublin, composing and directing. This would have made him happy and perhaps preserved his fortune.

With Garret dead and Richard the second earl, Lady Mornington—a dowager while relatively young—had five children yet to raise. William was launched, and though Richard would opt to leave Oxford without a degree, everything that could be done for him had been done. That left Anne, age thirteen; Arthur, age twelve; Gerald, age eleven; Henry, age nine; and Mary, age eight. They laid their father to rest in Grosvenor Chapel on Audley Street with great ceremony and at great expense. This was Richard's decision, and spending £80 on the funeral was his first, but far from last, extravagance.

2

Richard Takes Charge

Because of Garret's benign and passive behavior as head of the family, his death did not seem an occasion for unease on the part of either his heir or his widow. They might be expected to carry on as they always had. However, this turned out not to be the case.

For Richard, the fact that he should decide to cut short his Oxford days was the first sign that his father's premature death left him sensing that his life had changed. He soon recognized that the earldom brought with it unconsidered responsibilities. There is no evidence that before his father's death he had been given the slightest hint of the Irish estate's compromised condition: the debts to be managed with much-diminished resources. He was twenty-one years of age, and he had to learn quickly how to squeeze an income from an estate that had hitherto provided what was needed. There was also his immediate future to consider. He had been educated to take his place in the political world as his friend Grenville was doing. But he was at a loss as to how to begin. The halcyon days at Eton and Oxford had not prepared him for this; he had expected a period of transition as he entered young adulthood. Such uncertainty was new ground, and to make matters worse, he could not ignore the fact that his mother, still a relatively young woman, had five children yet to raise. What would be his role in this?

That point brings us to Lady Mornington. Her husband's death left her more anxious than mournful, as she had to face the uncertainties created by her own ambition. There was the generous jointure of £1,600 a year, yet she could not help but wonder where that money might come from and for how long. And while she could manage on such a sum, raising the children would be problematic. Naturally she expected Richard to help. In point of fact, he had no obligation to do so; she would have to rely on his sense of familial obligation. Is it any wonder, then, that the first weeks after Mornington's death found her in the grip of panic? By her own account, she sent scolding letters to Richard, complaining of her straitened means and challenging him to do something about them. There was little time for grieving. Richard proved up to the task. In July, he sent his mother £800, half a year's jointure, along with £15,000 left by Garret for the younger children in the hope that interest on the sum would meet their needs until they were educated, at which time the principal could be used to launch them into careers or marriage. Richard also asked that all outstanding bills be sent to him. Lady Mornington, who doubted whether £15,000 would be sufficient, informed her son that she would need more than his father had provided.[1]

If Richard anticipated an independent life for himself, Anne soon put that notion to rest. Her life, twenty-two years after her marriage, was entirely different from what she had expected. Mrs. Delany's critical assessment in 1759 of the newlyweds Anne and Garret had proved percipient: they had planned their lives very badly. As a widowed mother of seven, only two of whom were independent, Anne could not begin to support the life she had promised herself and her children. That she had seen the reversal of fortune coming did not make it any easier. Surrender, however, was out of the question. Tough and determined, Anne insisted on getting what she felt was rightfully hers and her children's. Richard was the key to the future, but that was as she had planned. She expected him to deliver on her investment.

Unfortunately, Richard, though he always proved reliable and generous in the support of his family, required acknowledgment of his good deeds. He resented his mother's presumption and never forgave her for it. He took her at face value as a cold, severe woman, without bothering to look behind that tough facade. She had, after all, given him what she thought was the best of everything, and she would do what she thought was best for the rest of her children as well. The girlish charm and enthusiasm of her youth were forever gone, and none of the Wellesley children ever warmed to her. As adults, they saw her as meddlesome and judgmental, and they failed to appreciate how much of her they had in themselves. They even maliciously suggested that there was mixed paternity in the family, but visual and circumstantial evidence argues against it.[2]

The estates, the mortgages, and the debts became Richard's responsibility. Anne's was the children. Gerald and Arthur were enrolled at Eton in early 1781 and were placed in the care of Mary Naylor, who had succeeded her sister, Mrs. Young, at the Manor House. No tutor is listed for Arthur, though he likely was attended by Joseph Goodall, who was Gerald's tutor.[3] Gerald proved a superb student, cut from the same mold as Richard but lacking his imagination. No one had much hope for Arthur. As all his biographers are at pains to note, he never volunteered much about his youth, a fact that is interpreted as a product of unhappiness. This is a reasonable assumption. Lady Longford (his most authoritative recent biographer), describes him as awkward, and the Reverend George Gleig (one of the duke's first biographers), as "dreamy, idle, and shy."[4] He was also a hesitant lad. We do know that Arthur differed from his siblings. There is no hint, for instance, that anyone in the family shared his fondness for music. As a youngster, this must have caused him embarrassment.

Lady Mornington never much took to Arthur. She saw him as the odd man out. A couple of curiosities in Arthur's early life help explain this attitude on his mother's part. That he bore the name of a deceased brother is not without precedent, but one wonders whether the second Arthur evoked a memory of the first. In addition, there is confusion over the date and place of his birth. No one seems to know whether it was March, April, or May, and at Dangan Castle or in Dublin. Until Arthur became the Duke of Wellington, no one bothered to set the record straight, and by that time, no one knew for certain.

Such details suggest the extraordinary indifference with which he was treated. Is it any wonder that he was taciturn and at times combative? His fights with Robert "Bobus" Smith and Blacksmith Hughes are a part of Wellingtonian lore, but they are never viewed as a manifestation of the young man's feelings and personality in that period of his life. The other Wellesleys were never in this sense physical. Richard would not have dreamed of physical combat at any point in his life, and such appears to have been the case with Gerald and Henry as well. William possessed a ferocious temper, and his brief stint in the navy must have exposed him to the rough and tumble of life his brothers did not see at that age, but he was not a violent person. How then does one account for Arthur's behavior? After all, throwing stones at a schoolmate while he was swimming and then punching him when he protested was hardly generous. The young Arthur clearly harbored anger attributable to his middle position in a large family and the fact that he was different from and not living up to the standards set by his siblings. Arthur was easy to ignore, and when noticed, it was the product of a misstep. Such a child could be excused for living up to his parents' low expectations. This defeatism manifested itself at school, which he did not like, and where, not surprisingly, he performed poorly.

Richard, seeking to give some direction to his life, retreated to Ireland to take his seat in the Irish House of Lords. Later, the family's seat at Trim would be taken by William, giving the Wellesleys representation in both houses of the Irish parliament.[5] Lady Mornington, meanwhile, traveled between Dangan Castle and London, keeping track of her widely distributed children. Richard found himself in the midst of interesting times in Ireland's history. Henry Grattan, who had come to dominate Irish politics, was in the midst of orchestrating legislative autonomy for the Irish parliament. This he cleverly managed through the gradual creation of an "army" of volunteers to protect the island while England busied herself with the American war.

In due course, London made concessions to Dublin, starting with the "free trade" issue in 1779–80. Next, Grattan and the other outspoken Anglo-Irish nationalist of the day, Henry Flood, led the assault on Poyning's Law and the Declaratory Act of 1720, which together made the Irish parliament subservient to Westminster. Public demonstrations on the part of the volunteers and political chaos in London combined to carry the day. In 1782 Parliament amended Poyning's Law and repealed the Declaratory Act. Grattan's personality and politics captured Mornington's imagination. The strange combination of conservative instincts, high-flown rhetoric, and liberal views towards Irish Catholics caught Mornington's attention.[6]

At the same time, Richard's Eton and Oxford experiences taught that Ireland was a sideshow; the real action was in London, and he took care not to lose touch with his friends there, especially Grenville. In July 1782 he wrote,

> We are all thrown into the utmost consternation by the apparent confusion in the British Cabinet, at this time instability of counsels will be absolute destruction. W. Pitt Secretary of State! and Lord Shelburne Premier! surely the first cannot be qualified for such an office, and the last is, in my opinion, little to be depended upon. . . . I am quite angry with your silence in Parliament; do you remember what Burke said on that head; that a habit of not speaking at all grows upon some men as fast, and is as difficult to be broken through, as a habit of speaking ill; and that he was not sure which of the two was the greater misfortune.[7]

This is an interesting letter for many reasons. First, it is clearly from one young man to another, full of well-considered opinions but exuding inexperience—pompous but enthusiastic. Second, it shows that Richard was as yet unappreciative of the younger Pitt's talents and the importance of Grenville's family ties to him. William Pitt, of course, would become Grenville's patron and Mornington's political patron saint. Finally, there is his pontificating on speech making. How curious it is to find him scolding Grenville just as he would be scolded in future years.

In the summer of 1782, Mornington learned that Grenville's brother, George Nugent-Temple-Grenville, Earl Temple, would be coming to Dublin as lord lieutenant and that Grenville himself would serve as chief secretary in London. Sensing opportunity, he wrote to Grenville in August, "You may consider me as one of your assistant secretaries, a servant though not a slave of the crown; and ready to fag with you at business as we used to fag at Lent verses and Episcopo-pastorals together."[8] Richard, despite his abruptly altered circumstances, was faring well. He enjoyed life in Ireland, thrived in the political environment, and looked forward to a partnership with his old friend: "I need not add that the zeal of my support will be highly increased by the warmth of my friendship for you. . . . I shall deem it a very small tribute paid to that constant, uniform, and ardent friendship which has so often assisted me in every shape."[9]

Realizing that he was but a small player in an important game, Mornington threw his unqualified support to the Grenvilles and the government. He would, in the immediate future, act as agent for the government, running between London (Grenville) and Dublin (Temple) for his friends. His work paid immediate dividends. One of Lord Temple's first responsibilities as lord lieutenant was to institute on behalf of the king a new Irish order of knighthood, the Order of Saint Patrick. Temple, hypersensitive to matters of honor, knew a kindred spirit when he saw one and nominated his young friend to the initial list of fifteen, raising many eyebrows in the Irish House of Lords.[10] Temple and Mornington both craved recognition in the form of awards and titles and in the process irritated friends and family with wails of wounded pride when such things did not materialize.

The times were not without controversy, and Mornington found himself caught up in it. In the aftermath of the great victory of 1782, Grattan began to have second thoughts about the volunteers. He believed that they had outlived their usefulness and had become a liability. Just as the volunteers had proved a double-edged sword to London, so too might they be to him. Further, Grattan was unclear as to his next steps; without articulated goals, a strategy for political action was unnecessary, and a tool for implementation even more so. Flood, by contrast, had clear ideas about what would come next—parliamentary reform—and the volunteers would help him accomplish it.[11] Reform, however, was an uncomfortable subject in Ireland because inevitably it involved discussion of Catholic enfranchisement. Strains between Catholic and Protestant were ever present in eighteenth-century Ireland and lurked behind everything said and done at College Green. Mornington would always be a proponent of Catholic rights and never understood the hyperdefensive mentality of the Anglo-Irish. No doubt this was a product of being educated in England, away from the fray. Still, he was interested in his homeland, and there is even a hint of commitment to it. When Grattan split with Flood over the issue of reform, one might be surprised that Mornington would not have been alienated from the former over his failure to promote Catholic rights. But Grattan could not abide elements of Flood's tactics, and Mornington agreed with Grattan's judgment. Most significant, of course, was the use of the volunteers. Flood lacked Grattan's subtlety, and under his direction, the volunteers appeared menacing. The issue came to a head on 29 November 1783. On that day, Flood introduced a motion in the Commons for the reform of Parliament. His backers astonished the house by wearing their volunteers' uniforms, a blunt reference to the armed units encamped on College Green. Such thinly veiled intimidation backfired on the heavy-handed Flood, with the resounding rejection of his motion. Two days later, in the House of Lords, Mornington added his voice to the Commons' rejection of Flood.[12] It was a clever, thoughtful speech, reflecting Mornington's passion for order—a passion shared by all of the Wellesleys—which would characterize his politics throughout his career.

Even while he was deeply engaged in Irish politics, Mornington's family concerns did not disappear. In 1783, Henry, the youngest of the Wellesley boys, enrolled at Eton, joining Arthur and Gerald under the watchful eyes of Mary Naylor and Joseph Goodall.[13] A bright and eager child, Henry was secure in his place at Eton. The same could not be said for Arthur. Lady Mornington could not support three boys at Eton, so, in consultation with Richard, she removed Arthur.[14] Arthur probably greeted the decision with ambivalence; only the uncertainty of his future could have given him pause. He departed Eton without an education or a friend. Removing Arthur from Eton was one thing, finding something for him to do quite another. Until that decision was made, Lady Mornington sent him to Brighton for a few months of tutoring by the Reverend Henry Mitchell. In early 1785, she packed her bags and left with Arthur for Belgium, one step ahead of her creditors and taking Mary and Anne with her.[15]

In Brussels, the Wellesleys lived with a Louis Goubert, and they were joined by the son of a wealthy Yorkshireman, John Armytage. The pace of life in Brussels must have been leisurely but dull. M. Goubert taught the boys but not well. Certainly they worked on their French, but in general the experience was aimless. Arthur played his violin and gave no hint of talents that might be turned to practical benefit. After a year, Lady Mornington and Richard agreed that the army, that bastion of aristocratic misfits, was the place for Arthur. She returned to London and sent Arthur to the French Royal Academy of Equitation at Angers.[16]

The year and a half spent at Angers proved the first positive experience of Arthur's young life. Angers was more than a finishing school for rich, young aristocrats; it was a thriving academy that took its responsibilities seriously. Horsemanship, fencing, and manners were high on the curriculum, but so were mathematics and the "humanities." Arthur would never be socially sophisticated, but what grace he did have, he acquired at Angers. He gained confidence and learned to speak French flawlessly.[17] As part of a large contingent of English and Anglo-Irish students, he enjoyed life. He even studied. He was, in short, growing up, and he was fortunate to have come of age at Angers and not under the scornful eye of his mother. Equally important, he became acquainted with the France of the ancien régime, and he liked it. All the Wellesleys despised the French Revolution, but their shared view was variously acquired.

Through 1783 Mornington found Irish politics satisfying. But if "all the world's a stage," Dublin most certainly was not the West End, and it was only a matter of time before he realized this truth. The year 1784 found him again traveling the long but gloriously beautiful road between Dublin and London on behalf of the Grenvilles. The responsibility must have yielded a sense of self-importance, because he detested the travel. He complained continuously to Grenville of fatigue and illness, especially seasickness, but in the voice of the true martyr, he assured his friend that "my object always will be the success of those to who [*sic*] I wish well, in preference to my personal interest."[18] The Grenvilles watched out for him but were uncertain as to what they might do. "Pray communicate a little with Mornington about your resignation, etc.," wrote William to his brother. "It will flatter him; and he is beyond measure disposed to you both in Ireland and *here,* to which he looks in a short time; but you must not let him know I have told you that."[19] Temple worked to find Richard a seat in the English House of Commons on Pitt's becoming prime minister, but Mornington, expressing sincere gratitude, declined the offer in expectation of the coming dissolution of Parliament. The strategy worked, and Mornington was elected by the rotten borough of Bere Alston under the patronage of the Earl of Beverley.[20] He had taken an important first step; with seats in both the Irish House of Lords and the English House of Commons, he was a valuable intermediary for the government.

In the autumn of 1784, Mornington exhibited the first signs of frustration with the status quo. The tone of his correspondence with Grenville began to change. He suggested that perhaps he should move to London, the inference being that Grenville should find something profitable for him to do there. A chatty letter reveals an idle man: "I am glad you have returned to Latin and Greek; I hope when I come to London to be able to form some plan with you in that way which may be pleasant and serviceable to both of us. I am grown an early riser, which gives me a great deal of time for reading." Then he gets to the crux of the matter. "I have known and admired, and

God knows, felt the two lines which you quote, *superanda omnis fortuna ferendo est,*"[21] but he continues, "You don't say a word about my quitting Ireland entirely, upon which I asked your opinion." Grenville had tried to be gentle, but Mornington missed the point. The contrast between his subtle, sophisticated understanding of Latin and his failure to pick up on Grenville's hint suggests that he did not want to hear what his friend was telling him. There was little that the Grenvilles could do for him at that time. William responded, stating directly that Mornington should stay in Ireland.[22]

In reality, this spoiled if brilliant man had nothing to offer his friends politically. His title was Irish and recent, his estates were mortgaged; in other words, he possessed neither wealth nor patronage (even in Ireland), facts made more consequential by the fragile political conditions of the time. While he contemplated his fate from the bleak outside, his friends steadily made their way into English political life. Not surprisingly, he was lonely. A letter to Grenville in April 1785 laments, "Pray give my love to Apsley and to all my friends. I wish to God I was with you, for here

> 'I have no mate, nor brother in exile
> Nor has old custom made this life more sweet
> Than that of painted pomp__ __.'[23]

A member of the privy council for Ireland, he continued to work closely with the Grenvilles, and through them he was introduced to Pitt. Finally in September 1786 the Grenvilles delivered; Pitt appointed Mornington a Lord of the Treasury.[24]

It is hard to feel sympathy for Mornington. The Grenvilles had been efficient in finding things for him to do, and they wondered whether they were wise to sponsor him. "I have pressed him most earnestly to make himself master upon the subject of the French treaty," wrote Temple (who had become the Marquis of Buckingham), "and to put himself forward in it; for I am, for many reasons, most earnest that he should justify his appointment."[25]

One area of concern was Mornington's private life. In his lonely commute between London and Dublin, he had discovered women. This should not come as a shock; he was, after all, twenty-six years of age and strikingly handsome. Neither tall nor well built, in old age Mornington would be described as small. In his prime, however, he was of average height and fastidious in dress, grooming, and personal hygiene. His eyes were his most prominent feature, as they were dark and penetrating and surmounted by enormous black eyebrows. With his elegance in manner and style, women found him attractive. Still, this is one of the great intangibles of Richard Wellesley's life. Proud, intelligent, and socially at ease with friends, he should have found that making the acquaintance of women of his station in life came easily. But there is no sign that this was the case. His friend Grenville also appears to have found the opposite sex daunting, and when he married, he did so quietly, taking Wellesley for one by surprise.

Perhaps as young university men they had avoided women and as a result never learned how to socialize with them. The closeness of this friendship inevitably gave rise to rumor, which both men ignored. Wellesley always dressed like a peacock, but the great show of feathers attracted none of his species. Not that he went completely unnoticed. In January of 1786, the *Times* reported: "Lord Mornington is in high request at Paris [he was there placing Arthur at Angers]; the ladies admire his Lordship, because he is a knight of the Order of St. Patrick, and are not at all surprised at his crest being a game cock!"[26]

All of this is significant because Richard Wellesley—unable, for whatever reason, to establish a relationship with a woman of society—turned to women well beneath him socially. A highly sexed man, all his adult life he found outlets among the lower levels of society. He is known to have had a woman in Devonshire, from which he was first returned for Parliament, and very likely had a mistress in Holyhead as well. While the transitory keeping of mistresses in the late eighteenth century was commonplace, his behavior is incomprehensible when measured against his ambition. With an eye to a distinguished political career, Mornington by 1786 had to have become aware of his liabilities. Still, he clearly believed that these could be overcome through his own talent and through connections. But one wonders why he never attempted to address some of the practical constraints facing him through the making of a good marriage. As obvious as this might seem, there is no evidence that he ever tried. True, we now know that he did not bring many assets to the table, but not many people were aware of this when he was a young man on the make. To all appearances he was a reasonably prosperous Irish nobleman, witty, charming, and with the right friends. One is surprised to find the gossipy *Times* following him closely. There appear in its pages regular accounts of his movements between London and Dublin, announcements concerning his health, and even admiring commentaries on his character. On 20 September 1787, the following appeared: "We would recommend to those sprightly, fashionable and amiable young men, who do not at present think of paying their own debts, an occasional attention to the superior character of Lord Mornington, who has been narrowing his public appearances, and circumscribing his pleasures, to discharge a debt of his father."[27] Clearly, political and social eyes were on him, and though a brilliant match was unlikely, a respectable and even advantageous match was certainly within reach. Mornington needed this beyond all else, yet he seems to have been indifferent to the possibility. It frustrated his friends and family, especially his sharp-eyed mother.

To make matters worse, he flouted the conventions of the day. In 1786 Mornington took up residence with Hyacinthe Gabrielle Roland (whom, in all likelihood, he met while in Paris). The daughter of a French actress, Hyacinthe Varis, and the Chevalier Fagan, an Irishman who had settled in France, Hyacinthe was raised in the home of a man named Roland, whose name she bore.[28] The young Hyacinthe joined her mother on the stage and always carried the epithet "daughter of an actress." Nothing is known of the origins of the relationship between Richard and Hyacinthe, but clearly it was infatuation at first sight. An intensely physical relationship ensued, but to Mornington's friends and associates, she was just another of his socially unacceptable women, and they were very concerned.[29] Buckingham wrote to his brother in August 1786, "I have received from Mornington a most affectionate letter upon his appointment, which has enabled me to answer him with much advice as to his future exertions, and with some advice as to the necessity of reconciling his *domestic life* to that public character which we both wish for him."[30] In September he wrote again, "I have a . . . letter from Mornington, very explicit as to *the point* upon which I have writ, and full of assurances."[31] "The point" and the need to reconcile his "domestic life" both clearly refer to Mornington's love life. Whether this means Hyacinthe or his women in general requires conjecture, but the timing points to Hyacinthe. His tastes in women might not have mattered among Foxite Whigs—they might even have been the source of some amusement—but they caused consternation among Pitt's party and did not go unnoticed by the prudish George III.

Mornington's obsession with Hyacinthe mattered more to him than the sage advice of his friend Buckingham, who at this point guided his political career. She was already pregnant with their first child, Richard. Three others would follow in rapid succession: Anne in February 1788, Hyacinthe in February 1789, and Gerald in May 1790. The last child, Henry, was born in 1794. At the same time, Mornington resisted marriage; one wonders whether he would have given up Hyacinthe had opportunity knocked. He was not doing much knocking on his own. He did, however, heed Buckingham's other bit of advice and began making preparations to defend the commercial treaty with France. He had spoken in the Commons before, but this would be his first major responsibility.[32]

There was another outstanding matter to be addressed. On his appointment to the treasury, Mornington had to stand for election. The Earl of Beverley refused to return him for Bere Alston, owing to "neglect of political claims."[33] He therefore stood for Saltash in a contested election that created several difficulties for him. First, he lacked the temperament for electioneering; the very thought of defeat terrified him. Then there was the problem of money. Contested elections were costly, and such an expenditure was ill-timed. To Grenville he wrote, "I tremble at the idea of a contest, and would rather be out of Parliament for some time than risk so heavy and perhaps fruitless expense."[34] Mornington was a man at sixes and sevens: consumed by ambition, desperate to make a name and place for himself in the world of politics and expected to do so by his family, yet vain enough not to accept the prospect of defeat and with financial liabilities that made protracted campaigning impractical. Here, for the first time, Mornington confronted his limitations, and he panicked.

The Grenvilles steadied him, and the election went forward. Though he won, the result was successfully challenged by his opponent, but not before Mornington spoke in the Commons in defense of the commercial treaty. He delivered the speech in February. In May he lost his seat, and Pitt scrambled to find something for him. George III delivered, suggesting in June that Mornington stand for Windsor. Accordingly, Richard presented himself at court on 25 June, and arrangements were made. He stood for election on 20 July, and on 29 November he took his oath for Windsor.[35]

Between June and November, Mornington socialized with Grenville's and Pitt's circle and attended to business in Ireland, neither of which he found particularly satisfactory. The Grenvilles, and everyone else for that matter, had given up on persuading Richard to separate from Hyacinthe. Still, these were uncertain times, and the autumn found him felled by fever. "The Earl of Mornington," reported the *Times*, "lately returned member for Windsor, lies dangerously ill of a fever at his seat in the county of Meath, near Dublin."[36] By October he was back in England, retiring to Buxton to convalesce.

The new year found him actively engaged in the new session of Parliament. As part of Pitt's clique, his mood picked up. Life with Pitt was stimulating. It meant late-night dinners and weekends at Holwood, the prime minister's country house, talking politics and planning strategy. On the evening of 12 May 1788, Mornington, Grenville, and Pitt were accosted on the streets of London by a drunk. The event must have created a stir because Grenville promptly wrote to Buckingham to assure him that all was well. "I am much obliged to your kind attention," Buckingham responded, "for relieving me from the anxiety which I should have felt at seeing your name, and that of Pitt and Mornington, at issue with a drunken madman."[37] The *Times* was more fascinated with Mornington's treatment of the encounter than the event itself: "Lord Mornington's manner of treating a late affront was truly consistent with that propriety and dignity of character which he has always preserved; it was not indicative of resentment, but of ineffable contempt."[38]

That summer he returned to Ireland to check on his crumbling estate and to see Arthur and William. In the autumn, the king fell ill with what historians have now identified as porphyria, a metabolic disorder that periodically deprived George III of his sanity. A political crisis of the first order ensued, and Mornington returned to London to lend his support.

Pitt had experienced some difficulties in his first years as prime minister, but by 1788 the worst had passed; his fiscal reforms were in place and working, and his majorities in the House of Commons were growing. In short, he seemed firmly entrenched and his rivals exiled to the political wilderness. Then came the symptoms of George III's nervous agitation, which would lead to mental incapacity. The king's illness manifested itself first in excruciating intestinal pain. As his strength waned, especially in his limbs, he was eventually forced to use a cane. For the normally robust George III, this was extraordinary. The progress to irrationality was first noted on 22 October 1788. Although he continued to carry on business from Windsor, he acknowledged during the first week of November that he could do so no longer. On 6 November, at dinner with his family, he collapsed completely. Clearly, with the king surrounded by a set of preposterous physicians, something had to be done.

For Pitt, this gave rise to a problem. If and when the king was judged incompetent, a regency would be required. Such responsibility would naturally be conferred upon the Prince of Wales, the future George IV, whose character and politics were at odds with those of his father. What this meant to Pitt, and everyone else, was a prompt change in ministries with the prince's ally, Charles James Fox, taking the lead. Pitt, therefore, sought to do two things: buy as much time as possible in the hope that the king would recover, and fashion a regency bill that by constraining the regent would limit the strength of Fox and the Whigs. The two goals were complementary, and Pitt's pursuit of them reveals him for the strategic genius he was.

The king's condition also gave rise to a dilemma for Mornington. He worried that a regency would not only snuff out his rising prospects but also lead to new elections, which he could ill afford. However, in such a critical situation he could hardly avoid making the investment. If he bowed out when his friends needed him, his career would be over. The prospect weighed heavily on his mind, and Grenville spoke of it to his brother. Temple, in turn, tried to help by offering one of his seats. Here too there were problems:

> If the King should remain in his present unhappy state of mind, and the Parliament be either dissolved, or expire by its natural death under the government of a Regent, I shall think myself, under those circumstances, bound, by my respect for the person who placed me at Windsor, to endeavour to preserve that seat for him; that he may find his own friends, where he was pleased to leave them, whenever he may happen to recover his reason. But I might fail in this attempt to maintain the trust reposed in me, and the expense of the attempt might be such as to disable me from purchasing any other seat; in that case your offer would be most acceptable.[39]

In the end, the king recovered and none of this transpired, but the correspondence provides a glimpse of Mornington's precarious finances and the impact they had on his career and attitude.

Mornington was deeply involved in the regency deliberations; at the same time, Grenville became Speaker of the Commons. The atmosphere, while intense, Mornington found intoxicating—especially his work on the Commons conference committee, to which Pitt had named him. The king recovered, of course, and thanked all who had supported him during his illness. But some benefited more than others from His Majesty's gratitude. Although Mornington could hardly expect much, in August he was reappointed to the treasury along with Pitt, Edward Eliot, Sir John Pratt, and Bathurst. Earlier in the summer, he had been given the post of joint paymaster. And when election time came around in the summer of 1790, the king again sent up Mornington for Windsor.[40]

In July 1790, Richard Wellesley, with no new political prospects on the horizon, set out on a tour of the Continent with Hyacinthe and his brother Gerald, leaving behind his young children. Passing over the same ground on which Arthur would find glory twenty-five years later, Richard observed, "There is not one inch of ground uncultivated; the whole has the appearance of a garden. It is hardly possible to believe it was ever the scene of war; and I could not help regretting that it should be likely to become so again."[41] He would spend the month of August at Spa, and his correspondence with Grenville suggests hope that political developments in London might require his return. However, news from that quarter convinced him that such hopes were futile, and he resolved to go to Italy. September found him in Paris—revolutionary Paris, which he described in some detail. Clearly struck by the changes he observed, Mornington, in a clever turn of phrase, wrote, "You are well able to judge how strange the contrast must be between Paris governed, and Paris governing; but it is so strange in so many ways, that I own I find great difficulty in attempting to answer your question of what strikes me most, for I am quite perplexed by the number and variety of ridiculous and absurd things, which I hear and see every where, and every day."[42] Parisians he found to be enduring economic hardship without much concern and expressing unqualified support for the changes taking place around them. The general breakdown of order frightened him, and he was especially taken aback by the revolutionary press. "The Attorney General's blood would boil," he reported, "at the sight of such audacious bowdlery. The object seems to be everywhere to mark a contempt for all former regulations."[43] The general contempt expressed for established institutions such as the clergy and the aristocracy mystified him.

There was not much for him to do: "The *Aristocrats* are melancholy and miserable to the last degree; this makes the society at Paris very gloomy; the number of deserted houses is immense, and if it were not for the Deputies, the Ambassadors, and some refugees from Brussels, there would be scarcely a gentleman's coach to be seen in the streets."[44] Consequently, Mornington entertained himself by taking in meetings of the revolutionary clubs and the National Assembly. He was much amused. "Have you been told," he asked Grenville, tongue in cheek, "that one leading principle of the club 1789 is a resolution to reform all the defective (that is in their opinion all the) Governments of Europe, and for this laudable purpose they have sent missionaries into many countries already, to preach the example of France, and to teach all mankind how ill they have been governed, and how preferable a state of anarchy and confusion is to the trammels of order and law."[45]

In the National Assembly, he found nothing but anarchy and mediocrity.[46] Even the celebrated count de Mirabeau and Antoine-Pierre Barnarve he considered unimpressive. Observers in the galleries only added to the confusion. Mornington reported that their numbers far exceeded those allowed in the Commons and that they conducted themselves as if they were at some sort of public spectacle. As for the royal family, he found the king and queen much changed: "I went to Court this morning at the Tuilleries, and a most gloomy Court it was; many of the young people of the first fashion and rank wear mourning always from economy. . . . The king seemed well, but I thought his manner evidently humbled since I was introduced to him before; he now bows to everybody, which was not a Bourbon fashion before the Revolution. The queen looked very ill; the Dauphin was with her, and she appeared anxious to show him."[47]

From Paris, Mornington proceeded south, healthy and in good spirits, invigorated by the extraordinary experience of passing the Alps on his way to Turin in October. The pass of Mt. Cenis left an indelible impression.[48] He found both Turin and Genoa worthwhile, but he was especially attracted by the agricultural life of northern Italy. The range of his interests is remarkable. Little escaped his eye, which was equally charmed by prosperous farms, towering mountains, and Renaissance paintings.

As he approached Rome, his pulse quickened. A glimpse of St. Peter's and his first encounter with the Tiber more than assuaged his

initial disappointment at the approach to the city: "Here let me do justice to old Pater Tyberius, who I saw for the first time; he is by no means so contemptible a stream as he has been represented to be; he is of a very handsome breadth, and his banks are so steep, and himself so rapid and noisy, that although it must be owned that he is rather a bilious complexion, I should not have thought him an ugly fellow, even if his name had not been Tyber."[49] He explored the great basilica and clambered about the ruins of old Rome.

His correspondence suggests that his purpose in making the trip was to follow Virgil's path. After falling sick for several days in Naples (and blaming his illness on damp winds), he was revived by a visit to Virgil's tomb. He presented the various arguments concerning its authenticity and concluded that the evidence supports his "wish that this should really be Virgil's tomb."[50]

Mornington's enthusiasm was dampened only by the fact that while he walked with the ghosts of ancient Rome, political life went on in London without him. To make matters worse, only Grenville kept him in touch with events. He learned of Grenville's continued advance up the greasy pole, and while he doubtless celebrated his friend's good fortune, he sensed that he was being left behind.

In the course of Mornington's return, he contracted malaria in Rome.[51] Never possessing a high tolerance for physical distress, he became very sick and by his own account did not fully recover until he reached Spa three months later. In later years he would repeatedly be laid low by fever; one wonders whether those occasions were revisits of the malaria. His discomfort did not dampen his enthusiasm for the Tyrolean Alps, however, which he passed through on the journey from Verona to Innsbruck. Traversing Bavaria on his way to the Rhine, he stopped in Mayence and from there followed the great river to Cologne. The order, security, and cleanliness of Germany impressed him, especially in comparison with Italy.[52]

While taking the waters at Spa, Mornington reacquainted himself with family matters and political affairs. He had had his fill of French émigrés, whom he saw as idle, vindictive, and stupid. It was just days since the Flight to Varennes, but Mornington was hard-pressed to feel any sympathy for the émigrés. He deemed their behavior no better than that of the revolutionaries. To his mind they deserved one another.

Mornington returned to London filled with a new sense of urgency. Ever eager to play a role in the political world, he felt an increased anxiety about his future. He knew that his mother and siblings saw him as their only hope for the maintenance of family respectability and the attainment of proper careers. Richard would never deal well with such pressure, and it was aggravated at the time by the fact that he had a substantial family of his own. He desperately needed to move up in the world to be in a position to better place his brothers and to establish another source of income so that he might provide for his mother and sisters and his own family. But Mornington's situation was more complicated than that. Driven to an uncommon degree by a need for recognition, he would always crave some sort of public confirmation that he was doing well. He believed that he could never be secure until he held high office and an English peerage. The attitude of the parvenu, which never escaped him (much to the mystification of friends and colleagues), can be explained only by an abiding sense of social insecurity, if not inferiority.

He found the troika of Pitt, Henry Dundas (later Viscount Melville), and Grenville still dominating the world of British politics and feeling their way through a series of challenging diplomatic problems that prevented them from enjoying the security derived from the king's recovery. A territorial dispute with Spain in North America, political upheaval in the Netherlands, war between the Ottoman Empire and an alliance of Russia and Austria, and the revolution in France caught Pitt off guard. Foreign affairs were not the prime minister's strength, and he struggled, along with his colleagues, in trying to develop a policy. But foreign policy by trial and error exposed the ministry to criticism and challenge in Parliament.[53] With every cabinet and subcabinet post critical to the stability of the ministry, Mornington again found his ambitions frustrated.

His liabilities were as obvious as his strengths. While his closest friends marveled at his wit and intelligence, his Irish properties were mortgaged and patronage remained a dream. While there was the family seat at Trim, to call it modest would be a gross overstatement. But too much can be made of these handicaps in explaining Mornington's stagnant career. Though undeniably he did not bring much to the table as far as Pitt was concerned, there was always room for up-and-comers. His friend Addington, after all, had become Speaker of the Commons, and Addington had nothing more to recommend him than the facts that his father had been physician to Pitt's father and that he had had the good sense to marry the daughter of Earl Bathurst (sister of his good friend Apsley). Mornington's constant whining to Grenville might suggest that he approached his other friends in the same manner. It should be kept in mind, however, that Grenville was like a brother to Mornington—and Pitt like a god. But at this stage of Mornington's career, he did not beg Pitt for employment. And while Grenville was certainly in a position to remind the prime minister of Mornington's usefulness, Pitt might very well have thought that he had put his colleague in a position to make himself indispensable.

Given Mornington's subsequent reputation for pomposity, imagining him as reticent or lacking confidence is difficult. However, his governor-generalship of Bengal is what gave him an exalted self-image and whatever confidence he might have had. The evidence suggests that Mornington, while at Westminster, was very self-conscious. Earl Stanhope, one of Pitt's earliest biographers, puts it clearly: "Lord Mornington at the Treasury did not for a long time do justice to himself. . . . Pitt once said of him that he was the animal of the longest gestation he had ever seen. His speeches, when at last they came were excellent and justly admired, above all for their classic taste, their graceful elocution, and their vivid style."[54] In other words, Mornington's slow progress up the political ladder is attributable to his own reticence. It is interesting to compare Mornington's early career with that of George Canning, who was shortly hard on his heels. Canning started out with fewer advantages than Mornington, but Canning possessed keen political instincts and a determined, bold personality. He never bothered himself with the questions of honor that preoccupied Mornington but simply forged ahead; Canning made it impossible for others to ignore him.

But this was not Mornington, and so he languished, preferring to blame others for his predicament rather than taking a long and critical look in the mirror. Meanwhile he stayed close to Grenville and Pitt, and his relationships with Addington and Apsley matured. Through this close circle of friends he became acquainted with the formidable Dundas, who would gradually replace Grenville as Pitt's closest confidant. Finally in April 1792, Mornington emerged from the shadows in the heated parliamentary debate over the slave trade.

Richard Wellesley's liberal views on key issues confronting Great Britain constitute one of the remarkable features of his career. He never wavered in his opposition to slavery and the slave trade, and he advocated Catholic emancipation without hesitation or qualification throughout his career. Despite opposing parliamentary reform in the 1790s, he firmly backed it in 1832. His entrance into the slave trade debate was not without risk. Henry Dundas, ever alert to political possibilities, opposed abolition. Pitt supported it, but challenging Dundas was never a happy event. Nonetheless, Mornington forged ahead. As the debate progressed, Dundas and his crowd maintained that the issue was not abolition per se but rather when and how abolition should come about. In other words, they attempted to redefine the debate from a moral to an economic one. Immediate abolition, they said, would be ruinous.[55]

Mornington jumped in and moved that the trade be abolished by 1 January 1793, a proposal that was defeated 158 to 109. Two days later, he amended a resolution from Dundas that called for abolition on 1 January 1800. Wellesley moved the date to 1 January 1795, claiming,

> He was sorry that so infamous, so bloody a traffic should exist for one hour. Upon the justice of it nothing could be said; upon the humanity of it nothing could be said. Being destitute of principle, being hated by all good men, and, as far as regarded its justice or humanity, abandoned by its own advocates, what could be said on the subject? . . . it was nothing but mean and sordid avarice that induced them to wish for the continuance of this abominable, infamous, bloody traffic—the commerce in human flesh—this spilling of human blood—this sacrifice of human right—this insolence to justice—this outrage to humanity—this disgrace to human nature![56]

As far as he was concerned, time was not a factor in this debate. "The force of truth being given, and the hardness of a planter's heart being ascertained," he asked, "in what space of time will the former be able to penetrate the latter?"[57] All to no avail.

The results were not negligible politically. Mornington had demonstrated that he could speak with conviction and force and that he would take a stand on principle. Pitt took notice; in the year following, he chose Mornington to take a role in the debate over parliamentary reform. In this case, Pitt's ministers were as one. In a preview of the Reform Bill of 1832, Charles, second Earl Grey, introduced the legislation. Mornington contributed neither uniquely nor remarkably to this debate. He focused on the integrity of the constitution and its perfection, suggesting that tinkering with something that worked well was foolhardy.[58]

The reform bill was ill timed, coming as it did just months after the execution of Louis XVI and the onset of war with revolutionary France. Britain was not in a liberal mood, and Mornington can be excused for sharing that sentiment. Yet his speech exhibits the same fluffy logic that he would hold in contempt thirty-seven years hence: "Whatever might be contended to be the defective state of the representation in theory, it is an undeniable fact, proved by daily and almost hourly experience, that there is no interest in the kingdom, however inconsiderable, which does not find some advocate in the House of Commons to recommend it to the attention of the Legislature."[59] Though Charles James Fox answered him with withering sarcasm, Mornington, on this occasion, found himself on the winning side and was rewarded by Pitt for his efforts. On 21 June he was sworn a member of the privy council and given a seat on the Board of Control for India.[60]

Mornington's interest in India had been piqued during the trial of Warren Hastings, and no doubt Pitt thought this a good assignment for his friend. It had the twin virtues of giving him something to do while matching him with the shrewd Dundas. Mornington approached his new responsibility in the manner that characterized his later career. He set about making himself thoroughly informed on the subject. The breadth and depth of his studies would become apparent when he arrived in Calcutta five years later as governor general. From the start, he proved himself a master of detail on Indian history and politics. At the same time, he did his best to avoid board meetings. It would be easy to say that Wellesley could not tolerate meetings and disliked teamwork. But he loved the nightly dinners with Pitt's group and the weekends at Holwood. These events, far from being social, involved real work, with hours of political chatter and strategizing. Mornington found this energizing. What then was the difference? The answer is simple—the people. Around his table, Pitt assembled an elite group; stimulated by good food and drink, brilliant minds interacted with ease. Committee and even cabinet meetings were not like this. Mornington had little patience for what he identified as the inferior mind, especially if it was not deferential. Because he could not control who sat in such bodies, he stayed away. In the case of the

India board, his presence or absence hardly mattered; Dundas brooked little discussion.

This reluctance to work in concert is one reason for Mornington's reputation for arrogance and pride. His closest friends did not see him in such terms, because in their company he was warm, witty, and congenial. Incongruously, Mornington was also socially awkward. He did not understand social niceties, probably because although he had attended England's best schools, he had not been exposed to the manners and habits of London society. School had been the only stable thing in his youthful life. Home was transitory—London, Dublin, Dangan—and his family lacked the resources to expose him to an elite social milieu. This might have had something to do with his inability to establish a socially and politically acceptable relationship with a woman. Except among his intimates, Mornington was generally ill at ease. Like Robert Stewart, Viscount Castlereagh, he hid behind an icy façade, a behavior that had long-lasting political consequences. He never found a way to work easily with others in the business of policy making and problem solving, a prerequisite for the effective politician. The tragedy is that he never realized it.

While his appointment as a privy councilor represented a step forward, Mornington viewed it as insufficient. August found him once again plagued with his "miserable nerves," and for relief he took to sea bathing at Brighton. At the same time, he kept a close eye on events just across the channel. Britain was then at war with revolutionary France, which had descended into the political violence of the Terror. Mornington was under no illusions when it came to the revolution. He had seen it firsthand during its moderate stage and had been unimpressed. As he followed events and made himself conversant with parties and personalities, familiarity bred contempt.[61]

Autumn found him back again with Pitt, holding forth on the revolution but worried about his future.[62] Addington humored him with what had to have been a conscious understatement: "You want a wider sphere; you are dying of the cramp."[63] The days leading up to the opening of Parliament in January 1794 were busy ones. The young George Canning, newly elected to the Commons, places Wellesley in Pitt's company on a number of occasions, and Canning would not have been included in most of the gatherings of this period. Canning gives us the best glimpse of Mornington in this setting, writing,

"Lord Mornington I knew before—but like him better now than I ever did—both because he appears generally very sensible and pleasant, and was very good-naturedly attentive to me. He is also a Lord of the Treasury and one of Pitt's most intimate friends."[64] Canning had seen two Morningtons—one remote and indifferent, one pleasant and attentive. From Canning we even have a diagram of the seating arrangements at Pitt's table; Mornington can be found between Grenville and Dundas, once removed from Pitt.

It was probably at or because of these soirées that Pitt chose Mornington to lead in the government's motion of thanks for the king's speech from the throne opening the parliamentary session of January 1794. This was Mornington's most important responsibility to date. Pitt expected the motion to pass, but the war and the revolution were subjects on which the opposition had definite and clear ideas. More important, they would be articulated by Richard Brinsley Sheridan and Fox, both of unchallenged eloquence. That the government should state its position confidently and convincingly, and equally important, avoid embarrassment, was crucial.

Mornington's preparations were meticulous. Unfortunately, we know nothing of his sources or the time he expended in making ready. We do know that the performance was remarkable. "At 4 o'clock the debate began," wrote Canning, "and lasted, as you will have seen by the papers, for thirteen hours, that is till 5 in the morning. It was to me one of the highest entertainments that can be conceived."[65] Estimates of the duration of Mornington's contribution are vague, saying only that it lasted hours; judging from the printed text, nearly four hours might be close to the mark. It was a remarkable intellectual and physical accomplishment.

The speech was a model of logic and organization. Mornington's challenge was this. The opposition had two points to make: that though events had taken a rather bad turn in France, what happened there was France's business alone, and that the war had been forced on France by the continental powers and did not concern Britain. A third theme had also emerged. With the war going badly for the allies, the parliamentary opposition concluded that it could not be won. With these things in mind, Mornington constructed his speech. He would ignore the claim that France had been obliged to make war and instead would focus on the fact that once the war began, France went beyond self-defense. Mornington would portray the revolutionaries as innately aggressive and claim that their moves into the lowlands made Britain's involvement unavoidable. France, in other words, had freely made a choice. He would go into excruciating detail on this aspect, and in a perceptive and clever move, he tied French foreign policy directly to French domestic affairs. He knew that the opposition wanted to avoid this discussion. Conceding the point that the Terror was not to be admired, they maintained that references to it only clouded the issue with emotion. Mornington waded right in. He knew he had some ugly stories to tell, and he spared little detail. Here again his tack is fascinating. He took the words of Jacques-Pierre Brissot to illustrate the violence and cruelty of the revolution—aware that everyone in his audience knew that Brissot and his group (collectively known as the Girondins) had been routed by the radical Jacobins (collectively known as the Mountain) the previous spring and the revolution had moved even further to the left.[66]

With an astonishing command of the facts, Mornington spoke with authority not only on the politics of the period, with special reference to the Stillborn Constitution and the Committees, but also on religion, on the *leveé en masse,* and most especially on finances. Here the discussion included taxation, confiscation, and regulation, and again he pointed to the irrationality and cruelty of the revolution. The inference, of course, was that such a regime threatened civilization and was therefore worth fighting. For many in Britain, Maximilien de Robespierre, architect of the Reign of Terror, was the eighteenth-century version of Adolf Hitler or Josef Stalin. But Mornington did not belabor this point, for he knew that the opposition could reply that if the French choose to murder one another, they had the right to do so. Instead, Mornington turned to French aggression. He showed that the revolutionary government survived only through foreign expansion and further confiscation. France, having exhausted its resources, had to look elsewhere in a self-perpetuating process that had to be confronted. Thus, after several hours of presenting evidence, he had built the case for French war aims being based on the foundation of an aggressive ideology and fiscal necessity.[67]

As to the point that the war could not be won, Mornington pointed to the self-consuming nature of the revolution. In time, he argued, the French might self-destruct: when the revolution reached the point of diminishing returns, its strength would begin to wane. If England persevered, the tide would turn. Once the aggressive onslaught into the

Continent was slowed and France was deprived of the resources required by its insatiable appetite, the revolution would wither and die. In the end, he maintained that the war must be prosecuted.[68]

When Mornington sat down, Sheridan rose to answer. There were no surprises. He accused Mornington of playing upon the passions of the British public rather than focusing on the point in question. Sheridan blamed French political behavior on Britain and her continental allies: "you have created the passions which you persecute; you mark a nation to be cut off from the world; you covenant for their extermination; you swear to hunt them in their inmost recesses; you load them with every species of execration; and you now come forth with whining declamations on the horror of their turning upon you with the fury you inspired!"[69] This was classic Sheridan but did nothing to detract from Mornington's case; nor did his subsequent attack on the smug complacency of Britain's landed and monied interests enhance his argument.

The opposition, which accused Mornington of sacrificing substance for form, denigrated his speech as noteworthy only for its rhetorical flourish. But he had staunch defenders. "The speech of his noble friend," answered Pitt, "had been styled declamatory; upon what principle he knew not, except that every effort of eloquence in which the most forcible reasoning was adorned and supported by all the powers of language, was to be branded with the epithet of declamation."[70] William Wyndham argued that Mornington "had recapitulated the conduct of France in a manner so masterly, so true, and so alarming, as seriously to fix the attention of the House and the nation."[71] Dundas was equally complimentary, and when the division came, the government found itself with an overwhelming majority—a great moment for an aspiring politician.

While Mornington made his way in the world, he had also been attending to his siblings. There was no system or grand scheme behind what Richard Wellesley did for his brothers. Because he had no sense of where he was going, there is little reason to think that he sought to place these men in positions that might augment or support his own career. He simply wanted to send them on their way so that he might eliminate distractions. He dealt first with Arthur, who at age seventeen had returned from France in December 1786. "Let me remind you of a younger brother of mine," Mornington wrote to the Duke of Rutland, "whom you were so kind as to take into your consideration for a commission in the army. He is here at this moment, and perfectly idle. It is a matter of indifference to me what commission he gets, provided he gets it soon."[72] A commission was found and purchased, and on 17 March 1787, Arthur became an ensign in the Seventy-third Foot. At this time, Mornington was much engaged in Irish politics and traveling between Dublin and London. He was, therefore, constantly on the lookout for other assignments for Arthur, who needed an income beyond that provided by an ensign's pay. Naturally, Mornington turned to his friends the Grenvilles. On 27 October he wrote to William, "I cannot conclude this letter without assuring you that I feel most sensibly the kind and anxious part you have taken in this business of Arthur's promotion, which, in the present moment, it would scarcely have been possible for me to have managed myself."[73] Then opportunity knocked. When the Duke of Rutland died, Mornington, in expectation of Buckingham's appointment as lord lieutenant of Ireland, suggested to Grenville that Buckingham should appoint Arthur as aide-de-camp, assuring his friend that he would arrange for Arthur to take the family seat for Trim. Buckingham delivered, adding ten shillings per day to Arthur's income. Mornington made it clear to Buckingham that Arthur would not let him down.[74] Richard had in the past complained about the problem of Arthur. But this was a new Arthur—much grown up and infinitely more personable.

There was, however, a complication. Mornington and his mother had not compared notes, and the latter had made application to the Grenvilles as well. A horrified Richard apologized: "My mother informs me that as soon as she heard of Lord Buckingham's appointment she could not refrain from writing to you in favour of Arthur. It is natural that her great eagerness to get him into Lord Buckingham's family should induce her to take such a step; but it was entirely without my knowledge, and you may judge by the tenor of my letter on the subject, whether I can approve of such an application."[75] One can only imagine the exchange that must have ensued between the thoroughly annoyed Richard and his mother. She had been rash and importunate, and she had challenged his familial authority. Beyond that, her independent action betrayed the despair she felt concerning her family; she must have frequently reminded her eldest son of his obligations.

In December, Richard purchased for Arthur a promotion to lieutenant in the Seventy-sixth Foot and no doubt felt that the matter was settled. Six challenging years followed as Arthur grew into manhood attending to a variety of responsibilities, enjoying an active social life, and experiencing success and failure. In addition to fulfilling his minimal duties as an aide-de-camp, he took his seat for Trim and did his best to take part in the debates at College Green. Furthermore, as Mornington and Wellesley-Pole (who took a seat in the House of Commons) spent more time in London, the task of supervising Dangan fell to Arthur. This was not particularly rewarding, as the estate labored under a heavy mortgage and increasing disrepair; in addition, it meant traveling back and forth from Dublin to Dangan, much as his father and grandfather had done.

As an aide-de-camp, Arthur served two viceroys: the Marquis of Buckingham and John Fane, tenth Earl of Westmoreland. Under Westmoreland the emphasis would be on society rather than politics, and Arthur made an easy adjustment. He joined the festivities, occasionally making an impression. Eventually he came into contact with the Honourable Katherine Pakenham, known as Kitty, the pretty young daughter of Lord Longford of Castlepollard in Westmeath. According to the Wellesleys' old friends, the so-called Ladies of Llangollen, Arthur cut quite a dashing figure: "A charming young man. Handsome, fashioned tall and elegant."[76]

To Kitty, Arthur revealed a serious side that few suspected.[77] He enjoyed himself while in Ireland, as exhibited by his debts, but also took to studying military science and reading. As Kitty was bookish, the attraction between them was both physical and intellectual. Arthur was not the type, then or later, to show his feelings. The lack of love poems and emotional declarations is no indication of a lack of attachment. Kitty returned Arthur's attentions, fueling his ardor. But the courtship was cut short by the suitor's lack of prospects; the Pakenhams doubted whether Arthur could support Kitty in the style to which she was accustomed.[78] Arthur, shaken, betrayed the naïveté that had also plagued Richard. That Arthur seems never to have considered the possibility of rejection reveals that he did not know the rules of Anglo-Irish society, just as Richard did not understand the unspoken rules governing Britain's political life. Arthur learned quickly, however; Richard did not.

Meanwhile, in April 1793 Arthur became a major in the Thirty-third Foot and moved up to lieutenant colonel in September. Both commissions were purchased through loans tendered by Richard. By that time Britain was at war with France, and Arthur concluded that as a soldier, he might as well be involved. He burned his violin, in whose smoke went the memories of youthful disappointment, and when his regiment was assigned to the expeditionary force led by the second royal son, the Duke of York, Arthur left Cork for Ostend in June 1794. As one might expect, Arthur's first military experience left an impression. It taught him what not to do, as he would say in later years. The expedition turned into an unqualified disaster, and Arthur found himself involved mostly in retreats and defensive actions. He met the enemy for the first time on 15 September 1794 in a minor engagement at Boxtel in the Netherlands. Subsequently he took up a position on the River Waal from October 1794 to January 1795. He returned to Dublin in March, having been part of an embarrassing episode in British military history.

Back in Dublin, he took up where he had left off, but the experience in the Low Countries convinced him that his future lay in the military, not in politics. He began to look for another assignment. One would be provided, but it was not of the sort that held out much opportunity—an expedition to the West Indies. Most soldiers viewed the West Indies, where malaria and yellow fever yielded an uncommonly high fatality rate, as graveyard duty. As luck would have it, a less serious fever delayed Arthur's departure, and when the regiment did sail, bad weather turned it back. In the interim, he had been reassigned to India.[79] There is no evidence that Mornington had anything to do with the change of plans, but there can be no question of his satisfaction with it. This was the opportunity for Arthur to make a career and a modest fortune. Mornington arranged the purchase of a colonelcy, and in September he bade Arthur good-bye, having no idea that in eighteen months they would be collaborators halfway around the world. One must remember that Arthur had yet to exhibit any signs of military genius. He had fought in only one campaign, which had offered few opportunities to demonstrate his ability. What had happened over the preceding six years was that the brothers had come closer together. Mornington no longer viewed Arthur as the family's problem child, and Arthur was grateful for all that his brother had done for him.

Gerald proved easier to launch than Arthur. Ordained as a priest at Lincoln Cathedral on 21 December 1794, he settled in as rector of Beachampton and chaplain at Hampton Court. Gerald possessed a scholarly temperament. Like all his brothers, he attended Eton; like Richard, he was a great success. He matriculated at St. John's College,

Cambridge, at Easter 1789, and in 1791 he interrupted his studies to accompany Richard and Hyacinthe on their grand tour. He returned to St. John's to complete an M.A. in 1792. Then he decided, in consultation with his brother and mother, on a career as a clergyman; he was ordained as a deacon at Ely in December 1793.[80] All the brothers were fond of Gerald, and among them he was the only one who became the object of gentle teasing. Humor was not a marked Wellesley trait, but Gerald, who was able to laugh at himself, provoked what little there was. The brothers did whatever they could to advance Gerald's career, beginning with the appointments to Beachampton and Hampton Court, which provided him an adequate income. Richard must have been instrumental in their procurement, though there is nothing in the correspondence to confirm this supposition.

Henry, the last of Garret and Anne's five sons, seems typical of younger children in large families: noncombative, warm, diplomatic, not overly ambitious. Throughout life, Henry (who never aroused jealousy in his peers) was the best liked. It can be argued that his famous and powerful brothers made his diplomatic career possible, but fifth sons were often lost and forgotten. Henry allowed neither to happen. Intelligence and integrity made him a success. Henry did what his brothers told him to do and usually did it well.

Henry, too, attended Eton, where he stayed the course. When he left in 1789, the family's finances were in ruin, and so Lady Mornington suggested a career in the army. Years later, Henry expressed regret over his inability to follow Richard and Gerald to university because "the two or three years passed there by young men previous to their entering into public life are of the greatest value, not only with the view to the acquirement of knowledge, but also to the forming of friendships and connections, which, once formed, usually continue through life."[81] This reflection came after he had observed how the "Oxbridge" network dominated British politics. Gentlemen attended these institutions, and gentlemen ran Britain. But his was the youngest son's fate; Mornington agreed that the military might be an appropriate career, so off to the German state of Brunswick he went.

The court of Brunswick was not an unlikely choice for exposure to and training in the military life. The Duke of Brunswick was an able soldier, and many young Englishmen went to Brunswick because the duke was married to George III's sister.[82] From all accounts, the duke and duchess treated these young men kindly. They invited Henry to functions at court and frequently to Sunday night dinners.

The duke and duchess were the parents of Caroline, the future wife of the Prince of Wales (who later became George IV). On the death of George III, the prince and princess would provide Britain with one of the country's most outrageous melodramas. Henry got a hint of what was to come, observing that Caroline had already established a reputation for flirtation:

> The Princess Caroline . . . was at this period very well looking. It was whispered that she had already betrayed a strong propensity to gallantry, and had entered into a correspondence with a young man of the Duke's household. The lover, getting alarmed, betrayed the whole correspondence to the Duke, was removed from Brunswick, and has not since been heard of. After this the Princess had two governesses attached to her who always appeared with her in public and were instructed never to lose sight of her. I saw enough of her at Brunswick to feel little surprise at her subsequent conduct in England and in Italy. Nor have I ever had the least doubt of the truth of the charges which were alleged against her.[83]

After a pleasant nine-month stay at Brunswick, Henry returned to England to take up a post with his regiment in expectation of war with Spain, a commission as ensign having been arranged for him. The war never materialized, and Henry secured a leave, presenting his brother and mother with the challenge of finding something productive for him to do. Thus he went to Brussels and took up residence with a family friend, Colonel Gardiner, who was at that time acting as British minister. The French émigrés who thronged Brussels taught Henry the Wellesley distaste for the revolution.[84]

Mornington, in the midst of his continental tour, had Henry on his mind. From Naples in January 1791, he informed Grenville that Henry had left Brunswick and was in need of employment. This was not an urgent plea, but Mornington did think that idle time in London could lead to trouble. Grenville as foreign secretary could help by attaching Henry to an embassy. Thus, he promised some sort of diplomatic appointment. More than happy, Mornington commanded his brother to join him in Spa, where they talked of his future.

Grenville in short order offered a post at either the Hague or Berlin. "I think I can venture to say," Mornington wrote, "that there will be no risk in sending him either to the Hague or Berlin. I prefer the Hague if it should be equally convenient to you, because Lord Auckland is an acquaintance of my mother's, and because I think Lord H. Spencer's example might be very useful."[85] This was a thoughtful response from a concerned brother. The only hitch was securing an extended leave from the army.

Grenville explained to William Eden, first Baron Auckland,

> There is a young man, a brother of Lord Mornington's, whom I wish to bring into the diplomatic line. But he is, as yet, almost too young even for a Secretary of Legation; and, besides, I think it would be better that he should get a little in the habit of that sort of business before he is put into any situation. I have therefore desired him to fix himself at the Hague, and should be particularly obliged to you if you would, in some degree, take him under your protection, and employ him, as far as you may find him fit to be employed, and put him in the way of rendering himself moreso. . . . I have a long and sincere friendship for his brother, and should be very glad to be able to be of use to him, as his situation requires some addition to his profession.[86]

Accordingly, Grenville dispatched Henry to the Hague. The more than cooperative Auckland went on leave before Henry's arrival, but he arranged for Henry Spencer to take charge. Henry got on well with Spencer, and the relationship paid off quickly.[87]

After six months at the Hague, Grenville gave Henry a real job as secretary of legation at the Swedish court. A leisurely journey found him spending six weeks in Berlin taking in the sights and society of the Prussian court. Then it was on to Stockholm, where he arrived in time to play his part in the scenario of a Verdi opera. On 16 March 1792, a disgruntled Swedish nobleman by the name of Count Ankarstroen shot the king, Gustavus III, at a masked ball. The king lingered for days in agony before dying. Some suggested a French conspiracy, the credence of which the francophobic Wellesley willingly accepted. After Gustavus IV ascended the throne at fourteen years of age, his uncle, the duke of Sudermania, became regent and swung Sweden towards France. Despite this uncertain political situation, the envoy, Robert

Liston, went on leave, trusting Henry to act as chargé d'affaires for ten months, during which time Britain went to war with France.[88] This situation seems extraordinary, given Henry's age (he was nineteen) and lack of experience, and suggests the relaxed character of the eighteenth-century diplomatic corps.

Inevitably the war changed Henry's circumstances. In June 1793, he received orders to join his regiment, which was proceeding to Flanders. An arduous passage to London ensued, with heavy seas causing delays and alterations of course. Though Henry makes no comment in his recollections, he was not a good sailor. On arrival, he met with Mornington, who secured reimbursement of the extraordinary expenses he had incurred during Liston's absence.[89] Subsequently he joined the army on its march to lay siege to Dunkirk. When the French victory at Hondscotte put an end to those plans, it also terminated Henry's military career. On his return to England, Mornington pestered Grenville for another diplomatic assignment, preferably at the Hague. But first he had to sell Henry's commission for the highest possible price. As completing the sale would take two to three months, Mornington sent the idle Henry to Lisbon to render comfort and assistance to his recently widowed sister, Anne.[90]

After what appears to have been an abortive love affair in 1788, the beautiful Anne had married Henry Fitzroy, the third surviving son of Charles Fitzroy, first Baron Southampton, on 4 January 1790. They would not have an easy time, as neither had any money.[91] They made do, however, and very quickly produced two daughters. By all accounts they were happy. Then Fitzroy came down with consumption, and he and Anne moved to Lisbon in the hope that a change of climate might provide relief. Alas, there he died. There is some confusion about the dates. Whereas Henry Wellesley claims that he left London in February 1794 to bring Anne home, Fitzroy did not die until March. Anne may have foreseen her husband's death when she sent pleas for help, or the precise timing might simply be confused. What is certain is that Henry and Anne boarded a packet for Falmouth in early April.

On the morning of 23 April (Henry is precise here), a French frigate appeared on the horizon and gave chase. With Falmouth only twelve hours away, the packet made a dash. According to Henry, they were making good their escape when a second frigate appeared, flying British colors. Shipboard relief proved brief. When the second frigate ran up the tricolor, the packet surrendered. Henry, whose francophobia seethes throughout this account, points out that even after the surrender, the French frigate fired a broadside.

Subsequent events left an indelible impression on the twenty-one-year-old Henry. Taking the packet as a prize, the French escorted it to Brest, where passengers and crew were brought before a member of the committee of public safety, one Jean Bon St. André. Taking the measure of his audience, St. André launched into a diatribe in which he called George III an imbecile and Pitt a scoundrel. Henry was appalled. "This speech," he recalled contemptuously, "addressed to a young woman by a man of good education and one of the highest functionaries of the Republic, affords a good specimen of Republican taste and feeling."[92] In the span of four years, the young Wellesley had looked closely into the eyes of two types of French political animal: the émigré of the old regime and the Jacobin of the new republic. The former he viewed as tame and civilized, the latter as wild and barbaric.

After assuring the prisoners that they would be treated well, St. André dispatched them to Quimper, where other English prisoners of war were being held in an old convent. Henry's protests that he and his sister were civilians traveling on a packet, not a ship of war, fell on deaf ears. The French were indifferent to such distinctions, and one gathers that his captors found him pompous. The convent in which they were confined was not an oppressive place, and the prisoners were allowed to keep their personal belongings, including their money. Occasionally, probably in fun, the French jailers threatened to throw Henry into a common jail and even took him to it to show him his cell. Otherwise the prisoners were treated well. There are no comments about bad food or physical abuse, and there was regular exercise.[93]

The emotional strain, however, must have been intense. Henry and his sister had fallen into French hands at the height of the Terror, and they knew what was happening outside the convent walls. They had to have feared for their safety. Given the times, the French could be said to have displayed remarkable restraint (despite the fact that Wellesley and his fellow passengers were innocent bystanders).

After nine months of confinement, Henry broke free. The escape plans took shape in January 1795 when the Convention decreed that female prisoners should be sent home. Henry could then pursue any course of action without worry of consequences for Anne. He requested and received permission to accompany her to Landeman, where she would board an American ship for the voyage to England. There, the captain offered to take Henry as well. Ever gallant, Henry declined, as he had given his word to return to Quimper, but asked whether the captain would wait while he returned to Quimper and then made his escape. The agreement made, Henry and a fellow prisoner, a Mr. Delaunay, turned themselves back in, subsequently bribed their guard, and headed back to the coast.

Delaunay was French by birth and Henry fluent, so language was not a problem. Still, they were on the run and at great risk. When they reached the appointed meeting place at nightfall and found that the American captain had not arrived, they made their way to an inn, where they had dinner and secured a room. Time was their enemy; their absence at Quimper was bound to be noticed. Delaunay suggested that they had no hope of escape unless the innkeeper was willing to help or ignore them. As it happened, the innkeeper proved a sympathetic host. He concealed them until they made their contact.

The captain arrived at two in the morning, with bad news. The French were searching ships; if Wellesley and Delaunay were discovered, his cargo would be confiscated and the women detained. They waited three days in the vain hope that the French would abandon their tight security. On the captain's recommendation, they then decided on another course of action. Henry purchased a twenty-three-foot sailboat and recruited three escaping English sailors to pilot the craft across the channel. Before they set out, Wellesley's party was joined by nine other English fugitives, bringing the total on board to fourteen. Overloaded, they crept out of the harbor on the evening of 11 January 1795. It would not prove a pleasure cruise. In the best of conditions, a winter channel-crossing could be hazardous, but this evening was stormy and bitterly cold. Warmed only by brandy and fear, they slipped through the guarded harbor mouth into the Atlantic, steering a northerly course into the English Channel.[94]

Entirely open and with only a three-foot draft, the boat did nothing to protect the fugitives from the punishment of the waves. The storm-tossed sea prevented them from steering a direct course, and the men kept busy bailing water. Panic eventually took hold of some, worsening in proportion to increasing personal discomfort. At midnight the inevitable occurred: one man fell overboard and was lost. Morning brought no relief and revealed yet another casualty, for one of the thirteen remaining had perished from the cold. Drenched and exposed to the wind, two more died by nightfall.

By this time the helm had been taken by an ex-smuggler, a Mr. Brockensha, who knew something of seamanship and navigation in those waters. This did not make their situation any less alarming. All provisions having been spoiled by seawater, the men took increasingly to the brandy. Drunkenness led to disputes and near anarchy, but Brockensha's steady hand brought them to a safe landing at the tiny port of Mevagissey, where Brockensha's family lived. There the fugitives nursed themselves back to health, and Henry and Delaunay were off for London.[95]

It was an extraordinary experience, and though the escape was foolhardy, it revealed a side to Henry that few would have suspected. He had displayed courage, fortitude, and initiative, and he returned to a very anxious family. Mornington had been busy pulling strings trying to arrange the release of his brother and sister, with no success.[96] In fact, there was little that could be done. Whether Anne or Henry reached London first is not known, but everyone was glad to have them back. The year had not been a good one for the Wellesleys. No sooner had Henry departed for Lisbon than his younger sister, Mary, died.[97] The cause is not known, but her death along with the detainment of Anne and Henry led to extraordinary stress for the family, particularly Lady Mornington.

Henry took his time recovering from the ordeal, and one can imagine this young man making the best of his story. It would have circulated far and wide in London and made him something of a celebrity. Meanwhile, his commission sold, Henry looked forward to a career as a diplomat. Employment came soon, again from Grenville, who employed Henry as a précis writer in the foreign office.[98] The demands of such a job were not great, and Henry had ample time to establish himself socially.

Mornington's situation had not changed much. His performance on the floor of the House of Commons had left him enthusiastic and optimistic. At last, it seemed, a place of real responsibility would be his. The dinners with Pitt, Dundas, and Grenville continued, but at this moment of promise, unique circumstances again thwarted him. As early as January 1793, the Whig opposition had begun to break apart. The date is significant because it marks the execution of Louis XVI, an event that caused many Whigs to lose their taste for the revolution. The leader of this group, William Bentinck, the Duke of Portland, had in his train several influential men, and in the spring of 1794,

Pitt tried to tempt Portland's party to join the ministry. It was an opportunity not to be missed, but it required cabinet shuffling and the sacrifice of current officeholders. For Mornington, the implications were clear. "I am very much afraid," he wrote to Addington, "from a variety of circumstances, that Pitt has no idea of altering my situation this year. I cannot tell you how much I am mortified by that and other symptoms, not of unkindness, but of (what perhaps I deserve) decided preference to others. I have serious thoughts of relinquishing the whole pursuit, and becoming a spectator, (not a very indifferent one, as you may believe, either to the success of the war or to Pitt's interest and honour) but I cannot bear to creep on in my present position."[99] Mornington, whose threats were never convincing, was being unreasonable. Unquestionably he was unlucky, but Pitt had no choice. With an ego badly bruised and being desperate for income, Mornington barely survived, for in addition to caring for his siblings, his own family of five made increasing demands. He began to suspect a conspiracy. In his mind, he had done everything possible to advance the cause of Pitt's ministry and it had yielded nothing. If perception is reality, then Mornington learned that he could count only on himself, that connections were valuable only under opportune circumstances. As usual, Mornington was only partly right.

Pitt, sensitive to his friend's disappointment and anxiety, reassured Mornington in July that something would be found for him soon. Again, Richard confided in Addington: "Pitt sent for me . . . and told me that in settling this treaty, he had positively stipulated that I should have the next office (to be held with the Privy Council) which should become vacant; and he further informed me that the Duke of Portland entered very readily into this arrangement, and said it was but reasonable that I should stand first for such a situation. This is, I own, more than I expected."[100]

But time moved slowly, as Mornington busied himself with Indian affairs and politics. His persistent worry about the French was exacerbated by Henry's and Anne's incarceration. He feared that as France consolidated its control over northern Europe, the French navy would incorporate conquered navies and marshal resources for a naval expansion. To him, the danger from French victories on land would be a threat to England at sea.[101] He often sought refuge in Brighton, which he found soothing on his "nerves." He had taken one step to bring order to his life; in November 1794 he married

Hyacinthe. A year later, he gave up his seat for Windsor, because the king had lost patience with him. "The total want of attention of Lord Mornington," he wrote to Pitt, "has rendered him really obnoxious to them [the constituents of Windsor]."[102] One wonders whether this was at all embarrassing to him. The king, after all, had a notoriously long memory. Another seat was found—the thoroughly rotten borough of Saltash. Electioneering, even in such a secure seat, caused Mornington great anxiety. This aspect of politics never came naturally to him and constituted another element in his basic misunderstanding of the parliamentary system.

It follows, then, that Mornington wished to be out of the House of Commons. This ambition came not only from an aversion to elections but also from vanity. He craved recognition; to him, recognition came in the form of titles of nobility. Sadly, he would repeatedly embarrass himself over this matter. He gave a hint of his grasping nature in 1796. "My wish undoubtedly would be to go to the House of Lords," he wrote to Addington; "but I have not said more to Pitt than what I have mentioned above, thinking that it did not become me to enter into any detail with him in this stage of the business."[103] Mornington had hoped that the death of the lord president of the council would open a space for him. Again he was disappointed; the position went to Pitt's brother, John, the Earl of Chatham.

Mornington's fortunes finally turned in the autumn of 1797 when Pitt appointed him governor general of India, to succeed Sir John Shore, who had held the post since the resignation of Charles, Marquis Cornwallis. The talk in 1796 revolved around Pitt's brother-in-law, Eliot, who supposedly had the backing of Lord Cornwallis. Eliot did Mornington the great favor of dying, but when Shore resigned in early 1797, attention again focused on the experienced Cornwallis. At the same time, Dundas decided to recall the governor of Madras, Robert Hobart (later Earl of Buckinghamshire), and he and Pitt offered Mornington the post, with reversion to the governor-generalship. It is impossible to reconstruct the series of discussions that led to Cornwallis's appointment, his resignation before going out, and Mornington's assumption of the governor-generalship. The private correspondence leaves one wondering whether it was all a ruse. To begin with, Mornington's pretensions make his acceptance of a subordinate post in India unlikely, though he did examine the income that he could expect from it. At the same time, his appointment to Madras required the recall of Hobart, and the two were friends. Clearly, Mornington did nothing to protect Hobart and was embarrassed by what appeared to be his complicity in the recall. Buckingham, another of Hobart's friends, wrote to Mornington on two occasions asking him to try to secure a pension and a peerage for their mistreated friend.

Mornington's actions were disingenuous; he knew that Dundas had lost patience with Hobart. Mornington had written two letters to Arthur in March informing his younger brother that he would be going out as governor general. The letters do not survive; the contents can only be surmised from Arthur's response. Richard appears to have warned Arthur that as the arrangement was tentative, he should not let on to anyone what was afoot.[104] Mornington, therefore, knew that he would soon be governor general before Cornwallis had even accepted the appointment (if the appointment was ever made), let alone resigned it. If this indeed was the case, then Mornington's actions—his willingness to sign on as governor of Madras, his reluctance to protect Hobart—make more sense. The question then becomes, Why not appoint Mornington governor general straight away? The answer to this can only be that Mornington's outright appointment would have been controversial and that the indirect path made it politically palatable.

The presidency of Madras would have been acceptable to Mornington because it offered the opportunity to increase his income. When the offer was made, he had little choice but to take it, and he was clever enough to negotiate good terms. Cornwallis, we must conclude, accepted the appointment in all seriousness, seeing it as his duty. Problems concerning his role as commander-in-chief in India dampened his none-too-great enthusiasm, however, and when the government suggested that his talents might be better utilized in Ireland, where invasion and revolution threatened, he jumped at the opportunity. Mornington, in turn, acquired the prize. Neither Pitt nor Dundas was unhappy with the turn of events. Certainly Pitt was pleased to offer his friend an important post, not only because he genuinely liked and respected Mornington but also because he would no longer have to endure the constant pestering (he would be proved mistaken on the latter point). Dundas, by this time, knew Mornington well and could count on a good working relationship.

The appointment as governor general brought another reward: an English peerage. This had been hard work for Pitt because George III was anything but enamored with Mornington. Pitt prevailed nonetheless, and Mornington became Baron Wellesley.[105] It was the ego-soothing gesture that Richard needed most of all, but he also claimed it as a political necessity in India. Status and station, he believed, were inseparable. The peerage also meant that when he returned to England, he could take a seat in the House of Lords. No more expensive elections for him.

Both the appointment and the peerage were announced on 4 October 1797, though they were well known long before. For his part, Mornington acknowledged his good fortune. "I knew how you would rejoice in my attainment of the peerage," he wrote to Addington; "it was to me an invaluable object, both public and private. . . . I suppose the door is now shut, not again to be opened—'with impetuous recoil and jarring sound.'"[106] At this point, anyway, Mornington felt that he had played out his hand.

Meanwhile, by late 1795, political talk had turned to peace. The overthrow of Robespierre had resulted in another constitution, and observers believed that the revolution had taken a turn to the right. Mornington hoped for greater stability in France, for without it, there could be no lasting peace. With the war becoming very expensive, everyone looked for a way out. While Mornington was hopeful, the manner in which the constitution was put into effect concerned him. Street riots and the "Whiff of Grapeshot" did not bode well for the future.[107]

Despite the ill omens, Pitt opted for negotiations in the autumn of 1796 and again in the summer of 1797. On both occasions, he entrusted James Harris, Baron Malmesbury, with the task, and on the second, Malmesbury included Henry Wellesley on his staff as secretary of legation, a splendid opportunity that proved a formative experience. The party left London on 30 June for Lille, which had been selected as the site of the negotiations.[108] Discussions would focus on territories captured and occupied by each side in the course of the war. The issues were not complicated, and success or failure depended simply on how badly each side wanted peace. The problem for Malmesbury's mission was deciphering the French point of view. In fact, the problem for the French was deciphering the French point of view: the Directory, presided over by five directors, found itself divided on the issue of peace. While Malmesbury was quick to present Britain's initial offer, the French were not forthcoming with a counteroffer. Instead, Malmesbury found confusion and obfuscation.

The negotiations proceeded nonetheless on a regular schedule. On 11 July 1797, Lord Granville Leveson Gower wrote to his mother,

> Morpeth, G. Ellis, Wesley and myself are all sitting round a table complaining of the impossibility of writing a private letter. Our life is really here so very uniform, one day exactly telleth another. We are employed in consultations abt. the negotiation, in writing dispatches and copying notes, and we amuse ourselves with a walk upon the ramparts, and with the Spectacle in the Evening. Nothing but the business itself being so interesting, and the society of the persons who compose the mission being in itself so agreeable, could make a Residence in this town tolerable. Ld. Malmesbury continues in good health, and all who have accompanied him are as pleased with him as he is contented with them.[109]

In fact, Lille was a small town offering little in the form of amusement. There was work and conversation—little else. Fortunately the members of the group were bound together by their amiable personalities and the importance of their task. Malmesbury was kind and gentle, and each of them believed that peace was possible and was determined to do what he could to facilitate it.

Just when it seemed the negotiations were going nowhere, Wellesley was approached by a Mr. Cunningham, an Englishman who lived in Lille, who presented him with a note from a Monsieur Pein, who was a friend of Maret, one of the French negotiators.[110] It was a secret overture, and Malmesbury responded by arranging a meeting between George Ellis and Pein. At this meeting, Ellis found that the Directory was divided over peace and that Maret was of the peace party.[111] The implication, of course, was that others taking part in the negotiations were not serious about drawing up a treaty. Malmesbury, confronted with the problem of dealing with two negotiations at once, would have to carry on as usual and at the same time cultivate the Maret group without betraying them to the French negotiating team.

This is not the place for a detailed examination of the negotiations; what is significant is that Malmesbury had to find a way to communicate with London and in turn receive instructions. The stakes were high, and Malmesbury knew that couriers were often searched, so he decided to shuttle his staff and rely on memory for the transmission of information. Leveson Gower was closest to Malmesbury and was clearly the most trusted, but Malmesbury chose Henry as his first emissary. It was a mark of confidence. Henry left on 30 July, and Malmesbury would shortly write to Grenville, "Mr. Wesley will have acquainted you with the secret channel of communication that has been opened here, and with such information as I had derived through it. . . . I have no doubt you found Mr. Wesley exact and accurate."[112]

By the time Henry returned to Lille in August, Mornington had been offered the appointment as governor general, and he wanted to take his brother along with him as his private secretary. It was an offer Henry could not refuse. "I shall regret Wesley," wrote a disappointed Malmesbury, "who gains upon my good opinion every day."[113] Given the camaraderie that had developed among the group, Wellesley no doubt had some regrets, but as it turned out, the negotiation was about to collapse. Henry left Lille on 30 August; on 4 September, with the support of General Pierre Augereau, sent from Italy by Napoleon Bonaparte, royalists and the peace party were expelled from the Directory and the Council of Five Hundred in what is known as the coup d'etat of 18 Fructidor. With it all hope of an acceptable peace settlement vanished. Malmesbury and his mission packed their bags and returned to London.

Henry Wellesley was twenty-four years of age when he went out to India with Mornington, but he had experience well beyond his years. His good fortune in managing affairs in Stockholm gave him a relatively low-pressure exposure to regular diplomatic operations. His experience at the hands of Jacobins and his escape showed him the value of courage and decisiveness. And his responsibilities on the Malmesbury mission forced him to absorb complicated diplomatic negotiations and subsequently to articulate them. Henry emerged as a reliable, intelligent, resourceful associate. Though he did not possess the imagination and ambition of either Richard or Arthur, Henry was without question a capable man. Lacking pedigree, wealth, and a talent for political intrigue, however, he would always have to be satisfied with playing a supporting role.

3

The India Adventure Begins

The lives of Richard, Arthur, and Henry Wellesley tempt one to view their service in India as a launching pad for one glittering and two distinguished careers. This would be a mistake, for their years in India were critical not only to their own development but also to Britain's emergence as a modern imperial power. At the time the brothers left for India, the trial of Warren Hastings had firmly placed the subcontinent in the public consciousness. Still, the war with France remained paramount, and the fact that India was an eastern culture, exotic and unknowable, prevented most Britons from embracing events there as critical to the security of the motherland. That said, the public generally assumed that despite the alien culture and climate, India was a land of opportunity for those with fortitude and imagination. This is what the Wellesleys recognized, but little did they suspect just how much they would accomplish, how dramatically their lives and careers would be transformed, and how important their relationship would be in this grand enterprise. None of the brothers would have dared even to speculate on such developments. Neither Richard nor Arthur nor Henry was prescient; each went to the subcontinent because it represented the best opportunity at the time.

For Arthur, India offered work and an opportunity to advance and acquire some wealth. It certainly was better than the West Indies, and Arthur, aware of the rules of his profession, knew that an unproved officer could expect little more than frustration if he stayed home. India was a different case. Even in periods of relative tranquility, soldiers and civil servants sometimes returned with fortunes—if they returned. Having been turned away from Kitty Pakenham's door, Arthur needed no reminder of the significance of his penury. He had little to lose in going out to India even if he had no reason to expect great success.

For his part, Richard chafed over his political stasis. He would rather have stayed in London as a member of Pitt's cabinet. But after years of unfulfilled expectations, he concluded that this promotion was not to be, leaving India as the best alternative. The governor-generalship would relieve his financial anxieties while placing him in a position of real political responsibility. To say that Mornington's finances were precarious would be understating the case, but he never much worried about them. As governor general he would receive a substantial salary and have the prospect of riches from other sources, but Mornington spoke of this only in reference to Hyacinthe, whose insecurity over her husband's debts weighed heavily on her practical mind. Mornington went to India seeking not fortune but a distinguished career; India would be his stepping-stone.

As for Henry, the most ambivalent of the trio, he was left with little choice. Henry did what his eldest brother told him to do, and India seemed as good a place as any to learn the craft of diplomacy.

So the Wellesley brothers went to India for various reasons, hoping for the best. As it happened, the best nearly blessed them all. They would leave India transformed and return to Britain better off than when they left. And (especially germane to this story) each was in part responsible for the success of the others. The Wellesley brothers learned to work with one another, despite some rough patches, and in the process their mature characters emerged.

Arthur went first with no hint that his brothers would follow. If he viewed the prospect of several years alone in India with bewilderment, one could hardly blame him. Hustled off by a family eager to see him go, he must have been lonely. Arthur's biographers are uniformly at pains to find signs of genius at every stage of his early life, but one must take Arthur as one finds him, and at this time he was nondescript. One of countless colonels, he possessed minimal military experience, and despite friends in high places, he had attracted precious little attention. That there was no reason to believe this situation would change made his assignment to India palatable. The venture got off to a bad start with Arthur again succumbing to some nameless malady. While he was confined to bed, his regiment sailed without him, though he would catch up with it at the Cape of Good Hope. The Wellesleys were prone to illness when under stress, so second thoughts may have laid him low. In any case, by February 1797 he was in Calcutta ready to work.

The India that Arthur found bore little political resemblance to anything he had known or experienced. If there was a European reference it was the Holy Roman Empire, for the old Mughal Empire had become a jigsaw puzzle of independent or autonomous states, each of which played its own brand of power politics to enhance its security, dominate its neighbors, or check growing European power. Britain had stepped into this fractured political environment in pursuit of commerce, but mercantile interest brought political engagement. The French joined in as well, but by the 1790s they had been marginalized, and Britain maintained the controlling interest. The great question of the day was how far Britain should or could press that interest. Was it Britain's responsibility to establish order in India by maintaining a balance of power among the Indian states, or was it Britain's destiny to rule India? Pitt, with his India Act, had sought to take the former tack. Britain, the act said, was in India for commerce, not conquest. At the same time, the interests of the East India Company had to be protected. The company ran its enterprise from Fort William outside of Calcutta. There the governor general presided, but other administrative units—presidencies—were at Fort St. George in Madras and in Bombay. As for the Indian states, Mysore in the south with its capital of Seringapatam, the dominions of the Nizam in central India with Hyderabad as its political center, Oudh in northeastern India, and the Marathas in the north were paramount. The Maratha Confederacy was a microcosm of greater India with the Peshwa symbolically presiding in Poona over a number of independent and competing chieftains.

This was the political milieu into which Arthur stepped, and he soon discovered that his status as Mornington's brother carried with it advantages at Fort William. Sir John Shore, the governor general, was sensitive to the fact that Richard sat on the board of control. Perhaps this explains Arthur's assignment to an expedition to Manila, a project that held out prospects for significant action and prize money as well.

Still, Arthur's first impressions of India were not positive; he saw chaos and treachery everywhere. "It seems a rule of policy here," he

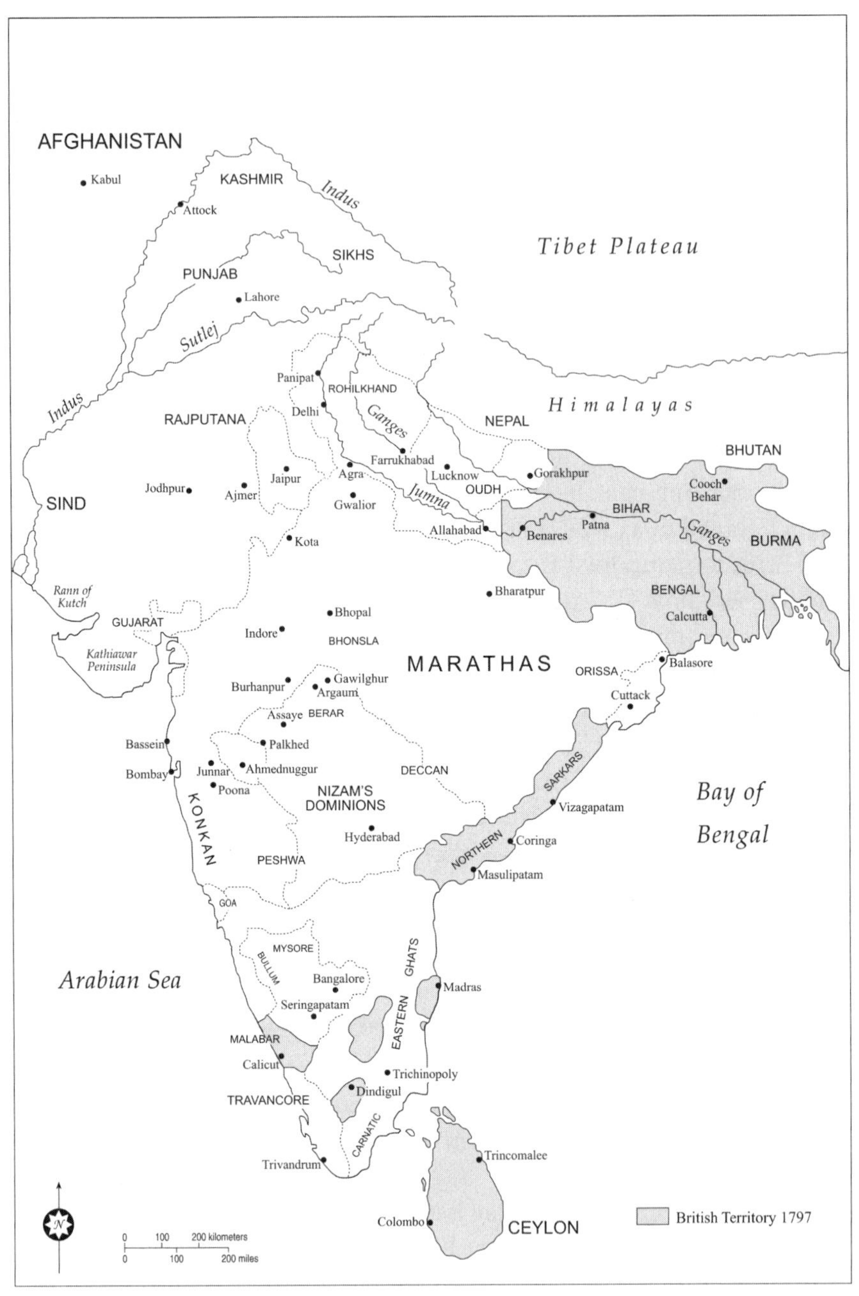

India before the Wellesleys, 1797

wrote, "never to give assistance to your friend when he stands most in need of it, and always to break your treaty with him at the moment when it would be most convenient to him that you should fulfill all its stipulations."[1]

A quick learner, Arthur had prepared himself well on the voyage out. He arrived with a good command of the history, geography, and politics of the subcontinent. Some things—such as the constraints of climate and weather on military operations, and the political behavior of Britons and Indians alike—he would learn on the job. Early on, he warned his brother of instability to the north in the state of Oudh, problems with the Nizam, and the threat from Tipu Sultan of Mysore. Like the rest of his family, he was paranoid about revolutionary France, and his discovery of French officers in various Indian armies alarmed him. He cautioned Mornington that as problematic as the French were at the time, the threat would grow more serious when the European war ended and French soldiers were free to ply their trade as soldiers of fortune.[2]

Arthur's early letters to his brother are direct and forthright, filled with intellectual energy. At the same time, the paucity of information from home left him downcast and lonely. He immersed himself in the Manila project, sending memoranda to the governor general and making detailed preparations.[3] In the midst of these preparations, Arthur received stunning news from his brother; Richard would be joining him. With a keen eye for opportunity, he saw potential benefits:

> I am convinced that . . . you will have the fairest opportunities of rendering material services to the public, and of doing yourself credit, which, exclusive of other personal considerations, should induce you to come out. . . . I shall be happy to be of service to you in your Government; but such are the rules respecting the disposal of all patronage in this country, that I can't expect to derive any advantage from it which I should not obtain if any other person were Governor-General. You may nevertheless be certain that I shall do everything in my power to serve you.[4]

Arthur was right; there were "rules respecting the disposal of all patronage in this country," but his claims that he could not expect to "derive any advantage" are disingenuous; he had already experienced the benefits of influence and preference. Clearly the brothers were already looking out for one another.

Arthur subsequently sailed with his regiment for Penang, which served as a staging point for the assault on Manila. He was there when Shore recalled the expedition owing to fears of an aggressive Tipu Sultan. He returned to Calcutta with the Thirty-third Foot but shortly thereafter traveled to Madras to examine the military preparedness of the presidency and become acquainted with problems in the Carnatic, which surrounded it. By this time, Arthur had come to agree with Shore that Tipu posed an immediate threat to the company's security. During the visit, he became acquainted with Major General George Harris, the commander in chief at Fort St. George who was acting as governor.

Richard and Henry, after several delays, departed on 8 November 1797, along with Rear Admiral Sir Hugh Christian, who was on his way to take command of the squadron stationed at the Cape of Good Hope. There is little to suggest that the event excited Henry. He would have the security of working with his eldest brother, but he had been doing well on his own. Saying no to Mornington, however, was not an option, so off to India he went. Mornington's state could best be described as agitated excitement. Six months of preparation had changed his view of the governor-generalship. Initially accepting the appointment because it represented the best opportunity at the time, he came to see it in a different light by the time of his departure. It then represented a high calling, not just an opportunity to prove his worth and pave a path to other appointments. This change came from the encouragement of those closest to him and to his own propensity to define what he was doing according to his self-image. Thus once he had decided that he must take up the challenge, his opinion of the governor-generalship escalated. Such self-indulgence is not unusual, but Mornington carried it to unusual heights. Life, however, is rarely simple, and Mornington was not allowed the luxury of unabashed enthusiasm for this new challenge. Standing in the way were a wife and five children. Without question, his relationship with Hyacinthe was passionate, and he looked with remorse on the prospect of several years apart from her, not to mention his young family. For her part, Hyacinthe—who shuddered at the prospect of several years without her husband—understood the opportunity that the governor-generalship represented. She had little or no appreciation for the political value of the appointment but clearly understood the financial ramifications; there was never any question but that he should go. Richard hoped that after he settled in, she would follow with the girls, leaving the boys at school under the watchful eyes of friends and family. This proved chimerical. Hyacinthe had no intention of going; she would not leave her children and was morbidly afraid of the sea.

Richard and Hyacinthe, therefore, became entangled in a web of their own spinning. Convinced of the necessity of Richard's going out to India, both were emotionally crippled by the prospect of separation. Their letters, written in French and translated and analyzed by Iris Butler, reveal them as devoted to one another. Through Hyacinthe, one is led to a very human, almost normal man in Richard Wellesley. This private correspondence reveals emotional sensibility, sexual tension, self-doubt, a vision of the future, jealousy, and anger. Absent is the pomposity that historians associate with Mornington's personality and his career. Even his earlier, grasping letters to Grenville were the product of an insecure man writing to a friend he could trust.[5]

Before Mornington departed, he placed most of his private affairs in the joint hands of Hyacinthe and his brother William Wellesley-Pole. Richard planned meticulously, and Pole, though he had always been cool towards Hyacinthe, took his responsibilities seriously.[6] In the years to come, Pole nearly made a career for himself in the management of his brothers' affairs. Apparently he was good at it, because none of them ever questioned him. Early on, he saw something special in Arthur because he attached himself closely to his younger brother long before Arthur's career soared. In return, Mornington's friends would look after Pole.

As Mornington's ship, *La Virginie,* pulled away from port, his heartstrings popped. He had not anticipated such a farewell, not knowing when, if ever, he would see his wife and children again. Still, he found his emotional bearings and his sea legs quickly and threw himself into the task of preparing for the challenge ahead. The letter diary that he would send to Hyacinthe reveals him as lonely but not preoccupied with it. He rose early and, weather permitting, took breakfast on deck. Having packed an extensive library to fill the long hours at sea, he occupied his days with study and conversation.[7] The books were not chosen idly. Included were several volumes on Indian history and geography, and clearly he mastered them. One of the remarkable features of Mornington's governor-generalship was his command of detail. Especially astonishing is how much he knew when he arrived, first in Madras and then in Calcutta. His seat on the board of control gave him a command of the essentials, but the depth of his knowledge suggests concentrated study as well as a copious intellect.

Mornington found Sir Hugh Christian an amiable companion, and he was much taken by the ship's navigator. Occasionally he had trouble sleeping, but generally the journey was pleasant. He was relaxed and optimistic. Laid low by a seasickness that he could not shake, Henry could not say the same; for him the journey was six months of agony. Not surprisingly, he was not a good companion, and Mornington lost patience with him. "Henry can do nothing," he wrote; "I have never seen anyone so defeated." Poor Henry. Knowing that his brother lacked the capacity to empathize, he tried desperately to activate himself when his symptoms subsided. They never left him, however, and he could not concentrate for long. Mornington mistook this for lethargy and began to wonder if he had erred in bringing Henry along.[8]

They stopped for refreshment at Madeira and then pressed on. On 28 January 1798, *La Virginie* put into harbor at the Cape to deposit Sir Hugh Christian and to make repairs. Richard and Henry enjoyed their visit with an old friend, Lady Anne Barnard, whose husband was chief secretary to the government of the Cape. Mornington made the most of his stay. Blessed with a marvelously temperate climate, the Cape served as a place where servants of the East India Company went for prolonged rest. It proved a tonic for the Wellesley brothers as well, but more important, it introduced Mornington to people who knew what was going on in India at the time. And because the Cape was a port of call for ships going to and from India, he had the opportunity to read dispatches sent to the board of control and the court of directors. Mornington became acquainted with Lieutenant Colonel William Kirkpatrick, resident at Hyderabad, who provided him with a picture of Indian politics.[9] Their conversations fired Mornington's imagination concerning the possibilities for involvement in Indian affairs.

Mornington's initial ideas came from his conversations with Henry Dundas, who presided over the board of control. Mornington respected Dundas and (as letters to Hyacinthe show) considered him a friend. We do not know what Dundas felt in turn. A cool-headed man and not the type to admire someone simply because of Pitt's endorsement, Dundas likely saw in Mornington a talent that could be tapped. He certainly treated Mornington and his family respectfully and kindly. In any case, the two had talked through Indian problems thoroughly before Mornington's departure. Whether Mornington knew or understood the assumptions underlying Dundas's views, however, is unclear.

Dundas believed that Britain's power and future rested on the firm foundation of empire. Britain's foreign policy therefore should be based not only on the preservation of that empire but also on shoring it up. Believing that peace with France was unlikely, Dundas questioned Britain's role on the European continent. He believed that Britain's ability to influence the course of events there was limited and saw the empire as the proper focus of the country's efforts. To his mind, this meant controlling shipping lanes, depriving European rivals of their colonial outposts, and enhancing the security of existing British dominions. It was a realistic and clearly conceived policy reflecting the subtlety of Dundas's mind. Accordingly, he directed Wellesley to preserve order in India and to minimize French influence wherever it might be found.[10]

This was fine with Wellesley, whose correspondence from the Cape of Good Hope vibrates with excitement. After spending three months contemplating the role he would play as governor general, he did not intend it to be passive. He had not given up family and friends to preside over the status quo—quite the contrary. He had long thought himself the equal of his old school- and university-mates Grenville, Addington, and Bathurst and believed that he had been deprived of the opportunity to demonstrate it. Now he had that opportunity. To make the best of it, he would have to be proactive; determining just how he would proceed must have troubled him as the *Virginie* plowed the waters of the Atlantic. His instructions spoke of maintaining a balance of power among the native states and of limiting European (meaning French) influence, the principles on which Pitt's India Act was based. The act, in an effort to stop a seemingly endless string of wars in the subcontinent that threatened both the prosperity and the security of the East India Company, forbade war as an instrument of policy; it could only be justified on the grounds of self-defense. The act was, therefore, restrictive, and Wellesley's predecessor, Sir John Shore, had followed it to the letter. So determinedly unobtrusive was Shore that he was prepared to abandon an ally unless there existed a clear case of its being the victim of aggression. Mornington did not intend to follow this course, and he realized that the caveat of self-defense allowed him some room to maneuver. He had every intention of playing a role in the politics of the subcontinent. Mornington and Dundas both recognized that a revitalized and hostile revolutionary France altered the political dynamics of India and that they needed to be prepared to deal with the French. Still, when Mornington went out, "caution" was the watchword. He knew that Tipu Sultan of Mysore gave cause for worry and that Zaman Shah perennially threatened from Afghanistan, but until he spoke with Kirkpatrick, he had no sense of how these factors might provide the means for a more active policy.

What Kirkpatrick described was a more extensive and pernicious French presence than had been thought previously. Particularly disturbing was French influence in the Nizam's army. To prove himself a man of action, Mornington needed something to act upon, and this would be it. In his hands, Kirkpatrick's information became the germ of a crisis. In describing the Nizam's French corps of ten thousand men to Dundas, he invoked all the proper code words: "The corps is recruited in the proportion of one-third of its total numbers, from our territories and from those of the Nabob of Arcot [Carnatic], and partly from deserters abandoning our service. The chief officers are Frenchmen of the most virulent and notorious principles of jacobinism; and the whole corps constitutes an armed French party of great zeal, diligence and activity."[11]

Mornington queried Kirkpatrick as closely as possible, thereby learning even more alarming news. The activities of Tipu Sultan had forced the recall of the expedition to Manila. The Marathas were disruptive, especially Daulat Rao Sindia, maharaja of Gwalior, causing concern for the Nizam. Malabar was in a state of chaos. And Zaman Shah once again threatened an incursion in the north, where political confusion made defense problematic. The frontier state of Oudh had experienced succession problems, and the nawab, Ali, was proving an ineffective ruler. Under most circumstances, such intelligence would have been cause for alarm; for Mornington it was music to his ears. To him it merely proved that Britain had lost the capacity to influence the course of events in the subcontinent. In a dramatic sigh, he wrote to Dundas, "I cannot shut my eyes to the diminution which our weight in the scale of the country powers has suffered, and is likely to suffer still more, if the means of checking the progress of the evil be much longer neglected." It was clear, he maintained, that "the balance of power in India no longer exists upon the same footing on which it was placed by the Peace of Seringapatam. The question therefore must arise, how it may best be brought back again to that state, in which you have directed me to maintain it." Mornington was calling for action, and the best part was that "I cannot receive your opinions for a long time. In that interval circumstances may compel me to decide some of these important questions upon my own judgment."[12] Decide he would, starting with the French corps of the Nizam.

Richard and Henry spent six weeks at the Cape while repairs were made to the *Virginie.* It constituted a refreshing interlude, one certainly welcomed by Henry, seeking to regain his strength after weeks of seasickness. Mornington, in turn, had plenty of time to digest all that he had heard. The great puzzle concerning Richard's early career is how he made the transition from an uncertain young politician to an aggressive, imaginative imperial leader. The process began through observation at Pitt's dining table, but the transformation occurred on the voyage out, especially in these weeks at the Cape. There Mornington began to recognize the possibilities and conceive of his modus operandi. His grasp of history, both ancient and recent, provided the reference points for his notions of leadership and imperial strategy. One can imagine then that the six-week crossing of the Indian Ocean seemed as long to him as the three months it took to reach the Cape.

The brothers arrived at Madras on 25 April 1798 to great pomp presided over by General Harris, who functioned as both commander in chief and interim governor. Arthur, excited over the prospect of seeing his two brothers, had preceded them to Madras in expectation of their arrival. After waiting in vain for two weeks, he returned to Calcutta, where they would eventually meet for the first time in two years. Entranced by all that he saw, Mornington wasted little time in getting down to work. He found the army in good condition and Harris a competent commander. He then attended to the problems of corruption and maladministration that plagued the Carnatic. When the nawab[13] proved uncooperative, Mornington chose to leave this problem to another day.[14] He was off to Calcutta and Fort William, landing there just days after Sir John Shore's departure. The British community he found was entrenched, tightly knit, and opinionated. They had their own ideas on how the company should manage its affairs and by all appearances lamented Shore's departure. Mornington, well aware of his predecessor's style of leadership, made clear from the moment he stepped ashore that things would be different. "Lord Mornington arrived . . . in the *Virginie* frigate," wrote William Hickey, "at once bursting forth like a constellation in all his pomp and splendour amongst us."[15]

Mornington had just settled in when he was presented with an unlikely turn of events. Circulating in Calcutta was the proclamation of one Anne Joseph Hyppolite Malartic, commander in chief and governor general of Isle de France and Réunion. "Citizens," he proclaimed, "Having for several years known your zeal and your attachment to the interests, and to the glory of our Republic, we are very anxious, and we feel it a duty to make you acquainted with all the propositions which have been made to us by Tipu Sultaun, through two ambassadors whom he has despatched to us. . . . In a word he only waits the moment when the French shall come to his assistance, *to declare war against the English, whom he ardently desires to expel from India.*"[16] The document perplexed Mornington and everyone else who first saw it. Such a negotiation, under normal circumstances, would be secret. For Tipu to show his hand or for his ally to betray a confidence made no sense. The proclamation was, therefore, received with some skepticism. At the same time, it fired Mornington's imagination, and he concluded that his best interest lay in confirming its authenticity. Thus an investigation was begun and the governor general got his confirmation, a fact later substantiated by documentation found in Tipu's archives.[17] Mornington's priorities promptly changed. Able to claim that Tipu intended to march against the company, he could respond aggressively within the guidelines of Pitt's India Act.

Mornington's thinking had been focused almost exclusively on the Nizam and the French-led corps in the Nizam's army, but with the proclamation it shifted to Mysore and Tipu Sultan. Mysore had long been a concern for the British, particularly threatening their interests in southern India. Three wars had been fought there, yet Mysore remained independent and formidable. Mornington's friend Lord Cornwallis had won the third war but had not chastened Tipu. For Mornington, then, this was a heaven-sent opportunity to prove himself; he would succeed where others before him had failed. On

9 June 1798, he ordered General Harris to begin preparations for war; it was his intention to bring the issue to a head as soon as possible.[18]

Like all governors, Mornington had been sent out with a mandate to economize. Never throughout his career would he take such matters seriously, and the politics of his new post gave him an excuse to ignore them. He portrayed a company under siege. There was Tipu to the south, Zaman Shah to the north, chaos in central India; nowhere did he find the company prepared to deal with the threats. This could be changed, but he could not be troubled with fiscal responsibility at the same time. Mornington had been through some of this with Dundas before he departed and believed that he would have support from Pitt's government. In any case, caution would get him nowhere. In many ways, Mornington's governor-generalship was an audacious gamble—one that, for the most part, he won. Meanwhile, he would disguise his intentions towards Mysore as best he could. He sent a letter to Seringapatam announcing his arrival, portraying himself as eager to negotiate outstanding issues, and making no mention of the Malartic proclamation; that he would do only at the critical moment. Certainly aware of the proclamation's existence in Calcutta, Tipu had his own game to play and did not attempt any sort of preemptive explanation.[19]

Mornington wasted little time establishing his authority. He used Harris's suggestions to Rear Admiral Peter Rainier for disposition of the fleet as the pretext. On 26 June 1798, Mornington wrote,

> The general protection of India belongs to me, and forms one of the most material branches of my arduous responsibility. In the discharge of this duty I shall always expect to be assisted by the co-operation of the other presidencies; but if they offer opinions to the commanders of His Majesty's squadrons with respect to the distributions of the naval force for the general purposes of defense, without reference to me, or any previous knowledge of my intentions, the utmost degree of confusion must be the result, and my views for the public safety must be wholly defeated. The public letter which I have sent to you in Council upon this occasion is intended as a general rule for the conduct of the Government of Fort St. George on all similar occasions, and I trust that you will have the goodness to recommend the observance of this rule both to your Council and your successor.[20]

One can almost see the smirk on Mornington's face as he penned this punishing letter.

The letter caused Harris less concern than the prospect of war with Tipu. The commander in chief faced many problems, among them the absence of reliable allies, the result of which would require the substantial reinforcement of Madras before any campaign could begin. Moreover, a siege train for the investment of Seringapatam would take several months to assemble. And then there was the monsoon, which would impede the movement of forces from Bombay and complicate the siege of Seringapatam.[21] Such problems would have been clear to any military man and to anyone who had spent time in India; neither applied to Mornington. The governor general found the delays frustrating and provocative, but before railing at Harris, he turned to Arthur.

Arthur must have been taken aback by his brother's request for an analysis of the company's ability to fight an immediate war, but it was a clear signal that the governor general needed input from someone he could trust. It also signaled that the familial connection would be a working connection; a governor general would not normally turn to the likes of Arthur for advice. Arthur had been on only one campaign (and then only briefly), and his experience of India was limited, to say the least. What must have been especially curious to Arthur was the fact that Richard had previously demonstrated little faith in him. Arthur knew full well that until only recently, his older brother had considered him more of a nuisance than an asset. These facts say something about Mornington's feelings and perceptions in his first months at the helm in Fort William. Placed in a strange, exotic, and perhaps even disorienting environment, surrounded by strangers for whom he had little respect, seeing them as members of a self-perpetuating bureaucracy, he turned to the familiar. His survival in India would not be unlike the Wellesleys' survival in Ireland: he had to be resourceful and flexible, and above all he had to rally the support of his family. In this way, Mornington forged a new relationship with his brothers; it was his good fortune that Arthur and Henry possessed abilities far surpassing anyone's expectations. It was part of the gamble.

Arthur had already given some of Mornington's questions serious thought. A series of memoranda assessing Tipu's intentions and capacities, problems to be confronted by the company in staging an offensive, and issues to be addressed with the company's allies (particularly the Nizam) flowed in rapid succession from his pen. In the end, Arthur confirmed Harris's analysis. He believed a fight justified but recognized that further preparations were required to undertake it. And while those preparations went forward, Tipu would have to be contained. Arthur's memoranda are extraordinary for their meticulous detail and the practical reasoning behind their conclusions. He had made himself an expert on the army and on India, and his confident style reflected his awareness that Mornington had come to consider him a confidant.[22]

Arthur's conclusions made Harris's more palatable. Those of Josiah Webbe, secretary to the government of Fort St. George, the governor general found problematic. Webbe thought Mornington's plans foolhardy. He considered a reasonably strong Tipu essential to the balance of power in India, a balance that included the Nizam and the Marathas. Equally important, he saw Tipu as more than a match for the company but, despite evidence to the contrary, unwilling to risk a war. "I have not studied to exaggerate any part of this memorandum," wrote Webbe; "but seeing that our resources have, by the mere operation of the war in Europe, been reduced to a state of the greatest embarrassment, and having no hope of effectual relief but in peace, I can anticipate none but the most baneful consequences from a war with Tipu."[23] Webbe thought Mornington out of his depth, and the condescension enraged the governor general.

No fool, Mornington took the advice of the experts he trusted; the objective did not change, he simply reworked the timetable. In fact, he found himself back where he had intended to start in the first place. Step one was to reconstruct the company's alliance with the Nizam and dismantle the French corps. At the same time, Mornington would deal with the Marathas, opening negotiations with the Peshwa in Poona and encouraging Sindia to move northwards. In the case of the Nizam, Mornington would invoke Tipu's threat, and in the case of Sindia, he would play the Zaman Shah card. Clearly, he envisioned solid British control over southern India as the end result. At this point, Mornington did not contemplate the annihilation of Tipu but rather the sultan's reduction and expulsion from the Malabar coast to cut him off from contact with the French. Mornington would force Tipu to admit a company resident and pay the costs of the war. Lastly, all Europeans would be required to leave Mysore.[24]

Mornington believed that success depended on the negotiations at Hyderabad. The Nizam had to be persuaded to disband the French corps. The governor general knew that the French officers would have to be replaced, and he decided to install British officers in their place to pull the Nizam into the company's orbit in alliance against Tipu. This was easier said than done, since the Nizam did not possess a wellspring of trust for the British. Nonetheless, Mornington proved lucky on several counts. First, the trusted brother of Colonel Kirkpatrick, Captain James Achilles Kirkpatrick, would handle the negotiations as interim resident at Hyderabad. Second, local politics would intervene to the governor general's advantage.

Tipu would be the trump card in these negotiations. Mornington instructed James Kirkpatrick to warn the Nizam that Tipu likewise maintained a substantial French influence in his army and that if the sultan went to war, his French mercenaries might induce treason among the Nizam's French. At the same time, Kirkpatrick would offer guarantees for the Nizam's security.[25] These were not particularly sound points for negotiation, so to succeed, Kirkpatrick would need help. He would find it in the Nizam's chief minister, Azim-al-Umra. The minister was closely involved in a succession struggle through his granddaughter who was married to the Nizam's eldest son, Secunder Jah, the heir apparent. However, a younger son maneuvered for his own succession and turned to the French for support. Azim-al-Umra made clear the price of his influence: Britain would support Secunder Jah as successor, British troops would be sent to support the expulsion of the French and the disbanding of their corps, and Britain would continue to act as arbiter between Hyderabad and Marathas. Mornington readily accepted these demands and instructed Kirkpatrick to move forward.[26] At the same time, he ordered General Harris to prepare his army for war and to make ready two regiments of infantry, consisting of one thousand troops to assist in the disarming of the French corps. Sensing hesitation at Fort St. George, Mornington turned the screws: "The true state of the question therefore is, whether by continuing unarmed and unallied we shall abandon the issues of peace, war, and certain victory, to the discretion of a vindictive enemy, or whether by resuming the power of meeting him in the field, we shall place in our hands the advantage now possessed by him."[27] General Harris did his best to demonstrate activity but at the same time was quick to make excuses: he needed specie, he needed reinforcements.

In turn, Mornington sent specie, but more important, he dispatched Arthur to Fort St. George with the Thirty-third Foot to replace soldiers sent to Hyderabad, along with orders to raise two more regiments for themselves. Arthur would also provide the governor general with eyes and ears in Fort St. George, where there existed a general fear that Tipu might launch a preemptive strike. Mornington had no patience for such thinking.[28] These men needed some backbone, and Arthur could provide it. Mornington tended towards paranoia in the best of circumstances; in this situation, he saw an enemy behind every tree. Harris's tone turned apologetic, and Mornington perceived evil elsewhere; he wanted his enemies in Madras identified and neutralized.

Negotiations in the north included the Peshwa, and the resident in Poona, Colonel William Palmer, would handle these. Mornington's goals there were more limited but pursued aggressively nonetheless. The ultimate goal was to bring the Peshwa into an alliance with the company in the hope that he might dispatch cavalry in a war with Tipu. At the very least, Mornington sought to neutralize any threat from that quarter. Equally important, he wanted the Maratha chieftain, Sindia, out of Poona and settled in the north to relieve the Peshwa while discouraging movements by Zaman Shah.[29] The threats of Zaman and the pernicious French were less convincing in Poona than in Hyderabad. Consequently, the negotiations dragged on inconclusively.

Meanwhile, the new governor of Madras, Edward Clive (son of the great Robert Clive, first Baron of Plassey), arrived at Fort St. George. Wasting little time, Mornington informed Clive of his plans, instructed the governor on the challenges awaiting in Madras, and established himself as the superior authority.[30] Meanwhile, Arthur arrived in Madras, and his correspondence suggests that he found Harris and Clive thoroughly bullied. He entered into frequent and detailed conversations with both, not only to acquire full knowledge of the ongoing military preparations but also to get a sense of the mettle of these two men. Clive was suitably cowed. "I cannot express to your Lordship the satisfaction I feel in the arrival of Colonel Wellesley," he wrote to the governor general. "I find him so easy in his manners and friendly in his communications, that I cannot doubt but that the more I have the opportunity of cultivating his intimacy, the more I shall rejoice at the presence of a person so nearly connected with your Lordship, and so entirely possessed of your views and intentions."[31] For Mornington, that response must have been welcome.

The prospect of war energized Arthur. Like his brother, he was in India to make something of himself, and the more quickly he took to the field the better. Knowing that he would play a major role in the coming conflict, he was eager to get on with it and did nothing to discourage the governor general. "The question is," he wrote in July, "are we or are the French to have superiority in the Deccan?"[32] Confirming Richard's view that the French influence in Hyderabad must be eliminated, he worried only that the governor general might provoke a war before diplomatic and military preparations were complete, and he suggested that the governor general maneuver Tipu into the rainy season to discourage a military initiative. This must have irked Mornington; he had no intention of provoking war. Did his brother take him for a fool?[33] Innocuous negotiations with Tipu continued. Because there appear in both Richard's and Arthur's correspondence references to resolving outstanding issues with Tipu through negotiation, one might conclude that Mornington opted for war only when other possibilities were exhausted. Such a notion cannot be taken seriously. The private and public correspondence makes the governor general's intent more than clear, particularly when combined with his actions on the eve of conflict. Mornington would have his war. References to a negotiated settlement were perfunctory—he knew it and Arthur knew it. Negotiations did serve a purpose, however, since they were designed to establish the time and place of the fighting.

As August melted into September, Mornington became impatient with the slow pace of negotiations in Hyderabad. His dispatches to Kirkpatrick betrayed a sense of urgency and not a little frustration. At the same time, Mornington received from the court of directors a dispatch announcing the departure of Napoleon Bonaparte's expedition from Toulon. Aware that an expedition was in the making, the governor general was not surprised. Mornington was, however, pleased to find that Dundas and the court of directors were concerned about the security of India. As far as they knew, Bonaparte had targeted either the eastern Mediterranean or India via the Cape. Both represented a threat to the subcontinent, and the court informed Mornington that reinforcements to number four thousand soldiers would be promptly dispatched to India.[34] Clearly, only a direct order to stop war preparations would have deterred Mornington at this point, but this sort of green light only stimulated an already energized governor general.

By the end of September, that the Nizam was moving towards a new treaty with the company had become increasingly clear. Writing to Clive on 24 September, Mornington proclaimed that "it cannot be denied that what we have already gained in point of influence was rather to be desired than expected; and if the moment had not been peculiarly favourable, we could not safely have ventured even so far as the limits of my instructions of the 8th of July." The influence came from Azim-al-Umra, and Mornington commented cynically in the same letter, "Azim ul Omra . . . is almost afraid of what he has done, and . . . still doubts whether he has enslaved himself or established his power on permanent foundations."[35] Three days later, the Nizam told Mornington that he would support an ultimatum to Tipu and go to war alongside the company if necessary.[36] There were details to be worked out, but Mornington's plans were nearing fruition.

Arthur found maintaining amicable relations between Fort William and Fort St. George his greatest challenge. Convinced that there was some sort of conspiracy in Madras designed to foil his plans, Mornington lectured both Clive and Harris regularly and railed to Dundas on the pernicious influence of Josiah Webbe. Arthur tried to put his brother at ease. Harris, he concluded, could be trusted, and together they would educate Clive. He saw Clive as a malleable sort and quite likable. His communications at this time reveal a mixture of confidence and insecurity. When writing about politics and military matters, Arthur was remarkably self-assured, but when it came to his brother, he was not altogether comfortable. He assured Richard, for instance, that he was working hard: "This is the third or fourth letter I have written to you or to Henry since my arrival; so that you see I have not been idle or inattentive to the objects which you recommended to me."[37] What concerned him politically was that Mornington's cajoling might become counterproductive. He instructed Henry that Clive could be trusted and that Mornington should just let the governor do his job.[38] The clear implication was that Arthur could control him: "Lord Clive opens his mind to me very freely upon all subjects. I give him my opinion, and talk as I would to M[ornington]." And in an example of extraordinary sagacity, Arthur noted, "My idea in this is to avoid disputes upon petty subjects, which have one effect only, that of erecting little men . . . into great ones."[39] As military preparations pressed forward in October, all of these issues were aggravated. On

23 October 1798, he again confided in Henry: "I don't think that it is advisable to let M[ornington] know that the Military Board have caused the delay in sending the train, as it will serve only to exasperate him still more against people here, which I don't think necessary." A day later, he wrote again: "I am . . . heartily sick of the business, and I wish I was anywhere else. . . . I don't wish that this should be mentioned to M[ornington]."[40]

Although Arthur enjoyed his influence, he remained uncomfortable with his position in Madras. "With regard to my staying here," he wrote to Henry, "I am perfectly satisfied to remain here as long as my presence may be necessary, although I consider my situation a very awkward one, and without remedy." What was awkward? Being the brother of the governor general apparently had its downside, most likely the gossip that attended it. Arthur had been thrust into the thick of important events for no apparent reason other than Mornington's favor. Whispers of that sort would have bothered the proud Arthur immensely, and so too would whispers to the effect that he was there only to spy. Careful not to complain to the governor general, he warned Henry, "I should not . . . wish M[ornington] to know that I feel it at all."[41]

It is hard to feel sympathy for Arthur. Whatever the difficulties of his position—perceived or real—Mornington had placed him well, and Arthur came to understand that while his relationship with the governor general gave cause for grief, the benefits far outweighed the liabilities. For instance, as he made preparations for assembling a supply train for the anticipated campaign, he abandoned without authorization (and in fact in defiance of standing general orders) the traditional requisitioning of bullocks in favor of hiring them. He could do this because he knew that Harris would not cross him. This is not to suggest that Arthur abused his privilege. He worked diligently, normally within the rules, and with great expertise. He impressed everyone around him with his reliability and his attention to detail. This was a man who left nothing to chance.

Henry's presence was crucial. He served as a sounding board and as a sponge, absorbing frustration and hostility. One can imagine that what Arthur said to Henry on paper he received in equal measure verbally from the governor general. The consummate listener, Henry was well suited for such a role. It was an interesting troika and one that must have intimidated those working with the Wellesley brothers. They watched out for one another and were absolute in their confidentiality.

Negotiations with the Peshwa and with Sindia progressed less satisfactorily than those with the Nizam, and the name Zaman Shah appears more frequently in the correspondence. The threat from the north Mornington viewed as secondary, but it was a negotiating tool and as such had to be made to look real. Had it been genuine, Mornington would not have moved so boldly in the south. Nonetheless, Zaman was not a figment of Mornington's imagination, and he used the shah first to try to separate Sindia from the Peshwa. Later, Mornington would use Zaman Shah to redefine the company's relationship with Oudh. All along, however, the key had been Hyderabad, where the dispersal of the French corps was critical. On 22 October, the Nizam finally ordered his French auxiliaries to lay down their arms. It all proceeded with remarkable ease; the French officers placed themselves under British protection without a hint of resistance. The only problem emerged from the rank and file, who were concerned over back pay.[42] This was negotiated, and Mornington had a diplomatic victory of the first order. Everyone knew it. "I should not even now have interrupted you," wrote Harris, "if the great and important news from Hyderabad did not compel me to congratulate you on it. Never was any event more completely the work of an individual, than that has been your Lordship's."[43] With that victory, the contest with Tipu Sultan could begin in earnest.

Mornington engaged Tipu by informing him of Nelson's victory over the French fleet at Aboukir Bay. After describing the barbaric nature of the French campaign in Egypt, he pointed out that the French were doomed, that the army would wither and die in Egypt and Tipu could expect no help from that quarter.[44] Serious engagement followed the light sparring. "It is impossible," wrote the governor general, "that you should suppose me to be ignorant of the intercourse which subsists between you and the French, who you know to be the inveterate enemies of the Company, and to be now engaged in an unjust war with the British nation." He proposed sending an envoy to Seringapatam, a Major John Doveton, to represent company interests.[45] This was followed by a dispatch to James Kirkpatrick asking how long it would take to put the Nizam's army on a war footing. Clearly, Mornington expected war and wanted to fight it before the middle of February. A nudging of Clive followed:

> For my own part I declare to your lordship, that I deem myself bound by every principle of duty and character to suspend every other consideration as secondary to the indispensable object of providing a large force in the field and an efficient system of alliance; and so entirely devoted am I to the exigencies of this duty, that my estimate of characters, and my sentiments of respect, and even of affection in this country, are regulated absolutely by the degrees of zeal and alacrity which I find in those who are to assist me in this great struggle.[46]

This stands as an extraordinary statement: either you support me or you are not my friend! Tipu, meanwhile, responded incredulously if insincerely, wondering why, if reports were true, the British were making military preparations. Tipu had parried the first blow. At the same time, Dundas once again inadvertently stoked the fire: "I think it . . . right to send the copy of a proclamation said to be issued by the governor of the Mauritius, and if it speak true, we are probably at this time at war with Tipu Sultaun."[47] Well, not quite.

Through a spy, Clive learned that Tipu expected war but was not yet prepared, with the citadel of Seringapatam undergoing repair and renovation. Tipu thus sought to buy as much time as possible.[48] Mornington by this time had decided to go to Madras to be closer to the action. This had been suggested earlier, but Mornington was loath to leave Calcutta in the hands of Sir Alured Clarke, the overall commander in chief in India. Arthur, however, insisted on Mornington's presence in Madras for a number of reasons. First, it would show that the governor general was serious about the ongoing negotiations—thus sending a signal both to Tipu and to the company's allies. More important, residency in Madras would dramatically shorten the time necessary for the exchange of correspondence. Convinced that Mornington wanted to fight, Arthur urged commencement of hostilities by the end of January. He also thought that managing his impatient brother might be easier in person, for Arthur worried that Mornington might alienate Clive and force him into the hands of others less well disposed to war.[49] The decision made, Mornington adopted a more aggressive tone in his correspondence with Tipu, who could not help but notice. Poised for action, Mornington talked negotiation but thought war, considering the situation nonnegotiable: "the course of our complaint against Tipu Sultaun, is not that he has seized a portion of our property which he might restore, or invaded a part of our territory which he might again cede, or violated a right which he might hereafter acknowledge; we complain, that, professing the most amicable disposition, bound by subsisting treaties of peace and friendship, and unprovoked by any offense on our part, he has manifested a design to effect our total destruction."[50]

With Mornington on his way to Madras, military preparations went forward with renewed energy. One question that remained unresolved was the role Arthur would play in the upcoming campaign. There was no question that he would have an important command; Harris, after all, was no fool. But just what the role might be carried some significance if there was a prize to be divided. Lady Longford maintains that Arthur did not share his brother's warlike intentions, but there is not much to support such a thesis. Certainly Arthur spoke of the benefits of negotiation, but so did Richard. The fact is, Arthur counted his pennies carefully, and with the court of directors cutting allowances to officers, they were flowing out faster than they were coming in. Moreover, he had not gone out to India to sit idly by. He was there to make himself solvent and perhaps a name in the process. Those objectives could best be reached through war. He was not so mercenary as to argue for an unjust war, but in this case his conscience troubled him not. To his mind, Tipu had done more than enough to provoke a British response, and as long as there was to be war, Arthur wanted to be a part of it. Mornington had no doubts about his support.[51]

Arthur proved lucky. His immediate superior, Colonel Henry Aston, had been assigned the task of organizing a force to march north, take charge of the Nizam's army, and lead it back to link up with Harris's main force. In the midst of these preparations, one of Aston's officers challenged him to a duel. The unfortunate Aston caught a bullet in the shoulder and a week later died. To fill the void, Harris turned to Arthur, who promptly set about completing preparations. As Christmas came and went, great optimism pervaded Madras. Clive reported Seringapatam to be in bad repair and predicted a six-week siege. Arthur too saw success on the horizon but expected to achieve it more slowly than the sanguine Clive projected, perhaps requiring two campaigns.[52]

Tipu, still trying to evade the charging Mornington, responded with a clever letter. He claimed incredulity over any doubt of Mysore's friendship. Everything was fine, so fine indeed that there would really be no need for Mr. Doveton to go to Seringapatam. After all, there was a treaty—peace and amity could be maintained simply by the observance of these treaties. He finished with a flourish, making disparaging remarks about the French.[53] The letter awaited Richard and Henry when they arrived at Madras on 31 December. It meant nothing other than the fact that Tipu was playing the governor general's game. The worst that could have happened at that point would have been a call for negotiations. In that unlikely event, Mornington was prepared to offer unacceptable conditions.

Clive welcomed the governor general and Henry to Fort St. George, and Mornington subsequently took control.[54] Tipu's next letter was friendly and typically evasive. Mornington stepped up the pressure. He sent a copy of the Malartic proclamation along with a clear and detailed explication of Tipu's hostile intent. If Tipu wanted peace, he could start by welcoming a resident to Seringapatam.[55] Mornington found Fort St. George in a state of high excitement. Gone was the uncertainty of earlier months; even Webbe had come round to his way of thinking. There was a reason for this. "The improvement of affairs here, the state of Lord Clive's mind, and the advancement of the preparations," wrote Mornington to Dundas, "are to be attributed principally to my brother, Colonel Wellesley. I must repeat my earnest request, that you will, as soon as possible, make him a major-general on the staff of India. He has been most useful to me. He is intimately acquainted with the affairs of this country, and universally beloved."[56] Universally beloved? This is hardly a description that one would associate with the future Iron Duke, but he was after all a young man and had been trying to play the role of mediator. The point is that the brothers were assuming direct management of the proceedings knowing full well that there would be resentment.

Mornington attempted to mobilize the Peshwa but without success. Still, by the middle of January, most pieces of the puzzle were in place. The Nizam's army had begun its march to join Arthur, who had moved north; the Peshwa at least made promises of support; the Carnatic mobilized to a state of readiness; and the navy moved into position off the Malabar coast. Even Zaman Shah appeared to be less of a threat.[57] With everything coming together and war all but a certainty, the suggestion was made that Mornington accompany the army on the campaign. The suggestion doubtless appealed to the governor general, who felt anxious and restless. Although a quick rejection would have been the proper response, Mornington opted for the next best thing. He asked Henry to secure Arthur's opinion. Not surprisingly, Arthur was unambivalent in asserting "it appears to me that your presence in camp, instead of giving confidence to the General, would in fact deprive him of the command of the army. . . . All I can say upon the subject is, that if I were in General Harris's situation, and you joined the army, I should quit it."[58] Mornington accepted his brother's advice with reasonably good grace.[59]

On 3 February, Mornington ordered the invasion to begin, with the object of capturing Seringapatam. Even at this point he did not expect total victory, and he provided Harris with terms for peace. They included an indemnity for all expenses of war, guarantees against future aggression, and territorial concessions.[60] He sent Henry to follow Harris's camp so that he would have a reliable source of information in addition to Arthur, who was in regular contact with the commander in chief. Then the wait began.

These first months in India saw the establishment of Mornington's agenda as well as his modus operandi. In terms of the agenda, the governor general left little doubt that he would be aggressive. Nothing in the record suggests that he had formed anything that resembled a comprehensive policy for India or even a vision for what the future might hold. If he had a policy, it was the advancement of the Earl of Mornington. He intended to show the political world back home that he was a man of action—a problem solver. To him that meant reacting to every opportunity. That said, it must be pointed out that Mornington was more than an opportunist. Well schooled in the history and culture of the subcontinent, he understood to a surprising degree the intricacies of Indian rivalries, internal politics, and personal ambitions. He had some sense of what could be done and what could not. Ambitious he was, but it was an ambition tempered by realism. He did not arrive in India with the aim of creating an empire.

The methods by which he would implement his policies were established in these first months. First and foremost, he would insist on absolute authority. His dispatches to Madras and Bombay make this clear: he would brook no dissent, and he expected prompt execution of his directives. To find a man with so little experience with leadership asserting himself so confidently is surprising, and one cannot help wondering whether it was contrived. Through his studies and the long months of contemplation on the voyage out, Mornington seems to have developed a sense for the type of leadership that worked and, more important, did not work in India. In his opinion, only strong leadership succeeded. Having reached this conclusion, Mornington viewed Shore's tenure as governor general as a disaster. It astonished him to find the presidencies of Bombay and Madras functioning autonomously; even more shocking, in Calcutta he found little respect for the governor general. The British in the city were "so vulgar, ignorant, rude, familiar, and stupid," he wrote to Grenville, "as to be disgusting and intolerable." He wasted little time in administering the remedy: "I am resolved to encounter the task of effecting a thorough reform in private manners here," he went on vividly, "without which the time is not distant when the Europeans settled at Calcutta will control the government, if they do not overturn it. . . . The effect of this state of things on my conduct has been to compel me to entrench myself within forms and ceremonies, to introduce much state into the whole appearance of my establishments and household to expel all approaches to familiarity, and to exercise my authority with a degree of vigour and strictness nearly amounting to severity."[61] The origins of Mornington's imperial style thus lie in expediency, or so he claimed. Unfortunately, he would overdo it and come to enjoy it too much.

In addition to establishing his authority, Mornington also sought a measure of security in the implementation of his policies. This he found primarily in his brothers. Again, with a retrospective understanding of what Arthur would become, one can be seduced into a knowing nod over Mornington's judgment. But Richard had no sense of Arthur's nascent talent, because that is precisely what it was—nascent. That Mornington gave Arthur so much responsibility so soon is a testament to Richard's insecurity, not his judgment. The scope of Arthur's activities in these first months seems beyond reason, but Mornington perceived an administration out of control in which individuals, having established their little empires, would seek to preserve them. The logical conclusion was that no one—other than those with a vested interest in the success of the governor general—could be trusted. Mornington also knew that the strategic placement of his brothers would provide him with a measure of control over important proceedings and a source of reliable intelligence. That Arthur and Henry were as well informed and clear headed as he was turned out to be an additional benefit that he could not have contemplated.

Additionally, there are issues of family ambition and comfort derived from working with people one trusted and loved. No evidence suggests that either Arthur or Henry appreciated their good fortune at the time, but in later years, both acknowledged their debt to the eldest brother.

4

Tiger Hunt

The Mysore campaign proved a catalyst in the career building of both Richard and Arthur. Each expected the campaign to go well, but neither dared to dream that Tipu's collapse would be complete. Such a contest had been in the back of Mornington's mind since he boarded the *Virginie* in the autumn of 1797, but the fortuitous nature of the opportunity in Mysore and the extent of his success left him ecstatic but off balance. He fell prey to the seduction of the moment and allowed himself to forget that his work constituted only a part of Britain's comprehensive foreign and imperial policy. In short, he lost his sense of scale; the duel with Tipu he equated with England's struggle in Europe, and while a case can be made for this assessment, the fact of the matter was that few at home perceived it in that fashion. India's isolation and the fact that Mornington surrounded himself with people who, from self-interest, shared his view, partly explains his reaction. More to the point, his propensity for self-inflation and self-deception accounts for his attitude: Mornington would see the victory over Tipu as monumental because he needed it to be so. For Arthur, the results of the campaign were more prosaic but important nonetheless; doors of opportunity opened that under other circumstances would have remained closed. Once he passed through them, expanded responsibilities, a place towards the front of the officer queue, and financial independence greeted him. Neither man adjusted well to these changes, but for Richard they proved especially problematic.

Arthur's transformation from an officer whose only mark of distinction was a fraternal relationship with the governor general to a confident, decisive, and assertive leader occurred in a period of approximately twelve months, beginning in late 1798. His assignment to Harris's army at Madras offered a great opportunity. The tasks of organizing a force to accompany the Nizam's and of planning, acquiring, and managing supplies and transport for the campaign were daunting, and Harris happily left these tasks to others. Left to his own devices, Arthur proceeded cautiously at first. He is solicitous and uncertain in his early correspondence with Harris, but he quickly found his footing. Leaving nothing to chance, Arthur methodically purchased rice and bullocks on the open market in preparation for the advance on Seringapatam. His keen eye for detail also fell on timber for carts and artillery carriages. The meticulous care that Arthur took in providing for the army and doing it without provoking resentment on the part of the local population (his trademark in the future) gave him confidence. Consequently, Arthur's correspondence with his superior became much more forthright, even presumptuous; what started out as healthy respect for Harris gradually turned to indifference. Harris's attitude, perhaps better described as benign neglect, grated on Arthur. But could it have been possible for Harris not to appreciate matters of logistics and supply? More likely, Harris—not wanting to court trouble with the governor general—left the field to Arthur. The general, who planned to retire from active service in India and return to England after the campaign, was anxious to get on with the war, take the spoils, and run. He was a tired man anxious to end his career without controversy. If the governor general wanted his brother in a position of responsibility, so be it. In fairness to Arthur, Harris recognized talent when he saw it and understood that Arthur was a safe gamble. The two men were in constant contact, and one suspects that Harris preferred not to hear detailed reports from the eager Wellesley. Arthur, however, interpreted this as sloth, and he became more outspoken as time went on.[1]

The first days of the campaign found nearly everyone anxious. For Mornington, the anxiety arose from knowing that when the armies marched, he lost control of events. To compensate, he wrote dispatches so numerous that they became redundant and annoyed the recipients. He worried that Tipu might outmaneuver him; through prevarication and delay, the Tiger of Mysore would attempt to avoid battle until the rainy season. Thus Mornington advised Harris that "no treaty can be safely concluded with Tipu Sultaun until your army shall either be in actual possession of his capital, or shall command the effectual means of securing its reduction."[2] Uneasy with his separation from the army and not one to leave anything to chance, Mornington's fertile and paranoiac brain came up with the idea of a commission to handle political matters associated with the campaign. Members of the commission included Arthur and close confidants Lieutenant Colonel Barry Close and Captain John Malcolm. The message to the commander in chief could not have been clearer; the governor general wanted to direct the course of events as best he could. Though nothing suggests that Harris took the commission as a personal insult, in a preemptive attempt to mollify him, Mornington explained that the commission would ultimately be responsible to the general and that it would relieve him of distractions from the primary responsibility of directing the army.[3]

Arthur, in the meantime, betrayed his own anxieties. In a fit of pique, he wrote to Richard complaining that Harris ignored him: "As in fact there is nothing to be got in the army but credit, and as it is not always that the best intentions and endeavours to serve the public succeed, it is hard that when they do succeed they should not receive the approbation which it is acknowledged by all they deserve. I was much hurt about it at the time, but I don't care now, and shall certainly continue to do everything to serve General Harris."[4] Of course he cared, and he conveyed his feelings in typically convoluted fashion. He need not have been so downcast; three weeks earlier, Harris had sent a glowing report to the governor general stating that "the very handsome appearance and perfect discipline of the troops do honour to themselves and to him [Arthur], while the judicious and masterly arrangements in respect to supplies, which opened an abundant free market, and inspired confidence into dealers of every description, were no less creditable to Colonel Wellesley than advantageous to the public service, and deservedly entitle him to my thanks and approbation."[5]

When writing to Henry, Arthur sounded an entirely different—positive and enthusiastic—tone. He described the campaign as proceeding smoothly and the Indian troops as performing reliably.[6] This discrepancy is curious; one wonders whether Arthur, in his complaints about General Harris, might simply be making certain that Mornington appreciated all that he had accomplished. This would prove a theme throughout his tenure in India. One could never describe as modest Arthur's communications with his eldest brother. By the end of March, his complaints disappeared. It had become clear to Arthur that the campaign progressed well and that Seringapatam would be taken. He based this appraisal on the facts that the approaches to the capital were unobstructed and that the army carried with it a more than adequate siege train. "I am very well," he told Mornington, "but not a little fagged."[7]

Meanwhile, as word circulated that everything proceeded on a successful course, doubters began to climb aboard the bandwagon. "I was early satisfied of the necessity of the vigorous exertions of the governor of this country," wrote Sir John Anstruther, the chief justice of Bengal, "and I am perfectly convinced, however forward the army may now be, that it would still have been at the gates of Madras had you not gone to that settlement."[8] Normally susceptible to flattery, Mornington exhibited no sign of taking it seriously at this juncture (that would come later). There was work to be done, and his attentions fell on the Peshwa, who had promised to support the campaign but did nothing. The campaign was unlikely to fail without Maratha support unless the Marathas supported Tipu. Mornington impatiently instructed the resident, Colonel Palmer, to bring the Peshwa into line.[9]

As the army approached Seringapatam, Tipu resorted to the tactics that Mornington had predicted. Feigning incredulity, he wrote to Harris: "I have adhered firmly to treaties; what then is the meaning of the advance of the English armies and the occurrence of hostilities? Inform me. What need I say more?"[10] Tipu had every reason to worry. Strongly positioned, neither Harris nor the political commission considered negotiation. Arthur, in a long and detailed description of the British position before Seringapatam, informed Mornington that there could be little doubt of the outcome. The army had time, supplies, and a siege train. Not that everything was rosy. He added, "The fatigue and heat of the weather (which is greater here than even at Calcutta) and bad water had given me a bowel complaint, which did not confine me, but teased me much. I have nearly got the better of it, and I hope to be quite well in a few days."[11] One can imagine the discomfort of a jungle campaign, and the intestinal complaint that Arthur described affected others as well. English uniforms alone would have rendered the climate unbearable. Nonetheless, Arthur did not let this malady distract him. In the midst of projects that engaged them, the Wellesleys proved resilient. In the absence of intellectual and emotional commitment, they collapsed under the pressure of physical and emotional distress. On this occasion, Arthur was not about to allow events to proceed without him.

Letters drafted in his tent after long days of vigorous activity flowed from his pen. One dated 5 April 1799 betrayed no anxiety over Harris's orders that he clear the area surrounding his post of enemy troops. The Thirty-third Foot had been in some action as the army closed the perimeter of Seringapatam and had fared well. Perhaps for this reason, the normally cautious Arthur acted with more hubris than forethought and found himself in a difficult situation. Unfamiliar with the ground and faced with impenetrable darkness broken only by hostile fire, disorientation and panic afflicted both the commander and his troops. Arthur called off the attack, and it was every man for himself as the soldiers felt their way back to camp. It was a minor setback, and Arthur made it right the following day. Nevertheless, it embarrassed him, both then and in the days that followed. While Harris was unconcerned, Arthur did not tell his brother of the experience for two weeks, and then he made the best of it: "On the night of the 5th we made an attack upon the enemy's outposts, which, at least on my side, was not quite so successful as could have been wished. The fact was that the night was very dark, that the enemy expected us, and were strongly posted." But a lesson had been learned. "I have come to a determination when in my power, never to suffer an attack to be made by night upon an enemy who is prepared and strongly posted, and whose posts have not been reconnoitered by daylight."[12]

By the end of the first week of April, with the British ensconced before the citadel, Seringapatam's fall was inevitable. Still, Tipu retained his composure, even when Harris responded to his entreaties with harsh demands.[13] Despite heavy rains, on 4 May Harris ordered the assault. The ensuing struggle was brief. Led by the impetuous and courageous general Sir David Baird, the British poured through a breach in the citadel's wall and occupied the city in the course of an hour and a half. Tipu fell in the fighting.[14]

Wholesale looting followed the fall of Seringapatam, and Harris again turned to Arthur, who took charge in the city and moved quickly and mercilessly to establish order. As Arthur explained, he "came in to take the command on the morning of the 5th, and by the greatest exertion, by hanging, flogging, etc. etc., in the course of that day I restored order among the troops, and I hope I have gained the confidence of the people." He soon discovered that it took more than one day to establish order, and as time went on, he looked to Harris for more precise instructions.[15] Arthur had not long to wait. Harris took careful note of his young officer's work and came to the conclusion that Arthur could meet the challenges of managing postwar Seringapatam.

Historians are in agreement over the manner in which Wellesley addressed the problems of managing a conquered city and a victorious army. He proceeded with energy, humanity, and integrity. At the same time, Arthur made certain that everyone understood his role. His first correspondence with Mornington, pompous and presumptuous, focuses almost exclusively on himself. In describing the fall of Seringapatam, he begins,

> A series of successful attacks upon the enemy's posts, particularly one which I made upon his posts close to the river and within about 400 yards of the fort on the 26th of April, enabled us to erect our breaching batteries at a very short distance, and to complete our breach in the place where it was thought most advisable to have it by the 4th instant. On that day, as you will probably have been informed by General Harris, the place was stormed, and was in our possession in about two hours after the troops first began to move out of the trenches. Tipu was killed in one of the gateways, and to complete our good fortune his body was found among the 500 others piled one upon the other in a very narrow compass.[16]

Admittedly, Arthur did not intend this letter to be a comprehensive account of the battle. But to give equal weight to the skirmishes designed to bring the batteries forward, a normal part of the process towards the actual assault (which, although brief, was remarkable), is rather self-serving. Even Mornington in his self-inflating account of the campaign took care to bring others to notice.[17]

What is more extraordinary is the hectoring, presumptuous manner in which Arthur outlined to his brother what he perceived to be the obstacles to peace making and his own proposals for a comprehensive peace. These are presented as between equals, which may have been what Mornington expected. Even so, the tone of their correspondence had palpably changed. "Many persons in camp, and particularly those about the General," Arthur advised his brother, "are exceedingly anxious that you should come here to settle everything. I am (as I was upon a former occasion) of a different opinion. That which is to be settled is a political question, of some consequence certainly, viz. whether you will at all, and in what manner, and in what proportion, take possession of the territory which has been conquered; but there is not information to be got here which can aid you in deciding that question: it can be done equally well, if not better, in your closet at Madras, and we here can execute your orders."[18] The point is that on the "former occasion," Arthur's advice had been solicited. Not that he offered bad advice: Alured Clarke, for one, agreed with him. Clarke, who warned Mornington that Seringapatam would be bad for his health, meant to persuade him to reduce his direct role in the conduct of political-military affairs once the war was over.[19] Mornington was fast becoming what now would be called a micromanager, and no one in the service of the East India Company was much enthused by that.

Mornington responded by appointing another commission, this time to oversee the settlement. The commission included Arthur, Henry, Barry Close, General Harris, and William Kirkpatrick. John Malcolm and Thomas Munro were sent as secretaries. Henry Wellesley and Kirkpatrick carried Mornington's instructions. The unexpectedly decisive victory and the manner in which it was won presented several problems. First and foremost, was there to be a Mysore in the future, or was it to be absorbed by the victorious allies? Arthur's analysis proceeded from the assumption that Mysore belonged to the East India Company by right of conquest. The problem with that assumption was that the Nizam would expect to be rewarded for his assistance, and if he were rewarded, then the Peshwa would expect to be. And so problem one bumped into problem two. The Peshwa had promised his support to the company but hedged his bets and did nothing. Consequently, he deserved no compensation, yet he could not be expected to stand back and watch his neighbor acquire additional territory. Seeing the conundrum, Mornington responded by leaving in existence a much reduced Mysore presided over by a restored Hindu dynasty.[20]

While these details were being worked out, another unexpected problem surfaced. The conquest of Seringapatam had made the city a prize. The army knew this, and to a man they eagerly awaited the division of spoils. Arthur, as usual, had advice for his brother—get on with it. He had reason to be anxious. Tipu's tremendous wealth challenged the order in Seringapatam that had been painstakingly established. Wearied by the responsibility and having been the cause of a dispute between Generals Harris and Baird over his selection for the command of Seringapatam, Arthur wished to satisfy the army's expectations as soon as possible. Baird, who had led the assault and had a reputation as a fearless, aggressive officer, claimed the right to command the city. To say that he was taken aback by Arthur's appointment would be an understatement. "Before the sweat was dry on my brow," Baird wrote, "I was superseded by an inferior officer."[21] While Harris had the right to appoint whom he wanted, Baird had reason to be angry over such obvious political favoritism. Even if Harris felt that he was doing the governor general's bidding, there is no evidence that Mornington leaned on him, and he had good reason to think the assignment fitted Arthur better than the impetuous Baird. Nonetheless, an unseemly correspondence ensued between the two generals.

Harris, correctly seeing bruised egos rather than a clash of principles, reminded Baird that he had not wanted command of the city until he became aware of Arthur's appointment. Harris felt little sympathy for Baird and did not take kindly to the questioning of his judgment: "I am . . . directed to acknowledge the receipt of the *very improper* letter which accompanied your report. . . . Lieutenant-General Harris is persuaded that an officer *who thinks himself authorised to remonstrate with his immediate superior, can never be usefully employed in the army he commands.* Should you, therefore, continue to hold sentiments so opposite to the principles of military subordination, you have his permission *to proceed by the first conveyance to Fort St. George.*"[22] This was the context in which Arthur commanded. The dispute had become common knowledge in the army, and that only Baird protested is perhaps fortunate, as there were several other officers senior to Arthur. Regardless, his sensitivity piqued, Arthur asked Richard to do or say something to assure the army that the men would get their spoils.[23] He implied that rumors in camp suggested that the Wellesleys were about to abscond with the prize money. The last point is worth examining, for it suggests that the brothers were seen as a cabal with the three brothers acting as one and viewing India as their own. Richard did not care; Arthur did.

More interested in Tipu's archive than his treasure, Mornington felt little sympathy for his brother. Beyond that, the punctilious governor general felt that the army presumed too much. "A little more eagerness than I could have wished has appeared in the army on the subject of the property captured in Seringapatam," he wrote to Dundas. "The army conceive that, as the place was taken by storm, they are of right entitled to what was found in it; this is certainly an erroneous opinion."[24] Mornington informed Arthur testily that all prizes belonged to the state, to be granted to the army as the state saw fit, a practice especially necessary in the case of such a huge prize. He suggested that half be given to the army immediately, the second half to be distributed at the discretion of the East India Company. Mornington assured his brother that he would recommend the distribution of the whole of the prize money. But as a bad precedent might be set if they proceeded in any other fashion, he issued a general order on 2 June 1799 that the distribution would be determined by the king's government.[25]

Arthur could hardly believe his eyes but knew instinctively that this was an issue of form and procedure and had nothing to do with the prize. He replied, explaining that the army believed it had the right to the prize according to precedent or custom. He warned his brother that while the army would take what it could get, it would only be happy with taking all. And, in a note of despair, he explained that he was suspected of being responsible for Mornington's decision. He had again been reminded that being the brother of the governor general was a double-edged sword. It brought preferment, but resentment and sometimes ridicule were in its company. Arthur acknowledged the second more often than the first. His discomfort was aggravated by concern for Mornington's good opinion: "If you had not mentioned my name, and alluded to a letter from me in yours to Henry of the 28th of May, I should have imagined that you had been informed that the army was in a state of mutiny on account of its prize-money, and that it had been recommended to you to yield to its unreasonable demands rather than to oppose them. I do not recollect to have said that I thought that the army had a right to the prize: if I had, however, that opinion would have agreed with Lord Cornwallis's, as given to the army in his general orders. . . . I should not have written again upon this subject," he explained, "only that it appeared to me that you had misunderstood what I meant, and had written with more than usual warmth about it."[26] The next day he dispatched another letter explaining that Harris based the army's claim on the precedent set by Cornwallis. The issue of the prize found Arthur caught between a rock and a hard place, with Harris taking one line and Mornington another. Mornington had already concluded that the pressure came from Harris, even though, to his annoyance, Harris had communicated nothing on the subject. That, however, made the situation no easier on Arthur, who did his best to reason with Richard. To him, it made no sense to irritate the army when in the end, as everyone knew, the prize in its entirety would go to those who had taken the city.[27] Ultimately, Mornington won out by reserving the assignment of the confiscated military stores and supplies for the king to determine. This decision would return to haunt him.

Mornington explained to Arthur why he had written with "more than usual warmth" on the subject. "If you were to read over your own letter, on which mine of the 28th May to Henry was founded," he pointed out, "I think you would agree that it was impossible for me to draw any other inference from it."[28] The Mysore correspondence provides an instructive glimpse into the developing relationships among the brothers. The frequency of their contact and the contrived nature of the "commissions" pieced together by Mornington all show that they derived great comfort from one another in that distant and alien land. This is more than simply family self-promotion. It betrays vulnerability and the fact that they were watching out for one another's blind side, though it was Mornington's blind side that was most often watched. The system worked best when they communicated honestly and clearly with one another, as they implicitly understood. The problem was that none of them took criticism well, even when it was invited and came from a trusted family member—perhaps especially then. Thus, when Mornington asked Arthur whether traveling with the army was a good idea and Arthur replied that it was not, Mornington claimed to have thought so all along. He saw no need to concede a sibling's wisdom. And when Arthur told Mornington how to handle the prize issue, he replied that it was not Arthur's problem, thereby wounding Arthur. It was indeed a delicate situation but one that they handled reasonably well, based on the shared recognition that they needed one another; they had to stick together and speak with a common voice because if the governor general failed, so did they all. Their sharing of one another's correspondence confirms that. Henry played the decisive role. Despite being involved in the planning of the conquest and settlement of Mysore, he had the time to shuttle between Madras and Seringapatam to mediate or clarify, whichever was necessary. The triangular correspondence continued with frequency throughout the summer of 1799.

The dust settled quickly on the matter of the prize because the portion split immediately was so large that nobody could complain of an injustice. Harris went home with the astonishing sum of £130,000, and the generals under his command benefited in proportion.[29] Arthur also did well, and on receiving his share, he offered to reimburse Mornington for the cost of his commissions. Mornington's response was fraternal, if a bit patronizing: "no consideration can induce me to accept payment of the sums which I have formerly advanced for you. I am in no want of money, and probably never shall be: when I am it will be time enough to call on you."[30] There would come a time when Richard did find himself in want of money, and he would then call on Arthur. By that time, however, Arthur had long forgotten this exchange.

Meanwhile, Mornington pushed for the conclusion of a treaty. The commission, applying principles outlined by the governor general, had begun to piece things together, especially after one of Tipu's Hindu lieutenants, Purnea, presented himself to Harris and offered to help with the reconstruction of Mysore. Purnea, who had at first advocated the installation of a Muslim government under one of Tipu's heirs, changed his mind when he realized that Mornington would object and instead called for the reestablishment of the old Hindu dynasty.[31] As the heir was only six years of age, Purnea's role would be decisive. And so Mornington found an active and able collaborator just as he had in Hyderabad, and the treaty began to fall into place. Claiming all by right of conquest, Mornington granted the maharaja territories mostly south of Seringapatam. The capital and its fortress were kept by the company; extensive territories along the Malabar coast and on the northern frontier were annexed as well.

The tricky part came when considering compensation for the Nizam and the Peshwa. In these deliberations, Mir Allum represented the Nizam, but the Peshwa had no spokesman. Initially Mornington proceeded on this ground cautiously and with a measure of deference. Within two weeks, however, his tone changed, for he had taken time to contemplate the Peshwa's failure to contribute to the war effort. Eager to consolidate what had been gained and seeing little point in worrying about the Peshwa's sensibilities, he instructed Colonel Palmer in Poona simply to inform the Peshwa that he would receive territory from Mysore, though he did not deserve it. In other words, as far as the Peshwa was concerned, the treaty was a fait accompli. The language of the treaty could not have been more clear in this regard: the Peshwa "has neither participated in the expense or danger of the late war, and therefore is not entitled to share any part of the acquisitions . . . [yet] certain districts . . . shall be reserved for the purpose of being eventually ceded to the said Peshwah . . . provided however, that the said Peshwa . . . shall accede to the present treaty."[32]

There were some tangential issues to be addressed, not the least of which was the fate of Tipu's family, immediate and extended, and his former ministers of state. The treaty provided for their support and security but required that they leave Mysore. For the delicate task of removing them, Mornington again turned to Arthur: "The details of this painful, but indispensable measure cannot be entrusted to any person more likely to combine every office of humanity with the prudential precautions required by this occasion than Colonel Wellesley."[33] The challenge came from the fact that Tipu's household included a harem, and its relocation was fraught with potential for scandal. Mornington's public display of preference for Arthur on this occasion, as on others, amounted to a resounding vote of confidence. True to form, Arthur brooked no criticism as he went about the task and responded indignantly to any suggestion that it might have been handled better.

Through the settlement, Mornington grabbed control of southern India. "Seringapatam," he boasted to Dundas, "I shall retain in full sovereignty for the Company, as being a tower of strength, from which we at any time shake Hindostan to its centre, if any combination should ever be formed against our interests."[34] In addition, he made no secret of the fact that he regarded both the raja of Mysore and the Nizam as puppets.[35] The Marathas, however, perplexed him. Mornington's bullying had gotten him nowhere with the Peshwa because the Peshwa had no real power. The lack of a central authority baffled Mornington, and though he understood the details of Maratha politics, he refused to acknowledge their importance. For advice he turned to Arthur, who did not disappoint: "I recommend it to you not to put the Company upon the Maratha frontier. It is impossible to expect to alter the nature of the Marathas; they will plunder their neighbors, be they ever so powerful. The consequence of their plunder of the Company's territories will be perpetual representations at Poona of grievances which it will not be in the power of Poona to redress, and a bickering which will have no end."[36] Arthur had the situation figured out, at least at this point, and the advice could not have been better. At the same time, Arthur implied that conflict with the Marathas was nearly inevitable. For Mornington, his anger over the Peshwa's failure to contribute to the war conflicted with the realization that he had little control over the Peshwa. Thereafter, he treated the Peshwa as an independent sovereign while working to make the fiction a reality. That, in turn, would certainly make conflict inevitable. How could Mornington blunder so badly with the Marathas? One reason might be the old problem of fitting square pegs into round holes. Mornington's temperament could not tolerate the status quo with the Marathas. All along he had seen the principles of the India Act as being based on faulty thinking. He believed that balance-of-power politics in greater India did not and could not work in the best interests of the company. It followed that the same held true with the Marathas. He could neither leave well enough alone nor negotiate on the basis of a balance of power among the independent Maratha interests.

These issues lay in the future, however; Mornington's attentions turned in another direction. He began to think about what the Mysore campaign might mean to him, and his expectations were high. He proceeded on the assumption that his victory over Tipu was the equivalent of a victory over France, not only because he believed this but because it suited him. To him, his was an accomplishment of the first order involving military, political, and diplomatic preparations of great complexity. The fact that this was the fourth Mysore war and obviously the last was proof enough. Having done what Cornwallis had not, Mornington reasoned that he would be rewarded accordingly.

To understand this part of Mornington's story, one should recall what the governor-generalship meant to him. After a decade of unrealized political ambition that left him in despair, India was his opportunity to prove himself, to penetrate the inner circle of Britain's oligarchy. Moreover, in the year that elapsed between learning that he would be going out to India and finally arriving there, he had ample opportunity to consider how he might play the role of governor general. He knew well the challenges he faced, and he had studied them on the voyage out. How he would deal with them had to largely be up to him, given the distance in time and space between Calcutta and London. And upon tackling the problem of Tipu Sultan, he had come away with a success that exceeded even his extravagant imagination. The longer Mornington contemplated what had transpired, the more intoxicated he became, and he let his mind wander in an unsafe direction.

Material gain never entered into Mornington's calculations. Instead he thought in terms of honors and public recognition (which, to him, the honors represented). He wanted his king and colleagues to tell him what a splendid job he had done and then convince the public of their pride in and appreciation of him by conferring high honors. As governor general, he had reason to expect a reward, but for Mornington, the issue was whether the reward would match the accomplishment. That, of course, depended on how one perceived the accomplishment. Mornington believed that it was first rate, exceeding the achievement of Cornwallis, who had walked away with an English marquessate. That was the reward Mornington wanted, and to that end he set to work convincing London of his merits. The primary vehicle for persuasion would be his correspondence with Dundas.

Early on, Mornington described to Dundas his self-perceived tenacity and genius. He made certain that Dundas and the court of directors knew the details of his negotiations with the Nizam and their results. Then came descriptions of the contest with Tipu, the subsequent restructuring of southern India, and the treaty with the Nizam. It is curious to find the governor general focusing not only on the diplomatic and military events but also on economic issues. One would be hard pressed to find something that interested Mornington less, but Dundas continually reminded him of their importance. "If the debt in India is allowed to increase so much as to become unwieldy and unmanageable," warned Dundas, "we are cut off from the means of extricating our affairs when peace shall have returned."[37] Accordingly, Mornington devoted much effort to explaining his campaign in economic terms, though such reasoning made no appearance in his dispatches leading up to the conflict. His points were painfully elementary, explaining that the destruction of Tipu would allow the company to reduce its military expenses in southern India. Moreover, future revenues from annexed territories would more than cover the campaign's costs: "Reasonable indemnification for our expense in the war," he explained, "and an adequate security against the return of that danger, which originally provoked us to arms."[38] The plodding nature of his discussion of economic issues gave way to exuberance when discussing strategic matters, in which he took comfort and exhibited great pride. Southern India was theirs, and more important, "the French influence in India, thanks be to God! is now nearly extirpated."[39]

While Mornington believed that he had accomplished something remarkable of benefit to England and India alike, he also knew in the back of his mind that there were grounds for criticism. Dundas's letters to him spoke of economy, and he understood the disposition of the typical shareholder in the East India Company. At the same time, he remained alert to the strategic issues that he and Dundas had analyzed at length and over which both continued to express concern. At the top of the list had been Tipu, and he had been removed. At this point in Mornington's governor-generalship, it was apparent (as Edward Ingram has brilliantly proven) that Mornington's view of India was one-dimensional whereas Dundas, always the wily politician, saw a bigger picture with an extraordinarily intricate landscape. Certainly Dundas saw India strategically. In fact, he was the first to define its relationship to the struggle in Europe and to Britain's future role in the world. Beyond that, however, he saw it in economic and political terms that he knew were inseparable. If the company did not yield a good return, there would be a political price to pay.

While capable of viewing the challenge of India in similar terms, Mornington was prevented by emotional turmoil from thinking objectively. He needed to prove his worth, he needed to advance, and he needed to demonstrate the import of his activities. His is the classic case of the inferiority complex. He could not leave it to others to compliment; instead he complimented himself and expected others to chime in with their agreement. No sooner had Seringapatam fallen than the governor general sought to make clear, to those who counted, that the success was his. On 16 May he wrote disingenuously to Dundas, "To me *alone* all the blame is imputable; and let the punishment fall on my head. But if the picture be reversed, I must claim the *sole and exclusive* merit of whatever is honourable, proud, and commanding, in our present situation in India."[40] The theme reappeared three months later in a letter to Pitt: "With these sentiments I may be allowed to say that I suppose you will either hang me or magnificently honour me for my deeds (mine they are, be they good or bad)."[41] Mornington believed that he had been the driving force behind the Mysore campaign and that without him, Tipu would never have been engaged, let alone defeated. Even William Hickey, no great admirer of the governor general, understood the singularity of the achievement. "This vigorous measure," he explained in his memoirs, "was adopted upon the sole responsibility of Lord Mornington in his capacity of Governor-General. . . . [He] turned a deaf ear to all the objections that were offered from different quarters, being determined to carry into effect the plan he had formed."[42] Still, Dundas and Pitt must have shaken their heads in amusement over such vanity. They might also have greeted such sentiments with sorrow over such insecurity. Regardless, Mornington awaited their responses with bated breath.

Mornington's efforts to draw attention to himself took even less dignified forms. He began to criticize everyone who might claim to share his glory, particularly Clive and Harris. His view of Harris had been mostly positive from the start, but he had viewed Clive's arrival as governor of Madras with skepticism; Clive's name alone brought great cachet that implied independent authority. Arthur removed Mornington's doubts about Clive, however, describing him as decent and steady if uninspired. Because Mornington considered Hobart's former staff at Madras a threat to his authority, he worked to ensure that Clive did not fall under the influence of the likes of Josiah Webbe. By the end of the Mysore campaign, all of that had changed. Mornington had come to see Clive as incompetent and a dullard, unfit for his job. Webbe was the real governor of Madras: able, diligent, and knowledgeable. Harris he described as tired and indifferent. Colonel Barry Close he described as the best man in the army and the real commander.[43] It should come as no surprise that both Webbe and Close were subordinates, several steps removed from the governor general. He could praise their contributions without obscuring his own glory. Iris Butler's suggestion that Mornington's negative views on Clive and Harris were a product of his anxiety (and the fact that he had nothing to do while the war progressed) does not explain the flow of postwar venom. Mornington's strategy appears to have been that of clearing the deck of all rivals.

So that there could be no confusion or misunderstanding concerning the Mysore war and his role in it, Mornington dispatched Henry to England to carry the information firsthand. Ostensibly the mission was intended to clarify the terms of the treaty, to discuss the next steps with Dundas and the cabinet, and to secure for the governor general an appointment as commander in chief. Except for the last point, such reasoning makes no sense. There was little that anyone could have done to clarify Mornington's lengthy and well-reasoned dispatches. Arthur had been Mornington's first choice as emissary, but Arthur's responsibilities and opportunities had expanded so enormously that to leave would be too great a sacrifice.[44] Consequently the task fell to Henry, who was suffering from an irritating skin ailment that Arthur diagnosed as ringworm. The youngest brother, therefore, found himself on the horns of a dilemma: remain in the jungle that caused him significant discomfort or face six months at sea and the seasickness that had laid him low on the voyage out.[45] But the decision was not his to make; Mornington wanted him to go, and go he would.

Henry sailed in August 1799 with detailed instructions concerning Mornington's expectations for a reward. An English marquessate would constitute an appropriate sign of a nation's gratitude, or perhaps the garter. To make his task easier, Henry sailed with a quantity of trinkets for the king, the Prince of Wales, the prime minister, Dundas, and various friends—trinkets confiscated from Tipu's palace. Dundas, Grenville, and Pitt needed no nudging. No sooner did news of Seringapatam's fall arrive in London than they got down to the business of a reward. None of them cared much for such rewards, but they knew their friend did, and they proceeded accordingly.[46]

Mornington had left instructions with his banker and agent, one Mr. Bernard, that if an award should be in the offing, Bernard should promote an elevation in the Irish peerage to a marquessate and should secure reversion to Mornington's office as chief remembrancer of the Irish Exchequer for his eldest son. Hyacinthe also knew this, and when word reached London about the conquest of Mysore, Bernard consulted Hyacinthe, and Dundas consulted them both. Dundas placed most of this information in the hands of Pitt, who saw no problem with the title but expected a struggle over the reversion. Dundas, in the meantime, proceeded on another course:

> Leaving these points to others, to whom they with more propriety belong, I confess my ideas with regard to your family run in a different course, and, from the peculiar situation in which your children are circumstanced [they were illegitimate], it occurred to me, that the most substantial mark of friendship I

> could bestow upon your Lordship, was to direct my attention to consider by what means I could put under your power a large sum of money, which, in the event of any accident befalling yourself, would leave those children in a state of independence. I mentioned my ideas to Lord Grenville and Mr Pitt, both of whom were exceedingly pleased with my idea, and they both concurred in thinking, that in whatever way I could accomplish the idea, it must of all things be most gratifying to you. . . . In the dispatch which goes by this conveyance from the secret committee respecting the booty to be given to the army, your Lordship will observe an order given to ascertain the value of the military stores captured at Seringapatam, and to report to the court of directors for their further instructions. . . . I have spoke on the subject to the chairman and deputy, and they enter warmly into my suggestions. In some shape or other the idea must be carried into execution.[47]

Two features of this letter deserve emphasis. First, on receipt of Mornington's news, Dundas moved promptly on the issue of a reward. Second, Dundas consulted all the right people when deciding what that reward might be—Hyacinthe, Bernard, Pitt, and Grenville. In other words, Dundas understood Mornington's character and sought to do what would satisfy him. In fact, in Dundas's letter, one can sense the excitement among Mornington's friends at having the opportunity to provide for him not only what he wanted but what he needed. They knew that he loved titles and honors but also knew, better than he, that financial rewards would go further. Dundas also anticipated objections that Mornington might raise to a monetary award by assuring him that the army would not be shortchanged.

Time intensified Mornington's anxiety, and while he can be excused his dreams, he cannot be excused for allowing them to obstruct his judgment. He continued to write disparaging comments about subordinates and colleagues, solicit increased powers for the governor general, and boast of his accomplishments. "I hope that the arrival of my brother Henry with the treaties of partition and subsidy has satisfied your anxiety respecting the settlement of Mysore," he wrote to Dundas. "It would have been impossible to have retained more of the territory without throwing the Nizam absolutely into the counsels of Poona: but if you will have a little patience, the death of the Nizam will probably enable me to gratify your voracious appetite for lands and fortresses. Seringapatam ought, I think, to stay your stomach a while; not to mention Tanjore and the Polygar countries. Perhaps I may be able to give you a supper of Oudh and the Carnatic, if you should still be hungry."[48] This is an impolitic letter indeed, treating serious subjects in a flippant manner and disguising anger as humor. It must have alarmed Dundas. Moreover, Mornington's bravado led him to make further suggestions that his powers be increased.

The fact is, the governor general was slowly coming undone. On 5 March 1800, he wrote to Dundas, "Although my health continues unimpaired, and the state of this government and of its vast dependencies is in every respect flourishing and prosperous, my separation from my family and friends becomes every day more painful to me, and frequently reduces my spirits to a state of melancholy, which is the more oppressive, because it must be concealed, and cannot be indulged, or even disclosed, without injury to the public service."[49]

Mornington had become a brooding man, and the absence of Henry did not make matters any better. That he missed his wife was undeniable, but this sort of plaintive lament is the product of worry. His wife, he had known for a long time, would not join him, and his reiteration of hope was nothing more than an attempt to cope. At the same time, since the end of the year, he had had hints that his reward would not be what he hoped. Letters to Hyacinthe reveal that he knew Bernard's request had been for an Irish marquessate, and he scolded his wife for not doing something about it. Surely family and friends understood that the magnitude of his accomplishment negated the instructions that he had left behind?

Mornington had not much longer to worry. In April came Dundas's dispatch with news of his reward, and he collapsed in nervous, irrational fury. To Pitt he wrote,

> With the warmest acknowledgment of the zealous and anxious interest which all my friends have taken in my success, I cannot describe to you the anguish of my mind in feeling myself bound by every sense of duty and honour to declare to you my bitter disappointment at the reception which the King has given to my services, and at the ostensible mark of favour which he has conferred upon me. . . . I will confess to you openly that as I was

> confident there had been nothing Irish or Pinchbeck in my conduct or in its result, I felt an equal confidence that I should find nothing Irish or Pinchbeck in my reward.

There were even threats: "You must . . . expect either to hear of some calamity happening to me here, or to see me in England; where I shall arrive . . . in perfectly good spirits, in the most cordial good temper with all my friends, and in the most firm resolution to pass the remainder of my life in the country, endeavouring to forget what has been inflicted upon me."[50]

Within a longer screed that went to Dundas, the newly created Marquess Wellesley sounded the same themes: the Irish marquessate did not adequately represent services rendered, and he would be the object of scorn and ridicule in India. He viewed the peerage as a mark of degradation rather than honor. Throughout his correspondence, there is a profound sense of betrayal and confusion. Dundas and Pitt were dumfounded by his response, and it is a measure of their friendship that they remained patient and understanding, though there would be precious little time left for them to deal with him. Both men, and Grenville, were convinced that they had done right by Richard and had expended time and energy in the process. They could not comprehend such rage. They had thought Richard would be overjoyed.

The marquessate was only half the reward. Dundas, as he had suggested, secured from the company an award of £100,000 and must have felt that Mornington could not find fault with this. But he did:

> Having stated my sincere feelings on this part of the subject, I am persuaded you will not deem me fastidious or capricious when I express an objection to the fund from which (if I understand the suggestion of your letter) this bounty of the E[ast] I[ndia] C[ompany] is to proceed. I understand that, if the reserved part of prize taken at Ser[ingapatam], consisting of stores and ordnance, sh[oul]d come into the possession of your c[ommittee], it is their intention to grant the whole to the army, reserving £100,000 to be hereafter granted to me. I am satisfied that upon reflection you will perceive, that my acceptance of such a grant w[oul]d place me in a very invidious and humiliating situation with respect to the army. The army w[oul]d feel that I had been rewarded at their expense: and they w[oul]d view the transaction with perhaps aggravated

> jealousy and contempt for my character when they recollected the effort, which I made in the face of their prejudices and popularity, to reserve these very stores for the ostensible purpose of saving the rights of the Crown.[51]

Therefore, he would accept pecuniary reward only through "some channel wholly unconnected with any prize taken by the army." This was the voice of the martyr, not the altruist. Wellesley knew full well that the army had gotten more than its due. In the course of his lecture, one even finds prevarication. He informed Dundas that his children would be well provided for through his Irish estates. This was not the case, and his entire political career was proof of it. Dundas knew it, Grenville knew it, and Pitt knew it; Mornington's straitened means were common knowledge.

So Dundas and Pitt had failed on two counts. They had done what they thought was right and good and had nevertheless come up empty-handed. Certainly they had to have wondered whether they could ever satisfy their friend. Nonetheless, the ever-patient Dundas attended to the task of devising another financial arrangement while both he and Pitt sought to find ways of soothing the marquess. Somehow, Wellesley would have to be brought to his senses. There was still work to be done, and no one would be well served if Wellesley quit. The self-centered Wellesley never realized, let alone appreciated, that he had caught his friends at the most delicate of times. They were preoccupied not only with Bonaparte's invasion of Egypt and the renewed conflict on the Continent but also with a political crisis at home. The Irish Rising of 1798 and the subsequent dissolution of the Irish parliament in favor of union led to trouble between Pitt and George III, who would reject Pitt's plea for Catholic rights. That Catholic rights formed an essential component of union was disclosed to the monarch only after the union was in place. In short, because Pitt would ultimately resign over the issue, the cabinet had precious little time to deal with Wellesley's pique.

A measure of Wellesley's addled emotions can be found in the fact that he thought he had expressed his disappointment delicately. "I have written to Pitt quite gently, even humorously," he explained to Hyacinthe, "but . . . I am infuriated and disappointed and really when I got Pitt's cold and unworthy letter I feared for my health, but I'm better now, and between friends these things can be forgotten."[52] Like everyone else, Hyacinthe was dumbfounded and thought her husband a fool. Especially perplexed and angered was she over his rejection of the £100,000. She realized that if her husband thought India would laugh at his "double-gilt potato," as he called the Irish marquessate, it would be nothing compared to the hilarity prompted by his rejecting such a gift. But while Wellesley's political friends sought to soothe him, she chastised him, and he did not take it well.[53] Hyacinthe was as fastidious with money as her husband was in matters of honor. In fact, the *Times* saw fit to note on one occasion, "The Marchioness of Wellesley's departure from Brighton is very interesting, and of admirable example, as the accounts from thence state, that she called in her bills, and paid them."[54] In short, she adhered to the quaint notion that one paid for what one received. Personal finances worried her, and for this reason she viewed her husband's rejection of a fortune as madness.

Wellesley's shrill and irrational responses suggest a man who had lost his balance. They also show him to be a desperate man who, when he went out to India, understood that his political career existed on borrowed time. The personal and public pressures on him were enormous, and when he saw that things were working out favorably, he exaggerated his accomplishment and conjured unrealistic expectations. His responses become even more perplexing given that he understood the system. Even if he believed that an English marquessate was a fair reward, he should have known that fairness had nothing to do with promotion. That he did not know this and was unprepared for disappointment is incomprehensible and points to an emotional imbalance. This theme appeared in his correspondence as early as three weeks after Seringapatam and accelerated through the summer and autumn. Sending Henry home was a product of irrational anxiety, and by the time he received the gazette, he had worked himself into a frenzy despite knowing what it was likely to contain. Beginning in April, his behavior turned manic. We would now describe this as a nervous breakdown, and those around him were aware of the change. In April 1799, Wellesley had written to Sir Alured Clarke, his commander in chief: "I entirely approve your judgment in referring so delicate and important a question to my judgment. . . . The main spring of such a machine as the Government of India can never be safely touched by any other hand than that of the principal mover." In other words, his council—like everyone else—deferred to his judgment at that time. In June 1800, it was an entirely different case.

Then, Wellesley complained to Dundas that "Sir A[lured] C[larke] has plainly intimated his expectation, that I should refer *all,* even the most minute details, political as well as others, to the council before I proceed to act in any instance; adding with *great politeness,* that it was *not unnatural that I should err.*" It is not conjecture to say that there was great concern over the governor general's state of mind. Wellesley did not ask himself why Clarke's attitude had changed. Instead, he dismissed the other man as a fool: "His character is a composition of low pride, and ridiculous vanity."[55]

Wellesley could not clear his mind. Later he would write to Lady Anne Barnard, the one person with whom he communicated confidentially and as an equal and a friend,

> This brief declamation will admit you to the secret agonies of my poor dear heart or soul, and give you some light to discover the causes of my ill health and of my declining, indignant, wounded spirits. But do not suppose me to be so weak as to meditate hasty resignations or passionate returns to Europe, or fury, or violence of any kind. No. —I will shame their injustice by aggravating the burthen of their obligations to me; I will heap kingdoms upon kingdoms, victory upon victory, revenue upon revenue; I will accumulate glory, and wealth, and power, until the ambition and avarice even of my masters shall cry mercy; and then I will shew them what dust in the balance their tardy gratitude is, in the estimation of injured, neglected, disdainful merit.[56]

There it is, the anger and spite of a wounded man. Wellesley's subsequent years in India (and even beyond) are impossible to understand without this context: he had been wronged, and he would get even. An already aggressive governor general would become even more so.

It is interesting that thirty years later, when Lord Wellesley supervised the collection and publication of his India papers in five volumes, he chose to omit his lengthy protests over the marquessate. It is as if this were an episode in his life that he had forgotten, and he had the capacity to purge his memory of uncomfortable facts (as did his brothers). He did, however, choose to publish his rejection of the £100,000, as he continued to believe that it was a point of honor—and a way of reminding the company of what Wellesley considered a great injustice. He and others had calculated that the difference between an outright cash award and an annuity of £5,000 per year over twenty years (which would be his reward) constituted at least a 50 percent loss. And so we read in the published correspondence, edited letters to both Pitt and Dundas. To Pitt he chose the following words: "The fund from which it appears that this grant is to proceed, will render it impossible for me to accept it. It seems to be intended to make the sum a charge on the military stores taken at Seringapatam. This arrangement will have the appearance, if not the substance of depriving the army of a part of their prize for the purpose of enriching me."[57]

Meanwhile, Wellesley ruminated in lengthy dispatches to the court of directors and to Dundas on the government over which he presided. These are curious documents indeed, and one has to take great care in reading them. Wellesley had a penchant for redundant detail and overextended arguments, and though his logic is sound and his style clear, he tends to put one to sleep. One wonders whether that was the intent, because important points lie buried under the mountain of words. Wellesley's concern through the spring and summer of 1800 was the acquisition of increased powers. This emerges especially from a July dispatch that includes an extended and pointless analysis of British constitutional theory as it applied to India. In the end, what Wellesley suggested was that his responsibilities had outgrown the administrative structure that he inherited: "To dispense justice to millions of people of various languages, manners, usages and religions; to administer a vast and complicated system of revenue throughout districts equal in extent to some of the most considerable kingdoms in Europe; to maintain civil order in one of the most populous and litigious regions of the world; these are now the duties of the larger portions of the civil servants of the Company."[58] He intended, therefore, to expand and redefine that structure, increase the number of civil servants, and create a college to educate them. Like many of Wellesley's other plans, this was both enlightened and self-serving. "Your servants are nominated to the highest stations of civil government," he pointed out, "without any test of their possessing the requisite qualifications for the discharge of these offices. No such test could now be required, none having been prescribed, and no means having been afforded to individuals of acquiring the necessary qualifications for public stations."[59]

With all of this, Wellesley aimed to consolidate power in his own hands. He craved independence so that he might proceed unimpeded.

His plans for reorganization included repeated complaints about the quality of personnel with whom he was forced to work. His mixed motives can be seen clearly in the midst of this flight of loquacious fancy: "The Civil servants of the English East India Company, therefore, can no longer be considered as agents of a commercial concern. They are, in fact, the ministers and officers of a powerful sovereign; they must now be viewed in that capacity, with reference, not to their nominal, but to their real occupations."[60] By "sovereign," of course, he meant the king, but with the knowledge that he represented the king in form and function halfway around the world.

By the autumn of 1800, Dundas knew that his friend was in trouble, and he gathered around him Henry and Gerald for advice and counsel on how to handle their irascible brother. With Henry about to embark for India, it was important that he and Dundas develop a clear understanding concerning both policy and the mental health of the governor general. Dundas had a high opinion of Henry, and there is every reason to believe that Henry and Gerald were frank in their discussions with Dundas. In any case, the result, a series of dispatches written over a period of three weeks, displays Dundas at his best—generous, patient, and wise. This is especially remarkable given the fact that the "Wellesley problem" could not have come at a more inopportune time, burdened as he was with the Irish problem and the conduct of the war. After addressing specific policy issues, Dundas jumped right into more difficult matters concerning power and feelings:

> I must so far interfere between your suggestions and that consideration, as to warn you of the propriety of applying in a particular manner to the government of India the old maxim, *that we must look rather to what is practically best, than to what in theory we think so.* There is another principle equally true in government and in legislation, and essentially necessary to be attended to in the administration of great concerns. *We must legislate and regulate public affairs, not on the hypothesis that the instruments of government are always to be the ablest, the purest, and the best, of men, but we must take mankind according to the general run of human nature, some better some worse, some able some less able,* and we must recollect, that in the general currency of

> human affairs the rulers and governors of India, like all other public men, must occasionally be selected from the heterogeneous mass of which the world consists.[61]

This remarkable advice shows that Dundas chose to see Wellesley as naive rather than corrupt; though paternalistic, Dundas was also gentle. He would later remind the marquess that absolute power was fine in the hands of an able person but disastrous in those of the less able. A classicist of Wellesley's ability should not need such reminding, but he did.

As for Wellesley's college, Dundas knew instinctively that the company would object because it would disrupt the existing system of patronage. Wellesley had expected this and pointed out that the college would train only company servants who had already been appointed. But one sees what he was up to. Just as he had clearly admitted that time and distance provided him with the opportunity to alter the company's instructions and procrastinate in their implementation, so too would the college allow him to alter and delay the placement of personnel.

Thus Dundas tried to settle the governor general, give him some focus, and reassure him. He secured Wellesley's commission as captain-general but informed him that control of naval operations was out of the question. As for the question of the reward, the peerage could not be changed, but Dundas would explore new ideas for compensation. This was a particularly irksome point for the Scotsman, who thought Wellesley ludicrously sensitive:

> The fact is, that in truth the army were considered to have got as much as any army ought to get in the way of pecuniary reward, but when it could be accompanied at the same time with a reward bestowed on the conduct of the first civil servant in India, the objection was a good deal removed. Under these circumstances your feelings are somewhat embarrassing; but I acknowledge with great frankness, that they are natural and honourable on your part, and I shall certainly turn my thoughts to some mode of suggestion to the Company, by which they may make good their intentions to you, without mixing them with any thing that can injure your feelings.[62]

Dundas, having said his piece in a cool, sensitive manner, sent Henry off to rejoin his brother. The break had been good for Henry, though not particularly fruitful. Still, it had brought him back into contact with his brother's influential friends, and they came away impressed. Henry had learned something else: "Both the Government and the Court of Directors were loud in their commendations of Lord Wellesley's proceedings in India," he wrote, "though I had then the opportunity of remarking what further observation has abundantly confirmed, that military successes, and indeed proceedings of all kinds in India, however important and advantageous, produce but little effect in England."[63]

Arthur's views on Richard's emotional collapse are unknown. He did not have Henry to confide in, and so there is no correspondence to consult. Moreover, responsibilities in Mysore kept him busy. There is nothing particularly unusual in the official letters that passed between Seringapatam and Calcutta, but Arthur would soon conclude that Wellesley's next steps lacked the clearheadedness of his first.

5

ARTHUR

From Mysore to the Maratha War

For Arthur to settle into his assignment in Seringapatam took very little time. The task required someone with steady nerves and a thick skin, and Arthur proved that he had the nerves. The appointment was undefined, which suited him, and drew on his conspicuous talents—organization and discipline. In these three years, he developed into a superb administrator and a talented field commander. These facts were not lost on his brother, the governor general, whose familial preferences grew as a result. Arthur's confidence soared, and along with it, his expectations. But while Arthur enjoyed tremendous success in the years that remained for him in India, he did not experience all smooth sailing. His expectations proved to be nearly as unrealistic as his eldest brother's, and eventually, perhaps even inevitably, he was disappointed. To his setbacks, he responded with the same type of irrationality and immaturity that characterized Lord Wellesley's response to the awards for the Mysore war.

Arthur assumed command in Seringapatam under difficult but not unusual circumstances. Sieges always brought out the worst in soldiers. The stress of battle and the lure of loot and fleshly reward created a heady potion. Normally the conditions of war made the rampage of an army through a captured citadel—raping, killing, looting—a brutal and inhumane event, but it was viewed as one of the regrettable but inevitable consequences of war. The victorious army eventually marched away from the site of the conflict and never looked back. At Seringapatam, where the British intended to stay, the conquerors had to learn to live with the conquered, and the army had to be brought under control as soon as possible. Indeed, the situation was even more complicated. If the East India Company retained possession of Seringapatam or even the whole of Mysore, or turned Mysore into a client state, then the country had to emerge stable, peaceful, and prosperous, with a cooperative as well as pacified populace.

Arthur thus faced a double challenge—to make the army obey and trust him, and to win the respect of the people. These would seem to be quite different challenges, but Arthur Wellesley proved the perfect man for the job. He threw himself into the task of establishing order among enlisted men through the selective use of capital punishment for looting: nothing like a few hangings to sober an army. Long-term order required more, including discipline and a clear chain of command in the officer corps. As he knew, the inhabitants of Seringapatam and Mysore were vulnerable not only to the capricious behavior of the rank and file but also to that of the officers, who might perpetrate all kinds of abuses, from usury to forced prostitution, from petty corruption to murder. These were the things on which Arthur would keep a keen eye.

Arthur's success in administering Mysore certainly resulted from intelligence and imagination, but superb organizational skills and sheer hard work mattered more. The breadth, depth, and quantity of the dispatches that flowed from his pen in these years are awe inspiring, considering Arthur's youth and lack of experience. His attentions fell on the law and judicial procedure, supply and transportation, hospitals, security, discipline, trade and the economy, and local politics. As for the army, he left little doubt that he was on the job and alert to missteps. Accountability was a watchword. For the people of Mysore, it brought security and stability. They could get on with their lives under a government subject to its own rules. They could farm, manufacture, and trade confident that they had every opportunity to see their work through to fruition. In other words, they could earn their livings in peace. For most of these people, their needs were simple. They did not require a leader sensitive to their emotional needs, only a governor both strong and fair. Arthur delivered on both, and his work did not escape notice. Both the governor general and General Harris took great satisfaction in all that Arthur accomplished. Both knew that the reorganization of Seringapatam might not have worked out in such a fashion. There had been nothing in Arthur's early career that revealed such talent—from Mornington's perspective, quite the opposite. Harris, aware of Arthur's superb administrative skills, could have known little of his leadership skills. This said, it is important to remember that Arthur, capable though he proved to be, found himself in this position only because of the influence of his brother.

The siege of Seringapatam had not been a shining moment for Colonel Wellesley. Aside from the failure of the evening skirmish outside of Seringapatam, Arthur had played a secondary role in the assault, and although he had performed well, his responsibilities did not allow for the demonstration of higher-order skills. Consequently, that he possessed military talent had been effectively hidden. Clearly he would have made a good quartermaster, but that was not a part of his plans. Then the command at Seringapatam appeared to be taking him along the road of the administrator, not the warrior. However, the fighting did not stop with the fall of the city and death of Tipu. Unrepentant Mysorean soldiers roamed the countryside, and the collapse of the established civil authority encouraged opportunists of all types to take advantage of the political transition. One such opportunist was Dhoondiah Vagh. This man had fallen afoul of Tipu, who had had him arrested and thrown into the city's wretched dungeons. There Dhoondiah had languished when the Mysore war began. In the chaos of the fall of Seringapatam, he escaped and fled the city. Subsequently, he gathered around him remnants of Tipu's army and an assortment of malcontents, desperadoes, and freebooters.

Dhoondiah's activities were not unlike those practiced by bandits since the dawn of humankind. Moving rapidly on horseback, he looted and pillaged and subjected villagers to extortion. His followers constituted a small army; because of this, his activities threatened the security and prosperity of northern Mysore, not to mention the territories of the Nizam and the Peshwa. He protected himself through threats and intimidation and the imaginative use of the dense terrain. The first word of his activities arrived in Seringapatam in June 1799.[1] By August, Harris considered Dhoondiah a serious threat and ordered Arthur to hunt him down.[2] Arthur in turn dispatched a force under the command of Colonel James Stevenson to the north in pursuit of the bandit. Although Dhoondiah's operations were much disrupted, he evaded capture by fleeing across the frontier into Maratha country,

Stevenson being under orders not to pursue.[3] At that point, Dhoondiah found himself surrounded by enemies, the Marathas being no more enthusiastic about him than the British were. Subsequently, Dhoondiah's army broke up, and Arthur turned his attention to other matters.

In September, General Harris was ready to return to Madras, in preparation for going home to Britain. On his departure, he gave Arthur full command of the army in Mysore. Subsequently, with Wellesley enterprise, Arthur moved northwards in support of Stevenson and in an effort to resolve differences with the Marathas over frontier issues.[4] In the course of this venture, Arthur moved with speed and decision, and the Marathas melted away from the disputed areas. These operations offered him the opportunity to survey a large portion of the country and to work with Purnea to pacify problem areas. An interesting characteristic of Arthur's, demonstrated clearly in this early assignment, is that he rarely wasted time or opportunities. As he marched southwards from the Maratha frontier, he took careful note of the terrain, the state of the countryside, and the potential for trouble. By November, he was back in Seringapatam and attending to the task of reconstructing the fortress.

Arthur's correspondence during this period makes for instructive reading. His attention to detail is remarkable, but the fact that he commanded such detail reveals more than breadth of knowledge and a powerful intellect. It tells the reader that here was a man who had put in place a sophisticated and efficient staff and an effective network of intelligence. All of this seems to have been instinctive with Arthur. He learned much from observation, but he had not been long in positions from which he might observe. Much of Arthur's attention was given to military concerns—matters of security, not only preparations for defense but also anticipation of future operations. "In the wars which we may expect in India in future," he wrote, "we must look to light and quick movements; and we ought always to be in that state to be able to strike a blow as soon as a war might become evidently necessary."[5] Arthur had concluded that the company must always be prepared to make a rapid show of force; speed and decisiveness would be more important than sheer power. This represents advanced thinking, as it suggests that Arthur perceived that as the company's political presence in India expanded, the potential for conflict increased accordingly. Great risks thus attended empire building, and although the company was capable of controlling the frontiers of its claimed territory, this would not be a practical endeavor. Consequently, the company should be prepared to deal with threats before they gestated into full-blown wars, and thus the nineteenth-century equivalent of the twenty-first-century idea of a rapid deployment force was developed.

The issue of settling Tipu's family and chief ministers of state continued to distract and frustrate Arthur. By February, he was hearing again about Dhoondiah Vagh, who was rumored to be planning to kidnap members of Tipu's family from under Arthur's ample nose. Not one to dismiss threats, regardless of their likelihood, Colonel Wellesley took steps to enhance the family's security. The importance of the issue lay in Dhoondiah's restlessness. Reports arrived in Seringapatam of his efforts to recruit followers in northern Mysore and along the frontier with the Marathas.[6] By April, he was again attacking Maratha villages, which alarmed Arthur even while seeming to offer a degree of cooperation from the Marathas.

At the end of the month, Arthur decided to respond. He sent three regiments of cavalry to reinforce the Seventy-seventh Regiment stationed at Chittledroog along with three battalions of sepoys. The activities of Dhoondiah and the response of the Marathas perplexed Arthur:

> The state of the case regarding this man is very curious. Having quitted the service of the Rajah of Kolapoor, he seats himself with an immense body of troops on our frontier, and he is not thought so worthy of attention as that the questions should be asked, to whom does he belong? and for what reason is he come? Surely, if the Maratha Government is anything but a name, it may be made either to crush this man, to allow us to destroy him, or to avow him. He either belongs to the Marathas, or he does not: if he belongs to the Marathas, they ought to remove him to a greater distance, as no state has a right to assemble on the frontier of another such a force as he has on ours; if he does not belong to the Marathas, and he is there contrary to their inclination, they ought to allow us to drive him away, and to join with us in so doing.[7]

Meanwhile, Arthur awaited orders from the governor general; to campaign against Dhoondiah, he needed permission to cross into the territories of the Peshwa. Richard, in a rage over the announcement of his Irish marquessate, remained silent. When word did arrive from him, it was not at all what Arthur expected. What he got was another sort of proposition. Wellesley (who refused as yet to use his new title) had received orders from the war department to capture the Dutch colony of Batavia and explained,

> The object of this letter is to propose to you a situation which I think it would be unjust not to submit to your option, although I entertain considerable doubts whether you will think it eligible with a view to your individual interest; and I am still more apprehensive of the difficulty of reconciling it with the exigencies of the public service in Mysore at this crisis. You will, however, exercise your own free judgment on the subject, and I have no doubt that you will decide in the manner most honorable to yourself and most advantageous to the public.[8]

The offer placed Arthur in a quandary and sent Madras into a panic. Josiah Webbe almost immediately tried to persuade Arthur to stay in Mysore. His tack was simple: Lord Wellesley's offer was not as good as it sounded. While Arthur would command the troops, Admiral Peter Rainier would have overall command. And if the Dutch at Batavia placed themselves under British protection, there would be neither fame nor prize money for Arthur. In Mysore, however, Arthur would be free "to pursue Dhoondiah Vagh wherever you may find him, and to hang him on the first tree."[9] Clive followed up on Webbe's appeal:

> I have deemed it my duty to represent, that it is not possible for you to quit your present command even for a few months, without the greatest detriment to the affairs of Mysore; and I have made it my earnest request that his Lordship will select some other officer for this service. . . . I have no hesitation in recommending in the strongest terms, and in requesting you, if I may be permitted so to do, to remain in a situation which I have long felt, and still feel, that you fill with singular advantage to our own country as well as to Mysore; a situation in which for the prosperous settlement of our new acquisitions, integrity and vigilance of conduct are indispensable; and in which your acquired knowledge and experience, especially in the event of active operations, must give you the advantage over other men; and in which I

> should find it not only difficult, but impossible to replace you to my satisfaction.[10]

Webbe agreed with Clive: Arthur was too valuable to be wasted at Batavia; the stakes were too high in Mysore. In the end, Webbe and Clive got the best of Arthur, who told his brother on 29 May that he would stay to finish off Dhoondiah Vagh. The decision neither surprised nor annoyed Richard, which is noteworthy given his state of mind. In a letter to his brother, the governor general heaped on praise: "Lord Clive has pressed for your continuance in Mysore with an earnestness so honourable to you, that I think you cannot accept the command of the forces destined for Batavia; indeed I suspect that you could not quit Mysore at present. Your conduct there has secured your character and advancement for the remainder of your life, and you may trust me for making the best use of your merits in your future promotion."[11]

Clive's and Webbe's appeals highlight the quality and importance of Arthur's work. What higher praise can there be than to be viewed as indispensable by those working most closely with you, who would be responsible for the results of your work? Arthur had arrived; he was no longer just the governor general's brother. Flushed with confidence, he began the pursuit of Dhoondiah Vagh.

As Arthur moved northwards for the chase, he received intelligence of Dhoondiah's defeat of the Maratha chieftain Goklah and of unrest within Mysore caused by Dhoondiah's supporters. There would be no negotiations with Dhoondiah, only victory over him in battle.[12] Arthur did not have long to wait for the first engagement. Dhoondiah's large, mobile striking force was designed to confront or evade an enemy while inflicting serious damage to the countryside. Arthur, therefore, knew that he had to be ready to answer anytime opportunity knocked. When he found himself in late July near Dhoondiah's baggage train, he decided to attack despite the exhaustion of his army. On 31 July at a place he identified as Pursghur hill, Arthur destroyed or captured most of the baggage, some artillery, large numbers of draft animals, and numerous camp followers. Arthur reported that he knew not whether Dhoondiah had been present, and because his army could do no more, he had to be satisfied with what he had accomplished and allow Dhoondiah and his main force to retreat. He had, however, managed to inflict a blow that compromised the integrity of Dhoondiah's army and put the enemy on notice that Colonel Wellesley meant business.[13]

Arthur questioned the wisdom of further pursuit. The company would never be free of nagging problems along the Maratha frontier, he thought, of which Dhoondiah was just one. "In my opinion," he wrote,

> the extension of our territory and influence has been greater than our means. Besides, we have added to the number and description of our enemies, by depriving of employment those who heretofore found it in the service of Tippoo, and of the Nizam. Wherever we spread ourselves, particularly if we aggrandize ourselves at the expense of the Marathas, we increase this evil. We throw out of employment, and of means of subsistence, all who have hitherto managed the revenue, commanded or served in the armies, or have plundered the country. These people become additional enemies; at the same time that, by the extension of our territory, our means of supporting our government, and of defending ourselves, are proportionably decreased.[14]

Arthur's analysis, though perceptive, is filled with holes. One suspects that it is as much the product of frustration and disillusionment as it is serious thought. All the Wellesleys were good at finding excuses for what might be perceived as failure. Arthur, not optimistic about eliminating the threat from Dhoondiah, would rather call off the pursuit than risk failure.

Despite the doubts concerning Britain's policy towards the Marathas throughout the Indian administration, Lord Wellesley retained faith in his brother: Arthur would determine the best arrangement on the Maratha frontier.[15] Colonel Wellesley took the hint and continued the pursuit of Dhoondiah. Dividing his army into three separate columns, he began a series of marches and countermarches that kept the bandit ever on the move with ever-decreasing options. Finally, on 10 September, he caught up with Dhoondiah well to the north in the territories of the Nizam. Though outnumbered two to one after having divided his forces, Arthur ordered an attack. Dhoondiah's demoralized and tired troops were quickly routed, with Dhoondiah falling in battle.[16] Arthur, who could not have hoped for a better outcome, was more relieved than proud: "The complete defeat and dispersion of the enemy's force, and, above all, the death of Dhoondiah, puts an end to this warfare. . . . At the same time I must inform you that all the troops have undergone, with the greatest patience and perseverance, a series of fatiguing services."[17]

The marquess welcomed Arthur's success as the one bright spot in a bleak summer. "There is the second chapter in the story of Seringapatam," he wrote to Hyacinthe. "This is a most important victory and has covered Arthur in glory."[18] To the court of directors, he was equally full of praise: "Colonel Wellesley's subsequent operations have realized every expectation which we were induced to form from our confidence in his professional knowledge, in his skillful management of his resources and supplies, and in his enterprising and active spirit."[19]

Arthur remained in Maratha territory for the following month in the hope that he might influence the company's fruitless negotiations with the Peshwa. He came to see the Peshwa as powerless, a conclusion borne out by later events, and to appreciate the growing problem of Sindia, who did not recognize the Peshwa's authority. In the end, there was little that Arthur could do, and he requested permission to return to Mysore. This Clive granted in early November. Arthur's campaign against Dhoondiah proved important not only for its political and strategic consequences, but also in demonstrating Arthur's capacities as a tactician and a leader of men: his military skills matched his administrative abilities. Lord Wellesley's faith in his brother soared, as did Arthur's sense of his own worth and his expectations. As Arthur settled back into his responsibilities in Seringapatam, the marquess formulated new schemes.

The governor general had called off the Batavia expedition in July on the pretext that events in Egypt had once again left the French in a position to threaten India. The French bogey again raised its ugly head. As early as March, Wellesley had warned Dundas, "If the war with France should be protracted, and Buonaparte continue at the head of affairs, I am persuaded that some attempt will be made by France against our Indian empire."[20] At about the same time, he had heard from the British ambassador at Constantinople, Thomas Bruce, the seventh Earl of Elgin, that the French position in Egypt was still strong and still threatening. Elgin anxiously solicited Wellesley's cooperation in an effort to dislodge the French, something that the governor general avoided either through obfuscation or outright rejection.[21] All of this gave Wellesley plausible justification for calling off the Batavia expedition, for which he had little enthusiasm. He informed Admiral Rainier that there existed the possibility that a French force would relieve Egypt through the Red Sea, which would in turn constitute a potential threat to India. Consequently, Britain's India forces needed to be kept on standby, and the fleet also needed to be ready to come to the defense of Britain's India interests.[22] Wellesley's thinking at this time is unclear. Edward Ingram, who has examined the situation more closely than anyone else, has concluded that Wellesley's real interest lay in protecting the forces at his disposal for use in various projects for expanding British influence in and control of the subcontinent.[23] Ingram believes that Wellesley never saw the French threat to India as real but needed to perpetuate the appearance of a threat to justify his own actions. There is scant evidence to support a counterargument. Wellesley's various activities at this time will be explored in a later chapter; what is important at this juncture is the impact of his fertile imagination.

On 18 October, the governor general wrote to Lord Clive announcing his intent to abandon the planned expedition to Batavia. He ordered Clive to send Arthur to Trincomalee, there to meet Admiral Rainier to consider "measures to be adopted for defeating any hostile projects which may be formed by the French."[24] Wellesley's dispatches reveal that he ordered Arthur to Trincomalee (without first asking his brother), subject to Clive's approval. Without telling Clive and Rainier, Wellesley had something very specific in mind. Shortly after he wrote these dispatches, one went off to Sir Roger Curtis, vice admiral at the Cape, asking for cooperation in transporting troops from the Cape for an attack on the Isle de France, now known as Mauritius, for either January or May 1801. A day later a missive went to Dundas asking for reinforcements for the same operation.[25]

Not until 5 November did Wellesley write to his brother, and he again gave Arthur little choice. Wellesley left no doubt of his intentions. There were three possible uses for the force to be collected at Trincomalee: to assist in the expulsion of the French from Egypt; to cooperate in the defense of the subcontinent wherever the French might threaten; and to attack the Isle de France, should the French not constitute an immediate threat elsewhere.[26] Clearly, however, Wellesley's eyes were focused on Mauritius. He knew full well that there was no evidence of a French threat to the subcontinent and that any expedition to Egypt would be part of a cooperative venture, the existence of which he had as yet no knowledge. Therefore, he was at liberty to plan the expedition to Mauritius.

The question then arises, why Mauritius and not Batavia? The answer is simple. The former was his idea, and, equally important, it would constitute a direct attack on France, which he believed would be more popular in London. There were sound strategic reasons as well. The island functioned as a base for French privateers operating in the east, and as it was France's only outpost in the Indian Ocean, from it any operation in the East would have to proceed. With Wellesley, strategic interests took second place to personal interests. He was looking for ways to make a splash, to prove the injustice of his double gilt potato, and carrying out orders dictated by London would not accomplish this end. As a result, he would find a way out of the Batavia expedition and define his own goals. At the same time, he wanted to retain control over the military forces available in India to employ them if he saw fit in Oudh, in the Carnatic, and at Poona.

Arthur's command at Trincomalee included the Eightieth, the Nineteenth, and the Tenth Infantry regiments along with a thousand volunteer sepoys and field ordnance consisting of four 12-pounders, six 6-pounders, and two howitzers. That Wellesley turned to Arthur certainly was a compliment, but one wonders whether the younger brother felt put out. After an arduous campaign against Dhoondiah Vagh and while trying to reestablish order in Mysore, he was directed to assume command of an army being assembled five hundred miles to the south. Wellesley had not bothered to consult Arthur on this occasion but relied on flattery. "Great jealousy will arise among the general officers in consequence of my employing you," he wrote; "but I employ you, because I rely on your good sense, discretion, activity, and spirit; and I cannot find all those qualities united in any other officer in India, who could take such a command."[27] Wellesley spoke with enthusiasm and urgency about the project, but Arthur, who had heard this sort of thing before, did not take him too seriously. "It is difficult to conceive the anxiety which I feel for the success of this enterprize against the Isle of France," the marquess wrote to Clive. "I look upon it, however, to be certain, if the Admiral shall act with cordiality, alacrity, and vigour, and I really expect to meet with all those qualities in him."[28]

Here was a problem. Wellesley, who had no control over Rainier, would shortly discover that the admiral was not well disposed to the expedition. The reasons were simple. First, Rainier saw no good reason for calling off the Batavia expedition, over which he had control and which promised greater rewards. Second, if the Batavia expedition were to be called off, he looked to the east, towards the Philippines, where the spoils of conquest would be enormous, and not to the west. Finally, none of Wellesley's arguments in favor of the expedition to the Isle de France, let alone the feasibility of the project, convinced Rainier. As a result, he would torpedo the project, if in fact Wellesley ever believed it practicable.[29]

Arthur was anything but enthusiastic, but he put the best face on the situation: "I think much better of the expedition than I did at first. The only doubt I have now is of the weather."[30] Arthur can be excused his doubts when one realizes that Wellesley was seeking advice from one Mr. Stokes, for whom the governor general had developed an attachment but whose only qualifications were that he was a navigator and had been held in confinement at the Isle de France for a number of weeks. But Arthur, who with hindsight months later would call the plan utter foolishness, was always willing to cooperate when there was something in it for him.

By the third week of December, Wellesley's plans were already beginning to unravel as he realized that he could not count on Rainier. The governor general conducted these proceedings in secret, instructing Arthur and others to be discreet, which leads one to believe that from the start he wished to leave open a line of retreat. He prepared Arthur for the worst:

> It is necessary that I should apprize you, that if circumstances should ultimately determine me to attempt the expedition to Egypt, that attempt will require so large a force as to occasion the necessity of my employing some one or two of his Majesty's General Officers in India. Under such circumstances, you will judge whether your best post would not be Mysore, after you shall have afforded me your assistance in collecting the army, and in giving me your opinion with respect to the general plan of its operations. Either Sir James Craig or General Baird, or both, would probably be employed on the service against Egypt; and I apprehend that in neither of these cases your situation would be very eligible.[31]

Wellesley's warning seemed casual enough, and in his own mind it probably was. If the army went to Mauritius, Arthur would command; if it went elsewhere, the command would be someone else's. Ingram sees this as a simple issue. The Mauritius campaign was to have been Arthur's, but that was becoming an impossibility. There was still Batavia, but that expedition belonged to Rainier. Because Arthur had previously declined to serve under Rainier, if the plan switched back to Batavia, the admiral would probably not accept the notion of Arthur directing the operation, and vice versa. Thus, in the unlikely event that Wellesley revived the Batavia scheme, there would have to be a change in command.[32] This all makes sense. However, the event of a supportive operation in Egypt is a bit more problematic. Wellesley's original orders to his brother included the prospect of an expedition to Egypt. So what had changed? Certainly Baird had protested, but Wellesley would have been willing to fight that battle if he thought it worth the effort. Obviously he did not; he evidently realized that Rainier would not cooperate in the Mauritius scheme and that an Egyptian campaign, which must have seemed only a remote possibility when he had mentioned it to Arthur, was becoming increasingly likely. With rumors about an Egyptian expedition rife, the governor general knew that he would have to use a senior officer. That Wellesley would offer to Arthur the eventual governorship of Mauritius should be considered as nothing more than a red herring, proof of the discomfort the governor general felt over disappointing his brother. At the same time, one must recognize that Wellesley had *appointed* Arthur to the task of organizing an expeditionary force; it was not something he *offered,* as it is often made to appear. Wellesley had done many things for his brother, and he probably never considered that Arthur would be wounded by being superseded. Moreover, Wellesley had offered an option: serve under Baird or return to Mysore. It was not as if Arthur would be left empty-handed. All the evidence suggests that Richard expected Arthur to do his bidding without protest. He was, after all, both the governor general and the patriarch. And, it almost goes without saying, he had many other irons in the fire.

More than wounded, Arthur felt betrayed. "I am sorry to observe that you have altered your mind upon this subject since the army was first assembled, and your first orders were given. It appears to have been intended that I should command the army at all events, however reinforced by troops to be supplied by the governments of

Fort St. George and Bombay; and in consequence I have put myself to a great expense, and have brought with me several officers who held situations which were agreeable to them."[33] The irony is that Wellesley, fresh from his own humiliation (as he perceived it), should have been insensitive to Arthur's feelings. In an attempt to regroup, Wellesley imagined all sorts of unrealistic options. As one possibility, Arthur would accompany Baird as the general's second in command in an expedition to Batavia, and when that reached a successful conclusion, he would command his own project against Mauritius.[34] However, should Rainier after all decide to go to Mauritius first, Baird would be in command but Arthur would have equal powers in the settlement of the island and have the option of staying on as governor.[35] Such thinking demonstrates the level of Wellesley's distraction, of which Arthur had little understanding. In any case, it proved an exercise in futility in the sense that nothing would pacify Arthur. And because neither event was likely, the marquess exposed himself to fraternal charges of disingenuousness.

By this time, Arthur knew that Baird had been dispatched to Trincomalee to assume command, and the prospect clearly drove him to distraction. His irrationality nearly equaled that of his brother's when presented with the Irish marquessate. He had for several days been complaining that Trincomalee could not support the troops assembled there. Issues of supply, so important to him, were on his mind. Then on 6 February there arrived in Trincomalee copies of dispatches sent from Fort St. George by Josiah Webbe. They contained instructions from Dundas to dispatch the forces assembled in Trincomalee to the Red Sea in support of Lieutenant General Sir Ralph Abercrombie's attack on Egypt from the Mediterranean. Arthur, certain that he would be superseded, panicked. Without orders he directed the army to board awaiting ships for transport to Bombay.

Arthur's friend, the Honourable Frederick North, governor of Ceylon, strenuously advised him to remain in Trincomalee until the arrival of instructions from Fort William. He would have none of it, however, and lectured North on the needs of the army, which, he maintained, could be acquired only in Bombay. He had, so he said, been forced to use provisions intended for the campaign just to maintain troops at Trincomalee. No matter what North believed could be done, Arthur could not take a risk. In an oft-quoted passage, Arthur took the high moral ground:

> Articles of provision are not to be trifled with, or left to chance; and there is nothing more clear than that the subsistence of the troops must be certain upon the proposed service, or the service must be relinquished. If there is a chance that by going to Bombay with the fleet we shall be late, is it not more probable that the provisions for which shipping must be prepared at Bombay will be late, and is there not a chance that the provisions will miss the fleet entirely, and that the troops will be in want? If the provisions are to be supplied from Madras or Calcutta, the probability of want is greater in proportion to the greater length of the voyage.[36]

Such an elaborate justification missed the point, and Arthur knew it; he had made a decision that was not his to make, and in so doing, he was guilty of gross insubordination. He was not thinking clearly, and his state of mind can be appreciated from a short, private letter to North: "I have received your letter upon the subject of my proceeding to Bombay, to which an answer will accompany this letter. I am concerned that you, or General Macdowall should have thought it necessary to write a public letter upon this subject, as I hope that I have always shown myself ready to attend to your wishes in whatever manner they may have been made known to me. The existence of your public letter upon the records of your government increases considerably my responsibility upon this occasion."[37] The truth of the matter is that he went to Bombay primarily because he loathed giving up command and felt humiliated by having to give it up to Baird. It was a case of what goes around comes around, and he did not like the prospect.

Arthur sent letters of explanation to Wellesley, to Rainier, and to Baird, but only when he was at sea. And then he stewed. Wellesley meanwhile sent the expected orders: Baird was to take command and Arthur was to either stay on as Baird's second in command or return to Mysore. There was some good news: Arthur had been promoted to major general in the army of Egypt. But the bad taste of his supersession he could not purge. And when he received another explanation from the governor general, it drove him to distraction. "With respect to your own situation," explained Wellesley,

> although I have more confidence in you than in any officer in India . . . you must know that I could not employ you in the

> chief command of so large a force as is now to proceed to Egypt without violating every rule of the service. I have no hesitation in saying that I should feel much more confident with you at the head of the army than with any other man; but this arrangement is impracticable; and although it was always my intention to employ you to assemble and prepare the army, I was aware that, if it came to act in Egypt, you must hold the second command.[38]

Arthur accepted none of this.

Meanwhile, Henry, who arrived back in India on 22 February 1801, did his best to mollify and mediate. Arthur sent him a series of letters at the end of March that unfortunately did not reach him until late April. They are almost pathetic in their tone. "I was at the top of the tree in this country," moaned Arthur; "the governments of Forts St. George and Bombay, which I had served, placed unlimited confidence in me, and I had received from both strong and repeated marks of their approbation. . . . But this supersession has ruined all my prospects, founded upon any service that I may have rendered."[39]

While Arthur complained, Richard and Henry conspired to clear a path of retreat. They sent word that Arthur was needed in Seringapatam and that if he wished to return there, he was free to do so. The choice was his; he could also go with Baird. "Act as you shall think best," wrote Henry, "without any apprehension of displeasing Mornington; for I am certain he will approve whatever step you take, upon full consideration."[40] At the same time, the governor general assured Arthur that he was forgiven for moving the army to Bombay without orders despite "the precedent which might be created by this step, unless guarded by the special exigency of the case, or rather (what is much safer) by your knowledge of my intentions and objects."[41]

Arthur, in good Wellesley fashion, collapsed physically under the stress. Complaining of a fever, he took to his bed and was ill when Baird arrived on 30 March. Arthur states that he intended to accompany Baird (who, to his surprise, was sympathetic) but was unfit to sail. However, he was not too sick to keep on grumbling. He could not put it behind him. After providing his associate, Colonel J. Champagné, with a drawn-out account of the unfortunate events, he wrote, "However, this is a matter of little consequence to any body but myself, therefore I say no more on the subject." For two or three sentences, he refrained. Then: "I see clearly the evil consequences of all this to my reputation and future views; but it cannot be helped, and to things of that nature I generally contrive to make up my mind."[42]

Just as his fever began to fade, he broke out in an excruciatingly uncomfortable rash, for which the doctor prescribed nitrous baths. This, like Wellesley's condition a year earlier, has all the earmarks of nervous collapse, though Arthur proved more resilient. Regardless, his maladies along with the call from Seringapatam led him to forgo the Egyptian campaign.[43] Baird's army sailed without him. This proved a fortuitous decision; the ship on which Arthur would have traveled struck a reef and sank with the loss of all aboard.

In the meantime, Henry, who held himself partly responsible for the mess because of his tardy return to India, worried about his brothers and thought that a breach might develop between them. He took responsibility, telling Arthur that the governor general's decision to appoint Baird could have been modified, if not prevented, but that in Henry's absence their eldest brother lacked a confidant comfortable enough to risk challenging his thinking. As Henry saw it, Wellesley should have ordered Arthur back to Mysore on the basis of his indispensability and not just presented the return to Mysore as an option. That Arthur would say or do something that might materially damage his relationship with his eldest brother also concerned Henry. In fact, he informed Arthur that he would not show Richard a letter of 21 March, because it "would only tend to irritate and distress him, without answering any good purpose." Most of all, he tried to assure Arthur that nothing had really changed: "I cannot think, my dear Arthur, that you have suffered in the slightest degree in your reputation in consequence of your being superseded in this command. You are still at the top of the tree as to character, and I declare to you (and I can have no wish to flatter you) that I never heard any man so highly spoken of, nor do I know any person so generally looked up to."[44]

Alas, Henry's counsel came too late. Arthur had sent a raging letter to Richard:

> To avail yourself of my knowledge and experience in the equipment of the expedition to be employed on the shores of the Red Sea is said to have been your inducement to call me away from Mysore; but, if this were the case, it was never so stated to me, and, if it had been, I should have requested you

> to employ in the drudgery that person who it was intended should reap all the honour of the service; and at least I should have refrained from incurring expense, and from taking officers from their situations to put them under the command of a man they all dislike.[45]

Arthur skated on thin ice; these comments represent an abuse of his relationship with the governor general.

Nonetheless, the response reveals much about the Wellesley character. In matters of pride, both Richard and Arthur were extraordinarily sensitive, so much so that each had difficulty recognizing this trait of character in the other. Richard's upset over his Irish title was so out of line as to be incomprehensible. So too was Arthur's upset over his supersession. The governor general could do what he wanted, and although that meant that he had the option of retaining Arthur as commander, there are times when strategic retreat served one's purposes better than holding the line. Arthur knew this but was unwilling to admit it. And while no one can deny that Richard handled the proceedings awkwardly, Arthur owed everything to him—certainly on this occasion he could have granted his brother some leeway. It perhaps came down to exhaustion and inexperience. Whereas Richard, to his credit, chose to ignore Arthur's indiscretion, Arthur never recognized or acknowledged either indiscretion or wrongdoing and was slow to forgive. Henry tried to calm both of them. "For God's sake," he wrote,

> try to forget what has happened. I am perfectly certain that whatever Mornington did was with a view to your advantage. . . . I know that Mornington has always thought, and still thinks, that his public duty obliged him to appoint a Major-General to the command of the expedition, and that the best thing he could do for you was to appoint you second in command to it. I am extremely sorry that he did so; but, at the same time, I am satisfied that your character is too well established to have suffered in the slightest degree from any part of the transaction.[46]

Henry was whistling into the wind. Incredibly and in juvenile fashion, Arthur wrote, "I am concerned that Mornington should be annoyed by any thing that I have written to him on this subject, as I certainly never intended to annoy him by my private grievances. . . . I only ask what would he have felt and have said if such a thing had happened to him?"[47] This is stunning stuff indeed and leads one to wonder whether Arthur had forgotten that his brother was governor general. His fever had crept into his brain. India did this sort of thing to those who served there. Inadvertently, Arthur revealed to Henry the source of the problem: "I know but one receipt for good health in this country, and that is to live moderately, to drink little or no wine, to use exercise, to keep the mind employed, and, if possible, to keep in good humour with the world. The last is the most difficult, for, as you have often observed, there is scarcely a good tempered man in India."[48] Arthur could count himself among the many ill-tempered men, and one wonders where he might have been without Henry nearby to discuss these matters with. Arthur continued to protest Wellesley's injustice occasionally for the next two years, always heaped with righteous indignation. Only when he marched to war against the Marathas did this theme disappear from his correspondence.

Arthur emerges from the episode looking much like a spoiled child. Nearly all of his biographers have tried to defend him. But why? Does such a personality flaw diminish his reputation? Certainly not. It reveals him as a real person, with imperfections. That he overcame many of them to carve out a brilliant career makes him even more remarkable. By contrast, Richard, who failed to come to grips with his flaws, never reached the summit of the career he sought.

6

Henry Steps Forward

Even before Wellesley received the notification of his elevation in the Irish peerage, news that enraged him and drove him towards even more aggressive actions, he had an eye focused on two areas: the Carnatic and Oudh. In both cases, he and Dundas had identified weaknesses that might threaten the security of British interests in India. Each perceived states in crisis in which wasteful, indifferent, or corrupt nawabs failed to meet their obligations either to the company or to the state. Both states had treaties with the company that bound them as allies and obligated the company to provide for their defense in return for payments to relieve the expense. The company considered them strategically vital, the Carnatic because it surrounded Madras and Fort St. George, and Oudh because it guarded the northwesterly approaches to Bengal and therefore Calcutta and Fort William. In other words, a case could be made that Britain's position in India would be compromised unless these powers were propped up. Here was a tailor-made opportunity for the ambitious Wellesley.

That the marquess looked for threats to British security that justified action, he had demonstrated in the case of Mysore. There he had constructed an elaborate scenario of French encroachment and Afghan aggression to bring to issue the long-festering feud with Tipu Sultan. He had proved quick to exploit the fears and sensibilities of his masters in London, particularly Dundas, who in the final analysis had to take Wellesley's word for what was going on in the subcontinent. However, the successful termination of the Mysore war made southern India stable: problems in the Carnatic were an annoyance rather than a threat. Similarly, stability in the south allowed the company to direct its attentions and its strength to the north to deter any ambitions that Zaman Shah might have in that quarter, thus making Oudh less problematic. But because this newfound security conflicted with Wellesley's ambitions, he chose to ignore it. Determined to enhance his reputation, he had decided, early on, to transform Britain's position. He had thought he had done so with the victory over Mysore, but the "double gilt potato" convinced him that he would have to do more. No one who knew Wellesley before he left for India could have imagined the scope of his ambition or that he would prove so difficult to control.

The dust had hardly settled in Seringapatam when Wellesley turned to these other projects, and in the process, he showed a remarkable ability to keep several balls in the air at the same time. If he caught the nawabs unaware, this should not come as a surprise; Wellesley's approach to governance could not have been more different from that of his predecessor, Sir John Shore. As he moved on Arcot and Lucknow, he would again employ his brothers. Arthur's role, because of his engagement in Mysore and involvement with the Batavian expedition, would prove inconsequential, but Henry would be called upon to emulate Arthur.

Wellesley knew the Carnatic well. Within days of his arrival at Madras in 1798, he had tried to negotiate a new treaty. In the process, he became acquainted with the personality of the nawab of the Carnatic, whose talent for obfuscation Wellesley could appreciate. On that occasion, Wellesley walked away from confrontation, preferring to focus on Tipu. He had, however, formed an opinion on what needed to be done. Because the nawab could not be trusted to deliver on his financial obligations to the company, some sort of territorial arrangement would have to be made to provide for them. Wellesley's mind had its own law of physics, and it always sought the moral and strategic high ground for whatever it concluded. In this case, Wellesley began by accusing the nawab of not living up to the treaty obligations and as a consequence jeopardizing the Mysore campaign.

In a letter written two weeks before the assault on Seringapatam, the governor general took another tack in his attempt to provoke action. He informed the nawab that according to the third article of the treaty concluded in 1792, in times of war the East India Company could take control of the Carnatic. The nawab, of course, needed no reminding of these particulars and, Wellesley knew, would find the reminder distasteful. The move constituted a threat. A bribe followed: such an extreme measure could be avoided if the nawab would make a new treaty, the provisions of which could hardly have caught him by surprise. All could be made right if "your Highness shall place under the exclusive management, controul, and authority of the Company, in perpetuity, a territory, equal to secure the receipts of the whole of your monthly payments into the Company's treasury, which payments are of course to cease from that time."[1] The nawab would retain only those territories surrounding his capital; the rest would go over to the company, making the nawab dependent on British support. This was Wellesley's version of the subsidiary treaty, which he did not invent but modified to his own purposes and for which he became famous. It allowed him to acquire territory without war and apparently without expense. Wellesley preferred to conclude the treaty peacefully, with goodwill intact. Nevertheless, his use of a threat together with a bribe provides a good definition for the term *extortion.*[2] The nawab knew at this point that Wellesley would not back away from confrontation a second time; his only hope lay in distraction and delay.

As luck would have it, events played into the nawab's hands. In a masterly letter dated 13 May 1799, he gave notice that his mind was subtle and supple as Wellesley's. The nawab began, appropriately, with flattery and an acknowledgment of the governor general's interpretation of the treaty of 1792. In the process, he countered Wellesley. If the company desired to take control of the Carnatic for the duration of the war, so be it. That was not what the nawab wanted, but treaties are treaties. This was a clever response. He conceded Wellesley's threat because the Mysore war was all but over and because he could remind the governor general that the company too was a signatory of the treaty. In other words, Wellesley had to concede the sovereignty of the nawab. Next, the nawab addressed the issue of the treaty needing revision, stating that "the treaty which is now suggested to be defective, has had a trial, my Lord, of more than seven years, and without a single exception, has been found for that period not only sufficient for all common purposes, but has secured the fulfillment of every engagement stipulated in it." One can only imagine the irritation with which Wellesley read this, and the nawab capped it off with flowery praise and a reminder that with the war's end, article three no longer applied:

> My Lord, Praise be to the Almighty God, that in consequence of your Lordship's wise and resolute measures, the strong Fortress of Seringapatam . . . has been captured, and the extensive country of Mysore restored to tranquility and safety, by the annihilation of the disturber of that country. . . . The victories which my friends have obtained by Divine favour, has given the greatest joy to me who am their ancient ally, I consider them as an auspicious omen of my own happiness, and am persuaded that your Lordship will manifest your kindness towards me, especially in support of my rights.

He concluded audaciously with a request for compensation in the form of the restoration of territories taken on previous occasions by Tipu Sultan.[3]

This was a dance that Wellesley wished to end. In the meantime, his attention was drawn elsewhere. In October he took control of the civil and military administration of Tanjore on payment of £40,000 to the raja. Then came Surat on the west coast just north of Bombay. Default on subsidies for its defense combined with the death of the nawab of Surat to prompt new negotiations. As a result, the company assumed full administrative responsibilities. Wellesley left little doubt that he was prepared to take advantage of any opportunity to extend the company's power and influence; whether the stakes were great or small mattered little. This attitude cannot be passed off solely as ambition. An eighteenth-century man (with a strong romantic streak), Wellesley craved order and symmetry. As Iris Butler puts it, he had a "passion for trimming ragged edges."[4] Whatever motivated him, he brought to the governor-generalship a dynamic new style.

In the ten months after the fall of Seringapatam, contrary thoughts consumed Wellesley. His writings show that he thoroughly enjoyed the afterglow of his victory over Mysore. At the same time, he agonized over how his work would be received in London. Though he spoke with great confidence over the significance of events in India, he had not totally convinced himself of the fact. This in part explains the futile gesture of sending Henry to London to press the point and his own emotional collapse when confronted with the reality of London's view. In the intervening months, he busied himself with his projects in Calcutta, overseeing Arthur's work in Mysore, and planning his next steps. Although his behavior during this period exhibits an almost frantic quality, he had not yet put on the mask of the bully. Some would say that he would remove the mask of the statesman to reveal the bully that he was by nature, but this is unfair. When confronted with the "double gilt potato" of the Irish marquessate, he lost his equilibrium, and he was not, at least for a year, a healthy man. Aggressive he would be, but a bully he was not. The bully intimidates and cajoles because he enjoys it, whereas Wellesley bullied to accomplish a desired end and because his emotions were out of balance.

Before leaving Fort St. George, the governor general impressed upon Lord Clive his concern over the Carnatic. Whether or not Wellesley directed Clive to find the means to pressure the nawab further on a subsidiary treaty can only be left to conjecture, but Clive's zeal suggests that he did. The catalyst for fresh negotiations (if that is what they can be fairly called) came from Tipu's archive, which Wellesley had all along considered more valuable than the treasury. In April 1800, Wellesley sent to Clive correspondence between Tipu and the nawabs of Arcot—father and son Muhammad Ali and Umdut-al-Umrah—going back as far as 1789, correspondence that appeared conspiratorial. Wellesley, of course, had made up his mind on the implications of this correspondence, but he insisted on the appearance of legal inquiry.[5] In other words, the nawab's guilt was clear, but the evidence should be put in order before he was punished for it. The correspondence was, in fact, anything but conclusive, because it was written partly in cipher and because it had the appearance of being collusive. Clive concluded the worst: "I have no hesitation in ascribing to His Highness a course of systematized councils fundamentally hostile to the interests of Great Britain in India."[6] The dates here are important because they come shortly after Wellesley's receipt of the marquessate, when he was at the height of his despair and anger, feelings that he transferred to his dealings with the nawab.

Discussions between the nawabs Muhammad Ali and Umdut-al-Umrah and Tipu had taken place through two ambassadors, Ali Riza and Gulam Ali Khan. Accordingly, Clive ordered the interrogation of the two men. He assigned the task to Josiah Webbe and Barry Close, who conducted the interviews separately in both time and place. They discovered nothing new. That discussions between the nawabs and Tipu took place could not be denied, but their purpose was open to interpretation. The two emissaries explained that as far as the nawabs were concerned, their aggressive neighbor could not be ignored or antagonized. If he wanted to talk, their best interest lay in humoring him, and if that appeared to be contrary to the interests of Great Britain, it was unfortunate. What were they to do? In addition, had the nawabs ever acted against the interests of the company? Discussion, as they pointed out, is quite different from action. Wellesley knew this but believed what he preferred to believe. While this might be human nature, in this case it would be accompanied by rather significant consequences for the unfortunate Umdut-al-Umrah. The eager-to-please Clive stoked the fire, stating, "I have no hesitation in recommending to your Lordship the immediate assumption of the civil & military government of the Carnatic."[7] In June, Wellesley informed the court of directors that he considered the nawab guilty as charged.[8]

Several months would pass before Wellesley acted. As he explained to Clive, he did not want to compromise delicate negotiations with Hyderabad. In other words, Wellesley—who knew exactly what he was doing—did not want to frighten the Nizam with such a high-handed gesture in the Carnatic.

The board of control and court of directors in the meantime put their stamp of approval on Wellesley's plans.[9] Encouragement and time gave rise to hyperbole that even for Wellesley was extraordinary. "The intentions of the nawabs Mahomed Ali, and Umdut al Umrah," he wrote with venom flowing, "have been uniformly and without interruption hostile to the existence of the British power in India."[10] Ready to strike, the marquess instructed Clive to begin negotiations with the clear understanding that the issue was simply *when,* not *if* the nawab would surrender. Clive could offer a generous pension along with a dignified retirement, but if the nawab should balk, then he should be made to understand that the company would assume control by decree, place the nawab on trial for treason, and expose his collaboration (as Wellesley understood it) to the world.

Such arbitrary and despotic treatment shocks, not because it had not existed in the past (even the immediate past of Wellesley's governor-generalship) but because Wellesley made no attempt to disguise his intentions. Wellesley entrusted Clive with a letter for the nawab that established the governor's authority and informed the nawab of what was about to transpire. Even given the excessive style of Indian correspondence, the nawab's response betrayed the seriousness of the situation. "Your Lordship's communications," he moaned, "have embittered my soul, plunged me with grief hitherto unknown & thrown over my infant prospects of Tranquillity & Happiness the gloomy mantle of Melancholy & Despair."[11] In the meantime, Wellesley learned that the nawab was about to die. That, he informed Clive, changed nothing; the conditions sent to the nawab were applicable in their entirety to any successor. Clive, however, found himself in an awkward position. The nawab's illness progressed rapidly, rendering him unable to conduct business. The governor decided to allow him to die peacefully while taking the precaution of ordering company troops into the palace "for the purpose of preserving order."[12] Umdut-al-Umrah died ten days later on 15 July 1801.

At that point, a new set of negotiations began. Clive dispatched Close and Webbe to the palace to deliberate on his behalf. There they were presented with the deceased nawab's will, which established as his heir Ali Hussein Khan, referred to by Clive as Umdut-al-Umrah's "reputed" son. As the boy was only thirteen, the will provided for a regency. Close and Webbe informed the regents of their charge and presented the appropriate documents. They then deferred discussion until after the nawab's funeral. The hiatus had no positive effect; when discussions resumed, the new nawab (on the advice of his regents) rejected the company's demands. Rather than proceed to an arbitrary seizure of government, Clive, taking advantage of existing doubt concerning the paternity of the heir and Wellesley's declaration that the company no longer recognized the legitimacy of Umdut-al-Umrah's family, opened negotiations with another party, Azim-al-Daulah, the nephew of the late nawab. This young man, unwilling to look a gift horse in the mouth, promptly signed off on the governor general's demands. Subsequently, he was installed as nawab and the company took control. Clive's summary of these dealings betrays both relief and pride.[13]

After tying up the loose ends, Wellesley apprised the East India Company of what had transpired, and, as usual, he made it seem as if he had done as the company wished, in a manner "highly creditable to the justice and moderation of the British character."[14] One doubts whether the new nawab (or anyone else in the Carnatic, for that matter) would have described Wellesley's actions as just and moderate.

Certainly the governor general displayed no regret; he had again added to the territories of the company in a very appreciable way. To the north, he was engaged in a similar feat.

There the object of his attention was the state of Oudh. The company's relationship with Oudh was a long and important one for the simple reason of geography. Oudh bordered Bengal and acted as a buffer to any threat from the north, particularly from the Afghans and the Marathas. Consequently, the company took an active interest in the affairs of the state, stipulating that the relationship should provide mutual support. Oudh would cooperate fully with the company, and the company, in turn, would defend the nawab from all threats. In practice, this meant that the company would maintain troops within the frontiers of Oudh and the nawab would provide for the expense. When Dundas appointed Wellesley governor general, Oudh was in a state of transition, with the ineffectual nawab Asuf al Daula on his deathbed. On reaching the Cape, Wellesley learned that the nawab had died and that a succession crisis had ensued, which in this case was a product of British meddling. On the old nawab's death, Sir John Shore had helped his son, Ali, to the throne. Shore soon found that Ali would not be the solution to Oudh's problems, which were a consequence of neglect, ineptitude, and corruption. Ali brought to the throne inexperience, a mean spirit, and a corrupt nature—which meant that he fit in nicely with the status quo. Consequently, Shore double-tracked, using Ali's questionable lineage to remove him and then installing the deceased nawab's half brother, Sadat Ali, in his place. The deposed Ali he moved to Benares. At the same time, Shore concluded a new treaty with the nawab that again provided for the stationing of British troops within the state and a prescribed subsidy from the nawab. The treaty left the nawab with complete control over the internal affairs of the state. The treaty of 1797 in essence guaranteed the sovereignty of the nawab in all things save defense.

Sadat Ali was not without merit. Shore found him intelligent, loyal to British interests, and well intentioned. He was, however, unable to summon the determination necessary to revitalize the state economy or to end corruption. This combined with the fact that the confusion over the succession factionalized the politics of Oudh, making dynamic leadership difficult, even if Sadat Ali had it to assert. Place seekers and established functionaries alike were quick to seek advantage from either Sadat Ali or his predecessor. Even before all this, Wellesley had concluded that Oudh was a state in decline. He and Dundas had agreed that something would have to be done, but because of the struggle with Tipu, resolution of the problem would have to wait. It did not alter the fact that for Wellesley this was fruit ripe for the picking.

Wellesley's first dealings with Oudh came not long after his arrival. The resident at Lucknow, John Lumsden, informed the governor general that the degradation of the nawab's army had reached the point where Lumsden viewed it as a liability. The company provided for the defense of the realm, but the nawab's army provided for internal security. It was without discipline and on the verge of mutiny. Here Wellesley perceived an opportunity. "In the place of the armed rabble which now alarms the Vizier and invites his enemies," he wrote, "I propose to substitute an increased number of the Company's regiments of infantry and cavalry . . . to be paid by his Excellency."[15]

Worried that the deposed nawab might attempt a coup, Wellesley issued orders to move him closer to Calcutta. At the time, the chief judge of the provincial court of circuit and appeal, George Cherry, who was responsible for keeping track of him, did so with the attitude of a parent. Cherry had handled the negotiations for the deposition, and he should have suspected that the erstwhile vizier might harbor some animosity towards him. In fact, Shore (who viewed Ali as nothing more than a brutal thug) had warned him that Ali could not be trusted. Cherry, deceiving himself, believed Ali to be a respectable sort who, if treated with patience and understanding, would mature into a fine young man. Ali murdered him at one of their regular breakfast meetings.

Ali's plans were bigger than the murder of Cherry. His bodyguard proceeded on a rampage of murder and mayhem until the arrival of company troops forced him to flee. Wellesley, hoping to evoke outrage, was dramatic in describing these events to the court of directors. By repeatedly linking Ali with Zaman Shah and the Maratha chieftain Sindia, Wellesley tried to build a case for reorganizing Oudh. In his opinion, these events spoke to the instability of the region, which could be remedied only through an enhanced British presence. Again, as in the case of the Carnatic, these initial steps occurred as Wellesley prepared for the assault on Seringapatam.[16]

In April 1799, Wellesley spoke of a conspiracy to overthrow Sadat Ali, reestablish Vizier Ali on the throne, and invite Zaman Shah to assist in expelling the British from eastern India. "But the complexion of this transaction," he wrote with a contrived sense of urgency, "leads to serious reflections on the condition of your possessions in Bengal and the provinces. The defective state of the police in the provinces and the several great cities will require immediate attention." In other words, management was the source of the problem, and that had to be dealt with through a redefinition of the nawab's powers.[17]

Wellesley's ideas concerning Oudh were evolutionary, based on the opportunity he perceived. In June 1799, after the Mysore war, his instructions to William Scott, Lumsden's replacement as resident at Lucknow, are not extraordinary. He speaks of the unpopularity of Sadat Ali and the necessity of working with him to minimize the problem. In the meantime, Scott was to exploit every opportunity to reduce the nawab's army, which both he and the nawab viewed as a liability. These instructions were just the first salvo, intended to be temporary measures until the governor general could give Oudh his undivided attention.[18] Dundas, in turn, did nothing to rein Wellesley in. "I have nothing very minute to suggest," he wrote, except "dispersing his useless rabble, and forming an army to be kept up and disciplined under our immediate superintendence."[19]

Wellesley's flair for the dramatic never flagged. He again invoked the specter of Zaman Shah in the north. The Afghan threat was especially convenient because it would have an impact on his negotiations—ongoing or pending—with the Nizam, the Peshwa, and the nawab of Oudh. When Wellesley reopened his direct contact with the nawab, he expected little opposition.[20] What Wellesley had in mind was the dismantling of the nawab's army to the point at which it became a police force and a ceremonial bodyguard. It is not difficult to figure out the governor general's reasoning. Without his own forces, the nawab would be left dependent on the British, not only for protection from foreign threats but also for internal security. The nawab had made the fatal blunder of informing the governor general that he could not rely on his army for security and in fact dreaded using it in pursuit of his rival, Vizier Ali, for fear that it might turn on him. Thus, Wellesley was able to describe Oudh as surrounded by enemies. He pointed out to the nawab that the seventh article of the treaty of 1797 required the company to "defend the dominions of your Excellency against all enemies." This he said he was prepared to do, but because of the conditions in India at the time, the thirteen thousand troops stationed in Oudh would not be sufficient to defend against "all enemies." That force, he pointed out, would have to be augmented, and he as governor general, by the provisions of the treaty, had the right to do so. As the augmentation would be costly, the nawab should meet the increased expense by dismantling his army. This argument, if ingenious, was frivolous, and Wellesley must have known that. It demonstrates that the governor general expected little or no resistance from the nawab. If he could supply his ally with a justification for giving way, the nawab would take it.[21]

Scott surprised Wellesley with the information that the nawab had had a change of heart. The nawab had informed the resident that his burdens had become too great and that he had resolved to abdicate. When pressed, he responded that he had never expected to be called to the throne and that he was by nature a private person. On taking the throne, he had found resentment and outright hostility all around him, conditions that he knew not how to resolve. He had, therefore, determined that the best course would be to abdicate in favor of one of his sons, to be selected by the governor general. Scott, unconvinced, suspected other motives. He knew that the nawab had removed his treasury to his harem, where it would fall under his private control. This fortune, which Scott estimated to be in excess of £1,000,000, could thus be carried away, leaving his successor penniless and unable to make subsidy payments to the company.[22]

The nawab's motives in threatening to abdicate are murky, but whatever he hoped to accomplish, he failed. Wellesley informed him that from the point of view of the company, nothing of a satisfactory nature would be accomplished by his abdication in favor of a son. First, none of his sons possessed the experience or maturity to govern with any expectation of success. Second, if the nawab retired with the resources of state, his successor would have to increase taxes to meet obligations. This would apply even greater pressure to a resentful citizenry, threatening even further the stability of government. Third, if he left Oudh with the treasury, he could not count on the protection of the company. This was Wellesley's trump card. He had perceived cowardice to be the nawab's greatest weakness. If Wellesley could increase the threat of physical harm, he could manipulate the nawab's mind. The nawab had also exposed another flank that Wellesley quickly attacked. If, as the nawab maintained, he could no longer govern, then it stood to reason that his heir, whoever that might be, could not govern either. Only the company could provide Oudh with good government. Wellesley suggested that the nawab turn over all responsibilities of state to the company. And so the stakes had increased, but, as Wellesley pointed out, the place to start was with the reform of the military establishment.[23]

Wellesley supposed that he held all the cards in the negotiations, which would soon be resolved. However, the nawab remained silent, perhaps because he had intended to relinquish the throne but had changed his mind. The reason for the change was the capture of Ali, who had been turned over to the British. This event did not alter the nawab's popularity or his ability to govern, but it did remove the threat of political violence. His repeated references to Ali as an assassin betray his fear.

Whether Wellesley thought of this aspect of the nawab's reasoning is not particularly important. He wanted results, and when he did not get them, he turned to threats: "The conduct of your Excellency . . . is of a nature so unequivocally hostile, and may prove so injurious to every interest, both of your Excellency and of the Company, that your perseverance in so dangerous a course, will leave me no other alternative than that of considering all amicable engagements between the Company and your Excellency to be dissolved, and of regulating my subsequent proceedings accordingly."[24] Despite having to threaten the nawab, Wellesley assured Dundas that all was progressing smoothly.

At this point there occurred a curious pause in Wellesley's negotiations with the nawab caused by the confluence of several events that drew the governor general's attentions away from Oudh: the arrival of the "double gilt potato" proved a distraction, and negotiations with the Nizam and the Carnatic had reached critical junctures. Consequently, Wellesley ignored the nawab of Oudh until January 1801, when the stalling of Scott's negotiations became clear. By then, Wellesley was in a demonstrably foul mood.

Near the end of the year 1800, Wellesley reinforced the company's troops stationed in Oudh on the pretext of providing its proper defense. He presented the nawab with the bill, knowing full well that payment would be difficult. Having nudged the nawab towards default, Wellesley then presented him with several options, the most important of which was the dismantling of his army, which had been Wellesley's goal all along. But there was more. Wellesley informed the nawab that the lack of money was attributable to corruption and inefficiency, to be remedied only by turning the administration of Oudh over to the British. Wellesley knew that the nawab considered this solution unacceptable, and so he offered another. The nawab could cede to the company territories with sufficient revenues to cover the expense of the augmented forces, as the Nizam had done.[25] It was a clever, ruthless maneuver that apparently had only just occurred to the marquess. There is nothing in the correspondence to suggest that this had been his idea all along.

Scott could get nowhere, partly because the nawab detested him—not that anyone else could have done any better. The resident began to suspect a conspiracy; his suspicions eventually fell on a British merchant in Lucknow, Gore Ouseley, whom the nawab had befriended. According to Scott, Ouseley busily advised the nawab to reject any and all British proposals.

The stalemate brought out the worst in Wellesley. "I . . . now declare to your Excellency in the most explicit terms," he raged to the nawab, "that I consider it to be my positive duty to resort to any extremity, rather than to suffer the further progress of that ruin, to which the interests of your Excellency, and the Honourable Company are exposed, by the continued operation of the evils and abuses actually existing in the civil and military administration of the province of Oudh."[26] As Wellesley pressed Scott, the nawab called the governor general's bluff because he had no doubt that bluff it was. Although Wellesley ordered Scott to move troops into position to take over the administration of designated districts, resorting to force would be in no one's best interests.

The nawab eventually submitted a counterproposal, which Wellesley treated as another effort to obfuscate and delay.[27] By July, in his frustration, he dispatched Henry (who had returned from his mission to London in February) to Lucknow to bring the negotiations to a conclusion.[28] The governor general did not intend to replace Scott but rather to reinforce his authority. The resident was to be a part of all negotiations and be a signatory to any agreement.

Henry's appointment was a mark of his brother's confidence. "The governor-general thought that, as his brother, I would have greater advantages in carrying on this negociation than could be possessed by any other individual in India excepting himself," he wrote modestly several years later, "and this was I believe, his principle reason for entrusting this important mission to me."[29] That was only part of the reason. While in London, Henry had proved himself a man of business and a person with whom people liked to deal. Dundas, no mean judge of talent and not one to flatter, reported to Wellesley, "I cannot allow myself to part with him [Henry] without assuring you that in the course of my life I never met with any person with whom I have had more satisfaction in transacting business than with him. He joins together one of the most amiable tempers to one of the soundest judgments I ever met with, and I trust opportunities will occur to enable him to prove to the world that my judgment of him is not erroneous."[30] Wellesley did not need Dundas's endorsement to turn to his youngest brother, but it certainly did not hurt. As for Henry, he could not have been surprised by his brother's decision. What he found on his return to Bengal was a governor general overworked, distracted, and in poor health, who was trying to salve Arthur's ego, wounded over Baird's appointment to command the Egyptian expedition. Too much was transpiring at one time.

On arriving at Lucknow, Henry discovered that he would have to deal not only with the nawab but also with Scott. The two problems were not unconnected. Scott, harried by the governor general and failing to persuade the nawab to buckle, came to resent the nawab and his friend Ouseley. Scott had ordered Ouseley to cease their regular meetings at the palace. The prohibition only heightened the animosity between the resident and the nawab.

Eager to break the impasse, Henry tried to signal a fresh start without undermining Scott. When the two met, Henry suggested a new way of handling Ouseley; as he could not be prevented from meeting with the nawab, it would be best to sanction the relationship on terms benefiting the company. Fortunately, Henry had leverage to exert. As the governor general's private secretary, Henry held the appointment of postmaster of the upper provinces. Technically, Ouseley, who served as deputy postmaster in Lucknow, served at Henry's pleasure. In meeting with Ouseley to discuss his friendship with the nawab, Henry was direct.

Henry accused Ouseley of having sabotaged the negotiations with the nawab, a charge he vehemently denied. Henry added that he and Scott would not try to prohibit the meetings with the nawab, so long as Ouseley did nothing to jeopardize the upcoming negotiations. Otherwise, Henry would ask Lord Wellesley to remove him from Lucknow. The point was made. This example of high diplomacy conducted on a low level worked as Henry had hoped. Ouseley became a collaborator, hoping to see his own career advance (he would eventually end up as ambassador to Persia). It was a good start.[31]

The nawab proved tougher going. Henry's first face-to-face meeting with the nawab came in September, although not before the governor general had again exploded in frustration over the nawab's tactics.[32] Wellesley's temper could not have helped matters, but Henry waded in. He confirmed his brother's suspicion that the nawab was receiving what was, for them, bad advice from some quarter. Other than that, the initial encounter pleased him. With Scott at his side acting as an interpreter, Henry presented the nawab with a précis of the negotiations and clarified that nothing would prevent their successful termination. He informed the nawab, who had called for a face-to-face meeting with the governor general, that that would not happen until the new treaty was signed and that he, the governor general's brother, represented the nearest thing to face-to-face negotiations.

For the first time, Wellesley perceived a glimmer of hope. "I have great satisfaction in communicating to you my entire approbation of the judicious manner in which you have opened the negotiation with his Excellency the Vizier entrusted to your charge," wrote the governor general; "and I rely with confidence on the continuance of this same judgment in the progress of your discussions which you have manifested in the commencement of them."[33] It was one thing for the nawab to put off Scott but quite another to reject proposals made by the governor general's brother. From this moment, Henry assumed responsibility for the negotiations and the marquess discontinued his direct correspondence with the nawab. There would be no more outbursts and no more threats. Certainly Wellesley's tactics had the effect of wearing down the nawab, but it should also be noted that the nawab did not give in into such treatment. It is as if he knew that the governor general might threaten a forceful takeover but would be loath to do so. Indeed, Wellesley must have known that such an action would be almost indefensible. And so, an honest and true negotiation ensued.

The nawab tried all of his tricks on Henry. He attempted to turn Henry against Scott, again threatened abdication, directed the discussion toward peripheral issues, and even offered a bribe—which Henry refused and said he "treated as a joke." Henry proceeded with great confidence and considerable skill, and in the end, perseverance paid off; the nawab agreed to proposals on 10 November 1801. By this treaty, the nawab retained sovereignty over a much-reduced state surrounded by territories ceded to the company for maintenance of its enhanced military presence. Perhaps Wellesley's gambit all along had been the threat of depriving the nawab of all responsibilities, as had been done in the Carnatic, so that he might feel better about giving up the lion's share of his domain. There has been considerable historical debate over Wellesley's policies and tactics concerning Oudh. His detractors point to his threatening, bullying manner in dealing with an ally who had always been cooperative. His defenders state that the nawab had inherited a political system that no longer worked, for it was mired in corruption, and had done nothing to fix it. In the process, the security of the state and the prosperity of the people had been compromised. In other words, Wellesley acted responsibly in the interests of all parties. Unquestionably, the governor general's methods were Machiavellian, but he had been pointed in that direction from the time he accepted office. That events transpired as they did resulted as much from the ineptitude of the nawab as from Wellesley's aggressiveness. There is something to Wellesley's own defense that he had been led down the garden path by the nawab only to find it blocked. His initial proposals to the nawab were more moderate than the last. Had Sadat Ali looked around at how the governor general operated elsewhere, he might have realized that to preserve the integrity of his state, he had to close a deal as quickly as possible. Instead he let the opportunity slip and led Wellesley to believe that he was deceitful at a time when Wellesley was in particularly bad spirits. Wellesley lost patience and decided to make the nawab pay for being obstreperous.

The terms of the treaty thrilled the marquess, who took great delight in his brother's success and his own inspiration in entrusting Henry with the task. So delighted was he that Henry's appointment as lieutenant governor of the ceded provinces followed. Wellesley seems to have given little thought to the political implications of the appointment, because he announced it promptly on receiving word of the treaty. He had little trouble justifying the decision: "The discretion, temper, judgment, and firmness which Mr. Wellesley has manifested, in the principal conduct of the negotiation with the Vizier have been the most efficient cause of its speedy, prosperous, and tranquil issue. These qualities, combined with the authority which he naturally derives from his near connexion with me, have induced me to consider him to be the most useful instrument which I can employ on this occasion."[34] Arthur, too, rejoiced in his brothers' success, believing it another gem in Richard's imperial diadem.[35] He was, however, suspicious of the subsidiary treaty; to him it only made a bad situation worse.[36]

Henry assumed his responsibilities as governor of the ceded provinces without much enthusiasm. This is apparent even in his memoirs written several years later. Nevertheless, his job was important, and he realized it. For the marquess, already under pressure for excessive spending, the last thing he needed was for Oudh to add to the burden.[37] Given the condition of many of the newly absorbed lands, that was a real possibility. Not that the area lacked potential. The land between the Jumna and Ganges rivers was some of the richest in India. That much of it lay idle was attributable to corruption and governmental neglect. Tax collectors, themselves in arrears, levied extortionate rates that forced many peasants off the land. The vicious cycle continued when opportunistic European entrepreneurs offered loans at usurious rates to make up for shortfalls. Bribery, place buying, and banditry followed as the administrative system ground to a halt. Everyone suffered, but none more than the peasants, who had no place to go and no incentive to work. Henry, as the year 1802 opened, had the unenviable task of bringing order out of disorder, prosperity out of poverty.[38]

Fortunately, he did not lack a sense of how to start. His experience in the administration of Mysore after the fall of Seringapatam proved invaluable, even though Mysore, unlike Oudh, had been a well-governed state. Henry had come to understand the Indian political system and Indian ways of doing business. The task of settling and reorganizing the ceded provinces would challenge both his intellectual and his physical resources.

Intellectually, he had to come up with a plan that reformed the existing system while preparing it for a permanent arrangement based on the administrative, judicial, and fiscal structures established by Lord Cornwallis in Bengal. This system, known as the "permanent settlement," while far from perfect, had been endorsed by Pitt and Dundas. Lord Wellesley therefore encouraged Henry to introduce it in the ceded provinces. The permanent settlement was known already to have caused disruption and hardship in Bengal. Therefore, Henry devised systems that moved towards the permanent settlement but fell short of complete implementation. Half measures are often counterproductive, but in this case, Lord Wellesley could not afford to risk in Oudh the collapse of the agricultural economy, which had attended the introduction of the permanent settlement in Bengal. This meant that Henry had to devise his own administrative and financial reforms at the same time as he reformed the military and the judiciary. The diversity and breadth of the task would tax his intellectual resources.

Henry would be required to travel extensively through the ceded districts to oversee the progress of his reforms, living out of tents and traveling on horseback, often in sweltering heat and humidity. After nine months of this, Henry had had enough. Like his brothers, when he grew tired or bored, his health deteriorated, and he used failing health as an excuse to move on. One can hardly blame him. Unlike his brothers, however, Henry had no fortune awaiting him for a job well done. In Oudh, he earned only his secretary's salary, and although he returned to Britain with money in the bank, India had not made him a rich man. It had given him valuable experience, the good opinion of his brothers, and status and recognition as a servant of the state.

While governing the ceded provinces during those long months, Henry was not alone in his work. The marquess, as he had done in Mysore, created a commission, this one consisting of Matthew Leslie, Archibald Seton, and John Fombelle, along with Scott, who remained in Lucknow as resident.[39] Henry was in charge and carried the title of lieutenant governor of the ceded districts. The first task would be the dismantling of the nawab's army in the ceded territories. This had been one of the primary objectives from the start of the negotiations, as these units were at best unreliable and many had become nothing more than freebooters. They operated outside the law, at their own whim. Scott would play an important role in this dismantling, working with the nawab on a comprehensive settlement. The nawab would retain a bodyguard and ceremonial troops, but by the terms of the new treaty, the company assumed responsibility for his protection. Scott and Henry coordinated their work with local rulers, and by the end of December, they were making real progress. As the nawab's troops were demobilized, they were replaced by company troops or absorbed into the company's units.[40] So important was this exchange that the commander in chief, General Gerard Lake, proceeded to the territories to observe it.

Equally important was the collection of revenues, not only because the company depended on it but also because reform of the system inevitably involved the whole administrative, judicial, and financial structure of the territories. Taxes in Oudh were collected by two sets of functionaries: the *zamindars* and the *amildars.* The zamindars were considered government officers, and their responsibilities included supervision of finance in their given departments and also, more importantly, superintendence of the land revenues. Their supervision of the collection of taxes was a right that they purchased from the state. The system resembled tax farming anywhere. These agents agreed to provide the state a fixed sum, established by contract, from a given district, and they kept sums in excess of the guaranteed revenues. The system had not worked well, because in their zeal to acquire contracts offered at auction (sometimes annually), the zamindars often overbid, which led to the evils of extortion and borrowing. The permanent settlement addressed this by offering permanent contracts that turned zamindars into local lords.

The amildars actually collected the taxes. They were unique in that they carried powers beyond those of collectors. They were given judicial and military powers as they went about their business. Often the amildars were at the heart of the military corruption in Oudh that made the army unreliable. They interacted directly with the populace, often capriciously and brutally. Their impact was devastating because the peasantry, rather than deal with them, often pulled up stakes and migrated. The cycle became self-perpetuating when zamindars and amildars resorted to whatever means were available to meet their obligations.

Henry Wellesley addressed the issue of the amildars first, by bringing in company collectors while creating a company-appointed judiciary. This decision was met with resistance, and therefore the military settlement went hand in glove with collection reform. Operating out of Bareilly, Henry introduced his reforms on a trial and error basis. The powers of the collectors were modified as Henry became acquainted with their modus operandi and as company magistrates made their recommendations. He soon saw that the company collectors were independent to a fault. Once in the field, they ignored both his directives and the system he put in place. Henry complained about them regularly to General Lake and to his brother, both of whom listened sympathetically. "I am sorry to hear you find your situation so unpleasant," replied Lake. "I know full well that neither the civil or military company's officers can brook controul, they have so high an idea of their talents that they imagine themselves superior to all the world. . . . If this letter is seen I shall be hung."[41] The marquess, who described the company collectors as arrogant and petulant, recommended judicial curbs.[42]

Henry faced real difficulties in dealing with the collectors, but there is more to his unease than simply the self-serving independence of these company servants. A competent and at times inspired administrator, Henry was not a good boss. He was much happier carrying out orders than giving them. Confrontation made him uncomfortable. His friend Merrick Shawe, who understood him, counseled, "I really cannot allow you to be right in vexing yourself so much about the conduct of others. You feel more sensibly than you ought that pain which your duty obliges you occasionally to inflict on the undeserving."[43] There were, obviously, times when Henry wished that his brother had not given him such extraordinary latitude. In their frequent correspondence, the marquess made recommendations but left decisions "to the exercise of your discretion on the spot . . . founded on a knowledge of local circumstances."[44]

There were countless details to be attended to, including moving the bureaucracy to Bareilly and reestablishing the currency. Here again Henry's mind raced ahead of realities. He knew what had to be done, but he would come to recognize that his goals could only be realized over time. The removal of the treasury, for instance, would take several months to accomplish, and his ideas for a uniform currency would be scuttled by local traditions. General organizational lines would be based on the administration of Bengal, but that did not make the task any easier. And there were the regular responsibilities of business—making appointments, seeing to salaries, reading reports, sending reports—it all began to take its toll on the unenthusiastic Henry. Yet even measured against his expectations, his efforts bore fruit quickly. In March 1802, he informed the governor general that revenues were up dramatically from the year before, that "tranquillity prevails throughout the Ceded Provinces, and that the change in the Government seems to have given general satisfaction."[45] Fatigue and frustration would have discouraged self-promotion at this time, so one must take Henry at his word.

If these responsibilities were not enough, Henry had to settle with the nawab of Farrukhabad. One of the political anomalies that popped up often, Farrukhabad was a quasi-independent state in the midst of the ceded districts. Because it was surrounded by British territory, it could not be considered independent, and its existence insulted Lord Wellesley's sense of symmetry—a "rough edge" that needed trimming. For Henry it posed problems more practical than aesthetic. "The Cession was rendered indispensably requisite to the safety and prosperity of the Company's contiguous possessions," he argued in a manner that pleased his brother, "by the total want of Police which has hitherto prevailed in the Province of Farrukhabad, and the frequent commission of Robberies and Murders."[46] And so Henry leaned on the nawab, Imdad Husain Khan, as he had leaned on the nawab Sadat Ali. The nawab would have to either transfer all authority to the company or cede provinces whose revenues would cover the expense of a dual administration, in particular the costs of civil and criminal courts.[47] The negotiations proved simple, as the helpless nawab accepted a pension and turned his state over to the company.[48]

Henry took great interest in the economic development of the ceded districts and toured the land to survey its potential. He promoted the establishment of trade fairs, fostered commerce, and even experimented (along with General Lake) with a horse-breeding enterprise. This topic is conspicuous in his correspondence, revealing that this part of India was already established as a center for the raising and training of horses. There was, of course, an ever-present need for horses—both military and civil—so his interest in the area's potential is no surprise. In the case of the trade fairs, Henry arranged for two a year to connect the hill people with the rest of the market. He provided military protection at the fairs so that all who attended would feel secure.

By the middle of the summer of 1802, Henry looked to move on. Believing most of the important work complete, he petitioned his brother for "permission to resign my present situation whenever it may appear that I can do so without injury to the public interests."[49] He claimed ill health but agreed to serve until the end of the year if necessary. The governor general agreed to the terms, and Henry prepared to leave Bareilly at the end of November.

By that time, Henry had developed his own opinion on the future of British India. "If the Indian Empire be a great stake to the Nation," he wrote, "it is time to look to it, thro' a very different medium; but the advantages which Great Britain ought to derive from what has been declared the brightest Jewel in her Imperial diadem, will never be realized, until the general Government of India shall be revised and general principles, shall supersede the miserable policy of temporary expedients. We may then hope to see the interests of the people of India more liberally considered, and on pervading power, watching over and directing the ways and means and their application."[50] There is more than a hint of bitterness here, but along with it is political insight and the clarity of thought typical of all the Wellesleys. The marquess meanwhile heaped praise on his brother.[51]

Henry resigned not just from the ceded provinces but from India. He had no desire to stay on. With his health and spirit broken, he preferred to go home, and his brother understood. The marquess would miss more than Henry's work; he would miss Henry's good company, his even temper, and his thoughtful advice. At the time of Henry's departure, Wellesley thought himself thoroughly in control of events, but he was mistaken, and in the challenges that lay ahead, he could have used Henry's stabilizing influence; Arthur would be the first to realize it.

Before Henry's departure, dispatches arrived in Calcutta from London, among them one from the court of directors annulling Henry's appointment as lieutenant governor. The court objected on the grounds that the appointment superseded "regular covenanted servants" of the East India Company. In other words, it got in the way of their patronage.[52] Much has been made of this, and it was an important decision, but not because it brought about Henry's removal. Henry had resigned long before arrival of the notice and had decided to return to Britain long before learning of the company's objections to his employment. The court's decision is important because it put the governor general on notice that he did not have a free hand. Wellesley's defense of his decision to appoint his youngest brother to the provisional government of Oudh states clearly how highly he regarded Henry's service: "No consideration inferior to the most urgent demand of the public service would have induced me to withdraw my brother from the management of my personal and domestic arrangements, in the conduct of which it must be perfectly evident, that the loss of his services must have been irreparable to my private interests."[53]

7

End of the First Act

The Maratha War

Lord Hobart once observed that Lord Wellesley's policies in India looked very much like those of Napoleon Bonaparte in Europe. He would not be the last to make such a connection.[1] The thesis is compelling. In both cases, one finds an ambitious man determined to make his way up in the world, eagerly and impatiently searching for the opportunity to do so. Conquest becomes the means to the end, and once a man is successfully launched on this course, his chosen destiny takes on a momentum of its own. Stasis is not possible for the parvenu who feels he must continually solidify what he has accomplished with more success. Driven in this way, each man would face adversity, and when he did, his course would be diverted. For Napoleon it would be the Peninsular War and the invasion of Russia; for Wellesley it would be the Maratha War. The argument is not airtight, but clearly, that Wellesley could not accept the status quo was attributable to the fact that he never felt comfortable with his place in Britain's political and social pecking order. The classic outsider, Wellesley idealized the world of which he so much wanted to be a part. Whether from a sense of inferiority, or anger over the injustice done to him by a random act of nature, or a hundred other such reasons, Wellesley desperately sought entrance into Britain's political clique much like Candide desperately pursuing Cunegonde. Unlike Candide, Wellesley never realized that the beauty of the goal he sought ran only skin deep. The point is, Wellesley set himself on a course that inevitably would be fraught with disappointment.

Does it follow, then, that war with the Marathas was inevitable? The standard interpretation is that once Wellesley had concluded his subsidiary treaty with Oudh, war with the Marathas was a certainty. If this interpretation is based on the supposition that the treaty constituted an enhanced threat to Maratha security or independence, it is erroneous, for such was hardly the case. The Mysore war and the subsidiary treaty with the Nizam constituted a greater threat than did the treaty with the nawab of Oudh, and, as Arthur had perceived much earlier, anytime the British extended their authority to Maratha frontiers, there would always exist the prospect of disputes. But that did not necessarily mean war. The treaty with Oudh represented Wellesley's need to consolidate the British position by extending the buffer zone around the Bengal presidency, something he had already accomplished with the Madras presidency. All of this made the British presence stronger and more permanent. However, it had not materially changed the company's relationship with the Maratha Confederacy. What made war with the Marathas inevitable was Wellesley's intervention in Maratha politics.

The Marathas had not been a politically unified people for decades, but that does not mean that they had lacked able leadership or that they had abandoned the concept of unity. They had once been an empire presided over by a strong ruler. Over time, the role of the monarch had faded, superseded by the peshwa, or prime minister. The evolution resembled Carolingian mayors of the palace superseding Merovingian kings in early medieval France. The peshwas took residence in Poona and presided over a great age of Maratha power and influence. Eventually, however, they encountered the same problems as the medieval French kings had. They found holding together a collection of competing local chieftains nigh impossible, and in time their devolving power became largely symbolic. There were, at times, able leaders among the chiefs who recognized that internecine warfare benefited no one and that there were benefits to a viable central authority. One of these leaders was the astute Nana Fadnavis, who did his best to prop up the peshwa. He was joined by a collection of chieftains who, while ruthless and opportunistic, understood that there were consequences to political chaos. Wellesley presided over the passing of these men, and the new generation proved far less able than the old. All of the important chiefs died in the 1790s, as did the peshwa. Nana Fadnavis followed in 1800, leaving a political vacuum. In the absence of wisdom and restraint, chaos ensued. The key players were the new peshwa, Baji Rao II; Daulat Rao Sindia, maharaja of Gwalior, who presided over territories in north-central and north-eastern India; Jaswant Rao Holkar, whose base was Indore; and the Bhonsle Raja of Berar, whose territories were in the south and east of the Maratha Confederacy, which spread across the northern half of India. Each of these men saw himself as the natural leader of the confederacy and sought to control or usurp the peshwa. A capable peshwa would have played the rivals off against one another, but Baji Rao II was not up to the challenge. A stupid, crude, opportunistic, and vicious man, he managed only to aggravate his problems.

Baji Rao brought on a crisis by ordering the assassination of Holkar's brother for no apparent reason. In the autumn of 1802, Holkar attacked and defeated the combined armies of the peshwa and Sindia, who had been leaning on the peshwa and actively manipulating events in Poona. Subsequently, Holkar occupied the capital and placed a puppet on the throne. Sindia fled south and east while Baji Rao sought the protection of Bombay.

As well as the marquess knew Indian history, he blundered badly in his reading of the Marathas. His sense of order led him to believe that the way to bring them under control and into an alliance with Britain was to prop up the peshwa under company sponsorship. He failed to realize that there was nothing there to support, that the figure of authority could not command it. Holkar, Sindia, and the raja all saw themselves in the role of peshwa, and so British support of Baji Rao II would simply undermine their own pretensions. Even with British support, Baji Rao intimidated none of them. In fact, the effect was quite the opposite.

Baji Rao's defeat at the hands of Holkar left him dependent on the British, and Wellesley quickly exploited that fact. Since becoming peshwa, Baji Rao had kept the British at arm's length, knowing full well that an alliance of any sort would mean trouble with the Maratha chiefs. However, at that point, he had no choice; when Wellesley presented a subsidiary treaty, he promptly signed. This Treaty of Bassein, ratified on 31 December 1802, looked much like Wellesley's other treaties. In return for the protection of six thousand company infantry, the peshwa ceded territories bordering Mysore and the lands of the Nizam. The Treaty of Bassein made the Maratha War inevitable because it not only threatened to put an end to the hopes of Holkar, Sindia, and the Bhonsle Raja of becoming dominant in Poona, but also appeared to threaten their independence. The obvious course to follow, and certainly one for which Shore would have opted, would have been to allow the Marathas to work out their rivalries on their own. The ensuing chaos, so went this line of thinking, could not have jeopardized British security. Obviously, Wellesley chose another view. As he saw it, if one man emerged a clear winner and consolidated his control over the others, there would be serious consequences. Wellesley knew that none of the Marathas had much love for the British and that all would exploit any opportunity to reduce British power and influence. Henry had experienced this in Oudh, where Sindia's agents attempted to raise troops among what they hoped would be a disgruntled populace.[2] Before that, Wellesley had observed Sindia's conspiring with Vizier Ali to overthrow British influence.[3] There were no easy choices for the governor general, given the place in which he had positioned British influence. Henry, for one, recognized the changing political dynamic, commenting that "the immense increase of territory, wealth, and power, which we have acquired within these few years" meant that the British would inevitably be drawn into local conflicts.[4] But this did not mean that every threat was of equal importance. Wellesley had steered the company onto a self-perpetuating course, but he still had choices, and in this case he chose to get involved because he believed he would emerge a winner. Success in the Maratha Confederacy would not only enhance his reputation but also strengthen his hand against the much-despised court of directors.

Meanwhile, Arthur had begun preparations to move northwards on Poona. Because of his familiarity with the land and people, he saw himself as the logical choice to command if the peshwa were to be rescued.[5] Accordingly, he mobilized supplies and transport and began plotting a strategy. He knew that Holkar would be a formidable foe and that pinning him down would not be easy, but that did not dampen the excitement in Arthur's camp as preparations went forward for the campaign.[6] Arthur clearly anticipated something like the Mysore campaign and even expected his brother to travel to Madras to be closer to the action.[7] Arthur encouraged this because he believed that

Clive no longer commanded much authority in Madras, and with Lieutenant General James Stuart taking the field, a political vacuum would result.

But although Arthur was eager to fight, he was confused about the objective. Full of doubt, he wrote to his friend John Malcolm, "I don't know enough of Maratha politics to be able to give an opinion as to the necessity of the great preparations which are making . . . [but] it appears to be imagined now that there is a chance that Holkar and Sindia will unite against us and the Peshwa, if we should interfere in his affairs. It is possible that the disunion of those chiefs may be more advantageous to us than any arrangement we could make with the Peshwa, and that we ought not to interfere in such a manner as to induce them to unite."[8] Such thinking was typical of Arthur at this stage of his career, when ambition and good sense often collided. He understood the issues but at the same time wanted to begin the fight. That is the luxury that one enjoys when not making the operative decisions. Arthur still smarted from Baird's supersession in the Red Sea expedition and eagerly awaited a return to action. Brilliant as he was as governor of Mysore, he was still a soldier and excited by the prospect of once again soldiering.

In this light, his presumptuous manner is not surprising. He would march on Poona because he was the best qualified, and no doubt he believed that the governor general would not undermine him on this occasion. Moreover, the military cast of characters had changed completely. General Stuart commanded in Madras, and General Gerard Lake presided as commander in chief in Bengal. Lake and Lord Wellesley worked closely together, and Arthur maintained a good working relationship with Stuart. All signs pointed to the fact that Arthur would enjoy independence in the coming operations.

The Marquess Wellesley had his own incentives. He had spent two long and stressful years heaping "kingdoms upon kingdoms, victory upon victory, revenue upon revenue" to prove to his friends in London the injustice of the double gilt potato. He had, however, impressed no one, either because everyone was too busy to notice, generally indifferent, or opposed to his policies. Much had changed at home in a short time, and the changes had a direct impact on India. Pitt's quarrel with the king over the issue of Catholic rights had come to a head. The prime minister, who had made political rights for Catholics a part of the union of the Irish and British parliaments, found the king unwilling to negotiate on the issue. Pitt opted not to challenge George III and resigned along with much of his cabinet, most significantly Dundas and Grenville.[9]

Wellesley's friend Henry Addington took the reins of government, and from outward appearances this did not seem to signal a radical departure from the policies pursued by Pitt.[10] But gone were the primary architects of Britain's foreign policy, which had been driven by the rivalry with revolutionary France, and thus an opportunity for a tired nation to negotiate a peace presented itself. Before long, terms were reached in the ill-fated Peace of Amiens, and hostilities ceased. This in itself would directly affect Wellesley, but what is more important is that Wellesley no longer had Dundas looking out for him. Not that he and Dundas were always on the same page when it came to Indian concerns, but the clever Scot always maintained considerable leverage over the court of directors. A gifted politician, Dundas knew how to maneuver Parliament to influence the composition of the court. Now he was gone, and to make matters worse, Addington's government had been erected on shaky ground. Lord Castlereagh, who eventually took the helm at the board of control, possessed little knowledge of Indian affairs. As a result, despite a friendly government, Wellesley would find himself confronted by a new set of directors determined to reverse the course he had set upon. These men, led by Jacob Bosanquet, were not impressed with Wellesley's work, seeing in it expanded control, increased obligations, and higher expense. The fundamental difference in philosophy between Wellesley and the company then came to the fore. The company saw India as an economic venture necessarily accompanied by political consequences; Wellesley saw the British presence as fundamentally political with economic consequences. Of course, the company had history on its side, but Wellesley could point to the fact that as the economic stakes grew throughout the eighteenth century and European and Indian politics alike evolved, the economic presence ultimately depended on a firm political presence. Conditions had changed, and to ignore the fact jeopardized the British investment. Wellesley viewed eighteenth-century assumptions about India as woefully out of date; stasis, to him, no longer served British interests, not to mention his own.

Wellesley was not without constraints. He did have to answer to the court of directors and to the board of control, and the court under Bosanquet promptly set about to make that point. The new court took it upon itself to counteract many of Wellesley's measures and to undo much of the administration with which he had worked so closely. To interfere in the day-to-day operations of the governor general marked a distinct change of course, and Castlereagh could do little to stop it. On 19 August 1802, the directors forwarded to the board of control their nullification of Henry's appointment.[11] The board of control knew the explosive potential of this step and advised the directors to delay sending the document until they had more information. Beyond that, the members of the board asserted their opinion that Henry's appointment appeared legitimate. Castlereagh's attempt to mollify in this case is almost laughable. In fact, his dispatch to the marquess of 27 September 1802 is a fascinating study of an attempt to congratulate and criticize at the same time. He makes clear that there were those in Britain who questioned the wisdom and the method of Wellesley's annexations in the Carnatic, Surat, Tanjore, and Oudh. He begs off of making a definitive assessment of his own, claiming that sufficient evidence had yet to arrive in London. And while he expresses these doubts, he also tries his best to flatter, because both the government and the court did not want Wellesley to resign as governor general at that particular juncture. It is all weak stuff, in stark contrast to the sure-handed Dundas.[12]

This was but one part of the struggle between the court and the governor general. Wellesley's first hint that something was up came when he learned that the court had decided to take advantage of Clive's resignation to revamp the government of Madras.[13] For Wellesley that meant the loss of not only Clive but Webbe as well; despite all the malicious things that he had said about them in the past, they had since become his allies. Knowing full well that he would not be happy with their replacements, Wellesley convinced Clive to stay on longer. This would not be easy for Clive, who had lost his zest for the job, because he would suffer the plight of the lame duck. In India, such a position was particularly compromising, as Arthur quickly detected: "Nothing can be so fatal to the respectability of government as the prevailing habit of treating the Governor with incivility, and the sooner it is stopped by the arrival of a man whose manners and character will command respect the better."[14] Wellesley could do nothing to save Webbe's seat on the governor's council, but he could keep Webbe actively engaged. Consequently, he appointed Webbe resident in Seringapatam, where he would work directly with

Arthur. Arthur for one knew the effect that all of this would have on his brother, and in writing to Webbe, he suggested that Wellesley would have to resign.[15] Clearly, if the court did not support the governor general, he could not possibly go on. To make matters worse, the court rejected Wellesley's College of Fort William, which he had established to train company servants in the languages and cultures of the subcontinent. This was one of Wellesley's most farsighted initiatives, and he took great pride in it. He had concluded that if Britain were to provide India with good government, it would have to be at the hands of trained civil servants and not a collection of adventurers and opportunists. This, of course, is an exaggeration, but Wellesley knew that the British could not govern well simply by superimposing the British system on the Indian. It was not only unwise in its basic concept but also promptly broke down even further in its practical application because there was no single Indian system of government and administration. Wellesley realized that governors needed to know something about those whom they governed, and they had to be able to communicate. From his own experience, he knew that relying on translators was cumbersome and unreliable.

The court rejected the college on the grounds that it disrupted the company's system of patronage, which was deemed crucial to the vitality of the East India Company. Wellesley would answer the criticism, but no one listened. The fact is that Wellesley's methods were as objectionable to the court as the idea itself was. Wellesley, as was his wont, proceeded with his project without consultation, which, given the investment, was inadvisable if not foolhardy. The cost of the college would be enormous despite Wellesley's assurances that he could find sources of income to finance it. Money would always be Wellesley's Achilles heel, and he never realized it. Unfortunately, everyone else did. Merrick Shawe (private secretary to the governor general), for one, worried about Wellesley's nonessential expenditures because he knew the court worried about it. As he told Henry Wellesley, ten lacs (roughly £100,000) on a college, ten lacs on a new government house, and ten lacs on a park were simply too much.[16] Those around Wellesley mirrored his lack of concern over the economic consequences of his political actions, but they knew that he set himself up for criticism with the rest of his spending. Even Hyacinthe recognized her husband as his own worst enemy: "I have an idea that a very strong cabal is forming against you among the Directors. They regard you as an enthusiast who will upset everything, and a man who is out to achieve a great reputation at all costs."[17] They were, of course, right on the last point. As for the rest, the directors were simply trying to justify their own view of Wellesley's expansive policies.

As for Arthur, the company's attitude towards Wellesley was embodied in its decision to replace his friend Webbe in Madras: he observed that "they will infallibly drive out of the country every man who wishes well to the public cause and who prizes his character. As soon as the old system of rapacity in the provinces is revived, and not only countenanced, but encouraged by the government, which will be the consequence of these changes, the greediness of the public servants will be as odious to the government as their dishonesty is at the moment."[18] Pressures from the court enraged the marquess, and this rage elicited his threat of resignation in January 1802, a resignation that Castlereagh anxiously sought to reverse. In writing to his friend Addington, Wellesley reiterated Arthur's point that the company pushed out men of talent for its own selfish ends. In this case, the talent was Arthur, who had seen his allowance for expenses reduced by company retrenchment. The consequence, suggested Wellesley, would be that "that excellent officer [Arthur] (whose high and noble Spirit of integrity can only be equalled by his valour and military skill) will spurn the indignity offered to himself and to his family by this unwarrantable suspicion, and will resign in disgust the command which he has exercised with such distinguished honour and advantage to his country."[19] The marquess's list of complaints went on for twenty pages, making it clear that the lines were drawn and that an extraordinary circumstance would be required to keep Wellesley in Bengal.

Throughout the spring and summer of 1802, Wellesley's entourage and the upper levels of government in India expressed concern over the company's adversarial position while conveying full support for the governor general. Arthur, for one, willingly expressed his opinion to whoever would listen. "All these measures," he wrote to Malcolm, "are aimed directly at Lord Wellesley, and he cannot remain in the government, and no *gentleman* can succeed to him, if means are not taken to prevent them in the future."[20] To another friend, Jonathan Duncan, he exclaimed, "In my opinion, the interference of the government at home in the disposal of the patronage of the governments abroad, and the encouragement given to controversy and opposition in the Councils, are directly contrary to the spirit, if not the letter, of the Act of Parliament."[21] In true Wellesley fashion, Arthur rallied to his brother's support, biographer Lady Longford's contention that he still simmered over Baird's supersession notwithstanding.

Other problems confronted the governor general. The change of ministries in London had brought with it peace with France. Richard and Arthur, and others, had anticipated this, though not with much joy. Peace with France would inevitably result in the restoration of some of the territories seized in the course of the war, along with territories formerly belonging to France's allies. This would be problematic in Asia, where a restored French presence would disrupt the established system based on British hegemony. Peace or no peace, if France were resurrected in Asia, rivalry would follow. Arthur began contemplating the implications as early as the summer of 1801, long before any word of the Peace of Amiens reached India. By the time he had been officially notified, Arthur had concluded that peace in Europe would destabilize India.[22] He believed percipiently that there existed no basis for a lasting peace in Europe and that an armistice only compromised British security in the East. As for Wellesley, he had no intention of conceding anything to the French. Skeptical from the start, he rebuffed any and all French overtures, claiming that he lacked instructions. Secretary for War Hobart exhibited little confidence in the peace, and given that fact, Wellesley made a unilateral decision to return nothing. When word arrived from Hobart in March 1803 that the peace was coming apart and that the governor general should turn no territory over to the French, Wellesley could assure him that he had nothing to worry about.[23]

Wellesley rose to the challenges of the occasion. Iris Butler, who has looked closely at the marquess's domestic troubles in the period, sees him in a continued state of nervous exhaustion. While that may well have been true as it applied to his wife, the scope of his activity and the careful, thorough, and even measured nature of his correspondence suggest that the governor general took some delight in the opportunity to proceed without concern for the opinions of the court. In fact, as early as the summer of 1802, Malcolm reported, "I never saw your brother in better health or better spirits."[24] A crisis provided Wellesley with the freedom of action that he craved and the authorities in London feared. In December, he informed the court of directors that he would not be returning to London as he had planned, that trouble among the Marathas required the attentions of an experienced hand. And as usual, he informed the court that the situation presented an opportunity for the company, which was precisely what they did not want to hear. Holkar meant to establish his dominance in Poona and the confederacy, and if the peshwa would not cooperate, the Maratha chieftain could find one who would. This, Wellesley pointed out, was good for the company. "The crisis of affairs appeared to me to afford the most favourable opportunity for the complete establishment of the interest of the British power in the Maratha empire," reported the governor general.[25]

Wellesley had it figured out. The peshwa needed British protection. Holkar would be unwilling to defy British arms, and Sindia plotted revenge against Holkar, not the company. Thus Wellesley believed that he could emerge the arbiter of Maratha affairs without risk of war, as he explained to Clive: "I entertain a sanguine hope of accomplishing the great arrangement of establishing a British subsidiary force at Poona, without proceeding to extremities with any party."[26] At that particular time, even Arthur believed that such a thing was possible.[27]

At the same time, the governor general made it clear to the Marathas that force remained an option. The army would move forward while his residents engaged the various chieftains in negotiations. Lieutenant Colonel Collins traveled with Sindia; to the raja of Berar, Wellesley sent Webbe from Seringapatam; and in Poona, Barry Close presided. Events did not evolve as the governor general had hoped, however. Wellesley made the mistake that politicians and diplomats have made with great frequency throughout history—that of assuming that one's adversary will make decisions based on one's own rationale. That Wellesley never fully understood the Maratha character is clear; what is less clear is whether he really cared.

As Arthur marched northwards, Holkar established in Poona a new peshwa, the son of Baji Rao's adopted brother, Amrit Rao. It was Arthur's responsibility to undo this and, according to the Treaty of Bassein, reestablish Baji Rao II in his capital. Neither Arthur nor Wellesley believed that Holkar would offer active resistance, but Arthur proceeded with care nonetheless. Typically, this included sensitivity towards Indians, friends and foes alike.[28] And as he prepared to cross the frontier from territories belonging to the Nizam to those belonging to the Marathas, he left behind the Indian soldiers of the Nizam's subsidiary force commanded by Colonel James Stevenson so that they would not ruffle the feathers of Sindia, or any other Marathas for that matter.[29] These were things that Arthur had learned in five short years, and they were invaluable. To Wellesley's credit, he not only realized it but also made certain that the court of directors understood the reasoning behind Arthur's appointment to preempt any further questioning, especially over his brother. "The extensive local knowledge and influence possessed by the honourable Major-General Wellesley," he wrote, "the personal intercourse established between Major-General Wellesley and the Maratha chieftains on the frontier of Mysore, and the confidence reposed by those chieftains in the approved talents, firmness, temper, and integrity of that officer, rendered him peculiarly qualified to discharge the complicated duties of the command of the detachment destined to proceed to Poona."[30]

Arthur would shortly present his brother with an example of the military skill. Soon after writing his dispatch to Stevenson, instructing the junior officer to leave the bulk of the troops within the territories of the Nizam, Arthur received word that Amrit Rao intended to evacuate and burn Poona. This intelligence was well known in Poona and Bassein, and it struck panic in both places. Believing that negotiations would serve no positive purpose, Arthur decided there was no time to waste. He set out on the evening of the 19th with his cavalry and a battalion of infantry on a forced march to Poona. Covering sixty miles in thirty-two hours, he surprised Amrit Rao, who promptly abandoned the capital and the intention to burn it. Arthur rode into a city untouched by the threatened violence.[31] After a few anxious days during which Holkar's intentions remained unclear, the peshwa entered the city. All appeared to be proceeding as the marquess planned.

An uneasy calm descended on the Maratha Confederacy. Holkar retreated northwards, and the raja of Berar joined Sindia on the Nizam's frontier. Wellesley remained hopeful but kept Arthur, General Lake, and General Stuart on notice.[32] In the meantime, Lord Clive prepared to depart for London. Clive's last months had been neither happy nor particularly fruitful, but for the marquess, that did not detract from a distinguished tenure, and the governor general was generous in his praise of Clive.[33] Lord William Bentinck, who replaced Clive at Fort

St. George, would work easily with the governor general, but this is understandable as he came at a time when his inexperience required that he play a passive role.

What then ensued surprised no one. The Maratha chiefs became restless, and because each presided over substantial armies, they returned to their marauding ways. As they threatened the Nizam, the British were forced to counter.[34] Wellesley's goal was to persuade them to return to their natural frontiers and, failing that, simply keep them on the move. Arthur informed General Lake that experience told him that if one kept the Marathas on the move and prevented them from pillaging and looting, eventually their armies melted away.[35] The peshwa, having second thoughts about the Treaty of Bassein, made the situation more complicated by entering into a secret collaboration with Sindia and the raja. This threat of an alliance redefined the situation and made peace less likely. "Divide and conquer" had been the foundation of Wellesley's policy, and that was coming undone.[36] By the end of May, Wellesley decided that he would no longer accept the status quo, and he resolved to bring matters to a head.

The governor general sent instructions to Arthur, who in turn instructed Colonel Collins to require from Sindia a declaration of intent. Would Sindia remain on the Nizam's frontier or retire to his home territories? Delay would be considered an intention to remain.[37] Arthur's concern stemmed from the fact that diminishing supplies of food and forage were forcing Holkar to move. In short, conditions were becoming increasingly unpredictable; the movement of one influenced the others. Arthur advised Collins that normally the Marathas considered compromise and moderation to be signs of weakness, which inevitably made them more aggressive. And while one might think that Sindia would understand the situation, Arthur advised Collins to take nothing for granted and warn Sindia that Britain was serious about his retreating from the Nizam's frontier.[38]

At this point, the collaboration between Richard and Arthur again became close. On 26 June the governor general granted to his brother, and later to Lake and Stuart, full powers to deal with the Marathas. Wellesley's granting to his commanders such extensive discretionary powers should not be construed as an abdication of his own responsibilities. The instructions he sent were explicit and characteristically thorough, and what they represent is Wellesley's realization that events would unfold quickly with the Marathas and that it was not in Britain's interests to pursue a cumbersome decision-making process that required time-consuming correspondence between the commanders and Fort William. Arthur had thought that his brother would take up headquarters at Fort St. George to be closer to the action as he had done in the Mysore war, and there had been discussion on this possibility. However, Wellesley opted to delegate responsibility. He did so because he realized that if war broke out, it would be fought on several fronts if it were to accomplish all that he desired. In other words, a Maratha war would not be solely Arthur's war. Consequently, moving to Fort St. George would provide him with little advantage over remaining in Fort William. Moreover, in Arthur, Lake, and Stuart, the marquess had men he trusted to act with good sense and (his favorite word) alacrity.

Arthur stood at the center of all this, and throughout the marquess's instructions, there exists the premise that Arthur understood thoroughly his brother's thinking. Another underlying assumption is that Arthur knew of and understood all existing agreements. This implies a closer working relationship between the two in the year 1802 than has previously been thought. Certainly a tremendous amount of information flowed to Arthur that did not come directly from his brother, but the symbiotic relationship is understood. The amount of responsibility thrown at Arthur was enormous. He was to be warrior and diplomat and prepared not only to negotiate for the company but to mediate between the Marathas as well.

Lord Wellesley's involvement in the Maratha War would be more extensive than in the Mysore war, and he exhibited an uncommonly calm demeanor throughout. His correspondence betrays none of the anxiety of the Mysore campaign. The reason lies in the fact that he had, in the interim, come to understand the nature of politics and war in India, and his opportunistic nature provided him with an optimism that he did not possess in 1798–99. To his mind, if he had to fight, he would fight for keeps. Sindia would be attacked on all fronts to reduce him to his traditional lands and to eliminate French influence in his army.[39] The French arrived right on cue. The resumption of war with France proved opportune for Wellesley because Sindia, like Tipu and the Nizam, employed French officers to raise and train his armies. Though this French presence had existed for a number of years, Wellesley had chosen to ignore it until it became a convenient justification for war. In fact, the French general Pierre Perron presided over a large and formidable force in the northeast. This force would be the focus of Lake's attentions.

That Wellesley should have been deeply involved in the military planning of this campaign comes as a surprise, but it illustrates the governor general's self-confidence. The instructions that he sent to his generals were detailed only in terms of strategy and goals. He knew what he wanted, and he clearly articulated himself on all points. The generals could fight in the manner they chose and would be free to make command decisions on their own so long as they kept the stated objectives in sight. Arthur had thought deeply about a war with the Marathas. After the contest with Dhoondiah Vagh, he wrote a detailed memorandum on how such a war would be fought. He based his assumptions on Dhoondiah's methods of fighting; although the campaign against Sindia would prove very different, much still applied. Most especially, Arthur had learned when and when not to fight. In India, there was a season for war, and success and failure depended on how well one predicted the onset of the appropriate season. In the case of the Maratha Confederacy, successful campaigning depended on water. In the north, filled rivers and an ample supply of drinking water were necessary for the British style of campaigning. Too much rain might hamper transportation but that would occur only at the peak of the monsoon, and then only if the rainy season hit with particular ferocity.[40] Wellesley learned these considerations from his brother and employed them in his thinking.

By the middle of the summer, Arthur still did not know what Sindia intended to do, but he believed that an alliance with Holkar was out of the question. Maratha jealousies remained as strong as resentment of British meddling. At the same time, an agreement with the company seemed no more likely. Still he did not despair of peace.[41] He saw the Marathas as motivated by either "fear of loss or hope of gain." In the circumstances of the moment, the British presence did not represent fear of loss, but it certainly stood in the Marathas' way of gaining a decided influence over the peshwa.[42] The problem then was one of convincing Sindia, Holkar, and the raja that the status quo was good for all parties. Until Wellesley's instructions arrived, Arthur seemed a bit confused on where things were going. "You will perceive by the late letters from Lieutenant-Colonel Close," he wrote to Collins, "that it is probable that the treaty of Bassein will not work as was expected even in the Peshwa's durbar [court]; and, on the other hand, the intelligence received from England in the beginning of June gives great reason to believe that the war with the French may have been renewed. Every circumstance, therefore, points out the necessity that, if possible, the war with the northern Maratha chiefs should be avoided."[43] Here he differed from his brother, who saw war with France as a positive event and that maintenance of the status quo certainly was not a goal.

Wellesley's instructions to Lake were as detailed and wide-ranging as those he sent to Arthur. Arthur's went out first because his contact with Sindia made that front the flash point. But in most ways, Lake's front was the more important. Wellesley and Lake had developed a close working relationship, and the governor general did not hesitate to confide in the commander in chief. In an extensive memorandum sent on 27 July, Wellesley granted Lake the full powers extended to Arthur and outlined his objectives. Here we find Wellesley explaining in detail the goals of the war, the plan of operations, and the outline of a peace agreement. Lake's primary goal was to eliminate Perron's army and then to move on Delhi. There the old Mughal emperor resided in degraded circumstances, but he symbolized the greatness of a bygone era, and for that reason he was to be treated with respect. When it came to protocol, Wellesley was at his best, and his treatment of the emperor would border on reverence.[44]

Meanwhile, Collins had engaged Sindia and the raja. As instructed, he made it clear that the British expected them to retreat to their capitals and that if they did not do so soon, there would be war.[45] The two Marathas typically avoided responding to Collins; as pressure began to mount, Wellesley expanded his thinking. Orders went out to Lieutenant Colonel Campbell, stationed in the east, to occupy Cuttack, which belonged to the raja.[46] What Wellesley was up to thus became clear. He intended to take advantage of this struggle to extend company territories in the north as a buffer to the ceded provinces, eliminate entirely French influence in India, link Fort William with Fort St. George through the acquisition of Cuttack, and enhance the influence of the peshwa through the reduction of the other chiefs.

Meanwhile, matters were coming to a head for Arthur. On 27 June, Wellesley instructed his brother "to demand an explicit declaration of the views of Sindia and of the Rajah of Berar, within such a number of days as shall appear to you to be reasonable, consistently with a due attention to the period of the season, and to the facility of moving your army, and of prosecuting hostilities with the advantages which you now possess."[47] Arthur instructed Collins to demand an answer and to clarify that if one were not forthcoming, silence would be interpreted as a refusal. Arthur considered the moment critical. Should Sindia and the raja decide to retire to their capitals, he believed that peace would be secured for a considerable time, for the simple reason that retreat would be a sign that the two chiefs viewed British power as paramount and resistance futile. In turn, that line of thinking would influence the rest of the Maratha Empire, and support for the recalcitrant chieftains would evaporate. Because such a decision would carry enormous consequences, Arthur did not think that they would arrive at it. Moreover, he believed that Sindia and the raja were unrealistic in their assessments of either British strength or their own: in the former case, they underestimated; and in the latter, they overestimated. Consequently, in all likelihood they would choose war over retreat. This being the case, Arthur believed that a quick and decisive blow by British forces would be necessary to sober them and to make a point to the rest of the Marathas that resistance was unwise.[48] That the Nizam was mortally ill made the situation especially critical. His imminent demise raised the specter of a succession struggle, which would be aggravated by instability among the Marathas and any show of weakness on the part of the British.

Once Arthur had received his brother's instructions, he moved with the decisiveness and focus that would characterize his entire career. His experience of the past five years had left him a confident, assertive man. Sensing that there no longer existed any hope for peace, he sought to bring matters to a head. He therefore instructed Collins to press the chiefs. Beginning in the last week of July, a vigorous and frequent exchange began between the resident and Sindia and the raja. Letters went back and forth, and two face-to-face meetings ensued. Sindia and the raja opted to play games by insisting that Arthur retreat first to Seringapatam, a suggestion that the general did not entertain for a second. Their goal was Tipu's in reverse. The sultan had sought to extend negotiations into the monsoon to make campaigning difficult if not impossible; the Marathas maneuvered to delay action beyond the monsoon so that their cavalry might roam at will. Arthur perceived the trick and made clear to Collins that there must be a deadline. Collins accordingly informed the two chiefs of his intent to leave camp on 30 July. Heavy rains delayed his departure, however, and as he waited on the weather, negotiations continued, with no results. On 3 August, he broke camp, and three days later the inevitable occurred; Arthur declared war.[49] "I offered you peace on terms of equality, and honorable to all parties," he wrote to Sindia; "you have chosen war, and are responsible for all consequences."[50]

The moment had arrived, and Arthur never doubted a successful conclusion. As it turned out, his campaign would be more difficult than he expected. If he was overconfident, there were reasons for it. The Mysore campaign had been decisive and short, and his pursuit of Dhoondiah Vagh had been a success. The latter event he believed to be especially informative, for he had concluded that the Marathas' fundamental weakness, like Dhoondiah's, was that they lived off the land and consequently had to be constantly on the move in any campaign. Speed was their strength, but if they were confronted during the monsoon, that strength would be neutralized. Then supplies became a serious problem. Arthur learned that if he kept the enemy moving and prevented his opponents from collecting food, forage, and loot, their armies would atrophy. Furthermore, in the case of Dhoondiah, when they met in battle, the enemy proved brave but undisciplined. Thus, when Arthur turned to the Marathas, he did not consider being outnumbered a matter for concern.

Arthur followed a clearly articulated campaign. He moved first on the fortress-city of Ahmednuggur. The city fell with little resistance and served as the gateway to the coming campaign.[51] Thus Arthur struck the first blow, but Lake was on the move as well and at the end of the month had his first encounter with General Perron. It too ended in success. In fact, Perron proved an unenthusiastic opponent who initiated discussions for his personal surrender and departure from India. Lake moved on to take the fortress of Allyghur, which in turn allowed him to move on Delhi. There on 11 September he defeated Sindia's army under the command of another Frenchman, Louis Bourquain. Overwhelmed, Bourquain looted the city and melted into the countryside with what was left of his army. Three days later, Bourquain and four of his officers surrendered to the commander in chief.[52] Lake's accomplishment was monumental. In one short campaign, he had accomplished two of Wellesley's most important objectives. He had destroyed the French-led army and French influence in Sindia's territories, and he had captured the old Mughal capital of Delhi.[53]

In the last week of September, it was Arthur's turn for glory. Throughout the month, he had been in hot pursuit of Sindia's and the raja's armies, which remained combined. This was all very familiar to him as he maneuvered to force battle. Meeting with Colonel Stevenson, his second in command, on the 21st, he resolved to engage the Marathas on the 24th. To that end, Arthur split the army to facilitate envelopment, with Stevenson proceeding on a westward route while Arthur took the easterly course. On the 23rd, to his surprise, intelligence informed him that while Sindia's cavalry had moved on ahead, the infantry remained encamped near the village of Assaye. This news presented Arthur with a dilemma: take advantage of the division of the Maratha's army and attack the infantry without Stevenson's support, or wait until the two armies had linked up and then fight a Maratha force that would also have had time to unite. Never one to let an opportunity slip, he opted for the first.

Accordingly, Wellesley marched on Assaye. There, to his surprise, he found the entire Maratha army—cavalry and infantry—adding up to enormous numerical superiority over his own. Discretion would have called for delay until Stevenson arrived the following day. But two factors argued against such a course. First, the element of surprise would be lost, a factor that General Wellesley felt to be especially important in India. Arthur's presence had not gone undetected, but the Marathas had not anticipated a fight. Because Arthur believed them to be an undisciplined force, they would not be able to assemble themselves in an effective line of defense. The second factor was psychological. If he chose to delay his attack, it would be perceived as a sign of weakness and Arthur would lose what he considered his moral advantage. Thus, against overwhelming odds he ordered an attack.

The story of Assaye has been well and often told. Some highlights, however, merit repeating because they have become a part of this modern Arthurian legend. One came as Wellesley maneuvered his army into position for the fight. After surveying the ground, he realized that his first obstacle would be getting the army across the river Kaitna and to get it across in a position to advance on the enemy's left, where the infantry had been positioned (the infantry and cavalry being separated). Again speed was of the essence, though intelligence told him there existed no natural ford in the area. But Arthur's keen eye had seen something that others had not. Looking down on the river valley, he noticed two small villages on either side of the Kaitna, and he concluded that they would not have been built in such proximity if a regular means of communication was lacking. In other words, there had to be a ford at that point of the river. He was, of course, correct in his reasoning, and he got his army expeditiously across.

His assessment of the Marathas' ability to react to his unexpected presence proved less reliable. They reacted quickly and surely and were ready when Arthur ordered his advance. Victory would, therefore, come down to who could fight better, and for a good part of the battle, the advantage remained unclear. The company's Indian soldiers withstood heavy artillery fire and advanced with courage and determination. But the Marathas acquitted themselves admirably as well. It was the famed Maratha cavalry that let Sindia down. They were effectively neutralized by the British cavalry despite their numerical advantage. Arthur put it succinctly: "I cannot write in too strong terms of the conduct of the troops [most of whom were Indian]; they advanced in the best order, and with the greatest steadiness, under a most destructive fire, against a body of infantry far superior in numbers, who appeared determined to contend with them to the last, and who were driven from their guns only by the bayonet; and notwithstanding the numbers of the enemy's cavalry, and the repeated demonstrations they made of an intention to charge, they were kept at a distance by our infantry."[54] Arthur felt the heat of battle. "The general was in the thick of the action the whole time," wrote Sir Colin Campbell, "and had a horse killed under him. No man could have shown a better example to the troops than he did. I never saw a man so cool and collected as he was the whole time."[55] Despite heavy losses, Arthur carried the day.

This was the victory the governor general awaited. While Lake's campaign was strategically more important, Arthur's had greater symbolic value. Sindia and the raja had to suffer personal defeat before their will to fight would be broken. The news therefore elated Wellesley, and he promptly turned it into a family event. He wrote to his brother with genuine admiration and pride, "I declare to you sincerely that you have infinitely surpassed all that I could have required from you in my public capacity, and have soared beyond the highest point, to which all my affection and all the pride of my blood could have aspired, in the most sanguine expectations which could be suggested by my sentiments of respect and love for a brother, who has always held the highest place in my heart."[56] Public praise was less emotional but no less effusive.[57]

Wellesley's comments to the court of directors, not surprisingly, dripped with self-righteousness:

> The conduct of Major-General Wellesley in the exercise of the extensive political and military powers, vested in him by the Governor-General in council, also deserves the highest approbation of your honourable Committee, and of the honourable the Court of Directors. . . . The transcendent victory obtained at Assaye in the Deccan, on the 23d of September, appeared to the Governor-General in council to demand a testimony of public honour, equal to any which the justice of the British Government in India has ever conferred on the conduct of our officers and troops in the most distinguished period of our military history.[58]

From Delhi, Lake proceeded to invest the great fortress at Agra. The garrison's surrender on 17 October gave Lake control of both banks of the Jumna and complete control of the Doab. In the meantime, the raja of Berar's distraction in the campaign against Arthur allowed British troops to occupy Cuttack, as Wellesley had planned. In a mopping-up exercise, Lake pursued remnants of Sindia's army in the north, determined to capture their substantial artillery. Hampered by rain, the pursuit resembled Arthur's in the west. March and countermarch finally bore fruit at Lasswary, where Lake destroyed what was left of the rebellious Marathas and confiscated their guns.

On 23 October, Arthur—intending to cooperate with Colonel Stevenson, who was about to lay siege to Gawilghur—signed an armistice with Sindia. Among the conditions of the armistice were that Sindia would retreat to the east. Sindia, however, took up position with the raja's brother and in the process created a substantial force that Arthur could not ignore. Sindia's ambassadors attempted to buy time, but Arthur rejected all overtures. On 28 November, he and Colonel Stevenson moved their armies into position before the combined Maratha army at Argaum. Wellesley intended to fight the following day but found the enemy vulnerably placed and ordered an attack late that afternoon. The results were overwhelming, with pursuit of the fleeing Marathas continuing well into the night.[59] At this point, Arthur moved on to besiege Gawilghur. The fortress was formidably situated on a mountaintop, guarding the headwaters of the Poona and Taptee rivers. Its value lay in the fact that it overlooked the northern approaches to the territories of the Nizam. Stevenson was to handle this venture, as he had planned it, but he was not up to the task. Arthur found himself engaged in the daily administration of the investment. Gawilghur surrendered on 15 November, and with it came what was left of Sindia's and the raja's armies. Arthur could then prepare for serious peace negotiations.[60]

Wellesley had already communicated his instructions for these negotiations that summer, but he followed up with details on 11 December. Wellesley's approach to peace making with the Marathas proved quite different from his previous dealings with the various Indian powers. It was as if he felt that in this case he had engaged a power that deserved more respect. Not that Tipu did not constitute a legitimate authority worthy of British respect, but in his case there existed so many years of animosity and continuing jealousy that Wellesley found magnanimity impossible. This was not the case with the Marathas.[61] In fact, by the time Wellesley's second set of instructions arrived, Arthur had concluded treaties with both the raja and Sindia. Nonetheless, they served as a yardstick for the general against which to measure his work, and he concluded that he had acted according to his brother's wishes and that nothing in his treaties would cause concern in Calcutta.[62]

If there was a problem with the treaties, it was that they were not sufficiently specific. Cessions of territories were defined along geographical lines rather than by specific lists of cities and territories, and this would lead to misunderstandings. Nonetheless, the cumulative results of the war with the Marathas were nothing short of spectacular, and everyone associated with that war understood the consequences. Wellesley had extended British power and influence to all corners of the subcontinent, and describing the British presence as an empire became fair at that point. Everything about this campaign of approximately six months' duration exceeded all that had preceded it. The Mysore campaign appeared as child's play in comparison. Wellesley justifiably took great pride in the accomplishment, but he also took great care to share the credit. He rather went overboard in his praise of Lake, however, and one wonders whether Arthur grew impatient with the accolades. Lake in turn heaped compliments on Wellesley.[63] Towards the end of his life, Wellesley would remark that the extraordinary feature of the Maratha campaign was that Lake and Arthur conducted it without a hint of jealousy. All evidence points to the accuracy of the observation, and that is in large measure attributable to the way Wellesley managed the situation. Perhaps he had learned something in the Baird affair. In the case of the Maratha campaign, he never led anyone to believe that anyone but Lake was in charge of the army. Neither Arthur nor any other subordinate had a problem with that. Consequently, Lake was left feeling secure. At the same time, Wellesley apportioned responsibility equally among the various commanders, providing them all with large measures of responsibility and independence. This was possible because of the geopolitics of the war; India was divided into distinct spheres of activity. Thus Arthur knew that he was responsible for the success or failure of his own campaign and that he could expect no help from another quarter. The same could be said for Lake, and this was the way both men wanted it. Arthur's comfort and confidence were at a high level largely because of his brother's confidence. Alas, nothing lasts forever.

The Maratha War caught London unaware, and there were those who viewed it with alarm. The court of directors, unsurprisingly, viewed it in a distinctly negative light. While they had legitimate reasons for their concern, it represented another front on which they could fight in their ongoing struggle with the governor general. There was, however, a political component to this duel. The Maratha War would be the first crisis that Wellesley confronted without the support of the government. Dundas had been ingenious in exerting a dominating influence on the court. But Dundas was gone and Castlereagh was a poor imitation. As a result, the court fell into the hands of "India men," who were primarily interested in preserving the rights and privileges of the company and in turning a profit. For them, that meant minimizing administrative expenses to free up capital for trade. The situation is complex; in essence, the court viewed India in economic terms while Wellesley saw it in political terms. These lines had been drawn earlier, on the demise of Pitt's administration, but the consequent struggle between the court and the governor general quickly became personal. Leading members of the court came to detest Wellesley, and he returned their feelings with equal measure—and then some. This quarrel was both unhealthy and irresponsible, but it continued to fester because the government proved too weak to modify the court's position. Previously the court had nullified Henry's appointment, ordered the disestablishment of the College of Fort William, and made appointments calculated to irritate. But these were merely tweaks. The struggle would turn to policy, and it was serious stuff.

The political problem centered on Addington's administration, which, for all practical purposes, had come to power because Pitt chose to give up his position. Its major accomplishment, the Peace of Amiens, had collapsed, leaving it in a politically precarious position. It depended on the goodwill of Pitt's followers and in some cases on the opposition. More to the point, with a small and unpredictable majority, it could not afford to alienate the India interests, which had a substantial constituency in Parliament. Therefore, even if the government agreed with Wellesley's policies, it could not always afford to press them in the face of court opposition. That this was the case had been made clear to the marquess by his brothers Henry, Gerald, and William, who kept him informed of political developments.[64]

That Wellesley's position had become increasingly perilous became clear in the aftermath of the war with Sindia and the raja. The results of the war were received with little enthusiasm in London. Wellesley could have lobbied for the coveted rise in the English peerage, but he did not. This was fortunate, since modest thanks came from both houses of Parliament but that was about all. Wellesley recommended rewards for Lake and Arthur; there would be forthcoming a peerage for the former and a knighthood of the Bath for the latter.[65] Still, Wellesley had every reason to worry, and he turned to Arthur for advice, sending one of Henry's more descriptive letters for comment. Arthur did not disappoint. As he saw it, Wellesley's position had been made untenable. The government, guilty of breach of faith and lackluster support, made it impossible for him to go on successfully. Arthur cautioned that Wellesley should not be duped by assurances of support from the likes of Castlereagh and Addington. They might say they cared, but they did not. In short, Arthur believed that his brother should leave India as soon as possible. Moreover, worried that Richard would be dismissed before he could resign, Arthur advised informing the court promptly of that intent. Anticipating an argument, he maintained that while an early departure would necessitate giving up unfinished projects, Wellesley's dismissal "would be more fatal to the public interests . . . [and] remaining in India after being informed that you were not to receive the support which you had always declared to be necessary to induce you to remain, would have appeared like an adhesion to the office."[66] Clearly, the state of affairs alarmed Arthur as much as it did Wellesley, and his advice reflects the warmth of their relationship at the time.

This is as it should have been. The war against Sindia and the raja had been a cooperative venture and had yielded impressive results. Each had good reason to appreciate the other. Richard was anxious for Arthur to come to Calcutta so that they might consult with one another in person. Arthur, in turn, contemplating a return to England, was eager to see his brother. There would be, however, one more disagreement between them before the Indian adventure came to an end; it concerned Wellesley's interpretation of the treaty with Sindia. Specifically, the controversy concerned Gwalior, Sindia's traditional capital. Wellesley labored under the impression that Gwalior had passed to the company in the general cession of territory identified in the treaty. Sindia, however, laid claim to the capital, pointing out geographical and political realities overlooked by both Wellesleys. The governor general refused to budge on the issue and in the process irritated an already unhappy Sindia. As far as Wellesley was concerned, Gwalior was one of several strategically vital fortresses guarding the Doab, which in the hands of Sindia would compromise the security of the region.

Arthur took blame for the misunderstanding, as much as Arthur ever took blame for anything. In retrospect, he acknowledged his error but explained that he had been duped by the cagey Marathan. In the course of the negotiations, Sindia's representatives misled Arthur on prior ownership of the area around Gwalior and therefore rights of possession in the peace. As far as Wellesley was concerned, that was just fine because he could fall back on intent and the general issue of good faith in negotiations.[67] The ever-defensive Arthur, embarrassed by his mistake, asserted that the issue was not worth an argument and the British should not risk exposing themselves to charges of negotiating in bad faith. This was a matter of pride—personal and national. It was not worth the renewal of war.

The question was made more complicated by the fact that the company's relations with Holkar were tenuous and that Sindia faced his own problems. Arthur pointed out that the beaten Maratha armies remained dangerous because they were unpaid and undisciplined and the state had not the means to change either fact. Therefore, there was a temptation to renew the fighting so that Sindia's army could move on to new territories to enrich itself. Essentially, Holkar faced the same problem. He had stayed too long in one place, and his army was restless. For this reason, Arthur urged his brother to put this matter behind him. "I am fully aware of the benefit to be derived from having forts, but I don't think that the possession of this or any other fort is worth the risk of renewed war." He did not fear a new war; on the contrary, he believed that the result would be as decisive as the last. But he saw that there would be a consequence for the marquess. Arthur advised with genuine concern,

> In relation to the state of affairs at home, I consider the renewal of the war to be the greatest misfortune that could occur. In the eyes of those who are to judge of your conduct, it would efface the glory of the last war and of your whole administration. Believe me that neither the Court of Directors nor the King's Ministers are capable of taking an enlarged view of the present state of affairs in India. Everything has been so much altered within these last five years that I doubt very much whether there is any man in England who understands our present situation.[68]

Clearly Arthur had his brother's interests in mind when offering this advice, and it is to be taken as a sincere expression of family solidarity. Still, Arthur could never resist the self-righteous pronouncement. "I would sacrifice Gwalior, or every frontier of India, ten times over," he wrote to Malcolm, "in order to preserve our credit for scrupulous good faith, and the advantages and honor we gained by the late war and the peace; and we must not fritter them away in arguments, drawn from overstrained principles of the laws of nations, which are not understood in this country. What brought me through many difficulties in the war, and the negotiations for peace? The British good faith, and nothing else."[69] This line of thinking is curiously absent from the letter to the marquess written two days earlier, for Arthur must have known instinctively that it would not be well received.

Meanwhile, things were heating up with Holkar, prompting the governor general again to delay plans for his departure. He wanted to leave India as soon as he gracefully could, but pride and ambition got in his way. There was always the loose end, and the marquess wanted to leave in a blaze of glory. At that point, Holkar stood in the way. Wellesley had given Lake responsibility for conducting the negotiations in January with the warning that Holkar was dangerous and war with him likely. Unfortunately neither the marquess nor his brother, and therefore few others, took this man seriously. And perhaps they were right that a quick campaign would put him in his place, if that campaign were as carefully planned and implemented as the one against Sindia.

In April, Lake warned the governor general that Holkar had grown more restless. Patience exhausted, Wellesley informed the general of his "determination to commence hostilities against Jaswunt Rao Holkar, at the earliest practicable period of time." Here indeed we find inevitability. Wellesley made no serious attempt to avoid war, and there exists again in his story something of the need to "trim the rough edges." Lake, for his part, made no effort to dissuade. War waited on an opportunity.

Clearly disappointed, if not alarmed by this decision, Arthur penned a lament to Henry in which with great insight he identified the marquess's weaknesses: "In fact, my dear Henry, we want at Calcutta some person who will speak his mind to the Governor-General. Since you and Malcolm have left him, there is nobody about him with capacity to understand these subjects, who has nerves to discuss them with him, and to oppose his sentiments when he is wrong. There cannot be a stronger proof of this want than the fact that Malcolm, and I, and General Lake, and Mercer, and Webbe, were of opinion that we had lost Gwalior with the treaty of peace."[70] There are points here that require comment. First, Arthur does not question Richard's integrity, and his criticism is respectful. He considered his brother an outstanding governor general, but often Richard was simply too clever by half. Arthur's numerous letters on the treaty with Sindia, like this one, point out that Richard was more than capable on any occasion of fashioning a cogent and tight argument to justify whatever he wanted. Lord Wellesley knew the power of his intellect. Unfortunately, in the process of constructing these arguments, he often lost sight of the central issue. The argument, in other words, became more important than the goal. This brings up a second point: the power of Wellesley's personality. In short, he intimidated with his intellect and probably, as an offshoot, with withering sarcasm. To keep him intellectually honest, he needed someone around him who had the confidence to bring him up short and tell him when he was playing intellectual games. That person would need more than brains; he would need courage bred from security and great familiarity. Arthur knew that only he and Henry fit the bill perfectly but that others such as Malcolm and Webbe at least had a chance. Implicit in Arthur's assessment is the sense that this was a family endeavor. He knew his own value, just as he understood the importance of Henry's presence in the governor general's entourage. That had been demonstrated when Henry first visited London and had become more evident with his permanent absence. There is no hint that Arthur suspected the eldest brother of being driven by self-serving motives; none of the family had the capacity for self-examination. It is interesting that when Arthur informed Henry that the war with Sindia added to his personal wealth, he treated it as nothing more than the consequences of soldiering, as if the prizes had been imposed on him. Finally, there is no bitterness in any of this, just concern.

Arthur, however, had had enough of India and applied to Lake for permission to return to England. He knew full well that his role in the struggle with Holkar would be peripheral at best, concluding that he could not hope to take his army into the field until after the rainy season; by that time, he believed, the war would be over. In Arthur's mind, Holkar was simply another version of Dhoondiah Vagh—chase him and be done with him. This line of thinking must also have extended to Lake, because he did not stand in Arthur's way despite the fact that he was again at war. Would a commander in chief allow his best officer to leave in the midst of a struggle if he were not certain of winning it?[71] But Arthur's request to leave India illustrates his propensity for finding excuses so that his motives might not be questioned. In this case, he stated that the Duke of York had avoided confirming his promotion to the rank of major general and to the staff of the presidency at Fort St. George. Arthur did not trust the royal duke and suspected animus, but had there been incentives to stay, these reasons would hardly have mattered. The simple fact is that Arthur had been in India for seven long years and he was tired and homesick. Richard, for one, understood. The question then becomes, why not say so instead of offering a lame excuse? One cannot help but conclude that Arthur knew that from all appearances, he had chosen to leave at a critical time. That he was ill placed to make any sort of positive contribution would not be obvious to the casual observer. And so he made the case that the powers that be did not appreciate him or trust him, and that being the case, it would be better for him to retire from India. Where and how Arthur acquired this sensitivity is a mystery, but the fact that he had it is not, and sometimes it was unbecoming.

Wellesley, meanwhile, requested Arthur's presence in Fort William so that they might consult before the younger brother's departure. Arthur's progress in that direction would be slow. In fact, he would never make it; instead, he ended up in Madras, from where he would sail on HMS *Trident* in March 1805. However, he never stopped working, continuing in his responsibilities to Mysore and doing his best to facilitate the war against Holkar. This involved a private correspondence with Sindia's court, in which he attempted to minimize the damage done by the quarrel over Gwalior. This was both unwise and insubordinate, and on the last point, Arthur knew it. He advised Webbe in June not to tell the marquess about the correspondence.[72]

The war with Holkar got off to a bad start when Lieutenant Colonel William Monson overpursued his prey, outdistancing his supplies and entering unfamiliar ground. In the process, he made a number of tactical blunders, which even the governor general recognized, and was victimized by the failure of support to arrive as instructed. A precipitous retreat ensued, with serious losses of personnel and armament. Arthur was appalled, viewing this as a gross failure of command and worrying that any kind of setback would encourage Sindia and the raja to join Holkar.[73] This did not occur, however, and there is no evidence of panic on the part of either Lake or Wellesley.[74]

In the case of Wellesley, an almost fatalistic calm characterizes his correspondence. He made no effort to affix blame for Monson's setback and instead focused on the future. His comments on Monson are almost moving in their moderation. One cannot imagine him writing in such a fashion in 1801: "I fear my poor friend Monson is gone. Whatever may have been his fate, or whatever the result of his misfortunes to my own fame, I will endeavour to shield his character from obloquy, nor will I attempt the mean purpose of sacrificing his reputation to save mine. His former services and his zeal entitle him to indulgence; and however I may lament or suffer for his errors, I will not reproach his memory if he be lost, or his character, if he survive."[75]

Redemption did not come quickly, but Wellesley was comforted by Castlereagh's announcement that Pitt was back at the helm in London.[76] Although political realities in London differed from Wellesley's perception, that was immaterial. That Pitt's administration was no stronger than Addington's and that he would prove no more aggressive in his defense of Wellesley would await discovery on the governor general's return in early 1806. For the time being, Wellesley labored under the impression that things would be better, and he retained his composure while awaiting Lake's victories at Dig and the Furruckabad on 13 and 17 November. These significant victories sent Holkar scurrying for cover.[77] Unfortunately they also filled Lake with a confidence that clouded his judgment. In January he proceeded to invest the fortress city of Bhurtpore, but he greatly underestimated Maratha preparation and will to resist. He would launch four separate and futile assaults before calling off the siege.[78]

Arthur celebrated his brother's ability to regroup and remained confident that the war would be brought to a successful conclusion, but as he prepared to depart Madras, a sense of foreboding descended on the brothers. Richard believed that Arthur would be well treated, but he stated,

> As far as relates to the general Policy of my Administration & to my individual services, I have been treated with the most intolerable indignity; not one line have I received from England since the month of June [he speaks here of the court of directors]; and then nothing but insult, and injury; nor has the crown intimated to me the slightest indication even of support, still less of approbation. I have therefore desired Captain Lambert to prepare his frigate for me (according to Admiral Rainier's orders) and I propose to embark as soon as the ship shall have been repaired after her late glorious action. The state of affairs here will make no alteration in my conduct; since the utter neglect of every public reference from me to England, and the virtual refusal of all support, have absolved me of all responsibility, and rendered me the least efficient Governor General, that could attempt to meet any difficulties or dangers, which may arise in India.[79]

Arthur departed with his Order of the Bath in hand and with the ample praise of his brother.[80]

Wellesley's mood by this time had changed, as he came to realize that nowhere would he find much support for what he was doing. The continuing problems with London (both court and board) stemmed from the fact that the government still rested on a feeble base and from the growing threat to British security from across the channel. Since the collapse of the Peace of Amiens, Bonaparte had been assembling his army on the channel coast and had managed to convince a large number of Britons that invasion of England was imminent. Pitt in the meantime scrambled to create the Third Coalition to confront Napoleon as national anxieties grew. The cumulative result was that Wellesley and India would suffer not only from the animus of the court of directors but also from public neglect. Not that Britons were uninterested, but they had more immediate concerns, and information from Asia was never much in abundance. The *Times* of London reported regularly what was available on Indian events but usually offered little comment. The public was not kept in ignorance, but often they had to work at keeping well versed. Henry had warned his eldest brother about this in 1801 and again after his return in 1803, so Wellesley should not have been surprised. Unfortunately, he never came to terms with the fact that for the general British public, European affairs were more important than Asian.

And so Wellesley's resolve to resign this time was firm; if ever there was a mutual parting of the ways, this was it. Arthur had been right to assume that if Wellesley had not resigned, he would have been recalled. In point of fact, both occurred. What surprised the marquess was the fact that his successor would be Lord Cornwallis.[81] Old and infirm, Cornwallis agreed only to a brief tenure until another governor general could be found. Arthur believed that Cornwallis's appointment amounted to public condemnation of Wellesley's policies. "As this letter may not reach you," he wrote from St. Helena,

> I will not enter into an enumeration of the circumstances which lead me to think that the appointment of Lord Cornwallis is intended as a mark of disapprobation. That opinion, however, is weakened in a great degree by a report in general circulation here that you are to be appointed the secretary of State for Foreign Affairs on your arrival in England, and that Lord Mulgrave holds the office only during your absence. If this should be the case, the arrangement will prove honourable to your character, and I should imagine that nothing more agreeable to you could be done than to send Lord Cornwallis to succeed you in India under these circumstances.[82]

Arthur had passed Cornwallis on the open sea.

There would be no animosity between Wellesley and Cornwallis, though they were very different men. The symbols of power that Wellesley had erected and for which he became identified meant nothing to Cornwallis. The old general preferred not to be bothered with ceremony and protocol and instead went about his business in a very simple manner. It is easy to ridicule Wellesley for his constant display and seemingly unending extravagance. For instance, he left Calcutta a changed city, the centerpiece of which was the new government house built in the neoclassical eighteenth-century style. He spent ten lacs on this structure, and, not surprisingly, he had his critics. He also built a retreat at Barrackpore—a great park outside of Calcutta that also ran to ten lacs. And there were the endless carriages, boats, servants, and retainers of various sorts. All this was and has been ascribed by some as needless and merely a product of Wellesley's vanity. Granted, much of what Wellesley built and concocted in terms of protocol seems unnecessary and frivolous, but an equal measure can be defended. Company facilities in Calcutta were woefully inadequate on Wellesley's arrival and needed upgrading. And after the marquess added immensely to the company's possessions and responsibilities, the need increased in proportion. In this sense, the government house was a good investment. The same cannot be said for Barrackpore. What must always be kept in mind about Lord Wellesley is the fact that though he was something of a parvenu, he firmly believed that image was important. This he understood from his Irish past. Ascendancy Ireland was built on image and form, and to Wellesley's eyes the British position in India looked much like the English position in Ireland. On his arrival in Calcutta, the manners of the British community appalled him. He described the behavior as familiarity and wondered how, if the British did not display a proper regard for authority, they could expect the Indians to do so. Perceiving society and government as slovenly, he set about establishing discipline. Unfortunately, the system he created seduced him. Intellectually he understood that protocol and ceremony had institutional value and that which people occupied the positions within the system made no difference; the system was what counted. But he came to admire his creation too much and came to see himself, rather than the system, as the key to its success. And so he became the object of ridicule when he returned to Britain filled with self-importance and unable to relinquish the

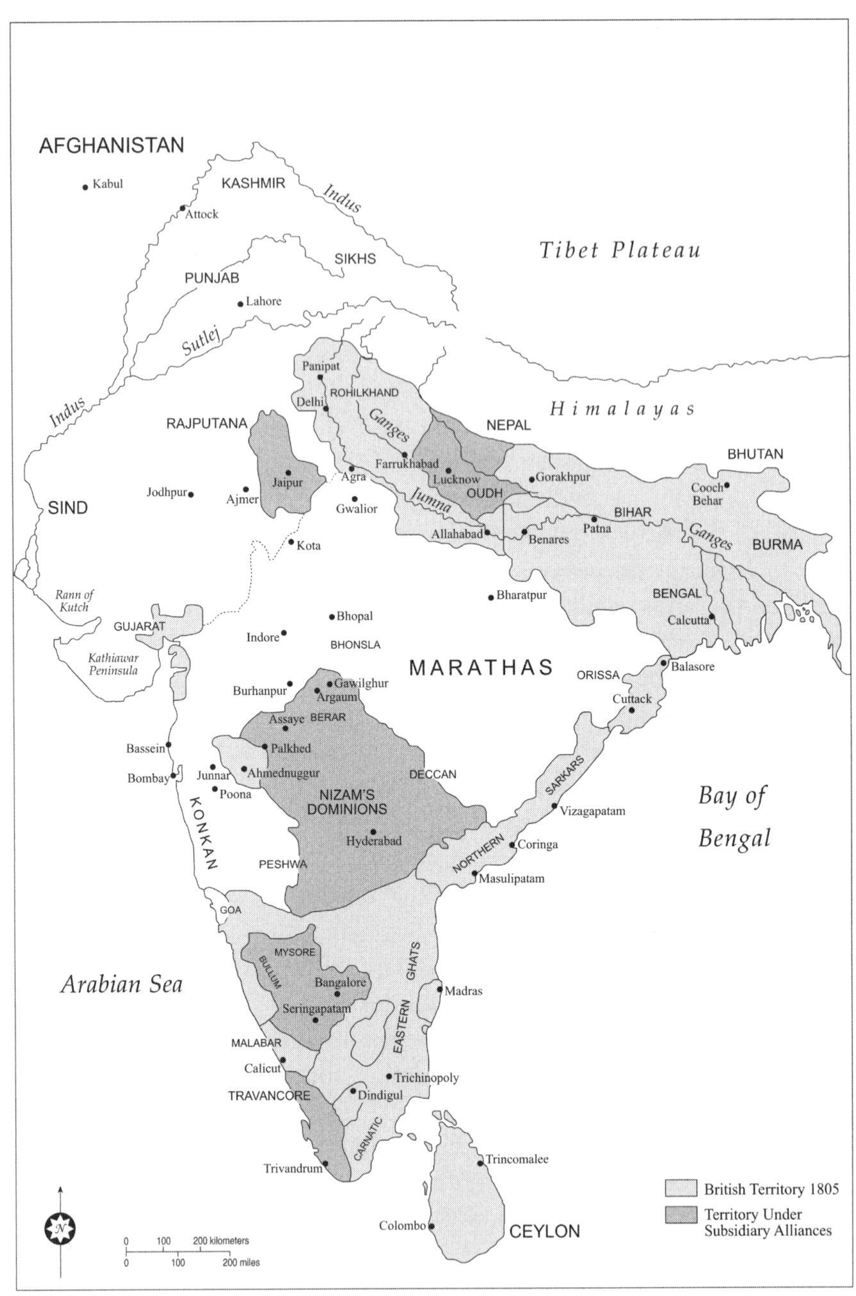

India after the Wellesleys, 1806

style of living to which he had become accustomed. He was a deeply flawed man, but a man of enormous talent—a man of brilliance lacking wisdom.

That said, his performance and behavior in the Maratha War are surprising. From 1803 to 1805, the pressures on Wellesley were enormous—public and private—yet he never buckled under the pressure as he had after the Mysore war. Problems such as Monson's retreat and Lake's failure before Bhurtpore he viewed simply as setbacks, not to be confused with failure or defeat. No matter how he looked at the sequence of events, he had won. Certainly his wars had been expensive and he had added appreciably to the company's debt, but that was a necessary evil that would yield enormous benefits in the future. He simply could not understand how anyone could continue to see Britain's presence in India as strictly an economic venture. Such thinking he viewed as preposterously outdated, and he had come to believe that Britain must consolidate its political presence in India or leave. The question is, how had he come to this conclusion? He had not gone out to India thinking in these terms. Rather, he had sailed with a list of problems and potential problems to solve, and he had fully intended to take them all on. There is no doubt that he was driven at that time by self-interest; somehow he had to break the political stasis in which he was mired. There were no dreams of empire. Instead there were dreams of cabinet posts, titles, and honors. India was simply a means to that end. At some point after the Mysore war, this began to change. Disappointment over the marquessate gave rise to spite and thus his determination to "heap kingdoms upon kingdoms, victory upon victory, revenue upon revenue." In the process, Wellesley's intellect and personality required that he develop a rationale for his actions that was not so crass. That is the point at which he began to think in terms of British paramountcy, what was even then called empire.

Arthur and Henry were eager collaborators. They too were men on the make, and they quickly came to see that their eldest brother's vision and largesse constituted ample coattails on which they could ride to fame and fortune. Each clearly saw Wellesley's many weaknesses—his vanity, arrogance, opportunism, precipitousness, and vindictiveness—and sometimes fell victim to them. But the weaknesses were balanced by determination, brilliance, and generosity, of which the younger brothers were always beneficiaries. They worked well together, and in this isolated setting of the Indian subcontinent, where time and space gave them extraordinary independence, they were allowed to develop their talents—talents that few others even dreamed they possessed. And while few in Britain viewed events in India as anything more than a sideshow, the Wellesley brothers presided over more people, more territory, and an infinitely more complex political culture than did the denizens of Whitehall. The Wellesleys, of course, recognized this and on their return to England were prepared to take up where they had left off.

8

Entr'acte I

When Wellesley embarked for Great Britain in the summer of 1805, he did so with mixed emotions and a large portion of uncertainty. His recent correspondence with home, official and unofficial, had been less than reassuring. The ongoing quarrel with the court of directors cast a pall over what he perceived to be a series of extraordinary accomplishments that had only strengthened the East India Company. Added to the ambiguities of his public life were his private concerns. Letters from Hyacinthe had turned challenging and cool, at times even desperate. Gone were the expressions of affection and loneliness that had characterized the first years of their separation. In their place came questions and interminable discussions of mundane, practical matters. There would be much for him to think about on the journey. He took with him aboard HMS *Howe* an entourage that consisted of some of the staff who had loyally served him, including Thomas Sydenham, Colonel Merrick Shawe, and John Forbes, names that would remain attached to his for many years. Wellesley kept no letter book on the return trip, and consequently nothing is known of what transpired during the long days and weeks on the open sea. No doubt these men spent their time congratulating one another on a job well done, revisiting an event-filled tenure in the subcontinent.

Awaiting the marquess were his brothers, eager to build on the India years but unwilling to proceed without him. In the coming years, opportunities would abound, but the brothers responded to them with varying degrees of success, as political developments and personal issues often confounded them. Marriage, health, and personal relationships proved as influential in the immediate future as did the instability and volatility of the British political scene. Richard, Arthur, and Henry would each face individual crises, and three years would elapse before the family established itself on firm ground, ready to take center stage in the great theater of politics and war.

There were, of course, five brothers. While Richard, Arthur, and Henry had been career building in India, William and Gerald had lived in the growing glow of their brothers' successes. William, whose ambition and pretense took root in these years, had been left in charge of family finances, including the Irish estates, which necessarily meant attending to political matters in Dublin. This appears to be the reason he gave up his seat in the Commons for East Looe that he held from 1790 to 1795. William left no diary or archive, but we do know that he traveled back and forth from Ireland when Richard, Arthur, and Henry departed. These were troubled times in Ireland's history; just how close to the action William found himself in the rebellion of 1798 is unclear, but from that time on, he never demonstrated much sympathy for the Irish. The union in 1801 meant the end of the Irish parliament and therefore less need for William to spend time in Dublin. Dangan had been leased, so that too was out of sight, out of mind. His own estates apparently required little attention, and William found a new seat for Queens, which he held from 1801 to 1821.

Arthur's and Henry's affairs required little attention, but Richard's were another matter. Not only did the eldest brother earn a handsome salary as governor general and acquire additional assets along the way, but he also had a large family whose interests had to be represented. This meant that William had to meet with his sister-in-law, Hyacinthe, to whom he could not help but condescend. For her part, the marchioness loathed him. Proud and clever, she could see through William, and she resented his doing what she felt she could do better.

Family and friends assumed that Pole was well off—in addition to the Irish estates he had inherited from his cousin, his wife, Catherine Forbes, had brought to the marriage a handsome dowry. But like Richard, William was careless with money and went through it with astonishing ease. Hyacinthe reported him near ruin. She is not to be trusted as a source on any of the Wellesleys (especially William), but although William was not bankrupt, by 1802 he was claiming to be short of cash. He looked with envy on those who had more than he, which caused him to lead a lifestyle that he could not afford. In the manner of the climber, he and his wife sneered at those whose social credentials they deemed inferior, particularly Hyacinthe, whom they viewed as nothing more than a courtesan. In Richard's absence, they treated her as one, or at least made clear to her that this was how they felt. They were not a likeable pair.

As Richard's trustee, William nosed his way into British social and political life, but he remained on the periphery. There are no glowing letters about Pole such as those sent by Dundas, Addington, and Bathurst about Henry. Curiously, though William wrote to Richard regularly, his letters contained scant political news of any value. William, though no fool, did not possess the subtle and sophisticated mind of his brothers but like them looked to Richard as his patron. One can imagine the panic that must have seized Pole when he learned to his surprise that Richard would return to London towards the end of 1805 or in early 1806. Strapped for cash, William had dipped into Richard's money pot to repay a loan that had come due. To his dismay, he found that he would be unable to restore the funds before Richard's arrival. There is little doubt that the marquess would have lent Pole the money, but he had taken it without asking, intending repayment at a later date, leaving no one the wiser. Caught with his hand in the till, he dashed off a letter filled with chitchat but also telling the marquess what he had done.[1] There is no record of Wellesley's response, but preoccupied with more important matters, he probably brushed it aside. The episode is more important for what it reveals about William if one accepts the notion that one's true character is revealed when no one is looking.

Gerald's life had been different. On Richard's departure for India, he served as rector at Beachampton and chaplain at Hampton Court, eagerly participating in what was known as pluralism. These were humble livings, but they were sufficient to maintain him. With the help of the bishop of Lincoln, as arranged by Richard before departing, he exchanged Beachampton for the vicarage of Staines in 1799, bringing his living to nearly £400 per annum, a respectable sum.[2] Gerald's personality could not have been more different from William's. Because he was quiet, pleasant, accommodating, sweet tempered, and naive, people were naturally attracted to him. Little was asked of clergymen in this age, and generally they returned what was asked. It is difficult to discover just what kind of priest Gerald was, but his peers respected him. He had chosen the right profession.

Even the hypercritical Hyacinthe liked Gerald, whom she described as gentle and kind. As was the case with all the Wellesley brothers, Gerald was handsome (perhaps the best looking of the bunch), and he was at ease around women. In a long letter to her husband, Hyacinthe related a conversation with the Prince of Wales, an inveterate gossip, who said of Gerald that he "was one of the greatest roués he had ever met, that he was infinitely amusing and knew all 'les filles.'"[3] Gerald moved in elevated social circles without the pretense or expense of the Poles, and he remained alert to both political talk and idle gossip, which he reported to Hyacinthe and the marquess. Eventually, as he moved from soirée to soirée, his eye fell on Lady Emily Cadogan, the eldest daughter of Earl Cadogan. The courtship moved swiftly; Gerald married Emily on 2 June 1802.

The liaison between the Wellesleys and the Cadogans would bring trouble and unhappiness, though the only possible hint of this in 1802 lay in the scandal that surrounded the Cadogans. The earl had divorced his second wife in 1796. Lady Mornington, who looked down on them, thought that poor Gerald had made a horrible mistake. But for Gerald the marriage had its benefits. The Cadogan family owned the living of St. Luke's, Chelsea, with an income of £500 and a marvelous house where the couple could live in style.[4] On 4 June 1805, Gerald exchanged the recently acquired living of Chaddleworth for St. Luke's, which along with the living of Staines and his prebendary of Westminster brought his income to at least £800—not bad for a humble priest.[5] That aside, Gerald was smitten with his young wife. "I long to introduce Lady Emily to you," he wrote enthusiastically to Richard, "and cannot help flattering myself you will like her."[6] Hyacinthe endorsed Gerald's judgment. She rather liked Emily, though one must understand that any enemy of Lady Mornington or Pole was a friend of hers. "Lady Emily . . . told me one day—in front of Gerald," she wrote, "that she considered Pole the ugliest man and with the most disagreeable manners she had ever met."[7] Children arrived regularly; as Gerald wrote to Richard, he got on "in the old parsonic way, that is, have a wife and one child, and am in daily expectation of another; am intolerably poor, but, that excepted, as happy as possible."[8]

Meanwhile, Henry arrived home, after a voyage no better than its predecessors. During the voyage, the war with France had resumed, which meant a threat from French frigates. As his ship, the *Sparrow*, entered the English Channel, a warship appeared on the horizon and fired warning shots. Images of his incarceration ten years earlier must have been vivid, but to his relief, the ship ran up a British flag and escorted the *Sparrow* to harbor. Henry limped ashore, deathly ill and emotionally spent—the shadow of his former self.

He promptly fell in with his brothers, especially Gerald, who introduced him to Charlotte Cadogan, Emily's younger sister. Cupid's arrow flew straight and true; to everyone's astonishment, within the year Henry was engaged. The astonishment arose from the fact that Henry, like Gerald, was a ladies' man and Charlotte, to many observers, did not seem much of a catch. Lady Mornington was succinct:

> The surprise, and, I must confess, vexation of dearest Henry's sudden determination to marry, and form the same odious connection that Gerald had done, affected my spirits beyond all description. . . . I believe Lady Charlotte is a good natured sort of person, 'tis impossible but she must love Henry and feel that she is in a situation infinitely beyond what she could expect. Therefore, I hope she will make it her study to make him happy, but *I* can see no charm of either person or manner. . . . and he certainly must be a better judge than I can possibly pretend to be, of what constitutes his own happiness.[9]

Though this was typical of Anne's acid view of humanity, she was not the only one perplexed by the match. By all accounts, Charlotte was a plain young woman who must have contrasted starkly with the women Henry had squired in the past. Perhaps Lady Harriet Cavendish had it right when she said of Charlotte, "She has very little beauty but I believe her powers of pleasing to have been uncommonly great and her Coquetry unfortunately in proportion."[10] She and Henry were married on 20 September 1803, the Reverend Gerald Wellesley officiating.

The evidence suggests that Henry's judgment at the time was not sharp. And is it any wonder? He had been ill for several weeks before leaving India, and though he felt better when embarking for England, he knew what lay ahead—a minimum of five months of suffering. What was he thinking when day after day he awoke with a tumbling stomach? Apart from sheer physical fatigue and a broken spirit, his mind probably played tricks on him.

Gloom certainly inserted itself into Henry's contemplations. Taking his lead from Richard, Henry thought how unjustly the court of directors had treated him as governor of the ceded provinces and how little they appreciated the hardships that he and his brothers had endured. Counterproductive as such thinking is, as Henry stepped from the boat, hope must have vied with anger for prominence in his mind as he looked forward to his first day free from nausea in months. He soon found that no one was much interested in India, let alone appreciative of what the Wellesleys had done there. London's bon ton were aware of Tipu's defeat, the developing war with the Marathas, and the dramatic growth of British power, but it was the knowledge of the dilettante acquired for the purpose of social discourse. There existed scant appreciation for the strategic and economic consequences. This must have been terribly frustrating for Henry, and one can imagine praise being heaped on him at social gatherings, followed by broad winks as he turned to walk away. His emaciated appearance must have initiated comments about his experience. One can imagine a condescending "Good show, old boy!" passing from unconcerned lips as Henry became reacquainted with London society. He quickly realized the insincerity and ignorance of it all and began to warn the marquess about it.

Henry quickly established a regular contact with Castlereagh, who kept him apprised of the official attitude at Ledenhall Street, where the court of directors presided over company affairs. These he duly reported to the marquess in a stream of letters sent in 1803 and 1804.[11] For his part, Castlereagh appreciated hearing the Wellesley perspective, for he knew full well that the marquess was a political force with which he would soon have to deal.[12] Castlereagh played a double game. He expressed appreciation for the marquess's work while knowing that politically he could ill afford to alienate the East India Company. He did not throw himself into the task of defending Wellesley; his qualified approval had the effect of moderating court criticism, not eliminating it. Castlereagh did, however, assure Henry that the court of directors looked favorably on his work and was about to award him £10,000. Such a sum would have left Henry and Charlotte starry-eyed.

Then, like a bolt out of the blue, Napoleon published in *Le Moniteur* a set of letters captured with the *Admiral Aplin,* on that ship's way out to India. Among them was a letter from Henry to the marquess dated 28 July 1803, a little over a month after Henry had returned home. In it he described the company's and the government's view of events in India. Some of his comments were rash. "Obstinate fools" he called the court of directors; Addington was "pompous" and "affected." Such comments, wrote an appalled Arthur, "Lord Wellesley would not have shown even to his private secretary."[13] Years later, Henry explained the letter in this fashion: "These mistakes may easily be accounted for when it is recollected, first, that my handwriting is not very legible, secondly, that the French are notorious for never copying English correctly, and thirdly, that my letter underwent two translations, first from English incorrectly given into French, and secondly, from French into English."[14] The rationale is unconvincing. A more plausible explanation lies in the facts that Henry, while exhausted, had discovered the controversial nature of Wellesley's administration and its likely bearing on his own career. The *Times* could not let the matter rest without comment: "Mr. Henry Wellesley's letter to his brother is curious. Is this a correct picture of Courts and Courtiers? To be abusing, in the severest terms, the Minister from whom he was soliciting a place? Alas! *Thomas Paine* (of excrable [*sic*] memory) never said anything more severe of the retinue of a Court, than this letter contains."[15] Suffice it to say, the £10,000 disappeared as if a mirage. Not that Henry lived in poverty. Like all company servants, he returned with a tidy savings off which he could live until he found employment.

Pitt, in the meantime, returned to office in May 1804; eager to secure a Wellesley alliance, he promptly appointed Henry a Lord of the Treasury after first offering a position in the Home Office. What Henry really wanted was a seat on the board of control that would enable him to defend his brother, but that was a political impossibility. The treasury job engaged the youngest Wellesley but did not stimulate him, and when, towards the end of 1804, he was asked to go to Spain as envoy extraordinary and minister plenipotentiary in relief of John Hookham Frere, he eagerly accepted and resigned his post at the treasury.[16] Henry's bad luck proved unrelenting. No sooner had he been appointed and begun preparations to embark than Spain declared war, leaving him without a job. He and Char (as she was called) settled into their house on Hertford Street, Mayfair, where their first son, Henry, was born.

While William, Gerald, and Henry attempted to make sense of their lives, Arthur prepared for his departure. He left India with few regrets. Though a man with few close friends, he saw his life in India as abnormal and was eager to return to something more conventional. Inevitably his mind turned toward marriage and the establishment of a household. One can hardly blame him. All the brothers were highly sexed, and for Arthur the years in India must have been a challenge. His biographers go to great lengths to dismiss rumors of Arthur's romantic conquests both before his marriage and then outside of it. The fact is, those rumors were legion, and though there is no concrete proof that his many acknowledged friendships were ever consummated, dismissing them entirely would be a mistake. Arthur was no saint, and like the rest of humanity, he rationalized and even prevaricated about his personal life. It is illogical to assume that this handsome, energetic, charming man, in the prime of life, far removed from social circles that might matter to him, and in a masculine environment that would have been quite uncritical of the occasional dalliance, remained celibate for ten years. While possible, it seems unlikely. Whatever the case, he deemed his personal life unsatisfactory, and he ached for something different. This explains his eagerness to get home as much as fatigue from the experience in India.

So Arthur boarded HMS *Trident* with a light heart, £43,000 in savings, and the freshly arrived Order of the Bath.[17] Life was good, and he intended to make the voyage home a restorative one. He packed a trunk full of romantic novels to occupy his time and set sail. Unlike Henry, Arthur developed sea legs, and the fresh, clean air must have acted as a great tonic. When the ship stopped at St. Helena for a month of refurbishment and resupply, the island's cool air had to have been especially welcome and perhaps explains Arthur's enthusiasm for the place. Napoleon's hatred for the island is just as easily explained; for Arthur, St. Helena represented liberation, for Napoleon, confinement. Moreover, Arthur had come from an unbearably hot climate and Napoleon from a temperate one. Not that these things entered the Duke of Wellington's head in 1815.

Arthur arrived at Dover on 10 September 1805 knowing that Richard was not far behind and that much work lay ahead concerning India affairs. Richard's policies were under attack, and though Arthur had his own doubts, he supported his brother to the hilt. He recognized that his own reputation would forever be connected to Wellesley's work, and like his brothers, he continued to look to the eldest for advancement. If Richard's career collapsed in a heap of scandal, then all of them would suffer. Richard had to be defended.

This meant that Arthur's life would be more complicated than he wished. Nonetheless, during the voyage, he had thought of Ireland and the person of Kitty Pakenham, whom he had unsuccessfully wooed ten years earlier. Kitty's friend, Olivia Sparrow, noting Arthur's success in India and concluding that the Pakenhams' objections would be removed, had taken it upon herself to bring the star-crossed lovers back into alignment. Finding both Arthur and Kitty amenable, she fanned the flames. Several factors combined to make Arthur especially vulnerable to Olivia's matchmaking. Most obvious is the fact that he was lonely and eager for female companionship of his own station. And who better than Kitty to provide it? Arthur remembered her as pretty, effervescent, and quick witted. The match still made sense—their similar backgrounds and shared social circles promised a comfortable reunion. Last (and to Arthur, most important), he could redress past failure. The Pakenhams' rejection had struck him to the core, and he had not forgotten the humiliation. Only this can explain his reluctance to consider the fact that much water had passed under the bridge in the past ten years: he and Kitty could not possibly be the same people they had been. Arthur's active life and challenging and diverse experiences had transformed him. Much is made of the notion that Arthur felt duty-bound to honor the promise he had made in 1793 or that he considered his proposal open-ended. This seems utter silliness and is used only to confirm notions of nobility of character, for no one took such a pledge seriously. His was simply the reaction of a bitterly disappointed and hurt young man. Rather, Arthur viewed Kitty as a symbol of the frustration and humiliation that he felt compelled to erase.

Kitty, despite her enthusiasm for Arthur, retained her equilibrium. She understood that because of the passage of time, they were treading on dangerous ground. Having recently rejected a proposal from Lowry Cole (whose future would be tied to Arthur's), she must have believed that her chances for making a suitable match were slight. One could excuse her for a hint of desperation when Arthur appeared on the scene, but even so she urged caution, pointing out the obvious—they had both changed. Arthur paid no attention: he would renew the proposal sight-unseen but not quite yet, for in the meantime, there was business to attend to. Arriving in London, Arthur met up with William, Gerald, and Henry but not his mother. Like the rejection of the Pakenhams, his mother's lifetime of rejection struck at his sensibilities. Unlike his future in-laws, Lady Mornington would not get a second chance. Henceforth, Arthur would place himself in the company of his mother only when he had to. There would be no knock on the door of Mornington House off Cavendish Square: Lady Mornington had to learn from others the news of her son's return.

Arthur promptly secured an audience with Castlereagh to discuss Richard. As he made his way to the office of the secretary for war and the colonies, Arthur cut an interesting and conspicuous figure. Slim, fit, carefully groomed, and well tanned, he must have turned many a head on Whitehall. The meeting with Castlereagh proved serendipitous for both Arthur and history. Waiting to see the secretary when Arthur arrived was Lord Nelson, there to say goodbye and to receive his last instructions before heading out to meet his destiny at Trafalgar. The story of this encounter is well known. A conversation with Nelson only two days after landing in England put Arthur on notice that he had stepped onto a new stage, one rife with anticipation.

Arthur's meeting with Castlereagh seems prosaic when juxtaposed with the weighty issues that must have been discussed between Nelson and the secretary. That is the point. At a crisis of the war, the Wellesleys' personal problems ranked low on the government's list of priorities. Unfazed, Arthur got right to it, and Castlereagh listened but, however sympathetic, could not be convinced that the Maratha War was unavoidable. While he did not consider Wellesley's policies irresponsible, let alone corrupt, he would not fully endorse them. Arthur had to be satisfied with that.

Following the meeting with Castlereagh, Arthur made the political rounds. He met with John Pratt, the second Earl Camden; Henry Bathurst; Robert Hobart, the Earl of Buckinghamshire; and most important, Pitt. The prime minister squeezed Arthur into a busy schedule by inviting him on the long ride from Wimbledon to Whitehall. In the course of it, Arthur aired all, informing Pitt of Wellesley's personal and public disappointment over the criticism of his administration. In the public sense, the marquess resented the government's silence because to his mind, silence implied agreement and represented gross ingratitude. In a personal sense, Wellesley could not believe that his oldest friends and political associates were not standing behind him. In Arthur's recounting of the conversation, much was left unsaid; no doubt he and Pitt talked about the marquess's extreme sensitivity. But that is beside the point. Perception in this case was reality, and Pitt promised to be more active.[18]

The attack on Wellesley's India policies was not all that concerned Arthur. He soon realized that the country's political life was in flux. On his way to Cheltenham, he stopped off at Stowe to visit his old friend the Marquess of Buckingham, Lord Grenville being out of town. The Grenvilles, having split with Pitt, were not members of the government, and Arthur needed to know where they stood. "Bucky is very anxious that you should belong to the opposition," he warned Richard. "He urged every argument to induce me to inflame your mind against Pitt, particularly that he had not given you the Garter. He told me that you might depend upon the cordial and active support of himself, his brothers, his son, and all his friends; that they had stipulated with Fox that they were to give you this support in any question that might arise on your administration." Worried that Richard would find himself between a rock and a hard place, Arthur's advice was clear and simple: "remain neutral for some time, and observe the course of events."[19] This done, he set out for Cheltenham, a spa in whose curative powers Arthur had great faith. There he met Olivia Sparrow, who had been chastising him for ignoring Kitty. He tried to explain to her the necessity of attending to business and his health before turning to personal matters; failing at this, he assured her that his feelings had not changed. Before the month was out, Olivia had coaxed a proposal out of Arthur, and the Pakenhams, seeing Arthur's situation much changed, had given the marriage their blessing.

The first week of November brought remarkable news: first Napoleon's victory over the Austrians at Ulm, then Kitty's acceptance of Arthur's proposal, and finally Nelson's glorious victory at Trafalgar at the cost of his life. Later that month, Arthur joined William, first Earl Cathcart, for an expedition to the Elbe in support of the powers of the Third Coalition. While sorting all of this out,

Arthur informed Kitty that he would not get to Ireland until the new year. In December he left for the continent, but before leaving, he took care to visit Hyacinthe and all of her children, a sensitive issue for her and for the marquess. In January Richard arrived, which brought a flurry of activity, and when Arthur returned from the Elbe (the expedition rendered futile by the battle of Austerlitz), he joined Richard to discuss their strategy. He returned as a colonel, having been given the Thirty-third Regiment in succession to Cornwallis, who had died shortly after succeeding Richard as governor general. Arthur had expected a promotion, but this one was especially gratifying, and it brought a hefty salary. On Castlereagh's advice, he secured a seat in the Commons for Rye on 1 April, after which he proceeded to Ireland with Gerald in tow to marry the long-neglected but ever-patient Kitty. Their meeting, so much anticipated, proved awkward. While Kitty was thrilled by what she saw, the same cannot be said for Arthur, who was taken aback by the discovery that Kitty was indeed ten years older. Not that she was unattractive, for her slight figure and fine features served her well. What Arthur found missing was the spark—the lively personality to which he had been attracted in the first place. To hear Arthur tell of it many years later, this reunion prompted the realization that he had not used good judgment. But this marriage was not about love (something Arthur conveniently forgot with the passage of time, if indeed he ever realized it); it was about redemption.

The marriage took place on 10 April 1806 at St. George's, Dublin. Gerald, as he had done for Henry, presided. The honeymoon was brief, with Arthur explaining to his bride that urgent parliamentary business awaited him in London. He left Gerald to escort Kitty to their home at 11 Harley Street. By this time, political events had taken on a momentum all of their own, much of which must be told as part of Richard's story. Arthur settled in with Kitty while attending to his political and military responsibilities. Meantime, he discovered that he and Kitty were very different creatures—he a man of business and she a woman of great sensitivity and compassion for whom the practical responsibilities of running a household held little interest. When unpaid bills landed on his desk, they caused great irritation; Arthur simply could not understand Kitty's personality and habits. In his mind, her responsibility was to make his life easier by relieving him of domestic tasks—not make it more difficult. As was his habit, he expressed this view very clearly.

Lord Wellesley's return was anything but a triumph either publicly or privately. His struggles with the court of directors had unnerved him and left him disillusioned. From his perspective, he had transformed India and solidified Britain's power and influence there for years to come. If his policies had led to an almost self-perpetuating state of warfare, then so be it—that was the price of empire. To his mind, his options were two: to preside over either expansion or contraction. This was not a choice for a great power engaged in a desperate struggle with a revolutionary, continental foe. Perhaps the choice was not obvious when sitting in London, but it was obvious in Calcutta. Even though Wellesley's capacity to mistake personal ambition for national destiny was superhuman, there was something to his argument. Even Arthur, who sometimes questioned his brother's judgment, recognized this.

If the political complications were not enough, his personal life careened towards disaster. Letters from Hyacinthe had become strident and hectoring. The years of separation had not been good for either of them. Hyacinthe suspected Richard of infidelity, and with good reason. There is little doubt that Richard strayed among Calcutta society, but there was no consistent woman in his life and this was what Hyacinthe feared most. Richard, of course, denied all and chastised his wife for believing the rumors that made their way back to London. Next on her list of complaints was Richard's failure to increase his personal fortune. His rejection of the company grant after Seringapatam was just one example. Though he would receive an annuity of £5,000 a year in its stead, this seemed to Hyacinthe a paltry substitute—as it was. Money was something that Wellesley rarely considered, in the sense that he never understood the relationship between income and expenditure. Although he did accumulate a small fortune while in India, he failed to explain this to Hyacinthe, probably because he was not aware of it himself.

The point of the matter is that Richard got from Hyacinthe exactly what he did not want and failed to get what he craved: an adoring wife, full of praise for his great work and a vehement defender in the face of criticism at home. They had been living in different circumstances, besides the obvious fact of geography. Hyacinthe dealt with the domestic concerns of raising a large family and dealing with difficult in-laws, while Richard dealt with great issues of state. And so their discourse occurred on entirely different levels and each passed the other by without acknowledgment. This would prove a great tragedy: it destroyed a strong and affectionate marriage and permanently altered the course of Richard's career.

Hyacinthe proceeded to Portsmouth with all her children in tow to greet the marquess. Nothing better illustrates their divergent views and personal needs than their preparations for meeting each other for the first time in seven years. Wellesley's voyage home had gone off without difficulty. Physically he arrived tired, and like everyone else who returned from the subcontinent, he complained of a variety of ailments. More important was his state of mind. As calm and reconciled to the court's view of his tenure as he appeared at the moment of his departure, he still hoped for some sign of approbation on his return. At the least, he expected to see some of his old friends waiting on the quay as he disembarked. He had sent instructions to Hyacinthe that young Richard alone should be there to meet him and escort him to a family reunion.[20] This suggests that he hoped to spend his first day accepting congratulations from admiring colleagues, revelling in the excitement of political talk, and reconnecting with old friends. Only then would he turn his attention to his family.

Hyacinthe disregarded the instructions in the belief that he could want nothing more than to bring together a family separated by half the world for seven years—seven very formative years. She ached for the physical and emotional contact that had been so much a part of their union prior to the Indian adventure. Politics and celebration could wait. One can imagine her as she prepared her children for this reunion. The younger ones, with no recollection of their father, would have had to be coached about him and how to respond to him. The days would have been counted, preparations in the house would have been meticulous, what to wear would have been discussed. For the family this was to be an extraordinary event. And going to Portsmouth only added to the excitement . . . and the stress. Reasonable as Hyacinthe's decision was, it proved a terrible miscalculation.

When HMS *Howe* slipped into the harbor on the afternoon of 7 January, the marquess scribbled a note to his wife: "We have just arrived and cast anchor. I am perfectly well. My journey has been unbelievably fortunate, in spite of all obstacles. I know nothing of your arrangements, but am dying to embrace you; however, I don't think I will be able to disembark before tomorrow morning. Farewell, *chère amie, toujours à toi et pour toi*—W."[21] This was less than honest. Wellesley, who had hoped for an official greeting, stepped ashore to find only the normal hubbub of a busy harbor and six happy faces eager for a warm embrace. He had been warned that no official greeting awaited him, not even old friends to reassure him of a job well done. He had, therefore, some time to digest this fact and he did not do it well. Angered and humiliated as only Wellesley could be, he lost sight of the fact that his family expected him to be happy to see them. Instead they found him distracted and enervated, and the "warm" reunion turned to ice. The trip back to London must have been bleak: the children puzzled and Richard and Hyacinthe nursing deep wounds. But while Richard tended to brood, Hyacinthe gave voice to her injuries. Chiding her husband for his pompous, self-centered ways did nothing but exacerbate the situation, sending the marquess deeper into self-pity. He had warned her of his state of mind and of his visceral reaction to her chiding letters, but she took no heed. Nor did Richard consider her needs, despite knowing her reluctance to part with him and her frustration over her prolonged isolation. Though they did not know it, by the time they reached the house on Park Lane, the marriage was over.

Rather than attend to his personal affairs, Wellesley tried to make sense of his political life. He discovered that he would have more to confront than anger from the court of directors and skepticism from the political establishment. While he was sailing home, the stakes had been raised, as the *Annual Register* clearly described: "Towards the close of the preceding session of parliament, Mr. Paull, a gentleman lately returned from India, had come forward in the House of Commons as the accuser of marquis Wellesley, and had obtained orders for the production of various papers to substantiate his charges."[22] With the example of Dundas' (then Viscount Melville) ruin by a similar inquiry and the specter of Warren Hastings' trial ever present, the marquess saw himself as fighting for his political life. In analyzing his political career, one can easily forget this. Wellesley's reaction to the Paull inquiry is usually seen as another manifestation of his insatiable need for public acclaim, but while he was indeed insatiable, this was something different. Should Paull succeed in securing a parliamentary censure, Wellesley's work in

India would stand publicly condemned and his career would be in ruins. His brothers, who were quick to recognize this, rallied to his defense without hesitation. As Richard went, so went they. In retrospect, the Wellesleys' alarm seems misplaced, but several factors combined to make the Paull charges especially problematic. First, Wellesley found himself in the midst of a political crisis at a time when his personal life was collapsing in a heap of ruins. This distracted him and clouded his judgment. Second, on his return, he had no idea where to turn politically for support, for much had changed and would continue to change.

Back in London on 9 January, he wrote to his old friends Pitt and Grenville, announcing his arrival, something that he must have found galling. In Grenville's case, he need not have bothered, for a letter of greeting passed his own.[23] At the same time, he made contact with his brothers and his mother. He quickly learned that Pitt was very ill, a fact of great political consequence. The letter that arrived from the prime minister on the 12th was probably the last he would write. In it, Pitt apologized to Wellesley for not coming to Portsmouth: his physicians had consigned him to bed away from London.[24] Wellesley lost little time in making his own pilgrimage, forgetting for the time being his own predicament. A very sad visit ensued because it was as clear to Wellesley as to everyone else that Pitt's days were numbered. When he called on Grenville next to report his observations, he became aware of the difficulty of his political position. Intellectually he understood that Grenville and Pitt were no longer political allies, but until he saw Grenville, he had not come to grips with the fact that there would be an emotional dimension to it. He found himself caught between Pitt, the public man he admired most, and Grenville, his oldest and best friend.

Pitt's death on 22 January did nothing to relieve Wellesley's anxieties. As the ministry could not carry on without Pitt, the king turned to Grenville, who put together a cabinet that included many of the old Whig opposition, including their head, Charles James Fox. Wellesley, who was uncomfortable with a coalition government, was in no condition or position to play an active part. Grenville knew this but assured his friend of support against Paull's charges even though Paull's few supporters sat on the government benches.[25] Grenville promptly delivered on his pledge, sending word to Paull through the

Prince of Wales that he would have to step back. Wellesley's self-absorption prevented him from appreciating the difficulties Grenville faced. First and foremost, events on the continent had transformed the war against France. Napoleon had followed up his defeat of the Austrians at Ulm with the rout of a combined Russian and Austrian army at Austerlitz on 2 December 1805. The Third Coalition was dead, and soon the Napoleonic hammer would fall on Prussia. Grenville would have to sort this out in the midst of an unsettled political environment. By comparison, Paull's charges must have seemed insignificant, as becomes apparent from Grenville's correspondence. He repeatedly assured Wellesley of his support against Paull. But by the middle of February, Grenville had decided that the charges would die through lack of interest and that he and the government would be best served by ignoring Paull. Grenville was right, but Wellesley was temperamentally incapable of such a tack. To him, the government's passivity signaled tacit agreement with Paull's charges.

Grenville understood Wellesley's state of mind but skirted the issue by busying himself with an ambitious agenda before Parliament. At the same time, he performed small kindnesses such as arranging the lease of Camelford House while the marquess searched for a house to buy.[26] Grenville continued to look for a way out, but Wellesley's paranoia got in the way. Writing to his good friend in March, the marquess betrayed his extreme uneasiness. Fox, he pointed out, had not lifted a finger in his defense in the Commons.[27] Wellesley felt caught in the flow of political events that only Grenville could direct. Sympathy from friends such as James Graham, third Duke of Montrose, only added to the despair: "I heartily regret the inconvenience you are put to, but the attacks made, & encouraged, by different descriptions of men; & fear with you that means are not taken to put a speedy end to this species of warfare."[28] Grenville could only assure his friend of his continuing support and enlist friends and family to make similar assurances. Even the recently disgraced but ever shrewd Melville assured Wellesley that all would end well.[29]

Wellesley's greatest comfort came from his brothers. His correspondence from the period contains numerous letters between them but especially from Henry and Arthur. Their support is unsurprising, considering the working relationships they had enjoyed in India and their familiarity with the issues at hand. The younger brothers hoped to establish what amounted to a "Wellesley Party" in Parliament to spearhead the marquess's defense and to provide them with some leverage with the government. To this end, Arthur stood for Rye, with Grenville's help, joining William, who already had a seat. Henry, meanwhile, organized the effort to secure allies through election. Arthur suggested soliciting the support of a newspaper: "It appears that the newspapers have at last made much progress in guiding what is called publick opinion in the country."[30] He also urged caution when dealing with the Grenvilles, knowing that the marquess could not afford to alienate them. For his part, the marquess set up an office from which he could direct his defense.

Political events took another turn when Fox died in September, which forced Grenville to reconstruct the ministry. For this Grenville engaged Wellesley's services, asking him to try, on Grenville's behalf, to bring George Canning into the government. When Canning refused, Grenville invited Wellesley to join the government, though one might question the sincerity of the invitation.[31] As Grenville expected, Richard declined, citing the pending charges. Grenville, more than ever dependent on Richard's support, kept in close touch with the family about Paull, whose challenge languished in Parliament owing to more pressing issues and to lack of interest.[32]

Meanwhile, George III dissolved Parliament and called for elections. Arthur and Henry sprang to action again. "I am ready to come into Parlt in any way you will think proper," wrote Arthur;

> but if it could be done I should think it most creditable to be returned independently of the Treasury. But that is only a matter of preference; & it is probably more important to be in the House of Commons at an early period, than to be returned for a place in which the Treasury has no concern. . . . I told you tht whether I was returned to Parlt or not I was willing to contribute 1500 £ for the purpose of defraying the expense of bringing into Parlt a number of persons who should be attached to you; being convinced that a Parliamentary following will facilitate the attainment of your object to get into office.[33]

While Wellesley made every effort to cooperate with Grenville, on Henry's and Arthur's advice he opted to bring his friends into Parliament separate from the government. Arthur on this occasion stood for St. Michael. William, it appears, was not much involved in the meticulous planning between the brothers. Writing to Richard in October, he was "anxious to hear whether anything has been arranged about that Reptile Paull—and what effect the scoundrel's late conduct in Westminster has had upon ministers."[34]

The elections on 19 December 1806 saw the defeat of Paull at the hands of Richard Sheridan. Subsequently Sir Francis Burdett, William Cobbett, and Horne Tooke took up Paull's charges, but they sparked little interest. The marquess felt confident enough to take his seat in the House of Lords for the first time on 31 December. Grenville's new ministry was short lived, falling on the Irish Militia Bill, to which the king objected. Thus Parliament dissolved again; after elections, the Duke of Portland pieced together a government made up of Pitt's friends in June 1807. Again, Henry and Arthur had been active. Henry found another seat for Arthur, at Newport. It could be purchased annually at a moderate price, keeping Arthur at the center of things until he found military employment. Henry stood for Eye, and the brothers pooled their money to bring in additional allies. Furthermore, they launched a pamphlet campaign refuting the claims against Wellesley in an attempt to mobilize public opinion. Richard is said to have lost his fortune in all of this, but that is not entirely the case. By Henry's calculations, these seats were bought for under £5,000. When all was said and done, after two years Wellesley was said to have spent £30,000, a substantial sum, particularly when this amount is combined with his personal expenses of £6,200 per year. He had to have felt the squeeze. Bankruptcy, however, would result from other causes.

The Duke of Portland made Wellesley's political position much more complicated. With Grenville out of office and Portland turning to Pitt's old friends, the marquess had to choose where he stood. Grenville was his oldest friend, the patron of his early career. At the same time, Grenville had had his chance, and years of opposition appeared to be his destiny. This was no place for the marquess, in either his mind or his family's. He had rejected offers of high office because of the scurrilous and unwarranted attack on his policies, an attack that finally appeared spent and nearing resolution. But if he attached himself to Portland, he forever separated himself from the Grenvilles. This would constitute a very big step. As one might imagine, the marquess began a series of intellectual gyrations to justify what seemed inevitable.

Portland, ever alert (if that term can be applied to the moribund duke) to potential support, knew that the marquess was vulnerable, and when assembling his cabinet, he offered Richard the Foreign Office.[35] Arthur believed Richard's time had come. Writing to his friend John Malcolm in February, Arthur explained, "A revolution is . . . in progress, slowly but very certainly, in the public mind, respecting the former system of government there [India]. . . . The Court of Directors are certainly less hostile than they were towards Lord Wellesley [and] . . . his mind is more composed, and he is more reconciled to his situation than he was last year."[36] Portland found himself on the same page with Arthur, recognizing that not only was it time for the marquess to leap into the political fire but also that Wellesley's presence in any government would be of great benefit. As the house secretary, Robert Banks Jenkinson (Baron Hawkesbury, the future Earl of Liverpool), put it to the king, "the appointment of Marquis Wellesley to the office of Foreign Secretary of State appears to be likely to be very advantageous to your majesty's service at this time, not only from Lord Wellesley's acknowledged talents, but likewise from its securing to your Majesty['s] government the active cooperation and exertion of all his family and connections."[37] Grenville, aware of all that was transpiring, did his best to head off the breach.[38]

Wellesley, who found all of this unsettling, he lost his nerve. He told Portland frankly that his friendship with Grenville was an obstacle to his accepting office in the new administration and suggested that if the king directly requested his services, it would relieve him of the responsibility for terminating this long-time political alliance.[39] Portland accordingly explained to George III that such a request would "effectually prevent the impressions which he [Wellesley] is exposed to by the incessant importunities of some of his earliest & most intimate friends who are jealous of seeing his talents employed in an Administration of which they make no part."[40] Even after the king agreed, Wellesley withdrew his name from consideration, again invoking the fact that the charges against him were unresolved. Canning, for one, knew the real reason: "Lord Grenville has shaken him to pieces. In such a state of nerves it is quite as well that he has not this situation to encounter. It is as well for us too, for he might fail us at a moment of need."[41] How the king felt about all of this is unknown, but one may safely conclude that he took note.

Wellesley made up for the inconvenience by delivering up his brothers, who were dismayed by his lack of nerve and worried that it might have repercussions for them. There was no reason to worry; Portland appointed Arthur chief secretary for Ireland, Pole a secretary at the Admiralty, and Henry a secretary at the treasury. Thus, while Wellesley himself remained separate from the government, everyone could see where his sympathies lay.[42] And his coattails, though somewhat tattered, still carried his brothers along. Both Henry and William needed the employment. As for Arthur, he found himself in a position that he could not have imagined two years earlier. Command of the Thirty-third Regiment already provided him with a comfortable income, especially when added to his personal fortune. As chief secretary, he found himself with an additional £6,566 a year. It was all a bit mind-boggling, and it took some getting used to. Arthur, who felt a little guilty, did not want anyone to think that he had turned his back on the Grenvilles for power and profit. Predictably, he wrote an elaborately contrived letter to Richard explaining his reason for taking the position and asking him to convey these thoughts to Grenville:

> When the change of Government took place, it was obvious that you could not go into opposition in aid of those who had always treated you ill, in the House of Commons, and against those upon whom you have principally relied and must rely for your defense. The only doubt I had therefore when this offer was made, was whether I should accept a civil office, the duties of which might take me away from my profession. I have consulted the Duke of York upon this point, and he has told me that he approves of my acceptance of the office, and that he does not conceive that it ought to operate to my prejudice; and the Ministers have told me that they consider me at liberty to give up the office in Ireland whenever an opportunity of employing me professionally will offer, and that my acceptance of this office instead of being a prejudice to me in my profession will be considered as giving me an additional claim to such employment. On these grounds therefore I have not thought myself at liberty to refuse an offer made to me under circumstances highly flattering in other respects.[43]

The letter was classic Arthur, justifying in exquisite detail a decision that might be construed as self-serving—which it certainly was. For his part, Grenville accepted defeat graciously, wishing Arthur and Richard well.[44] There were those in the Grenville camp, however, who were not as generous. William Fremantle, in writing to Buckingham, expressed his opinion quite clearly: "One of the things which has hurt me most in this whole business, is the conduct of Lord Wellesley—I am really quite vexed when it came across me; it disgusts one with mankind."[45] Wellesley felt badly about separating himself from his old friend. Writing to his son nearly a month later, he was still trying to convince himself: "The Grenvilles, I suppose, are as angry with me as I ought to have been long ago with them: *n'importe,* the whole world now acknowledges that it was impossible for me to take any other part than I have taken."[46]

The Wellesleys then became the focus of political attack from some on the opposition benches. Despite the marquess's reluctance to take office, the Wellesleys clearly had become a potent political force, like the Grenvilles but without pocket boroughs and a rich family tradition. Such success aroused suspicion and jealousy, and it frustrated those eager to humiliate the marquess in the House of Commons. The result was not only a lot of spiteful and sometimes malicious gossip but also a resolve by the most hostile towards the marquess to keep the India question open for as long as possible. They knew they could not win—in fact, they knew they could not come close to winning—but they could make life miserable for the prickly marquess simply by stretching out the proceedings.

Wellesley hoped the parliamentary session of that summer would bring a successful termination to the charges against him. Other business held sway, however, putting off the inevitable until the following year. On 9 February 1808, in a carefully planned attack, Lord Folkestone rose in the Commons to open the debate on Oudh initiated by Paull in 1805. After a long and critical speech, the diarist Thomas Creevey moved that the documentary evidence was so voluminous and so complex that referral to a committee was required. The strategy was obvious, especially to the Wellesleys: to prolong the agony. Arthur rose in defense of his brother, stating that

> it had always been his wish, and that of all the friends of the noble marquis, that the house should come to a decision with

> as much speed as was consistent with due consideration. His noble relation was in a most unpleasant situation. Four years had now elapsed [an exaggeration] since the subject was first introduced, and it was nearly two years since the noble lord had moved for papers. It must be painful to the feelings of any individual to have such charges hanging over his head for an indefinite length of time; and the consequences which he thought would be likely to proceed from appointing a committee would be, that the house would be four years longer before it came to a decision.[47]

The debate continued without resolution until suspended for a fortnight, when it resumed only to be suspended again without resolution. On this occasion, Pole impatiently interjected, "was it forgotten that it had been in discussion repeatedly, ever since 1805."[48] But Creevey persisted. "He did not care," he claimed unconvincingly, "how that committee was formed. He had no objection that the three brothers of the noble marquis should be members of it."[49] On 15 March 1808, Sir John Anstruther, one of the Wellesley parliamentary family, challenged Creevey and forced a vote.[50] The resolution was decisively rejected, and Anstruther then moved, "That it appears to this house, that the marquis Wellesley, in carrying into execution the late arrangements in Oudh, was actuated by an ardent zeal for the public service, and by the desire of providing more effectually for the prosperity, the defense, and the safety of the British territories in India." The motion passed with an overwhelming majority of 180 to 29.

Thwarted in their efforts, Wellesley's antagonists moved to plan B; on 17 May, Sir Thomas Turton introduced a motion of censure over Wellesley's actions in the Carnatic. The debate proceeded in much the same fashion as the previous one but attracted far less interest. There would be a hundred fewer members in the house to follow what was clearly seen as a vendetta. Again the brothers rallied to their patron.[51] As the debate continued, the opposition wondered why no one from the government had bothered to defend Wellesley. With this, Castlereagh stood and condemned those who persisted in recklessly attacking the honor and integrity of a government official. To his mind, the question had long been decided; what was occurring amounted to the humiliation of Parliament itself. When put to a vote, the motion went down to defeat 15 to 124; a motion approving

Wellesley's actions in the Carnatic carried 98 to 19. With that the proceedings came to a close.[52] The decisive votes explain the puzzlement of Wellesley's allies at his extreme sensitivity to the charges: everyone knew that the debate was going nowhere.

Meanwhile, Lord Wellesley's private life turned sordid. He and Hyacinthe had moved into the more spacious quarters of Camelford House. The larger the house, the less likely they were to run into one another; they communicated largely through notes and third parties. Only at dinner did they spend time together, but even then there was very little to talk about. Each complained that the other was neither sensitive nor attentive to the needs of the other. Hyacinthe, strong willed and temperamental, would not give in, insisting that as she had deferred to Richard for the duration of their marriage, now it was his turn. Richard, driven by vanity, could not imagine anyone's emotional and physical needs being greater or more important than his own. He refused to meet Hyacinthe on her turf. There were times when they had to meet, such as arranging their daughter Anne's marriage to Sir William Abdy. Even the marriage brought no joy to the marquess, who had to come up with £11,000 for her dowry.[53]

Throughout 1806 and 1807, Wellesley's animosity and petulance grew as he attended to his self-image both in Parliament and in the toilette. He purchased Apsley House from Lord Bathurst in 1807 for £16,000—which was £4,000 less than the asking price two years earlier, when Hyacinthe had explored the possibility—and hired James Wyatt to make renovations. Towards the end of 1807, after a particularly bitter exchange with Hyacinthe, he left Camelford House and went to stay with the Poles. Arthur and Henry, who had infants in their houses, could not provide appropriate and convenient refuge. Talk began of legal separation. When the lease ran out on Camelford House, with Apsley House not ready, a small house was leased for Hyacinthe while the marquess moved into a hotel. At this point, Wellesley's behavior took a turn. Out of spite or lust, Wellesley took up with a courtesan named Sally Douglas.

Wellesley's indulgence grew into obsession; he was seen everywhere with her. Nothing is known about her, but it could be that she belonged to Harriette Wilson's circle. Wellesley's infidelity amused much of London society but not all, and certainly not some of the new Tories. Hyacinthe saw Sally Douglas as nothing more than a whore "dragged from the mud of the London streets." Though the relationship probably started as a means to punish Hyacinthe, it came to dominate Wellesley's life, and he did not use good judgment in pursuing the affair. Hyacinthe counterattacked by telling Richard that he had become a laughingstock. "Up till now," she wrote, "I have refrained with great care, from telling you of your reputation for debauchery and the jokes that are made about it."[54] Even if she exaggerated, Wellesley had become the subject of gossip that continued long after he ceased such ill-judged public behavior.

The brothers worried that the marquess might destroy his career and compromise their own. As men on the rise, they wanted Richard to get on with his political life. Arthur and William had grown close. Together they had toured Ireland in the summer of 1806 and afterwards corresponded regularly when separated. Whether William recognized the future in Arthur and was backing his hunch, one can only speculate. But they had a genuine affection for one another. The same could be said for Richard and Henry. As for Gerald, everyone loved him. All the brothers were closely connected, and they must have discussed Richard's behavior. They were not above moralizing. Lady Longford quotes a letter to Arthur from William in which he comments, "Sydenham was discovered viewing Blenheim the other day with a whore—they went by the names of Mr. and Mrs. Thompson—O the Profligacy of the Age!!!" This smacks of hypocrisy, given that gossip once surrounded both William and his wife. Whether Pole was bothered by the fact that Sydenham was in the company of a courtesan or that he was *seen* in her company remains unknown, but one has to suspect the latter. The same would hold true with Arthur, whose life in India was attended by gossip and who was acquainted with Harriette Wilson. To these men, discretion was the name of the game. Arthur would always be discreet in his adulterous relationships, whether he needed to be or not. Which brings us back to the point that the brothers worried that Wellesley—not the wretched Paull—would be the architect of his own demise.

In the public arena, events on the Continent were conspiring to provide another stage on which the brothers might act together. In 1806 and 1807, the emperor Napoleon followed up his great victory at Austerlitz by running roughshod over the Prussians and Russians. He occupied Berlin and in the summer of 1807 met with Tsar Alexander to carve Europe into spheres of influence. Napoleon's Berlin Decrees of the previous year (closing European ports to British trade, with Russia's cooperation) seemed a real threat. The new foreign secretary, George Canning, also learned of Napoleon's intent to take Denmark, along with the powerful Danish fleet, into his sphere of influence. Since Trafalgar, Britain had not considered a French invasion feasible, because France lacked the requisite fleet. The Danish fleet might supply the means. Under the circumstances, Canning opted for a preemptive strike. Admiral James Gambier assembled a fleet along with an invading force commanded by Lord Cathcart.

Arthur had been in Dublin since the middle of April, and he was mired in innumerable requests for patronage. He had become reacquainted with Irish issues and the challenges of ruling an alien land. The aggravation of Ultra Protestants, the innate unfairness of the tithe, the problem of absentee landlords, and defense against a potential French invasion all came to the fore in just two months. Then came word that the government planned an expedition to the Continent; Arthur wasted not a second in telling Castlereagh that he would not be left out. At the end of June, he was back in London, protecting his interest in the upcoming expedition. The nature of this expedition remained secret; Arthur kept even Kitty in the dark. On 24 July 1807, he formally requested permission from the lord lieutenant of Ireland, Charles Lennox (fourth Duke of Richmond), to take part in the expedition, and on the 31st he sailed aboard HMS *Prometheus* as a brigade commander.

The army landed on 16 August and besieged Copenhagen. Cathcart selected Arthur to cut off a relieving militia force, which he managed with dispatch. Bombardment of Copenhagen ensued, and while not done in earnest, it provided reason for surrender on 5 September. As part of a commission of three, Arthur negotiated the terms. Although this action was little more than a skirmish, Lady Longford contends that it was important for Arthur because he became associated with service on the Continent.[55] This seems an exaggeration. Not only was the engagement trivial, but Arthur's selection as chief secretary proved that he was already being taken seriously. He was back in England on 30 September and in Dublin in October.

The only thing that had changed in Ireland was another rumor of imminent invasion, which had little effect on Arthur's routines—for routine they were, and they bored him. There would be distractions. Kitty gave birth to their second son, Charles, on 16 January 1808, and the following April brought promotion to lieutenant general, making

Arthur Wellesley the youngest general in the army. Arthur returned to London in February to take part in the debates on the Copenhagen expedition, the occasion on which Richard emerged from political hibernation to speak for over an hour. That this would be the occasion should come as no surprise. Arthur had figured prominently at Copenhagen and what was good for Arthur was good for Great Britain and, more important, for the family. Richard spoke only when personal interests were at stake, and he did so in a measured, careful style, without the flourish of a Pitt or a Fox but effectively. Wellesley always had command of the facts and presented them in clear and cogent fashion, buttressing a vigorous argument. In this case, he expressed incredulity that anyone could doubt the wisdom of the government's decision. He put to rest doubts over the legality and morality of capturing the Danish fleet, outlining with stark clarity Napoleon's designs, the means he possessed to accomplish them, the concurrence of Denmark, and the imminent danger that threatened Britain.[56] The result of the debate was never in doubt. The government received overwhelming endorsement; the army and navy, the thanks of the nation.

This was good for Richard and for Arthur. For Richard it demonstrated that he had gotten over his guilt for splitting with the Grenvilles and was ready to reenter politics. His personal life remained problematic, but his political course seemed set. It rested on the belief that the war against France had to be fought with vigor. On this the brothers spoke as one, and as one they recognized that only in the remnants of Pitt's party could their point of view find a comfortable home. The old Whigs, whom the Grenvilles had joined, were too mixed a bag. For Arthur, Parliament's endorsement of the Copenhagen expedition confirmed for him that the country had not tired of the war. For a man anxious to pursue his military career, this was good news. He had had enough of political life.

With the will to war established, what remained was opportunity. This had been the problem for policy makers since the onset of the war in 1793. Where and how would Britain engage the French with some chance of success on the Continent? Pitt and Grenville had never come to grips with the constraints on British war policy, among them that the British army was and would always be substantially fewer in number than the French, let alone the French army in alliance with others and that even if a respectable army could be assembled, delivering it to and supplying it on the Continent would be a logistical nightmare. Consequently, Pitt and Grenville had dabbled,[57] leaping before looking into whatever limited opportunity presented itself. Their efforts were designed to support the actions pursued by one continental ally or another and failed to live up to expectations. The Copenhagen expedition had succeeded because it was limited in scope and had merely tried to deprive Bonaparte of an additional resource. Under Grenville's Ministry of All the Talents, military expeditions to Egypt, Calabria, and South America had all come to naught.

Thwarted in Denmark and always restless, Napoleon had turned his attention to Iberia, where he wanted to close Portuguese ports and seize the Portuguese fleet. In the autumn of 1807, when General Jean-Andoche Junot marched an army across Spain into Portugal with that object in mind, Great Britain could do nothing to save its old ally, but it could save the fleet and the monarchy. The British ambassador, Percy Smythe (sixth Viscount Strangford), persuaded the Portuguese king, João VI (regent at the time), to take flight along with his court and his fleet, under British protection, to Brazil. When Junot entered Lisbon on 30 November, he found an empty palace, an empty treasury, and an empty harbor; the king and his court had sailed away the day before. Once again Canning had deprived Napoleon of a naval prize, but that was small consolation. France controlled the coastline of Europe from Naples to St. Petersburg, leaving Britain no opportunity for military engagement. Arthur Wellesley would have to wait.

9

Toil and Trouble

Eighteen hundred and eight found the Wellesleys on firmer ground. Richard, relieved of the threat from Paull, began to address his political future. William sat in Parliament and occupied a secretary's seat at the Admiralty, Arthur served as chief secretary to Ireland, Gerald thrived with his rich living in Chelsea, and Henry, in the Commons for Eye, filled a comfortable position as a secretary of the treasury. That the whole family had been well accommodated was not lost on some partisan observers. The Wellesleys were proving an easy bunch to dislike, and there were those, especially in the radical opposition, who were eager to knock them down a rung or two. The months ahead would provide that opportunity.

The family's attentions shifted in 1808 from Richard to Arthur, who found himself again on the field of battle. Having made clear to the Duke of Richmond, Castlereagh, and the Duke of York his desire to be considered in any and all plans for military engagement, he waited on an opportunity. It came in the spring of 1808 when South American revolutionary General Francisco Miranda arrived in London to solicit British assistance against the Spanish in Venezuela. Canning, eager to strike a blow against Napoleonic France, no matter how indirect, took up the challenge, and in June Arthur found himself in command of 9,000 troops destined for South America. This was hardly the theater of operations he had hoped for; unenthusiastic about fighting for a revolutionary cause, he accepted the assignment as better than nothing. But as these decisions were being made, events in the Iberian Peninsula took a dramatic turn. Napoleon, in orchestrating the invasion of Portugal, contemplated the political reform of Spain. Though Spain was his ally, Napoleon viewed Charles IV's monarchy with contempt and considered the government unreliable at best. Consequently, he filtered French troops into Spain on the heels of Junot's passage to Portugal. When troop levels approached 100,000, he dispatched Marshal Joachim Murat with an army of 40,000 troops to Madrid. Before Murat's arrival, a palace coup on behalf of Crown Prince Ferdinand deposed Charles IV in the hope of staving off occupation. This made little difference to Napoleon, who viewed Ferdinand as no better than his father. In the confusion that followed the coup d'etat, Napoleon summoned both Ferdinand and Charles to a meeting in Bayonne. There Charles IV surrendered his rights to the throne, and Ferdinand, intimidated by the emperor, followed suit. By the Treaty of Bayonne, signed by Spain's leading noblemen, all those in the line of succession likewise renounced their claims. Napoleon installed his brother Joseph as the new king.

Six weeks later, simmering hostility towards the new arrangement erupted in violent revolt on the streets of Madrid. Murat ruthlessly suppressed the uprising (the events of which are brilliantly memorialized by Francisco Goya), but Dos de Mayo became a signal to the rest of Spain, and people took to the streets in towns, villages, and hamlets. The enthusiasm for resistance subsequently grew when the Spanish forced the surrender of Henri Pierre Dupont's army at the battle of Baylen. Across Spain, junta governments emerged to organize and coordinate resistance to the French.

Such unprecedented popular defiance of French power aroused interest in Britain, where the *Times* suggested that the government could not stand by idly.[1] It was a bandwagon on which most were eager to ride, government and opposition M.P.'s alike. On 6 June, two representatives from the province of the Asturias arrived in London to solicit assistance, followed in July by one from Portugal. With Spain up in arms and Portugal cut off by the insurrection, the requests were too tempting for the Portland government to ignore. Caught in a wave of emotional enthusiasm for the beleaguered Iberians, the government ordered Arthur to prepare for a Portuguese expedition.

The decision enraged Miranda, but the government had little choice, as the *Times* impatiently pointed out:

> Never was there a period when the way to immortal honor and permanent security lay so open to the councils of this country, as it does at the present; and most anxiously do we wish that we may adequately avail ourselves of so favorable a juncture. But let us be fully aware, that it is not merely by praising the Spaniards, or stigmatizing their Oppressor, that we can support their cause—a cause the most glorious in the defense of which man ever bled: no, if they fight the enemy of every human right, we must fight him too, or we cannot hope either to partake of their glory or promote their success.[2]

Arthur found himself, as he had many years earlier, the beneficiary of a fortuitous change in course, though he and his brothers would hardly think so by autumn. The new orders provided Arthur with the opportunity he had desperately sought since his return—a campaign against the French on the European continent. Here was a new stage upon which the Wellesley troupe might perform. While the task gave him pause, Arthur addressed it with the vigor of his days in India. The nine thousand soldiers, assembled in Cork, would form the main body of his force, and to it would be added five thousand under the command of Sir Brent Spencer. Although this seems a modest operation, Arthur voiced no complaint. To the contrary, he knew that the army in Cork consisted of first-rate soldiers, well trained and well disciplined. There were, however, some danger signs that escaped him. The government's decision resulted less from forethought and long-term planning than a simple need to do something. Amid the hubbub lurked indecision, a fact reflected in the decision to leave Arthur in his capacity as chief secretary. The fact that no one suggested Arthur give up the post as chief secretary implies that either his command was seen as temporary or hopes for the expedition were not high. That Arthur, whose sensitivity to such things was keen, did not understand this is hard to believe. Regardless, John Wilson Croker served in his stead as chief secretary, and Arthur attended to his Irish duties as best he could throughout the campaign. One measure of his maturity is the fact that, even while caught up in the excitement and challenge of the campaign, he found time and interest for Irish affairs.

Arthur embarked on 12 July, heading first for Corunna and then Oporto. In both places he found high excitement. At Oporto he addressed issues of logistics and supply, and he made arrangements for a Portuguese force to join him for the march on Junot. He then sailed to confer with Admiral Sir Charles Cotton on a secure place to land. They chose Mondego Bay, north of Lisbon. At this point, the government's confusion caught up with him. Castlereagh sent word that owing to intelligence suggesting that Junot occupied Portugal with far greater numbers than was first thought, the invasion force would be doubled in size. In practical terms, this meant more generals, the list of which found Arthur on the bottom in order of seniority. Commanding would be Sir Hew Dalrymple with Sir Harry Burrard as his second.

This situation sounded much like his supercession in India, and therefore one can imagine Arthur's anger and frustration on receipt of the news. Still, he was no longer the young officer who sulked when superceded by Baird; instead, he forged ahead in hope of engaging Junot before his superiors arrived on the scene. The army disembarked beginning 1 August and on the 10th marched towards Lisbon. At Roliça on 17 August, Wellesley met General Henri de Laborde's four thousand troops, dispatched by Junot to delay the British advance. Laborde offered stiff resistance but in the end retreated with heavy losses. Arthur knew this to be merely a preliminary engagement: Junot's main army awaited, but so did four thousand British reinforcements and Sir Harry Burrard. These troops made their way to shore in the course of the next three days, and on the evening of the 20th, Sir Arthur met Sir Harry. Burrard listened to Arthur's plans to move on Junot but, aware that Sir John Moore was on his way with additional reinforcements, ordered Arthur to wait.

This might have been the end of Wellesley's active command had not Junot intervened. The French commander had marched his army from Torres Vedras and on the dawn of 21 August stood in front of Arthur's left flank at Vimeiro. Wellesley subsequently repositioned his army, and when the vaunted French columns advanced, he countered with disciplined lines of British infantry and administered a sound thumping to the inept Junot. By noon the French had opted for flight, and Arthur turned to Burrard for permission to pursue. Sir Harry responded with an emphatic No! In his defense, he had not a clue what was going on or what the disposition of the French army might be. Nor did he have much appreciation for Arthur's abilities. One wonders why Arthur even bothered to ask. He had the ability and the imagination to deprive his otiose commander of any choice. But that is beside the point. Arthur could only lament a lost opportunity. Still, he had won a battle; he had beaten the French. On the 22nd, he wrote to William with unabashed enthusiasm and appreciation for his good fortune:

> We gave the French an unmerciful beating yesterday. Sir Harry Burrard arrived on the evening of the 20th, & I did every thing in my power to induce him to march on; which he resisted till he should be reinforced by Moore; a decision with which I was not pleased any more than I was with the manner in which it was made. Sir Harry did not come on shore that night; & as I am the 'Child of Fortune' & Sir Harry did not chuse to march towards the Enemy, the Enemy came to us with his whole force & attacked us in our position; & we gained a most compleat Victory; Sir Harry not being in the field till one of the attacks was compleatly beaten off, & the other begun & all the dispositions made for defeating it.[3]

While Wellesley fought, London anxiously awaited news. The euphoria of the send-off had been replaced by a pessimism born of years of disappointments. The *Times* reminded its readers, "The public anxiety to hear some account of the progress of Sir Arthur Wellesley hourly increases. Those who are unacquainted with the real strength of the French force at Lisbon confidently speculate upon the immediate surrender of Junot. We are not of this opinion. Junot is an officer of great energy and decision, and will most probably defend himself to the utmost. He has had sufficient time to render his position very formidable, and to provide the means of a vigorous and protracted defense."[4]

The news of Vimeiro finally reached London the first week of September; not surprisingly, enthusiastic celebration followed. Arthur's victory contrasted vividly with previous expeditions in which even the occasional success, such as Copenhagen, either had been tainted by controversy or had seemed inconsequential. With Vimeiro, everything seemed right. The public were united on the goal, and the victory had been achieved over the French rather than one of their surrogates.

To the surprise of some, attached to the victory was the sepoy general, Lieutenant General Sir Arthur Wellesley, K.B.; he had proved himself worthy by fighting and winning on European soil.

The family had followed events closely. Richard received regular intelligence on the campaign and had kept Kitty informed along with his brothers.[5] The eldest, in fact, took great delight in Arthur's "most glorious and splendid success" because he saw it as an affirmation of them all. "The enthusiasm of this Country in his [Arthur's] favor is not to be described," he wrote smugly to his son, "& the discovery is at length made, that some advantage is to be derived from the employment of those intriguing knaves the Wellesleys in the Public service."[6] The gloat would be short-lived.

Sir Hew Dalrymple strode onto the scene on 22 August, superceding Sir Harry. It was the one-eyed leading the blind. With neither man predisposed to taking risks, and with the battle having been fought and won, Dalrymple proceeded to negotiate an armistice with Junot's representative, General François Kellerman. The terms, which were later ratified as a convention, the so-called Convention of Cintra, left Great Britain in control of Portugal while providing for the evacuation of the French army and its baggage on British ships. These terms were negotiated exclusively by Dalrymple and Kellerman, though Sir Hew asked Arthur to comment and in the end it was Arthur who signed the armistice for Great Britain. Dalrymple ratified the final convention on 31 August. Arthur knew instinctively that the convention signaled trouble, but he wrote to his friend Malcolm, "I must say that I approve of allowing the French to evacuate Portugal, because I see clearly that we cannot get them out of Portugal otherwise."[7] At this point, his mind was fixed on his supercession, not the consequences of Cintra.[8]

Arthur, however, was a quick study, and he came to realize that his name had come to be attached not to a victory but to an embarrassing peace. "I have only to regret that I put my name to an agreement of which I did not approve and which I did not negotiate," he moaned to Malcolm. "If I had not done it, I really believe that they would not have dared to make such a convention as they have made."[9] On this he was mistaken. The convention, as he had recognized, was inevitable, and to protest it in the face of his superiors would not have been worth the risk to his career. But his views on his superiors had turned from indifference to disgust, and in a letter to William, he pulled no punches: "These People are really more stupid & incapable than any I have yet met with."[10]

The convention hit London like a bomb. Euphoria turned to rage in the wink of an eye. Regardless of the logical basis for the terms and the fact that Britain had achieved its immediate goals, the public concluded that the army had been hoodwinked and called for heads to roll. So loud were these cries that the government prepared to launch lifeboats: the generals could go down with their ship alone! Sir Hew, Sir Harry, and Sir Arthur were recalled to face a court of inquiry. "This Convention must be directly ours, or our commanders'," an outraged Canning declared. "We must judge them—or the public will judge us."[11]

This abrupt reversal of fortune shocked the Wellesleys, but they allowed themselves no time to mourn. Instead they mobilized their resources for Arthur's defense just as they had done for Richard. The marquess sensed disaster and steeled himself for the onslaught. With his gift for hyperbole, he explained to his son, "It is yet impossible to know to what course the conduct of the gov't may drive me. But you will have anticipated my determination never to abandon the cause of my brother, who has saved Portugal, & is now to be sacrificed to those who have undone the consequences of his victories. Such a cause never existed in the world, & you may be assured that I shall not relinquish it, for the sake of sheltering the gov't or any other person."[12] The lesson he had learned from his own problems was that friends could not always be counted on when political careers were at stake, and in this case he could see that the government did not know which way to turn. Energized by all that had transpired, he allowed his excitement to steer him towards the inevitable self-congratulation that had become a large part of his character. "Your entrance into public life will of course be made under the auspices of your Father," he wrote to young Richard with not just a little bit of hubris, "and no dishonor or disgrace can fall upon you for acting under his opinions, & together with the whole body of his family, who never take a step without the opinion of their chief."[13]

Arthur arrived back in London on 5 October bewildered but calm. "I don't know whether I am to be hanged, drawn & quartered, or roasted alive," he wrote to Richard. "However I shall not allow the Mob of London, to deprive me of my temper or my spirits; or of the satisfaction which I feel in the consciousness that I acted right."[14] The convention and Arthur's role in it dominated newspapers and public conversations, and before long, political partisanship raised its ugly head. Dalrymple and Burrard were variously quoted as attributing the agreement to Arthur, who in turn refused to be drawn into the discussion. This is not to suggest that nerves did not beset Arthur. While he wisely avoided public debate, he wrote to all his friends providing lengthy descriptions of the negotiations leading to the convention and his role in them. These letters, all similar, betray great anxiety.[15] Then, to everyone's shock, he left London for Dublin in his capacity as chief secretary. This was a shrewd move, but it unnerved his brothers, especially William. No sooner had Arthur departed than Pole sent a letter after him stating that on good authority he knew that Dalrymple was laying full responsibility at Arthur's feet. The brothers wanted him back. "No person can act for you in this affair," pleaded William; "you must conduct your case yourself." Richard chimed in, "I . . . entirely concur with William in the necessity of your immediate return to London." He added, "Sir Hew's line of conduct is so extraordinary, that it is impossible for any other person than yourself to meet it."[16] Pole followed up with lengthy letters offering advice for Arthur's defense and again urging his return. William's panic must have seemed mildly amusing to Arthur, perhaps even suggesting that things were not as bad as he had thought.

As news filtered in and the public tried to make sense of all that had transpired, sentiment against Arthur grew. Throughout the last days of October until the convening of the court of inquiry, the Wellesleys found their most ardent allies in a surprising quarter, the Grenvilles—Buckingham, his son Richard (Lord Temple), Lord Grenville, et al. The brothers were taken aback by such uncommon political generosity, and the marquess in particular was much affected by it. Clearly, however, the Grenvilles were reacting to what they perceived as an injustice rather than to the old friendship. In any case, Buckingham's correspondence provides vivid descriptions of how each of the Wellesleys responded to the new crisis. "H. Wellesley," Buckingham is told in poetic terms, "is still in the country, and is taken ill on this business; his fibre is of the most irritable nature, and he cannot bear up against this severe stroke upon his family importance, who were sailing before the wind with every sail set, and have struck almost in the harbour's mouth." Henry apparently saw his own future on the line. As for William, his nerves and intemperate personality led to "cursing and swearing, and talking over it to every body." Not surprisingly, he could not avoid his own judgment on Arthur's role, stating pointedly that Arthur was "wrong to have signed these preliminaries." Pole, throughout his life, had the irritating habit of judging the decisions of others when he never had to make any of public consequence. The marquess, we are told, "bears up very well; his present view of things is to make a *pièce justicatif* of the whole of Sir Arthur's case; and if Lord Castlereagh refuses to give it to the King, that he will himself."[17] In the midst of all this, the marquess still found time for his paramour, spending much time at his love nest in Ramsgate.

Arthur's weakness and his strength lay in the fact that as chief secretary for Ireland, he was a member of government. This meant that even if the fires of public criticism on his role in the Cintra matter became hot, to jettison him out of political expediency would be difficult. If that did happen, however, his career as an officer and a politician would be much compromised. The fact that the marquess was not a member of government allowed him room to maneuver. He knew that those who viewed his family as "intriguing knaves" were eager to sink their political teeth into this wounded flesh. Samuel Whitbread spoke what was probably the most common sentiment among members of the opposition when he said, "I grieve for the opportunity that has been lost of acquiring national glory, but am not sorry to see the Wellesley pride a little lowered."[18] But then there were those such as William Cobbett who truly detested the family. "Now we have the rascals on the hip," he exulted; "It is evident that he [Arthur] was the prime cause—the only cause—of all the mischief, and that from the motive of thwarting everything *after he was superseded.* Thus do we pay for the arrogance of that damned infernal family. But it all comes at last *to the House of Commons.*"[19] To combat such sentiment, Richard would rally his friends in Parliament and then lean on the government to make certain that neither of Arthur's careers was threatened. The fact that Richard was still outside the government gave him more leverage than if he were in it, since ministers courted him. Regardless, Wellesley stood on dangerous ground; if he failed to influence the government, then he and all his brothers would find themselves on the outside looking in. In short, this was a high-stakes game being played out in the last months of 1808.

The court of inquiry sat from 14 November to 22 December. What was said behind closed doors and how the government developed a strategy for inquiry are unknown, but the Wellesley interests prevailed;

the court adopted procedures whereby all parties would receive a full hearing. Confident that if Arthur told his story in full there would be no problem, the brothers had urged precisely this. Pole delivered the good news on 28 October, leaving Arthur confident.[20] The brothers attended the hearings only when they had to, and when they ended, Arthur set off to Dublin to resume his work there.

The court's decision exonerating all concerned came on 22 December, and its report followed in January. This was an innocuous document that Arthur greeted with unexpected contempt. To his mind, it did not do him justice. "I shall say nothing of the opinions it contains, as they, like colours, are now matters of taste," he wrote to family friend John Villiers, "but as far as it respects me, the evidence is falsely reported, garbled, or represented in false colours."[21] Similar notes went to his other friends. Still Arthur acknowledged that he had emerged with his honor and reputation restored. Even the press, which he had condemned at every opportunity, he saw as treating him in the end with justice. The brothers had again weathered a great political storm, and the following year found them more confident than ever.

Arthur returned to London in January to take his seat in the Commons, joining William and Henry; Richard took his in the Lords. Together they awaited debates on the Portuguese campaign of the previous summer and the inevitable questions that would come from the opposition benches. Events intervened to deflect public interest from the Convention of Cintra: one concerned developments in Spain and the other a scandal at the Horse Guards. In the Peninsula, events had taken an ominous turn. Command of the British expeditionary force had fallen to Sir John Moore. Moore, along with Arthur, was one of the rising stars in the British officer corps, and his appointment received Arthur's hearty endorsement. The unfortunate Moore promptly found himself engaged in a hopeless campaign in Spain. On the surface at least, he had inherited a favorable military situation. The Spanish victory at Baylen and the evacuation of French forces from Portugal had placed the French on the defensive. Thus, Moore entered Spain to join in a broad Spanish offensive.

Cooperation proved a difficult task: the Spanish were hard pressed to coordinate their own activities, and Spanish leaders, though enthusiastic, often lacked good judgment and were given to exaggeration. Even when Napoleon, alarmed at the course of events in the Peninsula, marched an additional 100,000 soldiers into Spain, the

Spanish remained supremely confident. The British representative to the Supreme Junta, John Hookham Frere, added to the problem. Frere zealously urged Moore into Spain, believing that a combined Anglo-Spanish force could halt Napoleon's advance. Much less sanguine, an agitated Moore wrote to Frere, "The movement I am making is of the most dangerous kind. I not only risk to be surrounded at any moment by superior forces, but to have my communications intercepted with the Galicias. I wish it to be apparent to the whole world . . . that we have done everything in our power in support of the Spanish cause, and that we do not abandon it until long after the Spaniards abandoned us."[22]

In spite of all his foreboding, Moore advanced through Salamanca to Valladolid. Napoleon, realizing that Moore had greatly overextended himself against overwhelming odds, ordered the French army northwards to crush the British. Moore, in turn, seeing the danger to which he had exposed his army, beat a hasty retreat to Corunna, where preparations had been made for the army's evacuation. Napoleon led the pursuit as far as Astorga, where Marshal Nicolas Soult took command. After a tortuous retreat, Moore arrived in Corunna and, while waiting for the fleet, gave battle to Soult. Soult was repulsed, but the British army sailed out of Corunna without its commander; Sir John Moore died in battle on 16 January 1809.

The Moore expedition left the British public doubting the future of the country's involvement in Spain. Gone was the dream of a quick, decisive Anglo-Spanish victory over France, and with it the enthusiasm of the previous summer. The political response mirrored the public response. Before the battle of Corunna, the opposition had been prepared to support the war; after Corunna, few of their number believed that the war could be won. The returning soldiers from Sir John Moore's army only reinforced this pessimism with graphic descriptions of Spanish cowardice and Anglophobia.

With good cause, then, the Portland ministry girded itself for an attack on the Convention of Cintra and the government's overall peninsular policy when Parliament convened. Yet Cintra disappeared as an issue with little discussion and still less controversy attending it. On 23 January, Liverpool, in the House of Lords, moved a vote of thanks "to lieut. gen. Sir A. Wellesley, K.B. for the Skill, valour, and ability displayed by him on the 17th and 21st of August, and particularly on the latter day, in the Battle of Vimiero."[23] In response, the opposition offered an amendment to include Sir Harry Burrard in the thanks. The house rejected the amendment and followed in unanimous assent, Lord Wellesley's vote among them, for the original motion. Two days later in the Commons, Castlereagh introduced a similar motion dressed in profuse praise for Arthur, who as he sat listening, recognized an ally. Again the opposition sought to include Sir Harry, and again they failed. When the thanks passed, Arthur rose to express gratitude, and all appeared to be over.[24] In part this was attributable to the fact that public attention was focused on an investigation into the Duke of York's management of the Horse Guards and the corrupt sale of offices through his unscrupulous mistress, Mary Anne Clark. The scandal had all the necessary elements to dominate public discourse for the next several months—sex, money, and the royal family—and in some ways it proved a godsend for the government. Still, there was the Moore campaign to answer for, and the debates concerning that would be difficult.

The government attempted to control the discussion by introducing votes of thanks to Sir John Moore and his army, first in the House of Lords. Lord Thomas Erskine, responding for the opposition, put the government on notice that this discussion would differ from that on Vimeiro. There was no question but that Moore deserved the heartfelt thanks of the nation, but had he been well served by the government? Francis Rawdon-Hasting, second Earl of Moira, thought not: "What! did our troops go to Spain only to make their escape? What was to become of those great interests the protection of which was the greatest boon that Providence could have bestowed on a sinking country. British blood and treasure, and the invaluable lives of British officers and soldiers, had been sacrificed to no purpose, and without in the least assisting the great cause which the country had been pledged to support. . . . To what but the ignorance and incapacity of ministers were all these calamities to be attributed?"[25] And so it went. In February, Lord Henry Petty (future Marquess of Lansdowne) attacked the government on the Convention of Cintra, followed by questions concerning the government's Iberian policy in general. In the Commons, George Ponsonby accused the government of incompetence in carrying out its policy, but in an even more significant statement, he claimed the policy to be ill advised. He focused on John Hookham Frere, pointing out that Frere had no military background and that his enthusiasm for the Spanish had blinded him to the realities of their military capacities. As for the Spanish, their corrupt sociopolitical system made them unworthy of British blood.[26] Castlereagh and Canning answered at length for the government. In a bitter retort, Canning accused the opposition of lying, overgeneralization, misinformation, and rumor. Furthermore, he charged them with rank partisanship, with avoiding the truth while seeking only to discredit the government. The ideological diatribe was what he found most objectionable. "To assist the patriotic efforts of the Spanish nation was the sole object," he pointed out, "and they did not wish to inflict upon that country any change as the price of that assistance. God forbid! that we should ever be so intolerant, as to make a conformity to our own opinions the price of our assistance to others, in their efforts for national independence."[27] Within months, Canning's words would ring hollow, but for the moment they accomplished the desired end, with the government defeating the motion for an investigation with ease. Still, the political line had been clearly drawn, and the Wellesleys in turn had decided on which side their future lay.

Despite Moore's defeat and all the problems exposed by it, Lisbon remained free, and Arthur believed that Britain could hold it. With Moore dead, Baird seriously wounded, and Burrard and Dalrymple discredited, Arthur would be the obvious candidate to command if there were to be another expedition. The marquess could see this as clearly as anyone; accordingly, he became an ardent proponent of British involvement in the Peninsula. With the opposition, including the Grenvilles, staking out quite the opposite position, Richard's political future with the government was irreversible, and he began to make known that he was ready to take an active role. The change in attitude came with Arthur's defense; as that effort had proceeded towards fruition, Richard's confidence had grown. This is made clear by the abundance of speculation about how room might be made for him in the cabinet. "Now the nation looks up to Lord Wellesley," an anonymous correspondent urged, stating that "he and Mr. Hastings were the ablest men who governed India; Lord Wellesley there proved his talents as a statesman, let him then take the station to which the King calls him, and let not the nation be disappointed."[28]

The debates of January and February revealed Castlereagh as Arthur's advocate, and with peninsular matters shelved in favor of the Duke of York, the two began to talk. Sir John Moore had maintained that if Britain could not sustain a viable presence in Spain, then Portugal could not be held. This was not the case, according to

Arthur. On 7 March 1809, he sent to the minister for war a memorandum outlining his view of the defensibility of Portugal. In it he established minimum requirements: an army of twenty thousand, including four thousand cavalry, a reconstituted Portuguese army, and some semblance of resistance in Spain.[29] For Castlereagh, who certainly wanted to maintain a presence in the Peninsula, this was precisely what he wanted to hear. It became his task to convince his cabinet colleagues and to persuade the king to appoint Arthur to command.

Meanwhile rumors swirled around Richard, and where Castlereagh was Arthur's patron, Canning took the role on Richard's behalf. Wellesley was far more problematic because unless he took a seat in the cabinet without portfolio, someone would have to go to make room. Moreover, the marquess had his eye on a secretaryship of state, making the situation even more complicated. The mercurial Canning, however, had a plan. As Pitt's favorite, he had long chafed at subordination, considering himself the rightful heir to his mentor's party. Canning, however, fit the mold of British political leadership even less than Wellesley. Brilliant and ambitious, he lacked any sort of pedigree and shouldered the social burden of having an actress for a mother. Like Wellesley, he had to create his own career path. The two got along well and enjoyed one another's wit, but their personalities could not have been more different. Where Wellesley was socially reticent and relied on friends to clear the way politically, Canning was social, aggressive, and bold in all aspects of his life. He waited for no one. Consequently, he was either loved or hated with great intensity.

More to the point, by January of 1809, Canning had become impatient over his place in the Portland cabinet. He had come to see Castlereagh as his great rival and began to plot his lordship's removal. He quickly identified Wellesley as the logical replacement and set out to cultivate their longtime association. This meant altering his attitude towards Arthur and towards the war in the Peninsula. The Wellesleys were a package: take one, you take them all. As a result, Canning could not help but accept the inevitability of Arthur's assuming command in Portugal. Canning would later take credit for setting Britain on the course to victory in Iberia, but between the Convention of Cintra and Arthur's second appointment, his views are suspect.

Meanwhile, at precisely the same time that Arthur and Castlereagh discussed Portugal, and Richard and Canning discussed the cabinet, the family's attentions were once again diverted by crisis, only this time of a very personal sort. On 6 March, Henry's wife, Charlotte, ran off with Henry Paget, the future Marquess of Anglesey, creating a great scandal and equally great consternation for the family. Lady Mornington would lay responsibility for this affair on Char, whose deficiencies of character the dowager had perceptively identified in 1803. But such a conclusion is oversimplified, for by all accounts the marriage had done well until Henry's appointment to the treasury in 1807.

The appointment had come as a great relief despite the fact that he still aspired to a diplomatic career. Though jobs of this sort were not particularly demanding, Henry was ready to work and did so conscientiously. Responsibilities at the treasury combined with those of an M.P. to engage his attentions. As a result, the routines of his household changed abruptly from the first years of his marriage, when Henry had no official responsibilities and was able to spend much time with his family. He and Charlotte were separated during the day and often late into the night. Not one to sit and feel sorry for herself, Charlotte pursued a normal London social life and in the process renewed an old friendship with the dashing Paget.[30] The Cadogans and Pagets had long been close, and Charlotte and Henry had known one another since childhood. Paget's attorney described their history in this fashion: "A considerable intimacy had, for a number of years before this unfortunate transaction, existed between the families of Lord Paget and Lady Charlotte Wellesley; they met frequently, and in the words of the Noble Lord . . . their early acquaintance unhappily decided the fate of their future lives. Their intimacy too soon ripened into what they deemed friendship, and afterwards by a progress which is the calamity and curse of cases of this description, gradually and imperceptibly increasing, assumed a different appearance before the parties were aware of their real danger."[31] Char surrounded herself with friends, including Henry's brothers, to create a kind of social screen.[32] Her efforts were of no avail. The occasions where she and Paget might run into one another socially were frequent, and flirtation became romance in short order. Eventually Paget suggested that he introduce Charlotte to the pleasures of riding, which conveniently allowed them time alone. Henry, it seems, proceeded blissfully unaware of anything amiss, but he might be excused his naïveté because Paget's wife, Lady Caroline Villiers (Car for short), was equally ignorant. Then again, she must have felt something like a broodmare, having produced three sons and five daughters in twelve years. She probably had neither the time, energy, nor inclination to keep track of her husband's activities. Eventually Henry became jealous of Paget's attentions, but then Char became pregnant with her fourth child.

Paget went off to Spain to fight with Sir John Moore, and Char went into confinement. In due course, Henry heard gossip and questioned Char about Lord Paget. She declared that Paget was nothing more than "a common acquaintance" who "liked my society last year but I have no reason to believe that he thinks of me in any way that can be objectionable."[33] Henry accepted his wife's explanation, and as he turned his back on reality, the relationship bloomed again on Paget's return from Spain. Charlotte entered the relationship knowing that the risks were great. First, in cases of divorce for adultery, English law conferred custody of children on the father. Second, if Paget could not obtain his own divorce—and he had no legal grounds for one—she would be either left alone or consigned to the life of a mistress. Thus one must conclude that her passion was genuine.

On 5 March 1809, after discovering correspondence between the two lovers, Henry again challenged his wife as to the nature of her relationship with Paget. A heated argument ensued, and Henry angrily demanded she sever all contact with Paget. Subsequently, on a cold and bleak March day, an agitated Char dismissed her footman while pacing through Green Park and then hailed a hackney coach. Minutes later she called at Park Lane, where Paget joined her, and together they disappeared into the heart of London, finding refuge with Paget's former aide-de-camp, who turned his rooms over to the couple and retired to a nearby hotel. Henry soon discovered Char's absence, and together with Charles Arbuthnot he launched a search. Discovery came easily, prompting one to think that the wayward couple was eager to resolve the issue. Henry pleaded with Char to return to her family. She rejected this desperate solicitation, though not easily, for there remained a strong affection between them. Only a stronger affection for Paget kept Charlotte from returning.[34] Paget too was under pressure from friends and family to return to his wife, and like Char, he resolved not to go back.

Meanwhile, knowledge of the elopement reached every corner of London society. The *Times* even reported a duel: "It is now stated that on Monday, Lady C.W. wife of the Hon. H.W. eloped with Lord P.; this has been generally affirmed; but what has been further added, viz. that Sir A.W., the brother of the injured husband, pursued and overtook the fugitives, and that a duel between Sir A.W. and Lord P. took place, in which his Lordship was mortally wounded, is contradicted. The high rank of both families will soon cause a full disclosure of all the facts, which the relatives of both may, for the moment, be desirous to conceal. The Lady has four children; her lover a wife and eight children."[35] It did not take genius to figure out who H.W. and Lord P. were; in fact, most already knew. Harriet Cavendish wrote to her brother on 8 March, "London is full of impenetrable fog and horror at Lord Paget's elopement—he went off the day before yesterday with Lady Charlotte Wellesley. It is in every way shocking and unaccountable."[36]

At this point, the various parties became reconciled to the situation, and Henry began divorce proceedings. The first step in the process was civil litigation. Charges of criminal conversation (crim. con. for short) were entered against Lord Paget, and a trial took place on 12 May 1809 before the undersheriff of the county of Middlesex. The jury of twelve considered an award of damages to Wellesley, not the guilt or innocence of Paget, because the latter had admitted guilt by not appearing at the trial. Therefore, Wellesley's legal counsel, in a polite sort of way, attempted to portray Henry as the innocent victim of Paget's treachery and Paget as the worst sort of male predator. To this end, a series of witnesses testified to the solidity and harmony of the Wellesley marriage. In his introduction, counsel Garrow took care to use sympathetic language:

> Gentlemen, I certainly have no inclination to wound the feelings of any one, but if I had any such wish, (the contrary of which I believe you all know to be the case) if I had any propensity to indulge in such topics, the still remaining constant affection, regard and kindness, which Mr. Wellesley feels for this unfortunate Lady would have placed a restriction on my voice. I am commanded to say nothing that can give her pain; his heart is bleeding for her distresses; and however high we may look at the character of the noble Lord who is the Defendant in the case, as a public and military man, we must forget these things when we are in a court of justice.[37]

Clearly, the counsel for the plaintiff felt that only Paget's reputation as a soldier could threaten his case. Therefore, he condemned Paget for intruding upon a happy marriage, exploiting the woman in question, and leaving a wife and large family in the process. These were not the actions of an officer and a gentleman.

The defense counsel argued not to absolve Paget of guilt but rather to confine the damage. Not surprisingly, his counsel portrayed Paget as generous and kind hearted, wracked by a situation over which he had no control. The Paget he described to the jury resembled a character in a Greek tragedy, and the pain that he had inflicted was claimed to be a sort that could not be assuaged by money. "I have again," his defense counsel professed,

> the positive instructions of the Noble Lord to declare that if he could flatter himself that any pecuniary satisfaction you can award under the circumstances of this case would heal or even mitigate those pangs of which he feels himself to be the guilty author, the question of damages, as far as concerns himself, is one upon which he would feel very little solicitude, but he deems much too highly of Mr. Henry Wellesley to suppose that his future peace and comfort of mind, can in any degree depend upon this pecuniary retribution which he is this day to derive from your verdict, although an action to recover damages was a step, in point of law, he was compelled to take.[38]

This, of course, was not a view that Henry Wellesley would take. He was not in the mood to play the role of the gentleman loser.

The defense then sought to show that Paget had done everything in his power to extricate himself from the situation, even to the point of recklessly risking death on the battlefield.[39] He stood publicly humiliated; was not that punishment enough? Apparently not. The case was sent to the jury with instructions that damages were to be determined according to the class of the parties involved. Accordingly, the jury returned with a decision awarding the astronomical sum of £20,000. Equating the purchasing power of this sum with today's currency is difficult, but one might estimate it as between $250,000 and $500,000. Stunning as the award must have been to Paget, he paid promptly. If that were not enough, May ended with a challenge from the Cadogans. This time Paget obliged, and on the morning of the 30th, he and Henry Cadogan met at Wimbledon Common. The encounter left both men unscratched; Cadogan missed the mark and Paget fired harmlessly into the air.[40]

The next step was to take the case to the Church of England, and accordingly, evidence was presented before the consistory court of the bishop of London. The court granted a divorce on 7 July, but the procedure did not end there. Left still was the matter of presenting a private bill in the House of Lords to dissolve the marriage and to allow Henry to marry again. In the meantime, Paget departed for the Walcheren campaign. Alone and miserable, Charlotte appealed to Henry, who, in a strange twist, agreed to take her under his protection, stunning the Wellesley family. Writing to Pole from Portugal, Arthur stated incredulously,

> I have heard some most uncomfortable stories about Henry & Lady Charlotte respecting which principally I write to you at this present moment. I understand that she is already under his protection; & it is probable that they will soon come together again in some form or another. I don't exactly understand however how her brother who I suspect has been the instrument of bringing this about, can reconcile his feelings & notions of Honour, to allow his sister to live & perform with a Man, from whom she has been divorced by the Church, & I conclude Poor Henry will again be dragged through the Mire, & will marry this blooming Virgin again as soon as she will have been delivered of the consequences of her little amusements.[41]

Arthur tended to view the family women—including his wife—as nothing more than a burden, but he loved his brother and was concerned that Henry might do something he would regret. Above all, he hoped that Henry would have the opportunity to recover from the emotional torture of the past several months: "We ought to avoid everything," he advised William, "which can add to his misfortunes. It is certain that nothing will make him more unhappy than to have any discussion with us upon this subject, or to perceive by our looks or our manner, that we are impressed with unfavourable Opinions upon his conduct."[42]

In fact, Henry had no intention of remarrying Charlotte. He was simply a kind man who could not deal with the pain of his children being without their mother. And because she was again pregnant and depressed over being separated from her children, he must have thought that taking her under his protection in Paget's absence was logical. Her stay with Henry may have lasted for several weeks. When they separated, Henry took the unusual step of allowing his three oldest children to go with their mother. Henry did not recognize the fourth child, Gerald Valerian, as his own. Gerald was taken under the protection of Kitty Wellesley, Arthur's wife. Gerald would go on to become Queen Victoria's beloved chaplain and dean of Windsor.[43]

On 25 January 1810, Thomas de Grey (second Baron Walsingham) introduced before the House of Lords "An Act to Dissolve the Marriage of the Right Honourable Henry Wellesley with the Right Honourable Lady Charlotte Wellesley his now Wife, and to enable him to marry again, and for other purposes therein mentioned." A second reading came on 9 February, and witnesses were examined. The bill passed and received royal assent on 22 February 1810, ending Henry's ordeal.[44]

Following the conclusion of Wellesley's divorce, Paget orchestrated his own. His was a more complicated situation in that he had no grounds to divorce Car. She apparently had such grounds, but by English law only the husband could obtain a divorce on the grounds of adultery. Fortunately for Paget, Caroline was as anxious to get out of the marriage as he. She had become romantically involved with the Duke of Argyll and was ready to get on with her life rather than devote herself to the task of making Paget's miserable. The two, therefore, took advantage of Scottish law, which allowed women to institute divorce proceedings against adulterous husbands. The only requirement was that they reside in Scotland a minimum of forty days. Accordingly, Caroline and Paget took up residence there. Next, adultery had to be proved; this was generally done by hiring a prostitute and then allowing a maidservant to catch them in bed so that she might give witness. Char would have none of that and disguised herself in such a fashion that the maid could not make a positive identification of the person in bed with Paget, only that it was a woman. A Scottish court granted the much-desired divorce in October 1810.[45]

Shortly thereafter, Char and Paget were married, as were Car and the Duke of Argyll. And thus the affair, which had captured public attention even to the exclusion of the Duke of York's problems with Mary Anne Clark, ended. Ironically, despite the pain endured by the various parties, all worked out for the best. Each subsequent marriage succeeded, though Charlotte was never totally accepted by "respectable" London society. Writing to his brother a year later, Paget commented, "My Lady and I have just calculated that she has cost me

£20,000 for the 1st divorce, £10,000 for the 2nd, and £1,000 a year for Her Grace [Car]—and I must admit I find her [Char] a good and cheap bargain notwithstanding."[46]

It all made for good theater, but this was vaudeville, not the serious stage the Wellesleys sought, and it concerned and distracted them. In addition, there was to be a very practical consequence. The elopement occurred just as Arthur prepared for his second peninsular campaign, and that meant that he could not possibly call upon Paget to serve under him. This deprived him of the services of Britain's best cavalry officer for the campaign's duration. He frequently could have used a soldier of Paget's talent, initiative, and valor. When preparing for the Waterloo campaign, however, Arthur would not turn his back on Paget (then the Earl of Uxbridge). By that time, the scandal was behind them both.

While Henry attended to his personal affairs, political developments opened new opportunities for Richard and Arthur. In March, debates began in Parliament that would define the government's foreign policy agenda and alter George Canning's immediate plans to reorganize the cabinet. The debates, not surprisingly, concerned Moore's failed campaign in Spain. The opposition's efforts to embarrass the government on this in the first two months of the year had come to naught, and rightly or wrongly they concluded that the Duke of York's troubles had something to do with this. With that incident settled, opposition leaders decided to renew the debate on the Spanish campaign.

It opened in the House of Lords, where Earl Grey moved that the papers of Sir John Moore and John Hookham Frere be laid before the house. In a tactical miscalculation, Liverpool resisted and was greeted by a barrage of complaints and accusations. The opposition accepted no justification for withholding what they deemed public papers and suggested that the government tried to hide the truth. And what was the truth? Governmental negligence and Spanish incompetence topped the list. The opposition intended to revisit the whole issue of whether the government had fully understood the military situation in Spain and whether it had provided the support Moore required. Inevitably this would lead to Frere, whose uncritical support of the Spanish was seen by some as Moore's undoing. An examination of Frere's dealings with the Spanish would in turn give rise to the question of whether the Spanish were worthy allies who could be relied upon in the future. Predictably, Liverpool's efforts to obfuscate and delay collapsed, and the government made available all relevant papers. The debate then began in earnest.

For the government, the first question to be addressed was Spain itself. To fold one's tent and abandon the cause was neither a politically nor a morally acceptable choice, but clearly Britain's role as an ally had to be redefined. This process had already begun at the first of the year when a treaty of alliance had been signed. Since the onset of the war in Iberia, Spain had expected from Great Britain an unlimited supply of monetary and material aid, and Britain had hoped that Spain would make such subsidies feasible by opening its colonial trade to British commerce. The treaty that was concluded in January contained provisions for neither. Spain, jealous of its colonial trading monopoly, refused to commit to open trade unless Britain agreed to a specific yearly subsidy. Canning refused to go this far, preferring to use British aid as a lever in his negotiations. As a result, Anglo-Spanish relations would be based on vague pledges of mutual friendship and cooperation. In practical terms, this meant that in 1809, Britain's commitment would be much diminished. This would not make the Spanish happy, but for the British government, it was politically realistic.

This realism coincided with Castlereagh's decision to adopt Arthur's advice to invest the bulk of Britain's peninsular efforts into the defense of Portugal. The debate that began in March made this a rather easy policy to sell, but Castlereagh, never one to take anything lightly, spent considerable time studying the situation with Arthur. There was never any doubt in Castlereagh's mind who would command; on 26 March, the king appointed Arthur commander in chief of the British expeditionary force to Portugal. Castlereagh delivered up the following instructions a week later:

> The defense of Portugal you will consider as the first and immediate object of your attention. But, as the security of Portugal can only be effectually provided for in connexion with the defence of the Peninsula in the large sense, his Majesty, on this account, as well as from the unabated interest he takes in the cause of Spain, leaves it to your judgment to decide, when your army shall be advanced on the frontier of Portugal, how your efforts can be best combined with the Spanish, as well as the Portuguese troops, in support of the common cause. In any movements you may undertake, you

> will, however, keep in mind that until you can receive further orders, your operations must necessarily be conducted with especial reference to the protection of the country.[47]

These instructions reflected good military sense, but they were also a reaction to the troubles that had beset Moore and the debate in Parliament. First, they clearly state that Portugal would be the focus of Britain's efforts but that Spain would remain a part of the overall strategy. At the same time, Arthur, as commander in chief, was given full authority to determine when, where, and how his army would be used both in Portugal and in conjunction with a Spanish operation. In other words, a John Hookham Frere would have no authority. Moreover, by declaring Portugal the priority, Castlereagh gave Arthur justification for any decision he might make. All of these terms might have transpired in any case, but the events of March had certainly hastened them. For Arthur, things had turned out extremely well, and as he prepared to embark, the court of inquiry must have seemed a remote event indeed. His previous experience in Portugal gave him a sense of the possible. He went out with high hopes, and this time he resigned as chief secretary.

When the debate resumed in the Lords on 18 April, the opposition launched into Frere.[48] Liverpool made little attempt to defend the envoy and focused instead on trying to rescue the Spanish and the government's decision to assist them. Here he acknowledged failure but claimed that it was a failure resulting from inexperience and administrative deficiencies in Spain that could not have been anticipated. Moreover, he maintained that the government had had little choice but to do what it had done, reminding the opposition of the impatience they had shown in the summer of 1808.[49] The opposition soon discovered that they could not touch the government on its handling of the war and the decision to maintain the commitment in the Peninsula. But Frere was another matter; they gave notice first in the Lords and then in the Commons that they would move for his recall.

The government thus found itself in a difficult position. Frere had at the very least been injudicious, and he was proving difficult to defend. But allowing the opposition to dictate his recall would be bitter medicine. As a result, the government looked for a way out. Canning had an answer: send Lord Wellesley to Seville with full ambassadorial status. The prickly Spanish maintained an ambassador in London and looked for equal representation in Seville. Therefore, the government could justify Frere's recall because he could not be promoted to full ambassador, and Wellesley would go out as "special ambassador," again emphasizing Spain's importance to Great Britain. This reasoning all seems a bit spurious, but the government was grasping and this extrication seemed relatively clean. Sending Wellesley would be attended by other benefits. He was without question as experienced a person as could be found and capable of dealing with situations where lines of authority were not clear and local customs and protocol often got in the way of quick and decisive action. Spanish discontent with Britain's contracted contributions required a skilled diplomat to smooth feathers. At the same time, that person would have to encourage the Spanish to carry out the military and political reforms that would be essential to any future cooperative venture between Britain and Spain. Wellesley seemed the perfect person for such a delicate task. And then there was the obvious; he was the commander in chief's brother, and this relationship, which had been productive in India, would prevent the kind of conflict and mistrust that had plagued Moore and Frere.

All then were agreed that Wellesley should go to Spain as soon as possible. The question then became, would he go? On the surface, his acceptance of such an appointment seemed unlikely. Here was a man who for three years had been repeatedly mentioned for a leading cabinet post, a man who had filled the governor general's office for seven years. Ambassador to the Supreme Junta in Seville sounded like a demotion. But Wellesley did accept, and there were several reasons why. First, he would have a chance to put Britain's alliance with Spain on sound footing and in so doing play an important part in the first substantial British military effort against France since the war had begun in 1793. Equally important, the creation of a healthier partnership with Spain would make matters easier for Arthur in the months to come. In fact, working again with Arthur had its own attraction. The nation's focus would again be on the Wellesleys. There is no question that the marquess saw destiny on the family's side. He took great pride in what Arthur was doing and did not yet fear being surpassed by his younger brother. Cooperation would only make success inevitable, and there would be plenty of glory to share. Curiously, there is no evidence of anxiety or panic at this period of Wellesley's life. One would think that two years in political limbo would have wrecked the marquess's nerves as it had in the years leading up to the India appointment. He seems to have remained relatively steady in the face of adversity, as if he knew that he would be joining the government sooner rather than later.

No one considered Wellesley's decision to go to Seville a long-term commitment. The "special mission" status made certain of that. Most in the know assumed that the time was not yet right to bring him into the cabinet but that that time would soon come. Few knew of Canning's machinations, let alone that they had stalled: the foreign secretary had gone to Portland in March and insisted that Castlereagh be removed from the War Office and replaced with Wellesley. Portland confided in Bathurst, and together they decided that while the cabinet could not stand without Canning, neither could it withstand wholesale reorganization in the midst of a parliamentary session. They urged their impatient colleague to defer implementing his plans until Parliament had been prorogued. Canning agreed reluctantly and so informed Wellesley.[50] This was the point at which Canning conceived the idea of sending Wellesley to Spain to keep him busy and out of the way while political negotiations went forward. It must all have seemed serendipitous: Frere needed to be recalled, the embassy needed a steady hand, Canning needed time, Wellesley needed something to do. The appointment was announced on 30 April 1809 and was greeted with a positive response. "We consider the appointment as an unequivocal pledge given to the nation by Ministers that they are resolved to adopt no half measures, to pursue no system of cold or timid precaution, to leave no outlets for irresolution or vacillation," wrote the *Times*. "Lord Wellesley cannot be an instrument for such purposes; he possesses one of the cardinal virtues, fortitude, which we would at the present moment place above the others, because it is that which the necessities of the hour render indispensable."[51]

Three months would elapse before Wellesley embarked for Seville. The many reasons for this include Wellesley's efforts to arrange for a new mistress, a woman referred to simply as Miss Leslie, to accompany him. Canning would put a stop to this without much consequence but only at the last moment. The timing suggests that Miss Leslie was merely a distraction and not a cause for delay. The primary reason was Canning's continuing political intrigue, which required Wellesley's presence in London. In May, Canning had again attempted to force cabinet reorganization on the hapless Portland. This time the prime minister went to the king, who was unhappy with the idea and procrastinated. On 31 May, Canning submitted his resignation, which the king rejected. Concluding that the problem was systemic rather than personal, George III suggested redefining the responsibilities of the war and foreign offices. While this certainly could not have been what Canning had in mind, he could not dismiss it out of hand; simultaneously, Portland, with the support of Spencer Perceval (chancellor of the Exchequer), urged patience, pointing to Castlereagh's deep involvement in the planning of a major military expedition to the Scheldt estuary, the ill-fated Walcheren campaign. Forced to agree, Canning saw no further reason for the marquess to remain in London.

In addition to a confused political situation, Wellesley left behind a marriage in ruins. That two Wellesley marriages, those of the eldest and the youngest brothers, collapsed at the same time seems odd. The latter, as we have seen, ended in a shocking and abrupt fashion, while the former died a slow, tortuous death. Richard's marriage had been dysfunctional for some time and, to Hyacinthe's horror, open to public view. There can be no question here as to fault. Hyacinthe may have handled the marquess poorly, but his behavior towards her was inexcusable. He, however, never came close to acknowledging this. The relationship had begun as an intensely physical one. That Hyacinthe was beautiful and sensuous and French had seemed to make the relationship easier for Richard. In the years before India, they had been good friends who conversed easily and honestly with one another, and they seemed to have found joy. It is significant, however, that Richard waited until after the birth of his children to marry Hyacinthe; one may conclude that Hyacinthe forced the issue. Marriage changed the relationship because it changed Hyacinthe's view of life, and she became in Richard's eyes a different person. Instead of the fun and games of the years before marriage, Hyacinthe sought the domestic life, looking after home and hearth and seeing to the children. None of this interested the marquess in the slightest, and before the two could adjust to and compensate for the change, he was off to India. In the interim, Hyacinthe had nothing but domestic responsibilities, and she (much like her mother-in-law) became obsessed with her children's futures. They were, after all, illegitimate.

When Richard returned from India, he imagined returning to a relationship that could no longer exist. Carefree conversation and socialization no longer attracted Hyacinthe, and she could not understand why Richard did not see life in a similar fashion. The point is that even by eighteenth-century standards, Richard had little sense of the institution of marriage. He wanted Hyacinthe attending to his every need and agreeing with his every word. She expected compassion and serious attention to family responsibilities. This difference was aggravated by the fact that Hyacinthe was by nature a practical woman who craved financial security, while Richard had not a practical bone in his body.

Despite the contrast between them, it seems strange that they could not have arrived at an arrangement whereby they lived essentially separate lives and cohabited on a basis of civility. Such a situation would certainly not have been uncommon for the times. It could not and did not happen for two reasons: Hyacinthe's insecurity and Richard's narcissism. Hyacinthe had always had to deal with social innuendo, sometimes perpetrated by Richard's own family, that she had been a courtesan. Though this was not the case, she lived with what she considered ever-present insult. Lurking in her mind was the idea that she could be cast aside like so much trash, along with her children. This, she determined, would not happen, and it colored her attitude towards the marquess. As for Richard, he was incapable of empathy and could not imagine let alone appreciate Hyacinthe's needs. He could see only himself, and he reacted with fury when Hyacinthe did not respond to his desires or anticipate his needs. But Richard's behavior goes beyond simple spite, becoming obsession. Once he had given up on Hyacinthe, he determined to punish her, and the best instrument for this was humiliation through his public squiring of known courtesans.

The two moved into Apsley House in April 1808, and for the rest of the year, a calm descended on the marriage. They occupied entirely separate quarters—Hyacinthe and the children upstairs, Richard and his entourage downstairs. Occasionally they dined together, but only privately. Whenever Richard entertained, he banned Hyacinthe from the dining room. Domestic concerns were handled by letters delivered by maids and footmen. Like the eye of a hurricane, this truce could not last, and in 1809 the storm resumed. The issues were unchanged: women, money, and children. Richard no longer paraded his mistress through the streets of London but had removed her to Ramsgate and traveled there regularly. This infuriated Hyacinthe for obvious reasons as well as the less obvious reason that she assumed that the arrangement was costly, cutting into family resources and compromising her future security and that of her children. She could never leave this issue alone. She chastised and ridiculed Richard with a morbid obsession that almost equaled his, and it provoked a predictable response. He made no attempt at discretion and at the same time struck back at his wife by depriving her of any control over her household. He knew that this was a sensitive issue, and he went after it with a vengeance. The correspondence between the two is dominated by household issues. He controlled the disbursement of money for her monthly allowance and for miscellaneous household expenses. He paid the household staff and determined the terms of their employment. At first glance, Richard's arrangements seem generous, and one may be tempted to question Hyacinthe's complaints. Richard, of course, knew this. He avoided any hint of depriving her of support appropriate to her station in life, but he turned her into a kept woman with little control over the details of her living arrangements. She was, in other words, not unlike Sally Douglas or Miss Leslie.

So they stabbed at one another, inflicting wound upon wound with retaliation as the order of the day. The only redeeming feature of Richard's behavior was that he never placed his children in harm's way. This cannot be said for Hyacinthe, but she found herself utterly alone with no one to look to for support. London society might snicker at Richard's behavior and his family might express moral indignation, but in the end they were all on Richard's side. Hyacinthe had neither family nor friends. The Battle of Apsley House, as Iris Butler calls it, neared its conclusion on Richard's departure for Spain. From HMS *Donegal* on 24 July, he informed his wife,

> Lord Wellesley has received Lady Wellesley's letter, which has only served to confirm the sentiments, which he has long entertained, of the absolute necessity of a separate establishment for their mutual happiness, or rather for the possibility of their mutual existence. It would now be painful, as well as useless to repeat the reasons, which have led to this conclusion. It is sufficient to declare (without resorting to the unpleasant expressions so often used by Lady Wellesley) that Lord Wellesley will not and cannot continue to suffer the misery, by which he has been long afflicted, in living under the same roof with Lady Wellesley, and that he is determined for the ease & independence of both, to take the necessary steps for a separate establishment.[52]

This private drama was about to begin its last act; the great public drama, after an intermission, would begin Act II.

One wonders just how much this domestic crisis affected the Wellesleys as a group. In addition, one must consider the pressures of the previous three years: the Convention of Cintra and court of inquiry, Henry's divorce and Arthur's disappointing marriage, the attacks in Parliament, the end of the Grenville relationship, and the negotiations for cabinet office. Somehow the brothers put all of this behind them, fully aware that they constituted a force to be reckoned with. They continued to work together closely, with one imperceptible change; Arthur was beginning to make his own way.

10

The Wellesleys in Spain

The First Phase

Arthur arrived in Lisbon on 22 April 1809 to find an anxious country. After pushing Sir John Moore's army out of Spain, Marshal Soult had followed with the occupation of Oporto. In central Spain, Marshal Claude Perrin Victor, operating from a secure base, threatened the Portuguese frontier to the south; many Portuguese citizens assumed that the French would again occupy the capital. For those who had greeted Junot's defeat with delight and had collaborated with the British to that end, this was not a happy prospect. Wellesley's return, promising immediate security and a renewed British commitment to Portugal and Spain, not surprisingly gave rise to celebration. Cautiously optimistic and well acquainted with the strategic challenges that faced him, Arthur wasted little time in concluding that Victor did not pose an immediate threat to the capital and that he would strike first at Oporto. The pace and decisiveness of his activity suggest that Arthur had given the situation in Portugal serious thought and that he arrived well briefed and well prepared, just as he had done in India. His correspondence is uncluttered with the niceties that usually attend the arrival of a new commander in chief; instead, it was all business, with no time to waste. This was the opportunity he had sought—an independent command in a European campaign.

The second of May found him in Coimbra overseeing the mustering of his army of seventeen thousand and combining them with six

The Iberian Penisula, 1808–14

thousand Portuguese troops. This would be done quickly but with care. Within days he marched, arriving before the gates of Oporto on 12 May. Soult had settled into the city. Anticipating a British threat, Soult had prepared for the city's defense but not with much urgency, for he believed that the British, when they did come, would approach by sea. Such a threat did not concern him, but if it proved necessary, he would have ample time to conduct a retreat. He ordered the bridge across the Douro destroyed and all boats either sunk or confiscated and moored on the city side of the river. These tasks accomplished, he settled back to await the British, never dreaming that Arthur would come from the south.

French military intelligence failed completely, and Arthur's army arrived undetected. Sizing up the situation, Wellesley concluded that he needed to strike quickly but recognized that he faced what appeared to be an insurmountable obstacle—a deep, broad river and an unusable bridge. A Portuguese barber saved the day. He told of four wine barges beached around a bend, out of sight and undetected by the careless French. A skiff could transport soldiers across the river to seize the barges and return them to the British side. While the operation proceeded under complacent French noses, Arthur assessed the far bank and developed a plan. His eye settled on the Bishop's Seminary, a stout structure halfway up the steep rise leading to the city. This would be his assembly point, and he could cover it with artillery from the far bank. And so while howitzers were moved into place, soldiers were painstakingly ferried across the Douro, and from the banks they moved to the seminary. The French took over an hour to respond but then attacked the building in force. With howitzers firing in support, the British would not be dislodged, and panic set in amongst Soult's troops. Working in concert, the British and Portuguese attackers took advantage of the chaos to secure additional barges, and the trickle of British troops landing on the French side became a torrent. Soult could not believe his eyes and ordered his unprepared army out of the city, leaving behind a thousand soldiers in hospital. That night and the following day, the British occupied the city and then began a pursuit. Spring rains prevented the coup de grace, but Soult lost much of his baggage train and artillery. This pursuit gave Arthur his first taste of the particular ferocity of this war. Unspeakable atrocities perpetrated by both sides marked the roads of northern Portugal.

Soult's failure to defend Oporto and conduct an orderly retreat is inexplicable, but there is no question that Wellesley's assault on the city was both audacious and well executed. He had liberated Portugal with the loss of twenty-three killed, ninety-eight wounded, and two missing. Having avenged Sir John Moore, he returned to Lisbon to plan a campaign against Victor. For this he received permission from Castlereagh, by then knee-deep in the Walcheren expedition. Paramount to Arthur were the related issues of money and supply, both of which would cause him concern for the war's duration. He had found, on his arrival in Portugal, that his treasury was lacking 75 percent of the promised funds. For him the implications were clear: no money, no supplies. But General Wellesley was determined that his army would pay for what it required. He had established this principle in India, and besides, the age-old alliance with Portugal made this an imperative; those whom he had come to help must be compensated for that which he took. The same would hold true in Spain. And so scolding letters to London, the first of many, were sent.[1]

On 24 June, Arthur began his march westward, and he crossed the Spanish frontier on 4 July. The proud, ancient, and infirm Spanish general Gregorio de la Cuesta awaited him while convalescing from injuries inflicted by the panic-stricken Spanish cavalry at Medellin, where they had been routed by the French. Like many of his compatriots, Cuesta scoffed at the reality of French military superiority, remaining forever optimistic that the next battle would bring victory; he professed eagerness to get on with the campaign. For his part, Wellesley sensed Victor's vulnerability. The young French marshal with his twenty thousand soldiers had advanced beyond the supporting forces of Joseph Bonaparte and General Horace François Sebastiani. Arthur believed that combining his troops with Cuesta's would bring success through sheer force of numbers; in short, he too was eager to begin the campaign.

Arthur did not come to the table with a positive view of the Spanish. He had followed Moore's campaign closely and had come to believe that he could not trust his Spanish allies. In many ways, the campaign became a self-fulfilling prophecy; he expected the worst, and to his mind the worst came to pass, beginning when Spanish promises for the supply and transport of his army failed to materialize. Almost from the start, then, Arthur doubted the wisdom of his decision. Yet he knew that his army was not yet at risk; his was not Sir

John Moore's predicament.[2] As Arthur moved forward with Cuesta towards Talavera, he realized that he had caught Victor woefully undermanned. On 22 July he advised his Spanish colleague that they should attack on the following morning. Cuesta balked, claiming his army needed to rest, and a dumbfounded Wellesley watched as Victor retreated into the embrace of Sebastiani's Fourth Corps and Joseph Bonaparte's reserves, swelling his army to 46,000 men. Sensitive to the axiom that timing was everything, he greeted Cuesta's suggestion to attack on the 24th with shocked amazement.[3] On the eve of the 24th, Arthur found that the news was all bad: he could not count on the Spaniards to keep his army supplied, and a doddering old fool commanded the army with which he campaigned.

Then he watched with dismay as Cuesta marched on Victor, rejecting British intelligence and advice. When he realized his error, Cuesta beat a hasty retreat to Talavera. Hard on the old Spaniard's heels, Victor launched an attack at dusk on the 27th. After two days of bloody fighting, Victor retreated, having suffered seven thousand casualties. Allied losses, mostly British, totaled five thousand. Cuesta, flush with victory, urged pursuit, but Wellesley, whose army had born the brunt of the fighting, advised restraint. In Arthur's judgment, the battle had been his most difficult to date, tougher than Assaye. For the moment, while he pondered the consequences of his victory and saw to the refreshment of his army, the French would be left to their own devices. Then came alarming news.

On 30 July, Arthur learned that a reconstituted French force under Marshal Soult was advancing on his rear, threatening to cut communications with Portugal. The information turned his attention from Victor and obliged him to make a short retreat. This maneuver, which should not have been complicated or problematic, brought to the fore the issue of Spain's failed promise to provide transport and supply. Arthur discovered that he had not the means to carry fifteen hundred sick and wounded soldiers to the new position. Cuesta agreed to care for them, but frustration consumed Wellesley and he became intemperate, chastising both Cuesta and the Supreme Junta.[4] The Spanish fired back, and a livid Arthur declared he would never again cooperate with the Spanish armies.

Meanwhile, HMS *Donegal* sailed into Cádiz harbor on 31 July 1809; the following morning, Lord Wellesley went ashore. The Spaniards provided a flattering welcome for the former governor general, whose reputation had preceded him.[5] Some thirty thousand citizens lined the harbor, there to witness "Lord Wellesley's approach from the ship to shore; and on stepping from the barge to the carriage, a French flag was so placed, that on first touching Spanish ground the French flag was trampled on."[6] Suitably impressed, Wellesley wrote to Canning in flowery terms of his reception.[7] This information, of course, he intended for public consumption. Wellesley fully appreciated the growing skepticism in Britain for the Spanish alliance, particularly Spain's will to fight. Anything he could do to portray this most unlikely alliance as a good investment for Great Britain, he would. The warm welcome, if not spontaneous, was certainly genuine and must have gladdened him.

Once he was ashore, however, the slap of reality hit him full force. Accompanying the good news of Talavera were Arthur's diatribes against the Spanish, and Richard knew that he had his work cut out for him.[8] Wellesley had sent his eldest son, Richard, to secure a residence in Seville and to survey the political landscape. Richard, who spoke Spanish, had been busy, but his father's residence was not yet ready to be occupied. So Wellesley stayed in Cádiz and in the meantime became acquainted with the details of the events of the previous month. Wellesley knew instinctively the role of an ambassador, but Frere's blunders in the Moore campaign clearly defined the parameters of diplomacy. It was not his job to fight the war but rather to facilitate a working relationship between the allies. Some scholars have suggested that he treated the Spanish as he had treated the Indians and that he would be satisfied with nothing less than another subsidiary treaty. There is something to this argument, but it falls short of congruence, mainly because this was Western-style diplomacy between Western nations and there existed a long history between the two, much of which had seen Spain dominant. Beyond that, Lord Wellesley had learned never to question Arthur's military judgment. He did not view his brother as infallible but appreciated Arthur's strengths: Arthur proceeded with great care, would not expose his army to unnecessary risks, and understood his commission. Moreover, he very much wanted Arthur to succeed and would do what he could to make that happen. His first instinct was to arrange a meeting with his brother, and he suggested that Arthur come to Cádiz or at least send someone who could provide a firsthand report. Arthur replied that he could spare no one and suggested instead that his brother send an emissary.[9]

Knowing that the general was struggling to keep his army fed and secure, the marquess was not certain that Arthur could appreciate fully the consequences of a fracture in the Anglo-Spanish alliance. From the moment Arthur first became involved in the Peninsular War in 1808, Richard viewed the struggle as another opportunity to promote the family. Therefore, he viewed the war broadly. Small, isolated victories were fine, but they would not do. He looked towards something much bigger: at the very least, the expulsion of France from the Peninsula. Accordingly, the alliance could not be allowed to founder. Even if Arthur retreated into Portugal, he would come back, and when he did, Spain had to be ready to receive him and work with him.

To this end, the marquess conceived his task as twofold: to help Arthur extricate himself from what was left of the Talavera campaign without fatally disturbing the alliance, and to work with the Spanish to remedy what Lord Wellesley saw as obstructions to the efficient prosecution of the war against France. Both goals were delicate but not extremely so. While there would always be a certain amount of tension between Richard and Arthur, they understood one another well, and each trusted the other's judgment in their respective spheres. As for the Spanish, Wellesley possessed an innate appreciation of their sensitivities. Not for nothing did the future George IV refer to him as a Spanish grandee grafted on an Irish potato. The marquess recognized pride when he saw it and knew the hurt of its injury. At the same time, he recognized obfuscation and incompetence when he saw them and did not hesitate to point them out. All the while, the marquess would keep one eye on London, where political support for the war remained tenuous.

Wellesley set out for Seville on 8 August in the dry, intense summer heat. The discomfort of the journey contrasted with its style. The Wellesley entourage consisted of four carriages, two caravans, two baggage carts, and twenty-eight servants. Still, the experience must have left the ambassador with an appreciation for the hardships Arthur's army was enduring.[10] By the time Wellesley settled into the city, relations between his brother and Cuesta had deteriorated even further, especially after Cuesta abandoned the British hospital he had pledged to protect. Smarting from Arthur's charges of incompetence and neglect, Cuesta accused the British of looting Spanish supplies. Arthur scoffed at the charge and as if in a schoolyard brawl, hurled his own battery of accusations at the Spanish allies. "It is useless to complain, but we are certainly not treated as friends, much less as the only prop on which the cause of Spain can depend," he wrote to his brother in great frustration.[11]

In Seville, Wellesley found an atmosphere quite different from that in Cádiz. The city's inhabitants, the numbers of which had been swelled by eighty thousand refugees, viewed with alarm the retreat of the British army and the city's consequent vulnerability to French attack. More important, in Seville sat the Supreme Junta, feeling equally vulnerable and very defensive. This body, numbering between twenty-four and thirty-five members, had come into existence the previous year on the heels of the battle of Baylen. Mostly because of factors beyond its control, it fell woefully short of providing the necessary leadership for a country involved in a life-and-death struggle.

In the face of quarrels with the provincial juntas and lukewarm public support, the Supreme Junta found even the most basic functions of government problematic. As if this were not enough, within the councils of the Supreme Junta there was division. Colonel Cochrane Johnstone warned the marquess accordingly in the spring of 1809: "Your Lordship will find upon your arrival at Seville that the Supreme Junta are split into different parties—their number is too great for the proper dispatch of business—a great deal of intrigue is going on."[12] Wellesley's primary contact with the junta would be the secretary of state for foreign affairs, don Martin de Garay. He found Garay easy to deal with, if not to trust, as his son Richard had warned: "You will find in Garay above all a pretended friend but in heart a rancourous enemy."[13] In the end, however much the junta saw itself as the representative authority of Spain, a variety of factors conspired to prevent it from functioning in that capacity.

This was the essential problem confronting the marquess. He could deal with the junta but could never rely on it. Arthur's problems with supply and transport were a case in point. Not only had Cuesta, in the face of French threats, abandoned the British hospital at Talavera but also his promises to supply the British army remained unfulfilled. "With the army which a fortnight ago beat double their numbers," Arthur raged, "I should now hesitate to meet a French corps of half their strength."[14] Charge and countercharge followed, but beyond his frustration with the Spanish and especially with Cuesta, Arthur conceded that the Spanish countryside had little to offer his hungry army. He resolved to return to Portugal to regroup and make plans for a French invasion, which every day looked more certain; Napoleon, again victorious over the Austrians at Wagram, could turn his focus on Iberia.[15] But Arthur could separate from the Spanish only with good reason, and the whole issue of supply and transport provided such a rationale.

This explains his repeated verbal assaults only partly. Lady Longford observed that Arthur's "practical judgments were cool and moderate but on paper imagination and temper were apt to take control."[16] Although this observation is true, lost is the historical context. Back in London, the juries of public opinion and the Horse Guards had not yet rendered a verdict on Sir Arthur. He was where he found himself largely because of his political connections and because there were few alternatives to his appointment. Beyond that, Arthur knew that the government approached the Peninsular War with great caution. This seemed especially apparent when one considered the fact that Castlereagh, while entrusting Arthur with command, was at the same time planning the Walcheren expedition, where the commitment in men and material exceeded that of the Peninsula. None of this left Sir Arthur very confident. From Sir John Moore's failure, he had learned just how quickly political opinion could turn. It is no wonder, then, that he would carefully chronicle the failures and follies of his allies. As he did on the field of battle and as he would do in the political arena, Arthur always provided himself a secure line of retreat. His dinner-table recollections of the Peninsular War, recounted years later by the likes of J. W. Croker, Harriet Arbuthnot, and Philip Henry Stanhope (the fifth Earl Stanhope), stress the military difficulties of the Peninsular War but contain little sense of the genuine political uncertainty which surrounded Arthur. As a result, only in his letters to Richard do we find some appreciation of the difficulties the Spaniards faced. This was a man who trusted few people but least of all politicians. Pole tried to reassure him, but Arthur remained skeptical.[17]

The marquess understood his brother and appreciated Arthur's predicament. There is no evidence that he ever doubted Arthur's assessment of the army's plight, but because Lord Wellesley wanted to keep the Spanish alliance alive, he would do his best to mollify without questioning his brother's judgment. Accordingly, he demanded that the junta act immediately to relieve Arthur's want of supplies, pointing out that there would be no hope of military cooperation until that was accomplished. Secretary Garay renewed Spain's promises, assuring Wellesley that steps had already been taken to improve the situation.[18]

When Arthur began his retreat to cover Soult's advance from the north, he clearly had had his fill of Spanish promises. Regardless of whether his immediate goal had been separation from Cuesta and future military cooperation, his supply problems intensified in proportion to his anger with Spain and the Spanish allies. More important, his mind had clearly turned to the defense of Portugal. In short, the supply problems became a justification for retreat, making experimentation to remedy the problem unappealing. Thus, the war of words would not go away. Richard thought that removing Cuesta might change his brother's attitude, and he engaged Garay in that discussion. This effort proved unnecessary; on 11 August, Cuesta suffered a stroke, prompting his immediate retirement. The junta chose the politically acceptable but mediocre General Francisco de Eguia, Cuesta's second in command, as the new commander in chief.[19]

For their part, the Spanish felt increasingly insecure. They could see that Arthur had lost interest in Spain, in effect leaving the Spanish armies to the mercy of the French, who, though beaten at Talavera, were already regrouping. It became the Spanish goal to embarrass Arthur into remaining attached to Eguia's army by taking away the supply excuse. In so doing, the Spanish junta employed three tactics. First, they claimed that the British were being supplied. Second, when that failed to convince, they claimed that the Spanish suffered more than the British and that in fact the British were confiscating supplies destined for the Spanish. And third, they maintained a steady stream of "new" proposals to deal with the problem while presenting plans for new offensives against the French. There is a certain desperation to all this, mainly because the junta's eyes were cast in two directions. They appreciated the real danger posed by the French, especially in the absence of British support, but they also sensed growing impatience among the people of free Spain, who saw in the junta nothing but failure. Consequently, if Sir Arthur could not be persuaded to remain with his army in Spain, then the British rather than the Supreme Junta would have to be saddled with the blame.

The marquess sensed much of this. "I have reason to believe that great exertion has since been made by this government for the purpose of giving speedy effect . . . to the commencement of an improved system of supply and movement for the troops in the field," he wrote to Canning. "But the impoverished state of the country, the weakness of the government and the inveterate defects of the military department in Spain render any speedy improvement impracticable, and induce me to apprehend great difficulty even in the ultimate success of any plan, which can now be suggested."[20] His task therefore was rather complex. He needed to support Arthur while preserving enough influence and goodwill to enable him to nudge the Spaniards towards reform in the government and military. This meant toning down Arthur's rhetoric while giving him what he wanted, and preventing the junta from transferring responsibility for the failed campaign to the British. It meant cultivating Spanish cooperation, if not goodwill, while leading the junta towards its own demise.

The urgency of the situation became clear to the marquess when on 21 August, after a bitter exchange with Eguia, who questioned his veracity, Arthur, sick and more impatient than ever, wrote pointedly to Richard, "These reports and insinuations against me may do very well for the people of Seville: but the British Army will not soon forget the treatment it has received."[21] This was a level of acrimony the marquess had not heard before from his brother, and as a result he sat down to devise a plan that he hoped would allow Arthur a graceful retreat while providing the Spanish government another opportunity to remedy the supply problem. By this time, Wellesley had been in Spain for three weeks, and he had a general idea of what the Supreme Junta could and could not do. What they could not do was appropriate supplies sufficient for both armies, let alone create the administrative structure to deliver those supplies even if such could be found. What they could do was deflect public ire over their own failings onto the British, specifically Arthur and his army.

From the information that crossed his desk, the marquess had to know at this point that the supply problem was irremediable; resources were simply insufficient. At the same time, however, he was willing to play the Spanish game so long as Arthur's army did not suffer in the process. And so, pen in hand, he formulated a plan that called for Arthur to retreat towards the Portuguese frontier, thus separating British and Spanish forces and deploying what was left of the Spanish army in a position to defend Seville. While this transpired, each party would establish a series of supply depots from which both armies would draw. Each army could draw from the countryside until the depots were ready for business. Wellesley's plan was cleverly devised because at the very least it allowed Arthur to withdraw to a secure position apart from the Spanish without appearing to be either fleeing Spain or abandoning the Spanish allies in a fit of pique. As for the supply business, there is little reason to see Wellesley as sanguine about it. If it worked, then both parties would be the better off for it, but, as was more likely, if it failed, then the Spanish could only look to themselves for blame.[22]

Arthur received his brother's plans with what could best be described as profound skepticism. He appreciated Richard's point that his remaining in Spain, short of the Portuguese frontier, would provide the junta with a certain amount of political cover and prevent an outbreak of Anglophobia in Seville. Taking up a position in and around Badajoz would also provide the type of immediate security that he desired. Still, there remained a problem. In the preceding three weeks, Arthur had accomplished the messy task of separating his army from the Spanish and had announced the termination of his cooperation. Withdrawing into Portugal would reinforce this reality.[23] Lord Wellesley's plan, in other words, smacked of reengagement, which, above all, Arthur sought to avoid. Still, realizing that Richard might have something else on his mind, Arthur announced that he would take no further steps until he had "received your Excellency's sentiments upon what I have submitted to your judgment."[24]

Wellesley responded to Arthur's reservations immediately by assuring him that the positions designated for each army were selected to ensure their separation and that these positions were not intended to be permanent. The purpose was to shift the diplomatic initiative back to British hands and to place responsibility for the failure of the campaign squarely on the Spanish. Wellesley's hope was that "under all the circumstances of the actual situation of the enemy's force, the position suggested might be safe, for a sufficient time, to enable you to try the result of the plan of supply for your army, which I had offered to this Government, and that the supplies which were provided in Portugal would at the same time be within your reach."[25]

All came to naught, but not as Wellesley had expected. The junta not only failed to respond in a timely fashion to Wellesley's plan but also failed to meet their own modest guarantees concerning supply and transport. Therefore, Wellesley informed the junta that he would advise Arthur to continue his retreat. At the same time,

Richard suggested to his brother that "the longer you can delay your actual passing the Portuguese frontier, the less will be the ill-temper and alarm in this quarter; that, if you can take up your position within the Spanish frontier, it will be more satisfactory here."[26] Not surprisingly, the junta reacted with alarm, issuing another desperate set of guarantees, which the marquess rejected out of hand while assuring the Spaniards that Arthur would take up a position in Spain near Badajoz.

While all of this transpired, Arthur received letters from London informing him he had been made a viscount as a reward for the battle of Talavera, which no longer seemed much like a victory. Portland extended his congratulations to the new viscount, but William was the one who informed Arthur of the details. In fact, because Arthur was out of the country, it fell to William to choose his brother's title. With the College of Heralds breathing down his neck, Pole selected "Wellington," a town in Somerset not far from Wellesley. He was, however, less than confident concerning this decision. "I long much to hear," he wrote, "that I ought not to be hanged for my arrangement."[27] Arthur was genuinely pleased: "I could not have been better off for a name if we had discussed the subject twenty times; but this is a strong instance of the effect upon men's minds of being engaged in the Publick Service. I have been for some time in the way at least of being made a Peer; and I don't recollect that one word ever passed between any of us on that subject, or on the title which should be given to me; nor do I believe it was ever thought of."[28]

The course of events had not come as a great surprise to the marquess. In the absence of a knockout blow at Talavera, which would have required close coordination and support from the Spanish, Arthur's retreat was inevitable; the French were simply too strong. Wellesley's challenge, therefore, was to manage the fallout from yet another failure—both in Spain and in Great Britain. Worse, from London came gloom and doom. Besieged by unfavorable publicity from the failure of the Walcheren campaign, the ministers were in no mood for unfavorable reports from the Peninsula. Canning, in particular, was noticeably discouraged by the failure of British arms, so much so that he was ready to give up on Spain. In a "private and confidential" letter to the marquess, the foreign secretary proclaimed that the best to be hoped for was keeping the British army intact behind the Portuguese frontier, and moreover,

> If the result should be that there is no mode in which the British Army can act in Spain, creditably and advantageously; the next object is to get creditably out of the difficulty. And I hope the instructions which I send you today will at least put that within your power. The refusal of either and still more of both of the conditions, if it is thought right to press them (at the risque of their being accepted) would afford a plain and strong ground, and one highly acceptable to this country, for withdrawing from the contest in Spain, and leaving the Spaniards to their own exertions. Whatever be the results of the discussions, I am persuaded that it is very necessary to let the Spaniards see, that, if they are not at once more active, and more tractable, we shall soon leave them to themselves. . . . my patience is put to a proof which I cannot stand.[29]

This was tantamount to dismissing the Spanish altogether, to cutting one's losses, because what Canning suggested as quid pro quo to Britain's continuing assistance was the garrisoning of Cádiz and the creation of a centralized command in the Spanish army with the new Lord Wellington as commander in chief. Canning knew as well as anyone that Spain would reject each out of hand.

By the time Canning's letter reached Wellesley, Wellington had already withdrawn to Badajoz, leaving Wellesley free to ignore the suggestions—not to mention that he was several steps ahead of the foreign secretary and light-years ahead in terms of the subtlety of his deliberations. The marquess attended to the task of repairing the damaged edifice of the Anglo-Spanish alliance. To begin, he sought to dispel growing rumors that behind Arthur's retreat lay sinister motives such as a desire to acquire Cádiz and Havana. Wellesley dismissed this notion in a public statement[30] and followed with a formal note to the Supreme Junta in which he explained that Britain's priority was Portugal's defense and that Spain's inability to keep the army supplied in the aftermath of Talavera compromised its security and therefore the security of Portugal. For this reason alone, Wellington had retreated to the Portuguese frontier.[31]

But this was simply part of an ongoing propaganda war; Wellesley knew that more important matters required attention.[32] Clearly the marquess had no intention of giving up on Spain; rather, he sought to transform it into a more effective war-making machine. In practical terms, this meant reorganizing the government and filling it with lackeys who would do Britain's bidding, not unlike in India, with the exception being that Wellesley never saw the new arrangement as permanent or Britain's presence in Iberia as ongoing. One must concede that the marquess did not appreciate the magnitude of the military undertaking and therefore the time and sacrifice involved in confronting the French in Iberia—that was Arthur's problem.

The topic of political reform first came up within days of Wellesley's arrival in Seville. Martin de Garay solicited the marquess's opinion on the appointment of a regency and the calling of the Cortes. Wellesley jumped right in, having already given the question serious thought. Efficiency would be the hallmark of any change, along with the mobilization of solid public support. Accordingly, Wellesley proposed the creation of a regency council consisting of not more than five members who would assume executive powers. These regents could come from the Supreme Junta or not, but those who did not serve would superintend the convening of the Cortes, which Wellesley believed would rally public sentiment behind the regents. The Cortes, he told Garay, must include representatives from the colonies. The regency's first act, he stressed, should be the reform of the military.[33]

Garay had cynical reasons for engaging Wellesley in this discussion, coming as it did in the midst of Arthur's retreat, and naturally it came to naught. Wellesley, however, took it for what it was, an opportunity to present his views. He knew that the junta would not willingly or easily surrender its powers. He also knew that many in Spain feared preponderant British influence, but to his mind this was unavoidable.[34] Wellesley's preoccupation with Wellington's situation in August meant that these issues would be temporarily in abeyance, but in September they again attracted his full attention. Garay then got a taste of the marquess's cool logic. The British army, Wellesley informed the foreign secretary, would not return to Spain until the Spanish military could cope with the various problems of logistics and strategy. This could not be effected until the executive power of Spain was reformed, and fully mobilizing the human and material resources of Spain would require that the people have a voice in government: in other words, create a regency and call the Cortes.[35] The marquess had found his footing; he finally knew what he needed to accomplish and how he would go about doing it. He understood implicitly that he would have to apply considerable and consistent pressure on the Spanish government, for only this would provoke movement. Accordingly, he scolded "the Secretary of State regularly twice a day."[36]

Wellesley's challenge in the pursuit of sweeping reform was the Spanish perception that Britain had no choice but to work with Spain. Napoleon's defeat of the Austrians and the Walcheren fiasco suggested to the Supreme Junta that Britain needed Spain as much as Spain needed Britain. This was, in fact, a misperception, as Britain had not concluded that Spain should be the site of the struggle with Napoleonic France. But perception is reality, and the junta ignored the ambassador's calls for reforms and instead solicited active military involvement to thwart future French operations in the south of Spain. This infuriated the marquess, but he kept his emotions in check, going even so far as to save the government from an attempted coup d'etat. The resulting goodwill dissipated quickly. "They were all gratitude for an hour," the marquess told Wellington, "but now that they think themselves secure, they have begun to cheat me again. . . . I told Garay this evening that I would not trust the protection of a favorite dog to the whole Spanish army. It is some satisfaction to abuse such miscreants, if you cannot reform them."[37]

And so a kind of standoff evolved, which Wellesley took as a matter of course while dealing with the day-to-day responsibilities of the embassy until 23 October, when the junta delivered a plan for reconstituting the government. While Wellesley took careful note of the effort, he quickly saw it for the half measure it was. The junta proposed an executive council made up of a rotation of junta members; it promised little change in the status quo, and he so informed the junta.[38] Still, the ambassador sensed unease and knew from whence it came. On 13 October, he had requested a ship to be made ready to transport him to London, where he would take up the seals of the Foreign Office. Spain's future, now more than ever, lay in the hands of the marquess.

Wellesley had been waiting for the call, but it came under odd and disruptive circumstances. Canning had agreed not to press for Castlereagh's removal until plans for the Walcheren campaign were completed. Accordingly, the cabinet proceeded in a business-as-usual fashion with Castlereagh blithely unaware of serious discontent—until 28 July, when the Walcheren expedition set sail. Canning then reapplied pressure. Portland responded, promising that Lord Camden would advise Castlereagh of what had been discussed. Camden failed at the task, and Portland stepped into the breach. But before he could meet with Castlereagh, the prime minister suffered an epileptic fit, which disabled him for several days. At this juncture, Canning found the rest of the cabinet unwilling to go forward in that all were convinced that Portland could not carry on and that they faced an inevitable restructuring of the government. Portland recovered but resolved to tender his resignation. At this point, Canning's plans changed because the timetable had changed. All along Canning had been engaged in building support within the cabinet, anticipating Portland's eventual resignation and his own assumption of the premiership. With Portland leaving, the time had come to make his move.[39]

Canning subsequently tendered his resignation. At the next cabinet meeting, Castlereagh took note of his rival's absence and queried Lord Camden about it. Camden finally revealed all that had transpired in the past months. Understandably, Castlereagh promptly resigned, and Canning readied himself for a contest with Spencer Perceval for the premiership. It was well known that neither would serve under the other. Perceval suggested a third person acceptable to both: the reestablishment of the status quo under someone other than Portland. Canning, not surprisingly, rejected the idea. In this uncertain political environment, Canning sought to solidify his relationship with Wellesley, and to that end he cultivated a friendship with Henry. This was what lay behind the foreign secretary's appointment of Henry as Britain's representative to Portugal. Henry eagerly accepted but upon Canning's resignation withdrew, explaining that the next foreign secretary should make the appointment. Though appreciative of Canning's gesture, Henry smelled the tainted aroma of political maneuver and coyly backed away from the fray until he had heard from Richard. William was not as circumspect. After the debates over the Convention of Cintra, he had moved into the Castlereagh camp. On the grounds that any enemy of Canning's was a friend of his, Pole declared his support for Perceval.[40] Pole and Wellesley's confidant Benjamin Sydenham were thinking of the marquess and had concluded that his future lay with Perceval, not Canning. The two would keep Wellesley abreast of events in London, and neither portrayed Canning in a flattering light. Neither the king nor what was left of the cabinet would support Canning, they explained, and therefore the marquess needed to clarify his arrangements with Canning so that

Perceval might freely appoint him to a secretaryship—either the Foreign or War Office.[41]

The struggle for Wellesley's favor resolved itself when on 19 September Castlereagh challenged Canning to a duel. Castlereagh, who had been nursing his wounded pride for several days, had decided that healing could be accomplished only by making Canning physically and therefore publicly accountable for his political sins. The challenge stunned Canning, who never gave such things as dueling and physical violence a second thought. Canning was a cerebral man; he had not been brought up in the world of hunting and guns and notions of aristocratic "honor." Still, he felt he had no choice but to accept his rival's challenge.

Wasting no time in trying to make the best out of a bad situation, Canning asked Henry to serve as his second. This was peculiar indeed in that one's closest confidant usually filled the role of second. "I have always been at a loss to account for Canning's motive for applying to me upon this occasion," Henry would write disingenuously, "for although I had known him all my life we had never lived in great intimacy—I have sometimes thought that he might have a political motive, and that he might think it of importance to him at this juncture to appear to be intimately connected to the Wellesleys—which, had I acted as his friend in this quarrel, the world might have been induced to believe."[42] Indeed! There was no mystery here, and Henry sensibly informed Canning that he could not serve as second but would serve in another capacity should Canning desire it. At the same time, he suggested Canning's closest friend, Charles Ellis, as the duelist's second. Canning explained that Ellis was unavailable because he was attending the queen at his estate, Claremont, and that a response to Castlereagh could not be postponed. Henry offered to go to Lord Yarmouth (Castlereagh's second), explain the delay, and proceed to Claremont to bring Ellis back to London. Canning agreed, and Henry embarked on his mission. Yarmouth graciously accepted his explanation. Once Ellis was found, he and Henry joined Canning. Henry witnessed Canning's will, and at five o'clock the following morning, the party set off for Putney Heath. The ride was as dreary as the day.[43]

Despite its potentially lethal consequences, the duel contained elements of farce. The bumbling Canning needed instruction on the use of firearms, and Castlereagh, consumed with rage, insisted on firing until he hit his target. On the second exchange, Castlereagh delivered a clean shot through the fleshy part of Canning's thigh. Though the wound required an extended convalescence, it provided Canning ample material with which to regale London society in the weeks to come. "It used to be difficult to get in [to government]—at all times," he wrote to a friend; "but I never knew that getting out again was a matter of so much difficulty."[44] He would need a sense of humor, for his political career, along with Castlereagh's, temporarily came to an end. Left standing was Perceval, who faced a considerable challenge. The Whigs, thinking Perceval's task hopeless, prepared for the king's call. George III felt no such desperation and commissioned the nondescript Perceval to form a ministry.

At this point attention turned to Wellesley, and his brothers worried that he might squander another opportunity. "Canning has claims upon your friendship," argued Wellington, "because he was willing to sacrifice his own situation in order to bring you into power; but it is a question deserving your consideration whether you alone of all his friends and colleagues are to support his pretensions to be *the First Minister,* and are bound to sacrifice yourself to attain that object."[45] Wellington's views reflected Pole's, as the two had been in constant touch. Wellington believed that Wellesley could not be better placed to advance himself than he was at that time and explained to William that "as things now are he has time to hear how matters are settled, & to consider what line he will take under the settlement."[46]

The brothers had no need to worry; Wellesley had already sorted things out for himself. To his mind, the situation in September differed significantly from that in March and April. Canning's goal had shifted from trying to strengthen the ministry to seeking the premiership for himself. Wellesley believed that he was under no obligation to "act under him [Canning] either in or out of office for the purpose of forcing him [Canning] into any particular station, against the wishes of his colleagues, of his party, of his Sovereign, and even against the opinions of all in my own favor."[47]

Meanwhile, conjecture in the London press reflected the political uncertainties of the moment. No one could quite figure out where Wellesley's sympathies lay, as both Perceval and Canning laid claim to them. In the end, the press concluded that Wellesley would be coming into government and differed only in their attribution of his motive for doing so. Some saw Wellesley as an opportunist who would jump at any opportunity no matter who offered it, while others gave him credit for more integrity. The ever-caustic *Morning Chronicle* led the way: "It is well known that the Noble Marquis *loitered* three months in London, after his appointment to the Spanish Embassy, in hopes of getting into the Cabinet through the secret arrangement of his *friend* Mr. Canning; and he is now expected to *hurry* home, that he may take advantage of the success of his *friend* Mr. Perceval."[48] The *Morning Post* countered by pointing out that high office had long been within Wellesley's reach and that on several occasions he had declined for altruistic reasons. "We hope, at least," the *Post* continued, "that if any sacrifice be made, the Noble Marquis will be more fortunate in obtaining justice for his motives, than he has been on other occasions, when everything that office and honours could confer was obviously within reach."[49]

Once Wellesley's decision to accept the Foreign Office became known, the discussion turned to his merits. Again the *Chronicle* led the attack: "That he [Wellesley] should appear a great man to his Majesty's present Ministers is exceedingly natural. All magnitude is relative. When Lord Wellesley comes to Downing-street, he will find himself back again in Lilliput, without having had the trouble of doubling the Cape."[50] A more accurate reflection of public opinion came from the *Times*: "Lord Wellesley's acceptance of office is regarded by the supporters of the Ministry as an event equally favorable to the future interest of the country and the permanency of the new arrangements. By his accession the keystone of the arch is supplied, which the current of public opinion, however violent or adverse its direction, can it is supposed, neither injure or undermine."[51]

In Seville, Wellesley officially informed the junta of his decision to take the Foreign Office and of his imminent departure. Until permanent arrangements were decided upon, Bartholomew Frere (brother of John Hookham Frere) would assume the responsibilities of the embassy as minister plenipotentiary. But before the marquess left, Wellington, fully aware of the significance of having his elder brother in the Foreign Office, traveled to Seville to discuss peninsular matters. He arrived on 2 November and then accompanied the marquess to Cádiz, during which time there occurred a wide-ranging discussion on peninsular affairs—the military situation, the political and economic state of Portugal and Spain, the political environment in London, and plans for the future. Out of this meeting came a memorandum written by the marquess that represented the Wellesley point of view. Its heart was a clear commitment to Spain and the war: "However the conduct of the Spanish Government may increase the difficulties of cooperation, alienate the spirit of the English from their cause, and even apparently justify a total separation of the interest of the two nations, yet it must never be forgotten that in fighting the cause of Spain, we are struggling for the last hope of continental Europe."[52] This was pure Wellesley—clear, decisive, forward looking, and self-serving.

One can only speculate on the motives driving this policy of fighting the Peninsular War to the fullest and to its conclusion. There can be no doubt that Wellesley saw this as the right policy for a variety of reasons, but one wonders whether he would have felt the same had not his brother's future been clearly tied to success in Iberia. Wellington was on a road from which there would be no return, literally and figuratively. The consequences of success or failure would be immense, and Wellesley knew it. He also knew that the family's future would be inextricably tied to the results. For this reason, Henry quickly became a part of his calculations.

Henry was still in the midst of his divorce, which had moved through the ecclesiastical stage and was about to be introduced into Parliament as a bill dissolving the marriage. The summer and early fall had not been pleasant. In addition to his own despair, he had to deal with his young children, who were puzzled and anxious over their mother's absence. When Paget embarked on the Walcheren expedition, Henry brought mother and children together under his roof to alleviate some of the emotional pain. Arthur's victory at Talavera brought some cheer to the youngest Wellesley, but then he found himself caught up in the political wrangling in London. Canning's offer of the embassy in Lisbon must have come as a great relief, only to be overshadowed by bad luck when the news broke that Canning had resigned. Henry knew full well that it was his duty to retract his acceptance in deference to a new foreign secretary. Then came the duel, which tested his diplomatic skills and put him on notice that he and his brothers would be sorely challenged in the days ahead. He wrote to Richard,

> I have . . . distinctly stated to Canning and to my personal friends on the other side that I beg to be considered as belonging to no party whatever, and that I am determined to await your arrival in England, being at present entirely ignorant of the

> line you may think to take. I have adopted this course from the dread of the [political] family being split into parties, which indeed has already happened in the cases of Pole and Charles Bagot, one of whom continues at the Admiralty with Mulgrave, while the other retires with Canning. It is difficult to conceive the violence which prevails on each side of the question, greater than I ever before remember.[53]

Given Henry's state of mind, this is a remarkable letter—clear, perceptive, detached, and selfless. He was eager to get on with his life, but circumstances and family loyalty told him to hold back. Still, waiting involved risk. As for the marquess, he appreciated Henry's thoughts, though he could hardly have been surprised by them. If Henry wanted Lisbon, that was fine, but Lord Wellesley had another idea. Certainly Portugal was as much a part of Britain's peninsular policy as Spain, if not more so, but Wellesley was comfortable with Britain's influence there and saw Lisbon as less problematic than Seville. He had learned in three short months that the Spaniards were an independent lot and highly skilled in delay and distraction. He had also learned that the political and social status of the British representative could influence Spanish attitudes. That he thought of Henry as his replacement in Seville is thus no surprise. As brother of the foreign secretary, Henry would have far more influence than any other potential representative, just as had been the case in India. Of course, there was more to Wellesley's reasoning than this. Placing Henry in Spain would create a military-diplomatic-political triad that would give the marquess an uncommon degree of control over events both in the Peninsula and at home. It would also create an atmosphere of security and comfort in which all three brothers could work in the midst of volatile and unstable political conditions in London. The marquess and Wellington knew all too well the capricious nature of British politics, especially when it came to foreign policy and war. Accordingly, on accepting Perceval's offer, Wellesley promptly wrote to Henry, "I advise you not to decide your own situation (unless you should be particularly desirous of going to Lisbon) until my arrival. You may rely on my using every effort to place you in a situation worthy of you, and acceptable to you."[54]

On arriving in London, the marquess made his proposal to his trusted youngest brother. Henry had little choice in the matter, but nothing in his response suggests anything but delight. He was eager to get out of London and on with a career. The Spanish posting offered just such an opportunity while presenting him with the chance to work in concert with his brothers once again. The official appointment came on 12 December, when he was made envoy extraordinary and minister plenipotentiary to Spain. Six days later, the king made him a member of the privy council "to give him greater weight in dealing with the Spanish."[55]

Modern ruins of Dangan Castle, County Meath. (Photograph by Peter Jupp; reproduced by permission.)

Anne, Countess of Mornington, by William Owen. (Reproduced courtesy of the Duke of Wellington, K. G.; photograph by Courtauld Institute of Art.)

Richard Colley Wellesley, Marquess Wellesley, by J. P. Davis. (Reproduced courtesy of the National Portrait Gallery, London.)

The Hon. William Wellesley-Pole, by John Hoppner. (Reproduced courtesy of the Duke of Wellington, K. G.; photograph by Courtauld Institute of Art.)

Lieutenant-Colonel the Hon. Arthur Wellesley, by John Hoppner. (Reproduced courtesy of the Duke of Wellington, K. G.; photograph by Courtauld Institute of Art.)

The Rev. the Hon. Gerald Valerian Wellesley. (Artist unknown. Reproduced courtesy of the Duke of Wellington, K. G.; photograph by Courtauld Institute of Art.)

The Hon. Henry Wellesley, by John Hoppner. (Reproduced courtesy of the Duke of Wellington, K. G.; photograph by Courtauld Institute of Art.)

William Pitt Speaking before the House of Commons, by K. A. Hickel. Richard Wellesley is fifth to the left of Pitt. (Reproduced courtesy of the National Portrait Gallery, London.)

William Grenville, first Baron Grenville, by John Hoppner. (Reproduced courtesy of the National Portrait Gallery, London.)

Henry Addington, first Viscount Didmouth, by Sir William Beechey. (Reproduced courtesy of the National Portrait Gallery, London.)

Henry Bathurst, third Earl Bathurst, by William Salter. (Reproduced courtesy of the National Portrait Gallery, London.)

George Canning, by Thomas Lawrence. (Reproduced courtesy of the National Portrait Gallery, London.)

Robert Banks Jenkinson, second Earl of Liverpool, by Thomas Lawrence. (Reproduced courtesy of the National Portrait Gallery, London.)

Robert Stewart, Viscount Castlereagh, second Marquess of Londonderry, by Thomas Lawrence. (Reproduced courtesy of the National Portrait Gallery, London.)

Henry William Paget, first Marquess of Anglesey, by Henry Eldridge. (Reproduced courtesy of the National Portrait Gallery, London.)

Duchess of Wellington (Kitty), by John Hayter. (Reproduced courtesy of the Duke of Wellington, K. G.; photograph by Courtauld Institute of Art.)

Duke of Wellington Looking Over the Field of Waterloo, by Benjamin Robert Haydon. (Reproduced courtesy of the Duke of Wellington, K. G.; photograph by Courtauld Institute of Art.)

Countess of Mornington surrounded by her sons. (Contemporary print. Reproduced courtesy of the National Portrait Gallery, London.)

Wellington in Old Age, by Count D'Orsay. (Reproduced courtesy of the National Portrait Gallery, London.)

11

The Wellesleys at War

Arthur's decision to go to Seville to meet with Richard tells much about how the Wellesleys viewed the situation in the Peninsula and their role in it. Arthur had declined a similar opportunity three months earlier because of his deep concern for the security of his army in the midst of a strategic retreat. With that army safely tucked away behind the Portuguese frontier and preparations for the defense of Portugal well under way, he could leave for a short time to bring his brother up to speed on his preparations, which he would certainly be loath to commit to writing. Moreover, the home government's skittishness over the war concerned him. Richard was about to join that government, so it was important that they talk.

Indeed there was much to talk about. Richard, with an eye ever poised on family interests, also saw the moment as critical. Here were two bright, ambitious men who understood one another well and who knew that the next two years would determine not only Britain's future course but also their own. They were united in their determination to fight the war to its conclusion in the Peninsula, but how this was to be done and what would be needed to accomplish it were unknown. Here one can surmise with some certainty that Arthur would have told Richard of his defensive works, the so-called Lines of Torres Vedras, and that—barring a massive French invasion of Portugal—Lisbon and the surrounding countryside could be defended. In other words, the British presence could and would be maintained in Portugal without putting the army at risk. Nonetheless, for at least the next year, the war would be one of attrition. Wellington believed that he could win that war if proper support came from London; if it were not forthcoming, he would pack up his army and return to Britain a failed soldier.

Richard, who never thought in detail about military matters, had already cast himself and his brothers in the role of Britain's saviors and must have relished Arthur's details about the "lines." The resourceful Arthur would wait out the French, test their resolve, and eventually let the land and elements force them to retreat. Here is where Richard came in. He knew that the British public would not respond well to Arthur's retreat into Portugal, and with the retreat coming on the heels of the failed Walcheren campaign, the government would be sorely pressed to generate support for continuing the fight. Richard would have to see to it. Once the French were beaten in Portugal, then the nature of the struggle would change; the hunted would become the hunter. That next stage would introduce other complications. An offensive against the French would inevitably be fought in Spain and just as inevitably would involve some degree of cooperation with the Spanish. Diplomatically, then, Spain could not be ignored, much as Arthur wished for such a course of action. Britain's goals were various. Above all, every effort had to be made to maintain the guerilla war that so compromised the French. Much of this would be done by Britain in the form of supplies and arms, but providing the guerillas with official backing from the Supreme Junta was also important. Beyond this, Spain had to begin reconstructing its own army into a reasonably effective fighting force under reliable and competent commanders. As in Portugal, this would involve some level of British involvement. Further, the Spanish government had to reform itself into an efficient, working entity that enjoyed solid popular support. These things, the brothers knew, would require an active and influential British presence in Seville, along with vigorous support from London, where perceptions of the Spanish allies were negative in the extreme.

These were points that Arthur and Richard discussed at length. As in India, each had his own role to play—Arthur with the army and Richard in Parliament and the Foreign Office. But the cast was not yet complete. Richard's decision to employ Henry surely brought a smile to Arthur's face. Richard as foreign secretary, Henry as envoy to Spain, and he as commander in chief. What could be better? They would succeed, or fail, together. It was an extraordinary arrangement, and one without precedent. After seeing Richard off on 11 November, Arthur wrote to William, "He went to England in high spirits, & determined to exert himself to make a strong Gov't. for the King."[1]

But things were never simple with the marquess. Before he sailed for Spain in the summer of 1809, he had discussed with the Duke of Portland the prospect of the king conferring on him the Garter should one become available in his absence. The resulting documents he left in Charles Arbuthnot's charge with instructions to present them to the prime minister, whomever he might be, in the event of an opportunity presenting itself. And so again one finds lurking in his mind this issue of rewards, image, and public perceptions. As it happened, Portland's Garter is the one that came available, and Arbuthnot did as instructed. Meanwhile, Wellesley had made clear in his negotiations with Perceval, even before learning of Portland's death, that he expected the prime minister to put forward his claims. This proved awkward, as Perceval had already contacted the Duke of Richmond concerning Portland's Garter: "I have no difficulty in saying that if your Grace should wish to succeed to the D. of Portland's Garter, as far as depends upon me it shall certainly be yours."[2] Beyond that, the new prime minister knew that the king was not keen on Wellesley. This the king had made abundantly clear in his assessment of a query Wellesley sent to Perceval concerning the latter's negotiations with Canning and the suggestion that if Wellesley were made prime minister, both Perceval and Canning might serve under him. This correspondence Perceval laid before the king, who interpreted it as Wellesley's rejection of the Foreign Office.[3] Perceval responded quickly to disabuse the king of this notion. His Majesty did not press the issue, but he had made his point; others might be enthusiastic about the marquess, but he was not. When Wellesley's official acceptance of office arrived before the king, George III responded tersely: "H.M. is glad to learn that Mr Perceval conceives that Lord Wellesley's acceptance of that office will have the effect of strengthening the Government."[4]

Meanwhile, Bathurst put Richmond on notice of what was afoot: "Perceval has beg'd I would lose no time in putting you in full possession of this, of which he was until this day perfectly ignorant, but he thought that in your conversations with Pole you should be aware of this claim. . . . Lord Wellesley . . . is so great a card at the present moment, and *so aware of it,* that I know not what to say. . . . (*Entre nous*—Lord Wellesley is not a favourite with his Majesty.)"[5] The situation was indeed awkward, as Richmond was an old family friend and Pole, as chief secretary, worked closely with the lord lieutenant.

Wellesley arrived at Portsmouth on 26 November unaware of the king's view of him and the offer made to Richmond. These were, of course, details that Perceval could not share, and so Wellesley promptly engaged the prime minister on the issue of the Order of the Garter. Fortunately, Richmond graciously withdrew but not before pointing out his belief that both Wellesley and Perceval were making a mistake: "The world will never be persuaded that the Garter was not the price Govt. offered and he accepted for his taking office; it will make him extremely unpopular, and consequently it will hurt Governt. People in general will think he can carry what he pleases and indeed it will be difficult to prevail on him not to join in this opinion."[6] In the end, Perceval convinced the king, though this success gave him no joy. Indeed, when Wellesley suggested that the investiture take place immediately, Perceval advised the marquess to keep his mouth shut.[7] It was not a good beginning to this new partnership.

The evidence suggests that Wellesley never took Perceval seriously and from the start looked for ways to focus public attention on himself. His inability to appreciate the fool he made of himself seems inconceivable. Richmond was right in predicting that there would be whispers; when word filtered out on these negotiations, as inevitably it did, some spoke of his vanity rather than his talent. One might say that he was indifferent to public opinion and that the Garter was simply a political card to strengthen his hand, but quite the opposite was true. His brothers never commented on all this, but no doubt they viewed it with wry amusement. Nevertheless, the general public perception of Wellesley was positive, and most viewed him as the dominant member of the new government.

Wellesley had not lost sight of the Peninsular War, and he got down to the business of placing Henry in the Spanish embassy. For the youngest Wellesley, his brother's assumption of the Foreign Office signaled an end to several years of personal chaos and disappointment. He had returned from India with high hopes for a distinguished diplomatic or political career, hopes that were soon dashed by unsettled political conditions in Britain and his own indiscretion and naïveté. Frustrations with his career were then aggravated by the collapse of his marriage. Here too he had been blindsided, thinking all was well.

To add insult to injury, Char's elopement exposed Henry to the ridicule of a judgmental and insensitive London society. Its debilitating effects on him soon became obvious to his brothers. Richard's offer of the Spanish embassy, fraught as it was with uncertainty, thus offered Henry a fresh start. It would set him on course for a career in the diplomatic service and would also get him out of London and society's critical gaze.

The month of January Henry spent getting his affairs in order and in meeting with Richard. There were still the distractions of his divorce, not to mention Richard's own marital problems, but the business of Spain and the war in the Peninsula was the family focus. No written record of his meetings with Richard exists, but there can be no doubt of what the eldest brother had to say, which concerned matters of both style and policy. The Spanish were a sensitive lot, and their innate mistrust of Britain meant that their initial response to any suggestions or requests would be negative or evasive, even in the face of what appeared obvious. They required patience. At the same time, the British representative needed to be persistent, firm, and proactive. Distance and time would preclude consultation with London in some and perhaps even many instances, and Henry would have to act on his own counsel. That was to be expected; he should only take care not to stray into areas outside his responsibility, specifically matters relating to the British expeditionary force. In this he would rely exclusively on Arthur's judgment.

Concerning matters of policy, Henry would attend to three major issues: political reform, military reform, and the pursuit of some sort of trade agreement. These would require all the resourcefulness Henry could muster, and his success would depend largely on the military and political conditions of the moment. Other issues to attend to included the removal of Spanish ships from vulnerable ports to safe harbors, the distribution of material and monetary aid, and securing licenses to export specie from the Americas.[8]

Henry sailed for Cádiz on 12 February 1810. It would be India all over again, with Richard calling the shots and Arthur and Henry playing supporting roles—at least, so it seemed. Arthur did not see it this way, and in fact, Richard was not his boss; that role fell to Lord Liverpool. Still, he would rely on Richard to build and maintain support in London for the great military enterprise on which he had embarked. The arrangement differed from India in that the setting had changed. This was main stage drama played before an alert and critical audience. That said, never before had three brothers played such a central role in the fate of a nation. England's great struggle with revolutionary France, which had been ongoing for nearly seventeen years, would be resolved in the Iberian Peninsula. From London, Richard would devise policy and promote it; in Iberia, Arthur would command; and in Spain, Henry would mobilize the resources of a reluctant and hobbled ally. Not only did Britain's future role as a European power hang in the balance, so too did the careers of the Wellesleys.

As the marquess wrote out and explained his instructions to Henry, events in Spain took an ominous turn. In October the Spanish military undertook an ill-advised offensive against the French. It began positively at the battle of Tamames, but this had the consequence of filling the Spanish military leaders with false optimism without appreciably altering the French strategic position. Consequently, the Spanish troops blundered into a series of devastating defeats that destroyed what was left of Spain's standing armies and rendered Seville indefensible. Wellington's friend the Duke of Albuquerque took what was left of his ragtag army and marched to Cádiz to provide for its defense against a certain French siege. The decision was fortuitous, because without him the city would certainly have fallen. Meanwhile, the collapse of the Supreme Junta accompanied that of the military, and a regency of five organized on the model suggested by the marquess was proclaimed in Cádiz. The desperate Spanish leadership subsequently requested reinforcements for Albuquerque, and on 7 February, British troops from Gibraltar reached the city and took up positions on the Isla de Leon to the south of the city, joined four days later by another two thousand soldiers dispatched by Wellington.[9]

This was the situation when Henry arrived on 28 February 1810, completely unaware that Seville had fallen and that free Spain consisted only of Cádiz. He found utter chaos. Panic, joined by opportunism, led to undefined or contradictory authority—politically and militarily. Specifically, there were competing political authorities: the newly established regency and the existing Junta of Cádiz. This, of course, was nothing new but it took Wellesley by surprise. The problem was that the junta presided over the city and the regency over the country, when in fact they were one and the same. The regency compounded the problem by taking up residence on the Isla de Leon rather than in the city, which to Henry's mind was absurd.[10] The problem was

Albuquerque, who had stationed himself in Cádiz. General Francisco Xavier de Castaños, who served as captain general of the army as well as a regent, believed that as long as Albuquerque remained there, the regents should stay on the isle to preside over the military. Henry ignored the irrationality of this and instead went to work on Albuquerque to transfer his headquarters to the isle, thus making room for the regency in Cádiz. After much squabbling between the general and the junta, this was accomplished, and on 22 March the regents moved into the city. While the essential conflict between the city and the regency would never go away, the authority of the latter slowly became recognized. As far as Wellesley was concerned, he dealt solely with the regents.

This done, Henry turned his attention to two other immediate problems: the vulnerability of the Spanish fleet and the dangers posed by French prisoners of war confined to barges, both sets of vessels anchored in the bay. He entered into discussions on these matters with the new secretary of state, don Eusebio de Bardaxi y Azara, shortly after his arrival; only after working with the Spanish leadership to establish political order and some semblance of command and control did he address the issues in earnest. At first glance these might seem to have been distractions rather than problems, but Henry knew full well that Britain had undertaken a controversial operation against Denmark to secure the Danish fleet lest it fall into French hands. The number of Spanish ships that lay open to the French in both Cádiz and Cartagena posed a far greater threat. As for the French prisoners of war, there were enough of them, should they escape, to alter the balance of military power at Cádiz. For Henry, then, this was serious business.

He soon discovered, as Richard had warned, that the Spaniards would question every solution he proposed: there was no place to move the ships or the prisoners, there was insufficient manpower to undertake such operations, moving either ships or prisoners would involve negative symbolism. Henry responded quickly to every claim, but to do so, he ended up making commitments that normally would have required confirmation from London. Specifically, he took responsibility for at least half of the prisoners of war, who would be transported to Britain, and he promised to provide some of the manpower to remove ships to a secure harbor. In the end, most of the prisoners were sent to Britain aboard Spanish ships of the line anchored in Cádiz, and Spanish sailors who had sought refuge at Gibraltar removed the Cartagena fleet to Ceuta. In doing these things, Henry revealed the kind of autonomy he possessed as brother of the foreign secretary. He knew full well that Richard would support him in London, and from Portugal came encouragement from Arthur.[11] At the same time, this was baptism under fire, instructing him on the extraordinary difficulties he would face in the months to come. The Spanish were like quicksilver, shiny and bright but hard to corral.

None of this was good news for the marquess, who faced the supreme challenge of generating political support for the struggle. Beyond this, Wellesley's return to England brought domestic challenges. When he departed for Spain, he and his wife lived separate lives in Apsley House, but it was his understanding that they would separate and, furthermore, that in his absence she would find for herself and the children a suitable place to live. Hyacinthe, despite the humiliation brought about by her husband's cavorting publicly with known courtesans, instead made a final attempt at some sort of reconciliation. Her expectations were low, with Hyacinthe hoping to maintain the status quo whereby they would continue to live together in Apsley House but lead separate lives. Wellesley would have none of it and told her so by letter while in Spain. On his return she again made what she believed to be an appeal to reason.[12] Wellesley, who expected her to be out of the house, responded bluntly and cruelly:

> I . . . request you on my arrival at Apsley House, not to attempt to see me; because in that House, I am resolved not to remain with you, on any terms, which could admit of my seeing you. . . . I shall therefore request you to see Mr. Lightfoot the day after tomorrow (Thursday) and to settle with him the general terms of our Separation: If you should consent to this Now most necessary arrangement, you will not experience any thing disagreeable. I must hope that you will no longer delay a settlement, which cannot be postponed without positive destruction of the whole family.[13]

But Wellesley had underestimated his foe. She had done her homework and knew her rights. "There is the Devil to pay at Apsley House," Pole informed Arthur. "Lightfoot says she is perfectly up to the Law of her case as any man in Westminster Hall."[14]

The question arises, why should Hyacinthe wish to remain with the marquess? The answer lies in her maternal instincts and in her extraordinary resourcefulness and determination, born of an uncertain and challenging childhood. She would do anything to protect her children, and as they were legally illegitimate, she feared that her husband might abandon them. This was the root of her desire to keep them in the same household. Alas, since that outcome was denied her, she would demonstrate her mettle. Once her husband had determined his course of action, she had no intention of allowing him to determine hers.

Very cleverly, Hyacinthe turned to Sir Samuel Romilly for counsel, not only because of his reputation as an attorney but also because he was a lifelong and determined Whig with little sympathy for Wellesley. She knew, of course, that Wellesley would hope to keep his private life separate from the political arena. Romilly's involvement therefore proved ominous; she knew it and Romilly knew it. She also turned to a capable solicitor, Mr. Vizard, and the banker Thomas Coutts. Meanwhile, things became very messy indeed. On 7 December, Hyacinthe went to see the marquess, claiming it was to "congratulate you on your nomination to the Ministry." Caught by surprise and certainly concluding that she had ulterior motives, Wellesley reacted violently, grabbing her by the arm and forcing her from the room, all in front of his daughter.[15] Hyacinthe reported this to her solicitors, and in the last weeks of December, they began drafting documents of separation. In the meantime, she stubbornly remained in Apsley House, to the consternation of her estranged husband.

Clearly Hyacinthe understood that she controlled the course of events. She knew that Wellesley wanted her out of the house, that he wanted everything settled before Parliament reconvened, and that the law was on her side. She would, therefore, drive a hard bargain. In the document of separation, she wrote pointedly,

> Lord Wellesley continuing to insist upon a separation between himself and Lady Wellesley without having and indeed without even alledging any serious cause of complaint against her and Lady Wellesley feeling and it being admitted by Lord Wellesley himself and known to his Family his Friends and the World that she has at all Times performed her duty as a faithful

> Wife to him and as an affectionate Mother to his Children cannot be induced by any threats or any conduct of his however violent to assent to such Separation but upon such Terms as are suitable to her Rank and as shall enable her to live in that style which as the Wife of the Marquis Wellesley she is entitled to support.[16]

The separation would cost the marquess £5,000 per year, not including provision for a suitable house with furnishings. Wellesley got what he wanted but at an expense from which he would never recover. Hyacinthe departed Apsley House on 19 February 1810. To her intransigent husband she wrote, "I will never see you again, save before the Supreme Judge. It is there that I, with a pure conscience, will summon you to appear, to receive with me, your judgment. As for that of man, it is already pronounced in spite of the newspapers which you pay with their weight in gold, and the flatterers whom you are reduced to buying with money, jobs and presents."[17] Pole followed this transaction as carefully as he could and kept Arthur apprised of its progress: "There never was such a Devil; nothing can be more handsome than Wellesley has been to her in all his conduct, or more liberal than his proposals. But she is as vindictive as a fiend, and as hard and indelicate as those of her old profession can be."[18] This was vintage William, for whom dispassionate analysis was an alien concept. London society took note, with the gossip mill running at high speed.

This distraction behind him, Wellesley turned to the weighty public issues facing him. To his surprise, he had discovered that his view of the war differed from the rest of the cabinet. The difference was that of scale, which in turn was tied to political and fiscal uncertainty. Wellesley's colleagues, who had experienced firsthand the collapse of the Portland administration and the unenthusiastic reconstruction of the new government, were unwilling to press what at that juncture was a policy with uncertain prospects. Wellesley, who viewed the war in terms of family fortunes as well as national security, thought moderation shortsighted, if not counterproductive. Naturally, he seized the moral high ground. This would prove extremely frustrating to his colleagues, who saw him as arrogant and politically naive. They viewed foreign policy in conjunction with domestic policy, in which fiscal concerns were paramount. Mounting debt, declining trade, and rising taxes were serious concerns that had political import. Wellesley had no sense for this, and in many ways it was the same issue that proved troublesome during his term as governor general. With India, the strong lobby of the East India Company interests had hounded the marquess; with the Peninsular War, it was the broader influence of the London merchant community. That Wellesley had no sense for the give and take of parliamentary politics begs the question, why? One explanation may be that he spent precious few years in the House of Commons; another is that early in his career he had observed the efficiency of Pitt and Dundas, and when things became dicey in English politics, he was away in India. More important is the fact that he spent his truly formative years in India, where he had to answer to no one. In any case, he had no appreciation for Perceval's position at the head of a tenuous and untested government.

Specifically, this government faced an opposition eager to deliver the *coup de grace.* By some twist, Wellesley rather than Perceval would be the focus of the opposition's hostility. "I trust the Marquis [Wellesley] will meet with the fate you predict for him," observed Lord Milton. "He is a great calamity inflicted upon England."[19] The king's speech, which called for continued support of the Peninsular War, was not the place for the opposition to begin, and solid support for it signaled to them that the going would be rough. "Lord Grey came in drunk from the Duke of York's where he had been dining," wrote the ever-acerbic Thomas Creevey. "He came and sat beside me on the same sofa, talked as well as he could over the division of the night before, and damned with all his might and main Marquis Wellesley, of whose profligate establishment I told him some anecdotes, which he swallowed as greedily as he had done the Duke's wine."[20] Grey was hardly one to mock the morality of a parliamentary colleague, but then as today, hypocrisy ran rampant.

The opposition opted for a tactic of hit and run, probing for vulnerability and a hot issue. They began with the battle of Talavera when the government introduced a motion of thanks to Wellington. In the House of Lords, Lord Grey, hoping to kill two birds with one stone, began by calling for publication of all correspondence and dispatches concerning Wellington's instructions and his course of action. Grey might thereby expose the government for either negligence or incompetence and at the same time question the motives and competence of the commander in chief. The government turned aside the motion for papers, but the discussion went on over the original motion of thanks, and the strength of feelings against the Wellesleys soon come to the fore. John Howard, the Earl of Suffolk, charged that Wellington had acted imprudently by placing himself in the position he did, that he should have had better knowledge of the strength of the French. Robert, second Earl Grosvenor, concurred. In Grosvenor's opinion, votes of thanks were to be granted not for valor and skill alone but should correspond to overall success as well.[21]

A frustrated and angry marquess, absorbing the rhetoric, sat on the front bench. He allowed the discussion to play out and then rose. To no one's surprise, he launched into a detailed defense of his brother, but he provided much more. Wellesley disagreed with his cabinet colleagues over their strategy for defending war policy. To his mind, there was nothing to hide; to the contrary, a full airing would only serve to strengthen the government's position. So, in this case, after presenting glowing praises of his brother, Wellesley embarked on a detailed analysis of the goals of Wellington's operation culminating in the battle of Talavera, the problems he had encountered in the pursuit of those goals, and the results. Wellington, he said, made the best out of a bad situation, for without Talavera, "it would have been impossible to prevent the enemy from over-running the South of Spain, or from making a fresh irruption into Portugal." This, coupled with the fact that Wellington had been able to withdraw to an advantageous position within the Portuguese frontier, fully justified a vote of thanks.[22]

Wellesley left the opposition empty-handed, and a subsequent vote carried the motion. The Whig hostess Elizabeth Vassal Fox, Lady Holland, who was sympathetic with the Peninsular War but no friend of the government, commented, "Lord Wellesley made his debut in the character of Minister upon the thanks of the House being moved to Lord Wellington. Some commend, and others disparage his speech; perhaps the middle line of praise would be nearest the truth. He was rather oriental in his style of praising his brother, but much may be owing to his feelings upon such a subject as that of his brother's merits undergoing a slighting review."[23]

Perceval, however, was in no mood to conduct in the House of Commons the debate that Wellesley wanted. "Because national uniformity was necessary," he explained naively to the House, "he would not introduce the over-all plan of the campaign or other peripheral topics, and concentrate solely on the battle itself."[24] This smacked of conceding that the campaign as a whole did not merit a vote of thanks.

The opposition agreed, many suggesting that Wellington fought at Talavera for the sole purpose of obtaining a title. The battle, they maintained, was exemplary of the commander's indiscretion, not his valor. Like the debate in the Lords, the government's position did not become secure until the strategy of the entire campaign was revealed and the results analyzed. Castlereagh, who was responsible for Wellington's orders, assumed that responsibility. He concluded that Wellington had carried on a reasonably successful campaign, under trying circumstances, without putting "himself in a situation from which he might not at any time have been able to regain his former position in Portugal."[25] The motion carried without a division, prompting a disappointed Creevey to comment, "All our indignation against Wellington ended in smoak. Opposition to his thanks was so unpopular, that some of the stoutest of our crew slunk away; or rather, they were dispersed by the indefatigable intrigues of the Wellesleys and the tricks of Tierney."[26]

Wellesley had little opportunity to gloat, for the opposition carried a motion of inquiry into the Walcheren campaign, which promised to be a bloody and uncertain ordeal. He remained convinced that the government could strengthen its position on the war in the Peninsula through a strategy of full disclosure. Such a tactic ran the risk of exposing the Spanish to ridicule and contempt and ultimately to the suggestion that they were not worth the effort, but here too Wellesley believed that the documentary evidence would suggest reason for hope and continued support. Moreover, he believed that the government had done nothing that could create embarrassment. Perceval, however, remained skeptical, asserting that the publication of papers would make the government more vulnerable. Wellesley, with the impatience of one who cannot understand anyone unable to appreciate his reasoning, sent a terse response: "The moment is now arrived. . . . If the Spanish and Portuguese papers are to be suppressed, I confess that it appears to me that we shall deprive ourselves of our main advantage in the conflict with the opposition. They will not be able to withstand the intrinsic and honest strength of our cause as founded on the information. But we shall be subject to every kind of prejudice, misrepresentation, and calumny if we refuse to produce evidence of what we must assert."[27]

Wellesley's instincts on this matter—in contrast to his normally flawed instincts on things political—were correct. A closer inspection explains this apparent contradiction. Although the marquess did not understand or appreciate the functions of party, he most certainly understood the elements of a good argument. Equally important, when he focused his formidable intellect, the result usually was something of high quality, and nothing focused his intellect quite like the promotion of family interests. Perceval gave way.

Unfortunately, events in Spain created problems for the government. The fall of Seville, the collapse of the Supreme Junta, and the French advance confirmed for many that Britain pursued a lost cause in Iberia. As the government prepared to introduce motions for subsidizing the Portuguese, they would discover the political impact of these events. On 22 February, Wellesley moved in the Lords to take thirty thousand Portuguese troops into Britain's pay at a cost of £980,000; this was a key component of Wellington's strategy. Though Wellesley's speech was uninspiring, the opposition could not mount an effective response, and the bill passed by a comfortable margin. Such was not the case in the Commons. The opposition struck with its standard argument, which, given recent events in Spain, seemed to contain greater credulity. Maintaining that the cause was hopeless, the opposition pointed to the massive French reinforcements pouring into Spain, the wretched state of the British treasury, and what seemed to be a lack of potential for success in the Spanish and Portuguese armies. Samuel Whitbread summed up the opposition point of view: "Spain has not done its duty—no matter from what cause—the people, had, however, some excuse—they had been under the selfish sway of an aristocracy, that only wanted to use them as an instrument to effect their own narrow purposes [and] abused by the blind bigotry of an intolerant priesthood."[28]

The government ignored the ideological tirades, pointing instead to the resilience of the Spanish and Portuguese patriots and Britain's moral responsibility to support them as long as a spark of resistance remained. In the end the motion carried, leaving Wellesley cautiously optimistic. The debate revealed that the government still had strong support for the war, but it also illustrated a growing apprehension on the part of many parliamentarians (opposition and government alike) over Britain's ability to finance the war. In Perceval and Liverpool, the marquess certainly detected such sentiment. Moreover, the opposition had become more convincing in its position that Spain could never be successful or even worthy of success in the war against France as long as the old social and political institutions remained. As a result, Wellesley's focus fell on the questions of Spain's granting commercial advantages in its American colonies for British merchants and of reforming Spain's government. The need for action of any sort became especially urgent because of the ongoing investigation of the failed Walcheren campaign, which emboldened the opposition, and increased pessimism within the cabinet. There existed a general fear that the situation in the Peninsula would deteriorate (as it would) and that parliamentary support for increased expenditure for the war would become problematic. Perceval therefore began to lean on his foreign secretary to press for trading concessions. "If such liberty is not speedily obtained, I do not see how we shall be able to pay our army out of the Kingdom," he explained.[29]

All of this tended to enrage the marquess, driving a wedge between him and his colleagues. He began to urge Perceval to reorganize the cabinet with an eye to its strengthening. This could have only one meaning—including Canning, Castlereagh, and Sidmouth in the fold. Richard would pester Perceval over this course for the next year and a half, though the likelihood of such a change was remote. Castlereagh and Canning were not ready to reenter government together, and Sidmouth would enter only with Castlereagh. Wellesley's real goal thus seems to have been to bring Canning on board in the hope of tipping the political balance towards an increased commitment to the war on Wellesley's side. At the same time, Wellesley's sincerity cannot be doubted. He would repeatedly offer to step aside as foreign secretary to bring in reinforcements. The situation for Perceval was complex. Wellesley was proving difficult to work with. He made no effort to hide his contempt for some of his colleagues, and he began to make a habit of absenting himself from cabinet meetings. At the same time, his public reputation remained high and Perceval could not rein him in. William, who was always quick to criticize, could not figure his brother out. Wellesley juxtaposed his brilliance in the House of Lords with rumors that he neglected the Foreign Office and tainted his public reputation with his private. Having jettisoned Miss Leslie, the marquess had taken up with one Moll Raffles, to the great glee of London cynics. But while Moll was certainly an embarrassing distraction, Wellesley's dispatches from the period give lie to the accusation that he ignored his responsibilities. This fact, however, does not excuse his lack of focus and his deeply flawed approach to parliamentary politics.

In any case, at this juncture, the government's decision to publish Wellesley's Spanish dispatches was being challenged in the Lords by none other than Wellesley's old friend, Grenville. Grenville based his opposition on the argument that the ministry violated several basic tenets of diplomacy by publishing the correspondence. He believed that Britain would betray the alliance by casting aspersions on the Spanish government and would compromise the safety of those whom the government held in confidence. He also maintained that Parliament had no right to investigate the ability and integrity of foreign army commanders, especially those of an ally—in this case, General Cuesta. Such action, Grenville added, would inhibit all future operations involving the combined allied forces. Most important, Grenville was certain that should the papers be made public, future British ministers would be shunned and all confidence in them withheld by foreign governments.[30]

The marquess struck at Grenville's specific objections, claiming them moot because of the extinction of the Supreme Junta. Then, using Grenville as a means of attacking the opposition, Wellesley charged his former schoolmate with ignorance and neglect. He castigated Grenville for exhibiting hypocrisy in referring to the Foreign Office's mismanagement of its affairs while being grossly uninformed. "What then is the cause," asked Wellesley, "which has thus disturbed the noble lord's temper, and perverted his judgement? The noble lord cannot have read the papers, or he does not understand them."[31] The Lords flatly rejected Grenville's motion, and the breach in a long friendship widened. The event caused a stir, as Pole reported: "What passed in the House of Lords between W. and Ld Grenville, has raised the former very much in general estimation. The Chancellor told me that he never heard a speech produce so great an effect and that he thought it beyond comparison the best Speech he had ever heard. I witnessed both Speeches and there certainly never was a more complete triumph. It depends solely upon himself whether or no He is to be the greatest man in the country."[32] This was the problem with Wellesley: just when he provoked despair, there came flashes of genius.

Despite his success in debate, taking on his old friend reminded the marquess of the polarized nature of British politics and of the fact that generating support for a controversial policy would not be easy. The reality was that nothing looked particularly promising. Spain was a mess, the French were gearing up for a new offensive, and Portugal appeared to be vulnerable. Wellington, who carefully supervised the construction of his Lines of Torres Vedras, remained confident of his position, but no one could yet appreciate the effectiveness of his preparations. Beyond these extraordinary defensive measures, Wellington also planned for a future offensive by increasing the size of the Portuguese army, but when he looked to London, all he received in return was caution. "The expenditure of this country has become enormous, and if the war is to continue, we must look to economy," wrote Liverpool. "I do not believe so great a continued effort has ever been made by this country, combining the military and pecuniary aid together, as his Majesty is making for Portugal and Spain. The respective governments of these countries should be made sensible of the truth of this position, and should feel the necessity of making extraordinary exertions for their own support."[33] Such thinking frustrated Arthur, who pointed out the obvious: "If we had a strong government in England, and the command of money, and arms I think we might still oblige the French to evacuate the Peninsula."[34]

Henry, meanwhile, having cleared his desk of early distractions, turned to more pressing matters. He addressed two issues: securing a license to purchase specie in America, and initiating negotiations for a general agreement on trade between Great Britain, Spain, and the Spanish colonies. Specie had become essential to the conduct of the war against France, particularly in the Iberian Peninsula. Wellington needed it to purchase transport and supplies, and the government needed it to subsidize its continental allies, including Spain. As Spanish America was the most reliable source of gold and silver, Britain logically turned in this direction. The challenge for Henry was securing favorable terms for such purchases and making certain the flow was steady. Not surprisingly, the Spanish were not always cooperative, claiming that their own domestic needs came before Britain's but really using the granting of licenses as a bargaining chip in their negotiations.

The trade issue posed greater problems. The alliance with Spain, born in 1808, had greatly complicated Britain's relations with Spanish America. Heretofore, Britain had carried on a clandestine trade that had proved a profitable, though incomplete, substitute for the European trade lost to Napoleon's Continental System. Once Spain and Britain became allies, Britain's illegal trade was supposed to stop. It did not, of course, though it certainly slowed. For British merchants and therefore the government, the alliance promised free and open trade to compensate for increasing losses on the Continent. From the British perspective, trade with the American colonies seemed a logical step. Foreign subsidies were dependent on Britain's overall economic health, which, largely because of the Continental System, was not good. Increased trade would allow for increased subsidies. The Spanish, however, saw the situation differently. Since the establishment of its colonial empire, Spain had jealously guarded trade with the colonies. Trade occurred only on Spanish ships through Spanish ports, and to Spanish eyes nothing had changed; opening trade to Great Britain was a slippery slope that would lead inevitably to the decline of Spain's commerce and the colonial system. Moreover, the British could afford subsidies for Spain, just as they had managed to subsidize the Austrians, Russians, and Prussians. This inclination to stonewall on the issue of trade certainly derived from the belief that Britain had little choice but to support Spain, but concepts of self-preservation were also at work. With the fall of Seville and the transference of Spain's political center to Cádiz, the attitude became ever more firmly fixed. Cádiz had long been the center of Spain's trade with the colonies, and a merchant community with little interest in sacrificing their livelihood to British interests dominated the city. Henry Wellesley soon came to appreciate this reality. "The city of Cadiz is more connected with South America than all the rest of Spain put together," he wrote, "and the establishment of our influence here will greatly facilitate any arrangements we may wish to make hereafter with South America."[35]

He addressed the matter of specie first because it was more straightforward and far less controversial. Nonetheless, the regents responded in a fashion that would soon become tiresome for the British envoy. The Spanish maintained that the Mexican treasury was short of funds and could not meet British demands. Henry countered by asking for all that could be spared. No answer. He renewed the request knowing that London would not take no for an answer. Persistence, it seems, was the key; the regency granted him license to purchase $10 million of specie on the open market, asking for 17 percent on the bills of exchange. Wellesley again protested and settled for 11 percent.[36] It was all very hard work for something that bore little consequence in Cádiz but was absolutely essential for Wellington's army and for paying subsidies to the regency government of Spain.

Henry then waded into the complicated issue of trade. The subject came up when Bardaxi informed him that Spain would shortly be in need of money to meet its basic obligations and looked to Britain for relief. Wellesley warned that with Parliament ill disposed toward Spain, delaying the petition for subsidy would be advisable. Bardaxi countered by suggesting that discussions on a trade agreement might make a difference. Henry wrote naively to his brother: "I am certain that the Spanish government and Bardaxi are anxious to meet me half way in any arrangement which may have for its object the mutual benefit of the two kingdoms. I shall therefore wait with anxiety for your instructions upon this subject."[37]

The marquess, however, was not particularly eager to engage the Spanish on this subject, for he believed that the most effective leverage in dealing with the Spanish was the disbursement of subsidies. Therefore, he rejected the idea of a reciprocal arrangement whereby Britain promised a set amount of aid annually in return for trading privileges in Spanish America. At the same time, he knew that Perceval would insist on negotiations, but Perceval's idea of a trade agreement was simply that of Spain opening her colonial ports to British ships because only through expanded trade could Britain finance the war in Spain. Well aware of the unrealistic nature of expecting the Spanish to give in on trade for vague promises of reciprocation, Wellesley was still willing to indulge the prime minister as long as the two issues of trade and subsidy remained separate.[38] In other words, at this point, Wellesley did not take the issue of trade seriously but ordered Henry to persist nonetheless.

The warning came too late: Henry had discovered that the marquess was right to assume that Spain responded only to fiscal pressure. Despite the fact that Henry had headed off a food crisis caused by the regency's neglect, the arrival of $7 million in specie from Veracruz relieved the Spanish government's anxieties, bolstered its sense of independence, and eliminated any hint of gratitude. Suggestions of a trade agreement dissipated, and to make matters worse, rumors were floated in the city that Britain intended to make Cádiz another Gibraltar.[39] It was a clever trick that Henry would encounter again. Whenever the Spanish leadership felt as if they were losing the diplomatic initiative, they turned to rumor and Anglophobia.

Meanwhile, Henry carried on a vigorous correspondence with Arthur, just as Richard had intended. Normally they sent packets each week on ships sailing between Cádiz and Lisbon, with Arthur always including copies of his reports to Liverpool. In this way, they kept one another apprised of what was transpiring in their respective theaters of operations. The correspondence also contained brotherly comments. Quite naturally the younger looked to the older for advice, and Arthur willingly offered it. In these months, Henry found his brother in a demonstrably foul mood. As Wellington supervised the construction of the Lines of Torres Vedras and observed the chaos in the French army forming before him, he concluded that Portugal could be preserved as long as the government continued to meet his needs. Unfortunately, he could not convince skeptics in London, who were tired of unrealized expectations. He fumed at the government's inability to construct any sort of consensus, and he lashed out at Richard, of whose desultory private life William provided ample detail.[40] "The account which you give of the state of affairs in England is not satisfactory," he responded famously to his brother.

> I wish that Wellesley was *castrated*; or that he would like other people attend to his business & perform too. It is lamentable to see Talents & character & advantages such as he possesses thrown away upon Whoring. Then the ruin to his Private Fortune which at his time of life is irretrievable, is as certain as the loss of character & the misuse of his Talents and the dereliction of his advantages; & the Injury which the Publick & his Party must suffer from this folly. This really gives me the greatest concern; & I really think that Sydenham & Shaw as they are the only persons who he allows to talk to him upon these subjects ought never to cease to represent to him the inevitable consequences of his perseverance in the system which he has adopted.[41]

William loved gossip, and although he probably spared no details and may even have embellished some, the simple fact is that Richard was behaving badly. He was, however, in contrast to William's account, also attending to his duties. He carried on a vigorous debate with Perceval over the Spanish papers, explored ways to strengthen the ministry, prepared legislation to bring the Portuguese army into British pay, considered political alternatives to the regency government in Cádiz, and continued in his correspondence with Henry. Moreover, June found him emotionally on firmer ground. He dropped his mistress Moll Raffles and began leading a more conventional lifestyle.[42] In this light, Wellington seems harsh, though certainly in public he was much more kind in his comments about Richard. Still, Arthur was working hard under extraordinary pressure, and he felt underappreciated by those who should have known better. Nonetheless, the moment is significant because Arthur had begun to see his own career as separate from Richard's. Unlike India, where Richard controlled his destiny, the Peninsula gave Arthur a stage upon which he knew that he would succeed or fail largely on his own. He had also concluded that Richard was no longer a safe bet.

In June 1810, Parliament prepared for a debate on the Peninsular War and in particular the affairs of Spain. This was an event the marquess looked forward to, but the timing could not have been worse. Napoleon had dispatched his best marshal, André Masséna, to chase the leopard into the sea (as the imminent fate of the British troops was portrayed), and he was about to lay siege to Ciudad Rodrigo. The *Examiner* spoke for many when it declared, "There can be little question, that the French are putting or about to put the finishing stroke to Spanish independence. The Paris papers inform us that Masséna is marching towards this consummation with 75,000 men, so that we may soon look out for the return of my Lord Wellington—and then *Exeunt omnes,*—the farce is ended."[43] The new debate over the battle of Talavera would sound much like that, with the Marquis of Lansdowne challenging Wellington's competence and the government's wisdom.

The marquess rose in defense. He conceded that although the results of Talavera had fallen far short of expectations, the battle was not a total loss. Hinting at his brother's activities in Portugal, he pointed out that the campaign had given that country a "breathing spell" and a chance to reorganize its army and defenses. Furthermore, had the Spanish not embarked on their ill-fated autumn campaign, southern Spain would have remained secure. That said, Wellesley launched into the heart of his argument: "The brightest prospect which had offered itself for several years of reasserting the independence of Europe, and with it the security of this country, opened at the moment when Spain magnanimously rose to maintain her legitimate monarchy, and to resist the most unprincipled usurpation of which history affords an example."[44] Iberia provided Britain with a front on which to operate directly against the French and thus served as an example that could stimulate similar uprisings against Napoleon elsewhere. There were, of course, obstacles to success—a product of Spain's unique situation—but these were remediable. Moreover, Spain was Britain's ally, and as long as that nation offered a spark of resistance, Britain was obliged to assist in the effort.

When Wellesley relinquished the floor, he found little enthusiasm for continuing the debate, confirming his view that the Spanish papers would validate the government's policy. What did follow was effusive praise for his work as ambassador. His old friend Sidmouth commended his "sagacity and judgement," regretting that "recourse had not been had earlier to the services of that noble marquis."[45] Though normally a critic, James St. Clair–Erskine, the second Earl of Rosslyn, agreed; he speculated that if Wellesley had been sent to Spain earlier, "the contest would have been much more favorable to the patriots."[46] The concurrence of Lord Holland, Henry Vassal Fox, came from the opposition benches. Still, when the vote came, the government's majority was a comfortable but hardly overwhelming thirty-two votes.

Wellesley knew that though the government had escaped censure on its peninsular policy, its majorities were less than solid, certainly of insufficient magnitude to embolden Perceval. The marquess had hoped to reinforce Wellington's army and to begin reforms in Spain's military, both of which would require a substantial increase in expenditure. He maintained that rapid reforms could be made in the Spanish army by placing it under British officers and bringing it into Britain's pay, much in the same manner in which General William Carr Beresford had reorganized the Portuguese army as its commander in chief. Wellesley estimated the cost of the plan at nearly £3 million per year.[47] This he considered reasonable but knew the prime minister would disagree. Even more frustrating was the realization that reinforcing Wellington would also garner little support. Liverpool, in fact, informed Wellesley that Britain would be unable to support Wellington's army at its present strength and even suggested that Spain contribute.[48]

Liverpool's assertion presented the marquess with what appeared to be an insoluble dilemma. It came at a time when Spain again desperately sought a loan, and although this was a legitimate request, the marquess could not respond. How then could Spain be expected to cooperate in the financing of British troops in Portugal when in fact the Spaniards could not support themselves and Britain was failing to grant even minimal financial assistance? Frustration set in. Besides being genuinely convinced that Britain needed to enlarge the effort in the Peninsula, he was still an autocrat, used to having his way. He again thought about ways to reconstruct the ministry that might strengthen its grip on Parliament.[49]

In Cádiz, Henry continued to wrestle with Anglophobia, aggravated by suggestions in British newspapers that Ceuta should be seized to protect British commerce in the western Mediterranean. As a result, commercial interests in Cádiz were ever more determined to oppose trading concessions, believing that these would only promote what they considered a British conspiracy to destroy the economic power of the city. Wellesley wisely set aside the trade issue and focused instead on the purchase of specie, which Arthur desperately lacked. Frustrated with the machinations of the regency, Henry investigated the feasibility of acquiring specie on the open market. He found that $500,000 could be purchased monthly, and forgoing permission from London, he proceeded to do so while urging Colin Campbell in Gibraltar to do the same.

Then, as quickly as the Spanish had turned against their ally, Henry found them on his doorstep hat in hand. The regency had run through the infusion of cash it had received in May. With no additional income in sight, the Spanish government turned to Britain for an immediate loan of £2 million. The solicitation, made both in Cádiz and in London, confirmed their desperation. Clearly, Henry was in a better position than the marquess and his colleagues to judge the urgency of the request and the dire consequences of its rejection.[50] Still, he proceeded cautiously, wary of Perceval's conservative fiscal views.

To Henry's eyes, the regency's fiscal plight had reached a point at which it could not support even the most meager of military activities. Meanwhile, Bardaxi announced that he was prepared to explore trading concessions in return for the loan. But as direct trade with the colonies was out of the question, Henry, per instructions from the foreign secretary, could not bargain. Bardaxi followed with the suggestion that Henry issue bills of exchange to the amount of $1.5 million on the condition that if a loan were not granted in London, the amount could be paid from the first specie received from South America. Lacking the authority to grant such a request, Henry again declined. Then, recognizing that the crisis would soon lead to the disintegration of the Spanish armies still in the field, Wellesley began to reconsider. The results would be particularly disastrous in the case of the marquis de la Romana's army, which, although not a potent force, occupied the attentions of General Jean Louis Reynier's Second Corps. With Romana gone, Wellesley assumed that Reynier would be at liberty to reinforce Masséna with the seventeen thousand men under his command. Such reinforcements could have disastrous effects on Wellington, and so on his own authority, Henry granted a short-term loan of $1.5 million under the conditions outlined by Bardaxi.[51]

Such independent action was, of course, precisely why Wellesley had put his brother in Cádiz, but it horrified Perceval. "I tremble for the effect of it," he informed the marquess, "as far as our exertions in Portugal & our Portuguese subsidy is concerned."[52] The prime minister suggested a reprimand, but the marquess turned him aside. Henry was, however, ordered to inform the regency that the loan could not be granted and to demand repayment of the advance out of the first shipment of specie received from the American colonies.[53] Henry then returned to the trade issue. He had come to believe that insisting on unrestricted trade would have serious consequences and that some middle ground had to be found. "I am apprehensive," explained Henry, "that any measure likely to prove injurious to their mercantile interest would contribute more towards the completion of the designs of the enemy upon Cádiz than all his own efforts and exertions of whatever descriptions they might be."[54]

Wellesley therefore presented a three-part proposal. First, he proposed that the cotton manufactures of Great Britain and the British colonies, along with raw materials and certain other manufactured products, be exported through Spain to South America. Second was the proposal that Spain modify duties levied in Spain on all British goods and that customs procedures be streamlined to eliminate delays. The third element was that Britain be allowed to export specie from South America duty free for the duration of the war. There would, Henry pointed out, be a commitment by both parties that a regular treaty of commerce would follow when circumstances permitted.

Bardaxi countered with several additions and alterations. Among them were demands that all trade be carried on Spanish ships and that colonial goods be allowed into Great Britain. More important, Bardaxi insisted that any agreement on trade be tied to one on subsidies. Specifically, Spain wanted a loan of £10 million and the use of forty naval transports and adequate escort to convey troops and military equipment to wherever the Spanish government deemed proper.[55]

This was like a splash of cold water bringing Henry to an abrupt realization of the complexity of the issue. First, the whole issue of separating subsidy from that of trade, which he could understand from his brother's point of view, the Spanish deemed unacceptable. Whether the Spanish negotiators were truly interested in an agreement or not, he did not know; if they were not, then insisting on a subsidy agreement was a convenient diplomatic tool. Certainly he would have liked to call the Spanish bluff, but this would never get past Perceval. Then there was the issue of reciprocity in trade. If Britain was to be given trading privileges in Spain's colonies, then why prevent the colonies from acquiring similar privileges in Britain? That logic ran head-on into London's merchant community. But how was that situation different from British trading privileges and Cádiz's merchant community? There was in fact no real hope for an agreement, and this apparently suited the marquess. In any case, Henry sent his proposals and the Spanish response on to his brother.[56]

In London the trade issue took on new urgency. On 19 April 1810, the city of Caracas in Venezuela declared its independence. In a case of diplomatic doublespeak, the Venezuelans declared continuing allegiance to the person of Ferdinand VII (the Spanish king, then in confinement), but clearly they intended to govern themselves. The revolutionary junta in Caracas then turned to the British military governor in Curaçao, asking for muskets, ammunition, and naval protection. In return, the Venezuelans issued a vague promise to cooperate with Britain in the war and to open Venezuelan ports to British commerce. The governor, who was certainly in over his head, consented to the requests without first consulting with London. "The manner in which the chief authority has been constituted in the persons of your highnesses," he gushed, ". . . must and will be the admiration of future ages."[57]

The revolution in Caracas came as no surprise to Wellesley or to Liverpool, whose offices were directly affected by the course of events. The Venezuelan revolutionary Francisco de Miranda had long used London as a base of operations and had often solicited British assistance, including the plan to send Arthur with the expedition that had been redirected to Portugal in 1808. The alliance with Spain born of the uprising against France had forced Britain to terminate subversive activities in Spanish America and to sever connections with Miranda.

Wellesley and Liverpool therefore moved quickly to control the damage, and the latter reprimanded the governor of Curaçao, stating that Britain sought only to mediate Venezuela's grievances in an effort to bring the state back into Spain's colonial system. Wellesley sent copies of the document to Admiral Ruiz de Apodaca in the Spanish embassy and to Henry for distribution to the regency.[58]

This was all a clear reminder to the marquess of his precarious position; on the one hand, as Spain's ally, Britain was obliged to support both Spain and Spain's colonial empire, but on the other, failure to support the revolutionaries would push them into the hands of France and the United States. Moreover, Wellesley knew that British commercial interests would never tolerate active assistance in suppressing the revolt, because it would jeopardize future dealings, not to mention some existing illegal arrangements, in the Americas. Clearly, Britain's best interest lay in resolving any and all disputes between Spain and the Spanish colonies, at least while the war with France was being fought.

Simple solutions were not to be found, and the foreign secretary knew it. Spain's colonial system was oppressive and prejudicial to colonial economic interests. He did believe that trade was the most problematic issue. Since the war's onset, commercial intercourse between Spain and the colonies had been drastically curtailed, compromising the dominant middle class, who found themselves largely deprived of their livelihood. Spain's rigidly enforced trading monopoly prevented recourse to other sources (specifically, Great Britain) creating great frustration and some despair. Given this analysis, for Lord Wellesley the solution was obvious—that Spain must open its ports to British trade. This would not only reduce popular discontent in the colonies but would also enhance Britain's capacity to support Spain. Wellesley, of course, recognized that this analysis suffered from oversimplicity, but he believed that open trade would postpone open conflict, at least until the end of the war, when the domestic aspects of trade would become Spain's problem alone. The turn of events highlights Wellesley's cynicism concerning the issue of trade and the alliance in general. As often as trade appears in his dispatches, there is no evidence that the marquess ever took it seriously. Like the Spanish negotiators, he too was skilled in obfuscation. He saw the pursuit of a trade agreement as a foolish distraction that, even if concluded on terms acceptable to Great Britain (which seemed unlikely), would not appreciably change anything in a timely fashion. Certainly the revolt in Caracas greatly complicated diplomacy, requiring him to engage in discussions seriously but without expecting to achieve an agreement. He saw absurdity on both sides—Perceval's and Spain's—but revolution was serious business, and it could not be allowed to distract the Spanish government from the primary task of fighting France.

The situation grew more complicated when on 11 July, two representatives from the junta of Caracas, Simón Bolívar and Luis Méndez, arrived in Britain to solicit British support. The marquess could not ignore them, but at the same time, he could not legitimize them by granting them an audience. Consequently, he attempted to steer a middle course first by dispatching his Spanish-speaking son, Richard, to talk with them and then by meeting with them informally, privately.[59] As he explained to the Duke of Albuquerque, he "considered the arrival of these deputies as a circumstance of great advantage, as it would enable H.M.'s Govt. to represent in the most expeditious manner to the authorities in the Province of Venezuela the erroneous view which they have taken of the state of Spain and to urge the expediency of reuniting that province to the authorities of the provisional Govt. established in the Mother Country."[60]

This done, the marquess drafted new instructions to Henry, whose account of his own negotiations was in Richard's hands. Wellesley knew that the circuitous trade proposed by the Spanish would be unacceptable to Perceval, but he also regarded it as no solution. Only direct trading privileges would suffice because anything less would inhibit rather than increase trade. Britain's growing illicit trade with the Spanish American colonies through free ports in the West Indies would be compromised by any agreement. As he explained to Henry, "If a formal convention were to be established limiting our intercourse with the Spanish colonies to the circuitous trade through the Port of Cádiz, it might be inferred, that His Majesty's Government might be bound by the obligation of good faith to prevent the commerce carried on."[61] This does not sound much like the marquess, who was quite capable of diplomatic deceit. If Britain was already illegally superseding the colonial laws of an ally, what difference would the conclusion of a trade agreement make to Britain's ethical sensibilities?

Regardless, Wellesley instructed Henry to resume efforts to reach an agreement opening direct trade on a most-favored-nation basis. He offered some wiggle room, and one wonders if this was cleared with the prime minister. Specifically, Wellesley would be willing to accept circuitous trade but only if it took place on British vessels. But this was a work in progress; two weeks later, the instructions had changed. Spanish vessels could be used in the circuitous trade if duties were lowered and if specie could be exported duty free. This new flexibility reflected growing impatience in London with the Spanish ally. "When . . . they are in no possibility of supplying South America themselves they will not allow us to do so but upon terms utterly inadmissible," wrote George Rose, vice president of the committee on trade; "one would almost be tempted to say, founded in idiocy or madness—thus wantonly punishing their colonies and only ally, and compelling the former to break their ties with the parent country to obtain supplies which they cannot do with out. Mules as they are, it seems hardly credible that they cannot be made sensible of the perverse folly of their conduct."[62] Conversely, the Spanish were becoming impatient with Britain's conduct, and this too influenced Wellesley's actions.

In Cádiz, Henry proceeded as instructed, and as expected, the Spanish rejected his overture. Bardaxi offered grandiose explanations, pointing out, "A nation that is fighting for the preservation of its liberty, and independence, ought never to depart from those principles, that constitute either of these privileges, and from the moment that it should do so, it would renounce for ever the glory of acquiring them."[63] Beyond that, he accused Britain of extortion by threatening to withhold subsidies should trade not be granted on British terms. Not only was this contrary to the spirit of any alliance, it seemed to him especially illogical given Spain's performance as an ally compared to the likes of Austria, Russia, and Prussia. Spain, according to Bardaxi, was a real bargain, and Britain failed to take sufficient advantage.

To a degree, Henry concurred with these sentiments and thought that there were those in London who could use a heavy dose of realism.[64] Complicating matters, he had to deal with the reaction in Cádiz to his brother's meeting with Bolívar and Méndez. Always suspicious of British activities in their colonies, the people of Cádiz commonly believed that Britain was complicit in the Venezuelan revolt. The marquess's open dealings with Bolívar and Méndez and the public adulation accorded them in London only confirmed these suspicions. The British press did not help matters by suggesting immediate recognition of colonial revolutions. When news came of a revolt in Buenos Aires, Spanish anger grew, and Henry withdrew from discussions on trade. Instead he smoldered, nursing his anger over being asked to pursue a policy that he deemed unwise and unattainable. He vented to Arthur: "Thus are petty British objects of commerce suffered to interfere with the great and interesting work of releasing this country from the yoke of France; and, unless the British Government takes the decided line of discouraging the spirit which has broken forth in the colonies, and that too in the most open manner, it will create such a jealousy here as never can be got under, and will probably be the ruin of the whole cause."[65]

Arthur sympathized, but he approached the issues of trade and colonial rebellion from an entirely different angle. On the issue of trade, Arthur had strong opinions that must have come as a surprise to Henry. "I hope the Regency will have firmness to resist the demand of a free trade with the colonies," he wrote:

> Great Britain has ruined Portugal by her free trade with the Brazils: not only the customs of Portugal, to the amount of a million sterling per annum, are lost, but the fortunes of numerous individuals, who lived by this trade, are ruined; and Cadiz will suffer in a similar manner, if this demand is agreed to. Portugal would be now in a very different situation as an ally, if our trade with the Brazils was still carried on through Lisbon; and I would only ask, is it wise, or liberal, or just to destroy the power and resources, and absolutely to ruin our allies, in order to put into the pockets of our merchants the money which before went into their treasuries, and would be now employed in the maintenance of military establishments against the common enemy?[66]

In fact, Richard might not have disagreed with Arthur, though he likely did not give the matter much thought. Heretofore the whole issue of trade had simply been something he had to concede to Perceval and do his best to appear to care. In other words, for the marquess, trade was a political issue rather than an economic one. The events in Venezuela had complicated the situation, and Richard was desperate to prevent the spread of colonial rebellion, which he believed inevitable, not because he thought it a bad thing but because it would distract the Spanish from the project at hand—the defeat of France. Two things could happen: Spain could divert its military effort to the Americas, or Spain could come to an agreement with Napoleon to preserve the empire. Not surprisingly, Arthur again saw this differently. "I agree entirely with you respecting the impolicy of the conduct of our Government regarding the Spanish colonies," he wrote to Henry. "From what I hear, I believe that they think in England it is impossible to prevent the spirit which has broken forth in Caraccas from spreading all over America. It is my opinion they are mistaken."[67] Arthur believed that Bolívar's rebellion was narrowly based and that when the colonials discovered this, they would undo the damage. Sensing political trends was never Arthur's strong suit; on this he proved utterly wrong.

In any case, there is no suggestion in Henry's correspondence that he perceived Richard's strategy for what it was, merely engaging and perpetuating the discussion on trade with no intention of concluding an agreement, and perhaps he was better off for it. Richard was caught between the proverbial rock and a hard place. Britain was bound by treaty to maintain the Spanish empire as it existed in January 1809, but if Spain refused to deal with the new revolutionary governments, they would turn to France and the United States for assistance, taking their trade with them. Britain therefore had to steer a middle course while an attempt was made to effect a reconciliation between the mother country and the rebellious colonies. But this only accounts for Spain. Richard also had to deal with a nervous prime minister who was eager to placate the commercial establishment while at the same time increasing public revenue.

Putting issues of trade to the side, Henry turned to pressing political issues in Cádiz. There the regency's popularity had plunged. The regents were blamed for a myriad of problems, including the ongoing fiscal crisis and a deteriorating military situation. But what particularly engaged public attention was the upcoming assembling of the Cortes and the sudden presence in Cádiz of the duc d'Orléans (Louis-Philippe, the future king of France). The marquess had warned about Orléans, and as instructed, Henry had told Bardaxi that Britain would not look favorably on the duke's employment in Spain.[68] His sudden appearance in the city, therefore, was a mystery, and Henry promptly began his own investigation. He discovered, to his chagrin, that the duke had been invited by the regents to take command of the Spanish army in

Catalonia. Bardaxi denied complicity, explaining that the junta on the recommendation of the British government had issued the invitation much earlier and that the regents were in no position to revoke it. He assured Henry that Orléans would not be given the command. Unconvinced, Henry warned Bardaxi that Britons and Spaniards alike would find the employment of Orléans offensive.[69]

There was no denying that the duke was a problem. At the very least, the episode could cause Britain much embarrassment, but it could even destabilize the regency government. Clearly, Henry had to respond, but he operated in an information vacuum. He hesitated to deny Britain's involvement when he did not know for certain that Britain was not involved. Still, common sense suggested that Bardaxi's assertions were false. First, Henry found it puzzling that the duke made no effort to meet with him, which, if Britain were his sponsor, was highly irregular. Second, Lord William Amherst, Britain's representative in Sicily, where Orléans resided, had sent nothing to Henry concerning the duke's determination to go to Spain. If Britain were involved, then certainly Amherst would have been party to it and so informed Henry. "There is something at the bottom of this transaction which has not come to light," Henry wrote to the marquess.[70]

Awaiting instructions from London, Henry advised the regents to ignore the duke and by all means make no commitments concerning his employment. As the situation deteriorated, Henry induced the regents to preempt the duke by appointing the marquis de la Romana to command in Valencia and Catalonia and General Joseph O'Donnell in Murcia. These actions lessened the tension, but the duke remained in Cádiz and his mere presence fed the general discontent. Instructions finally arrived from Wellesley authorizing Henry to remove Orléans quietly from the city. Without delay Henry met with the duke, advising him that his services in the Peninsula would not aid the common cause and that he go to London to discuss his employment elsewhere. The duke responded in a fashion that would have done even a Spaniard proud: he would comply with anything consistent with his rank and dignity. Henry concluded that he would not leave Spain without an official request from the regency to do so. Strangely, this was not forthcoming. "The Duke of Orleans is intriguing to a much greater extent than you are aware of," he wrote to Richard. "It is wonderful that he does not feel the impossibility of his being employed here. I am persuaded that the first intelligence of his employment would occasion an insurrection. I fear it will require some strong measure to drive him from hence, for I have no hope of being able to get him away, excepting by an official application to the government."[71]

Finally Bardaxi came clean. The regents had in fact invited the duke to take command of an army in Catalonia, but that invitation had been issued at a time when conditions were favorable to such an event. In this light, the regents believed that if they ordered Orléans to leave, he might expose their role in bringing him to Cádiz, which could lead to such a public uproar that they might be forced from office. For this reason, Bardaxi requested Henry's assistance in removing Orléans. Though disturbed with the regency's deceit, Wellesley agreed, responding with a public statement declaring Britain's opposition to the duke's employment in Spain in any capacity. The regents hoped that Orléans would leave without exposing their role in the misadventure. To their dismay, this was not to be; the duke countered by publishing the regency's letters inviting him to Cádiz.[72]

Public discontent with the government intensified. The old issues—the static military situation and the chaos in Spain's finances—remained unresolved, and added to them was the embarrassment of Orléans. This antagonism, combined with the indignation created by Britain's tacit recognition of the colonial revolutionaries from Caracas and Buenos Aires, made the political situation in Cádiz highly volatile. Spaniards began clamoring for the Cortes, originally scheduled to meet in March and then postponed to August. A second postponement to September made many feel that the regents were engaged in a desperate act of self-preservation.

In fact, there was no conspiracy on this occasion. Instead there was turmoil over the elections. Liberals complained that the indirect mode of elections—a progression from the parish to the town to the district and finally to the province—favored the established classes, resulting in the election of a large number of priests and nobles. Even louder complaints came from conservatives. They objected to both representation based on population and a single-body legislature. Historically, the Cortes had been organized along the same lines as the old French Estates General, with representation divided among three groups: the clergy, the nobility, and the commoners. That system ensured a conservative majority, which, conservatives maintained, was necessary, or a "revolutionary spirit would introduce itself into that assembly, which would produce all the evils which had desolated France."[73] They argued, as French nobles had argued, that only the Cortes could alter the form of its representation and that any enabling decree by either the junta or the regency was invalid.

Besieged by complaints from all sides, the regency could not come to a conclusion on the other issues that were delaying the Cortes. In particular, the regents had to decide how to provide representation for those provinces whose deputies, because of French occupation, could not get to Cádiz, and for the American colonies. In late August, the regents finally ruled that these areas would be represented by provisional deputies elected from natives of those provinces and colonies residing in Cádiz. This accomplished, the date of 24 September was set for the opening session.

The announcement did little to settle the political atmosphere. Henry discovered in August that there existed a faction that sought to establish doña Carlotta, the princess of Brazil, as regent, and still another that favored the duke of Orléans. For this reason, the duke refused to leave Cádiz until the Cortes assembled, resulting in continuing public outrage with the regency. Henry feared that Orléans, recognizing he had little support, would strike a deal with supporters of the princess whereby he would back her pretensions in return for a command in the army. Both events Henry viewed as potentially disastrous. If the princess became regent, he wrote to Richard, it would weaken British influence in the Peninsula and "would place the Army of Portugal in some measure at the disposal of the Spanish Government, and would probably expose the Commander in Chief of the British Army to the interference of the Spanish Government in military points, from which he is now entirely free."[74] This conclusion was naïve, but it demonstrates the depth of Henry's concern. From Lisbon came advice from Wellington: "The Spanish politicians have only one object in the measure, and that is, to get hold of the resources of this country, as they are afraid of forcing the people of Spain themselves to submit to the privation and inconveniences to which they must submit, if ever they mean to form an army."[75]

Henry met with several influential delegates to the Cortes and outlined Britain's objections to either the princess or the duke becoming regent and suggested instead that if a new regency was to be formed, it should be composed of men from the Cortes. He also acquainted the Portuguese representative in Cádiz of Britain's opposition to the claims of the princess. The public announcement of Britain's position lowered the level of political tension, and the Cortes assembled on 24 September amidst calm.

The autumn brought more than the Cortes. Shortly after taking the fortress cities of Ciudad Rodrigo and Almeida, the French moved into the heart of Portugal. There on 27 September, Wellington fought and won a battle against André Masséna on the heights of Serra de Bussaco, providing Britain with its first good news from the battlefield since Talavera. Arthur's victory could hardly be described as smashing, but the end of the day found Masséna short 4,487 men while Wellington counted only 1,252 casualties. Bussaco was a battle that Arthur knew he had to fight for political as well as strategic reasons. His retreat from the field reminded some of Talavera, but this was Masséna's last chance to defeat the British before the allied army took up positions on the Lines of Torres Vedras. Moreover, the battle proved to Arthur and to the government in London that the Portuguese army had become a reliable and valuable component of the army.

Bussaco lifted a cloud from the marquess. Defeatism in London had become rampant even within the councils of government. For Richard, ever confident of ultimate success, this was hard to counteract given the reports from Ciudad Rodrigo and Almeida. But Bussaco revived lagging enthusiasm and infused Richard with energy. His mind turned to the future, envisioning a heightened British effort in Iberia and from there to central Europe. "I entertain great confidence respecting Portugal," the marquess exulted in a note to Perceval, "and if we should succeed, according to our real merits, in that quarter, a new & great scene may be expected to open in Europe."[76] The idea of extending the war against France reflected a comprehensive grasp of the importance of the conflict in the Peninsula and the nature of the war against Napoleonic France. Richard believed that overall success could be achieved only when the people of Europe rose in national revolts against French power. The Peninsular War would provide the model. "The wisdom of maintaining the war in Spain and Portugal," he wrote after Bussaco, "has been fully proved by the shade it has cast on the military and political character of Bonaparte."

The days following the news of Bussaco witnessed the delivery of generous shipments of military stores to Spain, reflecting at least some level of renewed confidence. Subsequent news of Wellington's strong position on the Lines of Torres Vedras only enhanced that sentiment, and Wellesley hoped that the convening of the Cortes would have the same effect for Spain. Richard had long believed that in the absence of the king, a representative assembly was necessary to overcome local jealousies and to generate public support for the government. Both the Supreme Junta and the regency had been able to control neither the provincial authorities nor their own generals, rendering coordination of the national effort impossible. Wellesley hoped that a regency ruling with the Cortes would strengthen the central government's authority, but in addition, the opposition's demand for a liberalization of Spain's political, economic, and social systems also motivated him. He viewed the Cortes as a visible first step in that direction. At the same time, he advised Henry to influence the Cortes against initiating what might be interpreted as radical legislation. Although Wellesley was intent upon silencing the liberal parliamentary opposition, he was not willing to do so at the risk of losing the support of the conservative majority. Wellington also worried that the Cortes might prove a double-edged sword: "The natural course of all popular assemblies, of the Spanish Cortes among others, is to adopt democratic principles, and to vest all the powers of the state in their own body; and this assembly must take care that they do not run in this tempting course, as the wishes of the nation are decidedly for a monarchy."[77]

It was on Henry that the responsibility for influencing the Spanish in the proper direction fell, and there were signs that this would not be easy. In one of its first official acts, the Cortes had declared itself Spain's sovereign authority, relegating the regency to a council of ministers. Henry, with good reason, worried that this would inhibit the decisive executive authority that was essential in times of war. Thus the specter of Spanish indecisiveness and inefficiency still loomed. To his credit, he remained optimistic. "Upon the whole," he wrote to Richard,

> with the exception of the decree by which the rank of the executive power is placed below that of the Cortes, their proceedings are extremely creditable to them, and justify a confident expectation that the most important consequences will be derived from this meeting. . . . In justice . . . to the motives of those who proposed the decree relative to the title of majesty being conferred upon the Cortes, and that of Highness of the Council of Regency, I must express my firm

> conviction that this does not proceed from any revolutionary feeling among the Deputies, many of whom declare both titles to be in conformity to ancient usage.[78]

As the year 1810 drew to a close, the Wellesley brothers found themselves in unsettled circumstances. In Cádiz, Henry encountered obstacles that he could not have imagined, though Richard had warned him to expect the unexpected. Matters of pride, petty politics, and cultural differences mixed with serious issues and conflicts of interest to stymie the youngest Wellesley's efforts to address urgently needed political and military reforms. Moreover, he believed that London asked the impossible of him in directing him to pursue the issue of trade. Not only had he come to view such a proposition as an impossibility, but he had also come to appreciate the Spanish point of view and resented the fact that trade greatly complicated his relations with the Spanish. Still, Henry had proved a quick study; he managed the embassy in Cádiz with great skill, ensuring the survival of the Spanish government while addressing British interests in a timely and conscientious manner. He worked with the assurance of support from Richard and the steadying hand of Arthur in Lisbon.

As for Richard, while often accused of neglecting political responsibilities in favor of personal interests, however ugly they might be, the record shows considerable activity and genuine concern for the government's course. The recognition that his was the lone voice in favor of an aggressive approach to the Peninsular War discouraged him while adding to his burden. One would be hard pressed to find two more different men than Wellesley and Perceval, and they found it difficult to work with one another. This was more of a problem for Perceval than Wellesley because the latter chose to ignore the former, a luxury the prime minister could not afford. Still, Wellesley spoke forcefully in the Lords in support of the war and especially Arthur's efforts, while urging the prime minister to strengthen the government. Unlike Perceval, Wellesley believed that pressing for a trade agreement was unrealistic and unwise. At the same time, he could not ignore the issue, first because of domestic political concerns and later because of the successful revolt in Caracas, but when he engaged in discussions on trade, he did so only for the purpose of discussion and little more. Instead he looked to Portugal, where Arthur had defeated Masséna at Bussaco and had then taken secure refuge behind the Lines of Torres Vedras. Better days lay ahead, and Wellesley urged the government to take a more ambitious stand.

Arthur, in the meantime, began to lose patience. "If *there was any Gov't.* or publick sentiment in England," he wrote, "if we thought of any thing excepting the saving of our shillings and six penses, if I could expect any thing but the gallows for making an exertion in which five lives should be lost, and which should not be followed by an immediate evacuation of the Peninsula by the French, I should say that we should yet make Boney repent his invasion of Spain. But alas! What can be done *for such a gov't.* and such a people?"[79] The government and the nation were not all that earned Arthur's criticism; so too did the army, as the "scum of the earth" theme made frequent appearances in his correspondence. Clearly, Arthur found himself under heavy pressure, and his nature led him to adopt a defensive posture. There would be many to blame him if he failed. This does not detract from his brilliantly conceived and executed scheme. The French stalled before Arthur's "lines," where they would suffer a horrific winter. Arthur had won the battle for Portugal, but no one yet knew it. The battle for Spain would begin in 1811.

12

Reversal of Fortunes

The distance of time makes it impossible to appreciate fully the accomplishment of the Lines of Torres Vedras, both in their conception and in their construction. This was defensive strategy on a grand scale. Wellington conceived it, Colonel Richard Fletcher of the engineers designed it, and the Portuguese constructed it. Oversight, labor, and secrecy combined elegantly to create something that no one—least of all Masséna—imagined, and they brought that brilliant soldier to a dead halt. This did not surprise the intrepid Arthur, but he also knew that few would understand that though he had retreated, he held all the trump cards. He had fought the battle of Bussaco not because he believed that he could put the French to rout but because London craved some sign of future success. Still, retreat from victory would conjure images of Talavera, and he prepared for the worst.

Grumbling arose first in Portugal among the "croakers" of his army and subsequently in London, but there were also those who anticipated and appreciated his strategy. Granville Leveson Gower wrote as early as 29 August 1810 to Lady Bessborough, "Do you not admire the Fabian Warfare of Lord Wellington? Any general who had not given such decisive Proofs of his willingness, when the occasion justified it, to engage in Battle could not have undertaken this species of War without incurring much clamour and abuse from the Public."[1]

Still, the public remained confused. My mother "amus'd me with her puzzle at the different readings of the news from Portugal," returned Lady Bessborough, who continued,

> At Mrs. Howe's it was explain'd to her as very good, and a proof of Ld. Wellington's good Generalship making Masséna retreat, and Mr. Long had betted . . . that Masséna without a battle would be forc'd to retreat into Spain before February. On her return home she met with Ld. Carlisle, who assur'd her Masséna had not retreated, but taken a better position, and plac'd us in a worse; that Ld. W. was no general at all, and fell from one blunder to another, and the most we had to hope was his being able to embark quietly and bring his troops in safety back to England, which he thought very doubtful.[2]

In short, unlike Jane Austen's rural gentry, London society speculated and gossiped incessantly about the war.

As always, Arthur chafed at even a hint of criticism and covered his political line of retreat by emphasizing the magnitude of his task. Days before the battle of Bussaco he had written to Pole,

> I have . . . terrible disadvantages to contend with. The army was, and indeed is still, the worst British army that was ever sent from England. Then, between ourselves, the spirit of party and of the times prevails in some degree here as well as elsewhere. There is a despondency among some; a want of confidence in their own exertions; an extravagant notion of the power and resources of the French, and a distaste for the war in the Peninsula, which sentiments have been created and are kept up by correspondence with England, even with Ministers and those connected with them.[3]

Nothing Arthur shared with William remained confidential for long; inevitably his views became a part of the public dialogue. Historians have repeatedly turned to such comments to demonstrate Wellington's contempt for his army, but while he may well have viewed it as a collection of rabble, he also knew that it functioned rather well. At work here, as on previous occasions, was the unflattering habit acquired in India of covering his tracks. He sought to convince anyone who would listen that he faced unfavorable odds. His claiming to have inadequate tools for the job meant that if he succeeded, the accomplishment would be magnified in proportion, and if he failed, well, that was to be expected.

Arthur's irritation never clouded his decision making. Bussaco, for instance, provided political cover, but there was much more to it and his soldiers figured prominently: "This movement has afforded me a favorable opportunity of showing the enemy the description of troops of which this army is composed; it has brought the Portuguese levies into action with the enemy for the first time in an advantageous situation; and they have proved that the trouble which has been taken with them has not been thrown away, and that they are worthy of contending in the same ranks with British troops in this interesting cause, which they afford the best hopes of saving."[4] This was Arthur's way of saying that Britain's investment in Portugal paid handsome dividends and that a similar investment in Spain might do the same. Unfortunately, that would require a major commitment from the government, and there was no sign that this would be forthcoming. Not all was gloom and doom, however; Spanish partisans continued to operate with devastating effectiveness in many areas of the country. That being the case, Arthur believed that while he kept Masséna fully engaged in Portugal, every effort had to be made to allow the partisans the opportunity to build their base and carry out their operations. And so while Lord Liverpool might be impatient for another battle, Arthur calmly informed the secretary for war that nothing good could possibly come of it and redirected the government's attention to supporting the guerillas. In the meantime, he looked to Richard not only to rally the government in support of his operations in Portugal but also to provide the resources necessary for Spain to undertake meaningful military reform. Henry would prepare the Spanish, politically and militarily, for the inevitable campaign to come.

After Bussaco the political challenge for Richard had grown more complicated rather than less. In retrospect it is difficult to appreciate Tory paranoia at this moment in Britain's history. Granted, government majorities on key issues were thin, but they were not razor thin, and although the Whigs appeared formidable, they were saddled with incompetent leadership and unpersuasive issues. None of this was apparent in 1810, however; few would have dreamed that nineteen years of unbroken Tory hegemony lay ahead. Since the collapse of Addington's ministry, the political world had been in the grip of palpable unease, and never more so than after Portland's resignation and the Canning-Castlereagh duel. This was largely attributable to the absence of obvious leaders and to the precarious health of George III at a time when Britain was mired in seemingly endless war. From the moment Perceval accepted the seals of office, London was rife with political speculation and maneuvering. No one expected the "evangelical prime minister" to last. As early as the spring of 1810, there were those who believed that the ministry would collapse on the ruins of the Walcheren campaign and that Wellesley, who was on record as having opposed that ill-conceived expedition, would step to the fore. Such fanciful musings were commonplace, and there is no evidence that the marquess took them seriously. What he did take seriously was the ministry's self-perceived weakness; he therefore continued to urge the prime minister to take steps to shore it up.[5]

An objective view of the political landscape leads to the conclusion that although Perceval was a less than inspiring leader, his position was stronger than it appeared, because those who found themselves in positions to challenge the government were not philosophically predisposed to do so. Canning, Castlereagh, and Sidmouth had little choice but to support the government on critical issues lest they expose themselves to charges of rank opportunism. But no one saw this until the Walcheren debate. Both Canning and Castlereagh—because in varying degrees they were authors of the event—weighed in on the government side while Wellesley, by agreement, remained silent. Success in debate bolstered Perceval's confidence but not sufficiently to proceed more ambitiously in the Peninsula. According to the Grenville coterie, the marquess emerged more dispirited than ever: "Lord Wellesley complains that he has no weight whatever in council—that there is nothing doing there which marks energy or activity—that the affairs of the country are quite at a stand-still, and are likely to remain so; . . . Add to all this, that he hates, despises, and is out of friendship, or even intimacy with every one of his colleagues at this moment."[6] Then came Bussaco; along with the convening of the Cortes, Wellington's success in the battle boosted political morale in London. But just as a new chapter appeared to be opening and Wellesley prepared to press his case, the king again fell ill. With the prospect of a regency in the person of the Prince of Wales, political speculation again ran rampant that the prince would dismiss government and turn to his lifelong political friends, the Whigs.

Discussions over the regency began in December 1810 and continued through the first of the year. Inevitably the government turned to Pitt's bill of 1788 as a model. This meant that the regent would be under restrictions for one year, preventing him from making basic alterations in the character of Parliament as left by the king. The prince and the Whigs, as was the case in 1788, argued vehemently against such restrictions and in so doing highlighted the political chasm that separated them from the government. It certainly brought no comfort to Wellesley, who knew where the Whigs stood on the war and that the prince was no friend to the family. On meeting the mercurial Prince of Wales shortly after Bussaco, he received not congratulations but an odd declaration delivered loudly from across the room: "I condole with you heartily, my dear Lord, upon poor Arthur's retreat; Masséna has quite out-generaled him."[7] It was the type of affront calculated to rankle the prickly marquess. Not surprisingly, the ministry adopted a conservative stance towards all things until it resolved the regency question. Wellesley understood this and bided his time while reassuring Henry that his job was secure. "I will not send this short note," wrote Wellesley, "without my most cordial congratulations on the character, which you have established by your very judicious conduct at Cadiz, in circumstances of the utmost delicacy and difficulty. This will be amply expressed to you, as soon as possible, in a formal dispatch. In the meanwhile, let me assure you, that even the opposition render you justice. . . . Whatever may be the result of the present melancholy condition of our good King's health, and whatever may be the fate of those now in office, your honor will stand unblemished."[8] As for Arthur, the distraction of the regency question certainly relieved him of some public scrutiny but at the same time deprived him of what he deemed adequate government support. Not surprisingly, he did not accept such neglect gracefully.

The Regency Bill proceeded through Parliament, with the most important debate taking place in the Lords, where the princes of the blood would join with the Whigs to oppose the legislation. Liverpool would lead, with the marquess and John Scott, first Earl of Eldon, prepared to support. Wellesley remained silent, however, provoking considerable speculation as to the reason, which included the possibility that he had sold his support to the prince. Such a notion was unlikely, however, at least then. In fact, he had met with the prince and pointedly informed the future regent that the government would have its way on this issue.[9] Wellesley never offered an explanation—probably because he did not see it as significant. As debate continued on the specifics of the bill, he took an active part. A final vote came on 5 February 1811, and the government carried the day. As the Prince of Wales took his oath as regent, everyone believed that he would oust the Tories and turn to the Whigs. It did not happen. The Whig grandees had assumed too much and overplayed their hand while the prince, struck by the weight of responsibility, used their impertinence as an excuse to maintain the status quo. Certainly those in the Tory government were pleased, but the capricious nature of the prince provided no comfort.

Arthur was among those who worried that the assumption of royal powers by the Prince of Wales could have only one consequence—a change of ministers and a termination of the war effort. He warned Henry, "In the event of a change of government in England, I don't think it likely that you will be allowed to continue in your office at Cadiz; but I recommend you to remain in it till you will be recalled."[10] Certainly that is what Arthur would do. Ever since taking command in the Peninsula, he had known that this might happen, and he could see that despite his avowed disinterest in "party," to everyone in London he was seen as a political appendage of his brother the marquess. Still, as he informed William, he had tried to establish at least some separation: "I have not written to Wellesley, because I have always expected that he would quit the government; at which period it would have been reported that he and I had been intriguing to increase the power of our family, and I wished to be able to say that I had not written him a line since he went into office."[11] This was not entirely true, but a more important question is, what possible difference could it make? One need only look at the correspondence of various opposition members to see that the Wellesleys were viewed as one. What is clear is that Arthur thought about this constantly and became fatalistic. Writing to Pole in January 1811, he explained that even if the government survived the creation of the regency, it would not "have the power, or the inclination, or the nerves to do all that ought to be done to carry the contest on as it might be."[12]

He was right. Weakness and uncertainty reinforced Perceval's natural inclination to hold back on the war, thereby perpetuating his struggle with the marquess. But Perceval was not the only problem Wellesley faced. Public opinion in Britain continued on its anti-Spanish course.

Various reports had reached London of debates in the Cortes on constitutional issues, annoying many who felt that its attentions would be better directed toward military reform. What was even more annoying was that Spain still refused to open the colonial ports. Additionally, there was the predilection towards Portugal. The prince regent's message to Parliament called for continued support for the Peninsular War in general but specifically for Portugal. In addition to the £1 million granted for 1810, the government requested an additional £1 million for 1811. Perceval introduced the formal motion in the Commons on 18 March, contending that the Portuguese had proved themselves effective and reliable and that the Portuguese government was doing everything in its power to support the resistance. By omission he suggested that the Spanish were not. The opposition argued that it all represented an exercise in futility.[13]

In the Lords, Wellesley again crossed swords with his old friend Grenville. While arguing the government's case, the marquess entered into elaborate praise for Arthur's accomplishment in Portugal. To his mind, it all pointed to future success and rendered the Portuguese worthy of anything Great Britain could provide. Lord Grenville answered in an equally tiresome manner: the Peninsular War had reached a point of diminishing returns, success in the Peninsula could come only when another front opened in Europe, and the treasury could no longer meet the demands of war. To no one's surprise, the government's motion passed easily.

Meanwhile the marquess continued to press the cabinet to increase the subsidy for Spain, and again he butted heads with Perceval. Indignation over Spain's performance ran high, but to Wellesley's mind, such concern missed the point. Yes, the Spanish might be stubborn, inefficient, and even incompetent, but they were fighting and in so doing led the way for the rest of Europe. In his view, France could be contained "only by creating so powerful a diversion in the Peninsula as might enable the powers on the Continent to oppose the views of France, according to their respective means, so that France might be reduced to the alternative, either of relinquishing her designs in the Peninsula or elsewhere, or of making an imperfect effort in two quarters."[14] Wellesley knew that there were cracks in Napoleon's system. Russia had had enough of economic hardship in the name of France. In this light especially, Wellesley viewed issues such as trade as mere distractions. End the war first and then deal with outstanding problems if they still existed. As for military reform, that could come only with a major infusion of money.

As for Henry, his challenge did not dissipate with the convening of the Cortes. In fact, the issue of executive authority hinted at a political struggle taking place in Spain, a struggle that from Henry's perspective distracted the Spanish from the war. Moreover, he detected the emergence of a nascent liberalism, which the Wellesleys feared for various reasons. With Spain's provisional government confined to Cádiz, mercantile and upper-middle-class interests held sway; they clearly recognized an opportunity when they saw one. While the war with France could not be ignored, to their minds neither could political reform. Spaniards of various political stripes appreciated the significance of the moment, but they pursued their goals in the Cortes in the guise of Spanish nationalism. This would prove frustrating for Henry because the Spanish often used the war and their relations with Britain as political tools. It was up to him to discover the political agenda, which was not always what it seemed.

Henry had welcomed the Cortes, believing anything preferable to the status quo. At the same time, he did not anticipate much change in his own situation, as he would still negotiate with and through the foreign ministry and the regency council, which in turn were responsible to the Cortes. The Cortes would appoint a new set of regents, but Henry was at a loss as to who they might be. He explained to the marquess, "It may perhaps appear extraordinary that after my repeated expressions of regret at the want of energy and activity in the present members of the Regency, I should, in my conversation with M. de Bardaxi relative to their sending in their resignations, have suggested anything calculated to prolong their continuance in power; but such is the extreme difficulty of supplying their places, that if the appointment of a new government were to be left to me, I should feel great embarrassment upon whom to fix my choice."[15] In the end, the Cortes elected a regency of three: General Joaquin Blake, don Gabriel Ciscar, and don Pedro Agar. Though unenthusiastic, Henry hoped for the best.

For Henry the issues remained unchanged. On the matter of military reform, in consultation with Arthur, Henry had, a few months earlier, proposed the creation of a Spanish corps of ten thousand men to be trained on the island of Majorca by the British general Samuel Whittingham. Britain would arm and clothe them, but they would be paid by Spain. He believed that this would benefit both sides, but to his surprise, the old regents rejected the plan. After recovering from the shock of what he saw as Spanish obstreperousness, Henry concluded that the Spanish government was punishing Britain for the reception given to Bolívar and Méndez in London. By October the time seemed right to reintroduce the plan. Henry's timing could not have been better. News of Wellington's victory at Bussaco had arrived in Cádiz at the same time the Spanish again found themselves in need of financial assistance. On this occasion, the Cortes cooperated and even conceded the training of an additional corps of five thousand in Cartagena under British colonel Philip Roche.

This was, however, one of the few questions on which the Cortes reached a decision, and Henry sat by while the assembly debated endlessly on matters of great import. There was no other direction to turn, as he explained with a great sigh to Richard: "I must observe however that whatever defects may exist in the Cortes, we can look to no other source for the salvation of the country, and it is therefore necessary that every possible degree of support should be given to them."[16] But when, in the midst of fiscal and military crises, the Cortes took up the issue of a constitution, Wellesley could hardly believe his eyes. A curt note of protest went to Bardaxi, who replied with equal irritation that "it was in vain to call to the people to enlist into their armies until they are assured, that after they had risked their lives to secure the independence of their country, they shall return to live under a government the abuse of which had been corrected."[17]

As much as he wished to do otherwise, Henry continued to work with the Spanish. He found himself in the midst of growing Anglophobia promoted by one of the new regents, General Blake. A nasty tiff over Whittingham's corps ensued, leaving the issue of wider, more comprehensive military reform problematic.[18] According to Blake, there was no problem with the Spanish military. Then, on cue, another joint military operation collapsed on Spain's failure to live up to its own promises. The event on this occasion was an expedition to Barrosa in an effort to relieve the siege of Cádiz. In a scene reminiscent of Talavera, the British commander, General Thomas Graham, engaged the French first while waiting in vain for support from his Spanish counterpart, General Tómas Lapeña. Although Graham took a pounding, he held his ground, and the French opted for a strategic retreat. Seething over Lapeña's failure to engage, Graham rejected the Spaniard's suggestion of a pursuit the following morning. Lapeña promptly claimed betrayal and brazenly took credit for the success of the day before. The battle of Barrosa was a relatively minor affair, but for Henry it confirmed his doubts on Spanish reliability. With Wellington about to enter Spain, the problem could no longer be ignored. Believing that Britain should have direct control of all military affairs in the areas of Spain in which British armies campaigned, on 15 March Henry formally asked the regents to confer on Wellington temporary command of the provinces contingent to Portugal. The Spanish response came as no surprise. The nationalistic character of the war, explained Bardaxi, "must necessarily suffer a very sensible change, upon the fact of seeing, that the command, although it should be temporary, of some Provinces, is confided to a foreign General."[19] In the Cortes, Blake's xenophobia overflowed: "They had begun the war with no other support than their patriotism and . . . ought to look to nothing else to carry them through it."[20]

Henry emerged from this experience convinced that the alliance would go nowhere until a new set of regents was installed, and he set about marshalling his resources to make it happen. After six months of contention, he had had enough. Meanwhile, the marquess attempted to mollify, reminding Henry to "avoid topicks which might wound the national pride, that sentiment (although partially injurious in its operation on some branches of the affairs of Spain) must be considered with esteem & respect as one of the sources of the independent spirit of the Spanish people and of their steadfast resistance to the designs of France."[21] Henry found himself handcuffed by the lack of meaningful financial support forthcoming from London. Instead he continued to subsidize the Spanish with small grants or loans for specific occasions or when he sought favor in return. It was never enough, and inevitably there came from Bardaxi a request for a loan of $500,000. First Henry rejected the plea, but the following day he acquiesced. "I have frequently had occasion to mention in my dispatches the pecuniary distress of the Sp. Gov't.," he explained to the marquess. "It is now arrived at its full height, the treasury is entirely empty, the Gov't. has not credit sufficient to raise a dollar in the town, nor is there any prospect of their soon receiving a supply from the colonies."[22] Henry had learned by this time that all deliveries of British assistance were accompanied by concessions of some sort. In this case, he required repayment in specie or receipts from the customs house in Cádiz, a license to export $5 million in specie from Mexico free of duty, and a guarantee that the money would be applied to the Spanish armies operating in Estremadura,

Murcia, and Cádiz. The Spanish agreed to all demands, news of which Henry promptly dispatched to Richard on 21 April 1811. Perceval did not bother to register a protest.

Meanwhile, in Portugal Arthur's army occupied the well-supplied Lines of Torres Vedras while Masséna's starved. The British had stripped the land bare as they retreated in front of the advancing French. Finally in March 1811, Masséna gave way and began the inevitable retreat. His army had suffered enormous losses, but it still represented a threat, one that would grow as it joined other French armies in Spain. And so Wellington followed cautiously, leaving the dirty work of dealing with French stragglers to Portuguese partisans.

On 10 April the last French troops crossed the frontier into Spain, and Wellington declared Portugal liberated, allowing Portuguese peasants to return to their ruined farms and villages. At the same time, he made plans for the next stage of the war. Arthur had known that any campaign in Spain would first require securing his lines of supply and retreat, and that meant the recapture of the border fortresses of Almeida and Ciudad Rodrigo, with the latter task looming especially problematic and time-consuming. Then came alarming news; the Spanish had surrendered Badajoz. It had been under siege for weeks but was well supplied and appeared able to hold out until relief came in the form of a British army out of Portugal. But a new commandant lost his nerve and negotiated a surrender on 11 March. An incredulous Wellington could hardly contain his fury. "I conceive the surrender of Badajoz at the moment, and in the manner it occurred," he wrote to Henry, "to be the most important event of the war in the Peninsula."[23]

One frustration recalled another. His anger with the Spanish military spilled over to the government, whose penury he saw as compromising the whole enterprise. He reminded Liverpool, "I shall be sorry if Government should think themselves under the necessity of withdrawing from this country on account of the expense of the contest. From what I have seen of the objects of the French Government, and the sacrifices they make to accomplish them, I have no doubt that if the British army were for any reason to withdraw from the Peninsula, and the French Government were relieved from the pressure of military operations on the Continent, they would incur all risks to land an army in his Majesty's dominions. Then indeed would commence an expensive contest."[24] Clearly these were unsettling times, and Arthur, who could sense ultimate victory, imagined it being snatched from him because of the government's timidity. As a result, his letters to London were as intemperate as they were frequent. Equally significant is that he wondered why Richard could not mobilize his colleagues. William told him one reason why: "His Colleagues complain that they never see him, etc., etc. and in the House of Lords, he seldom takes any part, by which he has lost much ground." Still, William continued, "Wellesley is certainly very anxious that the War should be carried on with vigor, and I believe always gives such council, but he has often complained to me that he cannot get his colleagues to do what he thought they ought."[25] According to Pole, Wellesley had again been spending more time with his mistress than on responsibilities of state, but what made this a matter of concern was the consequent lack of focus. Like everyone else, William believed that for Wellesley, personal issues trumped public responsibilities. There is truth to this, and in it was the first sign that the marquess was again coming undone. Wellesley's correspondence and the accounts of others confirm that he was very much a part of and involved in an unusual political environment. The marquess, however, talked a better game than he played.

In April, Parliament began discussing Wellington's success in defending and liberating Portugal, and great effusions of praise came from both sides of both houses. Even the *Examiner* found itself, almost embarrassingly, in agreement: "Let such of us, then, as have doubted the prudence and ability of that General, do justice at once to him and to ourselves, and shew him that we have not withheld our praise because he deserved it, but because we were ignorant of that desert."[26] Even so vociferous an opponent of the war as Samuel Whitbread sent a note of congratulations. Clearly taken aback by Whitbread's gesture, Wellington returned ironical thanks.[27]

Still there was no money for Spain, and the situation there grew desperate, leaving the marquess more despondent than ever. Not surprisingly, he took out his resentment on his colleagues for (what seemed to him impossible) appearing to be unappreciative of the stakes:

> With respect to the ultimate result of the proposed system, the advantages, which it holds forth to England, if successful, are equally manifest and important. It will rescue the Peninsula and its colonies from the dominion of France; it will place the Peninsula and its colonies, from a natural union of interest, under the influence of Great Britain; it will relieve an extensive

> country, full of resource, military, naval, and commercial, possessing the richest and most extensive colonies in the world, from an oppressive Government, and establish in its room a Government of well-tempered liberty, formed upon the model of our own constitution; it will secure to us a great and efficient ally on the very border of France, and will enable us to impose a stronger restraint upon France than was ever before in our power. Such are the probable results of the system, if it be admitted that it be carried into effect.[28]

This was overstatement, but Wellesley clearly kept a view of the future as he pondered the present. There is not much evidence that similar foresightedness existed elsewhere in the cabinet.

As Arthur struggled in western Spain to secure the border fortresses on the heels of Masséna's retreat, Richard and Henry conspired to deal with the troublesome issue of Spain's rebellious colonies. But the Spanish were digging in, and to make matters worse, they stepped up their efforts to secure a substantial increase in financial assistance. A request for a loan of £2 million was summarily dismissed by Perceval as "totally out of the question and impossible," and far more modest requests were also blocked. It constituted a bitter potion; Henry described "a very bad spirit prevailing here, and that it is increasing daily, and I am sure I know not what to do to correct it. I do not see how things are to go on here unless England furnishes some pecuniary assistance."[29] Wellington, of course, weighed in:

> My opinion has invariably been, that in all the concerns of Spain, Great Britain ought to take the liberal line of policy, and to lay aside, at least during the existing war, all considerations of mercantile profit; and it appeared to me that, in this question of the colonies particularly, this line would suit equally with the military policy and the mercantile interests of Great Britain, and add greatly to the general estimation of our character. . . . Knowing what I do of the Spanish Government and its means and resources, and the employment for them, I am certain that they have not the power to reduce to obedience even one of the weakest of the colonies which is disposed to separate. I am equally certain that to make the attempt would be the grossest folly and misapplication of means; and I will go further, and declare, that I believe that Great Britain could not in justice

> to the greater object in the Peninsula, give assistance from which any good can be expected.[30]

Wellington's observations in no way contradict those of Wellesley's, but they fail to take into account the politics of the issue.

In May Arthur began a chess match with the French in the north around Almeida and Ciudad Rodrigo and in the south around Badajoz. The results were two battles and the surrender of Almeida. While the allied armies prevailed over the French at the battles of Fuentes de Oñoro and Albuera, both were bloody affairs from which Wellington took little satisfaction. Albuera, where Beresford commanded, was a blood bath that left the normally steady Beresford shaken. Indeed the losses were heavy, but Wellington consoled his general and then ordered Beresford's dispatch rewritten to put the battle in a more positive light. The last thing he needed was to report a victory that looked like a defeat when for the first time since the beginning of the war, a sense of optimism had begun to grow in London.

Meanwhile, great confusion reigned among the Wellesleys concerning the desirability of Arthur's taking command of Spanish armies. The brothers agreed that only under British command did the Spanish stand a chance of improving their armies, but this in turn would require capital investment that the government was not yet ready to put forward. While Richard and Henry pursued this angle, Liverpool instructed Arthur to reject any offers of command. A confused Henry wrote, "I was very much surprised and concerned to find by your letter that Lord Liverpool had directed you to refuse any command in Spain which might be offered." He went on, "Had I known of this, it certainly would have saved me from much trouble and anxiety; but Lord Liverpool's orders to you are in direct contradiction to his own sentiments . . . and to every private communication which I have received upon the subject."[31] The two brothers would not have been wrong to wonder whether the marquess ever exchanged ideas with Liverpool.

In any case the issue was, at least for the moment, moot. Great political capital had been made in Cádiz after Albuera, where Spanish soldiers under the command of Blake and Castaños acquitted themselves well, in the sense that they had stood and fought. Wellington, in fact, officially complimented them, but in private he continued to seethe over his Spanish allies. "What a pity it is that the Spaniards will not set to work seriously to discipline their troops!" he wrote to Henry.

"We do what we please now with the Portuguese troops, we manoeuvre them under fire equally with our own, and have some dependence on them; but these Spaniards can do nothing, but stand still, and we consider ourselves fortunate if they do not run away."[32] Henry, of course, could not have agreed more, but he faced an even more obstreperous Blake, who used Albuera as proof that the Spanish could manage their own military affairs. Henry again retreated from an intended request to put Wellington in charge of Spanish forces operating in coordination with British.[33] Wellington understood: "I have no doubt whatever, that the Spanish Government will not comply with this requisition; and from all that I can see and hear, I am convinced that the demand will tend to interrupt much of the harmony and good will which exist amongst us at present."[34]

Clearly, Anglo-Spanish relations had reached an impasse. With the Cortes engaged in issues of its own interest, management of the war fell to the regents. Here there were several issues. Like their predecessors in the junta and the first regency council, Blake and his cohorts sought to remain as independent of British influence as prudence allowed. For them this meant retaining control of the army and maintaining the monopoly on trade with the colonies. These conflicted precisely with British goals. However, Henry understood that the Spanish leadership relied almost entirely on Britain for financial support and that public opinion, in this case that of Cádiz, might be mobilized for fear of losing everything to the French should the British effort fail. A kind of public relations war had always to be engaged by both sides in this odd relationship. In a sense, then, a high-stakes verbal game occupied the statesmen involved.

Blake played the game audaciously, unintimidated by the British. This irked the Wellesleys, who fought to maintain the initiative. For this reason, the issue of colonial rebellion in Spanish America proved especially problematic. The marquess had been working to neutralize the issue but had found it impossible. The colonies were considered Spain's lifeblood, and the Spanish could not imagine a future without them. For many Spaniards, the colonial issue was as important as the war with France, if not another aspect of it. Consequently, resentment ran high concerning Britain's connections to these events, and the Wellesleys knew it. But the marquess found himself with room to maneuver. News of colonial rebellion was music to the ears of Britain's merchant community, which anticipated splendid opportunities on the horizon. Wellesley perceived something different: a long-term trend that would signal the end of Spain's empire. The revolt in Caracas simply marked the first domino falling. He found nothing alarming in this; for him the opportunity was political as well as economic. That Símon Bolívar turned first to Britain for support signaled a primary role for Britain in the future. And so to Richard's mind the clock of history could neither be stopped nor turned back.

Wellesley also recognized the problems that the push for independence presented for Britain's relationship with Spain. The Spanish would insist that Britain take a stand against the rebels. This the marquess could not do, and so he obfuscated, insisting that he would employ his influence to mediate the dispute. There is little to suggest that this fooled anyone, least of all the Spanish. At the same time, while Spain might complain about Britain's failure as an ally, the marquess left the Spanish leadership without concrete evidence that Britain was in any way facilitating rebellion. What he wanted most of all was simply to keep everybody talking; he might have hoped that the revolutionary fervor would temporarily subside and the Spanish would do nothing rash. What he feared most was that Spanish alarm would lead to an attempt to subdue the rebels. This would have at least two serious consequences. First, it would distract Spain from the war in the Peninsula and fragment Spain's military resources. Second, it would provoke a vigorous response from British merchants and traders, with serious political ramifications.

Consequently, Wellesley pursued mediation, offering Britain as a conduit for the resolution of outstanding issues between Spain and the colonies. The Spanish, sensing a sham, would submit to mediation only if Britain promised to "break off all communications with the colonies, & moreover assist Spain with her forces, in order to reduce them to their duty" if mediation failed.[35] Wellesley could never agree to such a stipulation but forged ahead anyway, sending to Cádiz a proposal of remarkable complexity.[36]

Wellesley's policy regarding Spanish America makes sense only when one realizes that he was never serious about resolving the issue, much as was the case in negotiating a trade agreement. His proposal merely constituted "talking points" designed to extend the discussion endlessly while avoiding real action of any sort. This, of course, explains Spain's repeated efforts to pin Britain down. Beginning with a denunciation of Britain's conduct towards the colonies, Spain's counterproposals contained little with which Henry Wellesley could agree. Moreover, the Spanish plan ended with a secret provision that called for Britain to "suspend all communications with the said provinces, and moreover . . . assist the Mother Country with her forces in order to reduce them to their duty."[37] In response, Henry argued that the mediating power had to maintain an appearance of strict impartiality. Neither side would budge, and shortly Henry got wind of a systematic effort to undermine his influence in Cádiz. A rumor spread that Britain was concerned only with the defense of Portugal and that its goal in Spain was simply to prolong the conflict so that when Napoleon completed his conquest, the country would completely be despoiled. The development left Henry dispirited. Arthur, while sympathizing with Henry, cut the Spanish no slack:

> Great Britain did not bring Spain into the contest. To the contrary, the war, in its commencement, and throughout its progress has been carried on by the Spaniards without reference to our opinions, and generally in direct contradiction to our recommendation; and then we are to be blamed and abused, because, contrary to our own judgments and the plain dictates of military expediency, we don't choose to enter upon wild and visionary schemes which we have not the means of accomplishing. . . . Are we to blame if the Spanish armies are not in such a state as that they can be opposed to the Enemy? or if the Cortes have neglected their duty, have usurped the powers of the executive Gov't. & have misspent their time in fruitless debates? Are we in fault because by the mismanagement of the American Colonies the world has been deprived of its usual supply of specie, & G. Britain in particular cannot find money to carry on her own operations, or aid the allies?[38]

Arthur's facile response was true to form; his observations were clear and to the point. They also failed to take into account the reality that somehow some semblance of organized resistance had to be maintained in Spain, and that meant dealing with the regency and the Cortes regardless of what one thought of their performance.

To Henry's dismay, Anglophobia continued to mount in Cádiz with a new rumor suggesting that Britain was sending more troops to the city under the pretext of a French threat but in reality to seize Cádiz as it had seized Gibraltar. This was too much for Henry, who took the extraordinary step of sending to Bardaxi a declaration and demanding that the regents post it: "In the name of the British Government and the whole British Nation, I most solemnly and distinctly disclaim all views of aggrandizement, of acquisition of territory or of property either in Europe or America, at the expense of the Spanish nation."[39] In September the Wellesleys' greatest fear came to fruition. Bardaxi informed Henry of the government's intention to send troops to America. Henry responded with a vigorous protest, pointing out that such an action contravened the proposal for mediation, which called for a cessation of hostilities, and that it compromised the war in the Peninsula. Unmoved, Bardaxi explained that the regency was entrusted with responsibility of both internal and external affairs and that mediation had yet to be agreed upon. Spain, he went on to say, could not continue the war without the unqualified support of the colonies, that men were not in short supply, and that the enterprise was being financed privately. Then, taking the opportunity to jab at his ally, Bardaxi asserted that "it is notorious that the succour hitherto granted by England to Spain, have not been so extensive as to admit of their being applied to other objects than those for which they were immediately solicited."[40]

In London, the marquess changed course. To break the stalemate over mediation, Wellesley decided to go forward on his own terms. He appointed three "commissioners of mediation"—Charles Stuart, George Cockburn, and Philip Morier—and instructed them to prepare to sail to Cádiz.[41] Wellesley's idea was to present the Spaniards with a fait accompli: either they would agree to sail to Spanish America to begin mediation on British terms, or they would be held responsible for the failure of the mediation. Again, the tactic was to extend the stasis, as Wellesley could count on the Spanish reaction to be one of talk, and even if the Spanish agreed to terms, a voyage of mediation to the colonies would begin an interminable process. This, of course, was far from obvious to outside observers and left even the *Morning Chronicle* befuddled: "What can be effected by Commissioners in South America, it is very difficult to conjecture, and we cannot but consider it impolitic to intermeddle in any way between Spain and her colonies, or rather perhaps, it may be said, after the events that have taken place, what were her colonies."[42] In fact, Wellesley could not stop the two ships from sailing, but he could do his best to see that no others followed. The best way to do this would be to confound the Spanish with an ultimatum to which the regents would be loath to respond.

Meanwhile, both Richard and Henry had had enough of the Blake regency and decided to seek an alternative. Henry had been thinking in these terms for some time but lacked the resources and opportunity even to explore the prospects for change. In fact, a change in regents was something that he could only encourage and even then very discreetly; the Spanish Cortes would have to be the instigators. On 8 July 1811, the marquess met with don Andres Angel de la Vega, a determined Anglophile and one of the first of the Spanish representatives to travel to London to solicit aid after Dos de Mayo. Preparing to return to Spain, Vega met with Wellesley for what were certainly wide-ranging discussions.[43] On arriving in Cádiz, Vega wrote to Henry, "The Cortes should take without loss of a moment the resolution of constituting a Regency, with competent and independent faculties to act, without being constrained in its operations, however, liable to be called to an account in due time."[44] Subsequently the two met, and Henry outlined his view of a future government. His ideas were hastily presented and contained several impracticalities, but the central premise, that of the need for change, was realistic; Vega responded to that premise, asking for Henry's suggestion of suitable regents. Henry recommended the duke of Infantado along with Henry O'Donnell, Pedro Cevallos, and Padre Gil, men whom he thought most likely to work closely with Great Britain. With these suggestions in hand, Vega went to work and promptly ran into roadblocks. "The choice of Regents brought into action private interests & personal animosities in such a manner that some weeks elapsed without any communication being made to Mr. W.[ellesley] on the part of Mr. Vega," reported Henry's secretary, Charles Vaughan.[45] The regents, in the meantime, continued on their independent and, at least in Henry's eyes, contentious course. When in November Vega presented Henry with a list of potential regents, he found the latter in no mood for compromise. Upon reading Blake's name on the list of potential regents, Henry recommended that the effort be abandoned.[46] For Vega, the meaning was unambiguous.

Richard, concluding that all had come to naught, instructed Henry to back away from direct discussions on a new government. At the same time, he enhanced Henry's position by elevating his younger brother to ambassadorial status, something Henry had long coveted. Then, surprisingly, there came a break. Dissatisfaction with the status quo combined with anxiety over British intentions to prod the Cortes to action. On 12 January 1812 came a decree calling for a change in government with the hope that Britain would be satisfied with the new regents. Ten days later, the Cortes announced the appointment of a regency of five to include the duke of Infantado, General Henry O'Donnell, Admiral Villa Vicencio, don Joaquin Mosquera, and don Ignacia Ribas. Finally, as a delighted Henry informed his brother, there was a government that "promises to afford to Great Britain the influence which she ought to possess in the Councils of Spain, and to be productive of that change of system without which it is in vain to hope for a successful issue to the contest in which we are engaged."[47]

Meanwhile, after Albuera, Wellington had attempted a second siege of Badajoz, but French strength obliged him to abandon the effort and he retreated back into Portugal for the winter. The winter of 1811 passed much differently from that of 1810. With Portugal free of French troops, Wellington used the time not only to plan but also to refresh. By the first of the year, he was again ready to assume the offensive. His first target was Ciudad Rodrigo, which he carefully invested. It surrendered on 19 January 1812, and in an uncommon gesture of allied good will, Wellington passed control of the city to General Castaños. Though he had practical reasons for doing this, the Spanish were overjoyed, and the Cortes promptly made Arthur a grandee of Spain with the title "duque de Ciudad Rodrigo," which he graciously accepted. From London came word that he had been made an earl with a pension of £4,000, a handsome raise of £2,000.[48]

Next, Arthur returned to Badajoz, which he knew would be a much tougher nut to crack. With one eye always fixed on the movements of the French, Arthur sought to complete the siege expeditiously. This, along with a paucity of proper equipment, made the task perilous. The fortress fell on 6 April but at horrific cost and was followed by an equally horrific rampage through the city by the victorious soldiers, a story that is now well known. Although the experience profoundly affected Arthur, he quickly moved on.

Control of the border fortresses put him in a position to strike at the French either to the north against Marshal Auguste Marmont or to the south against Soult. He chose to move northwards. Such a campaign required as great a concentration of troops as possible, and accordingly, Arthur assembled Portuguese regiments to augment his British army. As for the Spanish troops, they were to garrison the border fortresses and to see to the repair and strengthening of those strongholds. Wellington's logic was simple: the Spanish could not be trusted in the field, where he needed every soldier under his direct command. On this basis he went forward, but before long, reports came of poor discipline and lethargy in the Spanish camps, particularly Ciudad Rodrigo. This sent Arthur into a fury. The reason for Spanish ineptitude as far as he could see was the simple fact that they disliked garrison duty. There would, however, be no changes: "I insist upon it," he wrote to Henry, "that Spanish troops are the proper garrisons for Spanish forts. If the Spanish Government differ with me upon this point, and insist upon my placing garrisons in these forts which we have taken from the enemy, and I have made over to them . . . I now give notice that I will destroy both Badajoz and Ciudad Rodrigo."[49] Enough said. Arthur proceeded towards Salamanca.

Throughout the spring and summer of 1811, the cabinet's failure to respond to what the marquess considered an obvious need to expand its support of Spain in the form of men, money, and supplies further alienated Lord Wellesley from his colleagues. Wellesley's absence from cabinet meetings became more frequent and his conduct of foreign affairs more independent. He maintained regular communication with Perceval, but these discussions also were characterized by disagreement. Perceval's timidity towards the war's financing so outraged the marquess that at times he became sarcastic, even insulting, in his dealings with the prime minister. When Perceval sent for comment his draft of the prince regent's speech to the closing session of Parliament in July 1811, Wellesley responded,

> As you wish for free observation upon it, you will not be offended when I tell you that I object to the whole plan of it which in my opinion is totally inadequate to the occasion. The great feature of the present session (with respect to the very existence of this Empire) is the effort, which Parliament has made to support the war in the Peninsula. And the principles from which that effort proceeded are, in my judgment, essentially necessary to be stated in the opening of the speech, quite distinctly from the success of our operation. . . . I really think that the general plan of the speech is far below the magnitude of the occasion.[50]

The tragedy of Wellesley's career is that he never understood the highly personal nature of politics and the fact that a parliamentary government's proper functioning required discourse and compromise among the several members of the ministry. Even the most imperious of Britain's past ministers recognized that they functioned as part of a group; they simply found ways to dominate. But Wellesley never took this extra step. He believed that he should dominate by right. He had seen collegial interaction at Pitt's dinner table, but he inexplicably refused to apply this experience to his circumstances. Instead of socializing with cabinet colleagues and participating in the greater social milieu of political London where he might be heard and in turn hear what others might think, he retreated to Apsley House, where he socialized with men of absolutely no import—his secretaries and aides. This would prove a fatal blunder because when the clash of political wills came, he would be repeatedly outmaneuvered. Merrick Shawe, Wellesley's perceptive and intelligent secretary, had seen it coming:

> I have often ventured to tell Lord Wellesley, when he complained of the stories told of him, that if he would live as other people, dine out, go to the opera, and mix with the world, they would not accuse him of keeping bad company when he was passing a quiet evening at home; and further, that if he would give his opinions fair play, by meeting his parliamentary and other friends often at his own table or theirs, and employing one-half the eloquence thrown away upon Sydenham, Smith, and me, in stating and enforcing his own view of public affairs, he would lead the country in spite of twenty such Juntas as were opposed to him.[51]

In any case, unable to persuade Perceval to place more money at Spain's disposal, the marquess decided to work through the prince regent. The two were longtime acquaintances but not close friends. Realizing, however, that they had much in common philosophically and stylistically and that the restrictions of the Regency Bill would run out in February 1812, Wellesley set out to change the relationship in the summer of 1811. By August he had become a member of the regent's inner circle, and it did not go unnoticed. Shawe maintained that Wellesley had at this point decided to retire from the field and that his overtures to the prince were merely an effort to develop an advocate to pursue the war with greater vigor. This hardly seems possible, given all that was at stake and the fact that though respected, Perceval lacked determined support. With an eye to the expiry of the Regency Bill, Wellesley no doubt hoped that the regent might in fact turn to him. Their relationship developed quickly; just as quickly, it became the subject of political gossip. The Duke of Buckingham was told "that, as the Prince is determined to make an administration, of which he is determined to be himself the framer, and to carry on the war in Spain on principles known to be adverse from those of Lords Grenville and Grey; and as Perceval will not go to the lengths, which, according to Lord Wellesley, are necessary to carry on the war with effect; and that Lord Wellesley, on whom everything turns, will not serve any longer with Perceval; therefore he, Lord Wellesley, will be the only person eligible to that high situation."[52] Pole followed all of this closely, and as early as February 1811, he reported to Arthur, "It is said, & I believe with some truth that Wellesley is a great favorite, & that Perceval & some others are also in H.R.H.'s good graces—York & Mulgrave certainly not. Many people think that Wellesley will be the man he will pitch upon to form a new administration."[53]

In addition to the war in the Peninsula, Wellesley also separated himself from Perceval on Ireland. Wellesley had long advocated Catholic rights, but George III's implacable opposition to that stance had been the undoing of first Pitt and then Grenville. The subsequent Portland and Perceval administrations had assembled on the guarantee that they would not bring up the issue. The marquess considered the war a matter of greater import than the Catholic question and therefore willingly joined Perceval on that basis. He came to consider the issues of Ireland and the war related. At a time when the government refused to give what he considered proper support for the Peninsula, he was annoyed by the fact that over seventeen thousand soldiers were employed in Ireland to maintain a peace that he believed could be achieved by merely granting Catholic rights. With the king indisposed and the regent long identified with anything the reverse of his father's thinking, proponents of emancipation saw an opportunity. Wellesley, for one, did not hesitate in expressing his opinion on the matter, hoping to draw a contrast with the anti-Catholic Perceval. Moreover, he would have considered that a liberal position on this issue might also be the basis of a coalition with the Whigs, if that proved necessary.

Thus Wellesley had determined his course, and when discussion in the cabinet began on the permanent regency settlement, he took the opportunity to champion the interests of the Prince of Wales. The central issues were the civil list, maintenance of the royal household, and payment of the regent's personal debt. The tight-fisted Perceval rejected the prince's requests and took the cabinet along with him—all except Wellesley. While he could not stand in the way of the government's decision, the marquess insisted that his objections be made public. This was done on 24 December 1811, and it served to alienate the marquess even further from his colleagues.

When Parliament reconvened in the new year, Wellesley seemed poised to assume leadership in a new ministry based on strong support for the war and Catholic emancipation. He hoped to coalesce with some of his old friends, such as Grenville and Canning, for he thought that Arthur's successes in the Peninsula would have softened the views of Grenville and other antiwar Whigs. Grenville dashed these hopes with a bristling antiwar speech in the opening session. Nonetheless, the marquess sought to bring matters to a head, and on 16 January, just three days before Arthur accepted the surrender of Ciudad Rodrigo, Wellesley informed the prince regent of his intention to resign. The following day Wellesley met with one of his few friends in the cabinet, Lord Bathurst. He explained that his resignation was not a sudden decision but rather one that he had been contemplating since October 1810 and postponed only because of the instability created by the regency question. His primary reason for retiring, Wellesley explained, was his being denied the leading role in the cabinet that he had been led to assume would be his when he accepted office in 1809.[54] He conceded that the habits he had developed as governor general had made him less receptive to discussion, but he honestly believed that in regard to the grounds on which he strongly disagreed with his colleagues—Spain and the Catholic question—there was only one valid point of view. Writing to Perceval, the marquess announced his intentions with the cordial but wholly untrue assurance "that my sentiments and my determination are entirely unconnected with any feelings of unkindness or disrespect."[55]

The prince rejected Wellesley's resignation, asking him to stay at his post until a successor could be found. To Wellesley this meant until the Regency Bill expired in February, but in fact he had erred badly, overestimating his importance and the reliability of the prince. Wellesley's resignation caused little consternation in the Perceval ministry; most were happy to see him go. At best they saw him as an anachronism, at worst a deceitful and unreliable colleague. In any case, the thoroughly acceptable Castlereagh replaced him. Castlereagh was as much one of them as Wellesley was not. Wellesley did not panic over the smooth transition and sat back to await the prince regent's call for a new government. This too proved illusory, as the prince, through Lord Eldon, curtly informed the marquess that the government would stay.

This turn of events stunned Wellesley; again one has to ask, how could he have been so naive? In fact, one might even conclude that Wellesley knew all along that his plans would come to naught and that these were simply the actions of a fatalist. However, the volume of Wellesley's correspondence at this time, particularly with Canning, along with the time and effort he invested in cultivating the friendship with the prince regent do not support this thesis. Neither do his all-consuming ego and his obsession with his brothers' continuing advancement. That he misjudged the prince is clear, and for this he stands condemned. There was ample evidence that the regent was not a man to be trusted. The Duke of Buckingham, for one, had experienced the prince's fickle loyalties firsthand and noted, "The Wellesley preference had set in with much too strong a tide to be lasting, and that brilliant but somewhat imprudent minister was never so insecure of his anticipated leadership, as when his royal master poured into his ear his confidence and his commendation."[56]

To put his political future in the hands of such a man was foolhardy at best. It reveals Wellesley as largely ignorant of human nature, and because of that ignorance, he was also less likely to know just how dispensable he had become in the eyes of his ministerial colleagues. That these men viewed him as outside the political mainstream he never truly appreciated. What Wellesley saw as his assets—intellect, knowledge, and experience—were not of primary importance to them. They were interested in those who could command a substantial following in Parliament and could be counted on to coalesce with the group. This was not Wellesley. He did have a following in the House of Commons, but it was not substantial. Canning, who shared many of Wellesley's liabilities, recognized his own shortcomings and sought ways to compensate. Wellesley never did. Through talent, force of will, and circumstance, he had made his way into the corridors of power. He discovered in 1812 that exit from those corridors was a much more facile task.

Meanwhile, these events caught Pole off guard, suggesting that he had little contact with the marquess. "Wellesley has never mentioned to me the subject of his resignation," William wrote in explanation to Arthur:

> I have however heard every thing from Sydenham—all the facts are the same as Perceval relates; but the impression of the Prince's sentiments are very different from Perceval's. . . . Sydenham's impression is that the Regent will call upon Wellesley to form an Administration, and that if HRH does, Wellesley is prepared to undertake the task. From every thing I have heard from all other quarters, I have no doubt upon my mind of its never having entered the Regent's mind to propose it to Wellesley to form an Administration and I am also clearly of opinion that he could not establish a Government that would last a week.[57]

Wellington remained remarkably detached from all this; he had already written off Wellesley as a key player.[58] Moral judgments apart, Wellington had tired of Wellesley and believed that his erratic brother had squandered too many opportunities to warrant sympathy. Pole, of course, had contributed to this view, and one wonders what game William played. By his own admission, he was fortunate to have been well removed from the marquess as Richard maneuvered against Perceval. When Wellesley resigned, Pole felt no obligation to follow him out of office.

In desperation, Wellesley spent March and April of 1812 trying to build public support by portraying himself as the victim of a conspiracy of unimaginative and weak-willed members of government. He focused on Perceval; the irony is that as 1812 progressed, Perceval's vulnerability lessened because of Arthur's success. The government was quick to take credit for Wellington's victories, but some in Parliament saw Richard as the author of the impending success in Iberia. It was indeed a cruel blow for the marquess. Still, the ministry was vulnerable, and the natural politician would have actively challenged it on a number of issues. Wellesley tried, but he did not have the instincts for it.

Urged on by Canning, Wellesley plotted Perceval's demise. Plans were made for Wellesley to deliver the fatal blow with a speech before the House of Lords. On cue, John Parker, Lord Boringdon, in making a motion for a more efficient administration, asked the marquess if he "would in the course of this debate explain the reasons which had enduced him to resign, at a moment when his services, with a view to the war in the Peninsula, were so very essential."[59] Pole described the scene:

> He [Wellesley] has not spoke since he surrendered the seals, but on Ld. Boringdon's motion, which is said to have been framed & brought on principally to give him an opportunity of making a speech, which all the Satellites [Wellesley's coterie] ran about London for a week saying would be such a display as never had been made, in the House of Lords & would blow Perceval, & his Administration at once to atoms, there never was seen so full a house, & literally all the House of Commons excepting Perceval & me & about four or five others were there, to hear him but he sat mute, tho' he voted with the opposition—From that moment I think all parties have given him up as a Public man. You can have no idea of the sensation his not speaking made. It is not pleasant to reflect upon it. He has been since out of Town, but he is now returned, & I hear, he is to speak on the Catholic Question. I do not think it much signifies whether he does or not for himself, for I fear he has lost the opportunity of being a Leader.[60]

In the aftermath of this debacle, there were those who sought to excuse Wellesley's silence by accusing Lord Eldon of not calling on the marquess when he rose. This is entirely plausible, given Eldon's notorious partisanship, but there is little corroboration to give it much credence. Rather, Wellesley appears to have simply lost his nerve, and his retreat from London seems to confirm this. Just when it appeared that all was lost for the marquess, an assassin gunned down Perceval in the lobby of the House of Commons. A political crisis of the first order ensued. Liverpool took over as interim prime minister, and the government attempted to hold on in the face of growing opposition. The ministry had never been particularly strong or confident, and the removal of Perceval, to most observers, seemed to portend major changes. Wellesley could hardly believe this sudden shift of fortune, and as if to confirm that it was not a dream, he, along with his son, accompanied the sculptor Joseph Nollekens to an examination of the prime minister's body.[61]

A sense of urgency and panic pervaded the flurry of political correspondence from mid-May to mid-June. Indeed, there was much at stake; political careers were on the line. Wellesley, therefore, firmed up his alliance with Canning and promptly staked out the political ground. His political principles would be defined first by the war; Wellesley and Canning would stand for an increased commitment in Iberia. Given the possibilities for a future government, this made sense. One likely option was that the prince regent would stay with what he had, a government led by Liverpool. Such a government, however, risked alienating the growing support for Wellesley and Canning. Moreover, many felt that the moment had come to put party aside and press the war with France to a successful conclusion. A broad-based government would be symbolic of this resolution. There was, therefore, every reason to believe that the prince would seek a coalition of the Wellesley-Canning group with the old Perceval cabinet. The trick here was reconciling enemies and sorting out the issue of leadership. Would Liverpool submit to Wellesley? Would Castlereagh submit to Canning? Would Sidmouth serve any combination? Could Wellesley and Canning be junior partners in anything? The combinations were endless.

There was another option. Wellesley and Canning might raid the Liverpool group, taking the likes of Bathurst, and combine this base with selected members of the opposition. In fact, this seemed to Wellesley the most logical course in that it might appeal to the prince regent by allowing the prince a graceful retreat from the embarrassing denial of his political past the previous February. To facilitate this, Wellesley and Canning announced that in addition to their stance on the war, they would call for Catholic emancipation. The only thing that seemed absolutely clear in May was that the prince would never turn to an exclusively Whig cabinet.

On 8 May the prince regent summoned Wellesley to Carlton House. Confused by the turn of events, the prince was antagonistic and accused Wellesley of conspiring against him. An angry exchange ensued, and peace was restored only when Wellesley threatened to leave the residence. In the end, the prince told Wellesley that he and Canning would have to consider joining Liverpool. In turn he would instruct Liverpool to include Wellesley and Canning. This, of course, was to no one's liking, at least for the time being. The following day, Liverpool met with Wellesley and Canning separately. Liverpool was conciliatory but unwilling to bow to his rivals. Specifically, he refused to admit that a proper effort had not been made in the Peninsula.[62]

Negotiations broke down and resentments ran high. At this critical juncture, Wellesley's insensitivity and lack of political finesse came into play. On 21 May there appeared in the various London newspapers Wellesley's recent correspondence with Liverpool. Wellesley authorized publication in an effort to justify his rejection of Liverpool's overtures and to build a case for his own leadership. There was nothing particularly unusual about this tactic, but Wellesley blundered by not extending to Liverpool the courtesy of prior notification. While this was a relatively minor matter, it confirmed for many of Liverpool's colleagues their belief that Wellesley was not a gentleman. Further confirmation, if indeed it was needed, could be found in that same day's edition of the *Morning Chronicle.* Appearing there was an overly long explanation for Wellesley's resignation from the Foreign Office in February. Such an explanation would have been a senseless exercise in March, let alone May; everyone knew precisely why Wellesley had resigned. But what would have been dismissed as old news in March became the source of angry discussion in May, as the memorandum contained a pointed and lengthy criticism of the recently assassinated prime minister, Spencer Perceval. This constituted not only gross insensitivity but a breach of political etiquette as well. In response, Liverpool and his colleagues signed a circular pledging to have nothing to do with Wellesley, whose actions had given them reason enough to exclude him, in defiance of the prince regent's express wishes. Wellesley always maintained that he had nothing to do with the publication, that it was the work of his overzealous staff. In fact, it was such an appalling blunder that one is tempted to accept this excuse; even Wellesley could have seen its inappropriateness and its marginal political utility. That said, all the evidence, and there is not much, points to Wellesley.

In any case, the political landscape had been dramatically transformed. Wellesley knew this but did not appreciate why. What the marquess had managed to do was cut himself off from his last but perhaps most viable political option—junction with the Liverpool group. At this point, he could only turn to the opposition with the hope of piecing together some sort of coalition. Accordingly, he and Canning polled Lords Grenville and Grey and others of the opposition: Holland, Moira, Erskine, and Sheridan. Wellesley subsequently informed the prince that Grenville and Grey agreed with him on the Catholic question but could not yet see themselves clear on an increased commitment to the war. Erskine, Moira, and Holland might cooperate. Then Wellesley told the prince what he already knew, that no one in Liverpool's group would have anything to do with him. Still it was not what the regent wanted to hear; he wanted to be done with Grenville and Grey, desiring instead a new ministry of Pitt's friends under Wellesley and

Liverpool. On 24 May, Wellesley and Liverpool both made visits to Carlton House. The meetings were contentious and accomplished little. The prince stewed for a week, and on 1 June he commissioned Wellesley to form a government.[63] The marquess again turned to the opposition, but he could move neither Grenville nor Grey on the issue of the war. What their strategy was at the time is unclear. Probably neither believed that the regent would seriously consider them for a new government, and they were unwilling to subject themselves to embarrassment from that quarter. Wellesley's efforts therefore came to naught. He had lost the political war through his ineptitude and Liverpool's skillful maneuverings.

On 3 June, Wellesley went before the House of Lords to report that his efforts to form a government had ended because of "the most dreadful personal animosities." The comment aroused the curiosity of bystanders and sent participants in the recent negotiations scurrying for cover. To whom was Wellesley referring? "That part of Lord Wellesley's speech in the House of Lords will be read with some surprize, where his Lordship speaks of 'personal animosity,'" reported the *Chronicle.* "The veracity of the Noble Lord cannot be called into question, neither can that of Lords Grey, Grenville and Liverpool; where then do these personal animosities exist?—It is not for us to answer the question."[64] Many speculated that the animosities were on the part of the prince regent, but Lord Moira, who was heavily involved in the negotiations, stoutly defended the prince. Consequently, on 8 June, shortly after Liverpool had put a government in place, the marquess cleared up the mystery. The phrase "dreadful personal animosities," he said, was "meant to apply to Lord Liverpool and his colleagues in the administration just formed, for it was their conduct that had rendered all his [Wellesley's] efforts impossible."[65] It was a sad end to an inglorious episode in British political history. The marquess clearly did not understand that his failure to achieve the premiership was largely a consequence of his own actions. He failed to recognize that his intrigues could only engender mistrust, that his insensitivity could only alienate, and that his judgment could only lead to miscalculation. Equally important, he did not recognize that he was considered an outsider and that political insiders would be less forgiving of his personality and methodology than those of one of their own. The *Examiner* perhaps put it best in writing of the marquess in May: "The Marquis Wellesley is very far from satisfying, as at all coming up, to one's ideas of a desirable Minister:—his private habits, his aristocractic pride, on the one hand, and courtliness on the other, his wasteful and Eastern notions of what is efficient as well as magnanimous in matters of policy, all give him an aspect very much the reverse of what is English, and very distinct from those great and simple qualities which have ever been esteemed the best security as well as ornament of this nation."[66] It bewildered the marquess. All that he could see in the summer of 1812 was that he had been right on the Peninsular War. He had stood on that platform and lost, and to add insult to injury, the war policy was being stolen from him. Was this justice? True, Wellesley was easy to dislike, but in this sense he was by no means unique. While one can understand why he was left out of Liverpool's arrangements, incomprehensible is the completeness of Wellesley's political demise. Once he had been broken, there was no effort to resurrect him.

13

WATERLOO

It would have been hard to imagine just how much would change for the Wellesleys in the three years that followed the marquess's failure to construct a ministry in June 1812. Wellesley's plan to grab the prize atop the greasy pole had fallen a hand short, and in his subsequent precipitous descent, he took Pole with him, leaving Arthur and Henry without a family advocate in London in what were still perilous times in the Peninsula. Arthur had enjoyed some success in the first half of 1812, but Napoleon had ordered a massive army across the Russian frontier in what looked like an inevitable French victory in the east. Certainly, an equally aggressive assault on Iberia would follow. As a result, Britain's war policy remained an open discussion with fiscal and economic troubles as a backdrop. The future could hardly have looked bright through Wellesley eyes, but one thing was certain—the cast had changed in this great family drama and the script would need rewriting for the next act. For most of their adult lives, the brothers had followed Richard's lead, but he was no longer in a position to help; that left the siblings, except for Arthur, at sixes and sevens. Ever the realist, he allowed himself no time for speculation or regret and simply forged ahead. In July he won a resounding victory at Salamanca. December found Napoleon back in Paris, his invasion of Russia a catastrophic failure. The change in the fortunes of war had profound implications for Britain and for the Wellesleys. With Napoleon unable to reinforce his armies in Iberia, Arthur could hope, on retiring to Portugal for the winter, that this would be his last retreat. In addition, the debate over the wisdom of pursuing the Peninsular War ceased, and Arthur became the focus of a new optimism in London. At the same time, his success rendered Wellesley politically superfluous. As the eldest brother's public role diminished, so too did his role as head of the family; William and Henry began to ride Arthur's coattails, not Richard's. The marquess's failure to adjust to these changes compromised his ability to function effectively in the political arena. Two and a half years and many battlefield victories later, Waterloo made Arthur an international celebrity and the marquess an emotional and political cripple.

June 1812 found Wellesley still searching for a path back into the political mix. Believing Liverpool vulnerable, he continued his collaboration with Canning. They were not alone in their assumption of the ministry's fragility. While the opposition remained incapable of mounting a serious challenge, there existed a broad, amorphous middle willing to consider another combination of Pitt's men. But first Liverpool had to be successfully challenged. In the summer of 1812, this became Wellesley's and Canning's goal. They chose as their vehicle the Catholic question, an issue on which both men had been perfectly clear and on which they were at odds with the prime minister. Canning fired the first salvo in the House of Commons. There he introduced a motion to refer the issue to committee with the object of removing all political disabilities for Catholics. Although this represented only a first step in the process of granting Catholic rights, its success would imply final victory. Canning held a strong hand because in the Commons the most eloquent voices on both sides of the aisle could be mobilized to speak in favor of the motion. The results were remarkable. On 22 June, Canning's motion generated a majority of 129 votes, a remarkable shift from an 85-vote defeat on a similar previous motion.[1]

The marquess followed nine days later in the House of Lords, where the results in the Commons heightened interest and anxiety over the promised debate. What most observers thought would be a ho-hum event had turned into high drama. Still, a formidable task faced Wellesley, for here sat not only an influential party of anti-Catholic lords but eighteen bishops as well. Still, he had the support of old allies across the aisle, particularly Lord Grenville.[2] He began with an interesting challenge:

> I rise, my Lords, to submit to your Lordships my promised resolution on the subject of the political disabilities to which the Roman Catholics of Great Britain and Ireland are subject. The question has been often agitated, but never fully, maturely, and deliberately considered. The ordinary maxims of state policy which have been applied to every other subject that has engaged your Lordships' attention, have in this instance been violated. The more important any question has been . . . so much the more deliberately, attentively and dispassionately has that question been usually investigated; but in regard to the disabilities to which the Roman Catholic subjects of the Empire are subject, this course has been inverted. The respectful claims of that great class of the population of the Empire have been met by passion rather than by reason and sound wisdom.[3]

Having gotten the attention of his colleagues, the marquess proceeded with the basic elements of his argument. He examined inconsistencies in the laws that subjected Catholics in England, Scotland, and Ireland to different standards. Having dealt with the basic illogic of the system, he then declared any restrictions as a violation of natural justice. But more than this, he explored the whole issue from a historical context. In this line of reasoning, he pointed out that the current restrictions had never been intended to be permanent, that they had merely been expedients reflecting the uncertainties of an extraordinary time. There no longer remained, he reminded his colleagues of the obvious, a serious Catholic pretender to the throne. Wellesley then proceeded to well-traveled ground, discussing the vicious cycle that intolerance generates.[4] This was not just political opportunism speaking; Wellesley truly believed all that he had said, and it caused a stir.

A spirited debate followed, but in the end, Wellesley found himself on the short end of a 126 to 125 division, proxies proving the difference. Remarkably, two of five royal dukes voted with him, along with three bishops. What lay behind this shift in sentiment can only be conjectured, but a pronounced shift it was, and Wellesley and Canning might have taken some consolation from it. Alas, one vote or fifty, they had lost, and Liverpool saw no threat to his government.

While Richard maneuvered in the Lords, Arthur maneuvered on the Castilian plains against the ever-cautious Marshal Marmont. An exhausting and tense game of cat and mouse ensued. At the end of

June, Arthur wrote to Pole, "I was never so fagged. My gallant officers will kill me. In the course of a fortnight that we were before Salamanca I don't believe I have been in bed, or rather laying down, altogether 48 hours. I am always on foot at 4 in the morning, and can't go to rest till 9 at night; and I am now writing under a tree while the troops are marching." Is it any wonder he had little patience for the marquess? In the end, Marmont erred in extending his lines, and on 21 July 1812, Wellington attacked outside of Salamanca. In his first open-field battle against a massed French army under capable leadership, he won a monumental victory, which resounded throughout the Peninsula and the United Kingdom. The subsequent retreat of the French army opened the door to Madrid; Arthur was quick to walk through it.

News of Salamanca found the marquess in a decidedly downcast mood. His defeat on the Catholic question left him keenly aware of the extent of his political ostracism, and he returned to the self-pity that had punctuated his years in India. Making matters worse, his dwindling political influence also compromised his position as family patron, though this he would be slow to acknowledge. With every success in the Peninsula, Arthur's name increasingly became a household word. Almost perversely, each victory also strengthened Liverpool's hold on the government, and Wellesley came to realize that success in Iberia dimmed his prospects as much as failure would have done. When news of Salamanca arrived in London, the ministry gathered to celebrate. Liverpool, Castlereagh, and Bathurst took the news to the Prince Regent at Carlton House, and then, in what was certainly a magnanimous gesture, they decided to send word to Wellesley before he read of it in the press. With relations between Wellesley and the government strained, they summoned young Richard to be the purveyor of good tidings.

Richard arrived at Apsley House just before midnight on the evening of 5 August. He found his father alone in the dimly lit dining room, picking at a late dinner and sipping port. Perhaps this should have been a sign that for Wellesley only no news was good news. In any case, the naive Richard, filled with excitement, assumed that his father would share his enthusiasm. After all, Arthur's successes only confirmed the wisdom of the policy that Wellesley had pursued for three long years at the Foreign Office. He was, therefore, unprepared for what ensued. After reading his brother's dispatch, the marquess launched an attack on his former colleagues. It was, he said, pure malice on the part of the prince regent and the cabinet to rub his nose in his brother's success. For over an hour young Richard would listen to the ravings of an angry, irrational man. The government was simply trying to elevate Arthur's reputation so that they would not have to credit Wellesley for the success of the peninsular policy. It was he who had devised the strategy, promoted it, and left it behind for his successors to direct. They, of course, would never acknowledge such a thing; to the contrary, they would do everything they could to dissociate Wellesley from the Peninsular War. According to the marquess, no one was willing to recognize that Wellesley was the one who had made Wellington what he was, a fact that even Arthur chose to ignore. What was he to do? He could not support these men who treated him ill; he could not join the opposition, whose view of the war was contrary to his own. No, he who was "*the only minister*" who had done "*any real service*" would be forced to abandon politics altogether or perhaps leave the country.[5]

Wellesley's twisted reaction to Salamanca reveals that there was more to his state of mind than politics. Jealousy of Arthur had begun to take root, though the marquess would attend public celebrations in the days following. In the autumn of 1812, Wellesley retreated to Cowes, on the Isle of Wight, as Wellington fell back to Portugal. From there he found a seat in the Commons for his son and attended to fleshly distractions. Arthur, in the meantime, maintained a lofty neutrality concerning his brothers and the Liverpool ministry. "Lord Wellington is determined not to mix himself up in politics, and still less in party-politics," wrote Thomas Sydenham. "He certainly regrets the present ministry should be on such bad terms with lord Wellesley and Pole, and it would give him great pleasure to hear that the ministers were reconciled to his brothers, and that his brothers could be employed in a manner satisfactory to their own feelings. He of course cannot conceal from himself that, commanding a successful army in the Peninsula, he is the main support of the present administration."[6] Pole had lost his post as chief secretary when Perceval died and Liverpool put together the new government. The new prime minister suggested Pole as secretary for war, but the prince regent rejected the idea as an insult to the marquess. Such a nomination would indeed have put Pole in a tight spot, and he likely would have declined the offer had it been made. Curiously, Wellington thought such brotherly notions of loyalty quaint and wished that Pole had stayed with the government.[7] Writing to

Henry in Cádiz, Sydenham sympathized with Pole and warned Henry to hold fast: "I do not know how Pole can with any consistency join the present administration without some arrangement being made for Lord Wellesley; and I do not see how Lord Wellesley can, under any circumstances, reunite himself to the present party. . . . Lord Wellington . . . is very anxious that you should not resign, and he told me that he should consider your resignation to be a public calamity."[8] The family was uncertain in this period of transition, and unease settled upon them. It is clear, however, that Wellington believed that Wellesley had made his own bed and the rest of the family need not sleep in it.

While Wellesley nursed himself at Cowes, Wellington regrouped in Portugal, having suffered a setback at Burgos after Salamanca. By this time, Arthur was beyond reproach, and he worried little about public criticism. Canning sensed this and tried to stir Wellesley by urging him to attack the government for failing to support Wellington adequately: "I think it can hardly be expected of you that you should refrain from explaining yourself fully on this subject on the first day of the session. I think it will be highly advantageous for you to do so—but (I still think) to do so, not as a determined opponent, but as a retired statesman taking a distrait, commanding, and unimpaired view of the state of the country."[9] Canning's view had changed. His thoughts were no longer framed in terms of overthrowing the ministry but rather in influencing it with the ultimate goal of joining it. Thus he urged the marquess to proceed cautiously in nudging the ministry while stressing the wisdom of his own statesmanship. In this way, Wellesley and Canning could march in tandem: "The tone which I *recommend* to you *I must adopt.* I can speak in no other, *yet,* than as regretting and admonishing. The difference between us in one respect, *viz.,* that *I* have not any prophecies to boast of, and *you* have, is in your favour, and will justify your going higher, and speaking louder and with less management than I can."[10] One can imagine the marquess viewing such sage advice as condescending, but he did begin to sketch out his thoughts on the government's failure to extend proper support to his brother's army.

With the troika of brothers directing the British effort in Iberia reduced to two, Henry, who felt the loss of his eldest brother intensely, searched for firm footing. Shortly after Wellesley's resignation, Perceval had secured for Henry a knighthood of the Bath as gesture of trust and goodwill, and Wellington's successes at Ciudad Rodrigo and Badajoz had provided the government with sufficient confidence to add £400,000 to the Spanish subsidy. Still, Henry felt anything but confident, and one can hardly blame him. While the spring of 1812 had seen the military initiative swing to the British, final victory remained anything but certain, and problems in dealing with the Spanish seemed as formidable as ever. Castlereagh's assumption of the Foreign Office brought no alteration of the British agenda; the issues of trade, subsidy, colonial rebellion, and military and political reform remained. Still, Henry recognized that he could no longer rely absolutely on the foreign secretary's support. In addition, just as Henry settled in with Castlereagh, a misunderstanding with Arthur arose that illustrates just how fragile Henry was. As Wellington prepared his army for its advance into central Spain, he called for control of all military subsidies intended for Spain. Henry interpreted this as a criticism of the manner in which he had handled the distribution of those subsidies, and he so informed Arthur:

> Your letter . . . has given me some pain, because it appears that you, in some measure, attribute to me the failure in sending supplies to Castille and Estremadura. . . . I look upon it that if the means of assisting the Spanish government were taken out of my hands, or the supplies conveyed through another channel, remonstrances or suggestions from me would cease to produce any effect; that I should lose all my influence; and that my continuance here as ambassador would be useless, and consequently not very agreeable. But in these times it is the duty of every public man to sacrifice his own feelings to what may be for the advantage of the public service.[11]

The quivering voice of the martyr stirred Arthur. He apologized for any insensitivity but suggested that Henry had misinterpreted his intent: "I never give an opinion on any subject not connected with my own business. . . . But you may depend upon it that I could not mean to impute blame to you; and I shall think very ill of any arrangement which is to remove your situation at Cadiz."[12] In fact, Wellington very much wanted a confident, assertive ambassador in Cádiz to control the Spanish.

London cleared up the matter by placing military subsidies alone in Wellington's hands while the general subsidy flowed through Henry's.[13] Meanwhile, correspondence flowed back and forth between Castlereagh and Wellesley concerning matters of trade and mediation of the colonial problem. Here nothing had changed save for growing impatience in Cádiz over the British attitude concerning the colonies. Generally the Spanish believed that Britain welcomed the revolts and would do little to see them suppressed. This was not far from the truth, and Castlereagh adopted Lord Wellesley's policy of engagement and delay in an effort to defuse the issue until war's end. That being the case, Henry could offer little hope for concluding any sort of trade agreement that might benefit British commercial interests. Liverpool's view on this situation was far less strident than Perceval's; as a result, Henry felt less pressure to engage the Spanish.

Then came Salamanca, which left Henry exuberant: "The raising of the Siege of Cadiz is not the least important consequence of the Victory of Salamanca, and will do more towards the restoration of tranquility in South America, particularly in Mexico, than the most decisive Victory which could be obtained over the insurgents. I can give your Lordship but a faint idea of the general joy which this event has occasioned among the Inhabitants of this place, who have thus been relieved from a siege of two years and a half's duration."[14] When Wellington subsequently entered Madrid, Spanish enthusiasm brought tangible rewards. Finally, the Spanish decided that Wellington could be trusted with command of the Spanish army. The Wellesleys approached this prospect cautiously, knowing that the devil was in the details, and Castlereagh concurred with their judgment. Curiously, in the midst of such good news, Henry still felt insecure. Writing to Charles Arbuthnot in September, he commented, "With respect to public business I naturally feel less confidence in myself, & act with less than I did when Lord W[ellesley] was in office, and (between ourselves) I do not believe that our Minister for Foreign Affairs has the same confidence in me that he, Ld. W. had."[15]

Negotiations began in earnest in the autumn, and Henry informed Castlereagh and Arthur that a variety of pressures would be brought to bear on the Spanish regency as it deliberated the powers that would accompany the designation of commander in chief of Spain's armies. Henry suggested that the result might be less than perfect, but given the changed military circumstances and the promise of a renewed offensive at the first of the year, Arthur should not quibble over minor issues. Castlereagh chimed in that he would accept whatever Wellington deemed appropriate, commenting, "It is impossible for me to express how much I have felt, in common with the whole nation, admiration, and I may say astonishment, at the extent & brilliancy of Lord Wellington's late operations. The whole campaign is a masterpiece."[16] Meanwhile, news from the east was good. Napoleon had been forced to evacuate Moscow. The retreat was on. On Christmas eve, Wellington joined Henry in Cádiz to finalize Arthur's commission as commander in chief. He got what he wanted: control over all important promotions, power to suspend officers for misconduct, control over the Spanish chief of staff and inspectors general, and the right to place political powers in the hands of corps commanders operating in the provinces. In the meantime, Napoleon arrived back in Paris a much diminished man.

When Wellington reemerged from Portugal in 1813, he did so with a new sense of destiny. The strategic advantage in the Peninsula had clearly shifted to him. Not only had he demonstrated superiority over the French the year before but also Napoleon's disaster in Russia meant that the French armies in Spain were on their own. But there was more to his buoyant attitude than this. Richard's political failures removed a shadow, allowing Arthur to bask in the full radiance of the sun of public attention. The timing could not have been better. Wellington would proceed boldly out of Portugal, marching four hundred miles in forty days through rugged terrain, forcing Joseph Bonaparte to give battle at Vitoria. The French were overwhelmed, but the distraction of loot among the French baggage allowed the erstwhile king of Spain to salvage a good part of his army. Nonetheless, Vitoria was a stunning victory, and it transformed Wellington from a national to an international figure.

The marquess clearly sensed the changed circumstances. He had managed after Salamanca to engage himself in Arthur's elevation to a marquessate, making suggestions for alterations to his younger brother's coat of arms.[17] These were ignored, but at least Richard avoided charges of spite, keeping his emotions largely private. Young Richard bore the brunt of his father's irritation. As usual the marquess mulled over another speech, but it came to naught.[18] The spring of 1813 found him at East Cliff, where he took to his bed in a state of emotional collapse. Wellesley ignored his family and his old political associates, and when summer arrived, young Richard reported that his father was becoming increasingly bitter as Wellington's successes mounted. He records a conversation of 9 June, before the battle of Vitoria, in which the marquess railed about his brother having become a government toady and that Arthur had done Wellesley every possible injury when what he owed was gratitude. Lord Wellesley even went so far to suggest that had it not been for him, Arthur would have been recalled from the Peninsula in the dark days of 1810.[19] Such fantasy was accompanied by threats on which he never made good. Equally significant, Pole at this juncture began to put distance between himself and his eldest brother.

Pole met with Wellesley and Canning in July 1813. At this meeting, the three agreed to dissolve their political association to pursue their political ambitions independently. In explaining to Arthur that they "parted very good friends," Pole made clear his eagerness to join Liverpool as soon as possible.[20] Ever the opportunist, Pole saw the future; it was a good time to change from a sinking schooner to a three-decker under full sail.[21] For his part, Wellington congratulated his brother for finally succumbing to common sense. Two months later, Pole was already complaining that he was still out of office, and by December his impatience had turned to animus for the eldest brother. His complaint was "had I known, as much as I do now, or as you knew then of the rooted habits & disposition of W[ellesley] I never should have sacrificed myself as I have done; however what is passed cannot be remedied and the wisest course to persue, is to look forwards, & if possible banish from my mind powerful reflections on what I have lost, retaining only respecting it the feelings that I acted from pure motives, and the consolation that I have not involved any one in my disappointments."[22] Pole possessed the maddening habit of interpreting hindsight as wisdom and writing precisely what his correspondent wanted to hear. The fact is, William and Arthur at that time had grown very close. Arthur commissioned him to begin looking for a country property and to take charge of the paintings seized from Joseph Bonaparte's baggage train. In other words, Wellington trusted Pole without question. The matter of the paintings is a great curiosity, as Wellington sent them to London for safekeeping thinking that they were of little value or importance. Some had, in fact, been used as tarpaulins to cover baggage. When they arrived in London, William recognized value and consulted the marquess, who in turn brought in experts. The paintings were, of course, invaluable; they hang in Apsley House today, a gift from the wretched Ferdinand VII. "I had no notion they were so good," Arthur wrote, "but I believe I was born with *Fortunatus* cap on my head. I thought the prints and drawings were the best."[23]

For whatever reason, the battle of Vitoria and Arthur's subsequent campaign in northern Spain revived the marquess. "You will have rejoiced in Lord Wellington's brilliant repulse of the revived French Army," he wrote to his son. "But if he be not greatly reinforced, he must retire." Wellesley mentioned little gifts sent from friends and associates and joked that he rather liked the attention: "the smallest donations will be thankfully received by me. . . . You may publish this proclamation in all languages."[24] Nonetheless, his mind continued to work overtime on the subject of political injustice. He informed his son that his arm was sore from throwing snails into the channel waters off East Cliff, suggesting long walks and difficult introspection. And in a tantalizing aside, he steered young Richard to a new novel, Jane Austen's *Pride and Prejudice.* One can imagine Wellesley seeing himself in Darcy, believing that misperceptions of his character distracted observers from his inspired genius. Still, he was unable to stir himself to action: "Sometimes I meditate a grand lecture on all things past, present, & future, but I fear it might be dull, ludicrous, & suspicious."[25] On that he was correct.

For his part, Wellington instinctively knew the impact that his success would have on the marquess. He kept his brother informed on his progress against the French almost as if nothing had changed and tried to engage Richard as if the eldest brother were still in the government. After the battle of Vitoria came a pleasant bit of chitchat: "I have been much concerned to hear that you have been unwell; but I learn that you are better, and I hope that the warm weather will re-establish your health entirely. I am quite well, but have occasionally the complaint of all old soldiers, the lumbago."[26] Letters also contained a variety of commentary. Arthur continued his lament on the Spanish, describing the Cortes as preoccupied with reform at the expense of the war effort.[27] Despite Arthur's best efforts, it all proved too much for the eldest brother, whose mood swings increased. A note from Pole did not help. He asked Wellesley to attend a great fête in honor of Wellington, advising that old political differences should not get in the way. Liverpool, said Pole, wanted Wellesley there.[28] Of course the prime minister did: a show of family unity would suggest that political wounds had healed. Wellesley participated but hardly with enthusiasm, for he knew that his circumstances would be no better for it.

Meanwhile, Pole found that the political road back was longer than he had anticipated. He had hoped to step quickly into Liverpool's government, but this did not happen. Despite his close relationship with Arthur, William was not someone people naturally warmed to. His good friend the Duke of Richmond, with whom he worked for several years, explained the problem in a different context: "Pole's unpopularity is against us. His manner is not conciliatory and even our best friends are often out of humour with him. You know before he was appointed [chief secretary to Ireland] I feared his warmth [temper] might do harm. I really have a great regard for him and should be sorry to do anything to prejudice you or anybody else against him, but it is impossible to conceal his extreme unpopularity."[29] Richmond's assessment stands in stark contrast to Pole's self-perception when responding to the suggestion that he take a minor appointment. William contended that in "considering the offices which I have filled, and the opinion which I know all those who have acted with me, entertain of my pretention & capacity (I hope I may say this confidentially to you without vanity) & moreover considering my connection with you, & the comfortable state of my private fortune, I am quite sure it would be a source of mortification to me, instead of gratification, to be placed in a subordinate station, & I would rather remain as I am."[30] William would have to wait; in 1815 he would be made master of the mint.

Wellesley attempted to make the same practical and emotional adjustment, but he had less success. Young Richard reported that his father and Canning had made it known that they would be willing to act with the government. Canning in fact threw in his lot and took the embassy in Lisbon. For his part, Wellesley did not expect a cabinet post but would accept an embassy. At the same time, his manner "was as usual, hot & irritable."[31] The early months of 1814 were filled with important military and diplomatic events. Castlereagh proceeded to the Continent to firm up the alliance while Napoleon mounted a brilliant defense of the homeland. On the advice of Charles-Maurice de Talleyrand-Perigord (the former French minister of foreign affairs), the allies eventually opted not to play Napoleon's game and marched straight on Paris, occupying the city on 31 March. Six days later Napoleon abdicated, a move that was followed on 10 April by Wellington's costly and superfluous victory at Toulouse. The war was over.

Like many others in Britain, Lord Wellesley found himself in something of a daze. Could it really be that the great crusade against revolutionary France was at an end? The marquess swelled with pride over his contribution to the successful conclusion of the conflict and looked around for confirmation of self-recognition. He imagined that the government would reward him with an embassy, and he looked to Paris, where the Bourbons were to be restored. Then news reached him that the government had offered Wellington the embassy and that Arthur had accepted. Wellesley erupted in a fit of rage. He had wanted the position and if Arthur had known it, he proclaimed to his son, his younger brother "would never be admitted into his house, never to be forgiven."[32] Although he could not shake his resentment over Arthur's fame, he still exhibited moments of clear thinking, as in a note to Countess Blessington in which he explained that "military laurels by common consent of mankind occupy the pinnacle of the Temple of Living Fame, and no statesman should envy a living hero, particularly if the Great Captain should happen to be his own brother. But the page of history is wide enough to contain us all, and posterity will assign the proper place to each."[33] In the midst of depression, he was his usual bundle of contradictions. On the one hand he expressed a desire to retire from public life and on the other he could speculate on negotiating a treaty with France.[34] It was all fantasy; the autumn of 1814 found Wellesley again isolated at East Cliff. "I have remained here," he told his son, "because, if in London I must attend the House, & being present, I could not be silent."[35] Under the circumstances, some self-delusion is understandable, but its persistence is not.

As for Henry, by the end of 1812, his insecurities had begun to dissipate following the news that Napoleon's Russian invasion had turned to disaster. This event, however, did not mean that the challenge of dealing with the Spanish leadership had diminished. Granted, the outstanding specter of imminent defeat no longer lurked, and some pressures eased. The prospect of success in Iberia, for instance, emboldened the British government to step up its subsidies. Castlereagh informed Henry that clothing and equipment for fifty thousand troops were on the way and that the £1,000,000 subsidy would be renewed for Spain along with £3,000,000–4,000,000 placed at the joint discretion of the Wellesley brothers. This indeed was extraordinary, and Henry could hardly miss the message. London could smell victory and was finally prepared to do what was required to secure it. At the same time, Castlereagh reiterated the perpetual hope that such a commitment might induce the Spanish to grant some concessions: "Spain ought to do something to conciliate the feelings of this nation: continued sacrifices, & no return, may shake the popularity of the war."[36] Henry administered a dose of reality; old suspicions remained.[37]

Castlereagh was well satisfied with Henry's work. The matter of negotiating conditions for conferring commander in chief status on Wellington had been handled expeditiously, and the ambassador had been firm and patient in representing British interests.[38] As a result, Henry was given more latitude in granting occasional advances to the Spanish, as he had done while Richard occupied the Foreign Office. There was no end to British largesse; supplies for fifty thousand troops were increased to a quantity suitable for one hundred thousand, as requested by Wellington.

Henry's greatest challenge proved to be political, as liberals in the Cortes continued their overhaul of Spain's political and social institutions, which had begun with what is known as the Constitution of 1812. He worried that the Cortes blundered in excluding the interests of the aristocracy and the clergy in framing the new government: "The Spaniards are naturally attached to their ancient customs and their peculiar Provincial privileges, and they have a respect for Rank and Distinction."[39] Wellington too was uncomfortable with this constitution, as he never failed to point out in his correspondence with his brothers, but he supported it. Whenever his armies entered towns and cities formerly occupied by the French, he declared the constitution in the name of the regency. But he feared that the Spaniards would get carried away, a fear confirmed when they turned their attentions to the Inquisition, voting unequivocally for its abolition. The Wellesleys viewed this as a mistake, not because they supported the Inquisition but rather because the vote added an element of controversy at an inopportune time. Arthur considered the move foolhardy and pointed out that the Inquisition would die a slow death on its own without help from the Cortes. By decreeing its abolition, the Cortes succeeded only in bringing supporters out of the woodwork, much as Napoleon had done in 1808.[40]

To complicate matters further, Henry viewed the liberal party as distinctly anti-British, which he attributed to the festering colonial issue. In February he wrote to Arthur of his concern: "There certainly is a violent spirit against us here; and it is to be attributed entirely to our conduct in South America. This is so much felt by our friends in the Cortes that they have given up all thoughts of changing the government until you shall have had some success against the French. This was told to me yesterday; but it seems a curious reason for continuing a bad government, that the English are unpopular."[41] This observation surprised Arthur because in his march through Spain, he had encountered boisterous support for his army. Moreover, he wondered if Henry was suggesting that the Anglophobia in Cádiz was actually antipathy towards Wellington and his army. Henry responded, "I never meant to say that our want of popularity (by which I meant the British nation, for I never alluded to you in any way) extended beyond the walls of Cadiz; but it certainly prevails here to a great degree, and influences the decision of the government upon every proposition that is made to them."[42] Henry saw political immaturity as the culprit, believing that the Spanish leadership had overindulged their enthusiasm for freedom of the press when they really did not understand the responsibilities that accompanied it.[43] His disillusionment led to threats that either the press be curtailed or he would leave the Spanish to their own devices, but this was an overreaction, and he quickly came to realize it.

Nonetheless, both Wellesleys were beginning to see that the Cortes, in attempting to lead, found itself too far out in front of the rest of Spain in its vision of the political future and that this would mean trouble—for Spain and for the alliance. Meanwhile, the Cortes moved to Madrid and began preparations for receiving the recently liberated Ferdinand VII. In March, Ferdinand's emissary arrived in Madrid with a letter from the king announcing his return as absolute monarch and suggesting his rejection of the Constitution of 1812. Henry saw real trouble on the horizon. He observed, "The Jacobins at Madrid are doing all in their power to raise a spirit against him [Ferdinand VII], and I am sure that their wish is that he should reject the Constitution. I think he has done wrong to delay his journey to the capital."[44] To Castlereagh he wrote, "In the actual state of Parties at Madrid the only safe line for the King to take is to accept the Constitution and to declare his determination to govern according to its regulations and without showing any particular partiality to either of the leading Parties in the Cortes, and to select his Ministers and advisers from among the ablest men on both sides. By adopting this line of conduct he will insure the good will and support of the Nation and may, by degrees, be enabled to effect such changes in the Constitution as are necessary."[45]

Alas, the odious Ferdinand was uninterested in British advice; he announced his intention to reject the Constitution of 1812 and to assemble a new Cortes in its ancient form. He then set about consolidating his position by attacking those whom he perceived to be his enemies regardless of their contributions in the struggle against the French, and to Wellesley's amazement, the actions appeared to make little impact on popular opinion.[46] Arrests were made, and all hopes of moderation and accommodation among the various parties disappeared. Alarm bells went off in London, and the decision was made to dispatch Wellington to Madrid to try to talk some sense into the monarch. This brought some relief to the beleaguered Henry, who was eager to see Arthur and to hear of all that had transpired in Wellington's campaign into southern France. Arthur announced that Pole might accompany him and added, "I believe I forgot to tell you I was made a Duke."[47] The extraordinary pressures of war explain Wellington's understated style, but once it was adopted, he clearly felt comfortable with it and exploited its novelty, perhaps because it contrasted vividly with the marquess's attitude. Wellington knew as well as anyone the significance of a dukedom: he had come to stand shoulder to shoulder with Marlborough in the pantheon of British war heroes.

Wellington arrived in Madrid on 24 May to great celebration but found only closed ears at court. True to form, Spain wanted money rather than advice from Britain, and the duke left after two frustrating weeks having accomplished nothing. It was not a happy time for Henry, who had hoped that with the military victory in the Peninsula and the restoration of the monarchy, things would change for him. Instead he found that he still had little influence over the course of events. To make matters worse, events had created for him a conflict of conscience. He instinctively felt little sympathy for the old Cortes and the Constitution of 1812 and believed that a more moderate constitution would better serve Spain. Therefore, Henry understood when the king and his party made quick work of the Cortes of Cádiz, but the ambassador then expected some sort of negotiation and accommodation. Instead he witnessed vitriol and hard-headedness. He looked for statesmanship from the Spanish court and found none. He rejected the Constitution of 1812 but could not support the monarchy. His complaints were numerous, and he gave Arthur an earful when his brother arrived in Madrid. The frustrations of dealing with the Spanish for four long years under trying circumstances had left him in need of a break, and he asked the duke to support such a request when circumstances permitted.

Wellington understood his brother's discontent and would do what he could for Henry when he met with Castlereagh in London. In fact, the Iron Duke was about to see England for the first time since 1809. This is an underappreciated fact; Arthur had not taken leave of his army for five years, something that few of his officers could boast. First he returned to Paris in June, and then in July he proceeded to London. The brief sojourn in Paris had been a tonic, what with an endless round of balls, dinner parties, and outings. The city had been filled with European royalty, including the tsar, the king of Prussia, and the emperor of Austria, along with various entourages. Wellington moved comfortably among them with a relaxed, understated ease that he would sustain for the rest of his life. No medal-bedecked uniforms for him. Rather there was the blue tailcoat, white trousers, white waistcoat, white stock, and round hat, which, ironically, had the effect of making him conspicuous among the peacocks of Europe. He assumed the attitude of an equal when socializing with these grand men, while honoring social distinctions when public occasions demanded. His extraordinary performance made him the talk of the town. He must have found the attention remarkable, but he never voiced annoyance or discontent. To the contrary, he enjoyed it.

What awaited in London would turn his head. Arthur knew that he returned the conquering hero and that he would be the toast of the town despite the distraction of European notables whose victory lap soon carried them to Britain. Complicating matters beyond this deluge of attention was the domestic reality of returning to his wife and family, on whom he had not laid eyes for five years. Neither his paternal nor his spousal instincts had ever been strong in the first place, but any affection he might have felt for Kitty was long gone. Resuming his place at the head of the household was hardly something that could have appealed to the great conqueror. Still, he braced himself and did what had to be done—just. He quickly concluded that he enjoyed the parties and invitations to country houses, although these made Kitty uneasy and she usually declined to attend. In the cavalcade of public and private engagements, the great and powerful stumbled over themselves to be seen in his company, and women swooned. In these brief two months, he stepped up his search for a country estate; he had £400,000 from a grateful nation with which to purchase it.

He also attended to Henry and found Castlereagh amenable to the ambassador's leave taking. Henry, Arthur realized, was desperate and appeared simply to want out of Spain. Arthur counseled caution. "Let me know when you will be coming here," he wrote from Paris. "I was sorry to learn from Pole, that in intimating your intention of returning to England, you had stated that your office would then be at Lord Castlereagh's disposal. I am quite certain that the Ministers are well disposed towards you; and I think you would do well to explain before you go home that you have no intention of resigning, if that is not your fixed intention."[48] For whatever reason, Henry had developed a paranoia concerning Castlereagh and never believed that the foreign secretary was satisfied with his work. Accordingly, Arthur did everything possible to protect Henry from himself. The duke later learned that Henry had hoped for a peerage; although he regretted that Henry had not informed him of the fact at the time, Arthur doubted that the government would have taken such a step, commenting that "the publick looked so little & the little they did look was with so evil an eye at Spain, that I did not think the Ministers would be supported by the publick opinion in the measure."[49]

Wellington, with official instructions as the new ambassador in hand, presented his credentials in Paris on 24 August. Kitty followed several weeks later, and they took up residence in the magnificent town house purchased from Pauline Bonaparte, which still serves as the British embassy. Nothing changed in terms of social demands, but Wellington had also to deal with serious issues. There was the slave trade, for instance, which had become a cause célèbre at home. But the real issue was the Bourbon monarchy and the perception that Britain (specifically, Wellington) was propping it up. The duke did all that he could to present an image of the generous victor, but for many of the French, this combination was too hard to accept. The Bourbons were lethargic and incompetent, and they symbolized the revolution's failure. Wellington, in contrast, looked the very essence of success and reminded the French of their defeat. These aspects, coupled with the fact that numerous veterans of the Napoleonic wars walked the streets of Paris, produced a volatile mix. Talk became violent, and before long, shots were fired in the direction of the duke.

It was all a bit much for Liverpool, who imagined the consequences of assassination or, even worse, the duke's being taken captive and held for ransom. It was time to get Wellington out of France, and in the late autumn, discussions began, concerning the means of doing so. In December, Pole and his wife arrived with Arthur's boys and their cousin Gerald, Henry's youngest son. By then the prevailing view in London was that Wellington should be sent to North America to take command of the military effort against the United States in the so-called War of 1812. Even Pole endorsed the idea. But Wellington rejected this proposal out of hand, not the least because he disagreed with the war in the first place. Next came the idea that he remain as ambassador but go to Vienna to advise Castlereagh. This seemed more palatable, but in Arthur's eyes the timing was not right.[50]

Circumstances resolved the dilemma when Castlereagh had to return to London to explain the Vienna proceedings to Parliament. The duke was the obvious person to fill his place. So the general-turned-ambassador then turned emissary. It was too much to take for Richard, who read about his brother daily in the London press. Aside from the fact that his younger brother was doing what he unrealistically had hoped to do himself, Richard had been utterly swamped by Arthur's fame. There appears in Wellington's *Supplementary Dispatches* a curious letter to Pole, instructing William to explore with the attorney general whether there were grounds for a libel suit against the *Times*, involving a question of honor. The offending article concerned Wellington's mission to Spain and its inference that Arthur had avoided applying much pressure on Ferdinand VII for fear of losing the honors conferred upon him by the Cortes. This was the sort of thing that set off the thin-skinned duke, and the fact that he followed the British press so closely is interesting. But the *Times*'s sin was compounded by the suspicion that the marquess had inspired the article. "I cannot drive from my mind that this paragraph comes from Apsley House," Arthur wrote to Pole. He continued, "There is in it such a knowledge of facts connected with Henry's transactions in Spain, & with the cause of his stay at Madrid after he had obtained leave of absence, which can be got only from his family. . . . God forgive me if I am wrong; and indeed the idea of such a thing is painful enough to carry with it its own punishment."[51] Given Wellesley's state of mind, Wellington's suspicions were well founded, though one must also take into account the fact that Pole was as capable of impugning a brother as was Richard. William was a scandalmonger of the first order who gave little thought to those about whom he gossiped. In any case, the unflattering episode reveals how much Arthur's meteoric rise had disrupted family relations.

Wellington left Paris in late January and arrived in Vienna on 3 February. At the time, the rift over the Polish-Saxon question was nearing resolution. Castlereagh had kept Arthur well briefed on the negotiations, so nary a step was missed in the transition. Wellington's forthright style prodded the negotiations forward. Then on 7 March came the unthinkable: Napoleon had escaped from his exile to Elba. Initially the delegates at Vienna seemed unconcerned; most believed that he had set his sights on Italy and that whatever his intent, it would be a futile gesture. Even Wellington saw little about which to be concerned. In a letter to Henry, he was dismissive: "You will have seen what a breeze Buonaparte has stirred up in France. We are all unanimous here, and in the course of about six weeks there will not be fewer than 700,000 men on the French frontier. I am going to take the command of the army in the Netherlands."[52] This was wildly optimistic, and he would soon realize it. Still, Wellington understood that Napoleon could only fail; he could not predict his own role in that failure.

Meanwhile, Richard lost his political bearings completely. The man who for four years had vigorously advocated full support for the war in the Peninsula, who had spoken of a reduced France, who had encouraged and supported resistance to France in central and eastern Europe, suddenly became an advocate of peace. That this was due to pique can hardly be denied, but one must concede that he had his doubts about the postwar settlement before Napoleon returned from Elba. He considered the Treaties of Paris and Fountainbleau and the proceedings of the Congress of Vienna to be disasters. In place of a stable and secure system that might ensure decades of peace, he saw vindictiveness and a blatant land grab. Conveniently, this interpretation of what was going on allowed him to mount a critique of the government that had failed to include him in their plans. As such, he began to consult with members of the opposition, including Grenville and Grey, though he never formally threw his lot in with them. Napoleon's escape and the Congress's subsequent decision to declare the erstwhile emperor an outlaw brought the issue to Parliament. On 7 April, the marquess rose in the Lords. He urged caution and deliberation, calling for negotiations with France instead of a knee-jerk declaration of war. A great power, he maintained, demonstrates its power through discussion. His logic then was that if Britain led a fresh renegotiation of the terms of the peace based on legitimate balance-of-power principles, then the French themselves would create a government that could accommodate to that new reality. On 12 April Wellesley rose again, charging the government with incompetence: "He would have granted a handsome—

nay, a noble provision to Buonaparte; but he would have taken care to make due provision against his return to power. There was not, however, one word in the treaty on this point."[53]

Wellesley's position left everyone scratching his head. Even Grenville supported resumption of the war. Liverpool, in writing to Canning, tried to make some sense of it: "Were you not surprised at Lord Wellesley adopting the peace policy and going with the Whigs? I hardly know how to account for it."[54] The simple fact is that Wellesley's argument was without merit and came despite Wellington's integral involvement in the course of events. Then again, maybe Arthur's connection to events are specifically what caused Lord Wellesley to stray so remarkably off course. One cannot help but see self-interest here: the marquess would deprive Arthur of another opportunity for glory even as he put himself forward as the font of wisdom. It was all ridiculous and in the end demeaning, and Wellesley found himself in the uncomfortable position of defending his views after Waterloo.

That defense exploited another tack—that even success in battle did not mean victory. Here Wellesley explained that removing Napoleon by force only increased the contempt of the French nation for Louis XVIII; the result would necessitate a British occupation force for many years to come, at great expense. He conceded that the war had ended more expeditiously than he had anticipated, but that fact did not change the greater reality of instability in France.[55] Liverpool was surprisingly calm about the marquess's political flip-flop, but Wellesley's argument was certainly not calculated to convince or please Wellington. Coming on the heels of his suspicions concerning the *Times*'s attack on his Spanish mission, it left Arthur viewing his brother as irrational and even a potential enemy. That he included Wellesley's lank justification for his point of view in the *Supplementary Dispatches* thus comes as no surprise.

While Richard brooded, Arthur found himself at the center of the growing crisis of dealing with Napoleon. With the mobilization of Russian and Austrian forces proceeding at a slow pace, Wellington and Field Marshal Gebhard von Blucher would have to contain the French until those forces could be drawn up. The duke traveled to Brussels to take charge of an army composed of Belgian, Dutch, German, and British soldiers, with little battle experience and no cohesion. As always, Wellington complained but in the end made the best of what he had. He carefully surveyed the ground between Brussels and the

French frontier and coordinated his plans with Blucher, whose Prussian army would prove decisive in the upcoming struggle. Although the duke wished for more veterans from the peninsular campaign, he maintained a calm, confident façade while awaiting Napoleon's advance. But one wonders what must have been going on in his mind and his emotional center. He believed that Napoleon would ultimately fail, but he also knew that battles would be fought and men would die. Wellington had thought that his fighting days were over. Readjusting to the military life—especially when that meant facing the greatest military talent of the age—would be no small task. That he did so without complaint demonstrates as clearly as anything his sense of duty and nerves of steel.

Napoleon cleverly disguised his intentions, and allied intelligence failed to provide even scant illumination on this point, but Wellington believed that Napoleon would have to strike at the lowlands before Russian and Austrian troops reached the frontier. In preparing for the inevitable conflict, Arthur knew full well that if he failed, greater carnage would follow. Moreover, the struggle would test all his resources. Having been in Paris, he knew that Napoleon could mobilize a seasoned army ready to fight and also had the advantage of choosing when and where to fight. In contrast, Wellington commanded a largely untested army with which he had to defend a variety of potential targets while taking care to plan for its retreat and disembarkation should he fail. With the Prussians as allies, he possessed numerical superiority, but they constituted a separate army with which he could only coordinate his plans rather than fight in concert. In short, the challenge was immense and the stakes high.

One must also take into consideration the fact that in the coming battle, personal reputations were at stake; Napoleon threatened to take the duke down with him. Arthur had experienced the heady phenomenon of celebrity, and he liked it. The role of hero came naturally to him; it put to rest the ghosts of a distant past and promised a brilliant future. Suddenly his reputation and celebrity rested in the balance, dependent on the outcome of one great battle. In fact, though he did not see it in this light, Wellington's future was at greater risk than Europe's. That he maintained an outward calm in the midst of this reality arose from the nerve-wracking years in the Peninsula.

At his headquarters in Brussels, Wellington did nothing to suggest much more than a normal concern. When the Duchess of Richmond asked whether there was any reason why she should not go ahead with plans for a great ball, Wellington urged her to proceed. The last thing he needed was to complicate matters with panic in the city even though he did not know when and where Napoleon would appear. Still, rather than focus on Wellington's demeanor, one would do better to appreciate the stress he clearly took upon himself. To believe that he did not feel it is absurd. At the same time, four years in the Peninsula had prepared him for this moment, and like a well-seasoned athlete, he knew what to expect. He knew that there would be surprises, even setbacks, but he was confident that if he planned thoroughly, he would succeed.

The first surprise came on the day of the Duchess of Richmond's ball. Napoleon crossed the Belgian frontier and captured the strategic position of Charleroi. With intelligence filtering in through the course of the afternoon and early evening, Wellington issued his orders, informed the Prussians of his plans, and late that evening proceeded to the ball. By the time he arrived, everyone in Brussels had learned, with varying degrees of accuracy, that the French were at hand. This was the first question to greet the duke when he arrived; he calmly affirmed that a battle was in the offing. Then he danced and joined the party at dinner. In the meantime, updated intelligence arrived at regular intervals until finally, shortly after 2:00 a.m., the Iron Duke excused himself. With the Duke of Richmond at his side, he consulted a map and then retired to his hotel for two hours of sleep. It was an extraordinary performance, although one wonders whether it was overdone.

The day of 16 June dawned clear and bright, and Wellington proceeded to Quatre Bras to oversee his army gathering in front of the French. He arrived near 10:00 a.m.; sensing that battle was still several hours off, he rode to Ligny to confer with Blucher. There he found Napoleon in a position to offer battle, but before Wellington departed, he assured his Prussian counterpart that he would come to Blucher's assistance if his own forces did not have to fight. By the time he got back to Quatre Bras, the French had arrived en masse and occupied the crossroads. The French, in fact, outnumbered the allied army, and had Marshal Michel Ney—hero of the Russian campaign—ordered an all-out attack, he would have sent Wellington reeling. But the French, unaware of their advantage, proceeded cautiously while Wellington played for time with well-placed counterattacks as he awaited reinforcements. Ney in turn waited in vain for the arrival of Marshal d'Erlon with a corps of twenty thousand. The affair at Quatre Bras was sharp and ended in a draw, which for Wellington was as good as victory; the duke retreated in good order to Waterloo, where the real battle would be fought. At the same time, the Prussians had been mauled by Napoleon's main force, but they too managed an orderly retreat. Blucher, battered and bruised, announced that he would reinforce Wellington. By late afternoon on the 17th, Wellington's army had reached Waterloo and began digging in. Their commander had chosen his ground carefully, not only for its defensibility but also because the location would allow the retreating Prussians to come to his aid. Without sustained sleep for nearly three days, knowing that he would soon face Napoleon in a decisive battle, and not altogether sure that Blucher could provide the promised reinforcements, Wellington continued to maintain the calm demeanor that had been evident in the days leading up to the campaign. That he was apprehensive would be confirmed by his activity on the field of battle on 18 June.

Napoleon once commented on the extraordinary physical and intellectual effort required in directing a battle. This was certainly the case at Waterloo, where the duke was on his horse for the battle's duration, directing his army from one vantage point or another. After a long night of heavy rain, Napoleon waited for the ground to dry before opening fire at about 11:30 a.m. That decision more than any other determined the outcome of the battle because it allowed the Prussians additional time to march in support of their allies. Still, there was much fighting to be done, and Wellington did it with energy and determination. Riding the length of his lines, he issued orders, exhorted his men, rallied them when they faltered, and cheered them when they took the offensive. His keen and quick eye identified key positions and discerned Napoleon's evolving strategy, making adjustments accordingly. With men and horses falling all around him, and riding from crisis to crisis, he never lost his nerve, maintaining a cool demeanor throughout the battle. The Prussians arrived in stages beginning in the late afternoon, and by 9:00 p.m., the French were in headlong retreat. Only then did physical and emotional exhaustion take over, leaving Wellington utterly spent. As the lists of dead and wounded were read to him, he wept, and when he sat down to write his victory dispatch, the result, while clear and succinct, hardly did the battle justice, not to mention leaving out a large number of participants who had distinguished themselves. Wellington would spend the rest of his life accounting for his oversights.

Nonetheless, it was over; Napoleon had been vanquished, Europe had once again been saved, and Wellington's reputation was intact.

He hardly had time to absorb the magnitude of the event, for there was a pursuit to make and Paris to manage. In the aftermath of Waterloo, Wellington drew most of the acclaim (though Blucher got his share) because Wellington's army rather than Blucher's was the one attacked on the 18th, and Wellington's forces bore the brunt of battle for most of the day. To the European public, the fact that Blucher turned near defeat into clear victory was a matter of indifference. As a result, Arthur, like the hero in a Greek drama, already the object of adulation and respect, was elevated to Olympian heights. His brothers basked in the radiance of his glory—all but the fatally flawed Richard.

14

Entr'acte II

Waterloo brought with it a realignment of European political forces and a variety of domestic challenges to victors and vanquished alike. The catharsis of a final battle proved a tonic, but it also released less attractive instincts such as revenge and gloating that made the conduct of international affairs a less than appealing business. Wellington, as commander of the occupying army, was left to cope with much of this in anticipation of more settled times to come. On the domestic front, peace brought celebration, but it soon gave way to the reality of economic stress and the attendant political pressures, which challenged the resourcefulness and resolve of all the victorious allies, especially Britain. Indeed, the world must have seemed a topsy-turvy place from the vantage point of Whitehall, and Liverpool's government can be forgiven if it felt hints of resentment over the fact that the tasks at hand allowed precious little time to enjoy the fruits of victory. A changed and changing world confronted the government. Britain had emerged from a generation of conflict a hegemonic power with little sense of what that might mean in terms of its role in the world. At the same time, the nation had entered the industrial age almost unnoticed, and this too required fresh thinking from its leaders. The Wellesleys likewise faced changed circumstances that challenged their long-established sense of family order. Most obviously, Arthur had ascended the social and political ladder almost as fast as Richard had slipped down it.

This had consequences for the whole family, and they struggled amid unforeseen events to make sense of it all.

Waterloo left the marquess like a punch-drunk fighter. The string of career-changing decisions that began with his resignation of the Foreign Office in February 1812 had run its pathetic course with his opposition to resuming the war when Napoleon returned from Elba. As the defeated emperor sailed for St. Helena, Wellesley took stock of the fact that he had squandered the last of his political capital, leaving him isolated on his own remote political island. Not surprisingly, he avoided the great celebrations that followed that summer. And as if the devil had not yet had his due, domestic peace proved equally elusive.

A family crisis involving his daughter Anne intruded upon the marquess's troubled little world and ultimately engaged the attentions of the extended family. Anne, well known for a sensuous, almost exotic beauty inherited from her mother, had married Sir William Abdy in 1806. From the start the match seemed unlikely, as Sir William was a quiet, dim-witted man who enjoyed only the manly pleasures of the hunt and the club. For him the London social scene held little interest, probably because he could not keep up with the rapid-fire social discourse of Regency society. The flamboyant Anne, in contrast, relished it. Much in demand for her beauty, wit, and charm, she found her tray filled with invitations and no reason to hold back. William was a wealthy man. The two lived in his town house in elegant Mayfair, but he maintained several country properties as well. Nearby lived his sister and mother, who made it their business to monitor the couple's activities. Clearly, Anne was more than William could handle, and there is every reason to believe that she bullied him with a fierce temper that she kept confined behind the closed doors of the Mayfair mansion. William conceded his wife's demands, allowing her to entertain and accompanying her to soirées, where he felt much out of place; mostly he retreated to the country and the hunt. There were no children from the marriage, and both families speculated as to the reasons why. Whether or not the relationship was emotionally or physically satisfying to either or both parties, it appeared comfortable; no one suspected a threat to it. Anne and William each derived something important from the match, and fashionable London society was filled with such arrangements. If nothing else, William and Anne were well amused.

Then in early September 1815, Sir William left London to hunt with a sister's husband in Cambridgeshire. These were exciting times for Anne. Her uncle Arthur's victory at Waterloo had been followed by a flurry of celebrations that were only beginning to die down. As the niece to the hero, she would have been in great demand, and one can imagine the emotional energy that consumed her and how starkly it contrasted with her husband's torpor. Although she attracted male attention as she made her social rounds, she managed to avoid gossip. In the early afternoon of 5 September, she announced to her servants that she would walk the dog. She proceeded down Hill Street to Park Lane. On cue a gig pulled up. She climbed in and rode off into the city. The event did not go unnoticed; passersby recognized both Anne and the driver, Lord Charles Bentinck, equerry to the prince regent and third son of the third Duke of Portland. When she failed to return home, it became clear that she had eloped.[1]

Sir William got word of his wife's desertion late that evening in a letter from Anne, who, in a panic, had begun to doubt the wisdom of her actions. William hurried back to London and discovered his mother and sister clutching an extensive correspondence that confirmed a long-standing liaison between Anne and Charles. The two busybodies, who had never much liked Anne, had been to the house and searched her belongings. It was all strangely reminiscent of Charlotte Wellesley's desertion of Henry six years earlier. Anne begged her husband's forgiveness, but her mother-in-law and sister-in-law were in no mood to be generous and Sir William was hardly the man to contradict anyone, especially these formidable women. They sent word of the event to Marchioness Wellesley, and a test of wills ensued, with Hyacinthe urging William to take Anne back.

Hyacinthe was in Brighton with her son Henry, a fact that greatly complicated any sort of negotiation, but in any case she was not the person to be charged with the attempt to bring order out of the chaos. The one to do this was her eldest son, Richard, but he too was out of town. It therefore fell to Edward Littleton, husband of her second daughter, another Hyacinthe, to hail Richard to London. To modern eyes, this all seems an amusing distraction, but the stakes were high for Anne and, in turn, her family. Richard and Edward understood this, as did Anne's sister Hyacinthe, who was pregnant at the time. From the start, the siblings were determined to effect a reconciliation, referring to Lord Charles as a villain. There was another problem—when and how to inform the marquess. Richard, well aware of his father's state of mind, decided to send a straightforward account without delay, and Wellesley responded in a fashion appropriate to a seasoned narcissist. He wrote with detached clarity and heavy doses of hypocrisy that must have brought a grimace to his son's face. For a man who had treated his own wife shamelessly, it was the height of conceit for him to write, "The calamity which your letter announced is among the most severe that can befall a family of honour; because in point of honour, it is irreparable."[2] However, the marquess endorsed Richard's view of the situation, which was to do all in one's power to bring about reconciliation. Wellesley, however, was less sanguine of success. Detached and alone, the marquess would direct this affair by proxy, and he instructed Richard to take steps should reconciliation fail.

First, and foremost, they needed to extract from Bentinck a formal pledge that he would marry Anne. If that could not be obtained, then prospects were grim indeed. But, assuming otherwise, then the case for divorce must be pressed. Eventually the young Hyacinthe made contact with Anne, and after considerable persuasion, the two of them set out to meet with Sir William. Abdy would have none of it, refusing to see them and suggesting that the publicity attending the event would make reconciliation a public humiliation. He would not be a cuckold. During the next few days, there would be some vacillation on this, and William and Anne would finally meet, but the parties could not agree to reconciliation.

Richard, as instructed, secured legal counsel in fashioning a pledge that Lord Charles should sign, guaranteeing that he would marry Anne on the conclusion of divorce proceedings. Anne reported Charles as ready to sign anything, that he could be relied upon to do the honorable thing. Then she descended to the type of behavior that must have driven her family and friends to distraction, observing that "yesterday I saw Sir William opposite my window in a state of phrensy. I flew out to him and did everything to calm and compose him. Oh Hyacinthe, if I had not been afraid of Lord Charles interfering I would never have left him." Her letter goes on singing of her affections for Sir William and his determination to take her back if only they could find some sort of respectable manner of effecting it. As in a soap opera, hysteria governed her thinking as she vacillated from one lover to the other. On close analysis, however, the passion seems manufactured. Anne created drama in her life because for her, drama was what made life worth living. In fact, neither William nor Charles was a man likely to elicit strong emotions from anyone. Neither possessed strong character or good looks, and there was no hint of supercharged sexuality in these events. Lord Charles Bentinck was no Marquess of Anglesey.

In any case, as Richard dealt with Charles, assuming the inevitability of divorce, Hyacinthe and Anne made one last effort at arranging reconciliation. William made it known that he would take Anne back only if some sort of foreign employment could be found for him. To his mind, the Wellesleys were a family of influence and should have no trouble arranging it. Accordingly, Richard wrote to his father to see if there was anything that could be done. Richard could have anticipated the answer, for he knew as well as anyone that Wellesley had no political cards to play. Wellesley, unwilling to acknowledge this, dismissed the suggestion as impractical and pointed out to his son that as time passed the whole transaction began to look farcical. Anne and William must make up their minds: reconciliation or divorce. If William could not come to a speedy decision, then Anne needed to, for she risked losing both men. Moreover, the longer this went on, the more difficult would be the proceedings in the House of Lords.[3] For his part, Charles was clear. Writing to Richard, he declared, "Sir, I hereby solemnly engage upon my honour that as soon as the forms of law will permit of it I will marry your sister, Anne, now Lady Abdy."[4]

Meanwhile William's solicitor drew up papers for divorce and filed them in the Consistory Court of Doctors' Commons. The citation would then be served on Anne. All seemed in place, but the Wellesleys asked for a delay of eight days because they had played one last card and needed time to see if it would take the trick. A letter had been sent to Uncle Arthur in Paris under Anne's name:

> I should not venture to address you if my unhappy situation and your uniform kindness towards me did not embolden me to apply to you in my present distress. . . . Sir William is willing to pardon the fault of which I have been guilty and to restore me to my station as his wife—if by obtaining some situation through your interest, he may be able to reside out of England for some years and may feel that his conduct has your support and that of our family against any reflections that may be cast upon him. I have no doubt that your great interest would succeed in procuring this appointment at an early period, and I most fervently hope that you may feel it to be in your power to exert it on my behalf. . . . I most earnestly beg your

> favourable compliance with my request and I shall await your answer with the utmost anxiety and impatience.[5]

Certainly Anne did not write this letter, for it is too calm and too measured to have been the product of her troubled soul. More likely, Richard and Edward drafted it, probably with the realization that Wellington could not help—nor, in the final analysis, would he if he could. Nonetheless, the duke was kind and gentle, and his advice clear: "I am quite certain, however, not only that I have it not in my power to prosecute Sir William Abdy's views of employment abroad, but that to attempt it at present would be highly injurious to his reputation and to yourself. I should not succeed because Sir William has, till now, had no experience in public business and it would naturally create suspicions in the minds of those to whom application should be made in his favour of the motive for making it, if it were brought forward at the present moment."[6]

Wellington's view of the matter was, of course, correct. What makes this extraordinary is that the siblings were willing to risk the solicitation in the first place and that William and Charles would wait on the matter. Hyacinthe shed some light on Anne's feelings. She believed that Anne's willingness to seek reconciliation was driven largely by concerns for her family, but "the very idea of going to bed with him again fills her with horror!"[7] In the end, both Anne and Lord Charles buckled under the pressure; they ran off again, leaving Sir William in the lurch.

Hyacinthe and Richard made no attempt to hide Wellington's involvement in these events from their father, despite the risk that the fury out of Ramsgate would know no bounds. The marquess responded calmly. He was complimentary and gentle with his daughter, praising all her efforts at effecting a solution. Still, he thought it all an exercise in futility, given the parties involved. Writing to Richard, he summed up his opinion:

> The conduct of these three parties is almost equally despicable and odious. What woman of sense, feeling or honour, would thus fluctuate between her seducer and her husband? . . . What injured husband could be so mean and so absurd, as to offer himself for a bribe to the family of the Adultress; and to imagine, that such a bribe would gild his disgrace; or would not accumulate upon him, with tenfold aggravation, the just

> sight of public indignation and private scorn? What seducer ever before sat quietly during the negotiation of such a corrupt bargain for the repurchase of the husband's goodwill?[8]

Still, the marquess was hardly the person to lecture on matters of the heart and honor, so it is no surprise that the women of his family chose instead to pour out their hearts to their uncle Arthur, who listened despite a schedule full of responsibilities, both political and social. He took particular care to console Hyacinthe: "I am not astonished at your feeling for your sister; but you must not allow these feelings to keep you out of the World or to make you believe that people will on that account think the worse of you; nor on the other hand should you regret any good-natured act you may have done by her, or be induced to abandon her in her misfortunes."[9]

The case went to court in December, with Lord Charles defended by the brilliant Lord Brougham. Sir William asked for damages of £30,000, but Brougham managed a more sensible £7,000 out of a skeptical jury. Eventually the case made it to Parliament, where the great family concern was over an exclusionary clause that would prohibit Anne from marrying Lord Charles. Proceedings began in May 1816, and as the marquess predicted, the Wellesleys faced some formidable opposition. Lord Wellesley had taken care of one potentially fatal opponent in the person of Lord Sidmouth. Though the two were estranged at the time, their ties went back many years.[10] Wellesley invoked the memory of this long friendship to persuade Sidmouth to hold his fire. That left Lords Lauderdale and Eldon, who were vigorous proponents of the exclusionary clause; the latter wielded immense influence as Lord Chancellor. In the end, however, no one wanted to expend political capital on such an issue, and when the final reading came on 18 June 1816, Waterloo Day, the divorce without exclusion passed. The duke, operating behind the scenes on behalf of his niece, provided formidable influence. One month later, Lord Charles and Anne were married, and a pathetic yet almost comical affair came to an end.

This episode does more than reveal a side to Wellesley family life that is generally unappreciated. All the brothers had some sort of difficulty with at least one of their children, and as fathers they were ineffective, indifferent, or inept. As uncles, however, especially Arthur, they were superb, and they always made time for their nieces and nephews, some of whom they adored. It is no surprise that Arthur, as put out with Richard as he was at that time, responded sympathetically and promptly to Anne's troubles. Nor is it a surprise that the marquess expressed no resentment at his brother's intervention.

This was not the last sex scandal to haunt the Wellesleys in the immediate post-Waterloo period. The year 1816 would see the desertion of Gerald by that other Cadogan woman, Emily. Letters and diaries from the period are remarkably quiet concerning this affair. Granted, Gerald was not of the bon ton, but he was a Wellesley and Emily was a Cadogan, so one wonders at the silence. Perhaps it was because Emily's behavior was beyond the pale even by Regency standards. According to Edward Littleton, who heard it from the duke, Emily had a brief affair with the Marquess of Anglesey, who was at the time married to Charlotte Cadogan, Henry's first wife. It is difficult to tell whether Anglesey was keen on comparing sisters or whether Emily was simply trying to confirm Charlotte's high opinion of the dashing hero's merits. In any case, Emily threw him off in favor of Joseph Henry, third Baron Walscourt, an Irish peer described by Littleton as "just of age, whom she had introduced into her house as a visitor to her daughter, but in fact for her own purposes."[11] Anglesey, not used to such treatment, promptly betrayed her to Gerald. This was hardly the kind of behavior one would expect of the wife of a canon of St. Paul's. It was all a terrible shock to poor Gerald, and Arthur promptly intervened in an attempt to assuage the cuckolded husband's wounded pride by securing for him a bishopric. One must conclude either that Arthur's political judgment at this moment was something less than razor sharp or that he simply did not appreciate the import of such proceedings for a cleric. In any case, an astonished Liverpool dismissed the request out of hand, refusing even to discuss it with the duke.

Wellington took offense. There were moments in Wellington's life when Wellesley pique and self-absorption burst free of the controlled veneer, and this is one of them. One need not search far to find an explanation. First, this was a man who had been commander in chief uninterruptedly for five years. He was not used to contradiction, let alone being simply brushed aside. Second, since Napoleon's first abdication, Wellington had enjoyed a celebrity that confirmed all opinions, all actions. Is it any wonder that he was miffed when his prime minister ignored him? Finally, and what is perhaps most important, the moral scandal that attended Gerald's circumstances Arthur could hardly afford to acknowledge, as he was in the midst of his own.

After Waterloo, Arthur had picked up where he had left off, as the object of adoration for a variety of women. For a man who had been on the field of battle for five straight years, he could hardly ignore the possibilities. Arthur's extramarital love life has always been rife with speculation. That he socialized extensively and often privately with many women has never been denied, but whether any of these relationships were consummated defies confirmation. Depending on the biographer, the duke has been tied romantically to Frances, Lady Shelley; Lady Frances Wedderburn-Webster; Lady Caroline Lamb; the Countess of Westmeath; Marianne Patterson; Lady Granville; Sara, Countess of Jersey; Lady Charlotte Greville; Harriet Arbuthnot; Olivia Kinnaird; Lady Georgiana Fane; and Lady Francis Cole. Given the circumstantial evidence, Lady Wedderburn-Webster, Marianne Patterson, and Lady Charlotte Greville seem the best candidates as lovers, but what is more important is that fact that we cannot be sure. The duke, if he did stray, certainly ranks among the most discreet philanderers in history—not to mention the fact that the women in his life were fond enough of him to protect his privacy whatever the reality. The exceptions to this were his dalliances with two women of the Paris stage, Giuseppina Grassini and Marguerite Weimer (better known as Mademoiselle George), and a tryst years earlier with the notorious Harriette Wilson.

Whatever the case, there is no denying the duke's status as a social lion or that he relished that status, especially in the heady years after Waterloo. Of course there were consequences for Kitty. The rumors about her hero husband pained her, and her friends bemoaned the fact that his reputation awaited a fate much like that of Nelson, whose affair with Emma Hamilton besmirched his legacy.[12] Eventually Kitty would join her husband in Paris, but she did not stay long, again clearing the field for the throng of admirers. Arthur would make trips to England, and this served to relieve some of the strain of social innuendo, but not much. In any case, he had the good sense not to pass moral judgment on Gerald's marriage, but he could hardly expect Liverpool to do the same. That he had this expectation confirms a propensity towards self-delusion. As a footnote to all of this, Arthur's anger with Liverpool had consequences for Henry and William. The duke refused to intervene on their behalf with the prime minister when Henry sought the embassy in Paris and William a seat on the board of control. The marquess, for all his faults, would not have done the same.

It was not all play and no work in Paris. As commander in chief of the occupying forces, Wellington spent much of the first weeks in the city restraining revenge-minded Prussians and Russians while playing the role of the generous victor. He did not want a repeat of the 1814 experience and did his best to build support for the Bourbons as they prepared to return in July 1815. But this was a heavy burden, and the duke had to do all in his power to remove the correct impression that the royal family was again being imposed upon France. Wellington established his headquarters at Cambrai, midway between Brussels and Paris, but maintained a residence on the Champs Elysées. As he shuttled back and forth, he found resolve in the belief that there was no option to the rotund, decrepit Louis XVIII. The duke remained well aware that the French were reminded daily of their status as a conquered people. Negotiations for another Treaty of Paris went on before their eyes and the eyes of a substantial occupying army. Wellington commanded that army and as such symbolized the tyranny of defeat. Once the treaty had been concluded, much of the responsibility for implementing it fell to the duke. First came the issue of the restitution of confiscated art. This was particularly troublesome because it was a public issue, involving the physical act of entering the Louvre, removing the art, packing it, and shipping it to the previous owners. Inevitably the process attracted crowds and led to protests and, in some cases, small riots. Especially large and cumbersome objects such as the horses from St. Mark's in Venice were problematic. Difficult as this was, Wellington went forward and absorbed the abuse.

The issue of punishing collaborators from Napoleon's Hundred Days, part of the so-called White Terror, also created a stir. Three senior officers were at the top of the king's proscription list: Colonel de la Bédoyère, General Lavalette, and Marshal Ney. Wellington opposed such foolish retribution but saw it as an internal issue and refused to be drawn into the controversy. Bédoyère and Ney were subsequently executed amid controversy focusing as much on Wellington as it did on the Bourbons. Three Englishmen—Sir Robert Wilson, Michael Bruce, and John Hely-Hutchinson, who arranged his escape—saved Lavalette. French authorities arrested all three, and the specter of their being tried for high treason prompted intervention from the reluctant commander in chief. Their punishment came in the form of slaps on wrists: three months' imprisonment. Not surprisingly, Paris again came to be a dangerous place, and the cabinet urged the duke to spend as little time there as possible. Louis XVIII, however, wanted Wellington in the city as a prop to the king's shaky regime. Wellington ignored pressure from both sides, choosing to reside where he felt he was most needed.

By 1817 the mood in France had become increasingly hostile towards allied occupation, and Wellington began to think it time to make some sort of gesture to ameliorate these feelings. He advocated a reduction in the occupying force so long as the French took steps to pay the indemnity called for by the Treaty of Paris. And so he began to work on two fronts: first, the political front, as he polled his own government and those of the allies concerning reductions in troop strength; and second, the financial front, as he opened negotiations between the French government and the Baring brothers and the Rothschilds for loans. It proved heavy going on both fronts, especially at home, where his views were greeted with skepticism. Eventually he prevailed, and the first steps were taken. In 1818 he concluded that the time had come to end the occupation entirely. Aside from the fact that he had been the target of more than one failed assassination attempt, he believed that nothing more could be accomplished by keeping allied troops in France. The loans were well subscribed, and the country had the appearance of tranquility. This was the situation as he prepared to leave for the first great postwar conference at Aix-la-Chapelle. Wellington won the tsar to his side, resulting in an agreement over the indemnity and the removal of all troops by the end of November.

His work done, Wellington returned to London at the end of the year, still a great hero. He would not, however, go into retirement. Anticipating the end of his commission, Liverpool's government recruited him as master-general of the ordnance. Meanwhile, he had made some decisions concerning where he would live. In July 1817, on Benjamin Wyatt's advice, Arthur had purchased from Lord Rivers an estate in Hampshire known as Stratfield Saye for £263,000, far less than the £600,000 allotted by the nation for his use. Wyatt had plans for a grand mansion on the property to replace the existing building, but Kitty found Stratfield Saye pleasing as it was, and when the duke came to spend time there, he too was satisfied. So there would be no equivalent of Blenheim for the hero of the new century, and that was appropriate.

As for a town house, there too he had taken steps. As negotiations proceeded on Stratfield Saye, he quietly purchased Apsley House from his brother for £42,000. As Wellesley had paid £16,000 for it, this seems an exorbitant price. The marquess had undertaken many improvements, but Wellington's generosity has another explanation. Richard's indebtedness had reached a crisis, and the Irish estates had been progressively mortgaged to sustain the marquess's mounting expenses. Wellesley gave precious little thought to all of this and spent himself into ruin. By 1817, however, it could go no further. With creditors of all sorts knocking on his door, some Irish lands were put up for sale. The details of the marquess's finances are too labyrinthine to straighten out and many of the details have been lost to time, so a clear understanding of the situation can never be gained. Iris Butler has given it as much analysis as anyone, but even her discussion gives rise to more questions than it answers. In any case, while Wellesley sought capital to pay down his debts, he turned to the duke for immediate assistance, lest he lose his furniture and staff. He requested £10,000. Arthur, who disapproved of his brother's lifestyle, responded by insisting that Richard provide proof that he had taken real steps towards reducing his expenses before considering a loan. Richard's appeal was not unexpected. As early as 1811, William had written of an impending crisis: "It is believed that he is entirely ruined—this I know is much talked of, and I have reason to think it is true, but at present his Establishment seems to go on as usual. I believe that all his Indian money is gone, that he owes his Banker £40,000 and that his allowance to his wife, sons, etc., etc. amounts to near 10,000 a year so you may guess what he has left."[13] One can only imagine the humiliation of going hat in hand to his brother, and it should not come as a surprise that the marquess did not respond when Wellington made him squirm with a caveat. But Wellesley's letter in response to Arthur's offer to repay the money advanced for his commissions must have still rung clearly in the duke's ears. He saved Richard from further humiliation with the generous offer for Apsley House.[14]

Wellesley's troubles did not end there. His son Richard provides the best picture of his father's financial situation in a letter to his brother Gerald stating that "he is so totally ruined in his fortune that not only are all his Estates in Ireland to be sold (the greater part have already been) but also his pension from the E. India Company, and his property is placed in the hands of Trustees for the payment of his debts."[15] That the marquess was desperate can best be seen in his behavior on the death of his wife in 1816. Hyacinthe, who had not been in good health, had in October gone to Staffordshire to visit her daughter

Hyacinthe at her husband's estate, Teddesley. The visit started off well, but after ten days, she fell ill. On 5 November 1816, she died in her daughter's arms.

All her children were grief stricken, and Richard took responsibility for informing his father. The marquess's response was correct, if wholly without sentiment or sympathy. Wellesley's first thoughts were to remind Richard (and through him, his siblings) of his father's authority. Not surprisingly, to avoid having to participate directly in any of the proceedings, Wellesley claimed illness and appointed Sydenham and Mr. Lightfoot as his legal agents. He wanted control of all Hyacinthe's papers, and he made that demand directly to Richard. Fortunately, the youngest son, Henry, possessed his mother's effects and would not be cowed by his father. There were, of course, many sensitive issues that the marquess wished to bury along with his wife, but he was most interested in the estate. Hyacinthe's premature death came as a boon because it meant that Wellesley no longer had to pay the annuity, which *Gentleman's Magazine* reported at £4,000 but was closer to £5,000. Hyacinthe had accumulated a tidy sum since her divorce through careful management, and she left it all to her children. The marquess desperately wanted to get his hands on that money, which he viewed as rightfully his, extorted by his vengeful wife. One wonders whether he wanted to get his hands on the will first so as to dispose of it, but certainly he knew that his wife would have taken great care to ensure its reading. In a fury over his inability to secure Hyacinthe's papers and the realization that the estate would not land in his hands, the marquess sulked. Not only would he not communicate with his children, but in addition, he attempted to stop the will's probate; then he cut off allowances to Richard and Henry.[16] The marquess had settled £11,000 each on Anne and Hyacinthe when they married, so they were not on his payroll. Neither was Gerald, who was making a good living in India.

It was all a tragically sordid affair that revealed the marquess's worst instincts. In the end, Wellesley would rely for income mostly on a sinecure, which yielded over £4,000 a year, but that amount could not support the style to which he had become accustomed. The humiliation of turning to Arthur for help confirmed their reversal on the family ladder, rubbing salt in the political wounds already inflicted. And so 1818 found Wellesley ruined and in control of no phase of his life: his career seemingly was broken, his family alienated.

His political life found him cooperating with the opposition as the country turned its attentions to the economic dislocations brought on by peace and industrialism. In such matters, a great gulf separated the marquess from the landed interests that he envied. The first question on which he took issue with the government concerned tariffs, specifically the Corn Laws. Logic told him that artificially inflating the price of bread when great suffering existed among the laboring classes made no sense. Beyond this, grasping onto eighteenth-century principles, he viewed a tariff on corn (grain) as a restraint of trade, and he thus established himself as an advocate of free and open commerce.[17] Implicit in his argument was the belief that high food prices would aggravate existing discontent and lead to further problems.

Problems did mount, though they were the product of a number of factors in addition to widespread resentment over the Corn Law, and the country was beset with protest and violence in the form of riots and machine breaking. In 1816 a huge public gathering took place in London at Spa Fields, and there the display of symbols from the French Revolution, including the tricolor and revolutionary caps, along with the recitation of incendiary slogans sent shudders through the ministry. The home secretary, Lord Sidmouth, responded with legislation to control such public meetings, including suspension of habeas corpus. Once again, Wellesley found himself opposing the government; this time he rose in the Lords to speak at length in emphatic and at times sarcastic terms. He pointed out that the government had done little to prepare itself for such events and nothing to discover the sources of public discontent. These, he insisted, were the proper first steps in response to what was clearly a growing threat to the state, rather than tampering with constitutional rights. Quite simply, the government was overreacting.[18]

Whether this stance made Wellesley at all uncomfortable after Sidmouth had generously supported Anne's case the year before cannot be determined. What is certain is that Wellesley sounded increasingly like a full-fledged member of the opposition, which could not have been lost on either Wellington or Liverpool. His manner certainly had not changed, as the cheeky Harriette Wilson reported:

> His lordship appeared the very essence of everything most recherche, in superfine elegance. He was in fact all essence! Such cambric, white as driven snow! Such embroidery! Such

> diamonds! Such a brilliant snuffbox! Such seals and chain! And then, the pretty contrast between the broad, new, blue ribbon across his breast, and his delicate white waistcoat! . . . Never before stood I in such presence, nor breathed I in such essence! What a pretty little thing too it would be, methought, if it were but once deposited unhurt in one's bonnet-box, and one could shut him down whenever the essence became too strong for one's nerves.[19]

When one realizes that Wellesley's efforts in the Lords correspond with Anne's divorce, Hyacinthe's death, and his bankruptcy, one realizes that reports of his lethargy were greatly exaggerated. While he continued to indulge his taste in courtesans, he did so out of the public eye and never at the expense of keeping well informed. The years 1817 and 1818 passed in relative quiet, but in 1819, laborers took to the streets again, culminating in the disaster in Manchester known as the Peterloo Massacre. This is not the place to examine the details of how an orderly afternoon gathering turned bad. What matters is that in the wake of ill-advised and incompetent efforts to disperse the crowd and arrest the speakers, eleven people lay dead and hundreds injured. To the public mind, it was an outrage, but for those sitting in Parliament, it looked like anarchy at best, revolution at worst. For our story, it marks a pivotal moment, in that the marquess again threw in his lot with the government, which responded with legislation known as the Six Acts to reestablish order. Indeed, in this crisis, Wellesley sounded like an entirely different man. In rejecting the course of action that he had advocated two years earlier, he "thought it their lordships' duty to proceed with as much dispatch as possible to the consideration of the measures which had been proposed by his majesty's ministers."[20] This speech, delivered on 30 November 1819, would prove the first step in a rapprochement with Liverpool that would revive Wellesley's moribund political career.

Meanwhile, Henry had taken his long-awaited leave, departing Madrid in August 1815. There exists no documentary evidence concerning his movements during the subsequent fifteen months. We do not know with whom he stayed or the general nature of his activities. Arthur was in France and Belgium for most of the period, and Richard alternated between Apsley House and Ramsgate. Henry likely spent time with his mother and with his brothers William and Richard.

What is clear is that he spent a good bit of time at Hatfield House, the seat of his family's friends the Cecils, because on 27 February 1816, he married Georgiana Cecil, eldest daughter of the first Marquess of Salisbury. This match certainly pleased the dowager Lady Mornington, whose best friend was Georgiana's mother. More important, it was a match that lasted and from all appearances brought Henry much joy. It also brought a child, Georgiana Charlotte, on whom the happy couple doted.

The prospect of leaving the charms and comforts of Hatfield House to return to Madrid must have been sobering indeed, but return he did in December 1816, and what he found could not have diminished his trepidation. In his absence, negotiations with the Spanish government over the abolition of the slave trade had reached a critical stage, and he had every reason to believe that they would acquiesce. Still, they never ceased to astonish, and Henry wrote, "Your Lordship is too well acquainted with H.M.'s [Ferdinand VII's] character to expect that he will be induced to consent to this measure upon any principle of justice or humanity, or from any sentiment of friendship for Great Britain, or feeling of gratitude for her past services, or from any motive whatever but personal interest."[21] The ambassador's worst fears were confirmed when he found himself engaged in a kind of bidding war with Cuban planters over the future of the slave trade. Ferdinand VII wanted £600,000, but Henry refused to be a party to this kind of blackmail, and he continued to wonder which was worse—Spain's ingratitude, incompetence, or avarice. In the end, he concluded an agreement, though its timing was not what he had hoped.[22]

This done, Henry watched as Ferdinand and his government proceeded to self-destruct. The king hired and fired ministers with bewildering frequency, banishing the old to the hinterland and hiring new based on their malleability.[23] Subsequently, the Spanish government prepared to send an expedition to the rebellious American colonies, but this project ran into a sequence of delays; in the meantime, opposition to Ferdinand VII began to take shape, first in the army. The cynical Ferdinand made an about-face, accepting the Constitution of 1812 in its entirety and agreeing to reassemble the Cortes. Not surprisingly, this action provoked skepticism, and Henry worried that violence might erupt. As sympathetic as he was to Spain's disillusionment with the king, he was troubled by the extralegal fashion by which events progressed, and he regretted the Cortes' taking measures that he believed would only complicate matters. In the summer of 1820, the Cortes again abolished the Jesuits and suppressed the monasteries, unwisely injecting religion into an already unstable political environment.

By the end of the year, Henry had had enough. On assurances from Castlereagh that he would be given the first vacant embassy, Henry Wellesley surrendered the ambassadorship to Sir William A'Court, and at the beginning of the new year, he and Georgiana along with their young daughter began their journey home via Paris. He had served in Spain for ten tumultuous years. The challenges and obstacles that he had faced in those years were complicated, and there were times when they nearly broke his spirits. Ambassador Wellesley has been lost in the history of this period, mostly because Spain's history has never attracted much attention, but his service in the cause of his country's struggle against Napoleonic France and subsequently the reconstruction of Europe was nothing short of heroic. Like his brother the duke, he never left Iberia until the war had been won, and clearly his efforts had exhausted him. He was even deprived of the opportunity to celebrate. Ferdinand VII had presented new, dispiriting challenges on the ambassador's return to Madrid, requiring Henry's full and immediate attention, and when he did take his leave in 1816, the Waterloo celebrations were over. As a result, it was all rather anticlimactic for the youngest of the brothers, who, as hard as he looked, could find little in his work from which he could derive real satisfaction. On his return to London, he hoped for a more civilized and stable assignment.

In the meantime, the pace of events in Great Britain proceeded briskly. The year 1820 brought the Cato Street conspiracy, the death of George III, and the squalid events surrounding George IV's attempt to divorce his wife, Caroline. The death of George III, though long expected, evoked great sorrow, as his reputation had been polished by the erratic and often embarrassing behavior of his son, the prince regent. However, because of his long illness and the regency, it represented no great change; as news it was quickly overtaken by revelations of a spectacular plot to assassinate the whole cabinet when it convened for dinner at the house of Dudley Ryder, first Earl of Harrowby, on the opening of Parliament. The home secretary, Lord Sidmouth, had first received word that something was afoot in December 1819. At that time, a decision was made to allow the conspirators to hatch their plot and to arrest the lot of them when they attempted to put it into play.

The distance of history tempts one to view this event as nothing more than farce, but one must place it in the context of the times. The Peterloo Massacre of the year before, which gave rise to fear and consternation, proved to be the last of a sequence of violent events. But to many in the ruling class, the country verged on anarchy, and plots of any description were not to be taken lightly. Beyond that, although members of government had had experience with unruly mobs, never before had there been a direct threat on their lives. For the most part, these were not physical men and their only experience with violent death concerned foxes, partridges, and pheasants. Consequently, the details of Arthur Thistlewood and his gang's plans for the government sent chills through the group. Small wonder they summarily dismissed Wellington's suggestion that they arm themselves and shoot it out with the conspirators when the would-be assassins arrived at Harrowby's town house. As it happened, most of them were arrested at their Cato Street headquarters, and those who escaped were captured the next day. Thistlewood and four others were tried for treason, convicted, and hanged. In the aftermath of this unedifying event, the government and public were relieved to discover that Cato Street was not the tip of a conspiratorial iceberg and that Britain was not on the verge of social and political collapse. Before long, tales of the conspiracy became common dinner table conversation, and as is often the case in such matters, tension gave way to mirth.

In any case, London was about to be consumed by another spectacle—the return of Queen Caroline and the king's determination to divorce her. No sooner had George III been lowered into the royal vault in St. George's Chapel, Windsor, than George IV began to think about his estranged wife. He closeted with his government and demanded that they initiate divorce proceedings in the House of Lords. When the cabinet proclaimed their united opposition to such a course, the king exploded in rage and threatened to dismiss them. Liverpool prevailed, convincing the king that Caroline should be bought off and left to herself on the Continent. The agreement fell apart when the queen returned with great fanfare on 5 June 1820. Panic-struck, the cabinet dispatched Wellington to negotiate on their behalf with the queen's counsel, Lord Brougham. The government offered Caroline £50,000 a year if she would live on the Continent and allow her name to be omitted from the liturgy. Tempting as this must have been, Caroline had a London mob rallying in her behalf, and on the advice of counsel, she rejected the offer. All of this clearly sickened Wellington, who had neither respect nor affection for either party, but when he reported the breakdown of negotiations, the king began to turn the screws.

On 5 July 1820, Liverpool introduced a bill of divorce in the Lords. Subsequently, something resembling hysteria gripped the city. That it was summer leads one in retrospect to view this as a form of mass entertainment, but that certainly was not how the ministers viewed it. For the first time in his life, Wellington found himself the object of public animosity, and although he bore up well, it certainly caused him discomfort and left him with a bitter taste for the legislative process and for the fickle nature of public opinion. In the midst of these desultory events that everyone found distasteful, there occurred an encounter with the mob that is variously attributed to Lord Anglesey and the Duke of Wellington. In either case, it accurately represents the sentiments of both men. According to popular accounts, an unruly crowd outside of Whitehall stopped a horseman (either Anglesey or Wellington) and demanded that he toast the queen. Came the retort, "God save the Queen and may all your wives be like her." The trial proceeded through the heat of August, was prorogued for September, and began again in October with Brougham's defense of the queen.

On the second reading of the bill, the government's majority had shrunk to twenty-eight, leaving the prime minister in despair. A third reading on 10 November found the majority further reduced to nine, allowing a much-relieved Liverpool to withdraw the bill. The king, not surprisingly, blamed his ministers for failing to carry the day, but all was not lost. Once the divorce bill had been withdrawn, the London mob declared victory and began to lose interest.

The government in turn began plans for a coronation that did not include the queen. Efforts to include her in the liturgy were easily turned aside, and to buy off an ornery king, the enormous sum of £243,000 was voted for the event. George IV remained a mass of irrational energy. On the eve of his coronation, he quarreled with the government and paced the floors of Carlton House. For whatever reason, at this unusual moment, he called for the marquess, which Brougham reported to Creevey: "there drove along the Mall furiously a carriage and four, which was followed by my informant and found to contain old Welles-ley in person. He was actually traced into Carlton House by the back door. You may make what you please of this, but the fact is undoubted, as Duncannon and Calcraft were the persons who saw him."[24] Brougham, like others, wondered whether a deal had been struck whereby the king would dismiss Liverpool and call Wellesley in the prime minister's place. In fact, the meeting had no political overtones. The king needed a friend to calm his nerves, and apparently George's physician, William Knighton, who had once served Wellesley, suggested his former patient. Wellesley informed Liverpool of the benign nature of his visit. The marquess had worked his way back into the good graces of the prime minister and would certainly not risk that at the hands of the mercurial king.

Coronation day went off without incident inside Westminster. Outside, however, the queen ran from door to door in a pathetic and futile effort to gain admittance. Three weeks later, she was dead, and in London, life returned to normality. England and the Wellesleys then embarked on a new era.

15

Encore for the Wellesleys

Just as the coronation of George IV marked a historical moment for Great Britain, so too did it mark a transition for the Wellesley brothers. The decade of the 1820s started with Arthur as Europe's most recognizable and Britain's most respected public figure. The transition from soldier to politician was one he had taken hesitantly, if not reluctantly. His public persona became that of a forthright conservative—inflexible and stern—often taken for narrowness of view by both friend and foe. As is often the case, the perception did not coincide with reality; regarding public concerns, Arthur generally thought broadly. One might not agree with his conclusions, but support for or defense of what he perceived to be the constitutional framework that made Britain great constituted the driving force behind his political actions. His views on the important issues of the day were formed with the big picture in mind. This did not always make him an easy colleague, a fact aggravated by a degree of political naïveté and simple orneriness brought on by impatience with human vanities and the distractions of family and ill health. That said, Arthur searched for his footing with a tenacity fed by twin senses of destiny and obligation, and the end of the decade found him as the king's first minister, shepherding through Parliament the nation's most contentious piece of legislation of the first third of the nineteenth century: Catholic emancipation.

Arthur's career remained closely tied to those of his brothers. Richard, his public and personal lives in ruin, required rehabilitation. Lord Wellesley had taken steps to reconnect with Liverpool, but the reality was that reentry into political life would have to come through the aegis of Arthur. Yet as the decade began, there was nothing on the horizon to suggest relief, let alone rehabilitation, for the eldest brother. Then, like a bolt from the blue, good fortune made an appearance. Unusual political circumstances resulting from the debacle of the king's divorce presented the marquess with the opportunity to again enter the political mainstream. Liverpool, after a complex series of maneuvers, appointed him lord lieutenant of Ireland. That Liverpool should have done so is extraordinary, and as usual, Richard failed to appreciate the gesture. That said, he would spend the better part of the decade in the political hotbox in Dublin known as the Castle. His tenure would be contentious, but Richard clung to the job because it provided him with financial relief and the opportunity to redirect Ireland's history. At the same time, the years would see his relationship with Arthur deteriorate to the point of complete alienation, and at decade's end, the two would look at one another from opposite benches in the House of Lords.

William and Henry were both well placed at the decade's start, with William in the cabinet as master of the mint and Henry at the embassy in Madrid. Here too change was in the offing. William, to his great disgust, would find himself an expendable pawn in the great political game that was ongoing in the first half of the decade. He did not respond gracefully, and he made life miserable for those closest to him, especially the duke. In the end, he bowed to the inevitable, moving from the mint to the ceremonial post of master of the buckhounds. Henry, wearied by the Spanish court, gave up the embassy in Madrid and returned to London on the promise that he would succeed Castlereagh's brother, Lord Stewart, in Vienna. This in fact would transpire, though not without some anxiety attributable to Castlereagh's suicide and Canning's assumption of the Foreign Office. The year 1823 found Henry in Vienna, where he would remain until the collapse of Wellington's ministry. Both William and Henry maintained good relations with the duke, and it paid off handsomely; each obtained a peerage before the end of the decade. As for Richard, both brothers remained actively interested in him, but Henry gradually lost touch because of distance and his own considerable responsibilities, and William never confused Richard's coattails for Arthur's.

Gerald—modest, even-tempered Gerald—continued to regroup from his wife's desertion. Though personally devastated, he remained professionally ambitious. As his brothers advanced, he looked to them for help, though he never grabbed in the fashion of his siblings. Arthur and Richard would do their best to realize their brother's ambition for a bishop's throne, but they failed. The attempt gave rise to family bickering and ill will between Wellington and Liverpool. Fortunately for Gerald, he was anything but destitute and continued to live a comfortable life, enjoying the powerful and interesting connections of his brothers. Eventually Wellington enhanced Gerald's situation, but his efforts fell short of the coveted bishop's throne

Britain's political landscape scarcely changed with George IV's ascent to the throne. As regent, he had long acted as king, secure in the knowledge that his mad father was well beyond hope of recovery. The new king, however, continued in his habit of snatching defeat from the jaws of victory with the ill-considered divorce proceedings. Everyone lost something in the process. Caroline died within weeks of the debacle, the king's popularity fell to a new low, and the government emerged battered and bruised, losing the services of Canning as well as its pride. Not surprisingly, when the dust settled, Liverpool set about to reinforce his government. To do so, he looked to the Grenvillites, with whom the marquess again cooperated.

Confusion reigned within the Liverpool ministry. The question was not whether it could govern but whether it could manage the king. As ever, George was the wild card. Liverpool needed a government that the king could not do without, and to that end he set out to limit the king's options. In practical terms, this meant tying to the government the opposition's potential allies, however slight that potential might be. Liverpool's maneuvers make sense only when looked at from this angle because the Grenvillites had been cooperating with the government for a number of years. Only on the Catholic question did they differ substantively with the prime minister, and in that, they were not alone. Because of its contentious nature, there was no party line on the Catholic issue. The Grenvillites seemed to be philosophically tied to the government and therefore did not exhibit any threat to bolt.

Liverpool derived no comfort from philosophical compatibility, however. He knew very well that ofttimes it proved unreliable, if not chimerical. No, factions were brought into a party through concrete measures, meaning seats in the cabinet and the dishing out of patronage. Lord Grenville had turned the party over to his nephew, the corpulent and foolish Marquess of Buckingham; thus he and his friends were the ones whom the prime minister would have to placate. But if new men were to be brought in, others had to go, and the prime minister turned to Wellington for help. This was just the sort of thing that the duke hoped to avoid. He disliked this part of the business of politics and preferred not to soil his hands with its grit. Nor did he appreciate the disruption of a pleasant routine.

It was, in fact, an unusually quiet time for the duke. With public protests and the Cato Street conspiracy but a memory, the coronation problem settled, and foreign policy in the capable hands of his friend Castlereagh, Wellington settled into the mundane business at the Ordnance and gave free rein to his sociable instincts. He enjoyed his life as venerable sage, presiding over dinners hosted by Britain's social and political elite and gossiping with his bevy of female confidantes. It was at this time that his relationship with Harriet Arbuthnot began to blossom into an intimate friendship. He enjoyed her conversation, her wit, and what he judged to be her good sense. This should come as no surprise, in that Harriet agreed almost always with him. Had he known that she kept a diary, the relationship might have faltered, but fortunately he did not, and through Harriet's eyes we are given a sense of the duke's private thoughts. One cannot help but wonder about a physical side to this remarkably close friendship. People certainly wondered at the time, so much so, that the two of them talked about and agreed upon how they should act in public to avoid rumor. Women who knew Harriet well dismissed such speculation, while Wellington's friends simply ignored it. From the evidence it is fair to say that Arthur, a highly sexed and attractive man, would have welcomed a physical relationship but that Harriet was not much interested. Pretty, even beautiful, Harriet attracted men, but she did not have a sensual nature. She married a much older man who had been married before and who had children from that marriage. From all appearances, this was not a highly charged relationship, and that suited Harriet. The duke, it appears, eventually came to terms with Harriet's nature, but until he did, one can imagine that there must have been uncomfortable private moments.

In any case, Wellington enjoyed his friends, traveled to house parties, and hosted his own. The brothers, especially Pole but even Wellesley, were often a part of this socializing. Pole visited Stratfield Saye often, eager always to take advantage of anyone's largesse. Henry returned from Spain at this time, and he made the best of a well-deserved rest. He and his wife divided their time between London and Hatfield House, the seat of his father-in-law, James Cecil, the Marquess of Salisbury. The Wellesley-Cecil connection was a close one, so Henry was never far removed from his brothers. As had long been the case, the Wellesley family adored Henry, and in political circles, he was appreciated as a levelheaded, reliable diplomat. "Sir Henry Wellesley came to see us this morning," wrote Mrs. Arbuthnot. "He arrived yesterday from Madrid where he has been as Ambassador for many years. He is Mr. Arbuthnot's greatest friend & is a most excellent, charming person, & I am delighted he is returned. He has not the same brilliant talents that the Duke has, but he is a remarkably sensible, well judging man & very agreeable."[1]

Liverpool, meanwhile, had business to conduct and with Castlereagh's help drew Wellington into the process. While the prime minister was eager to keep the duke comfortable in the cabinet, his plans would have an adverse affect on another Wellesley. Liverpool had decided that Pole was expendable and suggested a peerage in exchange for his stepping aside. Wellington's job would be to put forward the offer. There is no evidence that Arthur objected to the plan, an indication that he regarded William more highly as a brother than as a public figure. In any case, Wellington did as asked, and it did not go well. William inevitably heard rumors, and when his brother broached the subject, he flew into a rage extraordinary even by Pole's standards. Mrs. Arbuthnot reported the duke's account: "Pole . . . was quite frantic at the proposal for his quitting the Cabinet. He abused the Duke furiously, said that he ought not to have allowed such a proposal to be made him; in short, was quite beside himself, positively refused to listen to the proposal & burst out of the room after declaring that the Duke owed his advancement in life to him!"[2] The experience left the duke shaken and angered, and Mrs. Arbuthnot did her best to smooth feathers. The magnitude of Pole's outburst bore fruit; Liverpool followed through with the peerage and left Pole, the newly elevated Lord Maryborough, in office. Arthur's support and genuine affection for his brother is sometimes hard to understand. William was the worst type of hanger-on in that he had been clinging to family coattails for so long that he had come to believe that his advancement was attributable to his own talent. Like most parvenus, he exhibited habits and attitudes that tended towards pomposity in the extreme. Still, Arthur liked him and consulted him in matters both public and private. William's correspondence is often postmarked from Stratfield Saye. Relations between the two returned to normality primarily because the idea of taking a seat in the House of Lords delighted the vainglorious William. Arthur, however, did not soon forget the unfortunate encounter. Not surprisingly, when Richard's name came up, Arthur stepped back, offering nothing to the discussion.

It seems astonishing that after nearly ten years away, the marquess found himself back in the political mix. In the past decade he had endeared himself to neither Liverpool nor Wellington, so the prime minister's decision to factor him into the political equation was certainly not out of friendship or personal obligation. Moreover, those who looked at him with a jaundiced eye, and there were many, saw him as indolent, unsteady, and pompous. But there was something about Wellesley that nearly neutralized such views. Uncommonly bright and in conversation able to discuss issues of political import with great clarity and perception, he possessed a kind of intellectual charisma that could make people forget who they were talking to. References to Wellesley throughout his life, and most were in some way critical, include the word "brilliant" when describing him. On this, all were agreed.

One might be tempted to think Liverpool calculated that Wellesley's being given high office might solidify Wellington's attachment to the government. This would be a misreading of the situation from both Wellington's point of view and Liverpool's. Arthur had long separated his political life from his brother's, and to say that it was of little concern to the duke what the marquess chose to do or who chose to employ him would be an understatement. If anything, Arthur doubted the wisdom of rehabilitating his erratic brother. Mrs. Arbuthnot, who tended to parrot the views of the duke, commented (at the time these decisions were being made) that "Lord W is notorious for a degree of laziness & sloth which prevents his ever doing any business. Ten years ago he had the Foreign Department & literally did nothing &, since that, ten years of complete retirement from public business is not a good earnest of much activity in his new situation."[3] As for Liverpool, he knew the marquess well and precisely what he would be getting if he made an offer. The worldly wise earl possessed a keen understanding of humanity. He accepted human frailties and focused on what one might have to offer. In the case of Wellesley, he would get clear and enlightened thinking even if he did not always agree with it. In addition, he would get a small collection of MP's who remained loyal to the marquess, a connection to Canning (who had long been a Wellesley ally), and a loose attachment to the Grenvilles. It summed up to a tidy little package. As for the Grenvilles, on that front Liverpool secured a dukedom for the Marquess of Buckingham and a seat in the cabinet for Buckingham's associate, Charles Wynn. It all seemed to make good sense.

Moreover, Wellesley filled a specific need. Liverpool had not considered the marquess for a cabinet seat; experience told him that that was out of the question. Instead he looked to Ireland, where conditions had deteriorated badly and begged a change in administration. There had been talk of sending Wellington, but he rightly pointed out that appointing a soldier might be provocative. More to the point, Arthur still did not regard himself a politician and enjoyed the Olympian heights of the very unpolitical office of master general of the ordnance. As Mrs. Arbuthnot succinctly put it, "it wd not be fair by the country to make him solely a politician."[4] Beyond that, as Castlereagh pointed out, one does not use one's big gun on a sparrow. Wellesley fit the bill, and for once he did not squander a splendid opportunity by quibbling over details and matters of manufactured principle. In fact, the marquess jumped at the offer with very few questions asked. There is in his correspondence no lengthy exchange of letters that would suggest a negotiation. The reason is simple: Wellesley desperately needed the money.

The government, no doubt with some input from the duke, had already worked out most of the ticklish issues. First, that Wellesley would not be asked to compromise his Catholic sympathies was understood. In fact, his long-time stance on Catholic rights represented his primary qualification. The Protestant government of Lord Talbot had not done well, and it was thought time for a lord lieutenant with Catholic sympathies. In fact, the real question was not over Wellesley's appointment but over who should fill the office of chief secretary. Here Liverpool had two requirements: he wanted a Protestant to neutralize Wellesley and a disciplined, managerial type to keep the lord lieutenant on task.[5] "On the whole," wrote Lord Harrowby, "Lord Wellesley was thought the best, *provided a very capable* secretary could be found. All with one accord cried out Goulburn."[6]

The marquess's enthusiasm for Ireland proceeded not simply from pecuniary embarrassment, as his critics claimed, but also from a genuine interest in and attachment to the unfortunate isle. For the whole of his political life, he had remained connected to Ireland and confirmed in his belief that Catholic rights were central to its pacification and ultimate integration into the empire. Lady Longford suggests that Wellington harbored similar feelings, but there is no evidence of this. Not that Arthur was indifferent. The duke understood that Ireland was a problem that would not go away and would require fresh and independent thinking. Nonetheless, his tie was of a practical rather than a personal sort, and though he possessed a remarkable ability to block out unpleasant memories, his Irish past proved difficult to forget. Kitty was a constant reminder of disappointing and humiliating times there. Richard, by contrast, had always acknowledged his Irish roots and kept abreast of events there. His liberality towards Ireland and the Catholic Irish, however, caused concern among the Protestant faction in government. Attaching Henry Goulburn to him provided a degree of mollification, but when the government announced the appointment, doubters became anxious. Sidmouth, the Protestant home secretary and Wellesley's friend, along with Castlereagh, a quiet supporter of Catholic rights, attempted to deal with them. The question they addressed was whether Wellesley would be an activist lord lieutenant and, if so, how his activism might be manifested. "I had a long conversation with Lord Wellesley," wrote Castlereagh (who had become Lord Londonderry), "and my impression is, that, after some further discussion, his views for the conduct of the Irish government will be such as will fall in with the course of policy which, you, the Duke of Wellington, and myself, would concur in approving."[7] More to the point, Sidmouth assured the Protestant lord chancellor of Ireland, Thomas Manners-Sutton (first Baron Manners), that "conciliation, not concession is absolutely necessary. In Ireland, the government, I am confident, will be conducted on this principle. Lord Wellesley knows that he goes to administer the laws, and not urge an alteration of them; and, in his conduct towards Catholics and Protestants, no distinction, but what is made by the law, will be made by his secretary."[8]

Catholic enthusiasm matched Protestant apprehension. Wellesley's appointment was seen as a sign of change, as a dramatic step forward, and expectations ran high. Wellesley's oldest friend, Lord Grenville, thought that Richard would "not undertake such a task, nor could anyone have ventured to propose it to you, but that in . . . the conduct of those things which pressed on the government, you are to be left at liberty to follow your own judgment."[9] There was truth to this assertion, but it ignored the power of inertia in the politics of Ireland and the fact that Liverpool had surrounded the marquess with loyal Protestants.

Meanwhile, Wellesley made preparations for his move, assembling his staff and holding meetings. He found his family delighted by his new prospects, though the reasons for the delight were various. Henry, genuinely pleased that Richard would again be contributing to the nation's political life, knew instinctively that this was the right appointment. "I know from experience," he wrote, "what may be expected from you when you have no colleagues *to contend* with, and when you are left to the free exercise of your own talents & judgment."[10] Like Grenville, Henry ignored some inconvenient realities of the broader Irish administration, but he made arrangements to meet with his brother to compare notes and to wish Richard bon voyage. The rest of the family were more mercenary. Letters began arriving from Gerald and Charles Culling-Smith (Wellesley's brother-in-law through his sister Anne) requesting posts on the lord lieutenant's staff for their sons. Such requests Wellesley could appreciate and meet, for this was business as usual. Less agreeable were Maryborough's efforts to find jobs for sons of friends. But in regard to Wellesley's recognized children, the marquess blundered badly, unfortunately exhibiting the folly of vanity that his closest friends always feared.

The question concerned who the marquess would take to Dublin as his personal secretary. The obvious choice in the minds of many was his eldest son, Richard, who had served well at the embassy to Spain. The great quarrel over Hyacinthe's papers and property had not been resolved, however, and Richard and his father rarely spoke. Still, Wellesley's friends were hopeful that young Richard would go with his father to Dublin. "Is it true that Richard Wellesley goes in some court place?" wrote Harrowby to Bathurst. "When I saw him in London he looked much more like a man going to his last home. I was quite hurt to see him such a wreck."[11] Regrettably, the marquess gave his sons by his former wife no consideration and settled instead on Edward Johnston. Johnston emerges as a great villain in this period of the marquess's life. He was Wellesley's bastard son, the product of a liaison with a woman Richard saw regularly when he sat in the Irish House of Lords. A devious and opportunistic man, Johnston established himself in his father's household through flattery and charm. He clearly had a sixth sense in regard to the marquess, preying upon Richard's many weaknesses. Unlike young Richard, Johnston did not fear the marquess. Johnston could be obsequious in a more subtle manner because he sought rewards of a tangible sort while Richard sought approval. As a result, Richard found himself on the outside looking in. He would have served his father intelligently and honestly. Sad to say, neither adverb would apply to Johnston, who used his position to be a purveyor of favors while convincing the marquess that he was his father's only friend.

Wellesley set out for Ireland on Christmas Eve, stopping in Llangollen to see his old friends "the ladies." The trek across Wales must have been bracing but beautiful, and he arrived in Holyhead to find a storm-tossed Irish Sea. Crossing on 28 December, he took up residence in the Castle and was sworn in on the 29th. Arthur remained reluctantly optimistic about all of this. It is clear from Mrs. Arbuthnot's diary that he talked of Richard's prospects frequently. By this stage of their lives, Arthur seems to have viewed Richard with something bordering on contempt, while at the same time never shaking the lifelong obligation that derived from his India career. Beyond that, he knew full well that Richard was capable of excellent work. For their part, William, Gerald, and Henry recognized that the marquess's predicted success could only affect them positively. With the Wellesleys, the old issue of career building never completely abated. And as had always been the case, the Wellesleys relied on raw political clout in the absence of more traditional means of influence.

Wellesley began his tenure with enthusiasm and energy. Nonetheless, his first official function revealed the difficulty of his task. The Protestants of the old government did not retreat gracefully. Chief Justice Saurin, who would be replaced by the pro-Catholic Plunkett, detested the very thought of Wellesley occupying the Castle, and Lord Chancellor Manners, despite Sidmouth's best efforts to pacify, refused to attend official functions, going so far as to gracelessly avoid the lord lieutenant's swearing in.[12] Wellesley took this all in stride, occupied as he was by the chaos and violence plaguing the island. Having diagnosed what he believed to be the root causes of its discontent, he arrived with a plan of action. He was, however, enough of a realist to understand that nothing could be done until order was established. Copious descriptions of the island's condition flew from his desk, putting the government on notice that he would necessarily have to use force. To that end, he requested passage of a coercion act and suspension of habeas corpus. In short, he demanded extraordinary powers. This should have caught no one by surprise, as it looked very much like India, where he had assumed the same type of flexibility.

While awaiting the government's decision on this matter, Wellesley learned that his old friend Sidmouth was resigning and that Sir Robert Peel would succeed Sidmouth at the Home Office. This marked a significant change for the marquess. Sidmouth, though a hard and fast Protestant, accepted the need for change and supported Wellesley. Moreover, he lacked the energy and resolve to monitor and manage the lord lieutenant, a fact that suited the marquess just fine. Peel would be quite different. A determined Protestant and an able and conscientious politician, he would keep careful watch on Ireland.[13] A clearer sign could not have been sent; there would be restraints on Wellesley's power regardless of coercion acts. Indeed, the new lord lieutenant would labor under odd conditions. While he enjoyed Plunkett's support, Goulburn, Peel, and Manners would keep watchful Protestant eyes on him.

The government pushed through Parliament the measures the marquess requested, but as the long arm of the law raised its sabre, Wellesley presented a catalogue of issues with which he was eager to deal. Ireland's essential problem, as he saw it, was clearly economic, involving a counterproductive system of landholding and absentee landlords—he conveniently ignored the fact that he was a part of this system. As if this were not enough, the tithe system, laws against distillation, and a growing population at the lower levels of society made matters worse.[14] Above all, Wellesley believed that the Irish labored under a judicial and administrative system heavily weighted against Catholics, which gave the impression of their being a conquered people with no hope for fair government. While Wellesley considered these things along with a course of action to subdue the violence, Goulburn and Peel adopted a lecturing tone, which irritated and offended him. Arthur, however, liked what he saw, believing in the necessity of the coercion act.[15] Maryborough sent praise, the sincerity of which must be viewed with a skeptical eye because William considered any political connection as fertile ground for jobbing. Still, others more detached than Maryborough were also pleased with the marquess's agenda.

By the end of February, Wellesley could report progress. Hunger remained endemic but pacification went forward, and Wellesley trumpeted the news. Nonetheless, the political atmosphere in Dublin could not be termed positive. The various Orange societies, made up of Protestant extremists, saw the lord lieutenant as the anti-Christ and were actively hostile towards him. In turn, the ever-paranoiac Wellesley saw them conspiring behind every corner and withdrew behind the Castle's walls, in the process missing the opportunity to build a solid basis of support among moderates. Actually, there was more to his withdrawal than this. First, the marquess shocked everyone by adopting a quiet lifestyle. Buried in a mountain of debt, he had resolved to take advantage of his enormous salary of £30,000 per annum to begin working his way out from under it. While this is entirely understandable, it ran contrary to public expectations. In fact, the large salary was to be used for public display and entertainment. The lord lieutenant was expected to act like a king in Ireland and to project the power and prestige of the monarchy in the fashion of the king. It is ironic that Wellesley should spurn an opportunity so in tune with his own inclinations when the consequences were significant. Rabid Orangemen attributed his reclusiveness to indolence and spread the word far and wide.

There was a second problem. Inside the Castle, Johnston increased the marquess's isolation by acting as the lord lieutenant's representative in public matters and in meeting petitioners. Consequently, almost all information that Wellesley received concerning the state of public opinion came secondhand. And Johnston, in a successful effort to make himself indispensable in the eyes of his master, painted a bleak picture. Talk about Orangemen was frequent and venomous, and it made its way out of the Castle through the staff. In turn, Orange societies depicted Wellesley as a threat to the established way of life.

All of this, of course, made its way back to London in various forms, either through the Protestant eyes of Goulburn, Manners, and Saurin or through the Catholic eyes of Plunkett, John Newport, and various members of Wellesley's staff. Clearly, Wellington heard more of the Protestant view. In the spring, Mrs. Arbuthnot recorded, "All parties agree in praise of Lord Wellesley, which only shows how little opinions delivered in that way are to be attended to, for in fact Lord Wellesley gives great dissatisfaction to all classes. . . . Lord Wellesley is a strange compound of brilliant talents & an unconquerable lazyness that renders all his great qualities completely worthless."[16] In other words, the duke was beginning to suspect the worst, and he was not all wrong in doing so. Wellesley, as had occurred often in the past when confronted with unpleasantries, fell sick—another flare-up of his "nerves." When this happened, he took to his bed and left business to others. Still, the charge that he did not write was, in April at least, spurious. Not all the news was bad. Colonel Shawe reported (in contrast to Mrs. Arbuthnot's opinion), "I cannot deny myself the pleasure of congratulating your Excellency on the effect of Mr. Plunket's speech on Monday night, and upon the general result of the Debate on Sir John Newport's motion. I conceive it to have been extremely important & advantageous to your Excly's Government, and to the cause of liberality and conciliation in Ireland."[17]

Once Wellesley had established a semblance of order, he began to implement a strategy conceived of many years of thought on the problem. Fully aware, as he had stated forthrightly to Castlereagh and Sidmouth, that he could not change the law in his capacity as lord lieutenant, in fact he had no desire to do so. But he could administer the system as he saw fit. His top priority therefore was to show Catholics that the law and the administration could work for them as well as for Protestants. In other words, he saw it as his duty to integrate Catholics into the system through the use of the system rather than simply employing the system as a means of control. In this sense, Wellesley was the first lord lieutenant in years to give serious thought to changing the course of Irish history rather than simply presiding over a piece of the empire.

On the surface, this appears a reasonable strategy, but reasonable or not, it required great care in its implementation. Extremist Protestants, represented by the Orange societies, proceeded on the assumption that any concession was tantamount to revolution and an end to life as they knew it. This was an illogical siege mentality but one that was firmly held. The Orangists seized the high ground by passing themselves off as upholders of the law, of the throne, and of the established church. They were unflappable patriots and always had been. From an English perspective, this assertion proved hard to deny, especially for the likes of Sir Robert Peel and Lord Liverpool. Goulburn was rumored to be a member of an Orange society; Wellington very publicly was not; Peel and Liverpool were more detached. Still, Protestants in the government had difficulty in countenancing anti-Orange policies when the Orangemen were the very people upon whom they relied in times of crisis. Wellesley needed to deal with these people gently and subtly to allay their fears while at the same time building a foundation of support for change among moderate Protestants and Catholics. Instead, he isolated himself and governed by fiat, writing off the Orangists and hoping that moderates would understand. Here was the marquess's fatal flaw. His critics then and since always pointed to his indolence, to put it gently, but Wellesley was not the first lord lieutenant or cabinet minister who could be characterized as occasionally neglectful. No, the problem was that Wellesley simply did not understand people and therefore had unreliable political instincts. Wellington for one knew what was happening because he had seen it happen before, and he had no patience for it. If that were not enough, Wellesley had managed in just a few short weeks to bring the Irish question to the forefront—always an uncomfortable event for any government, as it made the governing process more problematic. Some ministers, among them Wellington, questioned whether the benefits derived from having Wellesley in that post were worth the trouble.

In the meantime, events took an unpredictable turn in London, and they had a dramatic effect on the government and ushered in several distracting and distressing months for Wellington. In the summer of 1822, his good friend Viscount Castlereagh slipped into a mania that was apparent to all of his closest associates, including the duke. Wellington's last visit with his stricken friend came just before he departed for the Continent to inspect fortresses in the Netherlands. At that time, he urged Castlereagh to consult his physician, Dr. Charles Bankhead, and then put their mutual friends on warning. It was all to no avail. Castlereagh tricked both his physician and his wife and slit his throat with a penknife. Wellington was aghast. As if a soldier needed any reminder, the suicide brought him face to face with human frailty, and it shook him.

Castlereagh's death deprived the duke of his closest friend in the government. There existed between them a degree of trust that Wellington shared with no other person. Their worldviews and political ideals were congruent. His death, therefore, left Wellington feeling alone and with an overwhelming sense of responsibility. Prone to cynicism in regard to political matters, the duke found himself fully absorbed in the life of the politician, whether he liked it or not. Until Castlereagh's death, Wellington had enjoyed the rather privileged assumption that he could take politics or leave them. But at that point, the government came to depend on him, a fact that became starkly apparent in the matter of choosing Castlereagh's successor.

The heir apparent to most in the political world, but especially to Liverpool, was George Canning, and this presented all sorts of problems both for the duke and for the prime minister. First of all, Wellington detested Canning and not because, as was often assumed, of Canning's pro-Catholic sympathies. Wellington's antipathies stemmed from Canning's duel with the revered Castlereagh. For Wellington, Castlereagh represented everything that was noble and good, and Canning was merely his dead friend's brash and unreliable counterpoint. The duke saw Canning as self-seeking and malicious, and the thought of having him as a colleague rankled. The king saw Canning in the same light but for different reasons. Canning had been the queen's lover (though "lover" might not be entirely apt) and had resigned from the government over the decision to go forward with divorce proceedings. This constituted a double sin in the king's eyes. Ironically, Liverpool turned to Wellington to persuade the king to accept a man as his foreign secretary whom they both detested. The logic of the situation, which was indisputable, made the task no easier.

Good soldier that he was, Wellington forged ahead, and the king gave way, though less than gracefully. Liverpool was right to believe that only the duke could cajole the king into acquiescence. But the persuasion came at a price; Arthur would never forgive himself. Moreover, serious physical discomfort exacerbated his emotional and intellectual ambivalence with Canning. While observing a demonstration of howitzers, he had stood too close to the guns, and their blasts left him with a persistent ringing in his left ear. After several days of aggravation, he called in a specialist, who applied a caustic of silver nitrate, a treatment that went badly awry. The acid penetrated the duke's inner ear, leaving him permanently deaf in that ear and in agonizing pain. All the expected side effects set in—dizziness, nausea, loss of appetite. That he survived is a wonder, but then again, it is a wonder that anyone survived the quackery that passed as medicine in the early nineteenth century. Such was Wellington's physical condition when called upon to mediate with the king.

This done, Wellington set off for the Continent to represent Britain at an international conference in Verona, proceeding under instructions drawn up previously by Castlereagh. It was an extraordinary undertaking considering his physical condition, and the subjects broached at the conference did nothing to lift his spirits. A readiness on the part of the continental powers to invade Spain in support of the Bourbon monarchy seemed sheer folly to the duke, and he did not hesitate to give the other delegates a piece of his mind.

Meanwhile, in Dublin, the marquess coped with his own crisis. On the evening of 14 December 1822, in one of his rare public appearances, Wellesley attended the Theater Royal for a performance of *She Stoops to Conquer.* As befit the lord lieutenant on such occasions, he went in state. His entrance into the royal box caused a great stir, and applause, interspersed with hisses and shouts, greeted him. Then the unthinkable occurred. The audience became unruly, and various objects were hurled towards Wellesley's box. Before order could be restored, a bottle whistled by the marquess's head, provoking gasps from the crowd. Wellesley remained calm, continuing to acknowledge friendly elements in the crowd, and eventually he settled in to watch the play. But while projecting an image of composure, beneath the façade he seethed.

The near riot at the theater punctuated a difficult summer and autumn. In July Wellesley had contemplated steps to reduce the visibility of the Orange societies and to defuse hostilities between Protestants and Catholics. One of these measures was the banning of public celebrations by the Orangists on the anniversary of the battle of the Boyne and the birthday of William of Orange. The first of these events took place in July, and Wellesley informed Peel of his desire to ban decorating the statue of King William in Phoenix Park. This was an all-day event that included parades and general celebration, and Wellesley saw it as a crass provocation of Catholic sensibilities and wholly unnecessary. To him these celebrations were nothing more than clear reminders to Catholics of who was in charge.

Peel informed the marquess that the cabinet could not support such a move, because it would only serve to heighten tensions throughout Ireland, especially in Dublin. The home secretary conceded that it was Wellesley's call but made clear that he would have to live with the consequences.[18] Wellesley was nonetheless prepared to go forward when Daniel O'Connell published an open letter to the lord lieutenant requesting just such an action. It was an ill-advised move in that it made any such policy impossible for Wellesley: had he banned public celebrations of the battle of the Boyne on the heels of O'Connell's letter, he would have confirmed Protestant suspicions that he was in the hands of the Catholics. Wellesley stepped back but with the determination to visit the issue once again.

For the rest of the summer of 1822, Wellesley remained in isolation, nursing real and imagined grievances and laying out plans for the future.

In the fall, he emerged with plans to reform the magistracy. He would cull incompetent magistrates and wherever possible replace them with Catholics who could legally serve in that capacity. This he hoped might eliminate some of the worst abuses of the judicial system and at the same time demonstrate to Catholics that the system could include them.[19] He followed this reform by going forward with the decision to prevent Orangemen from decorating the statue of William III on 4 November, the occasion of the king's birthday. The pronouncement came through the lord mayor's office, but there was little doubt as to its source.[20] This time Wellesley did not ask for permission or support, and O'Connell kept quiet.

What followed was a melee as Orangemen tested the lord lieutenant's resolve. Wellesley proved true to his word, dispatching armed police to the streets to control any protests. At the same time, he asked for cooperation from Catholics, particularly the clergy, not to aggravate the situation by forcing confrontations with the Orangemen. Peel publicly rendered his support, but there can be no doubt that he thought Wellesley a fool to pursue at such great risk what the home secretary considered a minor issue. Wellesley gave Peel no time to rest, however; a dispatch outlining the lord lieutenant's ideas for reforming the tithe followed.[21] The problem with all of this was that it had to be taken up in the cabinet, where it was certain to provoke a quarrel.

The theater incident, therefore, could not have caught Peel by surprise. Nonetheless, it caused great consternation both in Dublin and in London. The king, who just a year earlier had been cheered wildly by Dubliners, was appalled that his representative could be treated in such a manner. There were those, including Lord Sidmouth, who sent letters of congratulations for the manner in which Wellesley had faced down the rioters: "I congratulate you not only on the failure of the late atrocious attempt, but, I will say, on the attempt itself, as its immediate effect upon you has served to add to the lustre and dignity of your character; and the feelings which it has universally excited will give an increase of strength and authority to your government."[22] All of this occurred as Wellington returned from Verona, and it had the effect of focusing public attention on the brothers once again. Newspapers reminded their readers of the Wellesleys' partnership in the Peninsular War and the debt owed by the nation to the family.

Unfortunately, urged on by Johnston, Wellesley once again displayed his knack for the misstep. He ordered the perpetrators arrested and sent before a grand jury on charges of attempted murder. This was folly indeed, for not only was "attempted murder" a stretch, but in addition, no one would step forward as a witness even on the charge of rioting. The jury dismissed the case; Wellesley had once again made himself a laughing stock, undoing the goodwill that had greeted his measured response to the attack itself.[23] Wellesley's fury is understandable, but he had no sense of proportion or appreciation for the fickle nature of public opinion. This was attributable as much to his own failings as to the misguided advice he received.

Wellington returned to this set of confusing circumstances and to the problem of Maryborough. The Verona conference had certainly reminded him of how much he missed his friend Castlereagh and how he regretted Canning's joining the ministry. If this were not enough, the duke had to reconcile himself to the fact that bringing Canning on board meant finding places for his key allies. That, of course, meant moving someone out, and eyes once again fell on Maryborough but also on the duke's good friend Charles Arbuthnot. Arbuthnot came out of the rearrangements in good shape and endured the process with better than expected grace, though not without some protest. Maryborough was another case entirely. Canning blithely suggested that Wellington break the news to Maryborough that he must vacate the mint.[24] This was a preposterous suggestion, and Wellington did not hesitate in making his position clear.[25]

Maryborough, meanwhile, dug in his heels. Liverpool suspected that Lady Maryborough was behind the obstructionism, but the irascible William needed no urging. Harriet Arbuthnot found it all amusing: "Lord Maryborough called on Mr. Arbuthnot yesterday. He is quite in a fury with Lord Liverpool. He says he is quite determined that nothing shall get him out of the Cabinet. That he considers the usage he has met with as quite atrocious & that he wd not accept of any office but the one he has. He talked . . . like a madman."[26] Of course, Maryborough did give way, and it was quite a comedown to be given the non–cabinet post of master of the buckhounds. Fortunately, the position satisfied his pretenses and those of his wife because it kept them in constant touch with the court of George IV. Peel confirmed this: "When I last saw Lord Maryborough at Windsor I scarcely knew how to accost him. It seemed rather odd to congratulate a man on going to the dogs, and yet to take no notice of it would simply mean that I did not think of a promotion. I therefore went boldly up to him, and shook him very warmly and earnestly by the hand, as if he had at length attained what he had long wished for and what suited him. I found I was quite right. I said to him, 'Mint or buckhounds, you are master wherever you go.'"[27] Maryborough had no idea that he was being mocked, but such is the price of vanity. In any case, it all put Wellington in a sour frame of mind. The appalling discomfort of his ear, the loss of Castlereagh, the ascent of Canning, and messy family affairs combined to make him impatient, sharp-tongued, and cynical. Fortunately, Henry's appointment as ambassador to Vienna encountered no difficulty. Canning, when told by the king of Castlereagh's intent for the Vienna embassy, promptly made the offer to Henry, who gladly accepted. Still, the rest was certainly poor preparation for what the duke saw coming out of Ireland.

For the marquess, Orangemen who detested him as much as he detested them were the real enemy. The best course of action would have been to ignore them as best he could, play to leading moderates, and work with cooperative Catholics. But this was not to be. Led by Manners and Saurin, the Orangists took the measure of their prey. Any opportunity to embarrass or harass they seized with glee. A newspaper, the *Daily Mail,* became their voice, and despite claims to the contrary, there can be little question but that the lord lieutenant read every word. In February at a meeting of the Beef Steak Club, a Protestant group not necessarily Orange in its membership, a toast was offered. Mrs. Arbuthnot reported it as "To the exports of Ireland, & may the first be the invaders of the Constitution." Creevey recorded a much more explicit message: "Success to the export trade of Ireland, and may Lord Wellesley be the first article exported."[28] Whatever the actual wording, Wellesley got the message; when told that members of his household had attended the dinner, he summarily dismissed them. Along with two aides de camp, Sir Charles Vernon was swept out the door. Vernon was a man of long service, and his dismissal was viewed as unfair and ill advised.

Wellington was among those who viewed the lord lieutenant's action in this light, but he remained confused in his opinion of his brother. On the one hand, he disagreed with taking on the Orange societies in the fashion the marquess had chosen. He did not agree with the Orangists, but like Peel, he saw these people as staunch supporters of the crown and therefore not to be taken lightly, let alone abused. Moreover, he believed that the marquess suffered from bad advice: "He is surrounded by blackguard people," recorded Mrs. Arbuthnot, "who repeat to him every thing that is said about him in the Society of Dublin, & there is also someone in the Castle who writes anonymous letters to the Chancellor & Mr. Goulburn repeating everything that he says."[29] Mrs. Arbuthnot's comments came from the duke, who had ample information on the matter provided, most significantly, by Wellesley's secretary, Colonel Shawe. Shawe knew that Johnston had to go but recognized the delicacy of the task. Clever and determined, Johnston would vacate the Castle only on receipt of a better offer. It was Johnston, said Shawe, who reacted to pressure from the Orangemen and then provoked Wellesley. "No opportunity is lost to goad, irritate and insult Lord Wellesley: a cooler temper," Shawe wrote, "might lose its balance." On the other hand, although all of this was undeniable, Shawe maintained that the Protestants had much responsibility to bear. Wellesley had attempted to work with them at the start of his tenure and had been rejected. Shawe saw Manners as the real problem; his views encouraged others, leading to open attacks on the lord lieutenant.[30]

Shawe's information seems to have moderated the duke's temper. There was in February a friendly, chatty exchange of correspondence between the brothers. Wellington informed his brother of his ear problems, talked about Verona, and offered some thoughts on Ireland. For his part, Richard extended his sympathies over the duke's ear and recommended his own course of treatment. Clearly, however, he had no idea of the severity of the problem, which suggests that he had limited access to social chitchat in Dublin. More important, he appointed Arbuthnot's brother as bishop of Meath and assured Arthur that things were improving in Ireland. Almost as an aside, he attributed his quarrel with the Orangists to a simple power struggle: Were they to run Ireland or was he?[31]

To the forthright duke, this was encouraging, but it begged the point. Wellesley had created problems where they did not exist, and in the process he had made governing in London more problematic. The delicate balance that existed in the cabinet, with Grenvillites and Canningites on the Catholic side, was under pressure. Peel expressed great frustration over Wellesley—so much, indeed, that Liverpool became alarmed. The lord lieutenant had hoped to take legal action against the Orange societies, which would raise the level of animosity among Protestants. Peel thought this course foolhardy. In this situation, Wellington informed the prime minister that he and Peel should deal with Wellesley as they saw fit.[32] Perhaps, Wellington noted, it was time for a general reassessment of the situation. The *Annual Register* recognized the problems: "Indeed Lord Wellesley stood in an entirely false position: friendly himself to Catholic claims, he was to administer Ireland according to anti-Catholic laws, and under an anti-Catholic cabinet. There was, therefore, a constant opposition between his own feelings and principles, and the spirit of the system on which it was his duty to act."[33] Wellesley, for one, did not see the situation in this light: he would prepare Ireland, Catholic and Protestant alike, for the inevitable granting of Catholic rights. This view, however, did not take into account the realities of cabinet politics in London. When Wellington thought of his brother, he certainly objected to what he felt was an incendiary policy towards Protestants, but what perturbed him more was the fact that Wellesley was making it more difficult to maintain the existing political arrangement.

Meanwhile, Henry made preparations to depart for Vienna, and the confluence of those preparations and the mobilization of French forces on the Spanish frontier led to extensive discussions with Canning. Canning's view of Britain's place in Europe had long been one of aggressive independence; he had little time for Concert diplomacy. By the time of his death, Castlereagh had concluded much the same. However, there was a significant difference in the attitude held by each of these two men: Castlereagh had mourned the demise of the Concert and had decided to let it die a dignified and slow death, while Canning chose euthanasia. Although one might conclude that dead is dead, the process of dying proved all the difference to the tone of diplomacy in the post-Castlereagh era. The problem was simple but irremediable. The former allies saw the Concert in different terms because of their divergent definitions of "security." To the monarchical powers of Russia, Austria, Prussia, and France, security was both a domestic and an international issue. By this accounting, any threat to the internal stability of any European state constituted a threat to international stability. And because the allied powers had agreed to cooperate on matters threatening international stability, they were obliged to restore internal political peace wherever and whenever it had been undone. In other words, they viewed themselves as pledged to maintain the status quo both within and between national frontiers.

Britain viewed the situation differently. Domestic politics and international relations were seen as two separate spheres, and in all but extraordinary circumstances, the former were seen as beyond the reach of the Concert. Canning had seen this divide coming as early as the Conference of Aix-la-Chapelle and had been outspoken about it in the cabinet. Castlereagh, however, held sway at the time, and though he could see the Concert fading, he was not prepared to turn his back on his friends and former allies. He had assumed the seals of office just as the war turned in the allies' favor, and as a result, he presided over Napoleon's defeat and the reconstruction of Europe. In the process, he became well acquainted with Metternich, Alexander, Frederick William, and Talleyrand, and they with him. Despite serious disagreements, these men ultimately succeeded in their task and in the process formed personal bonds based on understanding and trust. And so to Castlereagh, international affairs were both personal and state matters. Canning saw this as sentimental claptrap and had no time for it. To his mind, it was time for Britain to call the shots. The Austrian statesman Prince Klemens von Metternich, for one, could see Britain pulling away from the Concert, but he, and others, saw this as a product of British public opinion rather than a change in attitude on the part of their friend Castlereagh.

Revolt in Spain proved to be the Concert's fatal wound. When liberal army officers imposed the Constitution of 1812 on their hateful and incompetent king, Ferdinand VII, the European monarchies saw revolution on the march. As if to confirm their point of view, similar uprisings occurred in Italy, provoking increased consternation and ultimately a response. Britain acknowledged the Italian situation as a threat to Austrian interests but would countenance no interference in Spain. Castlereagh, in fact, refused even to talk about the matter. Meanwhile, another revolution took place in Greece, which had the effect of persuading the foreign ministers to meet in Verona. This was the situation when Castlereagh died and Wellington went to Verona carrying Castlereagh's instructions, which Canning had confirmed. Britain would have nothing to do with any sort of active intervention in Spain. As for Greece, Wellington was to prevent Russian interference in that part of the world. The duke did as he was told. In fact, talk of invading Spain appalled him. Aside from the principle involved, he could hardly believe the allies' short memory. Had not Napoleon proved that invading Spain was not to be taken lightly?

Still, the spirit of Verona could not be described as overly antagonistic, at least not until Canning intruded. This was the situation when Henry sat down with Canning to talk. The new foreign minister positively seethed over the prospect of a French army marching into Spain, though he preferred it to a Russian army. He detested Metternich, whom he believed had hoodwinked Castlereagh. Although Canning's attitude towards revolutionaries was conservative, he saw no threat to international stability in Spain and instead saw intervention as a means for the continental powers to threaten Britain's vital interests in Portugal and America. Consequently, Canning instructed Henry to stop in Paris on his way to Vienna to discuss Spain with the French foreign minister, François-René de Chateaubriand.[34] As for Greece, that was a different matter entirely. There British interests lay with the Ottoman Empire, which would be compromised by a successful Greek revolt. Protecting the Turks involved restraining Russia, something that Canning hoped to accomplish without Metternich's help.

Off to Paris went Henry; there Chateaubriand informed him that Britain was much mistaken to believe that the revolution in Spain posed no threat beyond that country's frontiers. To the contrary, Spanish revolutionary cells were in touch with French revolutionary cells, and success in Spain could not help but encourage imitation in France. The tone of Henry Wellesley's account of his conversation with Chateaubriand suggests that he sympathized with the French. However, he was all too familiar with the vagaries of Spanish politics and the absurdity of the royal family not to think that the French were making a terrible mistake.[35] The message to Canning was that the French would probably invade. Indeed, by the time Wellesley reached Vienna, their army had crossed the frontier. Canning, incensed by his helplessness, informed the Commons that Britain would remain neutral but wished the Spaniards success. Thus it was that the continental powers got their first taste of the Canning style, and they found it bitter.

Henry arrived in Vienna to a warm welcome from Metternich and the emperor Francis. His experience in Vienna would be far different from that in Madrid. Paris might still be Britain's first embassy, but in terms of political importance, the action was in Vienna. Moreover, Vienna was a splendid city, a cultural center with a pleasant climate, and Metternich went out of his way to make Wellesley feel a part of the European fraternity of statesmen who had won the war. Henry knew, of course, that his relationship with Wellington provided him with an automatic entrée wherever he went, but he can be forgiven if at times he conveniently overlooked that fact. There is no evidence that he ever took it for granted. That said, Metternich manipulated him from the start. With Castlereagh gone, the prince saw Wellesley as a conduit around the hated Canning to Wellington, whom he knew and trusted. Unwittingly, Henry would be complicit in this attempt, though it was of little import because Metternich did not appreciate the differences between a constitutional and an absolute monarchy. Still, the fact of the matter is that Henry was nearly overwhelmed by his new post, which was quite different from Spain.

By Henry's account, his first days in Vienna found him socializing regularly with Metternich, who shared with him stories of the Congress of Vienna and the various clashes of personalities. Then the prince began to jerk the ambassador's chain. For Metternich, the Spanish situation was a sideshow, albeit an important one. Greece, instead, occupied him because it involved Russia and the principle of maintaining the status quo. Thus, on the topic of the French invasion of Spain, the prince played both sides. On the one hand, he sympathized with the French, acknowledging as legitimate their concern that revolutionary principles allowed to take root in Spain would inevitably drift into France. On the other hand, he agreed with Wellesley that France had overplayed its hand in Spain and that it was time to pull France back.[36] Conceding this point meant nothing in that France had already accomplished what Metternich desired: the snuffing out of revolution in Iberia.

Greece posed a greater threat. There the nationalistic aspirations of the Greeks created a dilemma for the tsar. The Greeks saw their struggle as a war of independence, while the Turks viewed it simply as revolution. In that it violated the status quo, Metternich agreed with the Turks and urged the tsar to treat it similarly; Metternich was also eager to discourage Alexander from any movement westward. As for the tsar, he had little sympathy for rising nationalism but could not ignore the fact that these were Orthodox Christians fighting Muslims. To thicken the sauce, one can stir in age-old animosity between Russia and the Ottoman Empire, and Russian territorial ambitions along the Black Sea coast. Somehow, Metternich had to convince the tsar that there existed only one choice and that was to support the Ottomans in accordance with the Concert's conservative principles.

Metternich hoped for consensus among the European powers, but Canning had already made clear that Britain would not cooperate. From the man who wished the Spanish all success, could the prince expect anything different with Greece? In fact, Canning had no interest in Greek nationalism, and he too wanted to contain Russia. The appearance of common ground, however, deceived. Canning would negotiate with the Russians on his own, beginning with an attempt to reconcile the Turks and the Russians. That meant resolving their differences over the Danubian provinces, which infuriated Metternich; he never failed to remind Henry that Canning made a colossal blunder in rejecting the Concert.[37] Adding to the annoyance was the fact that the Greek independence movement had captured the imagination of the British public, leading to popular support for the Greeks in both tangible and intangible forms. Responding to Metternich's impatient protests, Henry pointed out that in Great Britain, the government had no control over public opinion. Certainly Metternich knew and understood this, but it did not stop him from demanding an explanation.[38] Above all else, Canning's rejection of the Congress system most irritated the prince.

Henry Wellesley's accounts of his conversations with Metternich clearly provoked the foreign secretary. In a heated retort to Metternich's presumptions and assumptions concerning the course of British policy, Canning railed, "The Austrian Minister prides himself, you say, upon being the champion and protector of ancient institutions, and the sworn and irreconcilable enemy of revolution. I flatter myself that I am no more a lover of revolution than Prince Metternich; and I have certainly passed near thirty years in fighting for old institutions in that House of Commons which Prince Metternich views with so much jealousy."[39] The tone of Canning's missive suggests impatience with his ambassador, whose own response to the prince lacked vigor.

At the same time, Wellington and Canning were locked in a rancorous and sometimes bitter political duel. They would fight over foreign policy and domestic reform, and in both cases Ireland intervened to make these issues especially complex. Rivalries can sometimes become especially intense when there is little from which to choose in the protagonists. This certainly was the case with Wellington and Canning, and because of it both men—but especially Wellington—were captives of their emotions. Canning understood this and used it to his advantage. For our story, this is particularly significant because the fact that Wellington was not a well man made him irritable. Anything that compounded that irritability tended to affect the duke's judgment. Ireland was one of those triggers, and because Wellesley was the lord lieutenant, Wellington came to view his eldest brother primarily as an irritant. The duke's relations with Henry, by contrast, were positive.

The year 1823 proved a bad year for the duke. His ear problems persisted, and he was visited on two occasions by serious illnesses. Several of his biographers, most recently Neville Thompson, speculate that these episodes were revisits of malaria or cholera, both of which he had contracted in India. All except those closest to the duke tended to minimize these maladies, primarily because the duke minimized them. They were, however, serious and debilitating.

Politically, Britain was in the midst of an awkward period. The opposition was weak, but ironically, so was the government. Liverpool presided over a Tory party in transition, and the change was not occurring smoothly. It was the product not only of a changing of the guard but also of a changing view of the world. Liverpool represented a generation of political men who had dominated British politics for twenty-five years but were old and in some cases worn out. Lord Grenville's attitude perhaps sums it up best: "I am done with politics, & never, I will venture to say, was any gladiator on that scene more truly delighted with his dismission from it. There is not a day, not an hour of the day, in which I do not rejoice to have nothing to do with those odious & disgusting contests, or with the still more painfull burthen of deciding, & answering to one's own mind, for the decision of questions involving the happiness of millions."[40] Perhaps Grenville took his responsibilities more seriously than others, but his was a generation that had seen its day. Sidmouth had retired, Bathurst was just behind, Castlereagh was dead, Liverpool and Canning had just a few more years to live. The list goes on. The likes of Peel, Melbourne, and Palmerston waited in the wings. It is extraordinary that Wellesley had another eighteen years ahead of him, Wellington twenty-eight.

In Dublin, Wellesley became obsessed with the Orange societies and looked for measures to deal with them. He suggested to Peel that Parliament might open a debate on the whole issue of seditious societies.[41] No one was particularly anxious to do this, in that it was sure to divide the cabinet. The spring of 1823 found famine and discontent again raising their ugly heads in Ireland. While the hardships did not represent a crisis, they gave voice to Protestants who were eager to demonstrate that Wellesley had failed. In May of that year, Daniel O'Connell put together the Catholic Association, which overnight changed the political dynamic in Ireland. With the Orangists on the far right and the Catholic Association on the far left, extremists seized the political debate. The Orangists portrayed themselves as upholders of order and attempted to form themselves into something resembling a militia. This all fell on receptive ears in London among the Protestant faction. Mrs. Arbuthnot's diary is full of comments, and one must conclude that at least some of them were products of discussions with the duke. In May, after a conversation with Sir George Hill, she observed that "a rebellion will very soon break out, & that Ld Wellesley has not the head to prevent it, that the Irish have no respect for him & that the Catholic population are ripe for any thing."[42] Wellesley, however, did not take the bait. Alarmed though he was over deteriorating conditions and the rising Catholic protest, he still understood that the Orangists were a serious problem. He certainly had no interest in seeing them on the streets as armed patrols, since that task belonged to the army.[43] To his credit, Wellesley made no attempt to dodge responsibility. His reports to Peel were forthright, expressing his keen disappointment in the turn of events.[44]

The lord lieutenant's remedy remained unchanged. He called for military reinforcements, impartial administration of the law, and economic relief. He also warned that rumor inevitably led to counter-rumor and action to counter-action. It was time to cool down.[45] By the summer, both Peel and Wellesley had expressed serious concerns over the rise of the Catholic Association. The dynamic O'Connell was building a potent organization and had secured support of the Roman Catholic clergy. What bothered Peel was the fact that O'Connell was raising money, collected by priests, which would ultimately give him the ability to arm his constituency. What bothered Wellesley was the inflammatory rhetoric to which the Orange societies responded in like manner. Perhaps, both men thought, it was time to rein in the two factions.[46]

The political jockeying and polarized talk coming out of Ireland combined with terrible personal health to put the duke in a foul mood. General infirmity, whether cholera and malaria or something else, along with his chronic ear problem, tried his patience beyond measure. Perhaps this explains his view of the marquess better than differences over policy, but there is no question that he saw his brother as anything but circumspect. Still, one is left aghast when Wellington's opinion was solicited by Charles Wynn from the board of control about a proposal from the court of directors to increase a grant to Francis Rawdon, Lord Hastings, for his work as governor general of India. The question was whether, if such a grant were decided upon, it would require a similar gesture towards Lord Wellesley.[47] One would expect the duke to stand by his brother and advocate on Richard's behalf, especially since Arthur's early career had been closely tied to Richard's. To the contrary, Wellington did not believe that Wellesley should in any way be tied to Hastings or in fact get in Hastings' way. The duke's reasons were fourfold: (1) Hastings had served longer in India than Wellesley had done; (2) Hastings, in contrast to Wellesley, had left the country in a state of prosperity; (3) Wellesley had been removed by agreement of the company and the government while Hastings had not, and (4) Wellesley had engaged in a disastrous war when India's finances were in a reduced state.[48] This is one of those occasions when Wellington astounds. The selectivity of his memory was at times staggering, though of course such behavior is a very human failing. This opinion on his brother's service would be as if someone suggested that Wellington had nothing to do with the capture of Seringapatam and that his great victory over the Marathas was a colossal blunder that turned lucky. Or that Wellington's advancement in India had nothing to do with Richard's patronage. Nothing, in other words, could illustrate more clearly just how out of sorts the duke was concerning the marquess.

The duke's opinions were aped by Mrs. Arbuthnot: "Mr. Vesey FitzGerald called on me in the morning. We talked about Ld Wellesley, and Mr. F said he made himself ridiculous to the Irish by his absurd pomp & assumption of all the attributes of Royalty."[49] That Mrs. Arbuthnot should lap up such talk testifies to the fact that she was willing to accept any negative commentary on the marquess, and this in part came from Wellington. Of course, much of what Fitzgerald had to say about Wellesley was no doubt true, but this was not exactly new knowledge. Everyone knew of his pomposity, and many of those who had known him the longest actually thought it funny. "The truth is," wrote Liverpool, "he is a great compound, and if one is to have the use of him it must be by making as little as possible of some of his absurdities. We have known him for thirty years. The acquaintance of Peel & Goulburn has been but recent, & they cannot therefore see as well as us that a man may be wise in some things & most foolish in others."[50] Nothing better describes the marquess or the political genius of Liverpool, who took people as he found them, used what talents they could contribute, and avoided becoming exercised over the negatives.

For his part, Wellesley dug in. Despite abuse heaped upon him by Orangists, he was equally concerned over the activities of the Catholic Association. O'Connell's rhetoric had not abated, and he was determined to do something about it. While all of this proved frustrating, it resembled what the lord lieutenant had initially thought his policies might produce. His was a policy of inclusion, playing to moderates on both sides of the religious line, and he knew full well that this would provoke radicals on both sides who had no interest in accommodation as a solution to the Irish problem. Though he never said so, Wellesley appears to have perceived early on that O'Connell's goals went well beyond Catholic rights. Ironically, the marquess had come to the conclusion that Catholic rights by this time were meaningless, so much so that he thought this should be made a nonissue by the government. Catholic rights would only enfranchise well-to-do Catholics, who, even if they won seats in Parliament, would not wish to effect any substantive change in policy. No, what Ireland needed, in Wellesley's opinion, was wholesale reform involving economic investment, impartial justice, and the elimination of absentee landlordism and tithes. Only then would Irish exceptionalism be eliminated and Ireland be integrated into the empire.[51] John Malcolm, Wellesley's secretary and longtime friend, attempted to portray the marquess in the best light while acknowledging his obvious weaknesses. "Lord Wellesley," he wrote to Sidmouth, "is really in good force, and if he is fully appreciated, and well supported, will do you good work. . . . He hates jobbing; and when satisfied with those who act with or under him, he gives a confidence, and infuses a spirit, that quite corrects the evils of delay and misunderstanding, that must, under other circumstances, arise from his own habits of business not being so regular as could be desired."[52]

Wellesley's decision to pursue the Catholic Association with as much vigor as the Orange societies protected him in London. Wellington's opinion notwithstanding, neither faction in the cabinet could persuade the other that the marquess was a liability. Goulburn assured the lord lieutenant in early 1824 that the government accepted most of his policies and were pleased with the state of Ireland.[53] This must have rankled with Goulburn, who found Wellesley unexplainable. Taking advantage of the relative quiet, Wellesley turned his attention to two emotionally charged issues: the tithe and the burial of dissenters and Catholics in Protestant churchyards. Goulburn pointed out that if Wellesley was looking for trouble, these would provide him with it. The tithe issue presented the greatest challenge, as it generated both practical and symbolic concerns for the Irish. Tithing itself was not in dispute, but what made it problematic for Catholic Irish was the fact that by law they were obliged to support the state church to which they did not belong, and by obligation to support that to which they did. For a people already impoverished, the tithe proved a significant economic hardship; moreover, they viewed it as just another means by which the English reminded them of their subservience. Both facts were often aggravated further by insensitive, petty clergymen who imposed the tithe without thought or flexibility.

Wellesley had long viewed the tithe as unjust, but, as was the case with innumerable things concerning Ireland, dealing with it created a dilemma. Reformers, such as the marquess, were intent on eliminating "Irish exceptionalism," but if the tithe was to be abolished in Ireland, then the reform itself perpetuated exceptionalism. Although Wellesley could live with such fine contradictions, he recognized their volatility in the hands of opponents. He therefore focused on reform rather than abolition, and he used as his model the tax reforms he had introduced in India. The idea was to level out the consequences of the tithe between years of abundance and years of dearth. The problem was that in years of scarcity, the tithe bore more heavily, and so the marquess proposed settling on a sum based on the average production over a period of ten years. In that way, the Irish peasant would know exactly what was expected of him from year to year instead of relying on the capricious judgment of the local priest. Other factors such as methods of collection and payment would also be addressed in the administrative restructuring of the system, but what Wellesley really hoped to do was simply lessen the burden.

Controversy attended all of this across the Irish Sea. Those who advocated the status quo, especially the leading clergymen, maintained that any change threatened the existence of the established church. Reforming the tithe would be followed by the granting of Catholic rights that would compromise the monarchy and ultimately lead to the demise of the church. Irrational fear coming from rational people was not uncommon, but on the heels of the age of revolution it seemed less irrational than it otherwise might. In any case, it was bound to provoke acrimonious discussion in the cabinet. As if this were not enough, Wellesley followed up his proposal for reforming the tithe with another to allow dissenters and Catholics to bury their dead with religious ceremony in Protestant churchyards.[54] This issue the lord lieutenant saw in the same light as the Orange parades of July and November—as Protestant tweaks at Catholic sensibilities.

Richard's plans for the tithe brought him into contact with Arthur once again. They would require a general survey of property, and Wellesley saw that as master of the ordnance, Wellington would be responsible. As was always the case, Wellington responded to his brother promptly and positively. The two were always careful to avoid uncomfortable arguments. On this occasion, Arthur carefully avoided comment on his brother's plans but promised to cooperate, beginning with the training of surveyors as soon as possible.[55] Wellington's position in the cabinet is not known, but what is certain is that in that arena, a vigorous exchange ensued. The result was a significant moderation of Wellesley's ideas concerning the burial issue. He had hoped to simply open up the churchyards to all Christian burials, but the government was unwilling to go so far. The cabinet insisted that the presiding protestant priest have complete control. Wellesley was not happy: "In my humble judgment, this plan constitutes no settlement of the question, but, without affording any definite regulation of the interests or prejudices of either party, places both in a state of perpetual & boundless conflict and collusion."[56] In short, the government's proposal would do nothing to establish trust between Catholics and the local Protestant clergy. The cabinet revisited the issue in light of Wellesley's comments but made no changes.

All of this proved awkward for the prime minister, as it occurred in the midst of several other contentious issues. Peel, who was in the center of the storm, expressed frustration, and Wellington, whose relationship with Liverpool had soured, urged the prime minister to act by his conscience. In fact, the duke was alarmingly blunt, suggesting that if Peel could not get along with Wellesley, then Liverpool should dismiss the marquess.[57] This was at least the third time in as many years that the duke had pointedly told his colleagues that he was indifferent as to the future of his brother. Part of his ill humor towards Richard can be attributed to his ongoing struggle with his ear problem. An equal measure can be ascribed to Wellington's failure to stop Canning in a quasi-recognition of the South American republics through the official establishment of trading relationships and the opening of consulates. The only thing that could irritate the duke more than a collision with Canning was a collision he lost. To make matters worse, Canning planned to escape the tensions of London in the early autumn with a visit to Wellesley in Dublin.

16

Irreconcilable Differences

For some reason, Canning's visit to Wellesley in 1824 provoked comment and discussion far beyond its import. Conservative Tories, Wellington included, conjured all sorts of reasons for it. Most common was that Canning sought support for becoming prime minister on Liverpool's retirement, which many observers considered imminent. The Canning-Wellesley connection went back to the 1790s, and though its legacy was without consequence, a reconstruction of that connection on the basis of Catholic rights seemed logical. Wellington for one was willing to consider political conspiracy at work. Mrs. Arbuthnot commented tersely, "Mr. Canning is going to Ireland to visit Ld Wellesley & to hold forth, I suppose, at Tavern dinners. The King is rather in hopes he may commit himself & enable him to turn him [Canning] out. I don't much expect that."[1] Canning did his best to defuse the situation, insisting that the visit was nothing more than a short vacation, a distraction from the worries of the past several months. He assured the king that there would be no speeches.

The visit proved pleasant for both Canning and Wellesley despite the apoplexy of Protestants in both London and Dublin. Canning, true to his word, did not make it a political event.[2] A graceless Mrs. Arbuthnot conceded nothing, suggesting that Canning kept his mouth shut out of intimidation: "Mr. Canning has been passing a week with Lord Wellesley in Ireland, in a manner I shd guess very unsatisfactory to himself . . . without attending one public dinner or making one Speech, a circumstance quite unaccountable (for he is no friend of Ld Wellesley's) unless we suppose that he intended to have held forth & made himself popular and had his tongue very disagreeably tied by the King's lecture, given when it was too late for him to renounce his journey altogether."[3]

For Wellesley, the distraction of a visit from Canning could not have been better timed. He had been preoccupied for weeks while enduring blasts of intemperate criticism from the *Evening Mail.* Day after day came a running critique of his policies, mockery of his habits and personality, and speculation on his dismissal.[4] That Canning's arrival should have been welcome is therefore understandable. The two had not always agreed, but each possessed a quick and nimble mind and enjoyed an entertaining exchange of self-satisfied wit.

November's arrival brought the always contentious issue of William III's birthday; once again Wellesley remained firm in his prohibition of the traditional celebratory decoration of the Protestant hero's statue. At the same time, he turned his attention to O'Connell and the Catholic Association. The crafty O'Connell had frustrated the lord lieutenant's efforts to control his activities by keeping within the letter of existing law, and so both Wellesley and Peel believed that it was time to introduce legislation that would allow the breakup of the association, along with the various Orange societies.[5] Then, on 20 December, Wellesley sent word that he had decided to serve a warrant on O'Connell. The occasion was a speech that Wellesley believed could be proved seditious.[6] Once again, Wellesley's timing could not have been worse, because the arrest of O'Connell exacerbated an already acrimonious debate between Wellington and Canning.

The occasion was Canning's decision to recognize the Spanish American republics—to call "a new world into existence to redress the balance of the old." This was something that Canning had contemplated for some time, and by the end of 1824, he had made converts of most of the cabinet, with the notable exception of Wellington. It almost goes without saying that the duke would have opposed anything coming from Canning even though his foreign policy could hardly be called radical and indeed was in line with most of Castlereagh's thinking. Wellington, however, believed that Canning deliberately and needlessly alienated the old continental allies, and the Spanish colonies were a case in point. To the duke's mind, recognition was unnecessary, and besides, it smacked of supporting revolution. Wellington had a vocal ally in the king; in fact, it would be more accurate to say that the king had an ally in Wellington. On this occasion, Henry Wellesley's view departed from Arthur's in favor of Canning's. Canning's decision to recognize the American republics infuriated Metternich, and Henry patiently listened to the diatribes. But Henry's memory of dealing with the Spanish on this issue was clear, and when challenged by the emperor Francis on Britain's chosen course, the youngest Wellesley responded, "That from the year 1810 up to the present period, the mediation of Great Britain had been repeatedly offered to Spain, and had also been solicited by the Spanish Government, but that the conditions proposed by us as early as 1811, although they would at that period in all probability have been accepted by the Colonies and would have secured to Spain the sovereignty over those possessions and a continuance of all the advantages she had ever derived from them, were indignantly rejected."[7] In any case, all arguments against recognition had run their course by December, and Canning appeared to stand on the verge of another great political success. Then came Wellesley's decision to arrest O'Connell.

The event that prompted it was a speech given by O'Connell in which he said, "If Parliament will not attend to the Roman Catholic claims, I hope that some Bolivar will arise to vindicate their rights." To the lord lieutenant, this could be construed as sedition, offering him the opportunity to strike at the Catholic Association, thereby proving to moderate Protestants that he dispensed with justice in an evenhanded manner. Wellesley does not appear to have made any connection between O'Connell's speech and the matter of recognition despite the fact that he knew Bolívar and was well versed in Latin American affairs. What is certain is that the king and Wellington perceived an extraordinary irony in the contradiction of prosecuting O'Connell for encouraging Bolivarian behavior while at the same time granting recognition to its product.[8]

Of course, the two situations were entirely different, and under different circumstances, Wellington would have been the first to acknowledge this. But he could never see through the emotional haze of his feelings towards Canning, and he stood firmly by the king. There was even the suggestion of resignation, but meetings with Liverpool and Peel changed his mind, and he beat a quick and inglorious retreat. And so the duke had brushed shoulders once again with his ambitious brother, and it had been even less pleasant than recent encounters. First, Canning's visit in September had placed the marquess in company Wellington loathed, and then, as if to heap insult upon injury, came the confluence of the arrest of O'Connell, precipitated by Wellesley, and the recognition of the Spanish American colonies. One can only imagine Wellington's private mutterings about his brother. As for Wellesley, he certainly believed that he was only doing what he had to do, and he had no clue of the duke's growing animosity.

The case against O'Connell came to naught, but Wellesley avoided a crisis. From the Orangists had come calls for the army in anticipation of a Catholic uprising on O'Connell's arrest and then the fears of a Protestant backlash on acquittal. The lord lieutenant refused to panic or treat the case as anything beyond the ordinary. As a result, Ireland remained calm.[9] Calm did not prevail in London, however, where Peel expressed a very real sense of urgency. The home secretary urged increased vigilance and promised legislation that would allow Wellesley to shut down the Catholic Association. Wellesley certainly did not disagree as long as he would be granted equal power to move against the Orange societies.[10] Ireland dominated the political landscape, and Catholic rights advocates readied another bill for the Commons. This time they took a step to the right, hoping to win over moderate Protestant backbenchers. The bill guaranteed the rights of the church and raised the Irish franchise.[11] Meanwhile, Wellington had been mulling over the question.

Wellington's views on Ireland are among the most misunderstood of the period. His public pronouncements always sounded firmly anti-Catholic, but they were molded by his views on public order. This, of course, was a very Wellesley trait; Arthur saw disorder and public riot as the greatest threat to a civil society, and under no circumstances would or could he condone it. The fact that Ireland had been almost perpetually in or threatened by disorder during his public life meant that he rarely said anything favorable about the island. This combined with the fact that he never believed in Catholic emancipation as a quick fix but only as a part of a more comprehensive reform. Moreover, he firmly opposed granting Catholic rights as a means to establish order. He saw the solution in quite the reverse equation: order first, rights to follow. This did not differ in principle from his brother's views, since Lord Wellesley had gone to Ireland hoping to establish order and trust in preparation for emancipation. But the two brothers differed in methodology. Wellesley believed that Catholic cooperation could be gained only by proving that the administration served all Irishmen equally. To this end he aggressively pursued extremists on both sides of the religious question, treating starving peasants caught up in the maelstrom of public riot with a certain amount of understanding and compassion, and appointing Catholics to the magistracy. Wellington saw the situation differently.

The Catholic clergy were, in Wellington's view, the key to pacification and ultimately emancipation. His analysis proceeded from his belief that change would have to come and that full Catholic rights would be a part of those changes. To him this seemed obvious. Military force had been used often and threatened perpetually to no effect, and there was no reason to believe that this would change. Britain could not continue in this fashion in the modern world. But to his mind, only the Catholic clergy had the necessary influence to create an atmosphere conducive to serious and honest reform, and they could be mobilized only by the pope. The heart of Wellington's proposal then was a concordat with the papacy. Here the duke proved naive. He failed to consider constitutional issues in entering into a formal agreement with the papacy, and he unrealistically measured the pope's willingness to give way on such sensitive issues as control of the clergy and the status of the church. Wellington's analysis of the problem and elucidation of his solution are contained in an immense document that he worked on from the end of 1824 through the first part of 1825.[12] As early as May 1824, Mrs. Arbuthnot recorded a conversation with him on Ireland. It was "a subject he said he considered of such importance that he said he really could hardly sleep for thinking of it."[13] Whether he intended to go public with his ideas is not known. He did show his analysis to his closest friends but in confidence. It is human nature to fall prey to pride of authorship, but Wellington was especially stubborn on this. When he invested time and intellectual energy into an issue, he tended to view his conclusions as irrefutable. He never much cared for contradiction (this is one of the reasons he disliked Canning), but on this point, he was especially sensitive. In part it explains his hostility towards Wellesley at this period of time. Arthur saw his brother as misguided in that Richard's policies missed the point and tended to either stir up trouble or exacerbate existing problems. Moreover, the duke tended to agree with Peel that alienating the government's most ardent supporters in the Orangemen was foolhardy.

The introduction of a modified Catholic relief bill stirred all sorts of emotions within the cabinet. Wellington saw it as reckless and provocative; not one to back away from a battle, he coalesced with Protestants in the cabinet, especially Peel. Identifying Wellesley as part of the problem, he once again suggested removing his brother, this time along with Plunkett.[14] The bill passed the Commons but failed in the Lords because of the vigorous efforts of both Liverpool and the Duke of York. Wellington, however, was still at sixes and sevens. He decried the bill as ill advised and poorly conceived but at the same time disagreed with the Duke of York, who proclaimed that he would never accept emancipation.

Wellington continued to exchange the occasional personal letter with Wellesley, and by all appearances they seemed to be on friendly terms. There was no political talk, as Wellington, true to his word, avoided the subject unless asked specifically for an opinion. Still, there was no hint of disagreement or animosity.[15] Then in October came a bolt from the blue; Wellesley announced his intention to wed the widow Marianne Patterson. One would think that this would have been good news, as Wellesley could use some positive influence outside his rather incestuous household circle. Unfortunately, Wellington's passion for Marianne remained strong. By all accounts, she was as beautiful and charming as when they first met, having returned to Britain after the death of her husband, in hopes of matching her sisters' successes in finding British husbands. Her first meeting with Wellesley came at a dinner at Stratfield Saye, and Wellesley appears to have invited her to visit him in Dublin in the summer of 1824.[16]

She visited again in the spring of 1825 and returned for the dénouement in the autumn. In the second week of October, she accepted the marquess's proposal. "You have triumphed," she wrote, "and I confess all that you wish."[17] Another letter, also undated, reveals her excitement and the fact that Wellesley had warned her not to believe all she heard or read in Dublin: "My dearest Lord, you make me love you every day more and more, as your noble and amiable character is developed. . . . I will obey you dearest and never look at a scandalous newspaper, and if possible never be annoyed at their attacks, but it is easier for one like you, of unquestionable superiority to despise them than for me a woman and a stranger." Wellesley promptly sent announcements to his siblings (though not to his children), and responses were quick, all except Wellington's. Letters of congratulations and approval from Maryborough, Culling-Smith, and Gerald arrived on the 14th, 15th, and 17th, respectively.[18] The duke's simmering hostility, however, reached a high boil. He wrote a scalding letter to Marianne, which he described to Mrs. Arbuthnot, who wrote,

> I have never seen the Duke more annoyed. His love for her has long been at an end, but he had a great interest for her, & he told me he had given her credit for more real good sense than to make such a preposterous match. I told him I was not the least surprised for that she had come to this country on a matrimonial speculation; that it was pretty well for the widow of an American shopkeeper to marry a Marquis, the Ld. Lieutenant of Ireland a Knight of the Garter, and that I was not at all surprised. The Duke said the honours were all empty ones and that the real facts were that Ld. Wellesley was a man totally ruined; when he quitted Ireland, which he must soon do, he wd not have a house to take her to, or money to keep a carriage; that he had not a shilling in the world &, moreover, was of a most jealous disposition, a violent temper & that he had entirely worn out his constitution by the profligate habits of his life. He says he is sure Lord Wellesley will never allow her to associate with him from feelings of Jealousy, and that he considers all intercourse with her entirely at an end.[19]

This account is flattering to neither the duke nor Mrs. Arbuthnot, and if one needed proof of Wellington's intimate attachment to Marianne, this would be it. In any case, the duke recovered his equilibrium and followed up with a cordial letter of congratulations to his brother expressing his feeling "that in disposition, temper, sense, acquirements and manners she is equal if not superior to any Woman of any country with whom I have ever been in Society."[20] There is no evidence that Wellesley ever saw the letter to Marianne; no doubt she burned it.

The marriage, which took place on 29 October, did have public import in that Marianne was a Catholic. While few viewed this with concern, the marriage ceremony was problematic. The festivities began with a state dinner at 6:15, followed by a marriage ceremony conducted by the Protestant primate of Ireland, the archbishop of Armagh. A second, Catholic ceremony followed, presided over by Dr. Murray, the archbishop of Dublin.[21] The presence of the Catholic archbishop at the Castle incensed the Orange party and its mouthpiece, the *Daily*

Mail. Of all the unforgivable things that Wellesley had done in his tenure as lord lieutenant, this was portrayed as the most unforgivable. Not everyone responded in partisan fashion, however. *John Bull,* in response to a flurry of criticism, commented coolly,

> The Marquess of Wellesley was married on Thursday to Mrs. Patterson, a Roman Catholic lady of great fortune. The remarks which we have received on this marriage are able and powerful, and in their spirit we perfectly agree; but since the appointment of Lord Lieutenant is only temporary we do not regard the affair in the serious light in which our correspondent considers it. It is as a private individual Lord Wellesley marries; and by the union secures at once possession of beauty, accomplishments, and a vast fortune; the difficulty of his Lordship's necessarily partaking of a Popish Sacrament, is one which every Protestant marrying a Papist falls into.[22]

All of this eventually subsided, but for Marianne the adventure was just beginning. No sooner had she moved into the Castle than quarrels broke out between the new marchioness and Edward Johnston. The details of this domestic power struggle are vague, but the fact that it existed was well known. It sufficiently shocked Marianne to prompt a desperate letter to Wellington, who acknowledged it and sincerely sympathized with her plight. At the same time, he sensibly counseled patience and took some comfort in the fruition of his warnings.[23] In time, Marianne persevered, and with the help of pressure from London to remove the odious Johnston, she prevailed.

Iris Butler believes that fraternal competition had much to do with this marriage, and she may very well be right. Nevertheless, while the marquess certainly envied the duke's success, he remained too proud to compete with Arthur; never in his own mind did he concede inferiority. Marianne was a gem Wellington wished to possess, and one might be closer to the truth in concluding that it was the duke who continued to compete with the marquess and not vice versa. What is germane to our story is that the marriage was another factor in the growing alienation between the brothers.

Meanwhile, the government succeeded in legally disbanding the Catholic Association. However, the clever O'Connell promptly reconstituted it as the New Catholic Association within the parameters of the new law. This caused great frustration for both Wellesley and

Peel. Letters flew back and forth, and the opinion of the attorney general was solicited. Convinced that the New Catholic Association constituted an unlawful assembly, Peel wanted to take action. At the same time, he worried about a fiasco similar to the previous prosecution of O'Connell. He certainly did not want to give the Irishman the satisfaction of embarrassing the government again. In late January, O'Connell's chief lieutenant gave a speech that both Wellesley and Peel viewed as seditious. They decided to prosecute.[24] Pressure mounted in Dublin, and Wellesley again found himself the object of Protestant ridicule. "It is manifest," commented the *Evening Mail,* "that the Protestants of England have become alarmed, in the same proportion of those of this country are disgusted, and that it is absolutely necessary for the safety of one, and the satisfaction of the other, that the experiments making should at once be discontinued."[25] Rumors were rife that Wellesley would be recalled, with some saying that he would be sent to India again as governor general. In fact, the idea had been brought up. Wellington thought it ludicrous, Wellesley being too old. His brother, he claimed, would not survive the trip out.[26] The marquess had other reasons for squelching the project. "I have naturally felt a wish," he moaned, "that my political career should not close, without some testimony of remorse on the part of the East India Company, for the great injustice which they have committed against me."[27] The editors of the *Evening Mail* would have to postpone their celebration.

At this point, Wellington's attentions were directed elsewhere. The government, at the urgings of Canning, had decided to send the duke to St. Petersburg to represent Britain at the funeral of Tsar Alexander, who had died in December. But the task was more than ceremonial; Canning also entrusted the duke with negotiations over the Greek Rebellion. Throughout the year 1825, there had been talk of an international conference over Greece. Metternich in particular favored such a course, arguing that only some sort of Concert consensus would provide the tsar with the necessary political cover to negotiate with the Turks with confidence. Canning opposed any sort of international conference. Henry Wellesley found himself in the middle of all of this. In fact, the international discussions came to naught, leading the Russians to conclude that something would have to be done. This is not the place to enter into an examination of the issues that complicated Russian and Turkish negotiations over Greece; suffice it to say that the tsar became increasingly frustrated and alienated from the international community. In short, he concluded that some sort of ultimatum would have to be sent to both the Turks and the Greeks, implying Russian intervention should negotiations fail to establish peace. It was precisely what Metternich hoped to avoid because no matter what the result was, Austria would lose. This was the situation when the tsar died unexpectedly in December 1825.

Political confusion followed in St. Petersburg, where the young Grand Duke Nicholas superseded his elder brother, Constantine, to gain the imperial throne. After putting down an ill-advised, ill-organized revolt of army officers, Nicholas turned his attention to matters at hand; he sensibly announced that he would follow those policies previously established by Alexander. The new tsar represented for Canning a fresh start in Anglo-Russian relations, and this opportunity led him to dispatch Wellington to St. Petersburg. Put off as he was with Canning's diplomacy, Metternich saw a ray of light in Wellington's journey. In a letter to Arthur, Henry explained that he had been instructed to inform Metternich that Britain's view of the Greek crisis and the collateral complications in eastern Europe had not changed—meaning the "fruitlessness of any formal conference on the subject" and the determination to avoid a Russian declaration of war. Henry then informed Arthur that although Metternich "still thinks that the united co-operation of the five powers would afford the first chance of bringing the Greek question to a satisfactory issue, yet he has desired me to say that such is his confidence in you, that he is quite prepared to enlist himself under your banners, and to leave the interests of Europe in your hands, satisfied that they cannot be placed in better."[28]

Metternich would be sorely disappointed, as Wellington concluded a protocol with the Russians under which Russia and Great Britain would offer to mediate between the Greeks and the Turks on the basis of Greece becoming a Turkish dependency. Implicit in the protocol was the use of force should the parties reject the mediation. While such a discussion was something Metternich favored, he clearly envisioned it as a five-party discussion rather than two, and with Austria controlling the agenda. Wellington is generally thought to have given away more than he should in his negotiations with Nicholas, but the results generally pleased Canning in that Metternich had been relegated to the sideline. Henry Wellesley expressed this point clearly to Canning in a dispatch dated 28 June: "You will recollect the satisfaction expressed here when the resolution of the Emperor Nicholas not to interfere in the Greek question was reported from St. Petersburg, and the concern and disappointment occasioned by the subsequent intelligence of the arrangement concluded between the Duke of Wellington and the Russian Government. There is no doubt that Prince Metternich was greatly mortified at the Emperor's departure from his first resolution, and at his apparent abandonment of the continental Allies to join with Great Britain in the aforesaid arrangement."[29] Henry would endure the consequences of Metternich's anger as the events in Greece played out, complicated by equally contentious issues in Portugal and Spain. These were trying times indeed, made more so by the deep antipathy between Canning and Metternich.

Meanwhile, after three months, Wellington returned physically spent and unwell only to find family issues once again on his doorstep. In the summer of 1826, Wellesley's mind had turned to his brother Gerald. The occasion was a vacancy in the bishopric of Cloyne. The brothers had long hoped to see Gerald on a bishop's throne and, of course, firmly believed that he deserved it. The marquess had discussed the matter in 1821 in the course of conversations with Lord Liverpool. At the time, Liverpool had objected, citing the scandal of Gerald's broken marriage as the reason, as only five years had passed since his wife had publicly abandoned her family. Gerald, who had no interest in marrying again and was sensitive to the scandal to which his children might be subjected, chose not to pursue a divorce. After a ten-year interval, Wellesley again petitioned Liverpool (and informed Arthur accordingly). Liverpool, not knowing that this would be the opening salvo of a bitter debate, responded clearly and coolly: "I can indeed not concur that any person standing in the relation in which your brother unfortunately stands, towards his wife, ought to be made a Bishop, but this relation is certainly aggravated in the Eyes of the World (however unjustly) by his never having sued for a divorce, by which his conduct as well as hers would have been fully before the World, and his abstinence in this respect, is set down to motives, which may be wholly untrue, but which cannot operate otherwise than injuriously to his former life." Moreover, the prime minister pointed out that the church in Ireland was under heavy criticism, which meant that all appointments had to be made with great care. Gerald's appointment would look like nepotism.[30]

Wellington, not surprisingly, supported Gerald's nomination enthusiastically and thought Liverpool's earlier objections spurious. He saw

Liverpool as narrow and shortsighted on Gerald's personal life, for which Gerald had more than compensated through good and hard work.[31] For whatever reason, the duke continued to ponder Gerald's fate; the more he thought about it, the more irate he became. "There is one view in which it has occurred to me that the continued neglect of Gerald bears particularly hard upon him," Arthur wrote in a highly agitated state. "His Brothers are all in power; one of them has in his hands the Patronage of the Irish Church, another is in the Cabinet; and two others in High Office under Gov't. Any other Man so situated would be provided for; yet he can get nothing as a Clergyman of the Church of England."[32]

On 25 August, after receiving Liverpool's reply, Wellesley promptly wrote to the duke. He carefully outlined the prime minister's reiteration of his objections and then threw the matter into Wellington's hands. Richard was clear about his reason for this; he told Arthur that he could not oppose Liverpool without a public conflict that would serve neither the parties involved nor the government. But Wellington could lean on Liverpool privately, and Richard anticipated that the duke would. He recommended that Arthur secure the support of the archbishop of Canterbury and the bishop of London. Moreover, he had the testimony of R. R. Blake, who said "that on a certain occasion he delivered (as it was his duty) a menacing message from the wife to her husband respecting the children, when the husband defied her, and said she might proceed in any court as she pleased." To Wellesley this was proof positive that Gerald did not fear exposure or recrimination.[33] Wellington followed with a blistering letter to Liverpool, with whom he no longer shared the close relationship of years previous. As if compelled to do so, Wellington refuted all of Liverpool's arguments. In the process he all but called the prime minister narrow minded and bigoted, and he ended with an appeal "to all our Colleagues, to his Majesty and even to Yourself in your cool moments, whether there is any Man who has served you more faithfully and zealously than I have. I now ask you nothing but justice, forbearance from prejudice and passion, and fair, candid, delicate inquiry previous to decision; and I am ready and willing to abide by the result."[34]

By this time, Liverpool had awakened to the fact that he was in the midst of a real battle that might have political consequences. He tried to be cordial and logical, but inevitably he resorted to seizing the moral high ground and reiterating his unqualified objection to the notion that a man living apart from his wife should sit on the Episcopal bench. At the same time, on the advice of Peel, he informed the duke that Wellesley had already agreed with the decision to bypass Gerald and that Liverpool had the correspondence to prove it. This did nothing more than provoke Arthur to new levels of rage. In his eyes, Gerald was utterly innocent; sin lay with the wife and everyone knew it. That Wellesley had signed off on Liverpool's decision was unfortunate, even embarrassing, but at this point, it did not alter the duke's views, and he accused Liverpool of hypocrisy.[35]

In a short time, the dispute became common knowledge, and fingers pointed in the direction of the marquess. Liverpool complained to his friends that the Wellesleys had lost their senses, that he had already done much for the family. Peel, Bathurst, and the Arbuthnots, among others, were appalled at the marquess's conduct, seeing him as sending the duke into battle even as he had negotiated the peace. They also sympathized with Wellington and realized that this was no petty squabble. "The Duke, I see, is excessively angry," observed Mrs. Arbuthnot, "& I am certain will not forgive it & tho' he will not quarrel upon this subject, it will make him disposed to quarrel at the first opportunity."[36] What is curious is Wellington's decision to leave Wellesley hanging. Richard had been forthright about his position and had told Arthur quite clearly that if they wanted to fight Liverpool on Gerald, then Arthur would have to do it. Wellesley believed that he had no choice but to acquiesce. Perhaps Arthur was surprised at the alacrity with which Richard bowed out, but he certainly knew that the marquess would not dispute with the prime minister. It is one of those rare occasions when Arthur seems to have been willfully dishonest, and it comes as a shock. It certainly speaks to the damaged nature of their relationship, though whether the marquess realized the extent of the chasm between them is unclear. To the duke's credit, when informing Gerald of all that had transpired, he told his brother that Richard had initiated the effort, a fact that Gerald graciously acknowledged: "The Duke of Wellington has informed me of the exertions you have been making to place me on the Irish Bench of Bishops & also of the little success that has attended them. I can with truth assure you that their failure does not diminish the gratitude towards you for your goodness to me."[37]

Wellesley continued to wrestle with Irish problems. Specifically, the activities of the Catholic Association bedeviled the Irish scene and presented the lord lieutenant with precious few options. The status quo he deemed unacceptable in that it allowed emotions on both sides of the religious question to rise, but O'Connell took great care to deprive the marquess of anything concerning the activities of the association onto which he might grab. Consequently, Wellesley monitored the speeches of O'Connell and his lieutenant, Shiels, hoping for a seditious slip of the tongue that might allow for a successful prosecution. This would all come to naught, leaving Wellesley looking helpless and ineffectual.

In London, no one really cared. There, political events would unfold with astonishing speed. By the end of 1827, Britain would have had three prime ministers and would be poised for a fourth. These events affected the duke directly and for a period of over three months left him looking foolish.

Before slipping into the political mire, Wellington resolved the problem of Gerald. In February, two vacancies in bishoprics set off a rotation of appointments that, with the duke's careful management, left Gerald superbly placed. Dr. Robert Gray, prebend of Durham and rector of Bishop Weamouth, became bishop of Bristol. Liverpool, only too happy to put an end to this rather shabby episode, could manufacture no objection to Gerald's assuming Gray's place as the prebend of Durham. The duke was delighted, but no more so than Gerald. Although the bishop's throne had eluded him, he had a comfortable living of £3,000 per year.[38]

Several days later, Liverpool suffered a stroke. Though six weeks would pass before he officially stepped down, the jockeying for position began immediately. Not surprisingly, the right wing of the ministry turned to Wellington as the heir apparent. The duke quickly put them off, resorting to the claim that he was a soldier, not a politician. Though this strained credulity in the minds of most observers, Wellington did in fact dominate the military life of the country. He not only sat in the cabinet as master general of the ordnance, since the death of the Duke of York in January, he also served as commander in chief. The fact of the matter was that the duke would have been interested in the premiership only as a means of depriving Canning of the position, and he did not deem that likely. He believed that the king would opt for someone under whom most ministers could continue to serve.

In retrospect it seems naive on his part to think that Canning would accept the status quo, but so factionalized was the government that a controversial leader could have split it asunder. Canning's appointment would provoke wholesale desertion by the Ultras, and the duke's selection would lead to defections on the left. With a Whig administration unacceptable to the king, only some sort of understanding among the existing ministers remained as an option. This was the duke's reality. Although it makes some sense, it completely fails to account for ambition and hard feelings, both of which he should have understood and perceived. In the interim, the government introduced Corn Law legislation that passed in the Commons. At the same time, a Catholic rights bill, introduced by radicals in the Commons, failed by four votes. Protestants hailed this as a great victory not only for the constitution but also over the Catholic Canning. In fact, Canning was the prime beneficiary of the bill's failure, and he knew it. Canning, always outspoken in his support of Catholic rights, was clever enough to realize that the Catholic issue was what stood between him and the king. He also knew that passage in the House of Lords was at that point futile but as long as there were prospects for success in the Commons, bills would make their regular appearance. What was important to him in 1827 was power. The defeat of the Catholic bill meant that Catholic rights would no longer be a pressing issue in the formation of a new ministry, at least in the mind of the king. And so while the likes of Mrs. Arbuthnot might jump for joy over the event, others were more somber; their ranks included the duke, who was apparently becoming testy. "The Duke of Buckingham is a dirty, shabby fellow," she wrote, "& I am glad the Duke wd have nothing to do with him, but still I do not like he should repulse them all so unceremoniously."[39] Richard was one of those who attracted Arthur's pique. Hearing Richard's name bandied about as a prospective member of a new government clearly annoyed Wellington. Mrs. Arbuthnot reported the duke's telling Lord Clancarty, a vigorous Protestant, "to say to the King any thing he pleased about Lord Wellesley without scruple."[40]

Things were not about to get any better, from Wellington's perspective. Canning made good use of the month of March, and when, at the end of the month, Liverpool informed the king that he could not go on, the foreign secretary found himself well placed. He began to lean on George IV while surveying the political landscape for potential allies. The enemy was clearly the looming, brooding Wellington. The king explored various possibilities for retaining as much as possible of Liverpool's ministry, but this proved an impossible task. Wellington and Canning were too far apart and Peel too averse to having a Catholic sitting as prime minister. Wellington's antipathies became fury when he heard that Canning had been making overtures to the Whigs. As a result, he was in an angry mood when the king charged Canning with forming a ministry based on Liverpool's.

One wonders what must have been going on in Canning's head as he pondered his approach to Wellington. Canning was not the type to fear confrontation, but the prospect of soliciting the duke evidently gave rise to considerable unease. The foreign secretary had been scheming and dealing for six weeks, and he knew that there would be uncomfortable questions from Wellington. Neville Thompson demonstrates this clearly in his study of Lord Bathurst, and if Bathurst could put Canning on the defensive, one can only imagine what the duke might do. Concluding that discretion was the better part of valor, Canning decided uncharacteristically to write to Wellington. The ministry would be formed, he declared, on the same principles as Liverpool's, specifically that the Catholic question would remain an open issue. There was in Canning's letter a significant omission; no mention was made as to who would head the new ministry. And so, Wellington posed the question. He could not make a decision unless it was made clear who would head the government. Canning, in turn, forced the king to clarify that it would be Canning. When that was done, instead of simply declaring the fact, Canning tweaked the duke by suggesting that "the King usually entrusts the formation of an administration to the individual whom it is his Majesty's gracious intention to place at the head of it."[41] Historians have dissected this exchange ad infinitum. They point out that Wellington had every right to pose the question and that there was ample precedent for the king's entrusting the formation of a ministry to someone who might not head it. In fact such precedents include one in which Canning responded just as the duke had done. However, given all that had transpired, the fact that Canning was in charge of the negotiations was a clear sign that he would lead; accordingly, Wellington's contentiousness deserved the responding sarcasm. The long and the short of it is that both men were spoiling for a fight, and they both acted badly. Wellington compounded acting badly by acting irrationally.

The duke, in a fit of rage, not only refused to sit in a Canning cabinet but also resigned as commander in chief. He offered up a detailed rationale, but an impartial observer has to conclude that his was an emotional decision, which the duke made clear in his explanation to the House of Lords several days later. In any case, the duke's departure cleared the ground for Canning as the Ultras followed Wellington in short order. Canning would piece together an administration of liberal Tories and moderate Whigs. Wellington, in a sulk at Stratfield Saye, came to regret his resignation as commander in chief, and Canning, once the flush of victory over his great rival died away, regretted the total loss of the duke's great prestige. Not surprisingly, efforts were made to find a way to bring them together. One even included the suggestion that Arthur replace Richard as lord lieutenant with Arbuthnot as chief secretary.[42] Wellington rejected this option out of hand—but if only for a moment, in his mind's eye, there must have flashed the image of Wellesley's face at being informed of such an event. Attempts to bring the duke back to the Horse Guards followed, but Wellington's condition of an abject apology from Canning proved insurmountable. From Vienna came support for the duke from Henry. "Your letter is the only one I have received upon the subject of the late changes," he wrote. "Canning has, as usual, overshot his mark. He has sacrificed without scruple the King's government to his own personal objects, but I cannot believe that it could have been his intention to establish a radical government in its room. I should think that he must bitterly repent of what he has done for I cannot conceive a more irksome situation than his must now be."[43]

In the summer, after Wellington torpedoed a Corn Bill in the House of Lords, efforts were renewed to restore the duke to the Horse Guards. On this occasion, Canning and the king turned to Maryborough to begin the process. The whole thing was of course futile from the start in that Canning and Wellington each knew that the other would not back down on issues of personal pride, but it is interesting from the standpoint of the king and Maryborough. The hyperemotional king had grown tired of the fact that the new political arrangements had separated him from the duke and made it awkward for them to meet privately. For this reason, any attempt to bring Wellington back to the Horse Guards, whether successful or not, had the virtue of renewing their relationship. The king, therefore, eagerly pursued any suggestion (short of an official summons) that might bring Wellington to him. As for Maryborough, he and his wife had settled comfortably into their position in the royal household, Maryborough as master of the buckhounds and his wife as companion to Lady Conyngham. The arrangement, initially fraught with ill will, suited the pretentious pair perfectly. Aware of the king's mercurial nature, they kept a low political profile and anxiously avoided anything that might compromise their situation. Thus, when Lady Conyngham suggested to Lady Maryborough that her husband arrange for the duke to visit the Royal Lodge to ask after the king's health, they were, no doubt, uneasy. Maryborough could anticipate the duke's response, which was that such a visit would appear unsolicited and would give rise to misrepresentation.[44] This having failed, the king dispatched Maryborough a week later. He carried the king's surprise that the duke "had never called upon him since he had resigned and particularly now, although he was in his neighbourhood." This time the duke decided that he must go to Windsor, a decision that certainly provided Maryborough with great relief.[45] A formal offer of the Horse Guards was not made, but the king had hinted broadly that it could be: "He proposed again to the Duke to resume the command of the army, which the Duke waived and avoided & abused Mr. C[anning] a good deal. The King declared that Mr. C had said again & again that he never meant to offend the Duke, to which the Duke replied, 'Sir, he has never said that to me.'"[46] By this time the question lacked urgency, as Canning was gravely ill.

In Vienna, Henry felt equally insecure, having come to the conclusion that Canning preferred to be done with the Wellesleys entirely:

> It seems settled that Lord Dudley is to keep the Foreign Office. I suppose that Canning would like to have this situation to dispose of; he has, however, never hinted such a wish, nor has he indeed written me a line since he quitted the Foreign Office. It is a remarkable circumstance that I have now resided here more than four years during which period much important business has passed through my hands and yet Canning has never once specified his approbation of my conduct; on the contrary he appears to have studiously avoided any expression by which I could infer that he was satisfied with my services. . . . His conduct to me is the more remarkable as I know he has been lavish of his praises to other persons who certainly did not deserve better than myself.[47]

This was Wellesley pique once again; Henry forever felt unappreciated, except when working for Richard.

In his dark, brooding moments, of which there were many, Wellington must have wondered what part the marquess might have played in Canning's maneuvers in the spring of 1827. At the very least, there was the question of what the eldest brother knew of Canning's plans and when he knew it. In fact, there is no evidence that Canning confided in the marquess at any point after Liverpool's death. There is no correspondence, and there seem to have been few rumors floating about the Castle. What the evidence does suggest is that being out of the loop frustrated the marquess. Canning wrote on 24 April, "I learn . . . that you complain of not having heard from me. If I could find time to describe to you my daily occupation for any one of the last ten days, you would be surprised, not that I have not written before, but that I write now. Except for a few hours of scanty and interrupted sleep, I have not been free from the necessity of listening or talking—occupations most unpropitious to correspondence with absent friends."[48] At the same time, Wellesley certainly did not feel threatened by the prospect of either Canning or his brother assuming the premiership, as he believed himself to be on good terms with both. Canning's letter of the 24th seems to confirm that perception, for in it, the new prime minister alluded to his efforts to secure Wellesley's appointment as governor general of India, and as for Ireland, he stated, "You have been entirely misinformed if you have been led to believe that your office has been offered to any other person, although it is perfectly true that, in discussions, the Lord-Lieutenancy of Ireland, like all other offices, has been talked over, with reference to future and contingent arrangements. How is it possible that a Government should fall to pieces, without entailing the necessity of considering every part of it with a view to its reconstruction."[49]

In the days that followed, Canning attempted to keep Wellesley apprised of all that transpired, particularly concerning his quarrel with the duke. On 22 May came some alarming news, tucked as inauspiciously as possible into a general accounting of the problems of cabinet making. Canning told the marquess that the king, given the preponderance of pro-Catholics in the cabinet, insisted on a more Protestant administration for Ireland. In short, it was time for a Protestant to replace Wellesley at the Castle. The prime minister then explained that Liverpool and the king had previously discussed such a change for January 1828 with the seating of a new Parliament. But Wellesley would not be left high and dry. Canning inquired,

> Shall I open the Embassy to Vienna to you by recommending Sir Henry Wellesley for the succession to Lord Amherst [the governor general]? Answer me this question frankly, and as soon as you conveniently can. I will do and say nothing, in the meantime, to commit you or myself or Henry Wellesley. I will not write to him till I have heard from you; nor then unless your answer is affirmative—for it is *only* on your account that I should think of the appointment. I have, however, reason to know that he [Henry Wellesley] would accept it if tendered to him; and I have reason to believe that I could obtain it for him.[50]

The marquess could hardly believe his eyes, but though it looked as if Canning had been heading in this direction from the start, Wellesley measured his response. Setting aside indignation, he coolly explained that if Liverpool and Peel had been contemplating change, he certainly was unaware of it. He explained that he had all along intended to stay on at least until January, at which time he would equal the Duke of Richmond's tenure as lord lieutenant, which was the longest of modern times. In a spirit of self-congratulation, he listed his many accomplishments and then offered the challenge, "I certainly little expected that any eagerness should exist to abridge my term here, merely on account of my supposed agreement with you on the policy of altering the laws respecting the Roman Catholic claims."[51]

This left Canning in a quandary in that the king was insistent and the prime minister had no interest in provoking the marquess. One angry Wellesley was enough. As a result, he did his best to be accommodating. He assured Wellesley that the marquess could stay on through the end of the year but that his replacement would be chosen during the summer. He then returned to the issue of the Vienna embassy, pointing out that it could be held open till Wellesley's return from Dublin but that Canning would need to know the marquess's interest so that he could proceed with Henry's appointment as governor general.[52] In the end, Wellesley informed Canning that the Vienna embassy did not interest him and that they should proceed with January 1828 fixed as the time of his return. This clearly was when he anticipated returning in any case, but he remained eager to avoid any suggestion of recall. Canning ended the negotiations with a letter from the king along with one of his own clarifying details; Wellesley got all that he wanted.[53] Not long after, Canning announced the Marquess of Anglesey, presumed a Protestant when it came to Ireland, as Wellesley's replacement.

Wellesley thought Anglesey ill suited to the task. "I heard from Ireland that Lord Wellesley did not at all like his own supersession by the Marquess [Anglesey]," wrote Peel, "and spoke of the Marquess as peculiarly unfit for the government of Ireland. He wants to stay two years longer, as does Lady Wellesley. She is most anxious to effect a thorough reconciliation and good understanding between the Duke of Wellington and Lord Wellesley."[54] Peel's comments reveal quite clearly that political gossip had Wellington increasingly alienated from his brother and that Marianne knew it. As for Wellesley, his jealousies were still active, but for his part, he certainly did not consider himself estranged from Arthur. They had continued to communicate on an occasional basis, and Arthur had done his eldest brother the courtesy of sending an explanation for his resignation as commander in chief.[55]

In the meantime, Canning died unexpectedly on 8 August; to everyone's surprise, the king opted to continue with Canning's ministry under the leadership of Frederick John Robinson, first Viscount Goderich. Within the week, the king and prime minister decided to offer the Horse Guards to the duke. According to Peel, Wellington's decision was a foregone conclusion: "I do not think that he could on any assignable public ground refuse the offer that was made to him," Peel wrote to Bathurst, "considering the grounds on which alone he retired from the command of the army, the reasons which he alleged to the King for not resuming it, but above all considering his military character and peculiar relation and obligation to the military service."[56] Mrs. Arbuthnot, in contrast, was anything but pleased. She scolded the duke for what she deemed at best bad judgment and at worst hypocrisy: "I told him it was all very well and that he had a right to accept the command of the army if he chose, but that it was ridiculous nonsense for him to stand up and tell me he was *no politician*; that I had known him intimately as a member of the Cabinet for nine years, that he had taken a most active part both in our home and foreign politics; that a large body in the State looked to him as their protector against the political economists, and that he must be quite aware that they did not do so on account of his military talents."[57]

For his part, the marquess refused to back away from his agenda during his last months in Dublin. In September he irritated Orangemen by refusing to attend a banquet for the new lord mayor because, as he explained, a toast would be drunk to William III. In November he continued the prohibition on decorating William's statue.[58] On 19 November, the lord lieutenant announced his resignation. Absent from the announcement was any mention of ceremony, and it became clear that he intended to leave quietly. The *Evening Mail* could hardly believe this, commenting tongue in cheek, "What, and is the great pacificator of Ireland, the champion of conciliation, the idol of a paid press, and the companion of Popish Priests, about to quit the scenes of heroic exploits and gallant achievements without pomp, pageant, or procession?"[59] From that point on, day after day, the Orange press offered scathing assessments of the lord lieutenant, that of 26 November perhaps being the best example: "Your Lordship, on coming to Ireland, brought with you some character as a statesman—and a load of debts. We trust that during your sojourn here you have got rid of the latter—for the former—we can answer, that it will be no encumbrance to you." Whether Lady Wellesley followed her husband's strictures and avoided reading the hostile press is not known, but certainly Wellesley read it, and it could hardly have saddened him on the eve of his departure.

Meanwhile, Goderich's ministry had come undone. From the start, the well-meaning Goderich had been in over his head, and he knew it. The king, however, insisted that he carry on with an administration which the skilled Canning had had a difficult time assembling. That Parliament was not in session allowed Goderich to limp along, but inevitably politics overwhelmed him. It was, however, too late to preserve his reputation. "To be sure," wrote James Maitland (ninth Earl of Lauderdale) caustically to Bathurst, "there never was anything so ridiculous as this business of Lord Goderich's; he does not appear to me to be fit to manage a poultry yard."[60]

The duke, and the Tories who looked to him as their natural (if not only) leader, anticipated change, but until the end of December, they had no idea which direction it would take. Wellesley too cast an eager but wary eye towards London. Three days after Canning's death, the marquess penned a memorandum outlining his view of the new political environment and his place in it. His thinking is astonishing both for its audacity and for what seems its lack of realism. He would become First Lord of the Treasury if asked. So too would he take up the seals of the Foreign Office. President of the council would be acceptable, but he would stoop no lower. As to whom he would serve under, that was easy—anyone. Lansdowne, Goderich, Wellington, and Peel were all acceptable, and these names covered the political spectrum.[61] At first glance, one wonders whether the marquess had taken residence in some fantasyland. Here was a man who had not held cabinet office for fifteen years. Could anyone seriously consider him for a leading role in the new arrangements?

Apparently they could. At the beginning of December, Goderich toyed with expanding the base of his administration by reaching out further to the Whigs. Rumors swirled that pointed to the inclusion of Lord Holland, who could be balanced by the inclusion of Wellesley. Frederick Lamb relayed the truth of the rumors to the ever-vigilant Wellington: "I equally believe that some days back Goderich proposed to the King to admit Lords Wellesley and Holland into the Cabinet, and to give an appointment to Brougham, and was refused. I have not this from the same undoubted sources as the first part of my intelligence, but I make no doubt of it."[62] Wellington confirmed this: "As far as I can learn the fact is that last Monday Lord Goderich wrote to the King to propose to him that either Lord Holland and Brougham, or Lord Wellesley, should be brought in to efficient offices of the Government." In addition, Wellington noted that "they have, it is said, sent for Lord Wellesley, not designating him for any office. It is reported that Huskisson says he will not serve under Lord Wellesley; as he has been in the Cabinet and Lord Wellesley serving under it."[63] No doubt this rumor infuriated the duke, who had to have wondered whether Richard had lost his mind or was simply incapable of restraining his ambition. In either case, the marquess was not to be trusted; from this point on, if not much earlier, Wellington ceased to consider his brother as part of the political equation. Lamb's news grew more ominous two days later when he reported that the king had sent for Lord Harrowby but that Harrowby was expected to refuse any commission to form an administration. That being the case, observers speculated that Wellesley might be asked to take the treasury and that Holland would be brought in along with him.[64] The duke did not take this seriously; Wellesley as prime minister would have constituted a great leap indeed. Bathurst read the situation much as the duke did, remarking, "You may be sure that Lord Wellesley will accept, whatever may be offered him, either to be at the head or home secretary."[65]

While Arthur had given up on Richard, he had not given up on Henry. Taking advantage of Goderich's goodwill and the confusion of the time, he petitioned the prime minister to support Henry's claim to a peerage. Given all that was on the duke's plate at this particular moment, his attention is a superb example of fraternal generosity, and Henry was deeply touched. "I received last night your letter of the 1st instant," he wrote. "I really cannot express how much I feel obliged to you for the trouble you have taken respecting my peerage and for the very satisfactory manner in which you have stated my pretension to the honor."[66] Arthur, however, had sized up Goderich accurately. The prime minister responded quickly and positively to the duke's request. Two and a half weeks later came the following good news: "Various matters have prevented me from giving an earlier answer (or at least an earlier specific answer) to your letter upon the subject of a peerage for Sir Henry Wellesley. Having, however, communicated with the King upon the subject I have great satisfaction in saying that His Majesty sets too high a value upon the services of Sir Henry Wellesley not to feel that the dignity of the peerage is a reward for those services to which he is entitled to look."[67]

Goderich had indeed been busy. Much of December had been spent trying to salvage his administration. All had come to naught, and the prime minister concluded that he would have to go. The king refused to listen and bullied the compliant Goderich to persist. In the meantime, the prime minister awaited Wellesley's arrival to see where he stood, but the lord lieutenant's departure had been delayed. Wellesley slipped out of Dublin on the morning of 22 December, well aware of the events unfolding in London and knowing that he figured prominently in the discussions.[68] Political logic, therefore, would suggest an expeditious journey back to the capital. Such was not the case. Wellesley stayed a night in Holyhead before proceeding on, claiming his wife's poor health as a reason, and then took more than a week for the journey to London. This was classic Wellesley behavior; just when the opportune moment arrived, he hesitated. Bathurst told the duke that the king had told him that the marquess was not being considered as chief minister or even home secretary for that matter and that to save face, Wellesley purposely delayed his arrival.[69] There is no evidence to support such an assessment, and subsequent events contradict it. A better explanation would be the failure of Wellesley's nerves.

A charged political atmosphere prevailed in London. Tension and rancor had filled the air since Liverpool's stroke and appeared to be reaching catharsis. Everywhere one looked, passions ran high. Whigs, liberal Tories, and Ultras all looked upon one another with distrust. No one hesitated to express a point of view. The king, in turn, viewed all factions with distaste. In short, the stakes were high as Goderich crumbled under the weight of it all. The anticipation must have been trying, even for seasoned politicians like Bathurst. By the time Wellesley reached London, any chances for his sitting in a new government were gone. He had played his hand badly, and his brother was prepared to make him pay the price. From all appearances, Wellesley had attempted to play both sides. He allowed himself to be figured into Goderich's calculations while thinking that if Goderich failed, Wellington would look to his eldest brother should he get the king's commission. This assumption was extraordinarily unwise and speaks volumes as to why Wellesley failed as a politician: he did not understand how the game was played. No doubt his vanity got in the way, but he was a much cleverer man than his political behavior suggests. His misreading of Wellington would also suggest that Wellington had never made clear his frustrations with his brother.

The only real question to be answered when the new year broke was when, not if, the king would call Wellington. Still, the king remained cloistered in the Royal Lodge, and the various parties, including Wellington, were anxious. Consequently, everyone paid close attention to Wellesley. How the king treated him would be a sign of the royal intentions. For Canningites, Whigs, and Wellesley, the news was not good. A keenly observant Wellington wrote to Bathurst on 2 January,

> Lord Wellesley having been a week on his road from Holyhead arrived in London on Saturday. When I went to Windsor on Monday he had seen nobody. . . . The King did not mention his name to me, and Lady Conyngham pretended that they had not heard of his arrival. He had written to Lord Conyngham, however, by messenger on Sunday to report his arrival, and to express his anxious wish to pay his duty to his majesty. I have not seen him this day; but he had certainly not received any message or even hint when I left town on Monday. From all this, upon which I think you may rely, you will form your own judgment.[70]

That was easy; the king wanted nothing to do with his former lord lieutenant.

Still, the longer the king delayed, the broader the scope for rumor became, and Lord Wellesley's name would not go away. While Wellington and Bathurst convinced themselves that the marquess's political capital was spent, others still worried. Croker on 2 January and then again on the 6th recorded rumors that the king had determined on Wellesley as his first minister.[71] A less than sanguine Wellesley sought reassurance. Marianne reflected the panic in Wellesley's camp, writing to young Richard of her concerns that her husband might be left out of the new arrangements.[72] In the midst of all the speculation, the *Morning Chronicle* provided a superb assessment of Wellesley and his pretensions for the premiership:

> What has Lord Wellesley done to justify expectations of those who so loudly rejoiced at his appointment to the Government of Ireland? All his merits are of a negative character—he has not unnecessarily aggravated Catholic irritation—he has not encouraged Orange procession, or toasted Protestant Ascendancy—he has not permitted the insolence, the injustice, of the favored few, not goaded the misled many into open rebellion. But has he the vigor of mind to direct the destiny of this mighty Empire; has he nerve to speak frankly to the King, and boldly to his colleagues; does he have the confidence of Parliament and the people?[73]

The questions were rhetorical. Goderich officially resigned on 8 January. The following day, the king called for Wellington and the process of cabinet making began.

The Wellesley camp remained anxious and unrealistic. Marianne wrote to her stepson, "From the list in the Courier, Ld Wellesley is not I perceive to form a part of the new Cabinet, as he is still L. Liet. [*sic*] of Ireland perhaps they wait until he is free to accept office. I cannot think the Duke would be so unkind to him, or impolitic, as to overlook your father's claims. I know nothing but I will not believe he can forget Ld Wellesley's merits and services."[74] To this concern, Richard responded, "I hope and trust that the Duke has not only remembered my father's claims, but has pressed them strongly on his colleagues & on the King. This would be but an act of justice, and of sound policy as regards his own character, for the world will with one voice condemn his conduct, if he neglects this proof of respect & of attachment to his brother."[75]

Cabinet making proved less easy and more unpleasant than Wellington had anticipated. The king instructed him to leave the Catholic question open but insisted that Protestants fill the key posts relating to Ireland. Beyond that, only Lord Grey was proscribed. Wellington objected to none of these conditions, but he came to realize that political realities imposed others that he found painful. With great reluctance, he included a number of Canningites, most of whom he did not trust, simply because he associated them with their dead leader. Only weeks earlier he had made the following observations on Canning: "There were other objections to Mr. Canning, principally of a personal nature: such as his temper; his spirit of intrigue; the facility with which he espoused the most extravagant doctrines of the Reformers and Radicals, although himself the great champion of Anti-Reform; and his avowed hostility to the great landed aristocracy."[76] Peel educated the duke on this reality, and in this way, the new government was put together. That there would be Canningites in the government, along with others outside Wellington's circle, such as Anglesey, Henry John Temple (third Viscount Palmerston), and William Lamb, meant that there would be some important omissions. The most significant was Lord Eldon's, but Wellesley's also caught some by surprise. As late as 13 January, *John Bull* still mentioned Wellesley as a possible First Lord of the Treasury. On 18 January, the king had put an end to Wellesley's hopes. He would not see the lord lieutenant but instructed the marquess to carry on as if he had. In other words, Wellesley could formally surrender the seals of office at a later date.[77] There could be no doubt that he was out.

Arthur sent Richard a long letter on 3 February explaining the reasoning behind his cabinet making. It must have been a thoroughly uncomfortable task, for though the duke no longer respected his brother's politics, the fact that he felt compelled to write suggests that he hoped to avoid a complete breach: "It would have given me the greatest Satisfaction if circumstances had permitted me to ask for your Assistance in the difficulties in which I found myself; and to have been the means of giving the King and His Councils the benefit of your Powerful Services and able advice."[78] For his part, Wellesley refused to let his brother off the hook, but at the same time he could not afford to completely alienate Arthur. He wished the duke success and then scolded, "Had your intimation reached me sooner it would have saved some anxiety and would have prevented unpleasant public observation, but I do *not* wish to complain of your silence nor to investigate its causes."[79] Still, the marquess could not contain his bitter disappointment. "Some one jocularly observed to the Marquess Wellesley," reported *John Bull,* "that in his arrangements of the Ministry, 'The Duke had thrown him overboard.'—'Yes,' said the Marquess, 'but I trust I have strength enough left to swim *to the other side.*'"[80] Whether or not he actually said this, it certainly sounds like Wellesley, and in fact it is just what he did.

There was, however, unfinished business of a personal nature with which the marquess needed the duke's help: Edward Johnston. Johnston again needed a job. This put Wellington in a quandary. On the one hand, he detested Johnston and would probably have preferred to see his brother's bastard son rot in poverty. On the other hand, he also realized that unless something were done, Johnston would remain a burden on his brother's finances and Marianne's emotional health. And so the duke would do his best, but finding a post would not occur quickly. Five months later he would write, "Indeed, vacancies to be filled are the only description of legacy which my predecessors in office have not left me."[81] By this time, Wellesley was clearly in opposition to the duke's government, so Arthur should be credited for continuing to help with this unpleasant matter.

In public, there was clearly a chill between the two brothers. On their first meeting in the House of Lords, the report was that "a stiff and stately, but slight inclination of the head [was] . . . the only recognition that passed between the Noble Brothers."[82] Explaining this fraternal schism is not easy. Evidence suggests that the duke had already lost faith in his brother and that in Wellesley's term as lord lieutenant, Wellington looked for confirmation of that judgment. The fact is that a sympathetic eye could easily see much to be admired in Wellesley's tenure. Wellington, however, relied on what he heard, and most of it came from the mouths of Protestants such as Mrs. Arbuthnot and Sir Robert Peel. There were good reasons why Wellington did not include his brother in the cabinet, but he could also have developed a compelling case to include the marquess. The simple fact is that Wellington excluded Wellesley because he did not want him, and the fact that the duke did so was a harbinger of Great Britain's entering a new political era.

What cannot be lost in all of this is the fact that Wellington's attitude towards Wellesley could and would be misconstrued as a disagreement over Ireland. When Wellington took office, the Irish problem was clearly coming to a head. The fact that the duke had packed key positions with Protestants and excluded the most public proponents of Catholic rights in the old Tory government left many, including members of his own government, believing that he would defend the Protestant position to the end. Such would not be the case.

17

View from Across the Aisle

At the age of fifty-eight, Wellington sat atop the greasy pole; Wellesley at sixty-eight appeared a spent force. Maryborough retained his position as master of the buckhounds, but, like Wellesley, in his sixties he could hardly expect to play a substantive political role in the years to come. Gerald, comfortably ensconced in Durham, ceased to covet a bishop's seat. Only Henry, newly created Baron Cowley, seemed still to have a career before him. In other words, the Wellesleys, having reached the pinnacle of power through Arthur, were well beyond middle age and at a time in their lives when they might put ambition aside and take pride in a job well done. As it happened, nothing changed. The harping, the place seeking, the competition continued unabated.

There is little to suggest that Wellington gave much thought to the personal implications of omitting the marquess from his government. While Mrs. Arbuthnot's diary and Wellington's correspondence (with Peel in particular) clearly show that the duke had scant respect for his brother's political weight, let alone Richard's personal habits, Wellesley viewed his relationship with the duke in starkly different terms. Their correspondence had betrayed very little tension during Wellesley's tenure in Ireland, and Castle gossip focused on Peel, not the duke. The marquess's refined ability to mold his perceptions to fit his expectations combined with his continuing presumption of family leadership to prevent him from thinking that Arthur might be displeased with him. Moreover, his revitalized sense of political self-importance must be excused, as everything that he heard and read placed him in the political equation no matter how it might be configured. Although the duke dismissed his eldest brother from his thinking with nothing even approaching regret, Wellesley emerged from the process humiliated and eventually angry—an anger built on what he perceived as betrayal. The marquess, unsurprisingly, decided that two could play that game.

As for Maryborough and Cowley, given the extraordinary turn of events that left Wellington as first minister, one would expect to find them more comfortably situated than ever. With Maryborough this was not so. True to form, he had hoped to find his way back to the cabinet, but, as in Wellesley's case, such a thing never entered Wellington's mind. William, like Richard, did not respond well. Unlike Wellesley, Maryborough, though loath to admit it, knew his limits and retreated—ungracefully, but he retreated. In contrast, Cowley could not have been happier. Arthur had gained him a peerage and stood at the head of government. No longer would Henry have to deal with Canning's legacy, and this relief could not have occurred at a better time, as events in southeastern Europe had reached a crisis.

Family fortunes would change rather quickly, however, as Wellington found every step of his journey as prime minister a challenge; by 1830, events had forced him to take an unfamiliar seat on the opposition bench. The reversal of fortune brought an end to Maryborough's tenure as master of the buckhounds and left Cowley without a job. Wellesley benefited from the change, first becoming Lord Steward of the Household and then resuming his post in Ireland. These changes solidified a great falling out between Richard and Arthur, a breach that would not be mended until 1837.

Wellington's approach to cabinet making might be said to mark the transition from old school to new school politics in Great Britain. For the first time, a prime minister, by choice and by necessity, ignored old alliances and family connections in constructing a government. The factionalization of British politics among Ultras, Tories, Canningites, Whigs, and radicals—made especially problematic by the Catholic question and an erratic and unpredictable monarch—necessitated the change. The abortive attempt to maintain the status quo through a caretaker prime minister in the person of Goderich put everyone on notice that change was in the offing. Still, it took a man of Wellington's stature to lead the way into the modern era as Tory and Whig morphed into

Conservative and Liberal. Only Wellington could have turned his back on his brothers and his good friend Arbuthnot, not to mention long-time fixtures in Tory politics such as Lord Eldon. He balanced Ultra and Canningite, Protestant and Catholic and emerged with an unsettled but workable government.

While the opposition press spared little in its critique of the new prime minister's ability to lead, Wellington was not without admirers. "The Duke is," wrote *John Bull,* "unquestionably, the fittest man in the world to be Premier at this crisis—the decision of his character, so well known and thoroughly understood by the Continental Governments, will give a death blow to diplomatic intrigue."[1] Firmness and prestige trumped political naïveté and an arbitrary nature. There were many who believed that the times called for someone who could maintain some discipline.

The duke proceeded with confidence, and his first few weeks as prime minister saw relatively smooth sailing. He guided British foreign policy on a decidedly centrist course, and proved extraordinarily effective on economic discipline. There were dicey moments, such as Lord John Russell's bill to repeal the Corporation and Test acts. These acts, remnants of the Restoration, were written to exclude dissenters from the political life of the country. In practice they no longer functioned as a deterrent because of annual parliamentary action, but their presence in the statute books looked both archaic and petty to reforming eyes. Wellington saw the acts differently and worried that the established church would be weakened by their repeal. Peel's efforts to beat back the bill in the Commons failed on 26 February, and the duke decided that the issue was not worth a battle. The government conceded in the House of Lords. While less than pleased, Wellington revealed a pragmatic side that few suspected. Maryborough for one expressed pleasure at the outcome: "I look upon what has happened to be a fair trial of the noble art of bullying and I am much mistaken if you may not have the gentlemen as long as you chance to help them."[2]

Subsequently, a Corn Law bill created acrimonious debate within the cabinet, but moderates brokered a compromise between Wellington on the right and the Canningite William Huskisson on the left. Then the issue of parliamentary reform made an unanticipated appearance on the political agenda. In question were the pocket boroughs of Penrhyn and East Retford. The question was not whether they should go but how: as Lady Longford put the alternatives, "through loss of identity or total annihilation."[3] Wellington favored absorption rather than the transference of representation favored by Peel. This was the argument on a small scale that would reappear as wholesale reform in 1831. As in the case of the Corn Law, a compromise eventually emerged from the divided cabinet. Execution of the compromise, however, proved problematic. The fate of each borough was written into a separate bill to be considered separately. To make short a complicated set of circumstances, suffice it to say that in the confusion, Huskisson and Palmerston, because of the wrangling occurring on the first in the House of Lords, refused to vote on the second bill. This public show of ministerial chaos brought dismay to both sides in the cabinet debate. Huskisson, bitten by remorse, apologized in peculiar fashion. In the early-morning hours of 20 May, he wrote to the duke,

> After the vote which, in regard to my own consistency and personal character, I have found myself, from the course of this evening's debate, compelled to give on the East Retford question, I owe it to you, as the head of the administration, and to Mr. Peel as the leader of the House of Commons, to lose no time in affording you an opportunity of placing my office in other hands, as the only means in my power of preventing the injury to the king's service which may ensue from the appearance of disunion in his majesty's councils, however unfounded in reality, or however unimportant in itself the question which has given rise to that appearance.[4]

No matter how one reads this, it cannot be construed as anything other than a resignation, but Huskisson did not intend it as such. Instead, he intended it as an apology and expected a soothing response from the duke. He did not understand the character and personality of his prime minister; Wellington, who throughout his career had paid little attention to the sensitivities of subordinates, sent the incredulous Huskisson an acknowledgment of the letter's receipt and further informed him that it had been laid before the king.

Negotiations between the astonished Canningites and the duke ensued with little effect, and on 26 May, Wellington appointed George Murray to Huskisson's place as colonial secretary. In turn the Canningites left the government en masse. Wellington, who had always been ill at ease with his Canningite colleagues, viewed their departure as something of a gift and failed to appreciate that his political base had narrowed; as a result, he would find loyalty in his cabinet but would have rough sledding in the Commons. All in all, it was not a particularly auspicious start for the prime minister.

While Wellington traversed this political morass, the Irish question reappeared in the form of a motion for Catholic rights from Sir Francis Burdett. On the previous occasion of such a bill, it had been narrowly defeated in the Commons. This time a slim majority stood in favor. The Catholic question remained an open issue in the cabinet and therefore not one on which the government would stand or fall. Moreover, there was little question but that the Lords would reject the bill. Still, the debate attracted much attention because it promised to put Richard and Arthur at odds in a very public forum. Since the formation of Wellington's government, the press had been following the activities of the brothers and speculating on what appeared to be a rift. Wellesley's vote with the Whigs on repeal of the Test Acts in particular had been noted, but many Tories had done the same. Biographers are generally at pains to date the acrimony that characterized the relationship in the later stages of the brothers' lives according to political differences and therefore to this particular moment—but the real split was yet to come, and it would come for a different reason.

In fact, in the months after the formation of Wellington's ministry, the brothers had been in frequent contact. Anglesey did not proceed to Dublin until February, and Wellesley therefore did not give up the seals of office until then. In the meantime, Richard and Arthur corresponded regularly over Irish matters, particularly on patronage issues. So concerned was the *Evening Mail* on this correspondence that it even speculated that the duke might change his mind and send Wellesley back to Dublin in Anglesey's place.[5] Of course, Wellesley was simply doing his job, and returning him never crossed Wellington's mind. They worked together responsibly and without rancor. Wellesley communicated amiably with Peel and even socialized with him. Additionally, there was the problem of Edward Johnston and the ongoing efforts to separate him from Wellesley's household. The point is, while there might not have been warmth between the brothers, they were cordial, which brings us to June 1828 and the introduction of the Catholic bill in the House of Lords.

On 10 June, Wellesley rose to support the bill. He proceeded in the cool and logical fashion that characterized his infrequent speeches in the Lords. Rather than return to the well-worn discussion over the injustice of the laws, the marquess focused on the practicalities or, as he viewed them, the realities of the situation. The laws, he pointed out, had been passed to protect the interests and security of church and state. Clearly they were ineffective; Ireland then, as previously, remained in a state of disquiet and discontent. The laws not only failed to accomplish their purpose but also were the source of instability. Good and honest efforts had been made to administer the island and to enforce the laws, but it was time to concede their counterproductivity. Wellesley acknowledged that there were other ways of looking at the issue, particularly from the constitutional angle, but he saw no contradictions. In a spirit of honest debate, he turned to the duke, saying that "he could not but derive sincere consolation from the temperate tone in which this discussion had been carried on. It was now nearly admitted by their Lordships—it was in effect admitted by one whom he had the honour of seeing opposite to him, and who was a near relative of his, that such a state of things as the present could not long continue; and his opinion was favourable to an alteration upon such conditions as might be adopted, and upon such as he would state."[6]

When Wellesley sat down, Wellington rose in response. In an atmosphere of intense curiosity, he opened with the statement,

> My Lords, I rise under extreme difficulty to address your Lordships on this most important subject. I feel particular concern at being under the necessity of following my noble relative, and of stating that I differ in opinion from him whom I so dearly love, and for whose opinions I entertain so much respect and deference. I cannot, however, consent to take the view which he has taken of this subject, but shall proceed to state my own opinions, hoping that, in the end, the views of my noble relation and myself will not be found to differ, in reality, from each other.[7]

This could hardly be read as inflammatory stuff!

The press chose to emphasize the divergence in opinion, however, and the showdown in the Lords became a topic of much public discussion. Young Richard wrote to his father, "It is with sincere pleasure that I have read the report of your speech on the Catholic Question; and with still greater satisfaction that I have heard from many quarters the general impression which it has made in the country."[8] The long and the short of it was that the duke sensed inevitability on the issue, as the perceptive Charles Greville understood: "The Duke of Wellington's

Speech on the Cath[olic] qu[estion] is considered by many to have been so moderate as to indicate a disposition on his part to concede emancipation, and bets have been laid that Catholicks will sit in Parlt. next year."[9] The press, most of the cabinet, and certainly all old, hard-line Tory Protestants did not see the speech in this fashion. Their prejudices prevented them from recognizing the essential message from the duke, which was that order and security, not Catholicism and the constitution, were the issue. So certain were they of the duke's position on the Catholic question that they never considered that he was ready to move in the direction of Catholic rights. As for Richard and Arthur, there was nothing to suggest open animosity between them.

Wellington, unaffected by this little tussle, remained optimistic. Writing to Henry in Vienna he explained, "We are going on well here. The government is very popular and indeed there is but little opposition. We shall get through our Greek difficulties, I hope, and that we shall see the peace of Europe again re-established, and resting upon some permanent basis."[10] For his part, Henry certainly got on well. He continued to find the embassy in Vienna a comfortable place. His correspondence reveals that friends and family found their way to the capital regularly, something that had not occurred in his days in Madrid. No sense of isolation plagued him or his wife, who settled into her role as a diplomatic hostess. In Vienna they raised their daughter. He had found working for Canning something of a challenge, harboring as he did personal hostility towards the mercurial foreign minister founded on their history and on increasingly divergent political thinking. Nine years in Vienna would transform Cowley from a moderate liberal much in the mold of Wellesley to a pronounced conservative more closely reflecting Maryborough. Certainly Metternich had much to do with this change.

Canning's death unquestionably brought as much relief to Cowley as it did to Metternich, but the continuance of John William Ward (fourth Viscount Dudley) in the Foreign Office brought little change in style or substance. Then came the good news of Wellington's assumption of the premiership. The idea of again working in tandem with Arthur must have awakened in Henry feelings of great pride over their last joint venture in Spain. For Cowley the transition could not have come at a better time, as things were becoming dicey in Vienna. While Goderich struggled to hold together his government in the autumn of 1827, an Anglo-French fleet under the command of Admiral Sir Edward

Codrington, whose primary responsibility was to blockade the Morean coast, collided with the Ottoman fleet and completely annihilated it at a place called Navarino. With that, the role of the alliance between Britain, France, and Russia changed. Its stated purpose was to mediate the dispute between the Greeks and the Turks, leading to some sort of arrangement whereby the Greeks would be independent but still recognize the suzerainty of the Turks. The feasibility of such a task is an open question, but what is certain is that the British position was particularly delicate. While the Ottomans were longtime allies, public sentiment in Britain sympathized with the Greeks. In any case, Britain had become involved primarily to control the Russians and to avoid the outbreak of a Russo-Turkish conflict. The balance was compromised, as the Turks were justifiably outraged by the naval defeat.

In the aftermath of Navarino, allied ambassadors left Constantinople, and Metternich's worst fear, that of a Russo-Turkish war, appeared inevitable. According to the prince, wrote Cowley, "any war with the Porte must terminate in the aggrandizement of Russia, and that the views of the Allies respecting Greece, even supposing them to be realized can only be advantageous to Russia. It represents the policy of the Russian cabinet invariably to have been directed to conquest and extension of territory."[11] Cowley's efforts to explain Austrian policy to Lord Dudley betrayed an uncritical view of Metternich's goals and ambitions that diverged not only from Canning's legacy but also, unbeknownst to the ambassador, from Wellington's growing impatience with the Austrians.

In the Crown's speech on the opening of Parliament, Wellington's government tried to play down the significance of Navarino: "Notwithstanding the valour displayed by the combined fleet, His Majesty deeply laments that this conflict should have occurred with the naval force of an ancient ally; but he still entertains a confident hope that this untoward event will not be followed by further hostilities, and will not impede that amicable adjustment of the existing differences between the Porte and the Greeks, to which it is so manifestly their common interest to accede."[12] The opposition promptly concluded that Wellington would concede the field to Metternich at the expense of the hapless Greeks. "He was too intimately and personally connected with the monarchs of Europe," reported the *Annual Register,* "to set any value on the rights of their subjects; and the policy of Mr. Canning to protect Portugal and rescue Greece would wither under his influence."[13] In fact, Wellington ignored Metternich's repeated laments and insisted on following through with allied agreements on Greece. The risk, of course, was that war between Russia and the Ottoman Empire would ensue, followed by the inevitable Russian victory and independence for the Greeks. Britain's primary interest would then be to limit Russia's gains in the Balkans and to preempt Russian influence in Greece.

War indeed did come, on 26 April 1828. To everyone's surprise, the conflict did not go as expected with Russia initially suffering setbacks at the hands of the better-prepared Turks. Efforts were made to encourage the Porte to take advantage of these favorable circumstances and negotiate a peace. Cowley saw Metternich as a key player in these negotiations. Writing to the duke in the summer, Henry explained the prickly nature of the prince: "You will easily conceive that Prince Metternich is delighted at the changes in England, and particularly so at the appointment of Lord Aberdeen to the foreign office. If you mean, however, to keep him steadily with us upon the Greek and Turkish questions you must be very communicative to him both in London, through Esterhazy, and through the diplomatic agent here, let him be who he may."[14] By October, the Russians had righted themselves with an important victory at Varna. Still the Turks refused to negotiate, and Cowley encouraged Metternich to nudge them towards the inevitable. This, Austria refused to do, at least in any meaningful way. The situation was such that Cowley put aside his plans to take a leave of absence. Curiously, as the war dragged on, interest in it waned in both London and Paris. In both capitals, public enthusiasm for the Greek cause abated, allowing both governments considerably more flexibility. The war persisted through the spring and summer of 1829, and in September, the Russians were at the gates of Constantinople. The sultan could no longer ignore reality, and on 14 September he signed the Treaty of Adrianople. Metternich feared the worst. Writing to Cowley in the spring, he saw the war as a "Trilateral affair" that was part of a "Russian game and that the Allies have merely held the ladder for the Russians to enter the sanctuary of the Ottoman Empire."[15] In fact, the Russians proved moderate, claiming Moldavia and Wallachia as protectorates and allowing the allies to present the Porte with an ultimatum establishing Greek independence.

In the midst of the Greek crisis, Lord Granville gave up the French embassy, and Wellington promptly offered it to Cowley, thinking Paris the more prestigious assignment. Henry, however, had no desire to exchange Vienna for Paris, primarily because the change would prove expensive. Furthermore, he explained, "I have no predilection for Vienna, I have indeed but little to say in its favor but as a diplomatic station it is (particularly at the present moment) to be full as important, though not as brilliant, as Paris." Of course he would do whatever Arthur wished him to do.[16] Wellington, happy to have a trusted brother in a position to relieve him of some of the anxieties of office, was indifferent to transferring Henry.

If Wellington was less engaged in foreign affairs than one might expect, there was good reason. The odd series of events that would ultimately lead to Catholic emancipation had already been put in motion when Wellesley and Wellington aired their views on the floor of the Lords. The duke had appointed Vesey Fitzgerald to fill the post vacated by Charles Grant on the Canningite exodus. This was part of a general reshuffle that also claimed the chief secretary of Ireland, William Lamb, along with Palmerston at the War Office. Fitzgerald had been chosen because he was a loyal Tory and because he was sympathetic to Catholic issues and popular in Ireland as a conscientious landowner. He would stand for county Clare and was expected to be easily elected. This was before Daniel O'Connell decided to challenge the status quo. O'Connell submitted his name on 24 June, knowing that although law prohibited him from taking a seat in the House of Commons, nothing prevented him from standing for election. It was a symbolic move but one that O'Connell believed might mobilize his countrymen and in the process provoke a crisis. Voting began on 1 July, and by the 5th, Fitzgerald knew that he had been beaten. The results were decisive; O'Connell had 2,057 votes to Fitzgerald's 982.

O'Connell made no immediate attempt to press the issue, as the parliamentary session would close on 28 July; he would give the duke time to digest the implications of the election and to formulate a plan to deal with it. Wellington needed no time to ponder. In consultation with Peel and with encouragement from trusted sources in Ireland, he had concluded that the time for emancipation had come. Denying O'Connell his seat would ignite an explosion in Ireland for which Wellington did not want to be responsible. Some saw the situation as more dangerous than 1797 for the simple reason that a moderate Catholic element no longer existed.[17] Wellington needed no prodding. The rest of the summer and all of the autumn would be spent preparing a Catholic bill in great secrecy. His problems were myriad, and the duke needed all his ducks in a row before making any sort of announcement. This included keeping Peel on board, convincing the king to allow both the discussion of emancipation in cabinet and then the bill's adoption should it pass both houses, and mobilizing support for the bill in the House of Lords. These were formidable tasks indeed; each was fraught with danger. George IV was especially problematic for a variety of reasons, not the least of which were the influence of his Ultra Protestant brother Ernest Augustus (the Duke of Cumberland) and George's own extraordinary unpredictability. Wellington would threaten resignation on more than one occasion in the coming nine months. Not to be deterred, the duke forged ahead with the zeal of a convert. As early as August, Charles Arbuthnot worried that Arthur worked too hard.[18]

In the course of Wellington's planning, the Marquess of Anglesey proved particularly troublesome. Anglesey had surprised nearly all observers by pursuing a decidedly pro-Catholic policy as lord lieutenant. In so doing, he pushed events too quickly for the prime minister while creating instability at a time that called for order. As part of Wellington's strategy, he decided that summer that the lord lieutenant had to go, and an acrimonious exchange ensued. Wellington accused Anglesey of creating unrealistic expectations and of dealing ineffectively with disorder. In the course of their correspondence, Anglesey raised the unwelcome specter of Wellesley. "You say that 'I am mistaken if I suppose I am the first Lord Lieutenant who has governed Ireland with an impartial hand,'" he wrote. "I really suppose no such thing, and I am sure there is not an expression in my letter that will bear that construction. In truth, I need only go back to the last administration of Ireland to the government of Marquis Wellesley, to discover that 'mine is not a novel mode of governing.' I observe in every public act of Lord Wellesley not merely the intention but the fulfillment of that principle of governing."[19] If Anglesey thought that referencing Wellesley might placate the duke, he was woefully mistaken. Wellington did not want to hear of his brother's virtues; he proceeded with the recall and sent Hugh Percy, third Duke of Northumberland, to take Anglesey's place. As occurred with many things that Wellington did, observers misunderstood his motives in this supersession. This was not the action of a hard-line Protestant but that of a man whose practical sensibility required order, especially with controversial change in the offing.

Wellington's care and hard work paid off. In the Commons, the Emancipation Bill floated through with a 176-vote majority; in the Lords, he achieved an equally impressive 104-vote victory. The lopsided victory betrays the tension that preceded the vote. Wellington would fight a duel with George William Finch-Hatton, tenth Earl of Winchelsea (though "fight" might be stretching the point), and Greville reported that the infamous Orangeman who had thrown the bottle at Wellesley five years earlier now lurked in the corridors of Parliament.[20]

Wellesley's views on the bill's success are unknown, but certainly they were mixed. On the one hand, he could not help but take some pride in his role in leading Parliament towards emancipation; on the other, he must have felt that he was again the victim of fate. Just as he had guided Britain towards victory in the Peninsula only to see others preside over it, so had he steadfastly urged emancipation only to see his brother get the credit. Several years later he commented tellingly to his son-in-law, Edward Littleton, "Arthur has been my evil genius; when I fall he rises, to adorn himself with the plumes which I shed."[21] That said, on this occasion there were no retreats to East Cliff or diplomatic colds. One must assume that he simply took satisfaction in the fact that Catholic emancipation was accomplished.

Emancipation was not the only drama confronting the duke. While orchestrating passage of the Catholic bill, Wellington engaged in a distasteful legal duel with his nephew, the infamous William Pole-Tylney-Long-Wellesley. The history of the disreputable Long-Wellesley is novelesque. The only son of Lord and Lady Maryborough, he had from his youth been a dissolute character. His befuddled parents sought help wherever they could find it, farming the young man out to both the marquess and the duke. The brothers' best efforts to employ young William and provide some early guidance came to naught. Wellington found him incomprehensible: "He appears pretty well in health but his is the most extraordinary person altogether I have ever seen. There is a mixture of steadiness & extreme levity, of sense & folly in his composition such as I have never met with in any other instance."[22] The men in his life frightened William; as a result, he kept clear of them and generally lived up to their very low expectations. Then, in March 1812, in the midst of Wellesley's resignation, William somehow convinced Britain's most eligible heiress to marry him. The young woman was Catherine Tylney-Long, and she brought to the marriage an income of £30,000 a year—an extraordinary sum by any standards.

Clearly the young Pole possessed charm. On his marriage, he took his wife's names and became the unwieldy William Pole-Tylney-Long-Wellesley. Pole, in writing to Wellington to inform him of the marriage, expressed great relief. Three children would come from the match—William, James, and Victoria—but any hope that marriage would lead to emotional growth in William, he quickly put to rest. Something of a caricature of Regency values and mores, he became a fixture in London's clubs and accomplished what seemed the impossible. He gambled away his fortune and left his family in despair. Eventually, creditors forced him to the Continent, where he compounded his troubles by eloping with Helena Bligh, the wife of a British officer. Wellington and Pole made every effort to effect a reconciliation but failed. Catherine, meanwhile, took her children and retreated to England to live with her sisters. William quickly realized that she took with her a lucrative source of income in the eldest child, and he began a hostile correspondence demanding that the children be turned over to him. Catherine, her health broken by the misery of her wretched marriage and the stress of battling with her husband, died not long after. Her dying request was that the children be made wards of Chancery. And so a crisis loomed over the future care of the three children; the Tylney-Longs turned to the duke.

Wellington stepped in without hesitation, confident that the case would be made that "Wicked William," as the family referred to Long-Wellesley, was an unfit parent. Arthur did not anticipate the fight that his nephew would put up. But fight William did, with the irrationality and desperation of a broken man. He publicly threatened to shoot his uncle should he lose custody, but friends talked him down. Instead he wrote and published an overlong pamphlet detailing the immorality of those who maintained that he was unfit. The list included his parents, the duke, and his sisters-in-law. Adultery and sexual deviancy highlighted this spectacular account, which found a salacious but skeptical readership. All of this occurred in the midst of the political chaos of 1827–28, yet Wellington remained focused and firm in his dealings with William—and proved amazingly forgiving. Arthur never ceased trying to convince William that he had opted for the wrong course and that it was not too late to make things right. In this matter, Maryborough deferred completely to his brother.

When Wellington became prime minister in January 1828, he recognized that he no longer had the time to devote as guardian of his nephew's children and therefore set about to create a more permanent situation. He opted for a dual guardianship, with Kitty assuming primary responsibilities. Finding the additional guardian proved problematic, as no one was eager to expose himself to the ravings of Long-Wellesley. Eventually Sir William Courtenay agreed to serve. Kitty devoted herself to the task at hand with the same care that she took with Cowley's youngest son, Gerald. The youngest child, Victoria, stayed with her aunts in Hampshire, but Kitty kept the boys. Eventually a tutor was found for the eldest, William, and James went off to Eton. Wicked William managed to lure James away from Eton, and Courtenay convinced the duke and duchess that nothing could be done about it. As long as Kitty lived, however, the young William refused to leave her care. In the end, Long-Wellesley won out, as both boys drifted into his orbit. The spending and gambling resumed but far from public sight and much faded from public interest. It had been, nonetheless, a great scandal and an unwelcome distraction for the duke. Remarkably, it did not seem to perturb him in the least, far less, for instance, than the activities of the marquess. Uncle Arthur remained unfailingly patient with his nieces and nephews and never resented the cost to his time and purse. In the years to come, he would willingly provide support for the victims of Wicked William's depravity.

The political arena was not so easily settled. Passage of the Catholic bill brought relief, but it also bought trouble. The Ultras, led by Lord Eldon, claimed betrayal. In great frustration, the duke had tried to convince them that his fundamental view of the Irish question remained unchanged, but they would have none of it. The best he could hope for was reconciliation once the bill passed. Here too he would be disappointed in large part, because emancipation did not bring peace to Ireland. In fact, emancipation came long after it might have made a real difference. By that time, Catholic leaders were moving on towards repeal of the union. Only then, in Irish minds, could real reform begin. The Ultras would not be appeased and searched for opportunities to punish their old ally.

Wellington's efforts to rebuild his base ceased on the death of George IV, but with the king safely in his grave, they began again in earnest. Elections were called in the summer of 1830, and the duke's ministry made every effort to defeat Canningite candidates. The returns created a Parliament fundamentally unchanged in terms of balance, leaving Wellington vulnerable. By this time, revolution in Paris had chased another Bourbon from the throne, sending shock waves through Europe. The revolution occurred amid general economic distress in Great Britain. With both agriculture and industry suffering, popular protests arose in many parts of the country, prompted by events in France. Wellington acknowledged the existence of serious problems, but he would not accept that they were either general or catastrophic. He toured various parts of the country and came away maintaining that relief was on its way, that what was happening was part of the natural course of economic life, that sound fiscal management would set things right. But there were those who believed that the duke wore blinders. "It really does appear from many representations," wrote Greville at the beginning of the year,

> that a notion prevails of the D. of Wellington's indifference to the state of the country, and of his disposition to treat the remonstrances and petitions of the people, as well as their interests and feelings, with contempt, which I believe to be most false and unjust. He has an overwhelming opinion of his own all-sufficiency and that is his besetting sin, and the one which, if anything does, will overturn his government; for if he would be less dictatorial and opinionated, and would call to his assistance such talents and information as the crisis demands, he would be universally voted the best man alive to be Head of the Government.[23]

The fact remains that this was Wellington's way of suggesting that anyone who believed that political change would affect the economic life of the country was sorely mistaken. To his mind, taking advantage of difficult economic circumstances to promote parliamentary reform was not only opportunistic but also irresponsible. Because this opinion stood in stark contrast to his views on Catholic emancipation, historians and biographers have long tried to explain Wellington's inflexible attitude on the issue of reform. A political explanation remains most common. Wellington knew that he was in for a struggle on reform; to fight it, he would need the support of the Ultras and would thus have to demonstrate to his former allies that they could rely on him to hold firm. The controversy must have irritated him immensely, for he viewed himself as always consistent, and throughout his life, suggestions that his actions were self-serving provoked hostility. On the Catholic question, he maintained that he had never declared himself unalterably opposed to it, and he was right. But perception is reality, particularly political perception. No matter what the duke did or said, he could never convince the Ultras that on the Catholic question he had not changed coats. Like it or not, he needed to assure them that on reform, this would not happen; there could be no ambiguity.

There is of course something to this explanation, but it does the duke a disservice. Everything he said in the run-up to what became known as the Reform Bill of 1832, he firmly believed; he did not conjure reasons for political expediency. On this issue, upon which even the Ultras were looking for some sort of compromise, Wellington saw apocalyptic consequences to any sort of concession. And unlike Ireland, where there had been a clear connection between existing law and public violence, he viewed public protest derived of economic hardship as totally separate from constitutional reform. In listening to Wellington with closed eyes, then, one might have thought it was Metternich speaking. Parliament opened on 2 November with a speech from the throne that made no mention of parliamentary reform, though there was little doubt that this issue would make an appearance. The Whigs responded but in a moderate tone. Lord Grey spoke of reform but presented no detailed agenda and in fact hinted of a willingness to work with the government. Just as no one expected the duke to compromise on Catholic emancipation, everyone expected him to come to terms with Grey. It was with that expectation that the assembled lords listened when Wellington rose in reply. He addressed foreign affairs and commented on the state of Ireland. Peers wondered whether he would ever get to the matter of reform. He did, and when his speech was over, he left his colleagues slack jawed. "The noble Earl has alluded to something in the shape of a parliamentary reform," he began,

> but I shall not hesitate to declare unequivocally what are my sentiments upon it. I am fully convinced that the country possesses at the present moment, a legislature which answers all the good purposes of legislation, and this to a greater degree than any legislature ever has answered in any country whatever. I will go further, and say, that the legislature, and the system of representation, possess the full and entire confidence of the country, deservedly possess that confidence, and the discussions in the legislature have a very great influence over the opinions of the country. . . . Under these circumstances I

> am not prepared to bring forward any measure of the description alluded to by the noble lord. I am not only not prepared to bring forward any measure of this nature, but I will at once declare, that, as far as I am concerned, as long as I hold any station in the government of the country, I shall always feel it my duty to resist such measures when proposed by others.[24]

His position was clear. Certainly he hoped that the Ultras would again take their cues from him, but in this he would be disappointed. They were no friends to wholesale reform, but neither were they as adamant in their opposition to change as the duke, and they still smarted from emancipation. What is more important is that the duke said precisely what he believed.

Increased public disturbance followed the duke's declaration, and the question became one of how the administration intended to deal with such disorder in the absence of political reform. Would the very symbol of order and discipline apply police power to an increasingly restive populace? Here again the public would be surprised. One week after the opening of Parliament, the lord mayor's procession and banquet was to be held. There the new king and queen would appear before the general public, joined by the king's ministers in a great public event. With popular orators whipping the London crowd into a frenzy, fears grew that the crowds would threaten the king and his prime minister. The lord mayor recommended a military escort in case matters got out of hand. Wellington brought the matter before his cabinet, and collectively they decided to advise the king not to go and for the government to stay home as well. In essence, they cancelled the event. The decision stunned observers, who had expected the prime minister to take on the mob. "It was," said the marquess in one of several cheap shots he would take at his brother in the coming months, "the boldest act of cowardice he had ever heard of."[25] What such facile comments failed to take into account was Wellington's innate caution in resorting to the use of force. The old soldier knew better than others that once released, force took on a momentum all of its own—letting the genie out of the bottle, so to speak. And to what end? Wellington believed that public discontent would run its course; he for one was prepared to wait in lieu of risking lives and property.

Still, Wellington came to realize the ship of state had sprung a leak; worse, when he looked around, he found only himself bailing. Peel in particular could summon precious little enthusiasm for the pending struggle over reform. Thus, when the government lost a vote over the king's civil list, Wellington seized the opportunity to make a strategic retreat. Though the vote surprised the prime minister, it was a defeat he could survive, and many ministerial MP's were not even present at the vote. Still, with the Ultras opposing him, Wellington chose resignation over potential humiliation and would let someone else grapple with the issue of reform. Wellesley had his own view of things: "The Division is most creditable to the New Parliament, & most disgraceful to this despicable Administration: The slight ray of understanding would have lighted their wavering steps to another course."[26]

Wellington's administration had lasted a month short of three years. They had not been easy years, and while history may not view the duke's stewardship as remarkable, it was not without merit. Catholic emancipation did not solve the Irish problem, but it was a necessary step and generally was viewed as such. In the long run, it signaled an end to British political stasis, a remnant of the war with France. Wellington abhorred the idea of parliamentary reform, but by presiding over the repeal of the Corporation and Test acts and the passage of emancipation, he paved the way for it. In this sense, perhaps he was the right man at the right time, maybe the only man who could have set Britain on its long nineteenth-century course of political evolution. Subtle is not a term that one would apply to Wellington's political leadership. While his firmness and certitude have given rise to criticism of Wellington the politician, it is only fair to take a closer look at who he was and what he faced. From the time the duke entered political life on his return from France, he maintained to friend and foe alike that he was not a politician. While historians cannot and will not accept this self-assessment, there is something to it. Yes, the duke willingly participated in the politics of the time, and one might even point out that he was a lynchpin of the Liverpool years, but his great prestige, not political ambition, is what made this possible. At that time in his life, he considered himself born to serve. As such, he could not simply walk away from a public life into a private one. Like it or not (and there is every reason to believe that he liked it), he could not abandon the political arena.

That said, he never occupied a critical cabinet post until he became prime minister. Master general of the ordnance, after all, could not be mistaken for a secretary of state, and there is no evidence that he was ever considered for one of these delicate posts. Until Liverpool's death, Wellington refrained from engaging in cabinet making or cabinet strengthening; that, he left to others and gave his opinions and support, even when he disagreed. And so he was not involved in the management of political men, many of whom were singularly unimpressed with the duke's political credentials. That he moved to the forefront can be explained by the fact that he lived through a period of generational transition. The old political coterie with whom he came of age was either retiring or dying off, and the new generation had yet to come into its own. Wellington thus led not because he wanted to but, in his mind, because he had to.

Lest we let the duke off the hook too easily, it should be understood that he was not coerced into taking the premiership. Once in the post, however, he resembled more the general than the politician, though that fact did not preclude a willingness to discuss and the occasional compromise. The Earl of Ellesmere, Francis Leveson-Gower, is especially perceptive on this point. "I can easily understand why the Duke's old military subordinates were shy of him," Ellesmere observed; "I must say that in civil matters the reserve of his colleagues was misplaced. I have combated his views and maintained my own with him over and over again, and never could detect in him the slightest trace of obstinacy of conviction or impatience of discussion. In any professional matter, once settled according to rule, he was adamant."[27] While not always an inappropriate course of action, at times military methods created problems that otherwise might have been avoided. Wellington could not control men as he once had, and as he said to John Wilson Croker, he had to take account of their feelings. This was something that did not come naturally to him, and he therefore did it poorly. He did not anticipate the Ultra rebellion on the heels of emancipation, something that would have been second nature to Liverpool. And so Arthur surrendered the seals of office to Lord Grey, and when the opportunity arose again to take them up, he deferred to the new generation represented by Peel.

Towards the end of Wellington's government, acrimony between Richard and Arthur became palpable. That the marquess genuinely disagreed with his brother on both the Catholic issue and parliamentary reform can explain a coolness between them as they staked out their respective ground. But the potshots that the marquess took in private, knowing that they would quickly become public, suggests hostility rather than disagreement. The origins of this conflict were decidedly personal rather then political. As Arthur had predicted, Richard, on his return from Ireland, found himself in increasingly difficult financial circumstances. The extraordinary salary that he received as lord lieutenant had allowed him to remain several steps ahead of his creditors. While there are no records to confirm this precarious financial position with certainty, circumstantial evidence points to this conclusion. Friends and foes alike commented on Wellesley's relatively quiet life in the Castle. Because this behavior ran contrary to the inclinations of a lifetime, the logical assumption is that he was economizing. While he managed to meet his creditors' demands, he could not retire his enormous debts, some of which had been left to him by his father but most of which he had taken on after his return from India. In fact, evidence suggests that Marianne provided the capital necessary to acquire a residence when they established themselves in London.

The great burden of debt would eventually demand action. In 1828, Wellesley (in consultation with his attorneys and bankers) concluded that he would have to sell what remained of his Irish estates. The duke, having both a personal interest in the family property and the money to buy it, appeared to be the best prospective client. Therefore, in December 1828, Wellesley's agent, William Stephens, sent Wellington a prospectus on the Meath property. Stephens told Wellington that appraisers set the property's market value at £130,000, a figure arrived at largely from yearly income derived from rents. The duke expressed interest and took the matter under advisement. After eight months of silence—not surprising, given Wellington's preoccupation with Catholic emancipation—Stephens again contacted the duke, stating that he needed a decision, as the marquess's situation grew increasingly desperate. A sale would have to take place.

Wellington responded by saying that he believed the asking price too high; he presented a counteroffer, the details of which are unknown. Stephens accordingly presented this counteroffer to Wellesley's trustees. Writing on 5 December 1829, Stephens informed the duke that his offer was too low, explaining,

> The trustees are placed in a difficult position. When the arrangement was made in 1821 the estates were valued at 130,000 pounds and the mortgages and other charges amounted to about 70,000 pounds. It was expected that there would be realized

> at least 60,000 pounds to be divided among the accountants. The accountants under the supposition that their monies would be returned to them released Lord Wellesley from their claims. Difficulties in selling the estate have mainly arisen from the difficulty of the trustees to pay the mortgages. They have not yet offered the estate to anyone for less than 125,000 pounds. However, they may be able to obtain 120,000 pounds and therefore cannot relinquish the estate for less.[28]

If the duke was still interested, Stephens would provide further information for consideration.

In response, the duke informed Stephens that he had in fact not made a formal offer. He had simply arrived at his own sense of value and asked whether it would be considered if offered—a classic example of the Wellesley inclination to split hairs. Wellington also informed Stephens that should he desire further information, he would send his own agents to Ireland to acquire it. But that was neither here nor there; "As the trustees will not accept the sum," he closed tersely, "the affair ends there."[29]

Of course it did not end there for Wellesley. There is no record of the marquess's response to all of this, but to his eyes it had to smack of opportunism on Wellington's part. The duke perceived a fire sale and made his offer accordingly. It is no coincidence that from this point on, Wellesley cooperated more closely with the Whig opposition. His relationship with Brougham matured into sincere friendship, and his correspondence with Grey increased markedly.

The completed sale of the Irish estates did not meet Wellesley's expectations, and he could look to the failed deal with his brother whenever he felt the pinch of financial pressure. How could he not reflect on his generous forgiveness of Arthur's debts many years before? Clearly, Wellesley's attitude towards his brother hardened very quickly in 1831, and unfortunately this schism came at a time of political disappointment and concern for Wellington. Just when he might look to his brothers for support, he found the eldest across the aisle whispering barbs that were manifestly unbrotherly. Blaming Wellington entirely for this course of events is of course unfair, since Arthur clearly had no obligation to bail out Richard after a lifetime of irresponsibility. Still, he must have known that his decision would have consequences. Even Marianne felt betrayed.

In the meantime, Cowley had his hands full in Vienna. Seeing the Greek crisis settled and the Russo-Turkish war ended, he turned his attention turned towards the July Revolution in France and the subsequent rebellion in Belgium. These events caused consternation in Vienna and challenged all of Cowley's diplomatic skills. Metternich kept a reasonably cool head, which may be attributable to the ambassador's powers of persuasion. The fact is, no one much sympathized with the impolitic Charles X, and as accounts of events in Paris trickled in, a general sense arose that Charles had gotten what he deserved. Louis-Philippe's ascent to the throne made the revolution more palatable to the cautious Metternich, but he nonetheless worried over the example set in Paris.

Wellington did not entirely lack interest in international affairs, and he would use them to redirect the political debate in London. Still, domestic challenges occupied most of his attention. In light of this, Cowley's performance in Vienna can be judged as good but not inspired. Henry remained far too inclined to take Metternich's point of view, but the fact remains that Austrian interests generally did not collide with Britain's. Austria kept a free hand in Italy, and Britain, on its own terms, managed Belgian independence in concert with France. With Wellington's resignation in November 1830, Cowley knew that his tenure in Vienna neared an end. Detailed summaries of Anglo-Austrian affairs were sent to Palmerston, the new foreign secretary, along with assurances that Henry was prepared to make room for the new government's choice to occupy the embassy.[30]

Such were the courtesies of the day, and when Palmerston failed to act in the first months of 1831, Cowley began to think that perhaps he would stay on. Then in May came his recall; in typical Wellesley fashion, he reacted with some indignation.[31] Within the month, Cowley was in London. As far as Wellington was concerned, the youngest brother's return came not a moment too soon. Before moving on, one should recall that Arthur made no attempt as prime minister to secure a bishopric for Gerald, though he had several opportunities to do so. Nor is there anything to suggest that Gerald still entertained such a hope or that Wellington even considered it. Just as political considerations led him to overlook Richard and William, so would they guide him on the question of clerical appointments. In later correspondence concerning Wellington's nephew (Henry's son, Gerald, whom Kitty had raised), there is a strong suggestion of regret that the men

Wellington had placed on bishop's thrones had displayed precious little gratitude.

Taking his place as leader of the opposition in the House of Lords, Wellington focused on the coming debate over reform. Seeing the marquess on the government benches came as no surprise. "All the Cabinet was there . . . Ld. Wellesley, his little eyes twinkling with joy," reports Greville on the transition from Wellington to Grey.[32] The marquess had landed the post as Lord Steward of the Household, while the marchioness joined the queen at her court. As the duke had spent several weeks quietly and in great secrecy planning for emancipation, so Grey would do with reform. Initially, there were many who believed that Grey could not govern with his motley coalition. Even Cowley reported from Vienna the widespread belief there that Arthur would weather the storm. Certainly Maryborough thought that Wellington would soon return to power. Writing to the duke on 3 February, William staked out a claim to a cabinet office in the next administration, reminding Arthur of his displeasure when forced to move from the mint to master of the buckhounds. He found the experience degrading and a consummate waste of his talent. Still, his prose dripping with self-righteousness, he did not complain and proceeded to fulfill his duties well. Should Wellington become prime minister again, master of the buckhounds would no doubt again be offered, but he could not accept, since the rewards were insufficient. Almost incredibly, Maryborough claimed that to prevent embarrassment, he had made no application to the duke during Wellington's government, but William wanted to be First Lord of the Admiralty. His name, he claimed, had been mentioned for any change at the Admiralty for several years.[33] One wonders just what the duke made of this. First, speculating on offices in a government that did not exist would have been as far from Wellington's habits of doing business as one could get, and Maryborough should have known it. But beyond this, Wellington could think only of parliamentary reform and a proper strategy for defeating it, not his brother's slighted feelings.

Wellington had hoped that Grey would address the issue incrementally, something with which, though far from satisfactory, he could live. He knew nonetheless that whatever the Whigs put forward he would not like; in expectation, his spirits ebbed and his temper quickened. In February, Mrs. Arbuthnot described an extraordinary scene to her husband. To set the stage, she had been attempting, with the duke's blessing, to mediate a disagreement between him and his elder son, Arthur, Lord Douro. After meeting with Douro, she reported the results to Wellington at one of their regular visits. Expecting an amiable discussion, she bore the brunt of something entirely different. "He got into one of his most furious storms," she reported,

> abused his son, spoke as if he wished him to go out of his house, & then fell to abusing me, who, he said, always took part against him, & never did him justice, & used him shamefully. I was so astounded I said nothing. I believe my silence made him more angry, & he snatched up his hat & was going out of the room. I caught hold of him by his coat, and he turned round. I said, "How can you say such things, you must know I don't care the value of my pocket handkerchief about yr. son except for yr. sake." I held it up as I spoke, he snatched it out of my hand, threw it upon the floor, swore a great oath, and rushed out of the room! I assure you he was like a madman, & if he had knocked me down I shd. not have been surprised. I was silly enough to sit down & cry, but since, it only makes me melancholy that he shd. give way to his temper so.[34]

This is extraordinary indeed. For the duke to turn on the person he perhaps loved more than any other is a clear sign that he was on the edge. While he had displayed little remorse in resigning the premiership, disappointment and anger remained just beneath the surface. The duke sent apologies later that day. Still, in light of this episode, one can only wonder at the intensity of his feelings when he looked across the aisle in the Lords to find the marquess. Though Wellesley did not play an active part in the debates on the Reform Bill, his views were well known, and he clearly stood with Grey.[35] The irony, of course, is that if one returned to Wellesley's speech against a similar bill in 1793, one would find language and reasoning that corresponded with the duke's. But that was nearly forty years earlier and in a time hardly reminiscent of 1831 and 1832.

Then came news confirming the duke's worst fears; Lord John Russell had revealed the administration's reform bill. Hopes for moderation dissipated in an instant. There would be a wholesale redistribution of seats and an expansion of the electorate. Wellington saw an end to civilization as he knew it. When the vote on a second reading returned a government majority of one, crisis loomed, and everyone knew it. Grey maneuvered for a dissolution and got it on 22 April. On the 24th, the duchess died. Although Kitty had never been particularly robust, her death caught everyone by surprise. What exactly Wellington felt on this occasion is difficult to discern. Clearly he did not hold her dear as he did Harriet Arbuthnot, but their lives had been long connected, and suggesting that the duke was indifferent to her death would be grossly unfair. The loss of his wife would have confirmed and accentuated the melancholy that had him in its grip. His world was dying, in more ways than one.

Wellington held a proper funeral for the duchess, attended by royal liveries and the whole family.[36] The congregation of Wellesleys would have been a wonderful sight indeed. There was, however, little opportunity for mourning as the duke got down to the task of fighting reform. Maryborough, however, continued his irritating ways. This time it was the issue of the king's coronation. William IV did not want one, which suited Grey just fine. Old-line Tories, however, William among them, were horrified. In a screed that was pretentious and presumptuous even by Maryborough standards, William lectured his brother on the importance of the ceremony.[37] While Wellington generally agreed with William, the king's coronation paled to insignificance alongside reform. To Arthur's mind, the very future of the country was at stake; a coronation, in comparison, was very small stuff. Nothing better illustrates the separation of the great man from the mediocre. Wellington possessed a sense of scale, a concept for which Maryborough had not the slightest appreciation. There would be a coronation, over the protests of the king, and it went off rather well and at one-tenth the cost of George IV's.

Meanwhile, Wellington, still beset by gloom and doom, mobilized his forces to confront reform in the House of Lords. "Publick affairs are now in a sad state," he wrote to Peel, "and I don't see how the country can escape the ruin threatened by the monstrous combination of the King, the Whigs, the radicals, the dissenters and the mob, against the bulk of the property, the Church and all the great establishments and institutions."[38] To the recently returned Cowley he wrote in July,

> The mob, the radicals, the dissenters from the Church of all religious persuasion hail the measure as the commencement of a new era of destruction and plunder. The ministers and their adherents in both Houses of Parliament alone deny its consequences. But they do so only in publick discussion. In private many of those who vote, and will vote for the measure

> lament its consequences; some even I know who are members of the cabinet. You will say that it is extraordinary that such a measure should be carried under such circumstances. Carried I hope it will not be. I think that the House of Lords will be true to itself and will enable us yet to save the country.[39]

With Grey's government strengthened after dissolution in April, the Reform Bill progressed comfortably through the Commons in the summer, and on September 22 it made its way to the House of Lords. Grey hoped for Wellesley's active participation in the debate, as he made clear in a letter that spring: "It gave me great pleasure to hear that your health was so far reestablished, as to attend the hope of your being soon able to appear in your place in the H. of Lords. We shall be in great want of your assistance there, upon many of the matters that will soon come under discussion; & I look forward with anxious hope to the effect of a powerful speech from you, on the question of reform."[40] The marquess, to no one's surprise, did not recover quickly, but Grey did not give up hope, and the two remained in close contact. In May, Wellesley reported that the duke had surprised him with two visits, but, he assured his friend, they were not to be construed as "political visits."[41] In the midst of all this, the family was again uncomfortably brought together, this time by the death of Lady Mornington. As he had done five months earlier on the death of the duchess, the king offered the services of his carriages. On this occasion, the duke politely declined, for he was not eager to make the funeral into a public event. "Lady Mornington," he explained, "lived quietly and expressed a desire for a private funeral. The family decided the best sign of respect to Lady Mornington was to abide by her wishes. Lady Mornington's sons and son-in-law will attend the funeral in their carriages. They have declined the offers of attendance from friends and relatives."[42] None of the Wellesley brothers much loved their mother, but certainly Wellington loved her least. There is nothing in the family correspondence that provides a glimpse of this event. No doubt the service at Grosvenor Chapel proceeded with dispatch. Wellesley certainly danced on Lady Mornington's grave; no longer was he responsible for the jointure, which he could ill afford. The irony is that these men were their mother's sons. In character they resembled her more than their father; longevity was not the only trait she passed on to them.

The debate on the Reform Bill proceeded as expected with great passion on both sides, and as expected it ended with its defeat in the Lords by a margin of 199 to 158 on 8 October 1831. In response, the Commons reaffirmed their vote and their confidence in the government. Public demonstrations followed. With the country seemingly on the verge of revolution, attempts were made at compromise. These came to naught. In December the government introduced the bill again in the Commons, and in March it passed the third reading with a margin of 116 votes. The Lords got the bill after attempts at compromise again failed. It passed the second reading by a slim majority, and in May the Lords again delivered the coup de grace. The matter came down to the king: either he would create new peers in sufficient numbers to pass the bill or he would form a new government.

Attempts were made to find a new government, but they foundered on Wellington's inability to create any kind of working majority in the Commons. It was all too much for the duke. He publicly defended his efforts before the Lords, then withdrew from the discussion on the Reform Bill. When the king promised to create enough peers to pass the bill, others followed the duke's lead, and the bill passed a sparsely attended House of Lords on 4 June by a vote of 106 to 22. The king refused personally to sign the bill into law, and so it was done by commission on 7 June. Lord Wellesley acted as one of the commissioners, a fact that the duke must have found particularly irritating. This, however, was the extent of Wellesley's contribution. That he never delivered a powerful speech prompted disappointment on the government benches. John George Lambton (first Earl of Durham) wrote to him on 11 June 1832 in frustration: "I am highly gratified by your approbation of the speech I sent you. Your argument respecting the fear of the deliberations of Parliament being overawed by the visage of a large Elective body is unanswerable. I wish it had been addressed during the late discussions. Why do you, who view everything so justly, & have greater powers of enforcing your views by reasoning than almost anyone, never take a part now in debate? It is a great loss to the country & the liberal cause."[43]

As for the duke, his mood turned particularly sour. Writing to his son not long after passage of the Reform Bill, Charles Arbuthnot described his friend in stark terms: "The Duke is out of sorts, & out of spirits, & seems to think that nothing can be done. When he had his great military difficulties he never thought so, but as one grows older one has less animation. His powers of mind are as great as ever, & I never saw him in better health, but he thinks the country is inevitably ruined."[44] Arthur may have found some comfort in Cowley and Maryborough, for Arbuthnot places the three brothers together often in this period. Ellesmere relates that all those close to the duke were concerned for his emotional well-being. "It was shortly after his resignation," he relates, "and when he was at the height of his unpopularity, that, calling one morning at Apsley House, I found him dressed for a *levee.* Lord Cowley, looking ill and dismal, was in the Secretary's room with my brother-in-law. Lord Cowley asked, 'Is my brother going alone?' 'Yes' 'I am sorry for it; I wish somebody would go with him.'"[45]

Meanwhile, Ireland remained troublesome. Grey had returned Anglesey as lord lieutenant with Lord Edward Stanley (the future Earl of Derby) as chief secretary. Anglesey found Ireland no less challenging than in preemancipation days. In fact, not much had changed. Certainly the Irish considered their plight unchanged. Representation brought little relief on issues critical to their well-being. Particularly troublesome were the tithe and its corollary, the established church. Daniel O'Connell, in fact, had simply shifted gears from emancipation to even bigger issues, with dissolution of the union looming in the future. Anglesey, while sympathetic to tithe reform, found O'Connell impossible. Brushing off Anglesey's pleas for moderation, O'Connell had Dublin on the verge of insurrection, prompting the lord lieutenant to order his arrest. Although the case against O'Connell was not strong, the introduction of the Reform Bill changed O'Connell's attitude. He entered into an agreement with Grey not to provoke Ireland over repeal while the bill was under consideration. Similarly, Lord Stanley, the chief secretary, instructed Anglesey to maintain order and not complicate an already difficult political environment. After the enactment of the Reform Bill, Anglesey grew frustrated with the government's reluctance to address the tithe and the church. Whig reformers, including Stanley, had challenged traditional institutions as far as they cared to and believed that it was time to consolidate. Consequently, Anglesey and Stanley quarreled, and Ireland suffered accordingly. To reestablish order, Parliament passed the Coercion Bill in early 1833, and along with it came promises for church reform. The marquess was very much involved in this issue, sending his Irish dispatches and memoranda to the prime minister as he and Lord John Russell put together a Tithe and Church Reform Bill.[46]

The bill that Russell introduced in the Commons proved an aggressive piece of legislation, calling for the elimination of ten bishoprics deemed redundant, the phasing out of clergy with no parishes, and the commutation of tithes, with residual funds to be directed toward secular projects. Wellington again found himself at odds with his brother, though he agreed with some aspects of the bill. His most serious criticism concerned the use of church funds for secular purposes. This he associated with theft, just as he had viewed the elimination of pocket boroughs. Property was property and it must be respected. For their part, Wellington and Peel had decided that they were not prepared to defeat the government until they were ready to create one in its place. Consequently, the duke worked to effect compromise. Russell's bill passed the Commons intact, but in the Lords, it experienced more difficulty. Eventually the government conceded to many of the duke's objections, and a watered-down bill became law. Russell would try again in the next session.

In the midst of the discussions over the tithe and the Church, Wellesley replaced Anglesey in the Castle.[47] Grey had already moved Stanley from the Irish desk to the Colonial Office and appointed Sir John Hobhouse to his place. Hobhouse resigned before settling in, and the prime minister turned to Edward Littleton, the marquess's son-in-law and Anglesey's neighbor. Littleton and Anglesey were good friends and worked in close harmony. But Anglesey had had enough; with Ireland in relative calm because of the Coercion Act, he felt that he could step down gracefully. He recommended Wellesley—the "little Magnifico," as he called the marquess—to take his place.[48]

Wellesley took up the charge eagerly, though there were those who had their doubts. Greville could hardly believe his ears when learning of the appointment:

> Yesterday the announcement of Lord Wellesley's appointment to be Lord-Lieutenant of Ireland was received with as great astonishment as I ever saw. Once very brilliant, probably never very efficient, he is now worn out and effete. It is astonishing that they should send such a man, and one does not see why, because it is difficult to find a good man, they should select one of the very worst they could hit upon. It is a ridiculous appointment, which is the most objectionable of all. For years past he has lived entirely out of the world. He comes to the H. of Lords,

> and talks of making a speech every now and then, of which he is never delivered, and he comes to Court, where he sits in a corner and talks (as those who know him say) with as much fire and liveliness as ever, and with the same neat, shrewd causticity that formerly distinguished him; but such scintillations as these prove nothing as to his fitness for business and government, and as he was quite unfit for these long ago, it is scarcely to be supposed that retirement and increased age and infirmities should have made him less so now.[49]

Greville spoke for many in this assessment. No one could dismiss the fact that Wellesley was seventy-three years old. For most observers, the most generous interpretation that they could make of the appointment was that Grey no longer cared about Ireland. As for Arthur, the appointment surprised him because it did not seem to make sense. "I believe that Lord Wellesley wished for the office," he wrote condescendingly to the Duke of Cumberland. "But I cannot understand what object his appointment to it can attain either in the way of gratifying any party or of acquiring strength for the government or even of administering the government of Ireland."[50]

Wellesley, of course, never questioned his ability to govern. The fact is, the marquess had remained in regular contact with Grey, and the prime minister in turn appreciated this loyalty and respected his colleague's views. Moreover, Wellesley still needed the money. The position of Lord Steward of the Household was not well compensated, forcing the marquess to borrow money on his most prized possessions, the Garter jewels. The appointment certainly required a change of habits. Wellesley had been a casual participant in the House of Lords, and he made the social rounds in the leisurely fashion appropriate to a man of his age. Curiously, he did not see much of his wife, who was a part of Queen Adelaide's household. The appointment to Ireland would reunite them. Wellesley took over in October 1833 with much support from the amiable Anglesey, and he surprised everyone with his activity.[51]

As Wellesley established himself again at the Castle (knowing how much his presence there annoyed his brother), Wellington received word that in anticipation of Lord Grenville's death, members of the Conservative party at Oxford had set in motion an effort to name the duke the new chancellor. This move caught Wellington both unaware and surprised, for he had never anticipated receiving this honor. First among his reasons was that he did not consider himself on good terms with the university, having withdrawn his sons in favor of Cambridge over a disciplinary dispute with Christ Church. Second, and more important, he was not university educated; simple logic would dictate that the chancellor should be a product of such an education—specifically, a noteworthy Oxonian. In response to overtures concerning the chancellorship, Wellington went to great lengths to point out this consideration. But he was flattered, and becoming chancellor would fill a gaping hole in his career. In addition, he knew instinctively that it would provoke Wellesley as nothing else could. Christ Church had been the scene of one of Wellesley's greatest triumphs: the Chancellor's Prize for Latin Verse. He and Grenville had been intellectual giants in their day, and certainly Wellesley at least entertained the prospect of succeeding the great friend of his young adulthood. Beyond that, academic achievement was one area in which Richard stood in clear superiority to his brother. Lady Longford quotes the duke as writing to Harriet Arbuthnot, "What will Lord Wellesley say?"[52]

There was, of course, more to the issue than that. Wellington soon discovered that Oxford's determination to make him chancellor was part of an effort to revitalize the Conservative party in the aftermath of the Reform Bill. It was in a sense an attempt to bury forever the old antagonism between the Ultras and the duke. Ellesmere certainly understood this, writing that "the Oxford Installation, was one from which I think the rally of Conservatism may be dated."[53] The installation took place in June and proved a three-day celebration, which lifted the duke's long-depressed spirits.

As for Wellesley, he had his hands full with Ireland no more tractable than when he left in December 1827. Picking up where he left off, he pursued the same basic principle of his first lord-lieutenancy, that of equal treatment for Protestant and Catholic. Well meaning and logical as this approach was, extremist parties fought him every step of the way, as if emancipation had never occurred. "I have [been] compelled to use both edges of the sword, committed to my hands," he reported to Lord Holland, "& I have struck at Orangemen & O'Connellite with equal justice and severity but this system is not deemed equal or evenhanded justice in this Country, when to please either party, you must oppress the other, & where the hope of pleasing both by an equitable course between them is utterly extinguished by their reciprocal animosity & violence."[54] While dealing with extremism, he needed to deliver on some basic reforms, most significantly the tithe but also capital investment and reform of the established church.[55]

Accordingly, Grey's government introduced a second church bill calling for various reforms including the transference of tithes to lay purposes. The legislation gave rise to an immediate crisis as the right wing of Grey's coalition defected. These defectors included Stanley, Graham, Ripon, and Richmond. This caught Grey by surprise; in June, he informed the marquess that although he had weathered the storm, he did not know how long he could go on.[56] The bill, as expected, produced another struggle in the House of Lords, and again Wellington conceded the field rather than create a crisis that he could not see through to its logical conclusion. As for Grey, his prediction proved prescient.

In June 1834, the government prepared to renew the Coercion Act, which had succeeded in bringing a semblance of order to Ireland. Encouraged by Lord Brougham, Edward Littleton, the chief secretary, decided that the church and tithe legislation would stand a better chance of success if the Coercion Bill were modified. "I clearly foresaw," he wrote, "that without a modification of the Coercion Act, by the omission of the Meetings clauses, I could never carry the far more important measures of the Tithe Bill, which we all considered likely, in its new shape, to give security to Church property, and to aid most effectively in tranquillizing the country."[57] The meetings clauses that he mentions concerned the prohibition of public meetings for the purpose of petitioning. Several members of the administration (especially Brougham) agreed with Littleton. But this is beside the point. An important decision concerning government legislation required open discussion in cabinet. Rather than address the issue forthrightly, Littleton and Brougham attempted to introduce it through the back door, and as usually happens in such circumstances, this strategy backfired on them.

Littleton wrote to Wellesley on 19 June to bring him on board and ask him to advise Grey accordingly. Brougham followed with his own letter. Wellesley saw the logic to their thinking and informed them that he had written to both Grey and William Lamb (second Viscount Melbourne), the home secretary. Littleton then brought the issue up with Melbourne, who informed the chief secretary that this was the first he had heard of it and that he had not received a letter from the marquess. Moreover, Littleton learned that Grey opposed eliminating the meetings clauses. None of this would have mattered except that Littleton had conspired with John Charles Spencer (Lord Althorp), the chancellor of the Exchequer, who supported removing the clauses. Littleton then met with O'Connell and cautioned against "any unnecessary excitation of the people in Ireland until he should have seen the new Coercion Bill, which would be renewed, but with certain limitations." Eventually the cabinet did meet on 29 June, and the decision was made to renew the bill without change. Grey maintained that his only contact with Wellesley on the issue involved renewing the bill in its current form.

When the matter came up in the Commons, a stunned O'Connell reacted with fury. He accused Littleton of breach of faith, and the opposition pounced, to the administration's great embarrassment. One cannot, even with a favorable eye, dismiss this fiasco as simple naïveté on the part of Littleton and Brougham. The latter, after all, was a seasoned politician. One can only see it as incompetence, mostly in the fact that Littleton involved O'Connell. As for Wellesley, he clearly gave none of this the attention it deserved. He made the preposterous assertion that he did write letters to Melbourne and Grey and that these were lost; later he claimed that Melbourne was well aware of his views and chose to ignore them. Moreover, he put far too much faith in Brougham, and in a letter dated 21 June 1834 to the lord chancellor, the marquess stated quite clearly that he would accept any changes Brougham thought appropriate in the Coercion Bill.[58] The incident did not much concern Brougham, who wrote glibly to Wellesley, "O'Connell will rave, & do all the mischief within his power; in which we will be aided by the unfortunate error of attempting to hold confidential intercourse with him. In this plan I had no share. But to misplace confidence, is the calamity of all generousity of mind; & ought therefore to be forgiven."[59] Certainly Grey did not see the matter in this light; though he desperately sought an excuse to retire in any case, the embarrassment convinced him that he had to resign. With him went Althorp.[60]

The king initially turned to Wellington, hoping that he and Peel along with Melbourne might piece together some sort of moderate coalition. No one was particularly interested in this option, and Wellington informed the king that he would have to stick with the Whigs. As a result, Melbourne became prime minister and Althorp returned as chancellor of the Exchequer. Littleton submitted his resignation, but Melbourne would not accept it; Wellesley remained as lord lieutenant. Meanwhile, the duke, after fighting off bills to allow Jews into the Commons and dissenters into the universities, retreated to Hatfield House for relaxation with the Salisburys and Cowleys. He was there when news arrived on 2 August that Harriet Arbuthnot had died of cholera. Though she had been sick for some time, her death caught him by surprise, and it shattered him.

Nothing better illustrates Wellington's character than his reaction to his friend's death. Instant, expressive grief descended upon him, and he briefly allowed himself that indulgence. He traveled the next day to be with her grieving husband; in the days and weeks that followed, he mourned with the correctness of a friend rather than an intimate, and he went about his business. Nevertheless, Harriet's death affected him profoundly, and he slipped once again into melancholy. Fortunately, Parliament prorogued on 15 August, granting him some leisure and privacy in which to nurse his much-stressed emotions. In the course of three years, he had lost his wife, his mother, and his closest friend—and although one might dismiss the emotional impact of the previous two, there is no question that the combined effect was nothing short of devastating.

The respite would last until November, when Earl Spencer died and set in motion a series of changes that altered the political landscape. Spencer's death meant that Althorp, his son, would move to the House of Lords, leaving the leadership of the House of Commons vacant. Melbourne moved quickly to pass the torch to Lord John Russell, the great reformer. The attempt proved too much for the king, who could not abide Russell, and he dismissed Melbourne and called for Wellington. The duke traveled to Brighton without delay in response to the monarch's summons. To no one's surprise, William IV asked Wellington to take the reins of power. Wellington turned him down, explaining that he had long concluded that any future prime minister would have to come from the House of Commons; Peel, therefore, would have to be prime minister. The king voiced no objection, but there was a problem—Peel was traveling in Europe.

Wellington offered a solution: he would preside over the government until Peel's return, at which time the prime minister could create the government he wanted. Wellington would make no appointments and in the meantime would preside over the essential departments of state. It was an audacious suggestion, but the king deferred to it, and Wellington became prime minister and secretary of state for the Home, Foreign, and War offices. The political world blanched, but the duke paid no notice and went about his business with the diligence and efficiency that characterized his whole public life. That he exposed himself to ridicule bothered him not in the slightest.

The sudden change shocked the marquess and confirmed his notion that the duke was the source of all his misfortunes. Of course he knew he must resign, and so he did, on 24 November.[61] The king took great interest in Wellesley because of Marianne's close relationship with the queen, and William IV suggested that the marquess be sent as ambassador to Naples so that he might "end his days in comfort."[62] Wellington ignored the suggestion, nor would Wellesley have been interested in it. Instead, the brothers attended to the business at hand. Dispatches flowed from Dublin, making every appearance of normality. From London came assurances that Wellington was in no hurry for the marquess to surrender the seals of office. On the 29th, Wellesley sent a note of thanks that seemed to portray a sense of goodwill between the brothers.[63] But Wellesley adopted quite a different voice with his Whig friends. To Brougham he wrote that "our principle of action must be, to attack the Tories on all sides. . . . To submit to any Tyranny is grievous; but to submit to the gross, brutal despotism of blockheads & blunderers, is not a case, in which the condition of the slave is graced by the dignity of the masters."[64] These are harsh words indeed, but they reflect the Whig point of view. Even Grey could not quite come to grips with what had transpired and the role Wellington had come to play. In a long, rambling, and bewildered letter, Grey tried to interpret the situation, closing incredulously with the comment "the manner in which it was at once dismissed 'a la militaire' by His Highness the Dictator, had never, I confess, offered itself to my imagination."[65]

Peel's return on 9 December did nothing to alleviate the ill will that prevailed in London. The Whigs firmly believed that the government had been hijacked, and indeed they had a case. Many years had passed since a monarch had dismissed a ministry that commanded a majority in the House of Commons. While Peel constructed his ministry, the Whigs formulated a plan of attack and continued to seethe over Wellington's role. "I wish you & yours very happy new years," wrote Brougham to Wellesley on 2 January. "In the word Yours—I do not include a 'certain Duke'—for to him I wish many returns not of the season, but of the session, which is approaching & which he will find worse than any one French or Mahratta general he licked."[66]

Peel knew that he faced an uphill battle and concluded that he would have no chance of success with the current Parliament, so he called for elections. The results were largely favorable but still left him four votes short in the Commons. The narrow margin, however, encouraged him to forge ahead with Wellington at his side as foreign secretary. Wellington decided to send Cowley to Paris. Curiously, Henry accepted the assignment with some trepidation in that his last encounter with Louis-Philippe had not been particularly pleasant. That, it might be recalled, had occurred twenty-five years earlier in Cádiz when, as ambassador, Henry had contrived to keep Louis-Philippe from acquiring a command in the Spanish army and then demanded that he leave the country. This had been an uncomfortable situation, and Cowley had not forgotten. With this in mind, he presented his credentials at the French court. It was, he wrote in his diary, "not a little singular that having witnessed his expulsion from Cadiz as an Intrigant, I should now have to present my credentials to him as King of France." All went well: "I must say that during the whole period of my residence in Paris the King treated me not only with great kindness and attention, but also with every mark of confidence."[67] Cowley had little opportunity to exercise his responsibilities as ambassador, presenting his credentials on 30 March and then documents of recall on 7 May.[68]

Peel's demise came at the hands of an aggressive opposition in the House of Commons that successfully amended key bills and generally frustrated Peel's agenda. By the end of March, the game was up, and on 8 April, Peel officially resigned. Wellington retreated quietly from this unfriendly arena while Wellesley prepared for his return to Dublin. In a matter of days, however, Melbourne delivered the shocking news that Constantine Phipps (Earl of Mulgrave) rather than Wellesley would go to Dublin. Instead, the marquess would be lord chamberlain. Wellesley blithely accepted the appointment, the import of the transition in power not yet having sunk in. "I am Lord Chamberlain," he wrote to Brougham, "& another man is sent to Ireland; But I am not discontented & I, like you, adhere to my fixed allegiance."[69] The Littleton fiasco of the previous July had convinced Melbourne that the marquess could no longer be trusted in a sensitive post; Wellesley was beyond his time. The prime minister was not the type to agonize over such a decision, and he delivered it in a typically detached manner but not without charm. It took Brougham to ignite Wellesley's sense of pride and indignation. He joked of Wellesley being a "superintendent of stage plays"; just like that, the marquess turned on Melbourne. On 11 May he sent his resignation to the prime minister. Then, as always, he nursed his injured pride while loosely supporting the government.

Wellesley's resignation gave rise to speculation that it was attributable to disagreement over Irish policies, and inevitably the question came before the House of Lords. The marquess refused to enter the discussion, explaining

> I do not feel called upon—I should not feel justified in entering, in the House, upon an explanation of the causes of my resigning the office of Lord Chamberlain. If your Lordships are of [the] opinion that I should enter on that explanation, let me be called upon in a distinct and regular manner; or, if you choose, institute an inquiry into the subject if you think it sufficiently grave. . . . My opinion on public matters will be formed with independence, industry, deliberation, and, I trust, with integrity. Further I will not go at the present moment in answering the question of the noble Lord opposite. I will not state the grounds of my resignation till I am called on to do so by your Lordships—till I am compelled by proceedings of this kind, or by your instituting an inquiry which shall render my doing so absolutely necessary. I shall then, and not till then, think fit to reply to those questions. I will not make any disclosures not called for in a regular manner.[70]

It was a performance worthy of the duke, who certainly took note.

Despite refusing to turn his dissatisfaction with the prime minister into some sort of political crisis, Wellesley continued to seethe, and by the beginning of 1836, he could contain himself no longer. In a letter to Melbourne, he declared his intent to support the government but stated that he wanted to talk to the prime minister about certain issues. Melbourne, naturally thankful that the marquess had steadfastly held his tongue, answered that he would come to Wellesley. The meeting did not go well, as Melbourne took the opportunity to explain his displeasure over the botched effort to modify the Coercion Bill two years earlier. Wellesley described the meeting in great detail to his wife: "You perceive, that Lord Melbourne's rude, unjust, & insulting imputation of imprudence, & his defense of the want of good faith towards me for nearly a year of apparent confidence, concealing the most hostile designs; gave the whole transaction a character & spirit so injurious to my personal honour, that I could not hold any further intercourse with him without disgrace & ignominy."[71] And with this latest tirade in a life filled with them, Wellesley retired from politics to begin a drift back to the right towards collaboration with his estranged brother.

18

The Final Years

All the brothers lived long lives, even by modern standards. Their last years brought battles with the infirmities of old age and in Wellington's case a heroic struggle with the ravages of stroke. At the same time, the brothers laid aside their competitive instincts and settled into a genial camaraderie that none of them had anticipated. The warmth generated by this restored fraternity energized them and gave direction to their declining years. Each remained active and in some cases remarkably productive. Wellington survived them all, but his last years were lonely and not always happy even as he emerged a revered icon.

Wellesley's blowup with Melbourne proved a catharsis that allowed him to retreat gracefully, at least in his own mind, into dignified retirement. That a man so self-absorbed could finally lay ambition aside is remarkable, but he did; in the place of ambition came reflection. Reminiscence has the advantage of being self-selecting, and this suited the marquess perfectly. For this reason, the last six years of his life were the happiest since his Eton and Oxford days. Good things came of it. For the first time in years, he engaged his scholarly intellect. He edited his India dispatches, publishing them in 1836 and 1837, and wrote Latin and Greek verse, which he also published. More astonishing, he became pleasant to be around, even for his children. He corresponded regularly with associates of all political stripes and reconciled with Wellington, which had the effect of revitalizing his relationships with

William, Henry, and Gerald. Eventually, public perceptions of him changed, focusing on his work rather than his personality and habits, and accolades followed.

When Wellesley returned to London in December 1834, he established himself in the Clarendon Hotel, believing that Peel's ministry would be short lived and that he would soon return to Dublin. When that all came to naught, Marianne found for him a lovely home along the Thames called Hurlingham (now an exclusive London club) with beautiful gardens and pleasant rooms. It did not come cheap, costing £1,000 a year, but it proved an idyllic setting in which to restore the soul. Marianne flitted in and out of his life, for she spent much time traveling and socializing with her lady friends. Their relationship proved remarkably successful in the sense that they were warmly attached to one another while at the same time they regularly provided what today one would call "space."

His correspondence does not specify when or why Wellesley decided to undertake the task of publishing the India dispatches, but his determination most likely followed from the fact that Arthur had begun to do so. Richard hired Montgomery Martin as his editor and proceeded with great deliberation. Much work had already been done, as the marquess had long before organized his papers and stored them. Thus, the great challenge was that of selection and, when necessary, securing materials not in his possession. This would require contact with Arthur. The brothers shared documents and in this way began melting the ice of their frigid relationship. The appearance of Wellesley's first volume proved a great awakening as Britons took stock of their imperial origins, which had been nearly forgotten in the distractions of Ireland and reform. Brougham wrote glowingly in the *Edinburgh Review*, "The result is a publication of extraordinary interest in many points of view, and although the first volume only has appeared, we have no hesitation in bringing the subject of it before our readers, rather than delay until the rest shall be published, not only because by far the most important part of the noble Marquis's long and brilliant administration is that to which this volume relates, but also because it is one involved in no controversy, and upon the merits of which no question has ever arisen."[1] Brougham's praise overwhelmed the marquess and provoked an uncommon reference to God's grace while flattering his flatterer: "In all our troubles & adversities, we feel that our secure repose is in the goodness of our God & I do most sincerely & humbly acknowledge his goodness to me, in having extended my life to this day, that I might now depart with the certain assurance, that my memory would be vindicated from stain & slander by the ablest hand, now existing in the civilized world."[2] The following year saw volumes two, three, four, and five reach the reading public, and the admiration for Wellesley's work increased accordingly. Brougham was no less laudatory in his opinion of these volumes, predicting that they were likely to find their way into every library.[3]

Brougham proved prescient. No sooner were the dispatches complete than the East India Company sent sets to all company servants. This marked a sea change in the marquess's tempestuous relationship with the company. Indeed, in a letter to Sir James Carnac, chairman of the company, Wellesley wrote, "The kind feelings which dictated the wish expressed by the Court at the close of your letter are well calculated to revive early and ardent impressions of sincere zeal, attachment, and affection. To whatever period of time my days may be extended, I can never forget my duty towards the East India Company."[4] Later, he wrote an elegant defense of Pitt for Brougham, reprised for John Wilson Croker, that evoked much comment and praise from old colleagues.[5] Buried in this recollection was Pitt's glowing assessment of the young Arthur Wellesley, which Wellington certainly read with great interest.

Wellington was, in fact, quite sensitive about his India years. When General Baird's memoirs were published, Arthur's close friends worried that the general's description of the siege of Seringapatam—and the recollection of his supersession—might prove distressing. The level of Arthur's sensitivity to such things we do not know for certain, but in this case, the marquess took no chances. Nary a word critical of the duke would emanate from Wellesley's pen.

The *India Despatches* brought tangible rewards as well. In the autumn of 1837, the court of directors created a trust of £20,000 "to be applied to the benefit of the Marquess Wellesley in such mode as shall appear to them to be best calculated to promote his Lordship's welfare."[6] The purpose of the grant was to remove the "pecuniary difficulties which greatly interrupt his personal comfort in the decline of life," but, as Iris Butler astutely points out, that could be accomplished only by solid stewardship, which Wellesley certainly could not supply for himself. The court would act as trustees, dispersing the invested sum at a rate of £3,650 per annum.[7] As thrilled as Wellesley was with the grant, the sentiment accompanying it pleased him more.

They "called me," he wrote to his secretary Ally Montgomery, "'the Modern Founder of the British Empire in India.'" Flattery always worked magic with the marquess.

In response to the company's largesse, Wellesley sent a letter of thanks written in grand style; published by the London newspapers, this letter provoked another round of congratulations. Maryborough, with uncommon affection and delight, commented as only a brother might: "May your Highness live a thousand years."[8] Wellesley's renaissance was nearly complete.

Political sensitivities still ran close to the surface, however. Displeasure with the government's Irish policy led Wellesley to declare to Brougham that "disclosures made in the House of Commons, and the conduct of His Majesty's Ministers towards me, have determined me to relinquish all connection with them, and to hold myself at liberty to act against them in Parliament."[9] The death of William IV and Victoria's succession changed all that. Wellesley called for national unity, even going so far as to forgive Melbourne. "Casting away therefore from my mind all remembrance of former injustice or injury," he lectured, "(however severely I may suffer under their pressure) I renew to your Lordship my sincere assurance of hearty support to the Government, & accordingly I shall take my seat in the House of Lords at the earliest opportunity."[10] This spirit of forgiveness would not last, however, and at the end of the year, Wellesley was describing the prime minister as "brutal, false & stupid."[11] Brougham, equally out of sorts with Melbourne, received such comments approvingly. By 1839 the line had hardened. Still, such feelings were no more than small distractions, as the marquess had mostly given up his political life, rarely attending sessions of the House of Lords, delivering his proxy instead to the appropriate hands. No longer strident in his views, Wellesley was on good terms with old political associates with whom he had had precious little contact in the previous decade. There are numerous letters to Peel and especially Sidmouth, with whom he again socialized.

The sweetness of these years reached its fullness with Richard's reconciliation with Arthur. This had been building ever since both men had begun work on their dispatches. Although no personal letters between them are extant for the period up to 1838, we do know that they shared materials, and there can be little doubt that each found satisfaction in the other's success with his project. And why not? The India adventure had been a family event, and each acknowledged his debt to the other. The key to the rapprochement was Marianne, who had long been using her charms and wiles to break the ice. Clearly, the family talked about the prevailing ill will between the two brothers and the discomfort that accompanied it. While in Paris in 1835, Marianne spent much time with Cowley and his wife and doubtless the subject came up. In 1836 and 1837, correspondence among Richard, William, and Henry picked up with letters of congratulations and inquiries on health that are typical of men increasingly cognizant of their age.

Still, circumstances had much to do with the willingness of the brothers to give up their well-nursed grievances. For Wellington, the source of his resentment was the condescension of the eldest brother, along with the carelessness with which Richard had conducted his personal affairs; for Wellesley, it was Arthur's ingratitude. Edward Littleton (the current Lord Hatherton), who got on famously with both men, confirms this: "W[ellington]'s mind had not lost the impression of his earlier years; that he [Wellesley] would treat him as an inferior."[12] The marquess was equally clear in his complaint. Littleton quotes Wellesley as saying, "Arthur has been my evil genius; when I fall he rises, to adorn himself with the plumes which I shed."[13] They had become old men, and although Wellington had several years left, his health was uncertain; though still central to the great game of British politics, he saw himself as more of a guardian than a leader. In other words, finally neither brother resided in the competitive arena, and with Marianne's guidance, they came to see the foolishness of their ways. The healing gesture of reconciliation happened in 1838.

Marianne never dated her letters, and establishing a precise sequence of events is therefore difficult, but sometime in late April or early May, she broached the subject with the duke. She found him without bitterness and ready to meet with his eldest brother. This suited the marquess, and as a result, the duke came calling.[14] That the younger brother went to the elder was a concession that the marquess certainly noticed and appreciated. What was said is not known, but two such men are unlikely to have wasted time going over old ground or to have needlessly expended energy on emotional apology. More likely, they exchanged opinions, assured one another of mutual admiration, and perhaps talked of how far they had come. Astonishingly, they had never before taken the opportunity to do so, even though that would have been entirely appropriate. Imagine, after their extraordinary careers and the extraordinary times to which they had decisively contributed, what they could have thought when given the time to look at one another in their declining years. Arthur, the indolent youth, and Richard, the cash-strapped and awkward genius, had made it to the top largely because of the assistance they had provided one another. It made no sense to nurse wounds inflicted in the heat of political battle and fraternal rivalry. Without one another, their lives were incomplete, and with some coaxing from Marianne, they had both come to that conclusion.

Clearly, judging by her giddy response, Marianne had not been certain that the meeting would go well: "I have just seen the Duke, he says nothing could be more gratifying than your reception of him— That he was delighted to see you, and looking so remarkably well. That you were the most brilliant, and wonderful person in the world. . . . I gave him your letter to read and he has kept it—he was much affected, and evidently highly pleased. . . . I thank God, that you are now on good terms, and that nothing will ever change it."[15] As it happened, nothing ever would change their restored relationship. For his part, the marquess was equally filled with joy and relief, and his first response was to send heartfelt thanks to his wife. "The beautiful manner in which you have expressed your affection and good opinion," she wrote in response, "has touched me deeply, and gives a thrill of joy to my hand that it has not felt for a long time."[16] Next Wellesley wrote to Brougham: "I send one line to tell you, what I know will give you pleasure. Arthur & I are cordially reconciled. He has been here and nothing could be more satisfactory, than our meeting."[17] From Maryborough came expressions of brotherly joy: "Nothing could give me greater pleasure than to hear, that you and Arthur had renewed the affectionate intercourse which had subsisted for so many years; and which from my Heart I pray may continue for the remainder of your lives."[18]

Meanwhile, the duke continued with an active political life, but he chose his battles carefully and like his brother became increasingly less partisan. The role of senior statesman suited him. William IV died just after Waterloo Day in 1837, bringing the young Victoria to the throne. Melbourne subsequently called for elections that narrowed his majority considerably, correspondingly increasing the optimism and activity of the Conservatives. But the duke found leading the opposition in the Lords a thankless task, since the Ultras were as shrill and inflexible as ever. That changed in 1837–38. First the king was gone, but more important, so was the Duke of Cumberland, who became king of Hanover. He could not leave too soon for Wellington's taste.

Then came the death of the Ultra patriarch Lord Eldon; with Eldon's demise, Wellington stood unchallenged, though he would still endure the ravings and impractical suggestions of Buckingham and of Castlereagh's brother, the new Lord Londonderry. At Victoria's coronation in June 1838, Wellington nearly stole the show, and the queen came to realize all that the duke symbolized in the public mind. The point is, Wellington remained as active as ever as a public man but in a new and different way. He became a symbol of the nation, venerated for all that he had done and for the wisdom that he contributed to the political discourse. Yet he clearly was aging. His hearing became ever more of a liability, and rheumatism (probably arthritis) cramped his movement.[19] His health was a regular topic of conversation in political and social circles.

In the summer of 1838, just when Arthur thought that all was well with his brothers, he found himself in the middle of a fraternal row of his own making. Anticipating a vacancy in the captaincy of Deal Castle, Wellington, as warden of the Cinque Ports, settled on making an offer to Maryborough. This decision made sense, given their long and close relationship. Furthermore, Maryborough and his wife clearly enjoyed the channel coast and spent much time with the duke at Walmer, the seat of the lord warden. This would be a great favor that Arthur could confer upon William with no political consequence or even concern over charges of nepotism. He had long used his influence to help his brothers, but direct largesse was something he had avoided. Deal Castle brought with it a charming residence and an annual stipend, and Maryborough (being a Wellesley) always needed more money. The duke thus made the offer, but to his surprise, Maryborough turned it down.

Wellington, as was his habit, made no effort to ask why or to convince Maryborough otherwise. Instead, he turned to Cowley, who had been without employment since 1831 (excepting the few weeks in Paris). Lord and Lady Cowley could hardly believe their good fortune and jumped at the opportunity. No sooner had they done so, however, than William changed his mind. Ignorant of what had transpired since his refusal, he approached Arthur at a wedding with the assumption that all would be set right. When Arthur delivered the bad news, William responded in characteristic fashion—he pouted. Wellington, seeing that he had created a mess, met with Henry, hinting broadly that the youngest brother should defer to William. Henry responded almost pathetically, opening with the salutation "My dear Arthur" and continuing,

> In consequence of our conversation this morning, I have consulted with Lady Cowley upon the subject of Deal Castle. I said when accepting your kind offer that it was the thing of all others we wished to have—indeed as long ago as the year 1834 when we were with you at Walmer we both agreed in wishing that such a thing might happen to us as having that residence. . . . Under these circumstances we do not think that we can in fairness be required to make this sacrifice by any person, yourself excepted but if you have any desire that we should make it, or feel any embarrassment upon the subject, we are ready to give the thing up.[20]

The duke agonized for several days, as angry with himself as he was upset over William's behavior. "Men are not very reasonable," he explained to Henry, "when they are suffering severe disappointment even though occasioned by themselves; & this disappointment is aggravated in this case by his having been informed that I had for some years felt a disposition to give him this office when it should become vacant."[21] Maryborough's temper and self-centered nature combined to focus his indignation on Henry rather than himself, the actual author of his disappointment. Knowing William's character, one might wish that the duke had been less indulgent, but he had botched the deal and wanted to set it right.

Rather than insist that Henry give up the appointment, the duke used logic and guilt as levers to pry Deal Castle from Cowley's clutches:

> I think that nothing could be more fair than your Course has been. The office was offered to you, & you accepted it. You were not informed that it was previously offered to Lord Maryborough: much less that it had been intended for him. The office suits you, & you very naturally feel indisposed to give up your Claim founded upon offer & acceptance; and I don't think that any right can be made out on the part of any other.
>
> However, in all cases of this description all the circumstances must be considered; as well those bygone; as the probable consequences. Adverting to all these & to the state of feeling which certainly exists, I should not recommend to you

> to give up your Claim in order that that of Lord Maryborough may be preferred, or that you should in any way recognize that you have given cause for complaint; but I do advise that in consideration of what passed heretofore, & of Lord Maryborough having so immediately after his refusal of the office altered his mind, you should desire that the whole arrangement should be considered as *non aversu*, & that I should hold the office at my disposition to appoint to it whom I should choose when it will become vacant.
>
> It is very painful to me to make this proposition, but I am convinced that it is the only road to insure future concord and affection.[22]

One can only imagine the thoughts running through the Cowleys' minds upon hearing that they should be the ones to step aside instead of the Maryboroughs and that their good and balanced natures should be the cause of misfortune rather than benefice. It must have rankled. They gave way, of course, but they did not make it easy on the duke. "I confess that upon full consideration," Henry pointed out, "I thought the pretension of Ld Maryborough so selfish & unreasonable that I did not feel myself called upon to give way to it. Now, however, that you have expressed a decided wish upon the subject, I have no hesitation in consenting that the whole arrangement should be considered as *non aversu.*" Then he forced Arthur to consider William's behavior in another light:

> I cannot however refrain from making one or two observations upon the conduct of Lord M in this transaction. The situation is first offered to him, and he declines it. It is then offered to me, and I accept it—after an interval of a week or more, Lord M changes his mind, & intimates his wish to have the appointment. He is informed by you, that it has been offered to and, accepted by me, and then instead of stating his wishes to me (as I certainly had a right to expect from the very confidential footing in which we have always lived) he puts me, my feelings, & interests, entirely out of the question, & endeavours through your influence to gain his ends, and he alters his whole conduct to me because I do not immediately give way to what I have already said I consider to be a most unjust & unreasonable pretension—Let me for a moment reverse the case—& suppose

> me to stand in Lord Maryborough's place—Would he for one moment have attended to my wishes & feelings? Or should I, upon his declining to accede to them, have felt & acted towards him as he has done towards me? I hope not—[23]

The duke understood William's nature and appreciated Henry's gesture. Wellington would redress the grievance three years later.

In February 1839, the duke suffered the first of a series of strokes that occurred over the course of the next two years. Accounts of these crises make for fascinating reading. Clearly they were serious, leading friends to predict his demise on each occasion. Again and again he recovered, a feat remarkable in itself but especially noteworthy for the speed of his recovery. Ten days after this first stroke, he was back in the House of Lords, looking wasted but ready to speak. In May, Melbourne's government fell, but because of the queen's unwillingness to dismiss her Whiggish ladies of the bedchamber in favor of Tories, Peel refused to form a ministry. Melbourne returned to preside over the first of many Chartist protests.

Wellington saw Chartism as the logical conclusion to the Reform Bill of 1832, and it caused him considerable worry. His analysis of it, given on the floor of the House of Lords, revealed the toll his stroke had taken. While he could still deliver a speech, the logic and judgment of his oration were much compromised. His comparison of the riots of the summer to the sack of Spanish cities following sieges in the Peninsular War left everyone bewildered. Nevertheless, he remained bold and determined, going so far as to attend a Chartist meeting unaccompanied. No harm came to this symbol of the new Conservatism; perhaps the Chartists admired his willingness to see for himself what they were about rather than rely on presumption. The orderliness of the meeting impressed him, but he came away unconvinced by the Chartists' arguments.

Wellington's friends treated him to a grand banquet in September, but in October, Frances, Lady Salisbury—his closest female confidante since the death of Harriet Arbuthnot—died of what was probably diabetes. Her death came as a shock, and although he carried on as always, the stress took its toll. In November came another stroke. William reported to Richard that Arthur had lost the ability to speak and the use of his limbs. Another death vigil ensued.[24] Again, the duke recovered in a matter of days, although at a privy council meeting he was reported as looking "very old, very feeble, and decrepit . . . but he was cheerful as usual, and evidently tried to make the best of it."[25] Neville Thompson superbly describes the impact of the strokes on the duke's personality: they made him impatient, excitable, and short tempered. One sees this often in the elderly, even those of the most genial dispositions, but here was a man of extraordinary independence and energy, used to being in the midst of anything and everything of importance. That he could hear only a fraction of what was said around him only made the situation worse.

In 1839 Victoria announced her engagement to Albert of Saxe-Coberg. While this was generally thought to be good news, Victoria took advantage of the initial enthusiasm over the match to change royal rules of precedence in Albert's favor. This, the duke thought, was going too far, and he steadfastly opposed it. The young queen fell prey to immature antipathies and threatened to exclude the duke from the wedding. Melbourne set her straight, and eventually all was forgiven, with the queen giving way to Wellington's ducal aura. February saw not only a royal wedding but also another stroke. The pattern remained the same: initial debilitation and then rapid recovery. In January 1841, Wellington would suffer another attack in the House of Lords. Looking back on this sequence of serious medical setbacks, one wonders how he survived, let alone how he lived an additional eleven years. But he did, and it says much for a lifetime of careful, abstemious but vigorous living.

From 1839 on, the brothers interacted with affection and concern, though Gerald rarely figured much into their correspondence. While Wellington could not avoid political responsibilities, the marquess focused on intellectual pursuits, publishing a short set of classical verses in 1839 and then a more substantial collection in 1840 that drew much attention. His niece, Lady Burghersh (Priscilla Anne Wellesley-Pole), provides anecdotal evidence of his keen mind. She described for Lord Mahon a visit with the marquess during which he quoted several lines from Dante. "She expressed her surprise at his powers of memory, when he answered that he really thought, if he tried, he could repeat nearly the whole of that canto; and on trying, he really did repeat to her above fifty lines of it. She was struck too, she said, at his pure and classic pronunciation of the Italian." Mahon then pointed out "that what enhanced the merit of these accomplishments was that they never could have proceeded from business or ambitious objects, as he had never any Italian mission to fulfill or Italian negotiation to conduct, so that love of literature must have been his only motive."[26] As for Maryborough, he and his wife settled comfortably into Deal Castle;

there they largely remained, looking in on the duke when he was at Walmer. Cowley divided his time between London and Hatfield House in equanimity despite the disappointment over Deal Castle.

Wellington's *Dispatches* reached press between 1835 and 1838, and as was the case with Wellesley's *Despatches,* they attracted favorable attention. Brougham, writing in the *Edinburgh Review,* was warm in his reviews. Commenting on the duke's years in India (which occupy the first volumes), Brougham took pains to demonstrate that the fields of India were a training ground for genius.[27] Wellington took great pride in his India dispatches, commenting during the editorial process, "I have just been reading them over, and was surprised to find them so good—they are as good as I could write now. They show the same attention to details—to the pursuit of all the means, however small, that could promote success."[28] One must add, of course, that humility was not a Wellesley trait.

Of the second part of the *Dispatches* (which concern Europe and complete the set), Brougham wrote, "No man ever before had the gratification of himself witnessing the formation of such a monument to his glory. His dispatches will continue to furnish, through every age, lessons of practical wisdom, which cannot be too highly prized by public men of every station; whilst they will supply to military commanders, in particular, examples for their guidance, which they cannot too carefully study, nor too anxiously endeavour to emulate."[29]

Wellesley carefully guarded his brother's reputation, and he advised Brougham, who was busy writing short biographies, "If you speak of Arthur's career in India you may say truly, that he was entrusted by me, to the highest degree not only in military command, but in all civil affairs relating to the management of our conquests." Richard pointed out that he considered the Maratha War a greater achievement than the Mysore War because in the former, Arthur and General Lake had cooperated without jealousy.[30] This sort of mutual support continued with these old men talking to one another of their health and their mutual esteem. They visited when one was ill and celebrated when the occasion called for it. Wellesley even wrote a poem in honor of Wellington's son and daughter-in-law, Lord and Lady Douro, on their marriage.

When Wellesley's volume of verse, *Primitiæ et Reliquiæ,* appeared in January 1840, warm words of praise inundated the marquess. Wellington expressed astonishment at the accomplishment on a number of levels. "I assure you that it has given me the greatest satisfaction to observe the activity, energy and clearness of your mind and powers upon all the occasions in which I have seen you," Arthur wrote. "God-send! That you may long preserve and enjoy the satisfaction resulting from the use of [illegible]. You may rely upon my not overfatiguing myself. Others may endeavour to make too much use of me. But I resist as much as I can; and I am in good health."[31] Brothers and friends were not alone in taking note of Wellesley's accomplishment. The *Quarterly Review* stood almost aghast:

> These verses, like all that we have quoted, and indeed all that we have not, are elegant and amiable—creditable to the scholar and the man; but of all our judgment assigns the palm to those on the *Salix Babylonica*; which would be remarkable for their elegance and spirit, their force and feeling, if written in the full vigor of youth, by one who made poetry his chief pursuit; but when it is recollected that they are the production of a statesman who has spent his life in such very different and absorbing occupation . . . and above all, that the piece is written in his eightieth year—it appears to us not merely one of the best productions of the *Musæ Anglicannæ*, but a literary curiosity almost without parallel.[32]

On at least two occasions, Maryborough saved the marquess from himself. Wellesley busied himself not only with verse but also with essays on the people and politics of his age. In most cases, his mind focused on the positive and he had only good things to say of old colleagues. But there were exceptions, such as with Sir David Baird and Lord Cornwallis, and Maryborough, having been asked his opinion, gave it willingly. In the summer of 1842, just three months before his death, the marquess wrote a scathing essay on Melbourne and the Whigs. William advised that such an essay would accomplish nothing of a positive sort, pointing out that it would prove nothing that was not already known and that it would only provoke anger and bring censure on the marquess at a time when he finally enjoyed the recognition for his work that he had long deserved.[33] Wellesley was touched and told his brother so: "But my affection & respect for you will live in full vigour & (as you say) freshness, as long as one spark of life remains to me. I adopt your advice with gratitude, and cordial kindness. And I shall follow it implicitly with a true sense of its wisdom & sound judgment."[34] He might have added, "Where were you in May of 1812?" Had he, the answer would have been simple: "You never asked!"

Wellesley still occasionally brooded on what he considered the injustices of the past. In August 1840, he penned an immense document outlining a lifetime of service to the state and pointing out the paltry rewards he had received for his efforts—all leading to an argument that he should be given a dukedom. Fortunately, this never got past his desk, as it would have generated much embarrassment. These were good times for him, and they reached a crescendo in 1841 when the directors of the East India Company voted unanimously to commission a statue of the marquess to be placed in the general court room of the East India House in recognition of "the important services . . . in establishing and consolidating the British dominion in India upon a basis of security which it never before possessed."[35] The rarity of the gesture came with the fact that it was done while the marquess lived; no one missed the point. This gives rise to the question, why this abundance of generosity from the court of directors at this particular time? The answer lies in the fact that the company was in the hands of men who either had gotten their starts under Wellesley or had been educated in the system Wellesley began with the College of Fort William.[36] Surging industry and trade of the early Victorian age also played a role, with Britons taking stock of their great commercial empire.

In any case, Wellesley accepted the honor with delight and wrote another classic acceptance letter, concluding,

> At my advanced age, when my public career must be so near its close, it would be vain to offer any other return of gratitude than the cordial acknowledgment of my deep sense of the magnitude and value of this unparalleled reward. May my example of success, and of ultimate reward, encourage and inspire all the servants of the East India Company to manifest similar zeal and devotion in the service of the Company, and of the British Empire in the East, and may their continued efforts preserve and improve to the end of time the interest of that great charge so long entrusted to my hands.[37]

Four days after the announcement, Cowley sent his congratulations, recalling their extraordinary days in India. "I am one of the few persons now living who can bear personal testimony to the great difficulties you had to encounter upon your arrival in India," the youngest brother wrote, "to the miserable conditions in which you found the Empire, and to the state of prosperity and security in which you left it, after a most successful administration equally remarkable for wisdom and energy, and for statesmanlike views."[38] Even dear old Gerald wrote from Durham, and William was especially succinct: "From the very bottom of my Heart I most eagerly congratulate you—and pray God you may live to enjoy the delightful feelings." As for Wellington, what pleased him "most was your own answer to the Chairman & Deputy Chairman. It is inimitable. Nobody could write such a letter but yourself in these times."[39]

When the anniversary of the fall of Seringapatam came round every May, Wellington would send Wellesley his congratulations, and on 18 June, Wellesley would return the favor. This correspondence is genuinely warm and sincere, and the two brothers never missed an opportunity to reminisce. They shared collected correspondence and continued to call on one another to talk of politics. When Melbourne fell and Peel finally became first minister, Arthur joined the cabinet without portfolio, and the marquess gave the duke his proxy. Much indeed had changed. The deference that Wellesley enjoyed in these years must have gladdened him, but he returned the kindnesses. When the new foreign secretary, George Gordon (Earl of Aberdeen), appointed Cowley as ambassador to Paris, the marquess sent congratulations. Back came compliments remarkable for brothers at their age. "Many thanks for your most kind letter," wrote Henry, "the latter part of which is more gratifying to me than all the rest, for it has ever been my pride to be considered as your pupil, and in all the public situations I have held it has been my chief endeavour to conduct myself in such a manner as not to discredit the affectionate interest you have never ceased to manifest towards me."[40]

Wellesley's health remained robust until August 1842. He complained of gout, urinary problems, and, as always, colds, but these complaints were almost part of his personality. But in his twilight years, even his comments on his health were given with a lighter touch. His gout, he explained to Lord Holland, "came upon me, not manfully & boldly . . . but . . . under false colours, sneaking, & shuffling, & cheating, & hardly perceptible until you feel the pinch or bite."[41] That he remained alert and clearheaded till the end, he greatly appreciated. At times he even boasted of his memory. But when he took to his bed with his final illness, his death was mercifully quick. There were those who might have suggested that it was too merciful, but most of them had preceded him to the grave. His secretary, Ally Montgomery, kept the brothers posted on Richard's status. At 2:45 a.m. on 26 September, he died quietly at his home in Knightsbridge.

The grieving Marianne turned to the duke, who comforted her and helped her with her finances. Meantime, Wellesley's funeral took place at his beloved Eton; his grandson, another Richard (it seems unfair to call him Richard III) carefully described the event of 8 October 1842. Wellesley's remains were brought to Eton's Election Chamber to lay in state. There the brothers and other mourners gathered. For whatever reason, there were delays, and the service got started an hour late. This did not sit well with Wellington, whose obsession with punctuality combined with frayed emotions to leave him irritable. His eldest brother's death had clearly upset him. His response to Ally Montgomery is nearly unreadable (though much of what he wrote at this stage of his life was difficult to read).[42] That night Mahon reported him as "much depressed throughout the evening, and said little."[43] Gone were the twenty years of antipathy; left behind were memories of the halcyon days of their early careers.

The assemblage of Wellesley men included William, Arthur, Gerald, and Henry, along with their brother-in-law, Charles Culling-Smith. They clearly impressed the young Richard Wellesley, a student at Eton. "It was melancholy," he wrote perceptively, "to see all the old brothers with their Wellesley faces so like each other—three peers come to mourn over a fourth."[44] William, who had become the third Earl of Mornington, acted as chief mourner, as he was the eldest. The chapel at Eton is not a large space and must have been mostly filled, because faculty and students were included. Richard reports the service as affecting and dignified; then came burial in a vault in the antechapel. It was here that fraternal emotions began to loosen. "Lord Mornington and Dr. Wellesley were much affected," wrote the youngest Richard. "The Iron Duke folded his arms and looked sternly on the whole scene, what he felt he was determined not to show."[45] One should not be surprised by Wellington's self-control; he had spent a lifetime honing it. One must look to his body language and not to his eyes to find his feelings. Here it is clear that he grieved as much as his brothers. The stiffness, the frayed nerves, and his determination to leave the proceedings the moment they ended betray a man anxious to be alone with his thoughts. Certainly there was much to regret, but there was also much to celebrate. The brothers had led extraordinary lives, and at least half of their successes had been experienced together. It had been a remarkable journey; for a man such as the duke, who clearly understood who he was and how far he had come, the passing of his great patron had to have been momentous.

Alas, we must return to the living, and it is to Henry, Baron Cowley, that we cast our eyes. Perhaps no one was more surprised than Cowley when Aberdeen announced his appointment to the Paris embassy in 1841. There were concerns over his health and, at sixty-eight, his age. Aberdeen had put a simple question to him: was he up to the challenge of the French embassy? Cowley avoided a direct answer, responding that he would do as asked; by his own admission, he had little enthusiasm for he did not expect that such a thing would come to pass. "Well," came Aberdeen's response, "I shall see Sir Robert Peel this evening, and will speak to him upon the subject. I am not aware that he has anyone in view for the appointment. In the meanwhile this will remain between ourselves."[46] There is no trail of documents that traces Henry's appointment to Arthur, but Peel clearly would have done whatever he could to emphasize the duke's importance to the ministry. Henry was the senior Tory diplomat in the foreign service, and so there was some logic to his appointment besides his connection to the duke. Still, this was a time of transition, and France had been problematic for Britain in the preceding three years; vigorous representation in Paris would seem necessary. Did Arthur talk to Peel? Did Peel consult the duke? Probably the answer to both questions is "yes." There can be no question that Wellington never forgot the botched appointment to Deal Castle, and this was his opportunity to set things right.

Cowley waited, thinking that he might be used at home in some capacity at the Foreign Office. Then, "after an interval of three weeks I received a note from him [Aberdeen] saying that he had announced my appointment to Count St. Aulaire [the French ambassador in London], and that he wished me to lose no time in making my preparations for my departure."[47] Aberdeen's cavalier attitude towards the ambassadorship can be explained by the fact that vastly more efficient means of communication had rendered the role of ambassador less critical, and that being the case, as long as the person was deemed sufficiently prestigious for the post and could be relied upon to be loyal to the ministry, that was enough. Cowley fit the bill on both accounts. Not long after

Cowley presented his credentials, one finds Aberdeen writing to Dorothea, the Princess Lieven, "I am afraid you find Lord Cowley rather infirm, and very deaf."[48]

Aberdeen arrived in the Foreign Office determined to change the course set by his predecessor, Palmerston, which he deemed reckless and provocative. Palmerston's handling of the second Egyptian crisis, while in the end successful, had been accompanied by tense moments and talk of war in Paris, where the French foreign minister, Adolphe Thiers, found himself outmaneuvered by the quick-witted British foreign secretary. Aberdeen favored rapprochement with France, what came to be known as the *entente cordiale,* and that approach found receptive ears in the king, Louis-Philippe, and his first minister, François Guizot. This would very much be diplomacy based on a personal relationship between Guizot and Aberdeen, and it therefore marginalized Cowley's role. At the same time, Aberdeen recognized that an entente with France would not be popular in Britain and that small issues could quickly become large ones under political pressure. Cowley would be responsible for dealing with such crises through personal intervention with the premier and the king. In the course of Henry's five years in Paris, several sensitive issues arose that tested his diplomatic skills; among them were the French failure to ratify the anti–slave trade treaty, conflict over British rights in Tahiti, and the Spanish marriages.

Cowley and his wife left London on 4 November and arrived in Paris six days later, armed with only a general set of instructions. Henry was to oppose any attempt by Louis-Philippe to make a marriage alliance with Spain, insist on Belgian neutrality, and allow France a free hand in Algiers.[49] There would be no embarrassing audience of introduction with Louis-Philippe on this occasion; the ambassador found the king in amiable spirits, happy that he no longer had to deal with Palmerston.

The French promptly engaged Cowley on the controversial Spanish marriages. The issue was this: after years of corrupt and incompetent government under Ferdinand VII, Spain, on his death, descended into civil war (the so-called Carlist wars), which ended with Ferdinand VII's daughter and anointed heir, Isabella, on the Spanish throne. Isabella, only ten years old in 1840, ruled under a regency. She had a sister two years her junior. The great question surrounding the Spanish monarchy became that of the succession, which meant that husbands had to be found for the young queen and her sister. The modern eye has trouble seeing this as an issue of any significance, but it certainly became one. Britain's view of the matter was that any candidate except one of Louis-Philippe's sons would be acceptable. Britain preferred a Bourbon match, and to this the French did not object in principle. The problem lay in the details. Spanish candidates were two: don Francisco and don Henry, cousins to the queen and her sister. The first was thought to be impotent (owing to what was then described as effeminacy), and the second was a notorious rake. There were Bourbon princes from the Neapolitan branch whom Britain considered acceptable, but the French viewed such matches as politically impractical, and Metternich rejected them out of hand. The British suggested a prince from the Coburg line, but Louis-Philippe vetoed this option. In other words, there existed no clear candidate for the queen's consort; as for the princess, Britain came around to the idea that she might be married to one of Louis-Philippe's sons if the queen married first and produced children. In short, the question provided the backdrop for Cowley's tenure in Paris.

Cowley moved with far greater certainty and confidence in Paris than he had in Vienna. For one thing, the issues were those on which he had expertise—particularly the Spanish marriages, but all things regarding the Eastern question he also understood well. More important, he had experience in dealing with Louis-Philippe. Certainly, Cowley's mind returned over and over to Cádiz and Louis-Philippe's intrigues to secure a command in the Spanish army. The duc d'Orléans could not be trusted then, and there was no reason to believe that the king could be trusted now. As for Guizot, Cowley had taken his measure: "His manners are repulsive, and so little calculated to inspire confidence that he can scarcely be said to have a friend among his associates."[50] One thing is certain: Louis-Philippe and his first minister were no Metternich. Moreover, Cowley clearly understood his role. Many Britons did not consider the French worthy allies, so while Aberdeen built the entente, Cowley worked to make rapprochement appear to be in England's interests while not provoking Anglophobia in France. This was not always easy.

With the Spanish marriage question ever present, other issues arose that proved awkward. One concerned the treaty abolishing the slave trade. Britain had resolved the question of slavery with a great national debate that lasted from the 1780s up to the final abolition of slavery in the 1830s. Once a leading slave-trading nation, Britain took pride in taking the lead in ending first the trade and then the institution of slavery. Palmerston had then managed to conclude an international agreement putting an end to the trans-Atlantic slave trade. The treaty had been signed by all the great powers (excepting the United States), but for practical reasons, its enforcement would fall to the British and the French. Only they had a significant naval presence off the western coast of Africa, and only naval intervention could stop the trade. The great issue in negotiating the treaty had been the concept of search and seizure, but this point had been resolved and the treaty signed. The French Chamber of Deputies, which could not stand in the way of the treaty's ratification, voiced objections mostly because it appeared too advantageous to Britain but also because private colonial and trading interests objected to it. Rather than confront the objecting parties, Guizot chose to avoid them and simply put off ratification. Cowley, knowing that this move would be poorly received in London, urged Guizot to reconsider.

Guizot turned to delay, making thin promises that he had no intention of keeping. "He [Guizot] said he had attended a Council at the Tuileries to-day where the subject was discussed," Cowley reported, "that the King was determined to ratify the Treaty but this could not be done at present—that he had, however, come out of the discussion in the Chambers reserving to himself the power to ratify."[51] The king proved no more cooperative than his minister, explaining that political pressures made ratification impossible at the moment but assuring the ambassador that the treaty would be ratified. As Cowley had expected, Aberdeen sent a vigorous protest that Guizot calmly accepted before suggesting alterations to the treaty that were designed to extend the discussion. This would be the nature of the discussion on the slave trade until 1845; it had the effect of making Cowley increasingly skeptical of French motives and veracity. Midway through his first year at the embassy, his diary begins to reflect impatience and some disillusionment.

For the French, rapprochement signified legitimacy in the eyes of the world. To make certain that the point would not be lost, particularly in central and eastern Europe, an exchange of royal visits was arranged with Victoria traveling to France in 1843 and Louis-Philippe returning the favor in 1845. State visits are elaborate affairs, and Victoria always proved demanding. Cowley therefore spent August of 1843 preparing for her visit; so too did Lady Cowley, who had become close to the French royal family, particularly the queen. Queen Victoria's yacht arrived on 2 September to great fanfare and much ceremony.[52] Subsequent talks centered on the future of the Anglo-French entente but mostly on the Spanish marriages.[53]

The visit went off without a hitch, and on the queen's departure, Cowley's attentions returned to the routines of the embassy. Minor issues in Greece, Panama, and Texas, Cowley quietly brushed aside, considering them mere sideshows. A more provocative problem arose in February 1844 when news arrived from the South Pacific that the French admiral Dupetit-Thouars had taken military possession of Tahiti and arrested a British citizen. Discovered in the eighteenth century in the various explorations of the South Seas, a remote place with no strategic or economic value, Tahiti was as yet of no consequence. In 1825 a British missionary by the name of Pritchard had arrived on the island and set up shop, working with little notice and less controversy with the native population. When two French Catholic missionaries tried to do the same more than a decade later, they were denied entry. Dupetit-Thouars first intervened then, imposing a treaty of friendship on Queen Pomaré, who also agreed to an indemnity for the aggrieved missionaries. On Dupetit-Thouars' departure in 1838, the Tahitian queen appealed to the British for protection, but her request went unanswered. Four years later, Dupetit-Thouars returned, offering French protection. When Queen Pomaré failed to respond, he declared the island annexed to France. Then he arrested Pritchard, who represented British interests as consul, charging that Pritchard had encouraged insurrection. This was a mistake. Claiming an island that no one much cared about was one thing, but violating the rights of a British citizen and a representative of the British government was quite another. Cowley recognized immediately that this was the kind of issue tailor-made for provoking xenophobia. Guizot came to see that he had stirred a hornet's nest, and Cowley attempted to provide an avenue of retreat.[54] Still, Guizot responded slowly and reluctantly, and Cowley pressed him toward action even while encouraging Aberdeen to meet the French halfway. In the end, cooler heads on both sides of the Channel prevailed, and Louis-Philippe sweetened the pot by personally paying a pecuniary indemnity to Pritchard. This proved the deal maker, and the affair ended. "God be praised," Cowley wrote, "the Tahiti affair has been amicably settled."[55] The resolution came not a moment too soon, as preparations were under way for Louis-Philippe's visit to Windsor.

The king left for Portsmouth on 7 October 1845 to be met by Wellington and Prince Albert, and together they traveled to Windsor. There, amid the warmth of mutual expressions of friendship, the slave trade issue was largely resolved. In August 1845, Cowley had taken a six-week leave and returned to Britain. He stopped to see Wellington; according to Henry, they talked politics. They also discussed the duke's recent obsession: coastal defense. In 1842, on the resignation and subsequent death of Rowland, Viscount Hill, the duke had returned to the Horse Guards. There he worked conscientiously but remained traditional in his approach to the army, often obstructing meaningful reform. Modern technology intrigued him, but with an imperfect understanding of it, he either dismissed or, in some cases, exaggerated its implications. The advent of steamships could be counted in the latter. He speculated endlessly on the possibility of a surprise attack on Britain's shores made possible by the new, more mobile ships powered by steam. Wellington believed that France could again challenge Britain's mastery of the seas, particularly in the Atlantic approaches to the English Channel. With this in mind, he eagerly questioned Cowley on the state of Anglo-French relations. "I found the Duke of Wellington much disturbed at the unprepared state of the country in the event of a War," wrote Henry, "upon which he had made the most urgent representations to the Government."[56]

Most certainly the two also discussed family matters, for another brother, William, Baron Maryborough and Earl of Mornington, had died on 22 February 1845 at the age of eighty-one. William had been diligent in supporting the duke in the years of Arthur's strokes, but in 1843, his own health had begun to fail. Wellington subsequently returned the attention and traveled regularly to Deal Castle for friendly visits. William's passing was not without notice, though hardly of the type one might expect. In reading the accounts of his obituaries in the *Gentleman's Magazine,* one may be left aghast. Instead of at least faint words of praise, there are biting critiques of his personality and character. A description of him as a speaker sets the tone: "Other speakers appeared at times to be under the influence of varied feelings, such as triumph or regret, surprise, joy, disgust, or admiration; but Mr. Wellesley Pole was simply angry—angry at all times, with every person, about everything; his sharp, shrill, loud voice grating on the ear as if nature had never intended it should be used for the purpose of giving expression to any agreeable sentiment, or any conciliatory phrase."[57]

The *Times* added that "it must be acknowledged that Mr. Wellesley Pole was an undignified, ineffective speaker, an indiscreet politician, and a man by no means skilful in the conduct of official transactions . . . he was deficient in that sort of practical activity which sometimes obtains for men in high office the reputation of being men of business."[58] As shocking as such comments might be, one is left with the sense of satisfaction that Maryborough had fooled no one.

He was buried in the family vault in Grosvenor Chapel. His wife, Catherine, followed in 1851 at the age of ninety-one. Lest one imagine that these two had no redeeming features, allow their daughters to have the last word: "To the revered memory of those beloved parents, who long lives were examples of uprightness, benevolence, and charity in its most extended sense this tablet is erected by their surviving daughters Emily, Harriet, Lady FitzRoy Somerset and Priscilla Anne, Countess of Westmoreland, in token of their affection, respect and gratitude." Add to that encomium the charming letters sent to his grandchildren, and one sees a different Maryborough in the bosom of his family.[59]

Cowley returned to Paris in September to find the question of the Spanish marriages unresolved and a crisis in North Africa heating up. There the French were preparing to invade Morocco in pursuit of an Algerian rebel. They asked the Moroccans to join in the enterprise but announced that with or without Moroccan cooperation they intended to cross the frontier. Cowley thought this ominous and disagreed with Aberdeen in the foreign secretary's decision to give the French carte blanche as long as they made no attempt to turn Morocco into a French protectorate: "We have, I think, shown too great a readiness to sanction this violation of territory on the part of France, and should their navy be employed and any of the Morocco ports be taken possession of, we shall be great sufferers."[60]

In December 1845, Cowley suffered a bad fall and dislocated both of his shoulders, not to mention the bumps and bruises attendant to such an event. His convalescence lasted several weeks, as would be expected of a man of seventy-two years, and he never really resumed his responsibilities at the embassy. Sir Robert Peel's government fell in June 1846, and Cowley in turn resigned. Within a matter of weeks, the French put an end to the Spanish marriage question. The queen married her cousin, don Francisco, and the Infanta married Louis-Philippe's son, the duc de Montpensier. Greatly relieved that he did not have to deal with the fallout from what everyone perceived as French duplicity,

Cowley and his wife returned to London. They did not stay there long, however, but journeyed back to France to make their home in Paris, partly because they found Paris less expensive and partly because Lady Cowley remained a confidante of Queen Amélie's.[61] At last a casual but interested observer of Anglo-French relations, Cowley viewed Palmerston with a skeptical eye. The bellicose foreign secretary seemed to him the reincarnation of Canning. Then again, Cowley had difficulty accepting the transition to a new generation of leaders and even criticized his queen. On learning of Victoria's public fury over a perceived snub of Albert during a visit to Prussia, he wrote, "Her Britannic Majesty had better stay at home than have these displays of ill-temper and parsimony in a foreign land."[62]

In the winter of 1847, the Cowleys visited the Salisburys at Hatfield House. On their return trip in February, Henry fell ill with what was probably influenza. After several days of violent nausea and fever, he gradually righted himself and appeared to be on the road to recovery. The flu, however, had taken its toll, and in March he came down with a cold that slowly crept into his lungs. "His recovery from his very severe illness appeared to be tolerably certain," wrote Charles Bagot to the duke, "though very slow, till the night before last, when his sleep was bad and he was very restless. Still there appeared no cause for immediate anxiety till late yesterday, and Lady Cowley had hoped all danger was over."[63] But as evening fell on the 27th, his symptoms grew worse, and at 10:00 p.m. he died. Bagot reported that Henry's wife and daughter were "in sad affliction but perfectly well."

The duke received the news with the same restrained grief that had accompanied the previous losses, events that were becoming all too common in his life. Arthur wrote immediately to Henry's youngest son, Gerald, who had been raised by Kitty, and with great care and sensitivity described his father's death. Arthur then urged, according to Lady Cowley's wish, that Gerald proceed to Paris to take charge of his father's remains and the planning of the funeral.[64] The Duke of Richmond wrote to convey his "expression of deep sympathy towards yourself [Wellington], and of sincere sorrow for the deprivation which so many, and none more than myself, feel of so excellent and amiable a man."[65] Cowley was, wrote Mrs. Charles Bagot, "the most charming of all that Wellesley family, and the most lovable." As close to his brothers as he was, Henry maintained an equally close tie with Lord Salisbury, his brother-in-law. Salisbury had looked after Henry's financial affairs and mentored his children during his years in Madrid and Vienna. After Cowley's death, Salisbury was the one who would look after his affairs, sparing Wellington the task.

The following year, it was Gerald's turn; he died on 27 October 1848. The *Gentleman's Magazine* outlined his progress through the church ranks, ending as prebend of Durham, which carried with it £391 a year, but as the magazine pointed out, "this gives no evidence of its real value." In addition there was the living at Bishop Weamouth worth £2,899. There was of course the obvious omission; he had not been a bishop. Nonetheless, the *Gentleman's Magazine* pointed out generously that "Wellesley was much respected by all classes of the community for his kind and conciliatory manners, and the unvarying benevolence of his disposition."[66] Gerald rather than Henry was the most lovable of the Wellesleys, if not the most loved. He died in Durham; there he lies in the great cathedral next to two of his infant grandchildren.

In old age, Wellington's infirmities made him unpredictably irascible. He suffered no more strokes after 1841, and his general health was good for another ten years, though rheumatism made him stooped. Friends, family, and political associates were used to and adjusted to his abrupt manner and insistence on independence. He did not agree with Peel's repeal of the Corn Laws but, as he had done on previous occasions, concluded that it could not be stopped and facilitated the bill's passage. When Peel stepped down, Lord John Russell asked the duke to stay on as commander in chief, an offer that both surprised and pleased him. He worked closely with Russell and often acted as intermediary between the prime minister and the queen. The public had come to view him as above politics, and as such, he became more revered than ever. The queen paid an official visit to Stratfield Saye in 1845, and her accounts attest to the strong attachment she had for him.

As commander in chief, he worried not only about national defense but also about public order, particularly in 1848, when Chartist protests threatened the capital. Here we find him in his seventy-ninth year attending to the challenge as if he were preparing for a great battle. He thought through the problem and then offered clear and thorough solutions. He left nothing to chance. Though the Chartist protests withered and died without serious incident in London, Wellington saw the threat as a part of a broader challenge to British security, and he stepped up his efforts to persuade the government of the need to expand the army.

In 1850 Charles Arbuthnot and Sir Robert Peel died within three months of one another, leaving the duke very much alone. Arbuthnot had been a part of Arthur's life for over thirty years and since his wife's death had lived with the duke. His quiet, genial presence provided Wellington a kind of domestic comfort that he could have found in no one else. "Gosh," as Arbuthnot was affectionately called, had listened appreciatively and sympathetically to the duke's daily woes and of course reminded Arthur of Harriet. Peel's death meant something else entirely. For whatever reason, the two giants of the Tory party had never developed the political intimacy that one would expect. In style and background they were quite different men, but they shared values. Wellington saw in Peel a kind of integrity and devotion to duty that he believed to be fast disappearing. It is, of course, a perception typical of a passing generation, but that hardly changes its significance for a man such as the duke. Certainly Wellington began to wonder whether old age was a blessing even when one retained physical and mental vigor.

And so the duke's last years were in many ways something of a burden. But he had always thrived on burdens, and his response was to keep working. His last great responsibility came in his capacity as ranger of the royal parks. Under normal circumstances, this designation would have been simply honorific, requiring little more than loose supervision of a self-sustaining agency. But 1850 brought construction of Sir Joseph Paxton's Crystal Palace in Hyde Park to house the Great Exhibition of Art and Industry scheduled to open in the spring of 1851. As with all things new and exotic, the whole project appeared foolish to Wellington at first, but as it proceeded he warmed to it. Still, this was work, and he took his role seriously, cooperating carefully and conscientiously with Paxton.

Making Wellington's responsibilities more challenging was the fact that the exhibition brushed up against his role as commander in chief. Planners expected visitors to the exhibition to number in the millions, mostly Britons but foreigners as well. This meant addressing the whole issue of crowd control, and Wellington planned for the worst. This comes as no surprise, as it was the habit of a lifetime, but one must keep in mind that the Chartist protests were still fresh in his mind and that 1848–49 had seen the great explosion of revolutions in continental Europe. Thus, the influx of visitors to London represented to the always-suspicious duke fertile ground for political incendiaries. And so at eighty-one, conceding nothing to age, he created another barrage of seemingly endless memoranda, carefully and intelligently constructed to deal with potential crises. One forgets the energy and concentration demanded by such an effort, in this case of a man always dealing with various levels of physical discomfort.

The exhibition opened smoothly on his birthday in 1851, and before long the duke became an enthusiast. Everything about it—from the setting to the exhibits to the endless lines of people eager to get in—intrigued him. As Neville Thompson points out, the duke became something of an artifact himself as visitors clambered to get close when he made one of his several visits. More important, the Great Exhibition went off without serious incident, in no small part because of Wellington's meticulous planning, and served as a fitting monument to his last years.

The great tragedy of the duke's life was his deafness in that it compromised his great sociability. He loved dinner parties and house parties, but as the years marched on, he could no longer keep up with the conversations that attracted him in the first place. When people had important things to say, they made certain that he heard, but the idle conversation that he so enjoyed was forever lost. Compensation for the loss had to come from individual friendships; with his brothers and Arbuthnot gone, male companionship disappeared, with the exception of the Marquess of Anglesey, to whom he had become warmly attached. They made quite a pair: two doddering old men barking into one another's ear. But Wellington was a ladies' man and always had been, and those females closest to him had died in bewildering succession. There remained his niece Countess Westmoreland (the former Lady Burghersh). In her and her children, he took great delight. The same held true with his daughters-in-law. None, however, filled the gap left first by Harriet Arbuthnot and then Lady Salisbury. Wellington had always been vulnerable to a young and pretty face, and advanced age only seemed to intensify that vulnerability. He had after Harriet's death stumbled into an odd relationship with Anna Maria Jenkins, who was so far removed from the duke's world that their connection could never amount to much more than curiosity or perhaps vicarious lovemaking. Compulsive letter writing often got him into minor difficulties, and such was the case with Miss Jenkins. The same would be true with Lady Georgiana Fane. In his last years, he attached himself to three young women, and in each case, tongues wagged. Least controversial was a new Lady Salisbury (the former Lady Mary Sackville-West), mother of the prime minister, who was clearly stepping into the shoes of her predecessor. Wellington enjoyed being seen with her, but she could never possibly be a confidante. The same would be true of Mrs. Charlotte Jones. Pretty and ambitious, she exposed herself as something of the predator, but the duke could take care of himself, and if he enjoyed the company of a young woman, that was his business.

His relationship with Angela Burdett-Coutts was something different. Heiress to a great banking fortune, she had turned to the duke for advice on various charities. She quickly became infatuated with him. And why would she not? He brought great celebrity, and he clearly knew how to treat women. Thomas Carlyle for one understood the attraction, describing the duke as "truly a beautiful old man. I had never seen till now how beautiful, and what an expression of graceful simplicity, veracity, and nobleness there is about the old hero when you see him close at hand. . . . Eyes beautiful light blue . . . the face wholly gentle, wise, valiant, and venerable."[67] For Wellington, Angela had the advantage of being rich and therefore not suspect on that account. But there is something odd and inexplicable to this relationship. Possessing a fortune, Angela would have been a great catch for some Victorian dandy, but there is no evidence that such suitors came around. Quiet and unprepossessing, she busied herself with the affairs of business and good works. And then she fell in love with Wellington. As usual, he did little to discourage her attentions, and before he knew it, Angela proposed to him. After careful thought, the duke explained (in a letter, of course) why this would be inappropriate for her and for him. Angela took him at his word, but the friendship continued until his death. Most of Wellington's biographers have seen this relationship as strictly platonic. Sir Christopher Hibbert, in his recent take on the subject, is not so sure. Such speculation is fruitless, and one would do better simply to focus on what it says about the duke's emotional state as his life drew to a close. He could never escape his sense of duty and labored to the bitter end in fulfilling it. Clearly he was addicted to work; although he might complain of the "burdens" he bore, he could not do without them. Pleasure, at this stage of his life, came only in the form of feminine companionship. That he had earned the right to choose his companions without reference to contemporary or historical judgment goes without saying. Old men have made greater fools of themselves. In the case of Angela Burdett-Coutts, Wellington's children certainly respected the relationship, including her in his funeral proceedings.

On the morning of 14 September 1852, the duke's valet opened Wellington's curtains, the usual signal that it was time to rise. He did not stir from his camp bed, but clearly he had awakened. Eventually Wellington concluded that something was amiss and requested an apothecary, who prescribed the normal quackery of the day. Then he asked for tea but shortly after suffered a series of seizures and fell into unconsciousness. He was moved to his favorite wing chair, where he remained quietly until 3:30 p.m., when, surrounded by doctors, servants, his second son, and his daughter-in-law, he died, the last of a remarkable generation of Wellesleys.

And so we arrive at the point at which we began, the great state funeral ordered by Queen Victoria for her beloved duke, to which Prince Albert added his flair for the high Victorian style. The queen's first decision was to delay the proceedings until Parliament reconvened in November so that the funeral would truly be a national event. The intervening weeks would be necessary for planning and for construction of the great funeral car and of temporary seating along the procession's route. Wellington's funeral would be the first great public memorial of modern times (though the return of Napoleon's body more than a decade before rivaled it as a public event), and it became the prototype for those that followed, most recently the funeral of Ronald Reagan. In the meantime, the duke's body was embalmed and remained at Walmer, where family and close friends paid their respects. On 10 November, the body was transferred to London, where it would lie in state at Chelsea hospital. There the public could pass by the coffin placed under the rotunda masquerading as a camp tent. After public notables including the queen and the royal family paid their respects, 235,000 people made their pilgrimage in honor of the great hero. They did so despite cold and rain.

18 November broke clear but cold, requiring a sacrifice of comfort for the teeming crowds that packed the streets and buildings along the cortege route to watch the procession of over ten thousand participants. There were mishaps; two people died of funeral-related accidents, the funeral car got stuck along the mall, and the mechanism for unloading the coffin failed, causing a one-hour delay in the funeral service. Still, the event went off rather well, and despite the irony of such grandiosity for a man who in his daily routine craved simplicity, most observers

considered the funeral a great success. Wellington would have appreciated the effort and understood the reasoning behind it.

The two months between death and burial allowed the nation to consider its fallen hero in essay, in verse, and in art. In the contemporary world, one has difficulty in imagining that anyone could reach the iconic level attained by Wellington in the last years of his life. Part of his prominence was attributable to the natural respect and tolerance that civilized societies bestow on the elderly, and Wellington's determination to concede nothing to age only enhanced this tendency. In the last ten years of his life, he continued to attend to his responsibilities with the same discipline that characterized his work in the prime of life. He continued to correspond with astounding regularity and in equally astounding volume. More important, he remained omnipresent in the precincts of Whitehall, though there were those who wished that he had been less conscientious. That he regularly rode from Apsley House to the Horse Guards made him a fixture in Piccadilly and on the mall. Legendary work habits took on visible form in these daily treks, and Londoners loved him for it. More to the point, his instability in the saddle confirmed the great effort that he put forth, during his last days, in the performance of his duty. While it all had the appearance of quaintness and charm, there was another side to his aging. He refused to accept help from anyone at any task, and to those who tried, he gave short shrift. He could be rude and short tempered, but that was allowed. He and Anglesey made quite a pair, usually walking arm in arm when together, Anglesey's wooden leg making him unstable, and Wellington's rheumatism creating the same effect. Mutual support was justified on the grounds that each thought he was helping the other.

Just as in Wellesley's case, Wellington's last years found Britons focusing on the legacy rather than the controversies of a bruising political career. One could look back with the benefit of a broad perspective. The war hero emerged from the vanishing point and grew very large very quickly as he proceeded to the foreground, wearing the laurels of a lifetime of achievements. Wellington had been a great man, and everyone knew that even if they could not articulate why. Even so keen an observer as Charles Grenville had trouble explaining the duke's greatness: "He was beyond all doubt, a very great man—the only great man of the present time—and comparable, in point of greatness, to the most eminent of those who have lived before him. His greatness, was the result of a few striking qualities—a perfect simplicity of character without a particle of vanity or conceit, but with a thorough and strenuous self-reliance, a severe truthfulness, never misled by fancy or exaggeration, and an ever-abiding sense of duty and obligation which made him the humblest of citizens and most obedient of subjects."[68] As an epitaph, this falls short and in some ways misleads. It ignores the toughness of the man, physically and emotionally, and his complexity. Wellington played the role of duke so well that in the public mind he was and is synonymous with British aristocracy. But one must remember that he was the third son in an obscure Irish family whose aristocratic pedigree was not only insignificant but only two generations old. As Mrs. Delaney perceptively pointed out, neither his father nor his mother had the slightest notion of what it meant to be an aristocrat or how to act like one. Wellington became what he was because of his talent, because he was ambitious, because he had help, and because he consciously determined who and what he wanted to be.

Wellesley is more difficult to assess. Unlike the duke, whose persona was steady and predictable—"transparent," as Elizabeth Longford says—Wellesley is a study in contradiction. Unlike Arthur, Richard grew up expecting to occupy a place in the upper reaches of the political and social world. He experienced an education that was both scintillating and posh but discovered that his pedigree and scholarly achievement attracted little attention and that a place in the ruling oligarchy would have to be earned. To be sure, he possessed advantages, but they were far inferior to what he presumed during his idyllic days at Eton and Oxford. Wellesley took several years to work his way into a position where Pitt and Dundas might find him useful. The disappointments of these years had a profound effect on Wellesley, and they manifested themselves in pretense. His pretentiousness masked insecurities that only those closest to him understood. Thus the private Wellesley was genial and witty, whereas in public, he was aloof and arrogant. He very much wanted to be what he had thought he was during his gilded youth and then had been told that he was not. Thus, he took on airs and often embarrassed himself in the process.

India was the family's turning point. In undertaking this grand adventure, Richard, sensing that he might be in over his head, embraced his brothers as collaborators. While William stayed home to look after the family's political and property interests and Gerald embarked on his career in the church, Arthur and Henry found themselves as both servants and guardians of the anointed one—Richard. Favoritism and nepotism were hardly rare in eighteenth-century Britain, so the Welleseys fitted in nicely. This was an extraordinary historical moment for the brothers, and no one could have dreamed that they would make of it what they did. The fact is, they were lucky in many ways. First, distance and time provided a level of independence that could be found nowhere else. Second, they went out at a critical time in Britain's political and diplomatic history, a fact that amplified their independence by distracting the powers-that-be in London. And finally, they arrived in the subcontinent to find a politically uncertain state of affairs—a condition that invited intervention. Richard, determined that he would wager all on this great gamble, took the offensive from the moment he landed. It was his good fortune that Arthur had already taken stock of the opportunities and could provide both guidance and encouragement. Neither Arthur nor Henry imagined that he was anything more than a loyal servant to his brother, but at the same time, Richard desperately needed unqualified support in this new and strange setting. Thus, Arthur and Henry were given opportunities that would never have come their way under different circumstances.

That said, both men, but particularly Arthur, made the best of the opportunities they were given. Success bred confidence, and before long, Arthur interacted with Richard almost as an equal. In fact, it is Arthur's supreme confidence, born at this time, that marks his character more than any other single factor. In India he developed habits that would serve him well for a lifetime. He learned that there was no substitute for meticulous preparation and hard work, that personal supervision was the key to success, that procrastination was a recipe for disaster, and that nothing good could be accomplished without a measure of risk. There was, of course, much more to his education, such as the fact that armies fought better on full stomachs and that cooperation from the local population greatly facilitated campaigning, but the former were qualities that shaped his thoughts and actions throughout his career. Moreover, as in the case of his experience with the Duke of York on his first campaign, India also taught him what not to do. In that, Richard served as a model. Although Arthur greatly admired his eldest brother, he saw serious flaws, most especially Richard's propensity towards extravagance and ostentation. Perhaps more significant, Arthur perceived an unwillingness in Richard to examine ideas and proposals that were not his own.

As for Henry, he learned the skills of administration and diplomacy, first through observation and then through experimentation as governor of the ceded provinces. Henry was less ambitious than his brothers but nonetheless was anxious to find a place in life that carried with it respectability and a chance for advancement. That could be gained only through the auspices of the eldest brother, and therefore Henry proved more compliant than Arthur. Henry, however, was far more personable than his brothers, and people (including both the great and the not so great) took an instant liking to him.

By the time the brothers returned to Britain, they had accomplished much, some of it controversial. They suffered from the fact that most in Britain still saw India as secondary to Europe in terms of the country's vital interests, but their successes could not be ignored. Moreover, they returned to a period of transition as the giants of late eighteenth-century politics—Pitt and Fox—-passed from the scene. For this reason, they found their services much in demand. Thus it was that the trio, joined by William, came to play a central part in the Peninsular War. This was career building at its finest. Ten years earlier, the Wellesley brothers had been nothing more than a footnote to the political and military life of Britain. In this latest drama, they were nearly ubiquitous; not everyone approved, as Arthur found out with the Convention of Cintra. The Wellesleys had risen very high very quickly, and their elevation provoked resentment.

The Peninsular War was to Arthur what India had been to Richard. Just as Richard had become Marquess Wellesley, so did Arthur become the Duke of Wellington. On this occasion, however, even as one brother rose, the other fell. While Arthur managed the war brilliantly, Richard mismanaged his political career. Having long sought a cabinet post, when he finally got it, Richard had not a clue as to what to do with it. Ill suited to the teamwork required in cabinet government, Richard quickly alienated his colleagues and in the process marginalized himself. This brought frustration, followed by desperation, and eventually he conspired to supplant his own prime minister, Spencer Perceval. It all came to naught, and in the summer of 1812, Richard found himself without influence, consigned to the political wilderness. Arthur attributed Richard's failure to the fact that the eldest brother had moved too quickly into the governor-generalship, where he enjoyed something approaching absolute power, and therefore never learned the basics of cabinet government by working his way up through the ranks. There is something to this premise, but it ignores the fact that Wellesley was ill suited, temperamentally, to political life. That he was an eighteenth-century man in the nineteenth-century world of politics is part of the story, but even in the eighteenth century, he would have been something of an outcast.

Wellesley's fall from political grace took a great toll. His personal and public lives in ruins, he collapsed, a nervous wreck. And while he fumbled about embarrassingly, Arthur rose to astonishing heights, particularly after Waterloo. As for Henry and William, they continued to benefit from their family ties: Henry remained in Spain as Britain's ambassador, and William joined the cabinet as master of the mint. Richard, once the family's leader, found himself the odd man out, and Arthur, who stood at the top of the heap, did not deal with the changed circumstance sensitively. Then, to everyone's surprise, Liverpool turned to Wellesley as lord lieutenant of Ireland, and the brothers found themselves colleagues again.

What neither Wellesley nor Wellington was willing to admit was that they could not put their pasts behind them and that in fact they were rivals—if not politically, then personally. Wellington disapproved of his brother, for the opportunities that Richard had squandered and for his licentious and wasteful lifestyle. Wellesley never realized either the disapproval or the reasons for it. Thus, the duke gave his brother only pro forma support and made known among his intimates that to his mind, Wellesley was expendable. Thus, throughout the 1820s, a coolness developed between them, and Wellesley realized the extent of it only when Wellington rejected the marquess as a member of the duke's government in 1828. For the next ten years, they communicated only rarely, and Wellesley took the extraordinary step of joining the Whigs in opposition to the duke.

The great Reform Bill debate made the split worse. Wellington viewed reform as foolish and dangerous and resented Wellesley's active support of it. Wellesley held offices under Grey and Melbourne, even returning to Dublin, and adopted Brougham as his closest confidant—all calculated to embitter the duke. Then everything changed. Wellesley (like Brougham) fell out with the Whigs, and Wellington became less strident in his own views. The softening on both sides allowed for conciliation, and Wellesley's second wife, Marianne, stepped in as mediator. Reconciliation was complete and unqualified, and it extended to all the brothers. As they slipped away, one by one, beginning with Wellesley in 1842, they did so in the bosom of the family, which had come far from its obscure origins in county Meath.

The Wellesleys were as complex as they were remarkable. Richard was vain, arrogant, and often mean spirited. He was also brilliant, perceptive, cultured, imaginative, and generous. One must concede that the negatives far outweighed the positives, but this may be attributed in large part to the expectations placed on him as a young man lacking the resources necessary to meet them. Beyond that, while he was ambitious, he lacked the personality and temperament to successfully pursue those ambitions. Arrogance and ostentation covered basic insecurities and shyness. That he would have been a superb academic is beyond dispute, but under the influence of his ambitious mother, such a thing never entered his mind as the eldest son of a landed family, albeit of an Irish and recently titled one. His character flaws, obvious to everyone, became more pronounced as he entered middle age and were irremediable until he gave up on politics. He stands as almost a case study of a failed political talent, often compared with Lord Curzon. At the same time, even as a spent force, he proved intermittently valuable for both Liverpool and Grey; the power of his intellect could not be ignored.

As for William Wellesley-Pole, Baron Maryborough (and finally third Earl of Mornington), his legacy is minor at best. His most important role was that of a trusted manager of his brothers' affairs while they attended to building their careers. After Waterloo, he and Wellington became inseparable, and over time, William tended to forget how much he owed both Wellesley and Wellington. He possessed an off-putting personality, and had it not been for his brothers, he would without doubt have settled into provincial Irish gentrification. Self-absorbed and self-deluded to the end, his only redeeming features appear to have been exclusively personal—that of husband, father, and grandfather. Still, he provides another view of this family and illuminates the political culture of Great Britain in the early part of the nineteenth century.

Gerald in some ways was the most engaging of the lot. Kind, amiable, intelligent, handsome, and charming, he lacked the ambition of his brothers. Only once, when his brothers suggested that he should be a bishop, did he flirt with pretense. Wellington was right in saying that with all of his brothers either well placed or in positions of real power and influence, Gerald would be warranted in thinking that he could have his share. But that was not to be, and Gerald got over the disappointment quickly and never brought it up again, even when Wellington became prime minister. He survived the embarrassing desertion of his wife and remained a loving and supportive father to his several children. Anyone who had anything to do with Gerald spoke highly of him. In him one finds some semblance of normality.

Much like Arthur and Richard, Henry lived a challenging and frustrating life. He grew up (as the youngest of five brothers) not expecting much, but Richard took good care of him, nurturing his talents and providing him with opportunities that could have come only through influence. Henry, Baron Cowley, made the best of every opportunity, despite the distraction of a failed marriage more embarrassing than even Gerald's. When he took up the embassy in Spain, he confronted problems almost without precedent in the diplomatic corps. The learning curve was steep, but he managed it admirably. Although his efforts were crucial to Arthur's success in the Peninsula, Henry derived little satisfaction from his accomplishments and attracted equally scant recognition from London. To his dismay, he would stay on in liberated Spain until 1821, enduring the contemptible and malicious Ferdinand VII for seven long years. His appointment to the embassy in Vienna seemed an appropriate reward for such thankless service, but while he enjoyed his years there, they were not particularly successful. This was attributable partly to the fact that he served Canning, a man he neither understood nor trusted, and partly to Metternich's manipulation of him. Henry never really found his footing in Vienna. The same could not be said for his last assignment in Paris. There he negotiated with confidence and independence and closed out his career with distinction. Out of this career came a peerage, a result of Arthur's direct intervention. Henry's second marriage, to Georgiana Cecil, proved a great success and provided him with great comfort. Like Gerald, Henry was much loved. He was steady and reliable but vulnerable enough to evoke the protective natures of his older brothers. He did not possess the quick Wellesley intellect, but he had solid common sense (which some of his brothers lacked).

Towering over the family, of course, was Arthur, who lived a life and pursued a career predicated on careful thought. Whether on the battlefield or in Whitehall, his decisions were based on a foundation of sound analysis, thorough preparation, bold engagement, and an established, secure line of retreat should he fail. Always he acted only in the pursuit of a clear goal, whether the liberation of Portugal and Spain, or in defense of the constitution. This is what made him unique and eventually won over the hearts of Britons, even if they disagreed with him. He was indeed steady, reliable, and predictable. A case can be made that on a number of occasions good fortune saw him through not a few precarious positions in the field, but in the end, he never lost a battle. The same cannot be said for his political career. While passage of Catholic emancipation was an act of great political courage, he was out of step on the issue of parliamentary reform. But even in defeat he remained formidable.

He, like his brothers, was not without faults. He was an indifferent and sometimes cruel husband and a demanding and unsympathetic father. Ironically, again like his brothers, he was a superb uncle—generous and understanding. He cultivated a carefully contrived image, the one observed by Charles Greville. "Perfect simplicity of character without a particle of vanity or conceit" is as far from the truth as one can get. From the moment of his first entry into Paris in 1814 until his death, Wellington relished the "great man" role he played. The outrageously flamboyant personalities of the age—the Prince Regent, Alexander of Russia, Metternich—led him into playing a quite different game. He adopted a style of dress that was simple and elegant, suggesting that this was a man comfortable in his own skin. His forthright manner of speech (fashioned during five straight years of campaigning) transferred easily to the negotiating table and to the salons of Europe's capitals, mostly because it was uncommon. Wellington had always been a keen observer; remarkably, he had done so with detachment and never aped the style or behavior of fashionable society. Just as he never betrayed fear before his armies, he never allowed himself to be impressed by mortal men. The same cannot be said for his view of women. The point is, the duke exhibited a good bit of vanity in choosing how to carry himself, and the decision reflects complexity of character, not simplicity.

When he discovered in the years between 1815 and 1819 just how convincing and attractive the image was, it became imbedded. And as if he needed more incentive, that the marquess lived a life of gaudy ostentation made the duke ever more determined to maintain the image. Mrs. Arbuthnot's diary clearly illustrates that the duke encouraged comparisons between the two brothers, and by the 1830s, the disparity between them had become common in social discourse. Lord Mahon commented in 1839, long after the duke had ceased to care, "I think that the most remarkable contrast that history affords is between the Duke of Wellington and Lord Wellesley,—the one scorning all display, the other living for nothing else."[69] This observation sounds remarkably similar to one by Lord Ellesmere: "It was certainly an extraordinary freak of nature," he observed, "which produced from the same stock two such men as Lord Wellesley and his brother Arthur, so eminent and so antipodean in the eminence. If Virgil and Caesar, Pope and Cromwell, had been brothers, the contrast could hardly have been more striking."[70] That Wellington should have encouraged such judgments reveals another dark side to his character. That he was a fiercely competitive man should not come as a surprise, nor should the fact that the competitiveness occasionally manifested itself in unattractive ways. This was just another side of his reluctance to admit error and to exaggerate the obstacles that he faced—on campaigns and in the political arena. Wellington could not stand the thought of failure. He need not have let a man so obviously flawed as Wellesley distract him, but one must remember that they were brothers; such behavior among siblings is more common than not. And in the end, both men let go of their jealousies.

The fact is, to lesser and greater degrees, these were imperfect men, and we should be thankful that they were. Their remarkable successes are ennobled by their weaknesses. That Wellington struggled with such character flaws as disappointment, insecurity, ambition, lust, self-righteousness, and vanity—as we all do—and still accomplished all that he did in such remarkable fashion makes his achievement all the greater. That the marquess could not control these impulses and ultimately failed where his brother succeeded in fact confirms the duke's place in history.

NOTES

ABBREVIATIONS OF ARCHIVAL COLLECTIONS

AHN	Archivo Histórico Nacional (Spain), Madrid
CP	Carver Papers, Hartley Institute, University of Southampton
PMW	Wellesley Papers, British Library (Papers of Marquess Wellesley), London
PRO	Public Record Office of Great Britain, London
RP	Raglan Papers, Gwent Record Office, Cwmbrân
WD	Wellington Dispatches (published)
WID	Wellesley's India Dispatches (published)
WND	Wellington New Dispatches (published)
WP	Wellington Papers, Hartley Institute, University of Southampton
WSD	Wellington Supplementary Dispatches (published)

CHAPTER 1. THE WELLESLEYS OF COUNTY MEATH

1. Brougham, *Historical Sketches,* 268.

2. The best discussions of Wellesley family history appear in Longford, *Wellington: Years of the Sword,* and Butler, *Eldest Brother.* Until the late 1790s, the family spelled its name "Wesley." For consistency, the modern spelling of "Wellesley" will be used throughout. Intending this project to be accessible to the general audience, I have chosen to be spare in my footnotes, citing mostly primary sources but listing published sources when possible.

3. Foster, *Modern Ireland* and *Oxford History of Ireland*; Becket, *Anglo-Irish Tradition*; Moody, Martin, and Byrne, *New History of Ireland.*

4. Becket, *Anglo-Irish Tradition,* 24; Foster, *Modern Ireland,* 12.

5. Foster, *Modern Ireland,* 29.

6. Butler, *Eldest Brother,* 26; Longford, *Wellington: Years of the Sword,* 7; Guedalla, *The Duke,* 9.

7. Foster, *Oxford History of Ireland,* 104–13.

8. Ibid., 100.

9. Ibid., 115–20.

10. Longford, *Wellington: Years of the Sword,* 6; Foster, *Oxford History of Ireland,* 132.

11. Foster, *Oxford History of Ireland,* 124; Longford, *Wellington: Years of the Sword,* 6.

12. Foster, *Modern Ireland,* 173–90; Foster, *Oxford History of Ireland.*

13. Butler, *Eldest Brother,* 26; Longford, *Wellington: Years of the Sword,* 6–7; Guedalla, *The Duke,* 9. See also Pearce, *Memoirs of . . . Wellesley,* 1:1–18.

14. Delany, *Autobiography and Correspondence,* 1:344–46.

15. Foster, *Modern Ireland,* 194.

16. Delany, *Autobiography and Correspondence,* 1:408–9.

17. Ibid., 2:501.

18. Young, *Tour in Ireland.*

19. Delany, *Autobiography and Correspondence,* 2:335.

20. Ibid.

21. Torrens, *Marquess Wellesley,* 1; Butler, *Eldest Brother,* 26; Longford, *Wellington: Years of the Sword,* 9.

22. Delany, *Autobiography and Correspondence,* 3:534–37.

23. Ibid., 3:546. Emphasis in the original.

24. Ibid., 3:534–37; pedigree of the families Wellesley, Cusack, and Colley, drawn up in 1770, PMW, Add. MSS. 13914.

25. Disraeli, *Disraeli's Reminiscences* (1976), 5.

26. PMW, Add. MSS. 37416.

27. Pearce, *Memoirs of . . . Wellesley,* 2:17–19; Butler, *Eldest Brother,* 32–34; PMW, Add. MSS. 37316; Richard Colley Wellesley, *Wellesley Papers: Life and Correspondence* (hereafter cited as the *Wellesley Papers*), 1:6–7.

28. Butler, *Eldest Brother,* 33.

29. Austen-Leigh, *Eton College Register,* xxv–xxxi.

30. Mornington to Grenville, 18 November 1798, Historical Manuscripts Commission, *Manuscripts of J. B. Fortescue,* 4:381 (hereafter cited as the *Dropmore Papers*).

31. Austen-Leigh, *Eton College Register,* 555.

32. PMW, Add. MSS. 13914.

33. Longford, *Wellington: Years of the Sword,* 14.

34. Wellesley to Montgomery, 22 September 1838, PMW, Add. MSS. 37316.

35. Lady Stafford to Granville, 14 May 1787, in Granville, *Private Correspondence,* 1:8.

CHAPTER 2. RICHARD TAKES CHARGE

1. Lady Mornington to Mornington, 13 July 1781, PMW, Add. MSS. 37416.

2. Disraeli, *Disraeli's Reminiscences,* 5. This rumor is generally attributed to Lord Wellesley, but Disraeli says the duke also suggested it. Wellesley's

son-in-law, Lord Hatherton, relates the story in his diaries, Hatherton Papers, Staffordshire Record Office.

3. Austen-Leigh, *Eton College Register,* xxvi–xxxi, 555.

4. Longford, *Wellington: Pillar of State,* 14; Gleig, *Life of Arthur,* 4.

5. Mornington to Grenville, 30 November 1783, *Dropmore Papers,* 1:225.

6. Mornington to Grenville, 15 September 1783, ibid., 1:220.

7. Mornington to Grenville, 12 July 1782, ibid., 1:162–63.

8. Mornington to Grenville, 1 August 1782, ibid., 1:163–64.

9. Ibid.

10. Temple to Grenville, 2 January 1783, ibid., 1:175–76.

11. Mornington to Grattan, 9 December 1782, PMW, Add. MSS. 37308; *Wellesley Papers,* 1:9–10; Pearce, *Memoirs of . . . Wellesley,* 1:24–27.

12. Pearce, *Memoirs of . . . Wellesley,* 1:29–30.

13. Austen-Leigh, *Eton College Register,* xxvi–xxxi, 555.

14. This is well documented in Gleig's, Longford's, and Butler's works. See also Austen-Leigh, *Eton College Register.*

15. Longford, *Wellington: Years of the Sword,* 17–19.

16. Ibid., 19–20.

17. Gleig, *Life of Arthur,* 7–8; Longford, *Wellington: Years of the Sword.*

18. Mornington to Grenville, 16 March 1784, *Dropmore Papers,* 1:225.

19. Grenville to Temple, 27 March 1783, in Buckingham, *Memoirs of the Court . . . of George III,* 1:209–11.

20. Mornington to Temple, 10 April 1784, ibid., 1:227; Pearce, *Memoirs of . . . Wellesley,* 1:32.

21. This passage translates as "All fortune is to be overcome by bearing."

22. Mornington to Grenville, 7 November 1784, Mornington to Grenville, 26 January 1785, *Dropmore Papers,* 1:246.

23. Mornington to Grenville, 1 April 1785, ibid., 1:250.

24. *Times,* 18 September, 7 August, 30 October 1786.

25. Buckingham to Grenville, 4 August 1786, *Dropmore Papers,* 1:264–65.

26. *Times,* 20 January 1786.

27. *Times,* 20 September 1787.

28. Gerald Wellesley II to Richard Wellesley II, 30 July 1822, CP, A751/10.

29. Again, the best work on this is Butler, *Eldest Brother.*

30. Buckingham to Grenville, 13 August 1786, *Dropmore Papers,* 1:264–65.

31. Buckingham to Grenville, 7 September 1786, ibid., 1:267.

32. Pearce, *Memoirs of . . . Wellesley,* 1:32–34; *Times,* 3 June 1786; *Wellesley Papers,* 1:15–16.

33. *Wellesley Papers,* 1:14.

34. Mornington to Grenville, 8 October 1786, *Dropmore Papers,* 1:220.

35. *Times,* 8 May 1787; George III to Pitt, 24 June 1787, in Aspinall, *Later Correspondence of King George III,* 1:306; Pitt to George III, 24 June 1787, ibid., 1:306; *Times,* 3, 6, 11, and 20 July 1787, 29 November 1787.

36. *Times,* 8 and 13 September 1787, 18 October 1787; Mornington to Grenville, 31 October 1787, *Dropmore Papers,* 1:287–88.

37. Buckingham to Grenville, 13 May 1788, *Dropmore Papers.*

38. *Times,* 13 May 1788.

39. Mornington to Buckingham, 15 November 1788, in Buckingham, *Memoirs of the Court . . . of George III,* 1:456–57.

40. Pitt to George III, 13 June 1790, in Aspinall, *Later Correspondence of King George III,* I:483; George III to Pitt, 12 June 1790, ibid., I:484; *Times,* 13 June 1789.

41. Mornington to Grenville, 25 August 1790, *Dropmore Papers,* 1:593–94.

42. Mornington to Grenville, 27 September 1790, ibid., 1:607–9.

43. Ibid.

44. Ibid. Emphasis in the original.

45. Ibid.

46. Ibid.

47. Ibid.

48. Mornington to Grenville, 4 January 1791, ibid., 2:3–6.

49. Ibid.

50. Ibid.

51. Mornington to Grenville, 3 July 1791, ibid., 2:117–20.

52. Ibid.

53. See Black, *British Foreign Policy.*

54. Stanhope, *Life of . . . Pitt,* 1:309.

55. Great Britain, *Cobbett's Parliamentary History.* This work precedes the *Parliamentary Debates.* The debates are divided into five series: one, 1803–20; two, 1820–30; three, 1830–91; four, 1892–1908; five, 1909 to the present. Each series is numbered separately. Butler, *Eldest Brother,* 73.

56. Great Britain, *Cobbett's Parliamentary History,* vol. 30.

57. Ibid.

58. Ibid.

59. Ibid., 7 May 1793.

60. George III to Pitt, 21 June 1793, in Aspinall, *Later Correspondence of King George III,* 2:53.

61. Mornington to Addington, 26 August 1793, in Pellew, *Life . . . of . . . Addington,* 1:103.

62. Mornington to Addington, 8 November 1793, ibid., 1:112.

63. Addington to Mornington, November 1793, ibid., 1:104.

64. Jupp, *Letter-Journal of George Canning,* 28–29.

65. Ibid., 48.

66. Pearce, *Memoirs of . . . Wellesley,* 1:72–119; Great Britain, *Cobbett's Parliamentary History,* 30:1009–74.

67. Great Britain, *Cobbett's Parliamentary History,* 30:1009–74.

68. Ibid.

69. Ibid.

70. Ibid.

71. Ibid.

72. Maxwell, *Life of . . . Wellington,* 1:54.

73. Mornington to Grenville, 27 October 1787, *Dropmore Papers,* 1:286–87.

74. Mornington to Grenville, 4 November 1787, ibid., 1:287.

75. Mornington to Grenville, 7 November 1787, ibid., 1:289.

76. Llangollen Ladies, *Hamwood Papers,* 27 January 1788, 72; Longford, *Wellington: Years of the Sword,* 32–33.

77. Longford, *Wellington: Years of the Sword,* 37–39; Gleig, *Life of Arthur.*

78. Longford, *Wellington: Years of the Sword,* 38–42.

79. Ibid.

80. Venn, *Alumni Cantabrigienses,* 406.

81. Cowley, *Diary and Correspondence,* 17; Henry Wellesley's Memoir, Cowley Papers, PRO, F.O. 519/67.

82. Henry Wellesley's Memoir, Cowley Papers, PRO, F.O. 519/67.

83. Ibid.

84. Ibid.

85. Mornington to Grenville, 4 January 1791, *Dropmore Papers,* 2:10; 3 July 1791, ibid., 2:117–20; 14 August 1791, ibid., 2:165.

86. Grenville to Auckland, 19 August 1791, ibid., 2:168–69.

87. Henry Wellesley's Memoir, Cowley Papers, PRO, F.O. 519/67; Mornington to Grenville, 4 September 1791, *Dropmore Papers,* 2:184; Auckland to Grenville, 12 September 1791, ibid., 2:189; Auckland to Grenville, 29 October 1791, ibid., 2:219.

88. Henry Wellesley's Memoir, Cowley Papers, PRO, F.O. 519/67.

89. Ibid.; Mornington to Grenville, 4 August 1793, *Dropmore Papers,* 2:411.

90. Henry Wellesley's Memoir, Cowley Papers, PRO, F.O. 519/67; Mornington to Grenville, 27 December 1793, *Dropmore Papers,* 2:486; Mornington to Grenville, 18 December 1793, ibid., 2:479–80.

91. Lady Anne Wesley to Ladies, 15 September 1789, Llangollen Ladies, *Hamwood Papers,* journal entries, 9 January and 15 January 1790, 245–46.

92. Henry Wellesley's Memoir, Cowley Papers, PRO, F.O. 519/67.

93. Ibid.

94. Ibid.

95. Ibid.

96. Mornington to Grenville, 15 July 1794, *Dropmore Papers,* 2:599; Mornington to Addington, 27 July 1794, in Pellew, *Life . . . of . . . Addington,* 1:124.

97. *Times,* 4 March 1794.

98. Henry Wellesley's Memoir, Cowley Papers, PRO, F.O. 519/67.

99. Mornington to Addington, 3 May 1794, in Pellew, *Life . . . of . . . Addington,* 1:123.

100. Ibid., 27 July 1794, 1:124.

101. Ibid.

102. Pitt to George III, 21 September 1795, George III to Pitt, 22 September 1795, in Aspinall, *Later Correspondence of King George III,* 2:406–7.

103. Mornington to Addington, 4 September 1796, in Pellew, *Life . . . of . . . Addington,* 1:174.

104. Arthur Wellesley to Mornington, 27 July 1797, WSD, 1:17–18.

105. Pitt to George III, 30 October 1797, in Aspinall, *Later Correspondence of King George III,* 2:626–27; Portland to Mornington, 5 October 1797, PMW, Add. MSS. 37308.

106. Mornington to Addington, 14 October 1797, in Pellew, *Life . . . of . . . Addington,* 1:196.

107. Mornington to Grenville, November–December 1795, *Dropmore Papers,* 3:149.

108. Henry Wellesley's Memoir, Cowley Papers, PRO, F.O. 519/67; Malmesbury to Grenville, 6 August 1797, in Granville, *Private Correspondence,* 1:167.

109. Granville to Mother, 11 July 1797, in Granville, *Private Correspondence,* 1:161.

110. Malmesbury, *Diaries and Correspondence,* 14 July 1797, 3:408.

111. *Dropmore Papers,* 31 July–6 August 1797, 3:338–45.

112. Malmesbury to Grenville, 6 August 1797, in Malmesbury, *Diaries and Correspondence,* 3:447; Mornington to Grenville, 29 July 1797, *Dropmore Papers,* 3:336.

113. Malmesbury to Canning, 29 August 1797, in Malmesbury, *Diaries and Correspondence,* 3:519; Grenville to Malmesbury, 27 July 1797, *Dropmore Papers,* 3:335.

CHAPTER 3. THE INDIA ADVENTURE BEGINS

1. Arthur Wellesley to Mornington, 17 April 1797, WSD, 1:4–5.

2. Arthur Wellesley to Mornington, 20 May 1797, ibid., 1:6–8; Arthur Wellesley to Mornington, 12 July 1797, ibid., 1:12–13.

3. Arthur Wellesley to Mornington, 12 July 1997, ibid., 1:16.

4. Arthur Wellesley to Mornington, 27 July 1997, ibid., 1:17–18.

5. CP, A751/113, translations by Iris Butler. See also Butler, *Eldest Brother.*

6. Pole to Mornington, 8 July 1796, CP, A751/14; Mornington to Pole, 31 October 1797, PMW, Add. MSS. 37416.

7. List of books taken to India, PMW, Add. MSS. 13899; letter book to Mornington's wife, written on the voyage out to India, CP, A751/1; Lady Anne Mornington (mother) to Mornington, 4 November 1797, PMW, Add. MSS. 37416.

8. Butler, *Eldest Brother,* 100–109; CP, A751/1.

9. Henry Wellesley's Memoir, Cowley Papers, PRO, F.O. 519/67; Mornington to Dundas, 28 February 1798, WID, 1:30. The original documents are preserved in the British Library as the Wellesley Papers.

10. See Dundas, *Two Views of British India.*

11. Mornington to Dundas, 28 February 1798, WID, 1:17–34.

12. Ibid.

13. A nawab is a Muslim king or chief, though the term is also used as a courtesy title unattended by any power.

14. Henry Wellesley's Memoir, Cowley Papers, PRO, F.O. 519/67; Correspondence with the Nabob of the Carnatic, WID, 1:35–39.

15. Hickey, *Memoirs,* 4:200.

16. WID, Proclamation at the Isle of France, 1:viii–x.

17. A search after the battle of Seringapatam found Tipu's political archives intact.

18. Mornington to Harris, 9 June 1798, WID, 1:54.

19. Minute, 12 June 1798, ibid., 1:54–58; Mornington to Tipu, 14 June 1798, ibid., 1:59–61.

20. Mornington to Harris, 26 June 1798, ibid., 1:66–67.

21. Harris to Mornington, 6 July 1798, ibid., 1:67–70.

22. Observations of Mornington's Minute, 28 June 1798, WSD, 1:52–55; memoranda, July 1798, WSD, 1:72–79.

23. Webbe to Harris, 6 July 1798, WID, 1:72–79.

24. Mornington to Dundas, 6 July 1798, ibid., 1:82–83.

25. Mornington to Kirkpatrick, 8 July 1798, ibid., 1:94–110.

26. Ibid.

27. Mornington to Harris, 18 July 1798, ibid., 1:135–43; Governor-General in Council to Ft. St. George, 13 July 1798, ibid., 1:234–35.

28. Mornington to Harris, 16 August 1798, ibid., 1:211–16; Secret Committee to Mornington, 10 July 1798, ibid., 1:214–16; Harris to Mornington, 22 July 1798, ibid., 1:145–46; Harris to Mornington, 29–30 July 1798, ibid., 1:148–49.

29. Mornington to Palmer, 8 July 1798, ibid., 1:117–25.

30. Mornington to Clive, 29 July 1798, ibid., 1:223–32.

31. Clive to Mornington, 22 September 1799, ibid., 1:267–68; Mornington to Harris, 16 August 1798, ibid., 1:211–12.

32. Arthur Wellesley to Mornington, 28 July 1798, WSD, 1:70–71.

33. Arthur Wellesley to Henry Wellesley, 14 October 1798, ibid., 1:107–8; Mornington to Dundas, 11 October 1798, WID, 1:288–99.

34. Court of Directors to Mornington, 18 June 1798, WID, 1:61–64; Mornington to Kirkpatrick, 11 August 1798, 14 August 1798, 31 August 1798, WID, 1:158–59, 209–10, 349–52, respectively; Mornington to Arthur Wellesley, 17 August 1798, WP, 1/7.

35. Mornington to Clive, 24 September 1798, WID, 1:268–69.

36. Nizam to Mornington, 27 September 1798, ibid., 1:270–72.

37. Arthur Wellesley to Mornington, 25 September 1798, WSD, 1:96–97.

38. Arthur Wellesley to Henry Wellesley, 7 October 1798, ibid., 1:104–5; Arthur Wellesley to Henry Wellesley, 14 October 1798, ibid., 1:107–8; Arthur Wellesley to Mornington, 15 September 1798, ibid., 1:85–90.

39. Arthur Wellesley to Henry Wellesley, 19 October 1798, ibid., 1:108–10.

40. Arthur Wellesley to Henry Wellesley, 24 October 1798, ibid., 1:118–19; Arthur Wellesley to Henry Wellesley, 23 October 1798, ibid., 1:117–18.

41. Arthur Wellesley to Henry Wellesley, 19 October 1798, ibid., 1:109–10.

42. Mornington to Dundas, 12 November 1798, WID, 1:339; Grenville to Dundas, 20 September 1798, *Dropmore Papers*, 4:319; Dundas to Grenville, 28 September 1798, ibid., 4:326.

43. Harris to Mornington, 29 October 1798, WID, 1:318; Arthur Wellesley to Henry Wellesley, 28 October 1798, WSD, 1:124–25; Malcolm to Arthur Wellesley, 12 October 1798, WP 1/7.

44. Mornington to Tipu Sultaun, 4 November 1798, WID, 1:321–22.

45. Mornington to Tipu Sultaun, 18 November 1798, ibid., 1:326–28.

46. Mornington to Clive, 14 November 1798, ibid., 1:344; Mornington to Kirkpatrick, 9 November 1798, ibid., 1:328–37.

47. Dundas to Mornington, 16 June 1798 (received 20 November 1798), ibid., 1:348–52.

48. Clive to Mornington, 29 November 1798, ibid., 1:361.

49. Arthur Wellesley to Mornington, 22 November 1798, WSD, 1:130–33; Arthur Wellesley to Henry Wellesley, 26 November 1798, ibid., 1:135; Arthur

Wellesley to Mornington, 19 September 1798, ibid., 1:88–92; Arthur Wellesley to Henry Wellesley, 26 November 1798, ibid., 1:133–35; Arthur Wellesley to Henry Wellesley, 14 December 1798, ibid., 1:139–40.

50. Minute of the Governor General, 12 August 1998, ibid., 1:159–208.

51. Mornington to Dundas, 26 November 1798, in Dundas, *Two Views of British India,* 112–13; Arthur Wellesley to Henry Wellesley, 12 October 1798, WSD, 1:106–7.

52. Clive to Mornington, 17 December 1798, WID, 1:380–81; Arthur Wellesley to Henry Wellesley, 2 January 1799, WSD, 1:152–59; WP 1/5, copies of letters between Aston and Picton; WP 1/7, Aston to Arthur Wellesley, 13 December 1798; WP 1/7, B. Close to Arthur Wellesley, 19 December 1798.

53. Tipu to Mornington, 18 December 1798, WID, 1:381.

54. Minute of the Governor General, 2 January 1799, WID 1:391–93; Clive to Mornington, 31 December 1798, ibid., 1:389–91.

55. Mornington to Tipu, 9 January 1799, ibid., 1:394–97; Tipu to Mornington, 2 January 1799, ibid., 1:393.

56. Mornington to Dundas, 12 January 1799, in Dundas, *Two Views of British India,* 119–20.

57. Mornington to Court of Directors, 13 January 1799, WID, 1:404–11.

58. Arthur Wellesley to Mornington, 29 January 1799, WSD, 1:187.

59. Mornington to Arthur Wellesley, 2 February 1799, ibid., 1:187–88.

60. Mornington to Harris, 3 February 1799, WID, 1:426–27; Mornington to Grenville, 21 February 1799, *Dropmore Papers,* 1:474–76.

61. Mornington to Grenville, 18 November 1798, *Dropmore Papers,* 4:382–84.

CHAPTER 4. TIGER HUNT

1. Arthur Wellesley to Mornington, 27 February 1799, WSD, 1:195–96; Arthur Wellesley to Mornington, 16 February 1799, ibid., 1:193–94; Arthur Wellesley to Mornington, 4 February 1799, ibid., 1:191–93.

2. Mornington to Harris, 25 February 1799, WID, 1:472–73.

3. Mornington to Harris, 22 February 1799, WID, 1:442–48; Arthur Wellesley to Mornington, 27 February 1799, WSD, 1:195–96.

4. Arthur Wellesley to Mornington, 27 February 1799, WSD, 1:195–200.

5. Harris to Mornington, 2 February 1799, WID, 1:425.

6. Arthur Wellesley to Henry Wellesley, 9 March 1799, WSD, 1:200.

7. Arthur Wellesley to Mornington, 25 March 1799, ibid., 1:206.

8. Anstruther to Mornington, 27 March 1799, WID, 1:506–8.

9. Mornington to Palmer, 19 February 1799, ibid., 1:439–41; Mornington to Peshwa, 24 February 1799, ibid., 1:466–68; Mornington to Palmer, 3 April 1799, ibid., 1:509–13.

10. Tipu to Harris, 9 April 1799, WID, 1:522.

11. Arthur Wellesley to Mornington, 5 April 1799, WSD, 1:206–8; Arthur Wellesley to Mornington, 25 March 1799, ibid., 1:206.

12. Arthur Wellesley to Mornington, 18 April 1799, ibid., 1:209.

13. Tipu to Harris, 28 April 1799, WID, 1:560; Tipu to Harris, 20 April 1799, and Harris to Tipu, 20 April 1799, ibid., 1:538.

14. Harris to Mornington, 4 May 1799, ibid., 1:568–69.

15. Arthur Wellesley to Mornington, 8 May 1799, WSD, 1:212–17.

16. Ibid.

17. Mornington to Court of Directors, 11 May 1799, WID, 1:577–78.

18. Arthur Wellesley to Mornington, 8 May 1799, WSD, 1:212–16.

19. Alured Clarke to Mornington, 28 May 1799, WID, 2:16; Mornington to Harris, 12 May 1799, ibid., 1:578–80; Mornington to Dundas, 19 May 1799, in Dundas, *Two Views of British India,* 154–57.

20. Mornington to Harris, 14 May 1799, WID, 2:9; Mornington to Kirkpatrick, 5 June 1799, ibid., 2:25–34; Mornington to Commission, 20 May 1799, ibid., 2:10–12; Mornington to Arthur Wellesley, 20 May 1799, WSD, 1:220–21; Arthur Wellesley to Mornington, 8 May 1799, ibid., 1:216.

21. Baird, *Life of,* 1:226.

22. Agnew (Military Secretary) to Baird, 8 May 1799, in Pearce, *Memoirs of . . . Wellesley,* 1:428; Agnew (Military Secretary) to Baird, 8 May 1799, in Baird, *Life of,* 1:238–39. Emphasis in the original.

23. Arthur Wellesley to Mornington, 23 May 1799, WSD, 1:219–22; Beatson to Mornington, 6 May 1799, in Pearce, *Memoirs of . . . Wellesley,* 1:302–3.

24. Mornington to Dundas, 7 June 1799, WID, 2:40–41. Concerning Tipu's archive: Mornington to Court, 19 May 1799, WID, 1:691–92; memoranda, WSD, 1:230–32; Arthur Wellesley to Mornington, 23 May 1799, ibid., 1:219–22.

25. General Order, 2 June 1799, WID, 2:34–35; Mornington to Arthur Wellesley, 30 May 1799, WSD, 1:236–38.

26. Arthur Wellesley to Mornington, 2 June 1799, ibid., 1:234–35.

27. Ibid., 3 June 1799, 1:236–41.

28. Mornington to Arthur Wellesley, 10 June 1799, ibid., 1:242–43.

29. Pearce, *Memoirs of . . . Wellesley,* 1:342–46.

30. Mornington to Arthur Wellesley, 19 June 1799, WSD, 1:246; Arthur Wellesley to Mornington, 14 June 1799, ibid., 1:242–46.

31. Harris to Mornington, 13 May 1799, WID, 2:7–8.

32. Mornington to Commission, 20 May 1799, ibid., 2:10–12; Mornington to Kirkpatrick, 5 June 1799, ibid., 2:25–34; Mornington to Dundas, 7 June 1799, ibid., 2:35–43; Copy of Treaty, ibid., 2:26–33; Mornington to Palmer, 23 May 1799, ibid., 2:12–14; Mornington to Palmer, 12 June 1799, ibid., 2:51–52.

33. Mornington to Commission, 4 June 1797, ibid., 2:18–21.

34. Mornington to Dundas, 7 June 1799, ibid., 2:38.

35. Mornington to Palmer, 4 July 1799, ibid., 2:68–69; Mornington to Kirkpatrick, 30 June 1799, ibid., 2:60–68.

36. Arthur Wellesley to Mornington, 23 June 1799, WSD, 1:250.

37. Dundas to Mornington, 18 March 1799, in Dundas, *Two Views of British India,* 130–35; Dundas to Mornington, 21 March 1799, WID, 2:106–10.

38. Mornington to Court of Directors, 3 August 1799, WID, 2:88–89.

39. Mornington to Dundas, 7 June 1799, ibid., 2:38.

40. Mornington to Dundas, 16 May 1799, in Dundas, *Two Views of British India,* 151–53. Emphasis in the original.

41. Mornington to Pitt, 8 August 1799, in Stanhope, *Life of . . . Pitt,* 3:191.

42. Hickey, *Memoirs,* 4:227.

43. Mornington to Dundas, 31 July 1799, in Dundas, *Two Views of British India,* 167–73; Mornington to Dundas, 8 May 1798, ibid., 45–46; Mornington

to Dundas, 6 October 1798, ibid., 86–90; Mornington to Dundas, 12 January 1799, ibid., 118–19.

44. Arthur Wellesley to Mornington, 23 June 1799, WSD, 1:250; Arthur Wellesley to Mornington, 24 June 1799, ibid., 1:251.

45. Arthur Wellesley to Mornington, 18 July 1799, ibid., 1:273; Mornington to Dundas, 29 January 1800, WID, 2:202–3; Henry Wellesley's Memoir, Cowley Papers, PRO, F.O. 519/67.

46. Arthur Wellesley to Mornington, 17 August 1799, WSD, 1:289; Mornington to Dundas, 29 January 1800, WID, 2:202–3.

47. Dundas to Mornington, 4 November 1799, in Dundas, *Two Views of British India,* 209–11; Mornington to Hyacinthe, January 1800, CP, A751/3, A751/113, translations by Iris Butler.

48. Mornington to Dundas, 25 January 1800, in Dundas, *Two Views of British India,* 214–18.

49. Mornington to Dundas, 5 March 1800, ibid., 253–55.

50. Mornington to Pitt, 29 April 1800, in Stanhope, *Life of . . . Pitt,* 3:232–33; Mornington to Pitt, 29 April 1800, WID, 2:264.

51. Wellesley to Dundas, 29 April 1800, in Dundas, *Two Views of British India,* 257–61; Wellesley to Dundas, 29 April 1800, WID, 2:262–63.

52. Wellesley to Hyacinthe, 28 April 1800, CP, A751/3.

53. See Butler, *Eldest Brother,* 219–30.

54. *Times,* 10 September 1803.

55. Mornington to Clarke, 17 April 1799, WID, 1:528; Wellesley to Dundas, 8 June 1800, in Dundas, *Two Views of British India,* 265–67. Emphasis in the original.

56. Wellesley to Lady Anne Barnard, 2 October 1800, in Lindsay, *Lives of the Lindsays,* 3:404.

57. Wellesley to Pitt, 29 April 1800, and Wellesley to Dundas, 29 April 1800, WID, 2:262–64. Arthur supported Richard but warned him that he might end up with nothing: Arthur Wellesley to Wellesley, 3 December 1800, WSD, 2:316–17; Wellesley to Arthur Wellesley, 1 December 1800, 2:316.

58. Notes on the Foundation of the College of Fort William, 10 July 1800, WID, 2:325–55.

59. Governor General in Council to Court of Directors, 9 July 1800, ibid., 2:323.

60. Notes on the College, 10 July 1800, ibid., 2:329.

61. Dundas to Wellesley, 4 September 1800, in Dundas, *Two Views of British India,* 294–95. Emphasis in the original.

62. Dundas to Wellesley, 26 September 1800, WID, 2:376.

63. Henry Wellesley's Memoir, Cowley Papers, PRO, F.O. 519/67; Dundas to Wellesley, 11 September 1800, in Dundas, *Two Views of British India,* 297–99; Malmesbury to Grenville, 29 July 1797, *Dropmore Papers,* 3:336.

CHAPTER 5. ARTHUR: FROM MYSORE TO THE MARATHA WAR

1. Harris to Mornington, 15 June 1799, WID, 2:53.
2. Agnew to Arthur Wellesley, 24 August 1799, WSD, 1:290–91.
3. Arthur Wellesley to Agnew, 31 August 1799, ibid., 1:303–4.

4. General Order of General Harris, 11 September 1799, WID, 1:41; Mornington to Court of Directors, 3 September 1797, WID, 2:117; Arthur Wellesley to Harris, 4 December 1799, WSD, 1:405.

5. Arthur Wellesley to Sydenham, 16 January 1800, WSD, 1:432–33.

6. Arthur Wellesley to Close, 14 February 1800, ibid., 1:450–51; Arthur Wellesley to Kirkpatrick, 9 April 1800, ibid., 1:509–11.

7. Arthur Wellesley to Kirkpatrick, 21 April 1800, ibid., 1:529.

8. Mornington to Arthur Wellesley, 13 May 1800, WID, 2:46.

9. Webbe to Arthur Wellesley, 24 May 1800, WD, 1:48–49.

10. Clive to Arthur Wellesley, 26 May 1800, ibid., 1:49–50; Webbe to Arthur Wellesley, 25 May 1800, WSD, 2:1–2.

11. Mornington to Arthur Wellesley, 6 June 1800, WD, 1:54–55; Arthur Wellesley to Mornington, 29 May 1800, ibid., 1:52–54; Close to Arthur Wellesley, 29 May 1800, ibid., 1:50–51.

12. Arthur Wellesley to Close, 3 July 1800, WSD, 2:47–48.

13. Arthur Wellesley to Close, 31 July 1800, WD, 1:58–60; Arthur Wellesley to Secretary of Government, 18 August 1800, WSD, 2:112–14.

14. Arthur Wellesley to Munro, 20 August 1800, WD, 1:64–66.

15. Wellesley to Clive, 23 August 1800, WID, 2:367–69; Governor-General in Council to Secret Committee of Court of Directors, 31 August 1800, WD, 1:66–70.

16. Arthur Wellesley to Kirkpatrick, 10 September 1800, WSD, 2:143; Arthur Wellesley to Munro, 11 September 1800, WD, 1:72–73.

17. Arthur Wellesley to Adjutant General, 10 September 1800, WD, 1:75–77.

18. Wellesley to Wife, 15 September 1800, CP #3; see also Butler, *Eldest Brother.*

19. Governor-General in Council to Secret Committee of the Court of Directors, 3 October 1800, WD, 1:79–*20. The asterisk denotes pagination discrepancy in the published volume.

20. Mornington to Dundas, 5 March 1800, WID, 2:225–49.

21. Elgin to Mornington, 16 November 1799, ibid., 2:143–45; Elgin to Wellesley, 5 February 1800, ibid., 2:205–6; Sidney Smith to Mornington, 9 November 1799, ibid., 2:139–41; Sidney Smith to Wellesley, 27 June 1800, ibid., 2:299–305.

22. Wellesley to Rainier, 9 July 1800, ibid., 2:311.

23. Ingram, "Geopolitics of the First British Expedition."

24. Wellesley to Clive, 18 October 1800, WSD, 2:263–64.

25. Wellesley to Curtis, 24 October 1800, ibid., 2:406–9; Wellesley to Dundas, 25 October 1800, ibid., 2:410–12.

26. Wellesley to Arthur Wellesley, 5 November 1800, WD, 1:*22–23; Wellesley to Arthur Wellesley, 5 November 1800, WID, 2:413–15.

27. Wellesley to Arthur Wellesley, 1 December 1800, WSD, 2:315–16; Wellesley to Arthur Wellesley, 1 December 1800, WD, 1:*36–37.

28. Wellesley to Clive, 15 November 1800, WD, 1:*25–27.

29. Ingram, "Geopolitics of the First British Expedition."

30. Arthur Wellesley to Wellesley, 19 December 1800, WSD, 2:305–6.

31. Wellesley to Arthur Wellesley, 21 December 1800, WD, 1:*46–47; Wellesley to Arthur Wellesley, 21 December 1800, WSD, 2:323–25.

32. Ingram, "Geopolitics of the First British Expedition."
33. Arthur Wellesley to Wellesley, 8 January 1801, WSD, 2:323–26.
34. Wellesley to Arthur Wellesley, 24 January 1801, ibid., 2:333.
35. Wellesley to Arthur Wellesley, 5 February 1801, WD, 1:*59–60; Wellesley to Rainier, 5 February 1801, ibid., 1:59.
36. Arthur Wellesley to Governor of Ceylon, 18 February 1801, ibid., 1:*69–70.
37. Arthur Wellesley to North, 18 February 1801, ibid., 1:*69.
38. Wellesley to Arthur Wellesley, 10 February 1801, WSD, 2:356.
39. Arthur Wellesley to Henry Wellesley, 23 March 1801, WD, 1:*82–83.
40. Henry Wellesley to Arthur Wellesley, 28 March 1801, ibid., 1:*85.
41. Wellesley to Arthur Wellesley, 28 March 1801, ibid., 1:*85.
42. Arthur Wellesley to Champagné, 11 April 1801, ibid., 1:*99.
43. Arthur Wellesley to Wellesley, 10 April 1801, WSD, 2:350–51; Arthur Wellesley to Webbe, 7 April 1801, WD, 1:*88–89.
44. Henry Wellesley to Arthur Wellesley, 22 April 1811, WSD, 2:364.
45. Arthur Wellesley to Wellesley, 16 April 1801, ibid., 2:362.
46. Henry Wellesley to Arthur Wellesley, 5 June 1801, ibid., 2:409–10; Arthur Wellesley to Henry Wellesley, 26 May 1801, ibid., 2:407–9.
47. Arthur Wellesley to Henry Wellesley, 4 June 1801, ibid., 2:424–25.
48. Arthur Wellesley to Henry Wellesley, 8 July 1801, ibid., 2:501–2.

CHAPTER 6. HENRY STEPS FORWARD

1. Wellesley to Nawab of Carnatic, 24 April 1799, WID, 1:541–54.
2. Ibid.
3. Omdut ul Omra to Wellesley, 13 May 1799, ibid., 2:1–7.
4. Butler, *Eldest Brother,* 207.
5. Wellesley to Clive, 17 April 1800, WID, 2:254–55.
6. Clive to Wellesley, 23 May 1800, British Library,India Office, Home Misc. Series 460.
7. Ibid.
8. Wellesley to Secret Committee, 9 June 1800, WID, 2:273.
9. Dundas to Wellesley, 4 September 1800, in Dundas, *Two Views of British India,* 288–89.
10. Wellesley to Clive, 28 May 1801, WID, 2:515–24.
11. Nawab quoted by Clive in Clive to Wellesley, 24 June 1801, British Library, India Office, Home Misc. Series 463.
12. Clive to Wellesley, 5 July 1801, WID, 2:546.
13. Clive to Wellesley, 20 July 1801, ibid., 2:550–51; Clive to Wellesley, 27 July 1801, ibid., 2:551–61.
14. Wellesley to Secret Committee, 21 October 1801, ibid., 2:590–93.
15. Wellesley to Lumsden, 23 December 1798, ibid., 1:386–88.
16. Wellesley to Court of Directors, 12 February 1799, ibid., 1:429–32; Wellesley to Palmer, 3 March 1799, ibid., 1:475–77; Wellesley to Clarke, 8 March 1799, ibid., 1:487–91.
17. Wellesley to Secret Committee, 22 April 1799, ibid., 1:535–36.
18. Wellesley to Scott, 18 June 1799, ibid., 2:53–56.
19. Dundas to Wellesley, 18 March 1799, ibid., 2:101–6.

20. Wellesley to Dundas, 22 September 1799, ibid., 2:119–21.
21. Wellesley to Nawab Vizier, 5 November 1799, ibid., 2:132–34.
22. Wellesley to Secret Committee, 28 November 1799, ibid., 2:154–56.
23. Minute by the Governor-General, 16 December 1799, ibid., 2:159–67.
24. Wellesley to Nabob of Oudh, 9 February 1800, ibid., 2:208–19.
25. Wellesley to Nabob of Oudh, 22 January 1801, ibid., 2:429–36.
26. Wellesley to Vizier of Oudh, 5 April 1801, ibid., 2:474–92.
27. Remarks on Vizier of Oudh's Propositions, 2 June 1801, ibid., 2:527–29.
28. Henry Wellesley's Memoir, Cowley Papers, PRO, F.O. 519/67.
29. Dundas to Wellesley, 11 September 1800, in Dundas, *Two Views of British India*, 297.
30. Dundas to Wellesley, 11 September 1801, Cowley Papers, PRO, F.O. 519/286.
31. Henry Wellesley's Memoir, Cowley Papers, PRO, F.O. 519/67.
32. Wellesley to Vizier of Oudh, 14 August 1801, WID, 2:561–65.
33. Marquess Wellesley to Henry Wellesley, 17 September 1801, ibid., 2:571.
34. Wellesley to Court of Directors, 14 November 1801, ibid., 2:605–10.
35. Arthur Wellesley to Webbe, 8 December 1801, WSD, 2:634.
36. Memorandum on Oude, n.d. (November 1801), ibid., 2:615–17.
37. Shawe to Henry Wellesley, 6 February 1802, British Library, India Office, European MSS. 176.
38. Wellesley to Court, 14 November 1801, WID, 2:605–10.
39. Notification of ratification of treaty, 14 November 1801, British Library, India Office, European MSS. 174.
40. British Library, India Office, European MSS. 173.
41. Lake to Henry Wellesley, 12 July 1802, British Library, India Office, European MSS. 175.
42. Wellesley to Henry Wellesley, 29 May 1802, ibid.
43. Shawe to Henry Wellesley, 17 May 1802, ibid., 176.
44. Wellesley to Henry Wellesley, 29 May 1802, ibid., 175.
45. Henry Wellesley to Wellesley, 23 March 1802, ibid., 180.
46. Henry Wellesley to Wellesley, 7 June 1802, ibid., 181.
47. Henry Wellesley to Wellesley, 4 May 1802, ibid., 180.
48. Edmonstone to Mercer, 21 March 1802; Henry Wellesley to Wellesley, 4 May and 7 June 1802; all in British Library, India Office, Home Misc. Series 582.
49. Henry Wellesley to Wellesley, 18 July 1802, ibid.
50. Henry Wellesley's notebook, December 1802, ibid., 366/2.
51. Governor-General in Council to Henry Wellesley, 1 November 1802, ibid., 582.
52. Court of Directors to Wellesley, 19 August 1802, ibid., 236/7.
53. Wellesley to Castlereagh, 12 February 1803, WID, 3:54–60.

CHAPTER 7. END OF THE FIRST ACT: THE MARATHA WAR

1. Most significantly, Edward Ingram developed this theme in his definitive studies of British policy in the East.
2. Henry Wellesley to Wellesley, 5 August 1802, WID, 2:666–67.
3. Mornington to Palmer, 3 March 1799, ibid., 1:475–77.

4. Henry Wellesley to Wellesley, 5 August 1802, ibid., 5:70–71.

5. Arthur Wellesley to Webbe, 12 November 1802, WSD, 3:381.

6. Arthur Wellesley to Stuart, 27 November 1802, ibid., 3:431–36.

7. Arthur Wellesley to Webbe, 1 December 1802, ibid., 3:444–45.

8. Arthur Wellesley to Malcolm, 11 December 1802, ibid., 3:461.

9. Dundas to Wellesley, 16 March 1801, in Dundas, *Two Views of British India*, 326–27; Wellesley to Dundas, 30 September 1801, ibid., 331–34; Dundas to Wellesley, 16 March 1801, WID, 2:571–72; Pole to Wellesley, 10 February 1801, PMW, Add. MSS. 37416; Grenville to Wellesley, 20 February 1801, Grenville-Wellesley Papers, PMW, Add. MSS. 70927.

10. Pole to Wellesley, 13 March 1801, PMW, Add. MSS. 37416.

11. British Library, India Office, Home Misc. Series H/236/7, Directors of the East India Company to Wellesley, 19 August 1802.

12. Castlereagh to Wellesley, 27 September 1802, WID, 3:36–41; Wellesley to Court of Directors, 1 January 1802, ibid., 2:614–616; Dartmouth to Wellesley, 9 April 1802, ibid., 2:634–36.

13. Clive to Wellesley, 18 October 1801, ibid., 2:594–96.

14. Arthur Wellesley to Webbe, 11 October 1802, WSD, 3:321–25.

15. Arthur Wellesley to Webbe, 8 December 1801, ibid., 2:634.

16. British Library, India Office, European MSS. 176, Shawe to Henry Wellesley, 6 February 1802. In 1800, 10 lacs equaled £100,000, an enormous sum.

17. Butler, *Eldest Brother*, 223; Hyacinthe to Wellesley, Letterbook 1797–1803, CP #18.

18. Arthur Wellesley to Webbe, 21 October 1801, WSD, 2:586–87.

19. Wellesley to Addington, 10 January 1802, WID, 3:iv–xxiv; Arthur Wellesley to Chief Secretary of Government, 20 January 1802, WSD, 3:36–39.

20. Arthur Wellesley to Malcolm, 20 April 1802, WSD, 3:150. Emphasis in the original.

21. Arthur Wellesley to Duncan, 4 June 1802, ibid., 3:191–92.

22. Arthur Wellesley to Macleod, 15 March 1802, ibid., 3:112–13.

23. Hobart to Wellesley, 17 October 1802/30 March 1803, WID, 3:72; Wellesley to Hobart, 20 April 1803, ibid., 3:84–85.

24. Malcolm to Arthur Wellesley, 20 June 1802, ibid., 3:226–37.

25. Wellesley to Court of Directors, 24 December 1802, WID, 3:3–12.

26. Wellesley to Clive, 7 January 1803, ibid., 3:27–29.

27. Arthur Wellesley to Baird, 25 January 1803, WSD, 3:555–57.

28. Deputy-Adjutant-General to Chalmers, 21 February 1803, ibid., 4:22.

29. Arthur Wellesley to Collins, 17 April 1803, ibid., 4:58–60.

30. Wellesley to Secret Committee, 19 April 1803, WID, 3:79–80.

31. Arthur Wellesley to Stuart, 21 April 1803, WD, 2:144; Malcolm to Clive, 24 April 1803, ibid., 2:145.

32. Wellesley to Secret Committee, 19 April 1803, WID, 3:72–83.

33. Ibid.

34. Arthur Wellesley to Adjutant-General, 14 May 1803, WSD, 4:79–80; Wellesley to Rajah of Berar, 22 May 1803, WID, 3:104–5.

35. Arthur Wellesley to Lake, 27 May 1803, WSD, 4:97–98.

36. Edmonstone to Close, 30 May 1803, WID, 3:106–19.

37. Arthur Wellesley to Collins, 4 June 1803, WSD, 4:105.

38. Arthur Wellesley to Collins, 9 June 1803, ibid., 4:108–9.

39. Wellesley to Lake, 8 July 1803, WID, 3:182.

40. Memorandum, 28 April 1801, WD, 1:111–20.

41. Arthur Wellesley to Montresor, 28 June 1803, WSD, 4:122–23.

42. Arthur Wellesley to Collins, 29 June 1803, ibid., 4:123–24.

43. Ibid.

44. Wellesley to Lake, 27 July 1803, WID, 3:230–33.

45. Collins to Wellesley, 6 July 1803, ibid., 3:175; Governor-General in Council to Secret Committee, 1 August 1803, ibid., 3:255–64.

46. Wellesley to Campbell, 3 August 1803, ibid., 3:268–72.

47. Wellesley to Arthur Wellesley, 27 June 1803, ibid., 3:153–58.

48. Arthur Wellesley to Wellesley, 25 July 1803, WD, 1:237–44.

49. Arthur Wellesley to Wellesley, 6 August 1803, WID, 3:273; Collins to Arthur Wellesley, 21 July 1803, WD, 1:244–46; Collins to Arthur Wellesley, 22 July 1803, ibid., 1:246; Collins to Arthur Wellesley, 24 July 1803, ibid., 1:249–50; Arthur Wellesley to Collins, 29 July 1803, ibid., 1:255–56; Collins to Arthur Wellesley, 26 July 1803, ibid., 1:256–59; Arthur Wellesley to Collins, 31 July 1803, ibid., 1:262–63; Collins to Arthur Wellesley, 30 July 1803, ibid., 1:265–67; Collins to Arthur Wellesley, 1 August 1803, ibid., 1:270–73; Collins to Arthur Wellesley, 3 August 1803, ibid., 1:275–76.

50. Arthur Wellesley to Sindia, 6 August 1803, WD, 1:287–88.

51. Arthur Wellesley to Wellesley, 17 August 1803, WSD, 4:153–54. The best modern account of the campaign can be found in Cooper, *Anglo-Maratha Campaigns*.

52. Governor-General in Council to Secret Committee, 31 October 1803, WID, 3:424–36.

53. Lake to Wellesley, 4 September 1803, WID, 3:291–92; Lake to Wellesley, 12 September 1803, ibid., 3:310–12.

54. Arthur Wellesley to Wellesley, 24 September 1803, ibid., 3:323–26.

55. Extract of a letter by Sir Colin Campbell, WSD, 4:184–86.

56. Wellesley to Arthur Wellesley, 27 October 1803, WSD, 4:187–88.

57. General Order, 30 October 1803, WID 3:422–24.

58. Governor-General in Council to Secret Committee, 31 October 1803, ibid., 3:424–36.

59. Arthur Wellesley to Wellesley, 30 November 1803, ibid., 3:472–75.

60. Arthur Wellesley to Wellesley, 15 December 1803, ibid., 3:517; Wellesley to Arthur Wellesley, 23 December 1803, ibid., 3:522–23; Arthur Wellesley to Wellesley, 18 November 1803, WSD, 4:289.

61. Treaty of Peace with Sindia, 30 December 1803, WSD, 4:221–63; Treaty of Peace with Rajah of Berar, 17 December 1803, ibid., 4:285–87; Memoranda, 10 November, 11 November, 21 November, 22 November, 23 November, 28 November, 1 December, 8 December, 11 December, 24 December, 26 December, 28 December, and 29 December 1803, ibid., 4:221–63; Wellesley to Arthur Wellesley, 11 December 1803, WID, 3:497–515.

62. Arthur Wellesley to Wellesley, 17 December 1803, ibid., 3:531–36; Arthur Wellesley to Wellesley, 30 December 1803, ibid., 3:557–63.

63. Lake to Prince, 23 October 1803, in Aspinall, *Correspondence of . . . Prince of Wales*, vol. 4, no. 1757.

64. PMW, Add. MSS. 37315.

65. Wellesley to George III, 22 December 1803, in Aspinall, *Later Correspondence of King George III,* vol. 4, no. 2820; Pitt to George III, 26 August 1804, ibid., vol. 4, no. 2927.

66. Arthur Wellesley to Wellesley, 31 January 1804, WSD, 4:334–38.

67. Arthur Wellesley to Malcolm, 30 January 1804, ibid., 4:333–34.

68. Arthur Wellesley to Wellesley, 15 March 1804, ibid., 4:355–60.

69. Arthur Wellesley to Malcolm, 17 March 1804, WD, 3:486–89.

70. Arthur Wellesley to Henry Wellesley, 13 May 1804, WSD, 4:383–86.

71. Lake to Wellesley, 12 May 1804, WID, 4:63–65; Arthur Wellesley to Lake, 23 April 1804, WSD, 4:376–77.

72. Arthur Wellesley to Webbe, 20 June 1804, WSD, 4:441.

73. Arthur Wellesley to Webbe, 11 September 1804, ibid., 4:464–65.

74. Lake to Wellesley, 21 July 1804, WID, 4:178–79.

75. Wellesley to Lake, 11 September 1804, ibid., 4:204–8.

76. Castlereagh to Wellesley, 18 May 1804/14 October 1804, ibid., 3:570–73.

77. Lake to Wellesley, 17 November 1804, ibid., 4:326.

78. Lake to Wellesley, 22 January 1805, ibid., 4:293–94.

79. Wellesley to Arthur Wellesley, 2 March 1805, PMW, Add. MSS. 37415.

80. Camden to Wellesley, 24 August 1804, ibid., Add. MSS. 37309.

81. Castlereagh to Wellesley, 18 January 1805, WID, 4:549.

82. Arthur Wellesley to Wellesley, 3 July 1805, WSD, 4:507–9.

CHAPTER 8. ENTR'ACTE I

1. Wellesley-Pole to Lord Wellesley, 1 July 1805, PMW, Add. MSS. 37309.

2. Lord Wellesley to Wellesley-Pole, 31 October 1797, PMW, Add. MSS. 37316; Lambeth Palace Library, Acts Book, p. 24, 23 February 1799.

3. Hyacinthe Wellesley to Lord Wellesley, 22 August 1800, CP #18.

4. Lambeth Palace Library, Porteus 34/11, 14 August 1805.

5. Ibid., Acts Book, 239, 24 June 1805.

6. Gerald to Lord Wellesley, 24 May 1804, PMW, Add. MSS. 37315.

7. Letter Book, 1803–1805, CP #19; CP #133, translations by Iris Butler.

8. Gerald Wellesley to Lord Wellesley, 24 May 1804, PMW, Add. MSS. 37315.

9. Lady Mornington to Lord Wellesley, 3 February 1804, Cowley Papers, PRO, F.O. 519/286.

10. Harriet Cavendish to the Marquis of Hartington, 9 March 1809, in Cavendish, *Hary-O,* 310.

11. These are contained in PMW, Add. MSS. 37415.

12. Castlereagh to Wellesley, 25 August 1803, WID, 4:39–41.

13. Arthur Wellesley to Duncan, 12 June 1804, WSD, 4:423.

14. Cowley, *Diary and Correspondence,* 42.

15. *Times,* 1 October 1804.

16. Harrowby to the King, 26 July 1804, in Aspinall, *Later Correspondence of King George III,* 4:257.

17. Arthur to William, 13 September 1809, RP.

18. Arthur Wellesley to Lord Wellesley, 21 December 1805, WSD, 4:538.
19. Ibid.
20. Lord Wellesley to Lady Wellesley, 21 May 1805, CP #4.
21. Wellesley to Hyacinthe Wellesley, 7 January 1806, CP #4.
22. *Annual Register,* 1806, p. 100.
23. Grenville to Wellesley, 9 January 1806, Grenville-Wellesley Papers, Add. MSS. 70927.
24. Pitt to Wellesley, 12 January 1806, CP #34; Stanhope, *Life of . . . Pitt,* 4:373–74.
25. Grenville to Wellesley, 23 January 1806, Grenville-Wellesley Papers, Add. MSS. 70927.
26. Grenville to Wellesley, 17 February 1806, ibid.
27. Wellesley to Grenville, 12 March 1806, in Buckingham, *Memoirs of the Court . . . of George III,* 4:26–27.
28. Montrose to Wellesley, 21 May 1806, PMW, Add. MSS. 37309.
29. Melville to Wellesley, 14 June 1806, ibid..
30. Arthur to Richard, 3 October 1806, ibid., Add. MSS. 37415.
31. Grenville to Wellesley, 14 October 1806, Grenville-Wellesley Papers, Add. MSS. 70927.
32. Arthur Wellesley to Lord Wellesley, 27 October and 30 November 1806, PMW, Add. MSS. 37415.
33. Arthur Wellesley to Lord Wellesley, 22 October 1806, PMW, Add. MSS. 37415.
34. Pole to Wellesley, 16 and 19 October 1806, ibid., Add. MSS. 37309.
35. Portland to Wellesley, 24 March 1807, ibid.
36. Arthur Wellesley to Malcolm, 23 February 1807, WSD, 4:590–92.
37. Hawkesbury to King, 23 March 1807, in Aspinall, *Later Correspondence of King George III,* vol. 4, no. 3408.
38. Grenville to Wellesley, 23 March 1807, Grenville-Wellesley Papers, Add. MSS. 70927.
39. Aspinall, *Later Correspondence of King George III,* vol. 4, p. 537n, from Harewood MSS. (George Canning).
40. Portland to King, 23 March 1807, ibid., vol. 4, no. 3410.
41. Quoted in Aspinall, *Later Correspondence of King George III,* vol. 4, p. 537n.
42. Portland to Wellesley, 27 March 1807, PMW, Add. MSS. 37309; Portland to King, 25 March and 28 March 1807, in Aspinall, *Later Correspondence of King George III,* vol. 4, nos. 3416 and 3418, respectively.
43. Arthur Wellesley to Lord Wellesley, 27 March 1807, PMW, Add. MSS. 37415.
44. Grenville to Arthur Wellesley, 29 March 1807, WP 1/166.
45. Fremantle to Buckingham, 3 April 1807, in Buckingham, *Memoirs of the Court . . . of George III,* 6:155.
46. Wellesley to Richard Wellesley (son), 2 May 1807, CP #34.
47. Great Britain, *Parliamentary Debates,* 1st series, vol. 10:411.
48. Ibid.
49. Ibid., 10:699.
50. Ibid., 10:202.

51. Ibid., 11:315–92.
52. Ibid., 11:947.
53. Wellesley to Abdy, 26 June 1806, PMW, Add. MSS. 37315.
54. CP #20 and 21 hold this correspondence, which chronicles the breakup of the marriage. Translations by Iris Butler.
55. Longford, *Wellington: Years of the Sword,* 135.
56. Great Britain, *Parliamentary Debates,* 1st series, 10:342–50; *Times,* 9 February 1808.
57. See Black, *British Foreign Policy*; and Muir, *Britain and the Defeat of Napoleon.*

CHAPTER 9. TOIL AND TROUBLE

1. *Times,* 1 June 1808.
2. *Times,* 16 July 1808.
3. Arthur Wellesley to Wellesley-Pole, 22 August 1808, RP.
4. *Times,* 26 August 1808.
5. Wellesley to Kitty Wellesley, 19 August 1808, PMW, Add. MSS. 37315.
6. Wellesley to Richard Wellesley (son), 7 September 1808, CP #34; Lady Mornington to Wellesley, 3 September 1808, PMW, Add. MSS. 37315; Buckingham to Wellesley, 2 September 1808, and Montrose to Wellesley, 6 September 1808, PMW, Add. MSS. 37309.
7. Arthur Wellesley to Malcolm, 29 August 1808, WD, 4:112.
8. Ibid.
9. Arthur Wellesley to Malcolm, 5 September 1808, ibid., 4:125.
10. Arthur Wellesley to Wellesley-Pole, 26 August 1808, RP.
11. Canning quoted in Gray, *Spencer Perceval,* 183.
12. Wellesley to Richard Wellesley (son), 30 September 1808, CP #34.
13. Wellesley to Richard Wellesley (son), 13 October 1808, ibid.
14. Arthur Wellesley to Wellesley, 5 October 1808, PMW, Add. MSS. 37415.
15. See WSD, vol. 6.
16. Wellesley-Pole to Arthur Wellesley, 19 October 1808, ibid., 6:164–65. Postscript by Lord Wellesley.
17. Letter to Buckingham, in Buckingham, *Memoirs of the Court. . . of George III,* 4:255–56.
18. Whitbread to Creevey, 25 September 1808, in Creevey, *Creevey Papers,* 1:89.
19. Cobbett to Folkestone, 9 October 1808, ibid., 1:89. Emphasis in the original.
20. Pole to Arthur Wellesley, 28 October 1808, WSD, 6:174–75. Castlereagh followed with a letter on 4 November 1808; ibid., 6:184.
21. Arthur Wellesley to John Villiers, 9 January 1809, ibid., 5:524–25.
22. Moore to Frere, 23 December 1808, in Moore, *Narrative of the Campaign in Spain,* 160–61; see also Moore, *Diary,* 2:374.
23. Great Britain, *Parliamentary Debates,* 1st series, 23 January 1809, 12:106–7.
24. Ibid., 12:144–58.

25. Ibid., 12:134–35.

26. Ibid., 12:1057–75.

27. Ibid., 12:1075–1105.

28. An Independent Englishman to Wellesley, October 1808, PMW, Add. MSS. 37416.

29. Memorandum Concerning the Defence of Portugal, 7 March 1809, in Castlereagh, *Memoranda and Correspondence,* 7:39–42.

30. Hildyard, *Trial of . . . Paget.*

31. Ibid., 10.

32. Aspinall, *Later Correspondence of King George III,* 5:3896n.

33. Anglesey, *One Leg,* 93–99; Hildyard, *Trial of . . . Paget.*

34. Anglesey, *One Leg,* 91–99.

35. *Times,* 10 March 1809.

36. Cavendish, *Hary-O,* 307–8.

37. Hildyard, *Trial of . . . Paget,* 10.

38. Ibid., 19–20.

39. Ibid., 24.

40. *Times,* 31 May 1809.

41. Arthur Wellesley to Wellesley-Pole, 16 November 1809, RP.

42. Ibid.

43. Longford, *Wellington: Years of the Sword,* 204.

44. *Journals of the House of Lords,* 47:466.

45. Anglesey, *One-Leg,* 110–11.

46. Ibid., 109.

47. Castlereagh to Arthur Wellesley, 2 April 1809, in Castlereagh, *Memoranda and Correspondence,* 7:47.

48. Great Britain, *Parliamentary Debates,* 14:121–50.

49. Ibid., 14:151.

50. Bathurst Papers, British Library, loan no. 57, vol. 4, no. 324; Butler, *Eldest Brother,* 400; Hinde, *George Canning,* 219; Severn, *Wellesley Affair,* chap. 2.

51. *Times,* 1 May 1809.

52. Wellesley to Lady Wellesley, 24 July 1809, CP #21.

CHAPTER 10. THE WELLESLEYS IN SPAIN: THE FIRST PHASE

1. See WD, vol. 5.

2. A. Wellesley to J. H. Frere, 24 July 1809, and to Maj. Gen. O'Donoghe, 16 July 1809, PMW, Add. MSS. 37286.

3. Ibid.

4. A. Wellesley to J. H. Frere, 31 July 1809, WD, 3:383–84.

5. Apodaca to Garay, 1 and 9 May 1809, and Garay to Apodaca, 25 May 1809, AHN, Sección de Estado, Legajo 5459; Apodaca to Canning, 1 July 1809, PRO, F.O. 72/84; Cevallos to Canning, 2 June 1809, ibid., F.O. 72/86.

6. See Knighton, *Memoirs of . . . Knighton,* 94.

7. R. Wellesley to Canning, 11 August 1809, PMW, Add. MSS. 37286; R. Wellesley to Canning, 11 August 1809, PRO, F.O. 72/76.

8. Ibid.; An Account of the Talavera Campaign, PMW, Add. MSS. 37288; A. Wellesley to J. H. Frere, 24 and 31 July 1809, PMW, Add. MSS. 37286.

9. A. Wellesley to Wellesley, 8 August 1809, PRO, F.O. 72/76.

10. Knighton to Wife, 13 August 1809, in Knighton, *Memoirs of . . . Knighton,* 1:105–12.

11. A. Wellesley to R. Wellesley, 12 August 1809, Cuesta to A. Wellesley, 10 August 1809, and A. Wellesley to Cuesta, 11 August 1809; all in PRO, F.O. 72/76. See also WSD, 6:318–19, 324.

12. Johnstone to R. Wellesley, 22 May 1809, PMW, Add. MSS. 37286.

13. R. Wellesley (son) to R. Wellesley, 13 August 1809, PMW, Add. MSS. 37315.

14. A. Wellesley to R. Wellesley, 8 August 1809, PRO, F.O. 72/76; WSD, General Order, 9 August 1809, 6:327.

15. Severn, *Wellesley Affair,* chapter 3.

16. Longford, *Wellington: Years of the Sword,* 184.

17. Correspondence can be found in the Wellesley Papers, the Wellington Papers, and the Foreign Office archives, PRO, F.O. 72/76.

18. Garay to Wellesley, 17 August 1809, PMW, Add. MSS. 37287; Severn, *Wellesley Affair,* 55–57.

19. Wellesley to Canning, 15 August 1809, PMW, Add. MSS. 37286; Garay to Wellesley, 21 August 1809, PRO, F.O. 72/76.

20. R. Wellesley to Canning, 15 August 1809, PMW, Add. MSS. 37286.

21. A. Wellesley to R. Wellesley, 21 August 1809, PRO, F.O. 72/76.

22. Plan of Supply, 21 August 1809, PMW, Add. MSS. 37287; Wellesley to A. Wellesley, 22 August 1808, and Wellesley to Canning, 24 August 1809, PRO, F.O. 72/76.

23. A. Wellesley to Wellesley, 24 August 1809, PRO, F.O. 72/76.

24. Ibid.; A. Wellesley to William Wellesley-Pole, 29 August 1809, RP.

25. Wellesley to A. Wellesley, 30 August 1809, PRO, F.O. 72/76.

26. Wellesley to A. Wellesley, 24 August 1809, WSD, 6:337.

27. Wellesley-Pole to A. Wellesley, 22 August 1809, RP.

28. Wellington to Wellesley-Pole, 13 September 1809, RP.

29. Canning to Wellesley, 12 August 1809, PMW, Add. MSS. 37286.

30. Wellesley to Garay, 8 September 1809, PRO, F.O. 72/76.

31. Ibid.

32. Wellesley to Canning, 2 September 1809, ibid.

33. Severn, *Wellesley Affair,* 71–75; Wellesley to Canning, 15 September 1809, PRO, F.O. 72/76.

34. Plan for the Future of the Peninsula, September 1809, PMW, Add. MSS. 37287.

35. Wellesley to Garay, 8 September 1809, ibid.; Wellesley to Canning, 15 September 1809, PRO, F.O. 72/76.

36. Wellesley to Bathurst, 19 September 1809, PMW, Add. MSS. 37314.

37. Wellesley to Wellington, 19 September 1809, WSD, 6:372–73.

38. Wellesley to Garay, 24 October 1809, PMW, Add. MSS. 37288; Proceedings of the Supreme Junta, AHN, Sección de Estado, Legajo 2.

39. Severn, *Wellesley Affair,* 89–94; Bathurst's Account of the Dissolution of the Portland Ministry, Bathurst Papers, loan no. 57, vol. 4, no. 324; Liverpool Papers, British Library, Add. MSS. 38243; Perceval Papers, British Library, Add. MSS. 49188.

40. Arbuthnot to Huskisson, 14 September 1809, Huskisson Papers, British Library, Add. MSS. 37737.

41. Sydenham to Wellesley, 16 September 1809, PMW, Add. MSS. 37295.

42. Henry Wellesley's Memoir, Cowley Papers, PRO, F.O. 519/67.

43. Bathurst's Account of the Dissolution of the Portland Ministry, Bathurst Papers, loan no. 57, vol. 4, no. 324.

44. Canning to Booth, 19 December 1809, Canning Papers, British Library, Add. MSS. 46841.

45. Wellington to Wellesley, 5 October 1809, PMW, Add. MSS. 37415. Emphasis in the original.

46. Wellington to Wellesley-Pole, 6 October 1809, RP.

47. Wellesley to Wellesley-Pole, 8 October 1809, PMW, Add. MSS. 37295.

48. *Morning Chronicle,* 4 October 1809. Emphasis in the original.

49. *Morning Post,* 5 October 1809.

50. *Morning Chronicle,* 25 November 1809.

51. *Times,* 25 November 1809.

52. Memorandum by Lord Wellesley, 4 November 1809, PMW, Add. MSS. 37288.

53. H. Wellesley to Wellesley, 27 September 1809, ibid., Add. MSS. 37295.

54. Wellesley to H. Wellesley, 30 October 1809, ibid.

55. Wellesley to George III, 17 December 1809, ibid., Add. MSS. 37288.

CHAPTER 11. THE WELLESLEYS AT WAR

1. Wellington to Pole, 16 November 1809, 27, RP.

2. Perceval to Richmond, 30 October 1809, in Aspinall, *Later Correspondence of King George III,* 5:464n1.

3. King to Perceval, 5 November 1809, ibid., 5:445–46.

4. King to Perceval, 24 November 1809, ibid., 5:451.

5. Bathurst to Richmond, 6 November 1809, ibid., fn 1, 5:464. Emphasis in the original.

6. Richmond to Bathurst, 4 December 1809, ibid., fn 1, 5:465.

7. King to Perceval, 1 December 1809, Wellesley to Perceval, 2 December 1809, PMW, Add. MSS. 37285.

8. Notes of Marquess Wellesley, 25 January 1810, PRO, F.O. 185/19; Wellesley to H. Wellesley, 4 January 1810, PRO, F.O. 72/93.

9. B. Frere to Wellesley, 11 February 1810, PMW, Add. MSS. 49981; Wellington to B. Frere, 5 February 1810, WD, 6:474–75.

10. H. Wellesley to Wellington, 9 March 1810, Cowley Papers, F.O. 519/34.

11. Hamilton to Vaughan, 29 March 1810, All Souls College Library, Vaughan Papers, C:48:2; H. Wellesley to Wellington, 2 April 1810, Cowley Papers, F.O. 519/34; Wellington to H. Wellesley, 15 April 1810, WD, 6:35.

12. CP #63; notes given to J. Severn by Mrs. Iris Butler Portal.

13. CP #63.

14. Wellesley-Pole to A. Wellesley, 2 August 1809, RP.

15. Ibid.

16. Ibid.

17. Ibid.

18. Butler, *Eldest Brother,* 430.
19. Milton to Creevey, 8 January 1810, in Creevey, *Creevey Papers,* 1:118.
20. Creevey, *Creevey Papers,* 24 January 1810, 1:123.
21. Ibid., 15:438.
22. Ibid., 15:145–52.
23. Lady Holland, *Journal,* 2:254.
24. Great Britain, *Parliamentary Debates,* 1st series, 15:277–80.
25. Ibid., 15:288–95.
26. Creevey, *Creevey Papers,* 1 February 1810, 1:127.
27. Wellesley to Perceval, 12 February 1810, PMW, Add. MSS. 37295.
28. Great Britain, *Parliamentary Debates,* 1st series, 16:10–11.
29. Perceval to Wellesley, 4 March 1810, PMW, Add. MSS. 37295.
30. Great Britain, *Parliamentary Debates,* 1st series, 16:305–6, 373–79.
31. Ibid., 16:379–84.
32. Pole to Wellington, 5 April 1810, RP.
33. Liverpool to Wellington, 15 December 1809, Liverpool Papers, Add. MSS. 38244.
34. Wellington to Huskisson, 26 April 1810, Huskisson Papers, Add. MSS. 38,738.
35. H. Wellesley to Wellington, 2 April 1810, Cowley Papers, F.O. 519/34.
36. H. Wellesley to Wellesley, 31 March 1810, PMW, Add. MSS. 49981; Apodaca to Bardaxi, 14 May 1810, AHN, Sección de Estado, Legajo 5461.
37. H. Wellesley to Wellesley, 7 April 1810, PRO, F.O. 72/94; H. Wellesley to Wellesley, 7 April 1810, PMW, Add. MSS. 49981.
38. Notes of Marquess Wellesley, 25 January 1810, PMW, Add. MSS. 37291; Perceval's observations, PMW, Add. MSS. 37295.
39. H. Wellesley to Wellesley, 22 April 1810, PRO, F.O. 72/94.
40. Pole to Wellington, 7 March 1810, RP.
41. Wellington to Pole, 6 April 1810, RP. Emphasis in the original.
42. Pole to Wellington, 13 May 1810, RP.
43. *Examiner,* 3 June 1810.
44. Great Britain, *Parliamentary Debates,* 1st series, 16:484–97.
45. Ibid., 16:499.
46. Ibid., 16:500.
47. Memorandum by Marquess Wellesley, June 1810, WSD, 6:550–52.
48. Liverpool to Wellesley, 15 June 1810, PMW, Add. MSS. 37295.
49. Memorandum, 13 March 1810, ibid.
50. H. Wellesley to Wellesley, 12 June 1810, PRO, F.O. 72/95; Apodaca to Wellesley, 17 June 1810, AHN, Sección de Estado, Legajo 5461.
51. H. Wellesley to Bardaxi, 5 July 1810, and H. Wellesley to Wellesley, 11 July 1810, PRO, F.O. 72/96.
52. Perceval to Wellesley, 14 July 1810, PMW, Add. MSS. 37295.
53. Perceval to Wellesley, 23 July 1810, ibid.; Wellesley to H. Wellesley, 24 July 1810, Add. MSS. 49979.
54. H. Wellesley to Wellesley, 13 July 1810, PRO, F.O. 72/96.
55. Bardaxi to H. Wellesley, 15 July 1810, ibid.
56. Ibid.
57. Layard to Junta of Caracas, 14 May 1810, PRO, F.O. 185/18.

58. Liverpool to Layard, July 1810, PRO, F.O. 185/18; Albuquerque to Bardaxi, 4 July 1810, and Wellesley to Albuquerque, 21 June 1810, AHN, Sección de Estado, Legajo 5462; Wellesley to H. Wellesley, 13 July 1810, PRO, F.O. 185/18.

59. CP #49.

60. Wellesley to H. Wellesley, 13 July 1810, PMW, Add. MSS. 49979; Wellesley to Albuquerque, 14 July 1810, Albuquerque to Bardaxi, 18 July 1810, and Apodaca to Bardaxi, 20 July 1810, AHN, Sección de Estado, Legajo 5462.

61. Wellesley to H. Wellesley, 24 July 1810, PMW, Add. MSS. 49979.

62. Rose to Bathurst, 8 August 1810, Bathurst Papers, loan no. 57, vol. 65, no. 83.

63. Bardaxi to H. Wellesley, 24 August 1810, PRO, F.O. 72/97.

64. H. Wellesley to Wellesley, 24 August 1810, Cowley Papers, PRO, F.O. 519/36.

65. H. Wellesley to Wellington, 31 August 1810, ibid.; H. Wellesley to Wellington, 31 August 1810, WSD, 6:583–84.

66. Wellington to H. Wellesley, 20 August 1810, WD, 6:351.

67. Wellington to H. Wellesley, 14 September 1810, ibid., 6:414.

68. H. Wellesley to Wellesley, 10 June 1810, PRO, F.O. 72/95.

69. H. Wellesley to Wellesley, 24 June 1810 (two dispatches), ibid.

70. Ibid.; H. Wellesley to Wellington, 26 June 1810, Cowley Papers, PRO, F.O. 519/35.

71. H. Wellesley to Wellesley, 1 August 1810, WSD, 6:566.

72. H. Wellesley to Bardaxi, 12 August 1810, PRO, F.O. 72/96; H. Wellesley to Wellesley, 23 August 1810, PMW, Add. MSS. 37292.

73. H. Wellesley to Wellesley, 11 July 1810, PRO, F.O. 72/96.

74. H. Wellesley to Wellesley, 17 September 1810, PRO, F.O. 72/97.

75. Wellington to H. Wellesley, 3 October 1810, WD, 6:456.

76. Wellesley to Perceval, 9 October 1810, PMW, Add. MSS. 37295.

77. Wellington to H. Wellesley, 4 November 1810, WD, 6:559.

78. H. Wellesley to Wellesley, 26 September 1810, PMW, Add. MSS. 49981.

79. Wellington to [?], 4 June 1810, PMW, Add. MSS. 37415. Emphasis in the original.

CHAPTER 12. REVERSAL OF FORTUNES

1. Granville to Lady Bessborough, 29 August 1810, in Granville, *Private Correspondence,* 2:362.

2. Bessborough to Granville, December 1810, ibid., 2:373.

3. Wellington to Pole, 5 September 1810, WSD, 6:588.

4. Wellington to Liverpool, 30 September 1810, WD, 6:444–50.

5. Sidmouth to Bathurst, 17 July 1810, in Pellew, *Life . . . of . . . Addington,* 3:27.

6. Dardis to Buckingham, 25 April 1810, in Buckingham, *Court . . . of George III,* 4:435.

7. Dardis to Buckingham, 1 October 1810, ibid., 4:458.

8. Wellesley to H. Wellesley, 9 December 1810, PRO, F.O. 185/24.

9. Pole to Wellington, 25 December 1810, RP.

10. Wellington to H. Wellesley, 31 December 1810, WSD, 7:11.
11. Wellington to Pole, 15 December 1810, ibid., 7:4.
12. Wellington to Pole, 11 January 1811, ibid., 7:40–42.
13. Great Britain, *Parliamentary Debates,* 1st series, 19:394–414.
14. Wellesley's Notes on the State of Europe, 15 May 1812, PMW, Add. MSS. 37292.
15. H. Wellesley to Wellesley, 24 October 1810, PRO, F.O. 72/97.
16. H. Wellesley to Wellesley, 10 November 1810, PRO, F.O. 72/98.
17. Bardaxi to H. Wellesley, 16 December 1810, ibid.
18. H. Wellesley to Wellesley, 12 January 1811, PRO, F.O. 72/109; H. Wellesley to Bardaxi, 14 January 1811, ibid.; Whittingham to H. Wellesley, 2 January 1811, ibid..
19. Bardaxi to H. Wellesley, 25 March 1811, PRO, F.O. 72/110; H. Wellesley to Wellesley, 25 March 1811, PMW, Add. MSS. 49983.
20. H. Wellesley to Wellesley, 5 April 1811, PMW, Add. MSS. 49983 (quoting Blake); H. Wellesley to Bardaxi, 8 April 1811, PRO, F.O. 72/110.
21. Wellesley to H. Wellesley, 18 April 1811, PMW, Add. MSS. 49980.
22. H. Wellesley to Wellesley, 15 April 1811, PRO, F.O. 72/110.
23. Wellington to H. Wellesley, 10 April 1811, WD, 7:442.
24. Wellington to Liverpool, 23 March 1811, ibid., 7:380.
25. Pole to Wellington, 20 April 1811, RP.
26. *Examiner,* 28 April 1811.
27. Wellington to Whitbread, 23 May 1811, WD, 7:585–86.
28. Wellesley's Notes on the State of Europe, 15 May 1811, PMW, Add. MSS. 37292.
29. H. Wellesley to Wellington, 26 July 1811, WSD, 7:187.
30. Wellington to H. Wellesley, 14 July 1811, WD, 8:101.
31. H. Wellesley to Wellington, 9 May 1811, WSD, 7:122.
32. Wellington to H. Wellesley, 22 May 1811, WD, 7:568.
33. H. Wellesley to Wellington, 25 May 1811, WSD, 7:140.
34. Wellington to H. Wellesley, 29 May 1811, PRO, F.O. 72/111.
35. H. Wellesley to Wellesley, 24 April 1811, PMW, Add. MSS. 49983.
36. R. Wellesley to H. Wellesley, 12 May 1811, ibid., Add. MSS. 49980; Present State of the Colonies, 12 May 1811, PMW, Add. MSS. 49982; H. Wellesley to R. Wellesley, 29 May 1811, ibid.
37. Bardaxi to H. Wellesley, 29 June 1811, PRO, F.O. 72/112.
38. Wellington to H. Wellesley, 2 August 1811, WD, 8:159.
39. H. Wellesley to Bardaxi, 5 August 1811, PRO, F.O. 72/112.
40. Bardaxi to H. Wellesley, 22 September 1811, ibid., F.O. 72/113.
41. Wellesley to H. Wellesley, 30 September 1811, PMW, Add. MSS. 37293.
42. *Morning Chronicle,* 2 October 1811.
43. Wellesley to H. Wellesley, 27 July 1811, PRO, F.O. 72/108; Apodaca to Wellesley, 8 July 1811, ibid., F.O. 72/117.
44. Vega to H. Wellesley, 4 September 1811, ibid., F.O. 72/113.
45. Vaughan's Notes, 2 November 1811, Vaughan Papers, E:3:1.
46. H. Wellesley to Wellesley, 18 November 1811, PRO, F.O. 72/114; H. Wellesley Memorandum, n.d., Vaughan Papers, C:118:15.
47. H. Wellesley to Wellesley, 22 January 1812, PRO, F.O. 72/129.

48. H. Wellesley to Wellesley, 3 February 1812, ibid.; Wellington to H. Wellesley, 21 January 1812, WD, 8:534–35; Wellington to H. Wellesley, 19 February 1811, ibid., 8:584.

49. Wellington to H. Wellesley, 3 May 1812, WD, 8:110–11.

50. Wellesley to Perceval, 20 October 1811, PMW, Add. MSS. 37295.

51. Memorandum by Merrick Shawe, WSD, 7:257–88.

52. Buckingham, *Memoirs of the . . . Regency,* 7:127.

53. Pole to Wellington, 22 September 1811, RP.

54. Bathurst Memo, 18 June 1812, Bathurst Papers, loan no. 57, vol. 5, no. 433.

55. Wellesley to Perceval, 18 January 1812, ibid., loan no. 57, vol. 5, no. 435.

56. Buckingham, *Memoirs of the . . . Regency,* 1:195–96.

57. Pole to Wellington, 12 February 1812, RP.

58. Wellington to Pole, 29 April 1812, RP.

59. Great Britain, *Parliamentary Debates,* 1st series, 22:45.

60. Pole to Wellington, 12 April 1812, RP.

61. Richard Wellesley's Diary, CP #54.

62. Minutes of Wellesley's Meeting with Liverpool, 18 May 1812, PMW, Add. MSS. 37296.

63. Richard Wellesley's Diary, CP #54.

64. *Morning Chronicle,* 5 June 1812.

65. Great Britain, *Parliamentary Debates,* 1st series, vol. 22.

66. *Examiner,* 24 May 1812.

CHAPTER 13. WATERLOO

1. Great Britain, *Parliamentary Debates,* 1st series, 23:711.

2. Grenville to Wellesley, 25 June 1812, Grenville-Wellesley Papers, Add MSS. 70927.

3. Great Britain, *Parliamentary Debates,* 1st series, 23:814–32.

4. Ibid.

5. Political Diary of Richard Wellesley, CP #54. Emphasis in the original.

6. T. Sydenham to B. Sydenham, 13 September 1812, WSD, 7:423–24.

7. Wellington to Pole, 29 June 1812, RP.

8. T. Sydenham to H. Wellesley, 9 September 1812, WSD, 7:415–23.

9. Canning to Wellesley, 19 November 1812, PMW, Add. MSS. 37297.

10. Ibid. Emphasis in the original.

11. H. Wellesley to Wellington, 12 March 1812, WSD, 7:329.

12. Wellington to H. Wellesley, 27 May 1812, WP 1/347.

13. Castlereagh to H. Wellesley, 2 June 1812, PRO, F.O. 72/127; Liverpool to Canning, 13 June 1815, ibid.

14. H. Wellesley to Castlereagh, 26 August 1812, PRO, F.O. 72/131.

15. H. Wellesley to Arbuthnot, 20 September 1812, in Aspinall, *Correspondence of Charles Arbuthnot,* 65.

16. Castlereagh to H. Wellesley, 19 October 1812, PRO, F.O. 72/127.

17. Bathurst to Wellington, 22 August 1812, WSD 7:406–7.

18. Wellesley to Richard Wellesley (son), 9 January 1813, PMW, Add. MSS. 13806.

19. Diary of Richard Wellesley, CP #54.
20. Pole to Wellington, 28 July 1813, RP.
21. Diary of Richard Wellesley, CP #54.
22. Pole to Wellington, 10 December 1814, RP.
23. Wellington to Pole, 29 February 1814, RP; Pole to Wellington, 9 February 1814, RP.
24. Wellesley to Richard Wellesley (son), 18 August 1813, CP #34.
25. Wellesley to Richard Wellesley (son), 24 October 1813, CP #34.
26. Wellington to Wellesley, 22 June 1813, WSD, 8:3.
27. Wellington to Wellesley, 3 September 1813, PMW, Add. MSS. 37415.
28. Pole to Wellesley, 12 July 1813, PMW, Add. MSS. 37310.
29. Richmond to Bathurst, 21 February 1811, in Bathurst, . . . *Report on the Manuscripts,* 155.
30. Wellesley-Pole to Wellington, 10 December 1813, RP.
31. Political Diary of Richard Wellesley, CP #54.
32. Ibid.
33. Wellesley to Lady Blessington, WP 11/3/1–9.
34. Wellesley to Richard Wellesley (son), 18 August 1814, CP #34.
35. Wellesley to Richard Wellesley (son), 15 November 1814, CP #34.
36. Castlereagh to H. Wellesley, 15 February 1813, PRO, F.O. 72/142.
37. H. Wellesley to Castlereagh, 16 February 1813, PRO, F.O. 72/143.
38. Castlereagh to H. Wellesley, 4 March 1813, PRO, F.O. 72/142.
39. H. Wellesley to Castlereagh, 7 September 1813, PRO, F.O. 519.
40. H. Wellesley to Castlereagh, 23 June 1813, PRO, F.O. 72/143.
41. H. Wellesley to Wellington, 4 February 1813, WSD, 7:546.
42. H. Wellesley to Wellington, 18 February 1813, ibid., 7:556.
43. H. Wellesley to Wellington, 11 April 1813, ibid., 7:604–5.
44. H. Wellesley to Wellington, 7 April 1814, ibid., 8:721–22; H. Wellesley to Wellington, 31 March 1814, ibid., 8:707.
45. H. Wellesley to Castlereagh, 24 March 1814, PRO, F.O. 519.
46. H. Wellesley to Wellington, 31 May 1813, WSD, 7:625–26.
47. Wellington to H. Wellesley, 22 May 1814, ibid., 9:100.
48. Wellington to H. Wellesley, 13 September 1814, ibid., 9:244–45.
49. Wellington to Pole, 12 September 1814, RP.
50. Wellington to Liverpool, 7 November 1814, WSD, 9:422.
51. Wellington to Pole, 8 December 1814, RP.
52. Wellington to H. Wellesley, 24 March 1815, WSD, 9:605–6.
53. Great Britain, *Parliamentary Debates,* 1st series, 30:546–65.
54. Liverpool to Canning, 13 June 1815, in Yonge, *Life of . . . Liverpool,* 2:180.
55. Memorandum by Lord Wellesley, WSD, 9:636.

CHAPTER 14. ENTR'ACTE II

1. The correspondence concerning the elopement can be found in PMW, Add. MSS. 37315, and in the Carver Papers.
2. Wellesley to Richard Wellesley (son), 17 September 1815, PMW, Add. MSS. 37315.

3. Wellesley to Richard Wellesley (son), 10 October 1815, ibid.
4. Charles Bentinck to Richard Wellesley (son), 9 October 1815, ibid.
5. CP #78–88.
6. Ibid.
7. Ibid.
8. Wellesley to Richard Wellesley (son), 18 October 1815, PMW, Add. MSS. 37315.
9. CP #41.
10. Wellesley to A. Wellesley, 16 May 1807, WP 1/166.
11. Hatherton Papers, Littleton Diary.
12. Longford, *Wellington: Years of the Sword,* 374–75.
13. Pole to Wellington, 20 April 1811, RP.
14. WP 11/3/1–9.
15. CP #38.
16. Ibid.
17. Great Britain, *Parliamentary Debates,* 1st series, 30:263–65.
18. Ibid., 35:566.
19. Wilson, *Harriette Wilson's Memoirs,* 1:134.
20. Great Britain, *Parliamentary Debates,* 1st series, 45:440–41.
21. H. Wellesley to Castlereagh, 15 January 1817, in Cowley, *Diary and Correspondence,* 84.
22. Ibid., 84–86.
23. H. Wellesley to Castlereagh, 16 September 1818, ibid., 87.
24. Brougham to Creevey, 19 July 1821, in Creevey, *Creevey Papers,* 2:16.

CHAPTER 15. ENCORE FOR THE WELLESLEYS

1. Bamford, *Journal of Mrs. Arbuthnot,* 6 May 1821, 1:92.
2. Ibid., 30 May 1821, 1:99.
3. Ibid., 6 December 1821, 1:129.
4. Ibid., 17 March 1821, 1:82–83.
5. Sidmouth to Grant, 29 November 1821, in Pellew, *Life . . . of . . . Addington,* 3:376–77.
6. Harrowby to Bathurst, 24 November 1821, in Bathurst, . . . *Report on the Manuscripts,* 522. Emphasis in the original.
7. Castlereagh to Sidmouth, 8 December 1821, in Pellew, *Life . . . of . . . Addington,* 3:378.
8. Sidmouth to Manners, 12 December 1821, ibid., 3:381.
9. Grenville to Wellesley, 4 December 1821, Grenville-Wellesley Papers, Add. MSS. 70927.
10. H. Wellesley to Wellesley, 2 December 1821, PMW, Add. MSS. 37415. Emphasis in the original.
11. Harrowby to Bathurst, 22 December 1821, in Bathurst, . . . *Report on the Manuscripts,* 525–26.
12. Bamford, *Journal of Mrs. Arbuthnot,* 13 January 1822, 1:136.
13. Peel to Wellesley, 17 January 1822, PMW, Add. MSS. 37298.
14. Graves to Wellesley, 20 February 1822, ibid.
15. Wellington to Peel, 27 February 1822, WP 1/700/13.

16. Bamford, *Journal of Mrs. Arbuthnot,* 22 April 1822, 1:157.
17. Shawe to Wellesley, 24 April 1822, PMW, Add. MSS. 37299.
18. Peel to Wellesley, 21 July 1822 and 18 July 1822, ibid.
19. Wellesley to Peel, 27 September 1822, ibid.
20. Wellesley to Peel, 27 October 1822, ibid.
21. Peel to Wellesley, 2 November 1822, and Wellesley to Peel, 18 November 1822, PMW, Add. MSS. 37300.
22. Sidmouth to Wellesley, 24 December 1822, in Pellew, *Life . . . of . . . Addington,* 3:384–85.
23. A. N. Blake to Wellington, December 1822, WP 1/754/4.
24. Canning to Arbuthnot, 10 January 1823, in Aspinall, *Correspondence of Charles Arbuthnot,* 38.
25. Arbuthnot to Liverpool, 12 January 1823, ibid., 40.
26. Bamford, *Journal of Mrs. Arbuthnot,* 30 January 1823, 1:210.
27. Peel to Bathurst, 26 August 1823, in Bathurst, . . . *Report on the Manuscripts,* 542.
28. Bamford, *Journal of Mrs. Arbuthnot,* 16 February 1823, 1:215; Creevey, *Creevey Papers,* 14 February 1823, 2:63.
29. Bamford, *Journal of Mrs. Arbuthnot,* 25 February 1823, 1:218–19.
30. Shawe to Wellington, 20 February 1823, and Lindsey to Shawe, 15 February 1823, WP 1/756/25.
31. Wellington to Wellesley, 21 February 1823, PMW, Add. MSS. 37415; Wellesley to Wellington, 17 February 1823, WP 1/756/19.
32. Bamford, *Journal of Mrs. Arbuthnot,* 27 February 1823, 1:220; Peel to Wellesley, 22 February 1823, PMW, Add. MSS. 37300.
33. *Annual Register,* 1822; CP #12, #55.
34. Cowley, *Diary and Correspondence,* 96.
35. Ibid., 95–96.
36. H. Wellesley to Canning, 6 July 1823, PRO, F.O. 519.
37. Cowley, *Diary and Correspondence,* 118–30.
38. H. Wellesley to Canning, 16 August 1823, PRO, F.O. 519.
39. Canning to H. Wellesley, 16 September 1823, ibid.
40. Grenville to Wellesley, 27 December 1824, CP #34.
41. Wellesley to Peel, 1 March 1823, PMW, Add. MSS. 37300.
42. Bamford, *Journal of Mrs. Arbuthnot,* 16 May 1823, 1:235.
43. Francis Andrews to Wellington, 10 April 1823, WP 1/760/10.
44. Wellesley to Peel, 9 April 1823, PMW, Add. MSS. 37301.
45. Wellesley to Peel, 27 April 1823, ibid.
46. Peel to Wellesley, 29 June 1823, ibid.
47. Charles Wynn to Wellington, 6 August 1823, WP 1/769/8.
48. Wellington to Wynn, 8 August 1823, WP 1/770/8.
49. Bamford, *Journal of Mrs. Arbuthnot,* 12 August 1823, 1:252.
50. Liverpool to Arbuthnot, 2 October 1823, in Aspinall, *Correspondence of Charles Arbuthnot,* 45.
51. John Malcolm to Wellington, 10 October 1823, WP 1/773/5.
52. Malcolm to Sidmouth, 26 November 1823, in Pellew, *Life . . . of . . . Addington,* 3:386–87.
53. Goulburn to Wellesley, 3 February 1824, PMW, Add. MSS. 37302.

54. Wellesley to Peel, 1 March 1824, ibid.

55. Wellesley to Wellington, 17 February 1824, WP 1/785/1; Wellington to Wellesley, 23 February 1824, WP 1/786/24.

56. Wellesley to Plunkett, 7 March 1824, PMW, Add. MSS. 37302.

57. Bamford, *Journal of Mrs. Arbuthnot,* 10 June 1824, 1:321.

CHAPTER 16. IRRECONCILABLE DIFFERENCES

1. Bamford, *Journal of Mrs. Arbuthnot,* 7 September 1824, 1:336.

2. Canning to Bathurst, 29 September 1824, in Bathurst, . . . *Report on the Manuscripts,* 573–74.

3. Bamford, *Journal of Mrs. Arbuthnot,* 24 September 1824, 1:337.

4. *Evening Mail*; Shawe to Wellington, 9 May 1824, WP 1/792/11.

5. Peel to Wellesley, 18 December 1824, PMW, Add. MSS. 37303.

6. Wellesley to Peel, 20 December 1824, ibid.

7. H. Wellesley to Canning, 17 January 1825, PRO, F.O. 519.

8. Peel to Wellington, 29 December 1824, WP 1/807/30; Wellington to Peel, 26 December 1824, WP 1/808/17.

9. Blake to Richard Wellesley (son), 25 January 1825, CP #46; Wellesley to Peel, 3 January 1825, PMW, Add. MSS. 37303.

10. Peel to Wellesley, 31 January 1825, PMW, Add. MSS. 37303; Wellesley to Peel, 3 February 1825, ibid.; Bamford, *Journal of Mrs. Arbuthnot,* 19 February 1825, 1:376–78.

11. Grenville to Wellesley, 4 March 1825, Grenville-Wellesley Papers (British Library), Add. MSS. 70927.

12. Memorandum on the Case of the Roman Catholics in Ireland, WND, 2:592–607; Bamford, *Journal of Mrs. Arbuthnot,* 20 April 1825, 1:387–88.

13. Bamford, *Journal of Mrs. Arbuthnot,* 31 May 1824, 1:317–18.

14. Ibid., 8 May 1825, 1:394, and 25 May 1825, 1:400–401.

15. Wellington to Wellesley, 9 September 1825, PMW, Add. MSS. 37303.

16. Patterson to Shawe, 31 August 1824, PMW, Add. MSS. 37302.

17. Patterson to Wellesley, n.d., PMW, Add. MSS. 37315.

18. PMW, Add. MSS. 37315 and 37316.

19. Bamford, *Journal of Mrs. Arbuthnot,* 20 October 1825, 1:421.

20. Wellington to Wellesley, 13 October 1825, PMW, Add. MSS. 37416.

21. *John Bull,* 6 November 1825.

22. *John Bull,* 30 October 1825.

23. Bamford, *Journal of Mrs. Arbuthnot,* 11 January 1826, 2:2.

24. Wellesley to Peel, 29 December 1825, PMW, Add. MSS. 37303; Peel to Wellesley, 3 January 1826, ibid., Add. MSS. 37304; Peel to Wellesley, 9 January 1826, ibid.; Wellesley to Peel, 30 January 1826, ibid.

25. *Evening Mail,* 11 January 1826.

26. Bamford, *Journal of Mrs. Arbuthnot,* 11 January 1826, 2:3.

27. Wellesley to Wynn, 31 January 1826, PMW, Add. MSS. 37304.

28. H. Wellesley to Wellington, 22 February 1826, WP 1/850/13.

29. H. Wellesley to Canning, 28 June 1826, PRO, F.O. 519.

30. Wellesley to Wellington, 15 August 1826, WP 1/860/14; Liverpool to Wellesley, 19 August 1826, PMW, Add. MSS. 37304.

31. Wellington to Wellesley, 20 August 1826, PMW, Add. MSS. 37304; Wellington to Wellesley, 20 August 1826, WP 1/861/16.

32. Wellington to Wellesley, 21 August 1826, WP 1/861/18; Wellington to Wellesley, 21 August 1826, PMW, Add. MSS. 37304.

33. Wellesley to Wellington, 25 August 1826, WP 1/860/22.

34. Wellington to Liverpool, 30 August 1826, PMW, Add. MSS. 37304; Wellington to Liverpool, 30 August 1826, WP 1/861/24.

35. Wellington to Liverpool, 1 September 1826, PMW, Add. MSS. 37304; Wellington to Liverpool, 1 September 1826, WP 1/861/26; Liverpool to Wellington, 31 August 1826, PMW, Add. MSS. 37304.

36. Bamford, *Journal of Mrs. Arbuthnot,* 1 September 1826, 2:45; Peel to Wellington, 2 September 1826, WP 1/862/2; Arbuthnot to Bathurst, 1 September 1826, in Bathurst, . . . *Report on the Manuscripts,* 614–15.

37. Gerald Wellesley to Wellesley, 15 September 1826, PMW, Add. MSS. 37315; Wellington to Gerald Wellesley, 2 September 1826, WP 1/861/28; Wellington to Wellesley, 2 September 1826, PMW, Add. MSS 37315; Liverpool to Wellesley, 4 September 1826, PMW, Add. MSS. 37304.

38. Bamford, *Journal of Mrs. Arbuthnot,* 16 February 1827, 2:80.

39. Ibid., 22 March 1827, 2:93.

40. Ibid., 25 March 1827, 2:95–96.

41. Wellington to Wellesley, 10 April 1827, PMW, Add. MSS. 37415; Bamford, *Journal of Mrs. Arbuthnot,* 10 May 1827, 2:1189; Wellington to H. Wellesley, July 1827, WP 1/894/1.

42. Bamford, *Journal of Mrs. Arbuthnot,* 2 May 1827, 2:110–13.

43. H. Wellesley to Wellington, 6 August 1827, WP 1/895/6.

44. Quoted in Arbuthnot to Bathurst, 15 July 1827, in Bathurst, . . . *Report on the Manuscripts,* 637–40.

45. Bathurst to Countess Bathurst, 22 July 1827, ibid., 641–42; Bamford, *Journal of Mrs. Arbuthnot,* 10 May 1827 and 5 August 1827, 2:118 and 2:130–31, respectively.

46. Bamford, *Journal of Mrs. Arbuthnot,* 5 August 1827, 2:132.

47. H. Wellesley to Wellington, 6 August 1827, WP 1/895/6.

48. Canning to Wellesley, 24 April 1827, PMW, Add. MSS. 37297.

49. Ibid.

50. Canning to Wellesley, 22 May 1827, ibid.

51. Wellesley to Canning, 2 June 1827, ibid.

52. Canning to Wellesley, 7 June 1827, ibid.

53. Wellesley to Canning, 13 June 1828, Wellesley to George IV, 28 June 1827, Canning to Wellesley, 12 July 1827, and George IV to Wellesley, 10 July 1827, ibid.

54. Peel to Bathurst, 21 August 1827, in Bathurst, . . . *Report on the Manuscripts,* 644.

55. Wellington to Wellesley, 13 July 1827, PMW, Add. MSS. 37415; *Evening Mail,* 11 June 1827.

56. Peel to Bathurst, 21 August 1827, in Bathurst, . . . *Report on the Manuscripts,* 643–44.

57. Bamford, *Journal of Mrs. Arbuthnot,* 21 August 1827, 2:137. Emphasis in the original.

58. *Evening Mail,* 26 September 1827 and 7 November 1827.
59. Ibid., 19 November 1827.
60. Lauderdale to Bathurst, 30 December 1827, WP 1/903/26.
61. Memorandum of the Marquess Wellesley, 11 August 1827, PMW, Add. MSS. 37305.
62. Lamb to Wellington, 14 December 1827, WP 1/903/11.
63. Wellington to Bathurst, 18 December 1827, in Bathurst, . . . *Report on the Manuscripts,* 649.
64. Lamb to Wellington, 16 December 1827, WP 1/903/169.
65. Bathurst to Wellington, 19 December 1827, WP 1/903/16.
66. H. Wellesley to Wellington, December 1827, WP 1/903/1; Wellington to H. Wellesley, 1 December 1827, WP 1/904/1.
67. Goderich to Wellington, 21 December 1827, WP 1/903/18.
68. *Evening Mail,* 24 December 1827; Holmes to Wellington, 22 December 1827, WND, 4:171; Fitzroy Somerset to Wellington, 20 December 1827, WP 1/903/17.
69. Bathurst to Wellington, 30 December 1827, WP 1/903/26.
70. Wellington to Bathurst, 2 January 1828, in Bathurst, . . . *Report on the Manuscripts,* 651.
71. Diary entries for 2 and 6 January 1828, in Croker, *Croker Papers,* 1:367–69.
72. Marchioness Wellesley to Richard Wellesley, n.d., CP #63.
73. *Morning Chronicle,* 9 January 1828.
74. Marchioness Wellesley to Richard Wellesley, n.d., CP #63.
75. Richard Wellesley to Marchioness Wellesley, n.d., PMW, Add. MSS. 37316.
76. Comparison between Mr. Canning's government and that of Lord Goderich, WND, 4:179.
77. Knighton to Wellesley, 18 January 1828, PMW, Add. MSS. 37310.
78. Wellington to Wellesley, 3 February 1828, PMW, Add. MSS. 37415.
79. Wellesley to Wellington, 3 February 1828, WP 1/916/6. Emphasis in the original.
80. *John Bull,* 27 January 1828. Emphasis in the original.
81. Wellington to Wellesley, 24 June 1828, WP 1/939/32; Wellesley to Wellington, 23 June 1828, WP 1/937/30; Wellington to Johnston, 7 February 1828, WP 1/920/20.
82. *Evening Mail,* 21 March 1828.

CHAPTER 17. VIEW FROM ACROSS THE AISLE

1. *John Bull,* 27 January 1828.
2. Pole to Wellington, 30 March 1828, WP 1/924/8.
3. Longford, *Wellington: Pillar of State,* 160.
4. Huskisson to Wellington, 20 May 1828, *Annual Register,* 15; Huskisson to Wellington, 20 May 1828, WND, 4:456.
5. *Evening Mail,* 19 March 1828.
6. Great Britain, *Parliamentary Debates,* 2nd series, vol. 18, np.
7. Ibid.

8. Richard Wellesley (son) to Wellesley, 13 June 1828, PMW, Add. MSS. 37316.
9. Greville, *Memoirs,* 18 June 1828, 1:211–12.
10. Wellington to Cowley, 25 June 1828, WP 1/939/34.
11. Cowley, *Diary and Correspondence,* 160.
12. *Annual Register,* 70:22.
13. Ibid., 13.
14. Cowley to Wellington, 13 June 1828, WP 1/936/27.
15. Metternich to Cowley, 18 August 1829, Cowley Papers, PRO, F.O. 519.
16. Cowley to Wellington, 13 June 1828, WP 1/936/27.
17. Fitzgerald to Wellington, 9 August 1828, WP 1/946/35.
18. Arbuthnot to Bathurst, 12 August 1828, WND, 4:597.
19. Anglesey to Wellington, 23 November 1828, WP 1/967/11.
20. Greville, *Memoirs,* 26 March 1829, 1:279.
21. Hatherton Journal, Hatherton Papers, D260.
22. A. Wellesley to Pole, 6 September 1808, RP.
23. Greville, *Memoirs,* 17 January 1830, 1:358.
24. *Annual Register,* 72:155.
25. Greville, *Memoirs,* 10 November 1830, 2:56.
26. Wellesley to Shawe, 16 November 1830, PMW, Add. MSS. 37310.
27. Ellesmere, *Personal Reminiscences,* 71–72.
28. Stephens to Wellington, 5 December 1829, WP 1/1060/16.
29. Wellington to Stephens, 6 December 1829, ibid.
30. Cowley to Palmerston, December 1830, WP 1/1185/15.
31. Cowley to Wellington, 23 May 1831, WP 1/1185/15.
32. Greville, *Memoirs,* 2:69.
33. Maryborough to Wellington, 3 February 1831, WP 1/1175/3.
34. Mrs. Arbuthnot to Mr. Arbuthnot, 17 February 1831, in Aspinall, *Correspondence of Charles Arbuthnot,* 139. Emphasis in the original.
35. Wellesley to Brougham, 22 November 1830, Brougham Papers.
36. Sir H. Taylor to Maryborough, 25 April 1831, WP 1/1182/20.
37. Maryborough to Wellington, 11 July 1831, WP 1/1189/16.
38. Wellington to Peel, 11 May 1831, WP 1/1186/8.
39. Wellington to Cowley, 15 July 1831, WP 1/1191/10.
40. Grey to Wellesley, 19 April 1831, PMW, Add. MSS. 37311.
41. Wellesley to Grey, 21 May 1831, ibid.
42. Wellington to Lord Munster, 13 September 1831, WP 1/1197/3.
43. Durham to Wellesley, 11 June 1832, PMW, Add. MSS. 37311.
44. Charles Arbuthnot to Son, 15 June 1832, in Aspinall, *Correspondence of Charles Arbuthnot,* 161.
45. Ellesmere, *Personal Reminiscences,* 73.
46. Grey to Wellesley, 21 January 1833, PMW, Add. MSS. 37311.
47. Wellesley to Montgomery, 2 September 1833, and Grey to Wellesley, 1 September 1833, ibid.
48. Anglesey, *One-Leg,* 276.
49. Greville, *Memoirs,* 6 September 1833, 2:415.
50. Wellington to Cumberland, 13 September 1833, in Wellington, *Prime Minister's Papers,* 1:295–96.

51. Anglesey to Wellesley, 3 October 1833 and 5 September 1833, PMW, Add. MSS. 37306.
52. Longford, *Wellington: Pillar of State,* 289.
53. Ellesmere, *Personal Reminiscences,* 74.
54. Wellesley to Holland, 17 November 1833, PMW, Add. MSS. 37306.
55. Wellesley Memo, 25 February 1833, ibid.
56. Grey to Wellesley, 3 June 1834, PMW, Add. MSS. 37311.
57. Littleton, *Memoirs and Correspondence,* 7.
58. Wellesley to Brougham, 21 June 1834, Brougham Papers.
59. Brougham to Wellesley, 8 July 1834, Brougham Papers.
60. Hatherton Diary, Hatherton Papers, D260.
61. Wellesley to Wellington, 24 November 1834, PMW, Add. MSS. 37415.
62. King to Wellington, 19 November 1834, in Wellington, *Prime Minister's Papers,* 2:35.
63. Wellesley to Wellington, 29 November 1834, PMW, Add. MSS. 37307.
64. Wellesley to Brougham, 20 November 1834, Brougham Papers.
65. Grey to Wellesley, 9 December 1834, PMW, Add. MSS. 37311.
66. Brougham to Wellesley, 2 January 1835, ibid.
67. Cowley's Diary, Cowley Papers, PRO, F.O. 519.
68. Cowley to Wellington, 10 April 1835, Cowley Papers, PRO, F.O. 519.
69. Wellesley to Brougham, 23 April 1835, Brougham Papers.
70. Great Britain, *Parliamentary Debates,* 2nd series, np; Pearce, *Memoirs and Correspondence,* 3:408–11.
71. Wellesley to Marchioness Wellesley, 26 January 1836, PMW, Add. MSS. 37316.

CHAPTER 18. THE FINAL YEARS

1. *Edinburgh Review,* 63:537–38.
2. Wellesley to Brougham, 14 July 1836, Brougham Papers.
3. *Edinburgh Review,* 66:151–55.
4. Wellesley to Carnac, 20 October 1836, PMW, Add. MSS. 37311.
5. Croker to Wellesley, 5 April 1838, PMW, Add. MSS. 37312.
6. Wellesley, *Wellesley Papers,* 2:331.
7. Trustees to Wellesley, 4 January 1838, PMW, Add. MSS. 37312.
8. Maryborough to Wellesley, 23 March 1838, PMW, Add. MSS. 37416.
9. Wellesley to Brougham, 10 February 1837, PMW, Add. MSS. 37311.
10. Wellesley to Melbourne, 21 June 1837, PMW, Add. MSS. 37312.
11. Wellesley to Brougham, 28 December 1837, Brougham Papers.
12. Hatherton Diary, Hatherton Papers, D260.
13. Ibid., 5 January 1935.
14. Wellesley apparently sent a long letter in return to his wife in which he wrote affectionately and admiringly of his brother.
15. Marchioness Wellesley to Wellesley, n.d., PMW, Add. MSS. 37316.
16. Marchioness Wellesley to Wellesley, n.d., ibid.
17. Wellesley to Brougham, 14 May 1838, Brougham Papers.
18. Maryborough to Wellesley, 15 May 1838, PMW, Add. MSS. 37416.
19. Wellington to Lady Wellesley, 24 May 1838, PMW, Add. MSS. 37415.

20. Cowley to Wellington, 2 August 1838, Stratfield Saye, Wellington Papers.
21. Wellington to Cowley, 25 August 1838, Stratfield Saye, Wellington Papers.
22. Ibid.
23. Cowley to Wellington, 29 August 1838, Stratfield Saye, Wellington Papers.
24. Maryborough to Wellesley, 19 November 1839, PMW, Add. MSS. 37416.
25. Thompson, *Wellington after Waterloo.*
26. Stanhope, *Notes of Conversations,* 170.
27. *Edinburgh Review* 68 (1838).
28. Stanhope, *Notes of Conversations,* 49.
29. *Edinburgh Review* 69 (1839): 348.
30. Wellesley to Brougham, 28 August 1839, Brougham Papers.
31. Wellington to Wellesley, 31 January 1840, PMW, Add. MSS. 37415.
32. *Quarterly Review,* 65:537.
33. Maryborough to Wellesley, 29 June 1842, PMW, Add. MSS. 37416.
34. Wellesley to Maryborough, 29 June 1842, ibid.
35. Wellesley, *Wellesley Papers,* 2:385.
36. Butler, *Eldest Brother,* 569–70.
37. Wellesley to the Directors of the East India Company, 18 March 1841, in Wellesley, *Wellesley Papers,* 2:386.
38. Cowley to Wellesley, 14 March 1841, PMW, Add. MSS. 37312.
39. Gerald Wellesley to Wellesley, 24 March 1841, Maryborough to Wellesley, 19 March 1841, and Wellington to Wellesley, 20 March 1841, ibid.
40. Cowley to Wellesley, October 1841, Cowley Papers, PRO, F.O. 519/285.
41. Wellesley to Holland, 13 November 1839, PMW, Add. MSS. 37312.
42. Wellington to Ally Montgomery, 26 September 1842, PMW, Add. MSS. 37415.
43. Stanhope, *Notes of Conversations,* 278.
44. Richard Wellesley to Edward Wellesley, 8 October 1842, CP #64.
45. Ibid.
46. Henry Wellesley's Memoir, Cowley Papers, PRO, F.O. 519/67.
47. Ibid.
48. Aberdeen to Lieven, 21 December 1841, in Parry, *Correspondence of Lord Aberdeen and Princess Lieven.*
49. Henry Wellesley's Memoir, November 1841, Cowley Papers, PRO, F.O. 519/67.
50. Henry Wellesley's Memoir, 8 May 1842, ibid.
51. Ibid.
52. Henry Wellesley's Memoir, 4 September and 15 September 1843, ibid.
53. Henry Wellesley's Memoir, 17 October 1843, ibid.
54. Henry Wellesley's Memoir, 12 August 1844, ibid.
55. Henry Wellesley's Memoir, 7 September 1844, ibid.
56. Ibid.
57. *Gentleman's Magazine,* new series, 23 (April 1845).
58. *Times,* quoted in ibid.
59. Letters to and from grandchildren, RP.
60. Henry Wellesley's Memoir, 16 October 1845, Cowley Papers, PRO, F.O. 519.
61. Ibid.

62. Henry Wellesley's Memoir, 20 September 1845, ibid.

63. Bagot to Wellington, 28 April 1847, ibid., Cowley Papers, PRO, F.O. 519/285.

64. Wellington to Gerald Wellesley, 29 April 1847, ibid.

65. Richmond to Wellington, 1 May 1847, ibid., 519/286.

66. *Gentleman's Magazine,* new series, 30 (December 1848).

67. Quoted in Hibbert, *Wellington,* 387.

68. Greville, *Memoirs,* 6:360–64.

69. Stanhope, *Notes of Conversations,* 137.

70. Ellesmere, *Personal Reminiscences,* 86.

Bibliography

When I began this project, I intended it to be accessible to a general audience. My approach is not that of a historical monograph. It is, rather, that of biography, and biography of a specialized sort. My goal was to put a human face on distant characters and to explore the impact of personal relationships on careers and vice versa. The details of British political, diplomatic, economic, and social life are important, but here they form a backdrop to the story rather than serve as the story itself. This being the case, the historian looks for a different kind of evidence. Having told the story of the Wellesleys' work in the Peninsular War, I found myself reading again documents I had seen many times before, this time searching not only for historical detail but for signs of attitude, sensitivities, and opinions. I have, therefore, chosen to be spare in my source notes, citing mostly primary sources to tell the story of the Wellesleys from the inside. I cite published sources when possible even when I have consulted the originals. This is especially true of the Wellesley Papers concerning India and also the Wellington Papers. My reading of secondary sources was comprehensive, but for Wellesley family history I drew largely on Iris Butler, Lady Elizabeth Longford, Neville Thompson, and several of the classic Wellington biographers. For Ireland I relied on R. F. Foster and J. C. Becket. On the vast topic of India I found essential the works of Edward Ingram, A. S. Bennell, P. J. Marshall, C. A. Bayly, and Randolf G. S.

Cooper. The works of Charles Esdail, Jeremy Black, and Rory Muir were especially helpful on the war with France. For British politics I leaned on John Ehrman, Norman Gash, Denis Gray, Wendy Hinde, Peter Jupp, and again Neville Thompson. The list is by no means comprehensive.

ARCHIVAL SOURCES

All Souls College Library, Oxford

Vaughan Papers

British Library

Bathurst Papers
Canning Papers
Grenville-Wellesley Papers
Herries Papers
Hobart Papers
Huskisson Papers
[Oriental and] India Office Collection
    European Manuscripts
    Home Miscellaneous Series
Lenox Papers
Liverpool Papers
Melville Papers
Paget Papers
Peel Papers
Pelham Papers
Perceval Papers
Vansittart Papers
Wellesley Papers

Foreign Office, Public Record Office (Great Britain)

Spain, F.O. 72
Great Britain and General, F.O. 83
Treaties, F.O. 93
Embassy and Consular Archives, F.O. 185
Cowley Papers, F.O. 519

Gwent Record Office, Cwmbrân

Raglan Papers

Hartley Library, University of Southampton

Carver Papers
Wellington Papers

Hatfield House

Salisbury Papers

Lambeth Palace Library, London

Fulham Papers
Howley Papers
Vicar General Acts Book

Sección de Estado, Archivo Histórico Nacional, Madrid

Cortes, Legajo 3002
Great Britain, Legajos 5459–64, 5488, 5608–14
Supreme Junta, Legajos 1–84, 3066, 3072, 3110
Regency, Legajo 3566
War of Independence, Legajos 2994, 3010

Staffordshire Record Office

Hatherton Papers

Stratfield Saye

Wellington Papers

University College Library, London

Brougham Papers

NEWSPAPERS AND JOURNALS

Annual Register
Edinburgh Review
Etonia
Evening Mail (Dublin)
Examiner
Gentleman's Magazine
Hampshire Chronicle
Hull Packet
John Bull

Le Moniteur
Morning Chronicle
Morning Post
Quarterly Review
Shrewsbury Chronicle
Times (London)

PUBLISHED SOURCES

Aldington, Richard. *The Duke: Being an Account of the Life and Achievements of Arthur Wellesley, First Duke of Wellington.* New York: Viking, 1943.

Anglesey, Marquess of [George Charles Henry Victor Paget]. *One-Leg: The Life and Letters of Henry William Paget, First Marquess of Anglesey, K.G., 1768–1854.* New York: William Morrow and Co., 1961.

Aspinall, A. (ed.). *The Correspondence of Charles Arbuthnot.* London: Royal Historical Society, 1941.

———. *The Correspondence of George, Prince of Wales, 1770–1812.* London: Cassell, 1963–1971.

———. *The Later Correspondence of King George III.* Cambridge: Cambridge University Press, 1962–1971.

———. *The Letters of King George IV.* Cambridge: Cambridge University Press, 1938.

———. *Lord Brougham and the Whig Party.* Manchester: Manchester University Press, 1927.

———. *Three Early Nineteenth-Century Diaries.* London: Williams and Norgate, 1952.

Austen-Leigh, R. A. *The Eton College Register, 1753–1790.* London: Spottiswoode, Ballantyne and Co., 1921.

Bagot, Joceline. *George Canning and His Friends.* London: John Murray, 1909.

Baird, Sir David. *The Life of General the Right Honourable Sir David Baird.* London: Richard Bentley, 1832.

Bamford, Francis (ed.). *The Journal of Mrs. Arbuthnot, 1820–1832.* London: Macmillan and Co., 1950.

Barrington, Sir Jonah. *Personal Sketches of His Own Times.* London: Colburn and Bentley, 1827.

Bartlet, C. J. *Castlereagh.* New York: Scribners, 1967.

Bathurst, Seymour Henry [7th Earl]. *Historical Manuscripts Commission: Report on the Manuscripts of the Seventh Earl Bathurst.* London: Historical Manuscripts Commission, 1923.

Becket, J. C. *The Anglo-Irish Tradition.* Ithaca, N.Y.: Cornell University Press, 1976.

Bell, Herbert C. F. *Lord Palmerston.* London: Hodder and Stoughton, 1922.

Bennell, A. S. "Wellesley's Settlement of Mysore, 1799." *Journal of the Royal Asiatic Society* (1952): 124–32.

Bessborough, Earl of, with A. Aspinall. *Lady Bessborough and Her Family Circle.* London: John Murray, 1940.

Bill, E.G.W. *Education at Christ Church Oxford, 1660–1800.* Oxford: Clarendon Press, 1988.

Black, Jeremy. *British Foreign Policy in an Age of Revolution, 1780–1790.* Cambridge: Cambridge University Press, 1994.

Blanch, Lesley (ed.). *The Game of Hearts: Harriette Wilson and Her Memoirs.* New York: Simon and Schuster, 1957.

Brett-James, Antony. *Life in Wellington's Army.* London: George Allen Unwin, 1972.

———. *Wellington at War, 1794–1815.* London: Macmillan, 1961.

Brooke, John. *King George III: A Biography of America's Last Monarch.* New York: McGraw-Hill, 1972.

Brougham, Henry, Lord. *Historical Sketches of Statesmen Who Flourished in the Time of George III.* Philadelphia: Lea and Blanchard, 1843.

Buckingham and Chandos, Duke of [Richard Temple Grenville]. *Memoirs of the Court and Cabinets of George III.* London: Hurst and Blackett, 1852–55.

———. *Memoirs of the Court of England during the Regency, 1811–1820.* London: Hurst and Blackett, 1856.

———. *Memoirs of the Court and Cabinets of George IV.* London: Hurst and Blackett, 1859.

———. *Memoirs of the Court and Cabinets of William IV and Victoria.* London: Hurst and Blackett, 1861.

Burghclere, Lady (ed.). *A Great Man's Friendship: Letters of the Duke of Wellington to Mary, Marchioness of Salisbury, 1850–1852.* London: John Murray, 1927.

Butler, Iris. *The Eldest Brother: The Marquess Wellesley, the Duke of Wellington's Eldest Brother.* London: Hodder and Stoughton, 1973.

Castlereagh, Viscount [Robert Stewart, 2nd Marquess of Londonderry]. *The Memoranda and Correspondence of Robert Stewart, Viscount Castlereagh.* London: William Shobrel, 1848–54.

Cavendish, Lady Harriet. *Hary-O: The Letters of Lady Harriet Cavendish, 1796–1809.* London: John Murray, 1940.

Chamberlain, Muriel E. *Lord Aberdeen: A Political Biography.* London: Longmans, 1983.

Chandler, David. *The Campaigns of Napoleon.* New York: Macmillan, 1966.

Clark, George Kitson. *Peel and the Conservative Party: A Study in Politics, 1832–1841.* New York: Archon Books, 1964.

Colchester, Lord [Charles Abbot]. *The Diary and Correspondence of Charles Abbot, Lord Colchester.* London: John Murray, 1861.

Colley, Linda. *Britons: The Forging of the Nation, 1707–1837.* London: Yale University Press, 1992.

Cookson, J. E. *Lord Liverpool's Administration, 1815–1822.* Edinburgh: Scottish Academic Press, 1975.

Cooper, Randolf G. S. *The Anglo-Maratha Campaigns and the Contest for Control of the South Asian Military Economy.* Cambridge: Cambridge University Press, 2004.

Cowley, Lord [Henry Wellesley, 1st Baron]. *The Diary and Correspondence of Henry Wellesley, First Lord Cowley, 1790–1846.* London: Hutchinson and Co., 1930.

Creevey, Thomas. *The Creevey Papers: A Selection from the Correspondence and Diaries of the Late Thomas Creevey, M.P.* New York: E. P. Dutton, 1905.

Croker, John Wilson. *The Croker Papers: The Correspondence and Diaries of John Wilson Croker, Secretary to the Admiralty from 1809 to 1830.* London: John Murray, 1885.

Delany, Mary Granville. *The Autobiography and Correspondence of Mary Granville, Mrs. Delany.* London: Richard Bentley, 1861.

Disraeli, Benjamin. *Disraeli's Reminiscences.* London: Stein and Day, 1975.

Dundas, Henry [1st Viscount Melville]. *Two Views of British India: The Private Correspondence of Mr. Dundas and Lord Wellesley, 1798–1801,* ed. Edward Ingram. London: Adams and Dort, 1970.

Edgcumbe, Richard (ed.). *The Diary of Frances, Lady Shelley 1787–1817.* London: John Murray, 1912.

Ehrman, John. *Pitt.* 3 vols. London: Constable, 1969, 1983, 1996.

Ellenborough, Lord [Edward Law]. *A Political Diary, 1828–1830,* ed. Lord Colchester. London: Richard Bentley, 1881.

Ellesmere, Lord [Francis Egerton]. *Personal Reminiscences of the Duke of Wellington by Francis, First Earl of Ellesmere.* London: John Murray, 1903.

Farmer, Hugh. *A Regency Elopement.* London: Michael Joseph, 1969.

Fedorak, Charles John. *Henry Addington: Prime Minister, 1801–1804.* Akron, Ohio: Akron University Press, 2002.

Forrest, Denys. *Tiger of Mysore: The Life and Death of Tipu Sultan.* London: Chatto and Windus, 1970.

Fortescue, Sir John. *British Statesmen of the Great War, 1793–1814.* Oxford: Clarendon Press, 1911.

———. *Wellington.* London: Ernest Benn, 1960.

Foster, R. F. *Modern Ireland, 1600–1972.* London, Penguin Books, 1988.

——— (ed.). *Oxford History of Ireland.* Oxford: Oxford University Press, 1991.

Gash, Norman. *The Life and Political Career of Robert Banks Jenkinson, Second Earl of Liverpool, 1770–1828.* London: Weidenfield and Nicholson, 1984.

———. *Sir Robert Peel.* London: Longmans, 1972.

———. *Wellington: Studies in the Political and Military Career of the First Duke of Wellington.* Manchester: Manchester University Press, 1990.

Gleig, G. R. *Life of Arthur, Duke of Wellington.* London: Longmans, Green, Reader and Dyer, 1865.

Glover, Michael. *Britannia Sickens: Sir Arthur Wellesley and the Convention of Cintra.* London: Leo-Cooper, 1970.

Granville, Lord [Granville Leveson Gower, 1st Earl Granville]. *Lord Granville Leveson Gower: Private Correspondence, 1781–1821.* London: John Murray, 1916.

Gray, Denis. *Spencer Perceval.* Manchester: Manchester University Press, 1963.

Great Britain. *Cobbett's Parliamentary History of England from the Earliest Period to the Year 1803.* London: T. C. Hansard, 1816.

———. *Hansard's Catalogue and Breviate of Parliamentary papers, 1696– 1834.* London: T. C. Hansard, 1953.

———. *Journal of the House of Lords.* London: T. C. Hansard, 1809.

———. *The Parliamentary Debates from the Year 1803 to the Present Time.* London: T. C. Hansard, 1820.

———. *The Parliamentary Debates, Series II.* London: T. C. Hansard, 1830.

Greville, Charles. *The Greville Memoirs, 1814–1860.* 8 vols. London: Macmillan, 1938.
Guedalla, Philip. *The Duke.* New York: Literary Guild, 1974 (1st ed., 1931).
Herrick, C. T. (ed.). *The Letters of the Duke of Wellington to Miss Jenkins, 1834–1851.* London: T. Fisher Unwin, 1924.
Hibbert, Christopher. *George IV: Prince of Wales, 1762–1811.* London: Longmans, 1972.
———. *George IV: Regent and King, 1811–1830.* London: Allen Lane, 1973.
———. *Wellington: A Personal History.* London: HarperCollins, 1997.
Hickey, William. *Memoirs of William Hickey.* Hurst and Blackett, 1925.
[Hildyard.] *The Trial of the Right Honourable Lord Paget, for Criminal Conversation with Lady Charlotte Wellesley.* London: E. Hildyard, 1809.
Hinde, Wendy. *Castlereagh.* London: William Collins Sons, 1981.
———. *George Canning.* New York: St. Martin's, 1973.
Historical Manuscripts Commission. *Report of the Manuscripts of J. B. Fortescue, Esq., Preserved at Dropmore.* London: Historical Manuscripts Commission, 1925.
Holland, Lady Elizabeth. *The Journal of Elizabeth, Lady Holland.* London: Longmans Green, 1909.
Holland, Lord [Henry Richard Vassal Fox]. *Further Memoirs of the Whig Party, 1807–1821,* ed. Lord Stavordale. London: John Murray, 1905.
———. *Memoirs of the Whig Party during My Time.* London: Longmans, Brown and Green, 1852–1854.
Hook, Theodore. *Life of Sir David Baird.* London: Richard Bentley, 1833.
Horward, Donald D. *The Battle of Bussaco: Massena vs Wellington.* Tallahassee: Florida State University Press, 1965.
Howard, Michael. *Wellingtonian Studies: Essays on the Duke of Wellington by Five Old Wellingtonians.* Aldershot, U.K.: Wellington Press, 1959.
Howarth, David. *Waterloo: A Near Run Thing.* London: Collins, 1968.
Hutton, William H. *The Marquess Wellesley.* Oxford, U.K.: Clarendon Press, 1893.
Ingram, Edward. *The Beginning of the Great Game in Asia, 1828–1834.* Oxford, U.K.: Clarendon Press, 1979.
———. *Commitment to Empire: Prophesies of the Great Game in Asia, 1797–1800.* Oxford, U.K.: Clarendon Press, 1981.
———. "The Geopolitics of the First British Expedition to Egypt," part 3, "The Red Sea Campaign, 1800–1," *Middle Eastern Studies* 31, no. 1 (January 1995): 146–69.
———. "The Role of the Indian Army at the End of the Eighteenth Century." *Military History Journal* 2 (1973): 216–22.
Jenkins, Brian. *Era of Emancipation: British Government of Ireland, 1812–1830.* Montreal: McGill-Queen's University Press, 1988.
Jupp, Peter. *The Letter-Journal of George Canning, 1793–1795.* London: Royal Historical Society, 1991.
———. *Lord Grenville, 1759–1834.* Oxford: Oxford University Press, 1985.
Kaye, Sir John. *The Life and Correspondence of Major-General Sir John Malcolm.* London: Richard Bentley, 1856.

Knighton, Lady. *Memoirs of Sir William Knighton.* London: Richard Bentley, 1838.

Lawrence, Sir Thomas. *Sir Thomas Lawrence's Letter Bag.* London: George Allen, 1906.

Lennox, Lady Sarah. *The Life and Letters of Lady Sarah Lennox.* London: John Murray, 1902.

Leveson-Gower, Granville. *Private Correspondence of Granville Leveson-Gower.* London: John Murray, 1916.

Lindsay, Lord [Alexander Crawford]. *The Lives of the Lindsays; or, A Memoir of the Houses of Crawford and Balcarres, by Lord Lindsay.* London: John Murray, 1849.

Littleton, John Edward. *Memoirs and Correspondence Relating to Political Occurrences in June and July 1834.* London: Longmans Green, 1872.

Llangollen, Ladies of. *The Hamwood Papers of the Ladies of Llangollen.* London: Macmillan, 1930.

Longford, Lady Elizabeth. *Wellington: Pillar of State.* New York: Harper and Row, 1972.

———. *Wellington: Years of the Sword.* New York: Harper and Row, 1969.

Lyte, H. C. Maxwell. *A History of Eton College, 1440–1875.* London: Macmillan and Co., 1875.

Malcolm, Sir John. *The Life and Correspondence of Sir John Malcolm.* London: John Murray, 1856.

———. *The Political History of India from 1784 to 1823.* London: John Murray, 1826.

Malleson, G. B. *The Life of Marquess Wellesley, K.G.* London: W. H. Allen, 1889.

Malmesbury, Lord [James Harris]. *Diaries and Correspondence of James Harris, First Earl of Malmesbury.* London: Richard Bentley, 1845.

Marshall, P. J. *Bengal: The British Bridgehead, Eastern India, 1740–1828.* Cambridge: Cambridge University Press, 1987.

Maxwell, Sir Herbert. *The Life of Field Marshall His Grace the Duke of Wellington.* London: Smith, Low, Marston and Co., 1899.

Melville, Lewis. *The Huskisson Papers.* London: Constable, 1931.

Mill, James. *The History of British India.* London: James Madden, 1840.

Moody, T. W., F. X. Martin, and F. J. Byrne (eds.). *A New History of Ireland, 1534–1691.* Oxford: Oxford University Press, 1976.

Moore, Sir John. *The Diary of Sir John Moore.* 2 vols. London: E. Arnold, 1904.

———. *A Narrative of the Campaign of the British Army in Spain, Commanded by His Excellency Lieut. General Sir John Moore, K.B.* London: J. Johnson, 1809.

Muir, Rory. *Britain and the Defeat of Napoleon, 1807–1815.* New Haven: Yale University Press, 1996.

Napier, Sir William, F.P. *History of the War in the Peninsula and in the South of France from the Year 1807 to the Year 1814.* London: Barthes and Lowell, 1886.

Oman, Carola. *The Gascoyne Heiress: The Life and Diaries of Frances May Gascoyne-Cecil, 1802–1839.* London: Hodder and Stoughton, 1968.

Oman, Sir Charles. *A History of the Peninsular War.* Oxford: Clarendon Press, 1902–1930.

Paget, Sir Arthur. *The Paget Papers: Diplomatic and Other Correspondence of Sir Arthur Paget, 1794–1807.* London: William Heinemann, 1896.

Parry, E. Jones (ed.). *The Correspondence of Lord Aberdeen and Princess Lieven, 1832–1854.* London: Royal Historical Society, 1938.

Pearce, Robert Rouiere. *Memoirs and Correspondence of the Most Noble Richard, Marquess Wellesley, K.G.* London: Richard Bentley, 1846.

Pellew, George. *The Life and Correspondence of the Right Honourable Henry Addington, 1st Viscount Sidmouth.* London: John Murray, 1847.

Raikes, Thomas. *Private Correspondence of Thomas Raikes with the Duke of Wellington and Other Distinguished Contemporaries.* London: Richard Bentley, 1861.

Rathbone, Julian. *Wellington's War: His Peninsular Despatches.* London: Michael Joseph, 1994.

Roberts, Andrew. *Napoleon and Wellington.* New York: Simon and Schuster, 2001.

Roberts, P. E. *India under Wellesley.* London: G. Bell and Sons, 1929.

Romilly, Samuel. *Memoirs of the Life of Sir Samuel Romilly.* London: J. Fairburn, 1847.

Rose, George. *The Diaries and Correspondence of the Rt. Hon. George Rose.* London: Richard Bentley, 1860.

Rose, John Holland. *William Pitt and the Great War.* London: G. Bell and Sons, 1911.

Scott, David. *The Correspondence of David Scott, Director and Chairman of the East India Company, Relating to Indian Affairs, 1787–1805.* London: Royal Historical Society, 1951.

Severn, John. *A Wellesley Affair: Richard Marquess Wellesley and the Conduct of Anglo-Spanish Relations.* Tallahassee: University Presses of Florida, 1981.

Shelley, Lady Frances. *The Diary of Frances Lady Shelley, 1787–1875.* London: John Murray, 1912–13.

Sherwig, John M. *Guineas and Gunpowder: British Foreign Aid in the Wars with France, 1793–1815.* Cambridge, Mass.: Harvard University Press, 1969.

Smith, E. A. *Lord Grey, 1764–1845.* Oxford: Oxford University Press, 1990.

———. *Wellington and the Arbuthnots: A Triangular Friendship.* Gloucestershire: Sutton Publishing, 1994.

Smith, Vincent. *The Oxford History of India.* Oxford: Oxford University Press, 1958.

Spear, Percival. *A History of India,* vol. 2. New York: Penguin, 1990.

———. *The Nabobs: A Study of the Social Life of the English in 18th Century India.* Oxford: Oxford University Press, 1963.

Spencer, George, Lord. *Private Papers of George, Second Earl Spencer, First Lord of the Admiralty, 1794–1801.* London: Navy Records Society, 1913–1924.

Stanhope, Philip Henry [5th Earl Stanhope]. *Life of the Right Honourable William Pitt.* London: John Murray, 1867.

———. *Notes of Conversations with the Duke of Wellington.* London: John Murray, 1938.

Stewart, Robert. *Henry Brougham: His Public Career, 1778–1868.* London, 1985.

Stocqueler, J. H. *The Life of Field Marshal the Duke of Wellington.* London: Ingram, Cooke, and Co., 1852.

Stone, Lawrence. *Broken Lives: Separation and Divorce in England, 1660–1857.* Oxford: Oxford University Press, 1993.

Teignmouth, John Shore [1st Baron]. *Memoirs of the Life and Correspondence of John, Lord Teignmouth.* London: Hatchard and Son, 1843.

Thompson, Neville. *Earl Bathurst and the British Empire.* London: Leo Cooper, 1999.

———. *Wellington after Waterloo.* London: Routledge and Kegan Paul, 1986.

Torrens, W. McCullagh. *The Marquess Wellesley, Architect of Empire.* London: Chatto and Windus, 1880.

Twiss, Horace. *The Public and Private Life of Lord Chancellor Eldon.* London: John Murray, 1844.

Vane, Charles (ed.). *The Memoirs and Correspondence of Viscount Castlereagh, Second Marquess of Londonderry.* London: Henry Coburn and Co., 1850–1853.

Venn, John. *Alumni Cantabrigienses: A Biographical List of All Known Students, Graduates and Holders of Office at the University of Cambridge, from the Earliest Times to 1900.* Cambridge: Cambridge University Press, 1922.

Virgin, Peter. *The Church in an Age of Negligence.* Cambridge: James Clark, 1989.

Webster, Sir C. (ed.). *Some Letters of the Duke of Wellington to His Brother, William Wellesley Pole.* Camden Miscellany. London: Royal Historical Society, 1948.

Weigall, Lady Rose (ed.). *The Correspondence of Lady Burghersh with the Duke of Wellington.* London: John Murray, 1903.

Weller, Jac. *Wellington in India.* London: Longmans, 1993.

Wellesley, Muriel. *The Man Wellington through the Eyes of Those Who Knew Him.* London: Constable, 1937.

———. *Wellington in Civil Life through the Eyes of Those Who Knew Him.* London: Constable, 1939.

Wellesley, Richard [1st Marquess]. *The Despatches, Minutes, and Correspondence of the Marquis Wellesley, K.G., during his Administration in India.* London: W. H. Allen, 1836–1837.

———. "A Further Confidential Letter from Wellesley to Dundas," ed. Edward Ingram. *Journal of Indian History* 1 (1972): 15–20.

———. "An Unpublished Paper of Wellesley on the Government of India," ed. W. H. Hutton. *Imperial and Asiatic Quarterly Review* 7 (1899): 29–48.

———. *The Wellesley Papers: Life and Correspondence of Richard Colley Wellesley, Marquess Wellesley, 1760–1842.* London: Herbert Jenkins, 1914.

Wellington, 1st Duke of [Arthur Wellesley]. *The Conversations of the First Duke of Wellington with George William Chad.* Cambridge, U.K.: Saint Nicholas Press, 1956.

———. *Despatches, Correspondence and Memoranda of Field Marshal Arthur Duke of Wellington, 1818–1832* (New Series). London: John Murray, 1867–1880.

———. *The Dispatches of Field Marshal the Duke of Wellington during His*

Various Campaigns in India, Denmark, Portugal, Spain, the Low Countries and France. London: John Murray, 1837.

———. *My Dear Mrs. Jones: The Letters of the Duke of Wellington to Mrs. Jones of Pantglas.* London: Rodale Press, 1954.

———. *The Prime Minister's Papers: Wellington, Political Correspondence I, 1833–November 1834.* London: HMSO, 1974.

———. *The Prime Minister's Papers: Wellington, Political Correspondence II, 1834–1835.* London: HMSO, 1986.

———. *The Supplementary Despatches and Memoranda of Field Marshal the Duke of Wellington.* London: John Murray, 1858–1872.

———. *Wellington and His Friends: Letters of the First Duke of Wellington to the Rt. Hon. Charles and Mrs. Arbuthnot, the Earl and Countess of Wilton, Princess Lieven and Miss Burdett-Coutts.* London: Macmillan, 1965.

Wellington, 7th Duke of [Gerald]. *The Collected Works of Gerald, 7th Duke of Wellington.* Glasgow: privately printed, 1970.

Wilson, Harriette. *Harriette Wilson's Memoirs Written by Herself.* London: Eveleigh Nash, 1909.

Wilson, Joan. *A Soldier's Wife: Wellington's Marriage.* London: Weidenfield and Nicolson, 1987.

Yapp, M. E. *Strategies of British India: Britain, Iran and Afghanistan, 1798–1850.* Oxford, U.K.: Clarendon Press, 1980.

Yonge, Charles Duke. *The Life and Administration of Robert Banks, Second Earl of Liverpool, K.G.* London: Macmillan, 1868.

Young, Arthur. *A Tour in Ireland with General Observations on the Present State of the Kingdom.* London: T. Cadell, 1780.

Ziegler, Phillip. *Addington: A Life of Henry Addington, First Viscount Sidmouth.* New York: John Day, 1965.

———. *Melbourne: A Biography of William Lamb, 2nd Viscount Melbourne.* London: Collins, 1976.

———. *William IV.* London: Collins, 1971.

Index